ENCYCLOPEDIA OF THE
AMERICAN ARMED FORCES

ENCYCLOPEDIA OF THE AMERICAN ARMED FORCES

VOLUME II

Alan Axelrod

Facts On File, Inc.

Facts On File, Inc.
132 West 31st Street
New York NY 10001

Library of Congress Cataloging-in-Publication Data

Axelrod, Alan, 1952–
Encyclopedia of the American armed forces / Alan Axelrod.
p. cm.
Includes bibliographical references and index.
ISBN 0-8160-4700-6 (hardcover set : alk. paper) —ISBN 0-8160-6604-3 (v. 1: alk. paper)—
ISBN 0-8160-6605-1 (v. 2: alk. paper)
1. United States—Armed Forces—
Encyclopedias. 2. United States—Armed Forces—Biography—Encyclopedias. I. Title.

UA23.A875 2005
355'.00973'03—dc22   2004020549

Facts On File books are available at special discounts when purchased in bulk quantities for businesses, associations, institutions, or sales promotions. Please call our Special Sales Department in New York at (212) 967-8800 or (800) 322-8755.

You can find Facts On File on the World Wide Web at http://www.factsonfile.com

Text design by Joan M. Toro
Text design adapted by Erika K. Arroyo
Cover design by Ana Alekseyeva

Printed in the United States of America

VB FOF 10 9 8 7 6 5 4 3 2 1

This book is printed on acid-free paper.

Contents

FLO

List of Entries
UNITED STATES MARINE CORPS

List of Entries

UNITED STATES NAVY

United States Marine Corps

Entries A–Z

A

A-3 Falcon   See AIRCRAFT, FIXED-WING.

A-4 Skyhawk   See AIRCRAFT, FIXED-WING.

A-6 Intruder   See AIRCRAFT, FIXED-WING.

A-12 Avenger   See AIRCRAFT, FIXED-WING.

A-25/SB2C Helldiver   See AIRCRAFT, FIXED-WING.

AAVC-7A1 Assault Amphibian Vehicle Command Model 7A1   See AMPHIBIOUS VEHICLES.

AAVP-7   See AMPHIBIOUS VEHICLES.

AAVR-7A1 Assault Amphibian Vehicle Recovery Model 7A1   See AMPHIBIOUS VEHICLES.

Act of July 11, 1798
The Act of July 11, 1798, was the first U.S. law organizing a "Corps of Marines" from the U.S. Navy's marines. It is titled "An Act for Establishing a Marine Corps" and provided for the three-year enlistment of 32 marines as ship guards. A major was to be chosen as COMMANDANT OF THE MARINE CORPS to administer the USMC. Thirty-two captains and lieutenants were authorized (no distinction was made between first lieutenants and second lieutenants). In addition, 48 sergeants and corporals were authorized, along with 720 privates, 32 fifers, and 32 drummers. While serving ashore, the marines would follow the Articles of War, the same regulations that governed the U.S. Army. Embarked at sea, however, the marines were to be governed by navy regulations. The 1798 legislation did not give the Marine Corps an organization or mission independent of the U.S. Navy. It did, however, provide that the president of the United States might use the USMC as he saw fit.

Act of June 30, 1834
The ACT OF JULY 11, 1798, established the USMC as a separate armed service and roughly put marines under the Articles of War when they served ashore but under navy regulations when they served aboard ships at sea. This left the USMC's role in the defense establishment of the United States rather nebulous. Commandant ARCHIBALD HENDERSON complained that the USMC was effectively isolated, with the army on one side and the navy on the other—and neither

friendly to the corps. Henderson and others agitated for a clearer definition and legal establishment of the USMC as a matter of the survival of the Corps. Congress responded with the Act of June 30, 1834, which specifically provided that "the Marine Corps . . . shall at all times be subject to the laws and regulations established for the government of the Navy, except when detached for service with the Army by order of the President." Not only did this make the USMC's position and governance clearer, it formalized its relationship to the U.S. Navy. For the next 113 years, until the National Security Act of 1947, the USMC was governed by the 1834 law. Only twice during this period did the president see fit to detach the USMC for service with the army: during the U.S.-MEXICAN WAR and during WORLD WAR I. In WORLD WAR II, the USMC functioned closely in coordination with the navy. By the time of the KOREAN WAR, its role had been definitively redefined, along with the roles of the other services, by the National Defense Act.

AD-1 through AD-7 Skyraider   See AIRCRAFT, FIXED-WING.

Advanced Field Artillery Tactical Data System   See INDIRECT FIRE SYSTEMS.

advance guard
A security element that operates ahead of the main body of a moving force. The advance guard operates within the indirect-fire-support range of the main body and is responsible for finding the enemy; for locating gaps, flanks, and other weaknesses in the enemy formation; for determining the enemy's intentions; for preventing the main force from running into an ambush or surprise attack; and for providing cover for the main body, if necessary. The advance guard may also engage and destroy enemy reconnaissance elements, repair roads and bridges, clear obstacles, conduct general reconnaissance, and secure key terrain features, such as high-ground positions.

advance party
A relatively small group of troops or specialists sent ahead of a larger unit to prepare a new site of operations.

African Americans in the USMC
Prior to WORLD WAR II, the USMC accepted no black enlistments. Pursuant to directives from President Franklin D. Roosevelt, however, the COMMANDANT OF THE MARINE CORPS appointed a commission to study how black marines could best be used. However, it was not until after the Japanese attack on Pearl Harbor, December 7, 1941, that actual enlistments were accepted, and a segregated training facility, Camp Johnson, was established outside Marine Corps Base Camp Lejeune. The first recruits arrived at Camp Johnson in August 1942 to make up the 51st Defense Battalion. Initially, DRILL INSTRUCTORS were white, but they were replaced by black instructors as soon as they were available.

African-American marines of the Third Ammunition Battalion ride captured bicycles on Saipan, June 1944. *(National Archives and Records Administration)*

The 51st Defense Battalion was brought to a strength of 1,400 and sent to the Pacific, first in the Ellice Islands and then in the Marshalls. They remained posted there throughout the war. A second black unit, the 52nd Defense Battalion, was established in December 1943 and dispatched to Roi-Namur and then to the Marianas. The black marines were used almost exclusively as stewards and laborers, not as combat troops. In all, 19,000 African Americans served in the USMC. Most had been drafted. No black marine was commissioned an officer during the war. In November 1945, a black second lieutenant was commissioned in the MARINE CORPS RESERVE, and in May 1948, a black man was given a commission in the regular force.

Despite President Harry S. Truman's 1948 Executive Order 9981, calling for an immediate end to segregation in all of the armed forces, the USMC remained segregated, with a 10 percent cap on black enlistments, until the secretary of the navy ordered complete integration of the USN and USMC in mid-1949. Since that time, blacks have been fully integrated as members of the USMC.

AGM-45 Shrike See AIR-LAUNCHED WEAPONS.

AGM-65E Maverick Missile See AIR-LAUNCHED WEAPONS.

AGM-114 Hellfire See AIR-LAUNCHED WEAPONS.

AGM-122 Sidearm See AIR-LAUNCHED WEAPONS.

AGM-123 Skipper II See AIR-LAUNCHED WEAPONS.

AH-1J SeaCobra See AIRCRAFT, ROTARY-WING.

aiguillette
Braided and looped cord that serves as a badge of office for officers who perform specialized staff duty for senior officers or for senior government officials. Presidential USMC aides wear gold aiguillettes, while USMC aides to other officials wear aiguillettes braided in red and gold.

AIM-7 Sparrow See AIR-LAUNCHED WEAPONS.

AIM-9 Sidewinder Missile See AIR-LAUNCHED WEAPONS.

aircraft, fixed-wing
The following fixed-wing aircraft are either currently included in the USMC inventory or are of historical importance in the service.

A-3 Falcon
A Curtiss observation biplane first flown in 1924, the A-3 version was designed for the army and USMC as an attack aircraft. Top speed was 147 miles per hour, and armament consisted of two .30-caliber machine guns firing through the propeller, with two more mounted under the wings. Twin Lewis guns were operated by an observer in the rear cockpit. The aircraft could also carry a modest antipersonnel bomb load.

A-4 Skyhawk
A single-engine daylight attack aircraft designed for the navy and the marines, the A-4 was developed in the 1950s and first delivered in 1962. The principal missions of USMC A-4s are to attack and destroy surface targets in support of landing forces and to escort helicopters. With a wingspan of 26 feet 6 inches, and a length of just over 40 feet, the A-4 can make 586 knots with a 4,000-pound bomb load and has a range of 2,000 miles.

Originally produced by McDonnell Douglas, the A-4 remains in use despite its age. Currently, USMC Reserve squadrons use the A-4M and a

An A-4 Skyhawk deploys ordnance over Vietnam. *(U.S. Marine Corps)*

training version, the TA-4F. Upon its introduction, the navy-version A-4 was the only nuclear-capable strike aircraft available for use in large numbers from aircraft carriers.

A-6 Intruder

Built by Grumman and introduced in 1979, the A-6 Intruder was a two-seat, subsonic, all-weather, carrier-based attack aircraft used by the navy and the USMC. It was designed as a deep-penetration aircraft, capable of night or daylight operation, and it was equipped with repeatedly upgraded avionics and highly advanced weapons-release systems, as well as a single, integrated track and search radar. The A-6E was equipped with a target recognition/attack multi-sensor (TRAM), as well as a chin turret containing a forward-looking infrared (FLIR) system and a laser designator and receiver. In its prime, the Intruder was one of the best all-weather precision bombers in the world. The aircraft was withdrawn from service in 1997.

The Intruder was almost 55 feet long, with a 53-foot wingspan. Crewed by two and powered by a pair of Pratt and Whitney J52-P8B engines, the air-craft had a top speed of 563 knots and a ceiling of 40,600 feet. The Intruder was capable of carrying a wide variety of ordnance, including: 10 2.75-inch Rocket Pods; 10 5-inch Zuni Rocket Pods; 28 Mk-20 Rockeyes; Mk-77 Napalm; 28 Mk-81 250-pound bombs; 28 Mk-82 Snakeyes; 13 Mk-83 1,000-pound bombs; five Mk-84 2,000-pound bombs; 20 Mk-117 750-pound bombs; GBU-10E Laser Guided Bomb; GBU-12D Laser Guided Bomb; GBU-16B Laser Guided Bomb; AGM-123A Skipper II; AGM-45 Shrike; AGM-62 Walleye; and AIM-9 Sidewinder.

A-12 Avenger

This aircraft was planned to replace the navy and USMC A-6 Intruder. It was conceived by McDonnell Douglas/General Dynamics as a subsonic, carrier-based attack aircraft with the most advanced stealth characteristics and was officially designated as an Advanced Technology Aircraft (ATA). The USMC was planning to purchase 238 Avengers, the navy 620, and the air force perhaps 400. Planned to cost $100 million each, the A-12 soon proved more expensive; on January 7, 1991, Secretary of Defense Richard Cheney canceled the program—the largest contract termination in the history of the Department of Defense.

A-25/SB2C Helldiver

The Curtiss Helldiver was first flown in June 1942 and was sent to the Pacific in November 1943. It was intended to replace the venerable Dauntless bomber (A-24) and was larger and capable of carrying more bombs than its predecessor. In the USMC, the Helldiver never completely replaced the Dauntless, although some bombing squadrons used it.

AD-1 through AD-7 Skyraider

The last single-engine, propeller-driven attack bomber built for the U.S. military, the Douglas Skyraider was first flown in March 1945, but did not see service until after WORLD WAR II. Although the aircraft came into being on the verge of the jet era, the Skyraider served in the navy and USMC for 15 years and was flown in attack missions during both the KOREAN WAR and the early part of the VIETNAM WAR.

Although it was designed to carry a single 1,000-pound bomb, its Korean missions often saw it loaded with some five tons of ordnance, an incredible load for this single-engine aircraft. Service ceiling was 25,000 feet and top speed 365 miles per hour. By the end of the Korean War, the USMC had 11 AD squadrons.

AV-8B Harrier II

The Harrier II is a vertical/short takeoff and landing (VSTOL) aircraft of British design used by the USMC for light attack and close air support. Using vectored thrust, the Harrier II jet can take off and land vertically, making it ideal for takeoff and landing from amphibious vessels as well as from unimproved ground landing areas.

The AV-8B replaced the original Harrier in 1984 and is crewed by a single pilot. The aircraft is a little over 46 feet long, with a wingspan of 30 feet 4 inches. Its single Rolls Royce F402-RR-408 jet engine delivers 23,800 pounds of thrust, which gives the aircraft a top speed of 661 miles per hour. Ferry range is 2,840 miles; its combat range is 165 miles with a full bomb load. Armament includes a GAU-12 five-barrel 25-mm cannon with 300 rounds. Six wing pylons on each wing can accommodate a total of nearly 8,000 pounds of bombs or other ordnance, including B-61 nuclear bombs, ADM-65 Maverick missiles, and AIM-9 Sidewinder missiles.

Boeing PW-9

A post–WORLD WAR I single-seat, all-metal pursuit plane first produced in 1926 by Boeing, the PW-9 was built mainly for the U.S. Navy and U.S. Army Air Corps, but was also flown briefly by the USMC. It was one of the last of the biplane fighters, with a top speed of 163 miles per hour and a ceiling of 20,000 feet.

C-12 Huron

This twin turbo-prop airplane is used by the USMC, as well as the army, air force, and navy, as a transport and utility aircraft. It is sometimes used to support attaché and military assistance advisory missions. The Huron is crewed by a pilot and copilot and carries up to eight passengers. Its length is almost 44 feet, its wingspan 54 feet 6 inches, and it is powered by two Pratt and Whitney PT6A-41 turboprops. Maximum speed is 333 miles per hour, ceiling is 35,000 feet, and range is 2,140 miles.

Dauntless Bombers

The Dauntless A-24 dive bomber, also built in a scout bomber version, was designed by Douglas Aircraft for the USN and USMC in the 1930s and served in the Pacific during World War II until it was replaced by the SB2 dive bomber from Curtiss in mid-1943.

The Dauntless was powered by a Wright engine and could achieve 255 miles per hour. Armament consisted of two .50-caliber guns firing through the prop and twin-mounted .50s operated by the radio operator/observer in the rear cockpit. Rigged for dive bombing, the Dauntless carried a single 1,000-pound bomb under the fuselage and two 100-pound bombs on wing racks. The USMC used the Dauntless at GUADALCANAL and in every USMC close air support–mission through the Philippines campaign.

EA-6B Prowler

The USMC flies the EA-6B Prowler primarily to provide airborne Command and Control (C^2) support to FLEET MARINE FORCES, including electronic attack (EA), tactical electronic support (ES), electronic protection (EP), and high-speed anti-radiation missile (HARM) defense. The aircraft collects tactical electronic order-of-battle data, which is immediately and in real time disseminated to field commanders. The data can also be recorded and processed for analysis after missions. Additionally, the aircraft provides a platform for active radar jamming support for assault aircraft as well as ground units. Using HARM missiles, the Prowler acts against enemy air defenses.

USMC Prowlers operate from land bases or from aircraft carriers. As of late 2003, the USMC inventory included 20 Prowlers in four active squadrons. General characteristics of the aircraft include:

> **Manufacturer:** Grumman Aircraft Corporation
> **Power plant:** two Pratt and Whitney J52-P408 turbofan engines
> **Thrust:** 11,200 lb per engine
> **Length:** 59 ft
> **Height:** 15 ft
> **Wing span:** 53 ft
> **Speed, maximum:** Mach .99
> **Ceiling:** 40,000 ft
> **Maximum takeoff weight:** 61,500 lb
> **Range:** Unrefueled—977.5 mi; Refueled— unlimited
> **Armament:** ALQ-99 Tactical Jamming System (TJS); High Speed Anti-Radiation Missile (HARM)
> **Sensors:** ALQ-99 On-board System (OBS)
> **Crew:** four

F2A Buffalo

This single-seat, single-engine fighter was built by Brewster Aeronautical and ordered by the navy and USMC in 1938 as a carrier-based fighter. In early combat with Japanese Zeros, the Buffalo was outclassed. Although speedy at 337 miles per hour, its slow rate of climb and limited maneuverability were lethal handicaps. The aircraft was considered obsolete well before the end of the first year of World War II Pacific combat.

F2H Banshee

This single-seat jet fighter was built by McDonnell Douglas and flown in prototype in 1947, then delivered to the navy and USMC in the early 1950s. The F2H-2, flown by the USMC, was powered by two Westinghouse engines, which propelled the jet to 600 miles per hour and a ceiling of 50,000 feet. Action radius was 600 miles. By 1953, the Banshee was obsolete.

F2T Black Widow

A twin-engine, twin-boom night fighter built by North American Aviation Company for the U.S. Army Air Forces, the aircraft was also used by USMC squadrons in the Pacific late in World War II. Radar equipped, the aircraft carried a pilot, gunner, and radar operator and was formidably armed with four 20-mm cannon and four .50-caliber machine guns.

F4-B Phantom II

The McDonnell Douglas Phantom II was adopted by the air force, navy, and USMC in 1960 and was produced through 1979. With a top speed of more than Mach 2, the Phantom II had an operating radius of 900 miles and could carry heavy weapon loads of eight tons, including Sparrow III and Sidewinder missiles. In 1966, the USMC took delivery of the F4-J modification, designed for ground attack. It was this version the USMC used extensively in the Vietnam War.

F4D Skyray

This Douglas jet was built for the U.S. Navy and intended primarily for carrier operations, but was also adopted by the USMC as a fighter and fighter-bomber. The first production model was flown in 1954 and was delivered to the USN and USMC four years later.

As its name suggests, the Skyray was a delta-wing design. Its Pratt and Whitney J57-P-813 turbojet engine with afterburner was capable of Mach 1.06, and it could carry ordnance loads of 2,000-pound bombs, Sidewinder (AIM-9C/D) missiles, and rocket pods with up to 19 rockets per pod. The aircraft was produced through December 1958.

F4F Wildcat

This single-seat Grumman fighter was introduced as a carrier aircraft in 1940 and went into service (version F4F-3) with the USMC in 1941. It was the principal USMC fighter from the beginning of World War II until 1943. Top speed was 315 miles per hour, with a service ceiling of 34,000 feet and a range of 925 miles. The plane was armed with six .50-caliber wing guns and could carry two 250-pound bombs on wing racks. The Wildcat was indispensable in many USMC Pacific operations, especially the defense of WAKE ISLAND and the GUADALCANAL campaign.

F4U Corsair

Built by Chance Vought, this single-engine, gull-wing, carrier-based fighter was used extensively by the navy and USMC during World War II. The first models were flown in June 1942, and production continued through the end of the war, until 1947.

The Corsair was an extraordinary fighter, capable of speeds in excess of 450 miles per hour and with a ceiling of 20,000 feet. The Corsair outmatched the Japanese Zero and other fighters, although USN aviators found it difficult to operate from carriers. USMC pilots, who flew from island bases, had no operating problems, and by the middle of 1943, the F4U was the standard USMC fighter. It also served as a bomber for close air support.

F6F Hellcat

The Hellcat was a navy and USMC single-seat fighter designed early in 1942, deliberately incorporating certain features of the Japanese Zero, which at the time was outperforming all U.S. aircraft. Designed and produced quickly, the Hellcat was first flown in August 1942 and was sent to the Pacific, first seeing action at Marcus Island in September 1943. The USN widely adopted the Hellcat, while the USMC used it along with the older F4U Corsair.

The Hellcat had a top speed of 375 miles per hour, a ceiling of 36,000 feet, and a range of 1,050 miles without drop tanks. Armament consisted of six .50-caliber wing guns, and it could carry a pair of 1,000-pound bombs. The Grumman Aircraft Corporation produced more than 10,000 Hellcats before production stopped in December 1945.

F8 Crusader

The Vought Crusader was first flown in 1955. The USMC flew the F8D version, introduced in 1960 and powered by a Pratt and Whitney turbojet that drove it to Mach 2. Operating radius was 600 miles. In 1967, the USMC upgraded the D version to the H version.

The F8D and F8H were equipped with state-of-the-art radar systems and armed with four 20-mm cannon and four Sidewinder missiles, fired from the side of the fuselage. The aircraft flew extensively during the Vietnam War.

F8C-5 Helldiver

This Curtiss two-seat biplane was put into U.S. Navy service in 1922 and first delivered to the USMC in the 1930s. Top speed was 140 miles per hour with a service ceiling of 18,000 feet. Built as a fighter, the aircraft was completely obsolete at the outbreak of World War II.

F9F-8 Cougar

The Cougar was a swept-wing version of the straight-wing F9F-1, the first jet aircraft produced by Grumman. Equipped with a J48 Pratt and Whitney engine, the F9F-8 had a top speed of 712 miles per hour and a service ceiling of 42,000 feet, with a range of 1,100 miles. Armament consisted of four nose-mounted, 20-mm cannon and wing racks for bombs, rockets, or Sidewinder missiles. The F9F-8 entered service with the USMC during the late 1950s and continued in service until the end of the 1960s.

F9F Panther

The Grumman Panther was a single-seat jet fighter first flown in 1946 and delivered to the USMC (as the F9F-2 series) in 1948. The F9F-5 version was adopted after 1950 and served as the first-line USMC fighter until the mid-1950s, when it was replaced by the FJ-1 Fury. The F9F-5 had a maximum speed of 625 miles per hour and a service ceiling above 50,000 feet. Armed with four 20-mm cannon, it was also equipped with wing racks for bombs, rockets, or napalm.

F/A-18A/C/CN Hornet

The USMC F/A-18A/C/CN Hornet is tasked with intercepting and destroying enemy aircraft in concert with ground or airborne fighter control and under all-weather conditions. In addition, the Hornet provides close air support in day or night conditions. Another mission is day and night deep air support, consisting of radar search and attack, interdiction, and strikes against enemy installations. Secondarily, the Hornet provides armed escort of friendly aircraft. USMC Hornets may be deployed from aircraft carriers, advanced land bases, and expeditionary airfields. The USMC F/A-18A/C/CN strike fighter was designed to replace the F4-B Phantom II.

As of 2004, the USMC had 168 of the aircraft deployed in 10 active and four reserve squadrons. The service first used them in Operation Desert Storm (PERSIAN GULF WAR). USMC Hornet squadrons flew more than 4,600 sorties without combat loss.

General characteristics of the aircraft include:

Manufacturer: Boeing-McDonnell Douglas
Propulsion: two General Electric F404-GE-400 afterburning, low-bypass turbofan engines
Thrust: 16,000 lb per engine
Length: 56 ft
Wing span: 37.5 ft
Cruise speed: high subsonic to supersonic
Ferry range: over 2,300 mi
Range, fighter mission: 460 mi
Range, attack mission: 661.25 mi
Armament: nine external wing stations, comprising two wingtip stations for an assortment of air-to-air and air-to-ground weapons, including AIM-7 Sparrows, AIM-9 Sidewinders, AMRAAMs, AGM-84 Harpoons, and AGM-65 Maverick missiles; two inboard wing stations for external fuel tanks or air-to-ground stations; two nacelle fuselage stations for either Sparrows or AN/AAS-38 Forward Looking Infrared Radar (FLIR) pods; and a center station for fuel tank or air-to-ground weapons. Air-to-ground weapons include GBU-10 and -12 laser-guided bombs, Mk-80 series general purpose bombs, and CBU-59 cluster bombs. An M61 six-barrel 20-mm gun is mounted in the nose and has a Boeing-McDonnell Douglas director gunsight.
Crew: one

F/A-18D Hornet

The mission of the USMC F/A-18D Hornet is to attack and destroy surface targets, day or night, under all weather conditions; to conduct multi-sensor imagery reconnaissance; to provide supporting arms coordination; and to intercept and destroy enemy aircraft under all weather conditions. The aircraft conducts day and night deep air support, in all weather. This includes armed reconnaissance, radar search and attack, interdiction, and strikes against enemy installations. Additionally, the F/A-18D conducts multi-sensor imagery reconnaissance, including prestrike and poststrike target damage assessment and visual reconnaissance. By day or night, the F/A-18D provides supporting arms coordination, including forward air control, tactical air coordination, and artillery/naval gunfire spotting. In concert with ground and airborne fighter direction, the F/A-18D intercepts and destroys enemy aircraft. Secondarily, the aircraft can provide battlefield illumination and target illumination and conduct armed escort of friendly aircraft. USMC F/A-18Ds operate from aircraft carriers, advanced bases, and expeditionary airfields.

As of 2004, the USMC maintained 72 aircraft in six active squadrons. The USMC first deployed these aircraft in combat during Operation Desert Storm (Persian Gulf War) in 1991. They were used to provide target location and identification, threat updates, and the overall battlefield situation. A single F/A-18D controlled as many as 20 strike fighters in a 30-minute period.

General characteristics of the F/A-18D include:

Manufacturer: Boeing-McDonnell Douglas
Propulsion: two General Electric F404-GE-400 afterburning, low-bypass turbofan engines
Thrust: 16,000 lb per engine
Length: 56 ft
Wing span: 37.5 ft
Cruise speed: high subsonic to supersonic
Ferry range: over 2,300 mi
Combat radius, fighter mission: 460 mi
Combat radius, attack mission: 661.25 mi
Armament: nine external wing stations, comprising two wingtip stations for AIM-9 Sidewinder air-to-air missiles; two outboard wing stations for an assortment of air-to-air and air-to-ground weapons, including AIM-

7 Sparrows, AIM-9 Sidewinders, AMRAAMs, AGM-84 Harpoons, and AGM-65 Maverick missiles; two inboard wing stations for external fuel tanks or air-to-ground stations; two nacelle fuselage stations for Sparrows or AN/AAS-38 Forward Looking Infrared Radar (FLIR) pods; and a center station for fuel tank or air-to-ground weapons such as GBU-10 and -12 laser-guided bombs, Mk-80 series general purpose bombs, and CBU-59 cluster bombs. An M61 six-barrel 20-mm gun is mounted in the nose and has a Boeing-McDonnell Douglas director gunsight.

Crew: Two

FJ1-FJ4 Fury

This series of North American aircraft were carrier-oriented versions of the F-86 Saberjet flown by the USAF in the Korean War. Five USMC squadrons flew the FJ2 during the Korean War, and the fighter remained the principal USMC jet fighter until it was replaced by the F8U Crusader late in the 1950s.

The FJ2 Fury had a top speed of 650 miles per hour and a service ceiling of 45,000 feet. Its range was 1,000 miles.

KC-130 Hercules

The four-engine Hercules cargo aircraft was designed by Lockheed in 1952 and has been modified for various cargo and transport functions and even as a gunship for close air support. The USMC uses a version modified as an in-flight tanker,

A USMC KC-130 Hercules   *(U.S. Marine Corps)*

including versions capable of refueling fixed-wing aircraft and helicopters. The version built to refuel helicopters, HC-130P, can also be used to retrieve parachute-borne payloads. All USMC Hercules are also capable of use for tactical transport.

The KC-130 is powered by four Allison T56-A-16 engines to a top speed of 362.25 miles per hour and a service ceiling of 30,000 feet. The aircraft is 97 feet 9 inches long, with a 41-foot cargo compartment. Wing span is 132 feet 7 inches and maximum takeoff weight is 175,000 pounds. Tanker capacity is 10,183 to 13,280 gallons, depending on configuration. As a tanker, the Hercules's range is 1,000 nautical miles; as a cargo carrier, it is 2,875 miles.

Mitchell PBJ

During World War II, the USMC flew this medium bomber (designated by the USAAF as the B-25) in its seven USMC bomber squadrons. Built by North American Aviation Company, the Mitchell was crewed by five and could carry 3,000 pounds of bombs in the bomb bay and another 2,400 pounds on wing racks. Top speed was 300 miles per hour with a service ceiling of 24,000 feet. Modified as the PBJ-15, the Mitchell employed radar to guide night rocket attacks against Japanese positions in the Marianas.

OE-1 Bird Dog

A single-engine Cessna introduced during the 1950s primarily as a reconnaissance and surveillance aircraft. OE-1 is the USMC and navy designation; the air force and army, which use the plane primarily as a liaison aircraft, designate it O-1.

Length is 25 feet 9 inches, with a wingspan of 36 feet and a gross weight of 2,399 pounds. Its powerplant is a single Continental O-470 piston engine making 213 horsepower and driving the aircraft to a maximum speed of 150 miles per hour. Range is 530 miles and ceiling 20,300 feet.

OV-10 Bronco

This twin-turboprop armed reconnaissance aircraft was used by the USMC in counterinsurgency operations; until 1993, it was also used for light

Until it was replaced in 1993, the Bronco was a USMC workhorse.   *(U.S. Marine Corps)*

attack, helicopter escort, forward air control, and general reconnaissance. The aircraft entered production in 1967 and saw extensive service in the Vietnam War.

Crewed by two, the OV-10 can carry 3,200 pounds of cargo, five paratroopers, or two litter patients and attendants. The USMC has modified some OV-10s as Night Observations Surveillance (NOS) aircraft.

The Bronco is 44 feet long, with a wingspan of 40 feet. It is powered by twin Garrett T-76-G-420 turboprop engines and can reach a top speed of 288 miles per hour. Its combat radius is 228 miles. Armament typically consists of two sponsons mounted on the fuselage, each of which houses four 7.62-mm machine guns. Additionally the sponsons are racked for two 600-pound bombs each, or for rocket pods or auxiliary fuel tanks. Other armament configurations are also possible.

In 1993, the USMC replaced the OV-10 with the F/A-18D Hornet for forward air control, light attack, close-support, and tactical air control missions.

PBY-5A Catalina

The USMC adopted this twin-engine Consolidated Aircraft design as an amphibious plane prior to World War II. Whereas the U.S. Navy used it mainly for long-range reconnaissance during the war, the USMC used the Catalina for logistics and for long-range VIP transport. The Catalina was slow, but it had a range of 2,500 miles.

R4D Skytrain

Better known by its U.S. Army designation, C-47, and its civilian passenger transport designation, DC-3, the USMC R4D was used in the Pacific theater for airborne supply and transport. All Skytrains were powered by two Pratt and Whitney R-1830 engines and had a cruising speed of 230 miles per hour and a service ceiling of 10,000 feet. The first DC-3 aircraft were produced in 1935. A surprisingly large number are still in service in civilian applications.

T-34C Turbo Mentor

Primary trainer used by the USMC and USN and nicknamed the Tormentor. The aircraft is a two-seat turboprop Beechcraft, based on a 1934 design updated in 1973.

Student and instructor sit in tandem. The plane is 28 feet 8 inches long and has a wingspan of 33 feet 4 inches. The aircraft is powered by a 715-horsepower Pratt and Whitney PT6A-25 turboprop, offset to the right and down from the centerline to give the aircraft a jetlike feel in preparation for the student's step up to a jet trainer. Maximum speed is 240 miles per hour, range is 345 miles, and ceiling is about 30,000 feet. Up to 1,200 pounds of weapons can be carried, typically for armament training.

T-44 Pegasus

A twin-engine light-transport aircraft modified from the Beechcraft King Air C90 for use in the advanced training of USMC, navy, and Coast Guard multiengine pilots. The plane can accommodate two crew and up to eight passengers. It is 35 feet 6 inches long, with a wingspan of 50 feet 3 inches, and is powered by two Pratt and Whitney PT6A-34B turboprops, each producing 750 horsepower. Cruising speed is 256 miles per hour, range is 1,474 miles, and ceiling is 28,100 feet.

T-45A Goshawk

A tandem-seat McDonnell Douglas jet trainer used by USMC and U.S. Navy pilots. Procurement of this carrier-capable aircraft began in 1988. Length is 39 feet 2 inches, wingspan 30 feet 8 inches, powerplant is a Rolls-Royce F-405-RR-400. The aircraft has a top speed of 620 miles per hour, a range of 950 miles, and a service ceiling of 50,000 feet.

TA-4J Skyhawk

An advanced jet trainer used by the USMC and U.S. Navy until it was replaced by the T-45 Goshawk beginning in 1988.

aircraft, rotary-wing

The following rotary-wing aircraft are either currently included in the USMC inventory or are of historical importance in the service.

AH-1J SeaCobra

This Bell Helicopter design is a version of the AH-1 Cobra series that was specifically designed for the USMC. The AH-1J has a twin turboshaft powered by an 1,800-horsepower PW T400-CP-400 engine and carries a night-vision system. Armament includes a three-barrel 20-mm cannon in a chin turret. An attack helicopter, the AH-1J can launch Hellfire, TOW, and Sidewinder missiles. Top speed is 141 miles per hour, ceiling is 12,000 feet, range 315 miles, endurance three hours. The helicopter is crewed by a pilot and copilot, who also serves as gunner, seated in tandem behind the pilot.

Bell introduced the Model 209 Huey Cobra in 1965. A single-engine AH-1G Huey Cobra was acquired for the U.S. Army, and the two-engine AH-1J SeaCobra for the USMC. Deliveries to both services began in 1969. In 1977, the USMC began taking delivery of the AH-1T Improved Cobra, and, in 1986, the AH-lW Super Cobra.

CH-37

Sometimes referred to by its army designation, Mojave, the CH-37 was a Sikorsky-built helicopter introduced in 1955 and powered by two 2,100-horsepower engines mounted in outboard nacelles affixed to wing stubs. The CH-37 could cruise at 130 miles per hour over a range of 145 miles, carrying 20 marines or 24 litter patients in addition to a two-person crew. Configured to carry cargo, the helicopter had the advantage of loading and unloading through a clamshell door in the nose or through a rear door.

CH-46 Sea Knight

Since 1964, the Sea Knight has been the primary assault helicopter of the USMC. As of 2005, the MV-22 Osprey tilt-rotor aircraft is slated to replace the Sea Knight.

The Sea Knight is a tandem-rotor, medium-lift helicopter, which can carry 10,000 pounds of cargo, 17 troops, or 15 litter patients. The craft is equipped with a rear ramp to expedite loading and unloading. The Sea Knight is amphibious and can land on land or water.

The Sea Knight is 46 feet 8 inches long, with a rotor diameter of 51 feet. It is powered by two GE T58-GE-16 turboshaft engines, can reach 166 miles per hour, and has an assault range of 173 miles (ferry range is 650 miles). The ship's operating ceiling is 14,000 feet. The Sea Knight ordinarily carries no weapons, although two .50-caliber machine guns can be readily fitted. The USMC inventory includes about six Sea Knights specially modified for VIP transport service; these are based at Andrews Air Force Base, outside of Washington, D.C.

View of a USMC CH-46D Sea Knight   *(U.S. Marine Corps)*

CH-53D Sea Stallion

This all-weather, heavy-lift assault helicopter can carry 55 troops with equipment (or 24 litter patients, with four attendants) or 18,500 pounds of cargo, including heavy equipment and vehicles. The helicopter entered USMC service in 1966 and has been continuously upgraded since.

Sea Stallion is used in assault as well as in mine-countermeasure roles, and two Sea Stallions have been specially modified for VIP transport with MARINE HELICOPTER SQUADRON ONE (HMX-1). Crew consists of a pilot, copilot, and crewman; the RH-53D mine countermeasures configuration has seven crew members. The helicopter is 67 feet long, with a rotor diameter of 72 feet 3 inches, and is powered by two GE T64-GE-412/413 turboshafts, which can drive the Sea Stallion to 196 miles per hour and a maximum ceiling of 21,000 feet. Ordinarily, the Sea Stallion is unarmed, but it can be fitted with two 0.5-inch machine guns. Also see CH-53E Super Stallion.

CH-53E Super Stallion

The largest helicopter in U.S. service, the CH-53E is flown by the U.S. Navy and USMC and is used in assault and heavy lift operation. Similar in appearance to the CH-53D Sea Stallion, the Super Stallion has three engines (General Electric T64-GE-416) instead of two, is longer, and sports a seven-blade rotor instead of the conventional six-blade rotor. The additional power gives the Super Stallion almost twice the lifting capacity of the Sea Stallion—16 tons—and can lift more than 90 percent of the heavy equipment used by a USMC division.

The Super Stallion is crewed by a pilot, copilot, and crew chief and can carry 55 fully equipped troops. Its length is 73 feet 4 inches, and rotor diameter is 79 feet. Top speed is 195 miles per hour, with an 18,500-foot service ceiling. Like the Sea Stallion, the Super Stallion is normally unarmed, but can be fitted with 0.5-inch machine guns. Additionally, it can be equipped with Stinger missiles and AIM-9L Sidewinders.

HH-1H Iroquois

This light-lift helicopter is crewed by a pilot and, optionally, a flight engineer. The USMC uses the Iroquois principally for rescue and utility purposes. Forty-two feet long, the HH-1H has a rotor

A USMC HH-1H Iroquois light-lift helicopter   *(U.S. Marine Corps)*

diameter of 48 feet 4 inches, weighs 9,500 pounds, can carry 2,400 pounds of cargo, and is equipped with a single Lycoming turboshaft engine, which propels the ship to 133 miles per hour. Its range is 345 miles, with a ceiling of 15,000 feet. The helicopter is unarmed.

HRP Rescuer ("Flying Banana")

This large, twin-rotor Piasecki-built helicopter was introduced at the end of WORLD WAR II, in March 1945, and flew with the navy and USMC as late as 1962. Dubbed by sailors and marines the "Flying Banana" because of its elongated shape and upturned aft portion, the HRP was produced in two versions, a fabric-skin HRP-1 and an all-metal HRP-2. The navy used the HRP mainly for rescue, while the USMC conducted extensive experimentation with an airborne assault role.

Length was 54 feet, rotor span 41 feet, top speed 104 miles per hour. The helicopter's twin rotors were driven by a single Pratt and Whitney 600-horsepower engine.

RH-53D

The mine-countermeasures version of the CH-53 Sea Stallion. The RH-53D is currently used by Marine Air Reserve units.

Tactical Bulk Fuel Delivery System, CH-53E (TBFDS, CH-53E)

The Tactical Bulk Fuel Delivery System, CH-53E supports the USMC's over-the-horizon concept—that is, the tactical ability to operate as an expeditionary force at great range. TBFDS, CH-53E is a three-tank, air-transportable fuel-delivery, forward area refueling, range-extension system consisting of four subsystems: three 800-gallon fuel tanks, a restraint system, an electrical fuel control panel, and a Forward Area Refueling Equipment (FARE) system. The system is ballistically self-sealing and crashworthy.

As configured together, the system allows the CH-53E Super Stallion helicopter to transport and dispense aviation fuel to aircraft or tactical ground vehicles at forward landing zones or Forward Area Refueling Points (FARP). The system's three internal fuel tanks can be rapidly installed and removed from the CH-53E's cargo area to transform any Super Stallion into a tanker. The installation procedure can be carried out by a crew of four in under an hour. Removal takes less than 40 minutes. This quick conversion allows for rapid mission changes, freeing up the helicopter for other missions as required. Also, the system is designed to permit one, two, or three tanks to be installed, as the need may be. The installed internal tanks may be refilled while on the ground or in flight. They can accept fuel through the helicopter's single-point pressure refueling adapter, the in-flight refueling probe, or via the tank manifold or filler opening in the top of each tank. The system is equipped with internal pumps, which can be used to transfer fuel to the helicopter's tanks, thereby extending its range, or dispensed to other aircraft or vehicles using the Forward Area Refueling Equipment (FARE). The FARE subsystem is two-point capable, with a combined flow rate of 120 gallons per minute, and 200 feet separation from the host aircraft to the aircraft or vehicles being refueled.

General characteristics of the Tactical Bulk Fuel Delivery System, CH-53E (TBFDS, CH-53E) include:

> **Contractor:** Serv-Air, Inc., Lexington, Kentucky (prime), Robertson Aviation, Inc. (subcontractor)
> **Capacity:** 2,400 gallons in three 800-gallon tanks
> **Tank length:** 62 in
> **Tank width:** 58 in
> **Tank height:** 64 in
> **Weight, empty:** 600 lb per tank
> **Weight, full (JP-5/8 fuel):** 6,100 lb per tank
> **Operating area:** Cargo area of the helicopter
> **Aircraft:** CH-53E Super Stallion
> **Ballistic tolerances:** Self-sealing and crash resistant
> **Crashworthiness:** 10 G forward; 7.5 G aft; 3 G vertical; 3 G lateral

UH-34/VH-34 Seahorse

The Sikorsky UH-34 helicopter was introduced in 1954 and was a large utility helicopter capable of transporting 18 troops or carrying eight stretchers. The VH-34 version was modified for VIP transport and could carry 12 passengers. Both aircraft have a top speed just under 100 miles per hour and a service ceiling of 9,500 miles. Range was short, at only 250 miles. The USMC made extensive use of the utility version of the helicopter in the VIET-NAM WAR and used the VH-34 to transport senior officials.

V-22 Osprey

This medium-lift, high-speed, rotary-wing V/STOL aircraft was designed and built by Bell-Boeing to replace the USMC's principal assault helicopters, the CH-46E Sea Knight and CH-53A/D Sea Stallion. Two 6,150-shaft-horsepower turboshaft engines drive two three-bladed proprotors, each 38 feet in diameter and mounted as tiltrotors, which can be angled forward to drive the aircraft as a conventional fixed-wing airplane or angled vertically, to fly it as a helicopter. Thus the Osprey combines the vertical flight capabilities of a helicopter with the speed and range of a turboprop airplane. The development program began in 1986, and the first operational test period took place during 1994. Unfortunately, the Osprey was plagued by accidents, some fatal, which have called into question the viability of the aircraft as built and perhaps even the design. USMC command placed such a high priority on the aircraft that some testing procedures were called into question; however, in 2004, the Osprey finally entered active service with the USMC.

The Osprey functions primarily in the amphibious assault transport of marines, equipment, and supplies from assault ships and land bases. The Osprey is 57 feet 4 inches long, with a wingspan of 84 feet 7 inches. Range is 200 nautical miles, carrying 18 to 24 assault-equipped marines. Cruise airspeed is 240 knots.

VH-3D Sea King

Marine Helicopter Squadron One uses the VH-3D and the VH-60N Seahawk for presidential transport and for other VIP transport. Built by Sikorsky, the VH-3D began service in 1962 and has been continuously updated. Crewed by three, the VH-3D is 72 feet 9 inches long, with a rotor diameter of 62 feet. It is powered by two General Electric T58-GE-400B turboshafts and can reach 160 miles per hour. Service ceiling is 14,700 feet.

VH-60A Black Hawk

This is the USMC version of the U.S. Army's UH-60 Black Hawk helicopter. The VH-60A is flown by the Executive Flight Detachment of Helicopter Squadron One, which is assigned to transport VIPs. The VH-60A is used for routine VIP transport as well as for emergency evacuation of government officials.

The VH-60A is crewed by two pilots and a crew chief and can carry up to 14 passengers. Fuselage length is 50 feet, height 16 feet 10 inches, and the diameter of the four-bladed rotor is 53 feet 8 inches. Two General Electric T700-GE-700/701C turboshafts power the aircraft, which can cruise at 145 miles per hour and with a range of 500 miles using auxiliary tanks. Ceiling is 19,000 feet.

VH-60N Seahawk

With the VH-3D Sea King, the VH-60N is used by Marine Helicopter Squadron One for presidential transport and for other VIP transport. Top speed is 184 miles per hour, and range is 320 miles. The aircraft seats 10 passengers in addition to a pilot, copilot, crew chief, and a communication system operator. The VH-60N can be folded in less than two hours for loading and storage onto a USAF C-5A/B, C-17, C-130, or C-141.

The VH-60N is a single main rotor, twin-engine helicopter produced by Sikorsky Aircraft Division of United Technologies.

air defense artillery

The following air defense artillery weapons are currently included in the marine inventory:

Avenger

The Avenger is an air-defense system used by both the USMC and the army. Typically mounted on a vehicle, the Avenger system employs a variety of sensors (including infrared, laser, and optical) to guide the fire of Stinger missiles or .50-caliber machine guns against low-flying, high-speed, fixed-wing aircraft and helicopters.

FIM-92A Stinger

This shoulder-launched antiaircraft rocket is designed to be fired by a single marine and provides passive infrared and ultraviolet "fire and forget" homing on low-flying aircraft. The FIM-92A is a 5-foot-long missile, capable of Mach 2, and loaded with a high-explosive warhead. Its range is in excess of three miles and it is designed to hit targets as low as 33 feet and as high as 15,750 feet. The FIM-92A is in service with the USMC, USA, USAF, and USN.

HAWK

This is an acronym for the MIM-23B "Homing All the Way Killer" medium-range surface-to-air missile system. HAWK systems provide medium-altitude air defense coverage for ground forces. The system was first introduced in 1960. Its homing system is semiactive, and has a two-stage solid-fuel motor capable of attaining Mach 2.5. The missile, 16.5 feet long and 15 inches in diameter, has a range of 24 miles and carries a 120-pound proximity-fuse warhead.

HAWK is fired by a specialized platoon, equipped with an acquisition and tracking radar as well as an optical tracking system. The typical platoon carries four launchers, each with three missiles.

Stinger Weapons System: RMP and Basic

Stinger Weapons Systems are close-in, surface-to-air weapons for the defense of forward combat areas, vital areas, and other installations against low-altitude air attacks. The Stinger is man-portable and shoulder-fired. It launches a guided missile, which enables an individual marine to engage low-altitude jet, propeller-driven, and helicopter aircraft.

The system was developed by the United States Army Missile Command as a follow-up to the Redeye Weapon System. The Stinger is a "fire-and-for-get" weapon, which uses a passive infrared seeker and proportional navigation system. Fired in the general direction of the target, its heat-seeking IR sensor homes in on the heat source, typically the aircraft's engine. The latest Stingers incorporate all-aspect engagement capability and IFF (Identification-Friend-or-Foe), as well as improved range, maneuverability, and significant countermeasures immunity.

The Stinger missile is packaged within a disposable launch tube. It is delivered as a certified round, requiring no field testing or direct support maintenance. A gripstock, separable and reusable, is attached to the round prior to use.

In addition to the shoulder-fired configuration, Stingers may be installed on the Pedestal-Mounted Stinger Air Defense Vehicle and the LAV-AD, the Light Armored Vehicle, Air Defense Variant. As of the end of 2003, the USMC had 13,431 Stinger missiles in its inventory.

General characteristics of the Stinger Weapons Systems include:

Manufacturer: General Dynamics/Raytheon Corporation
Propulsion: dual-thrust solid fuel rocket motor
Length: 5 ft
Width: 5.5 in
Weight: 12.5 lb
Weight fully armed: 34.5 lb
Maximum system span: 3.6 in
Range: 1 to 8 km
Fuzing: penetration, impact, self-destruct
Ceiling: 10,000 ft
Speed: supersonic
Crew: two enlisted marines
Guidance system: fire-and-forget passive infrared seeker
Warheads: high explosive
Rate of fire: one missile every three to seven sec

The Stinger was introduced to the USMC inventory in 1982. In 1989 the USMC began fielding an improved Stinger, equipped with a reprogrammable microprocessor (RPM), a modular enhancement that allows the Stinger to engage and destroy more sophisticated air threats.

air-launched weapons

USMC aviators use the following air-launched weapons systems.

AGM-45 Shrike

The AGM-45 Shrike is an air-to-surface antiradiation missile, which homes in on hostile antiaircraft radar. It was developed by the navy's Naval Weapons Center at China Lake in 1963 and is still used by the USMC, USN, and USAF as well as by the air force of Israel.

General characteristics of the AGM-45 Shrike include:

Propulsion: solid-fuel rocket
Length: 10 ft
Weight: 390 lb
Diameter: 8 in
Warhead: conventional
Span: 3 ft
Guidance: passive radar homing
Platforms: A-4 Skyhawk, A-6 Intruder

AGM-65E Maverick Missile

The AGM-65E Maverick is an air-to-surface missile designed expressly for use against tanks. The AGM-65E version has been especially adapted as the USMC laser Maverick weapon for use from USMC aircraft. The USMC also uses Maverick versions with electro-optical or infrared guidance.

General characteristics of the AGM-65E Maverick missile include:

Propulsion: solid-fuel rocket
Length: 8 ft, 6 in
Weight: 630 lb
Span: 2 ft, 4 in
Diameter: 12 in
Guidance: laser (AGM-65E version only)
Warhead: conventional, with 300-lb blast/ penetration
Platforms: F/A-18A/C/CN Hornet, F/A-18D Hornet, and AV-8B Harrier II

AGM-114 Hellfire

This air-to-ground missile system provides heavy antiarmor capability for attack helicopters. The first three generations of Hellfire missiles use a laser seeker, while the latest, fourth-generation missile, Longbow Hellfire, uses a radar frequency seeker. The first-generation missiles constitute the main armament of the U.S. Army's AH-64 Apache and USMC's AH-1W Super Cobra helicopters. The missiles were introduced in 1982 by Martin Marietta and Rockwell International.

An AGM-114B Hellfire missile roars off the rails of a U.S. Navy SH-60 Seahawk helicopter toward a laser designated surface target during training off the coast of San Clemente Island, California, on August 25, 1999. *(Department of Defense)*

The AGM-114K Hellfire II missile incorporates dual warheads for defeating reactive armor, electro-optical countermeasures hardening, semiactive laser seeker, and a programmable autopilot for trajectory shaping. The planned Longbow Hellfire missile will provide an adverse-weather, fire-and-forget, heavy antiarmor capability for attack helicopters.

The Hellfire missile is 5 feet 4 inches long, weighs 99 pounds, and is propelled by a Thiokol TX657 solid-propellant rocket motor. Its range is more than three miles.

AGM-122 Sidearm

The AGM-122 is a small, supersonic anti-radiation missile carried on the army AH-64A/D Apache and USMC AH-1W SuperCobra attack helicopters for self-defense against antiaircraft guns and SAM radars. The AGM-122 uses an AIM-9C Sidewinder guidance section modified to detect and track ground-based enemy radar, to home in on that radar, and to attack it.

The Sidearm retains the Sidewinder's original Mk-17 motor and WDU-17 warhead, but substitutes a DSU-15 active fuse and a modification of control electronics to provide a dive attack on the target radar.

AGM-123 Skipper II

Developed by the USN, the AGM-123 Skipper II is a short-range precision attack missile, consisting of a Paveway II laser guidance system and a small booster rocket attached to a Mk-83 bomb. Built by Emerson Electric, it was introduced in 1985 and, as used by the USMC, was launched from the A-6 Intruder.

The Skipper II's wingspan is 5.25 feet, its length 14.1 feet, and its maximum range 15.5 miles.

AIM-7 Sparrow

The AIM-7 Sparrow is a radar-guided, air-to-air missile with a high-explosive warhead, which is deployed on airforce, navy, and USMC aircraft. Manufactured by Raytheon Systems, the missile was introduced in 1976. It is powered by a Hercules Mk-58 solid-propellant rocket motor, weighs about 500 pounds, and carries an annular blast fragmentation warhead.

AIM-9 Sidewinder Missile

The AIM-9 Sidewinder is a short-range, heat-seeking air-to-air missile, which uses an infrared seeker to find its target. The AIM-9 incorporates an enhanced warhead and an enhanced guidance system, which permits all-angle attacks. The most widely used air-to-air missile in the West, the USMC is one of many military users.

General characteristics of the AIM-9 Sidewinder missile include:

Primary function: Close-range, air-to-air missile
Length: 9 ft, 6 in
Weight: 186 lb
Span: 2 ft
Diameter: 5 in
Propulsion: Solid-fuel rocket
Guidance: Infrared homing
Warhead: Conventional
Speed: Mach 2.5
Platforms: F/A-18A/C/CN Hornet, F/A-18D Hornet, and AV-8B Harrier II, and AH-1J Seacobra.

Air-to-Ground Missile Systems (AGMS)
See AIR-LAUNCHED WEAPONS.

American Revolution
The USMC was created as the CONTINENTAL MARINES during the American Revolution, on November 10, 1775, when the Second Continental Congress authorized two marine battalions for service aboard ships of the newly formed U.S. Navy. Under its de facto commandant, Captain SAMUEL NICHOLAS, the marines saw some action during the war, beginning with a landing on New Providence Island in the Bahamas on March 3, 1776. Two hundred thirty-four marines under Captain Nicholas took Britain's Fort Montague there and captured powder and arms. Three companies of Continental

Marines accompanied General George Washington in the triumphant assault against Trenton (December 26, 1776) and the follow-up action against Princeton.

The last significant marine action of the war was an assault on Fort St. George on Penobscot Bay, Maine, on July 28, 1779. The landing and advance proceeded briskly until a quarrel between the overall commander and the commander of militia brought the operation to a standstill. During the delay, a British frigate arrived, prompting the commanders to scrub the assault altogether.

Both the USN and the USMC were disbanded, even before the conclusion of the 1783 Treaty of Paris, which formally ended the war.

amphibious assault

A USMC specialty, an amphibious assault is an offensive operation in which troops and equipment are landed on an enemy shore by LANDING CRAFT, AMPHIBIOUS VEHICLES, helicopter, or some combination of these.

See also AMPHIBIOUS OPERATION; AMPHIBIOUS WARFARE SHIPS.

amphibious operation

An attack launched against an enemy shore from the sea by forces embarked on ships. The AMPHIBIOUS ASSAULT is the culmination of the operation, which begins with planning and proceeds through embarkation, rehearsal, and movement. Marines specialize in amphibious operations.

See also AMPHIBIOUS VEHICLES; AMPHIBIOUS WARFARE SHIPS; and LANDING CRAFT.

amphibious vehicles

Amphibious vehicles are wheeled or tracked vehicles that can operate in the water or on land. They transport troops and equipment from ship to shore during the AMPHIBIOUS ASSAULT phase of an AMPHIBIOUS OPERATION. The AAVP7 vehicle, described below, is the primary USMC amphibious vehicle.

AAVC-7A1 Assault Amphibian Vehicle Command Model 7A1

The AAVC-7A1 is an assault amphibious fully tracked landing vehicle that serves USMC mobile task force commanders as a communication center in water operations from ship to shore and to inland objectives after arriving ashore. The vehicle's communication center system consists of five radio operator stations, three staff stations, and two master stations. The command comm system contains equipment to provide external, secure radio transmission between each AAVC-7A1 vehicle fielded and other vehicles and radios. The vehicle was prototyped in 1979, and the first production vehicle entered USMC service in 1983.

General characteristics of the AAVC-7A1 Assault Amphibian Vehicle Command Model 7A1 include:

Manufacturer: FMC Corporation
Weight, unloaded: 46,314 lb
Weight, combat equipped: 50,758 lb
Fuel capacity: 171 gal
Cruising range, land at 25 mph: 300 mi
Cruising range, water at 2,600 rpm: 7 hr
Cruising speed, land: 20 to 30 mph
Cruising speed, water: 6 mph
Maximum speed forward, land: 45 mph
Maximum speed forward, water: 8.2 mph
Maximum speed reverse, land: 12 mph
Maximum speed reverse, water: 4.5 mph
Engine: Cummins Model VT400, 4-cycle, 8-cylinder, water-cooled, turbocharged
Fuel Type: multifuel
Cargo compartment length: 13.5 ft
Cargo compartment width: 6.0 ft
Cargo compartment height: 5.5 ft
Cargo compartment volume: 445.5 c ft
Total vehicle capacity: 21 combat-equipped marines
Armament: 7.62 machine gun
Crew: three

AAVR-7A1 Assault Amphibian Vehicle Recovery Model 7A1

The AAVR-7A1 is a fully tracked armored assault amphibious vehicle designed to recover in the field

An amphibious assault vehicle belonging to Delta Company, 2nd Amphibious Assault Battalion, speeds toward the enemy during an assault by marines of Kilo Company at Camp Lejeune, North Carolina.   *(Department of Defense)*

and under combat conditions vehicles of similar or smaller size. In addition to recovery, the AAVR-7A1 serves as a platform for the performance of field repairs and support. It carries a full set of basic maintenance equipment for this mission. The vehicle was prototyped in 1979, and it was first fielded by the USMC in 1983.

General characteristics of the AAVR-7A1 Assault Amphibian Vehicle Recovery Model 7A1 include:

Manufacturer: FMC Corporation
Weight, unloaded: 50,113 lb
Weight, combat equipped: 52,123 lb
Vehicle load capacity: 21 combat-equipped marines or 10,000 lb of cargo
Fuel capacity: 171 gal
Cruising range, land at 25 mph: 300 mi
Cruising range, water at 2,600 rpm: 7 hr
Cruising speed, land: 20 to 30 mph
Cruising speed, water: 6 mph
Maximum speed forward, land: 45 mph
Maximum speed forward, water: 8.2 mph
Maximum speed reverse, land: 12 mph

Maximum speed reverse, water: 4.5 mph
Engine: Cummins Model VT400, 4-cycle, 8-cylinder, water-cooled, turbocharged
Fuel type: multifuel
Generator: 120 VAC Output
Air compressor: 145 PSIG to 175 PSIG
Welder: Miller Maxtron 300
Hydraulic crane: 6,000-lb capacity
Crane winch: 23,000-lb breaking strength
Winch length: 85 ft
Armament: M60D machine gun
Crew: five

AAVP-7

The USMC uses this amphibious assault vehicle to transport troops and equipment from assault ships to areas beyond the shore. The vehicle is fully tracked and can carry 21 troops and three crew. Highly versatile, it is capable of operating in rough seas and in surf up to 10 feet high. On land, top speed is 40 miles per hour; on water, 8.4 miles per hour. Land range is 300 miles at 25 miles per hour; water range is 55 miles, near its top 8-mile-per-hour speed. Regular armament includes a .50-caliber machine gun and a 40-mm grenade launcher.

The vehicle has been refurbished repeatedly to extend its useful life, most recently in 1999, as the AAVP-7A1, using engines and parts adapted from the U.S. Army's M-2 Bradley Fighting Vehicle. AAVP variants include a command vehicle (AAVC-7) and a repair and recovery vehicle (AAVR-7).

DUKW

Pronounced "duck," this 2.5-ton, six-wheel-drive amphibious vehicle was put into service with the USMC and U.S. Army in 1942. Built on a truck chassis, the DUKW could carry 25 fully equipped troops. Clumsy and slow, DUKWs were little used by the USMC in the Pacific during WORLD WAR II, although a USMC DUKW company saw action at IWO JIMA. Most DUKWs were used by the army in the European theater.

LAV-25

An eight-wheeled light assault vehicle, also used as a personnel carrier. Crewed by three—commander, driver, and gunner—the LAV-25 carries six combat-ready marines. The vehicle is equipped with gun ports, enabling marines to fire from within the cargo hold of the vehicle. A periscope is placed above each port. The LAV-25 is relatively lightly armored, able to withstand 7.62-mm armor-piercing rounds, and it is equipped with an M-242 Bushmaster 25-mm turret-mounted chain gun.

The LAV-25 has been developed in six major variations: a command and control vehicle, an antitank vehicle (carrying twin TOW II missiles), a mortar vehicle (equipped with an 81 mm mortar), a recovery vehicle, an air-defense vehicle (equipped with Stinger missile launchers and a 25 mm GAU-12 Gatling gun), and the standard LAV (armed with the 25-mm chain gun).

The vehicle is 21 feet long and 7 feet 2 inches wide. Its empty weight is 19,050 pounds, and its power plant is a turbocharged diesel, capable of driving the LAV up to 60 miles per hour. Its range is 485 miles. Like most USMC assault vehicles, the LAV-25 is amphibious. Top speed in water is 6 miles per hour.

LAV-C2 Light Armored Vehicle– Command and Control

The USMC's Light Armored Vehicle–Command and Control (LAV-C2) is used primarily as a mobile command station to provide field commanders with all necessary resources to control and coordinate light armored units in all assigned roles. The vehicle operates on all terrains and in all weather conditions and also has night-operation capabilities. It can be transported by air, using the KC-130 Hercules or other fixed-wing cargo aircraft, as well as the CH-53E Super Stallion helicopter. In its combat-loaded status, the LAV-C2 carries 200 ready rounds and 800 stowed rounds of 7.62-mm ammunition. Additionally, there are eight ready rounds and eight stowed rounds of smoke grenades. The vehicle can be made fully amphibious within three minutes.

General characteristics of the Light Armored Vehicle–Command and Control (LAV-C2) include:

Length: 253.5 in
Height: 110.0 in
Width: 98.4 in
Weight: 24,840 lb
Combat weight: 27,060 lb
Range: 410 mi
Speed: 62 mph
Swim speed: 6 mph
Crew: seven, consisting of driver, vehicle commander, two radio operators, two staff members, and battalion commander
Armament: M240E1 7.62-mm machine gun
Communication equipment: two SINCGARS AN/VRC 92 radios; one VHF/UHF AN/VRC-83(V)2 radio; one UHF position location reporting system; one HF AN/GRC-213 radio; one VHF AN/PRC-68 radio (stowed)

LAV-L Light Armored Vehicle–Logistics

The USMC's Light Armored Vehicle–Logistics (LAV-L) primarily functions to supply ammunition, rations, and POL (petroleum, oil and lubricant) as required to sustain operations of first-line armored vehicles. The vehicle operates on all terrains and in all weather conditions and has night capabilities. It can be transported by air, using the KC-130 Hercules or other fixed-wing cargo aircraft, as well as the CH-53E Super Stallion helicopter. In a combat-loaded condition, the LAV-L carries 200 ready rounds and 800 stowed rounds of 7.62-mm ammunition. Additionally, there are eight ready rounds and eight stowed rounds of smoke grenades. The vehicle can be made fully amphibious within three minutes.

General characteristics of the Light Armored Vehicle–Logistics (LAV-L) include:

Length: 254.6 in
Height: 109.0 in
Width: 98.4 in
Weight: 22,960 lb
Combat weight: 28,200 lb
Range: 410 mi
Speed: 62 mph
Swim speed: 6 mph
Crew: three, consisting of driver, vehicle commander, and crewmember
Armament: M240E1 7.62-mm machine gun
Payload: 5,240 lb

LAV-M Light Armored Vehicle–Mortar

The USMC employs the Light Armored Vehicle–Mortar (LAV-M) to provide indirect fire support to light infantry and reconnaissance forces and to provide high-explosive area fire, covering smoke, and illumination for first-line units. An all-terrain, all-weather vehicle with night capabilities, the LAV-M can be transported by air, using the KC-130 Hercules or other fixed-wing cargo aircraft, as well as the CH-53E Super Stallion helicopter. In its combat-loaded configuration, the LAV-M holds five ready and 94 stowed 81-mm bombs as well as 200 ready rounds and 800 stowed rounds of 7.62-mm ammunition. Additionally, there are eight ready rounds and eight stowed rounds of smoke grenades. Stowed within the vehicle is the base plate and bipod for a ground-mounted mortar. The vehicle can be made fully amphibious within three minutes.

General characteristics of the Light Armored Vehicle–Mortar (LAV-M) include:

Length: 252.6 in
Height: 110.0 in, reducible to 98 in
Width: 98.4 in
Weight: 22,750 lb
Combat weight: 26,700 lb
Range: 410 mi
Speed: 62 mph
Swim speed: 6 mph
Crew: driver, mortar crew, and commander
Armament: M252 81-mm mortar, M240E1 7.62-mm machine gun

LAV-R Light Armored Vehicle–Recovery

The USMC's Light Armored Vehicle–Recovery (LAV-R) provides the tactical mobility to reach and recover or support disabled vehicles. Like the USMC's other LAVs, the LAV-R is an all-terrain, all-weather vehicle with night capabilities and can be airlifted aboard the KC-130 Hercules or other fixed-wing cargo aircraft, as well as the CH-53E Super Stallion helicopter. Combat loaded, the vehicle holds 200 ready rounds and 800 stowed rounds of 7.62-mm ammunition. Additionally, there are eight ready rounds and eight stowed rounds of smoke grenades. The vehicle can be made fully amphibious within three minutes.

General characteristics of the Light Armored Vehicle–Recovery (LAV-R) include:

Length, crane forward: 21.3 ft
Length, crane aft: 24.16 ft
Height, crane forward: 8.83 ft
Height, crane aft: 9.08 ft
Width: 109.0 in
Weight: 26,220 lb
Combat weight: 28,320 lb
Range: 410 mi
Speed: 62 mph
Swim speed: 6 mph
Crew: Three, consisting of driver, vehicle commander, and rigger
Armament: M240E1 7.62-mm machine gun
On-board equipment: one boom crane rated at 9,000 lb (4,086 kgs); flood lights; one

winch rated at 30,000 lb; 230-volt three-phase or 120-volt single-phase power; 10-kilowatt hydraulic-driven output; and one welder.

LVT and LVT(A) Landing Vehicle, Tracked

The LVT was developed for the USMC in 1940 and was intended to be launched from ships, sail through surf and negotiate coral reefs, then move forward on tank tracks once landed. The LVT-1 was replaced in 1942–43 by the Water Buffalo (LVT-2), which was more powerful than the LVT-1 and had a suspension system that provided far greater traction and maneuverability. The LVT-2 was also larger. A total of 1,225 LVT-1s were built, and more than 3,000 of the LVT-2 and LVT(A)-2 models were produced. They were extremely valuable for landing troops inland, rather than exposing troops on foot to fire on a beachhead. The only drawback these vehicles suffered from was the lack of an off-loading ramp. Marines clambered over the sides—an action that rendered them vulnerable to fire.

amphibious warfare ships

Familiarly called "amphibs" or "gators," these are vessels expressly designed to transport troops from bases to landing beaches in AMPHIBIOUS OPERATIONS. The ships are operated by U.S. Navy personnel and include the following types:

LST (Landing Ship, Tank). This vessel runs right up to the beach and is equipped with a bow ramp, which is lowered so that land vehicles can drive off. A stern ramp may be used to launch AMPHIBIOUS VEHICLES.

LSD (Landing Ship, Dock). These vessels incorporate a well dock, which can be flooded to float landing craft and amphibious vehicles out through a stern gate.

LPD (Amphibious Transport Dock). Like the LSD, these incorporate a well dock, which can be flooded to float landing craft and amphibious vehicles out through a stern gate; in addition, they have a flight deck for helicopter operations.

LKA (Amphibious Cargo Ship). These vessels are for off-loading cargo necessary to the AMPHIBIOUS ASSAULT.

LPH (Amphibious Assault Ship). These carry helicopters and can land 2,000 marines and equipment (battalion strength).

LHA (General-Purpose Assault Ship). These are larger versions of the LPD.

LHD (Multipurpose Assault Ship). These vessels operate air-cushion vehicles as well as helicopters.

LCC (Amphibious Command Ship). Used as a seaborne command post during the amphibious assault.

See also LANDING CRAFT.

AN/PAQ-3 Modular Universal Laser Equipment (MULE)   See WEAPONS, INDIVIDUAL AND CREW-SERVED.

AN/PAQ-4A/4C Infrared Aiming Light

See WEAPONS, INDIVIDUAL AND CREW-SERVED.

AN/PSN-11 Precision Lightweight GPS Receiver (PLGR)   See PERSONAL AND MISCELLANEOUS EQUIPMENT.

AN/PSS-12 Metallic Mine Detector   See PERSONAL AND MISCELLANEOUS EQUIPMENT.

AN/PVS-4 Individual Weapon Night Sight

See WEAPONS, INDIVIDUAL AND CREW-SERVED.

AN/PVS-5 Night Vision Goggles (NVG)

See WEAPONS, INDIVIDUAL AND CREW-SERVED.

AN/PVS-7B Night Vision Goggle (NVG)

See WEAPONS, INDIVIDUAL AND CREW-SERVED.

antiarmor weapons

The following antiarmor weapons are currently included in the marine inventory:

AT-4 Light Antiarmor Weapon

The AT-4 is a shoulder-fired light antiarmor weapon designed to be effective against main battle tanks. Manufactured by FFV Ordnance of Sweden and Alliant Techsystems of the United States, the weapon measures 40 inches in length and weighs 14.75 pounds. Its bore diameter is 84 mm, and it has an effective range of 984.3 feet. At this range, the AT-4 is capable of firing a projectile that penetrates 400 mm of rolled homogenous armor. Time of flight is under one second, and muzzle velocity is 950 feet per second. The ammunition for the weapon is a rocket with a shaped-charge warhead.

Dragon Weapon System

The Dragon antiarmor weapon system has as its primary mission engagement and destruction of armor and light armored vehicles. Secondarily, the Dragon Weapon System is effective against such hard targets as bunkers and field fortifications. This man-portable weapon system makes it possible for a single marine to defeat armored vehicles, fortified bunkers, concrete gun emplacements, and other hard targets. The launcher consists of a smoothbore fiberglass tube, breech/gas generator, tracker and support, bipod, battery, sling, and forward and aft shock absorbers. Additionally, a day or night sight—not integral to the system—is required. Essentially, the system consists of the launcher, the tracker, and the missile, which is installed in the launcher during final factory

A marine sets up a Dragon antiarmor weapon as his spotter/loader watches for movement during an assault by marines of Kilo Company at Camp Lejeune, North Carolina. *(Department of Defense)*

assembly and is received by the USMC ready to fire. The launch tube functions as a storage and carrying case for the missile as well as its launcher.

The predecessor of the modern USMC Dragon was a Dragon weapon developed for the army and first deployed in 1970. It required 11.2 seconds flight-to-target time. The weapon was improved in a USMC program in 1985 and designated Dragon II, using a retrofit of warheads to the first-generation Dragon missiles already in the USMC inventory.

General characteristics of the Dragon Weapon System include:

Manufacturer: McDonnell Douglas Aerospace and Missile Systems and Raytheon
Length, launcher: 45.4 in
Length, missile: 33.3 in
Weight: 33.9 lb (Day Tracker version); 48.7 lb (Night Tracker version)
Maximum effective range: 3,281 ft
Time of flight: 11.2 sec
Armor penetration: will defeat T-55, T-62, or T-72 tanks

Javelin

Javelin is a portable antitank weapon manufactured by a Raytheon/Lockheed Martin joint venture. It can be shoulder-fired or installed on tracked, wheeled, or amphibious vehicles. Development began as a replacement for the M-47 Dragon II, and the weapon entered full-rate production in 1994; it was first deployed in 1996.

The Javelin system consists of a Command Launch Unit (CLU) and the round. The CLU incorporates a passive target acquisition and fire control unit with an integrated day sight and a thermal-imaging sight. The round is a Javelin missile and the ATK (Alliant Techsystems) Launch Tube Assembly. The range of the missile is 8,200 feet, and the weapon is "fire-and-forget"; it locks on to its target prior to launch and has automatic self-guidance. The missile has a tandem warhead fitted with two shaped charges, one (the "precursor") to initiate explosive-reactive armor, and another (the "main") to penetrate base armor. The Javelin is propelled by a two-stage solid-fuel motor.

In contrast to conventional wire-guided, fiber-optic cable-guided, or laser beam-riding missiles, Javelin is autonomously guided, allowing the gunner to reposition or reload immediately after launch. This makes the gunner far less vulnerable to retaliatory fire.

M-3A1 Antitank Gun

This 37-mm gun was developed in the 1930s to replace World War I–era artillery. A towed weapon, it fired a 1.6-pound shell 500 yards. By the time the United States entered World War II, German tanks were sufficiently well armored to render the weapon obsolete. In the Pacific and against the Japanese, however, the USMC still found the gun highly effective, because Japanese tanks were much less well armored. Marines also used the guns against pillboxes and against banzai charges by infantry troops.

M-47 Dragon II

A disposable antitank weapon used by the USMC as well as the army. The Dragon II can be fired by a single marine, although a crew of two is ideal. The Dragon II weighs 32.6 pounds and has a range of 195 to 3,000 feet. It is equipped with a tracker system capable of tracking targets moving at 30 miles per hour. The fiberglass launch tube is discarded after firing, but the tracking system is retained and refitted to another tube and rocket.

During the 1990s, the M-47 was in the process of being replaced by the Javelin.

M-151 TOW

A long-range, tube-launched, optically tracked, wire-guided antitank missile, TOW is used by the USMC and army. TOW launchers may be fitted to helicopters and to armored vehicles. Infantry units may be equipped with tripod-mounted portable TOWs.

The TOW system consists of a launch tube, missile guidance set, optical sight, traversing unit, and missile. Weighing 280 pounds, the TOW system is operated by a three-person crew.

TOW has a reliability factor of 95 percent over a maximum range of 2.3 miles. Its 6-inch-diameter missile is subsonic (625 mph) and is guided by signals transmitted along wires that deploy as the missile travels toward its target. The latest iteration of the TOW is the TOW II, which includes a 21-inch probe that detonates the target's reactive armor, allowing the main warhead to penetrate and destroy the enemy vehicle.

Saboted Light Armor Penetrator (SLAP) Ammunition

The USMC developed .50-caliber SLAP ammunition during the mid- to late 1980s. It first saw combat service in 1990–91 during Operation Desert Storm (PERSIAN GULF WAR). The structure of this armor-penetrating ammunition is unique. A reduced-caliber, heavy metal (tungsten), .30-inch-diameter penetrator is wrapped in a plastic, .50-inch-diameter *sabot* (shoe). This renders the saboted ammunition much lighter than the normal ball .50-caliber ammunition, so that velocity is significantly and safely increased in an unmodified M2-HB Browning machine gun. The result is a very fast round with a very flat trajectory that significantly increases hit probability.

Maximum velocity of SLAP ammunition is 3,985 feet per second. Effective range is 4,921.5 feet against 3/4-inch-high hard armor.

Tube-Launched, Optically Tracked, Wire-Guided (TOW) Missile Weapon System

The Tube-Launched, Optically Tracked, Wire-Guided (TOW) Missile Weapon System is a vehicle- or tripod-mounted guided-missile weapon system widely used by the USMC. Its primary mission is to destroy enemy armored vehicles, especially tanks. Secondarily, the TOW system is used to destroy other point targets, including non-armored vehicles and crew-served weapons and launchers.

First fielded in 1970, the TOW was and is primarily used in antitank warfare. It is a wire-guided line-of-sight weapon, which will operate in all weather conditions. The TOW 2 launcher,

the most recent launcher upgrade, is compatible with all TOW missiles and consists of a reusable launcher, a missile guidance set, and a sight system. Although the system can be mounted on a tripod, it is sufficiently heavy that it is more usually mounted on the High Mobility Multipurpose Wheeled Vehicle (HMMWV) (M-998 Truck) or on a Landing Vehicle, Tracked (LVT and LVT[A]).

The earliest TOW missiles were 5 inches in diameter and had a range of 9,850 feet. The Improved TOW (ITOW), delivered in 1982, also has a 5-inch diameter warhead, but incorporates an extended probe for greater standoff and penetration and an enhanced flight motor, which increased the missile's range to 12,300 feet. The TOW 2 series of improvements includes TOW 2 Hardware, TOW 2 Missile, TOW 2A Missile, and TOW 2B Missile. The TOW 2 Hardware improvements include a thermal beacon guidance system, which enables the gunner to more easily track a target at night, and many improvements to the missile guidance system. Warhead diameter was also increased to 6 inches. The extended probe introduced with ITOW is also included in the TOW 2A. The TOW 2B introduces new fly-over, shoot-down technology.

General characteristics of the Tube Launched, Optically Tracked, Wire Guided (TOW) Missile Weapon System include:

Manufacturer: Hughes (missiles); Hughes and Kollsman (night sights); Electro Design Manufacturing (launchers)
Diameter, TOW 2A Missile: 5.87 in
Length, TOW 2A Missile: 50.40 in
Diameter, TOW 2B Missile: 5.8 in
Length, TOW 2B Missile: 48.0 in
Maximum effective range: 2.33 mi
Time of flight to maximum effective range, 2A: 20 sec; **2B,** 21 sec
Weight, launcher w/TOW 2 mods: 204.6 lb
Weight, missile guidance set: 52.8 lb
Weight, TOW 2 Missile: 47.4 lb
Weight, TOW 2A Missile: 49.9 lb
Weight, TOW 2B Missile: 49.8 lb

A tube-launched, optically tracked, wire-guided (TOW) missile hurtles out of its launcher mounted on a U.S. Marine Corps Humvee at the Marine Corps Air Ground Combat Center, Twentynine Pines, California. *(Department of Defense)*

AN/TPQ-36 Firefinder Radar   See INDIRECT FIRE SYSTEMS.

AN/TTC-42 (V) Automatic Telephone Central Office   See COMMUNICATIONS EQUIPMENT.

AN/TVS-5 Crew-Served Weapon Night Sight   See WEAPONS, INDIVIDUAL AND CREW-SERVED.

AN/USQ-70 Position Azimuth Determining System   See INDIRECT FIRE SYSTEMS.

assault craft
General term for LANDING CRAFT.
        See also AMPHIBIOUS WARFARE SHIPS.

AT-4 Light Antiarmor Weapon   See ANTIARMOR WEAPONS.

AV-8B Harrier II   See AIRCRAFT, FIXED-WING.

Avenger   See AIR DEFENSE ARTILLERY.

B

Barbary pirates

For a long time, the Muslim rulers of the so-called Barbary States—Morocco, Algiers, Tripoli, and Tunis—sanctioned piracy against the vessels of Christian nations plying the Mediterranean near the coast of North Africa. The so-called Barbary Pirates demanded tribute—protection money—in return for allowing shipping to be conducted unmolested. In its early years, the United States, a struggling young republic in no position to wage war against the Barbary Pirates, concluded tribute treaties. However, in May 1801, a new bey assumed the Tripolitan throne, demanded a more exorbitant tribute, then declared war on the United States in an effort to get it. In 1803, during the course of the war, the bey's navy captured the USN frigate *Philadelphia*. Lieutenant Stephen Decatur, USN, led a daring raid, which included marines, to set fire to the *Philadelphia* while it was in harbor, thereby depriving the bey of his prize.

In 1804, while the U.S. Navy blockaded the harbor of Tripoli, a mixed force of Egyptians, European troops, and eight U.S. Marines under the command of Lieutenant PRESLEY O'BANNON incited a revolt against the bey. O'Bannon and his marine detachment led the force 600 miles across the Libyan desert and attacked and took Derna on April 27, 1805, defeating superior forces. Shortly afterward, the bey concluded a favorable peace treaty with the United States—and presented O'Bannon with a jeweled MAMELUKE SWORD, which became the model for that worn by USMC officers on ceremonial occasions. O'Bannon's victory was also the source of the reference to the "shores of Tripoli" in the MARINE HYMN.

Barnett, George (1859–1930) *Marine Corps commandant*

Barnett was the 12th COMMANDANT OF THE MARINE CORPS. He graduated from the U.S. Naval Academy in 1881, served as a midshipman in the USN, and was commissioned a second lieutenant in the USMC in 1883. He served at sea during the SPANISH-AMERICAN WAR and in PANAMA, the Philippines, and Cuba. Barrett briefly commanded the MARINE BARRACKS in Washington, D.C., then served on legation duty in China before returning to Cuba during 1911–13. Barnett succeeded General WILLIAM P. BIDDLE as USMC commandant on February 25, 1914. A conflict with Secretary of the Navy Josephus Daniels prompted his resignation in 1920, and his last assignment was as commander of the newly created Department of the Pacific.

bases, camps, and other installations

The principal USMC installations include the Marine Barracks in Washington, D.C., seven air stations, five major bases (three of which are also known by their earlier designation as "camps"), two logistics bases, and two recruit depots.

Marine Barracks

"Marine Barracks" has two meanings as used in the USMC. It denotes a special guard unit assigned to ensure the internal security of major U.S. Navy shore stations, including the protection of USN nuclear weapons. It is also the name of the ceremonial and special security unit assigned to Washington, D.C., and located at 8th and I Streets (often nicknamed "8th and Eye"). Established in 1801, the MARINE BARRACKS is the oldest USMC post. Since 1806, it has included the residence of the COMMANDANT OF THE MARINE CORPS and is considered the "spiritual home" of the USMC.

The site of the Marine Barracks was selected with the personal approval of President Thomas Jefferson because it lay near the Navy Yard and was also within easy marching distance of the Capitol. The only remaining building that dates from the earliest days of the Marine Barracks is the 1806 Commandant's House at the north end of the Barracks quadrangle. The rest of the present Marine Barracks was built between 1900 and 1907.

Originally, the Marine Barracks was the principal site for training new USMC officers and recruits. Until 1901, it was also the location of HEADQUARTERS MARINE CORPS. From the beginning, the Marine Barracks has also been home of the U.S. MARINE BAND. Today, marines based at the Barracks undergo light infantry training, participate in ceremonies, and perform presidential support duty. The barracks is also home of the Marine Corps Institute, a training center responsible for all USMC nonresident military education programs.

Further reading: Marine Barracks web site: www. mbw.usmc.mil.

Marine Corps Air Station Beaufort

Located in Beaufort, South Carolina, the air station is the home of the USMC's Atlantic Coast fixed-wing, fighter-attack aircraft assets, Marine Air Group 31, which consists of seven USMC F/A-18 squadrons. Two U.S. Navy F/A-18 squadrons are also based at "Fightertown." The base is home to some 3,400 marines.

Further reading: MCAS Beaufort web site: www. beaufort.usmc.mil.

Marine Corps Air Station Cherry Point

Construction of the 8,000-acre Marine Corps airfield at Cherry Point, located in Craven County, North Carolina, between New Bern and Morehead City, began in summer 1941 and the site was commissioned as Cunningham Field during WORLD WAR II, on May 20, 1942, in honor of the first USMC aviator, Lieutenant Colonel Alfred A. Cunningham. The facility was redesignated Marine Corps Air Station, Cherry Point.

During World War II, Cherry Point was a training center as well as a base for anti-submarine operations. During the KOREAN WAR, it trained not only aviators and air crewmen but also maintenance and support personnel. During the VIETNAM WAR, Cherry Point deployed three A-6 Intruder squadrons to the Far East in addition to carrying out training functions. Cherry Point contributed to Operation Desert Storm during the PERSIAN GULF WAR, supporting the deployment of three AV-8B Harrier squadrons, two A-6E Intruder squadrons, one KC-130 Hercules squadron, one EA-6B Prowler squadron, and provided headquarters detachments from Marine Air Group 14, Marine Air Group 32, and the 2nd Marine Aircraft Wing. Cherry Point marines and sailors participated in operations in Afghanistan following the terrorist attacks of September 11, 2001, on the United States.

Further reading: MCAS Cherry Point web site: www.cherrypoint.usmc.mil.

Marine Corps Air Station Futenma

Located in Futenma, Okinawa, Japan, MCAS Futenma is home to MARINE AIRCRAFT GROUP 36 and Marine Air Control Group 18.

Further reading: MCAS Futenma web site: www. futenma.usmc.mil.

Marine Corps Air Station Iwakuni

MCAS Iwakuni is located on the main island of Honshu, Japan, about 25 miles south of Hiroshima.

It was originally a Japanese naval air facility, built in 1940, and, after World War II, was used by the British Royal Air Force, the Royal Australian Air Force, the U.S. Air Force, and the U.S. Navy. It was reassigned to the USMC in 1958 and is home to Marine Aircraft Group 12, Marine Wing Support Squadron 171, Combat Service Support Detachment 36, and the Japanese Maritime Self-Defense Force. The base deploys F-18 Hornets, AV-8 Harriers, EA-6 Prowlers, and the CH-53D Sea Stallion.

Further reading: MCAS Iwakuni web site: www.iwakuni.usmc.mil.

Marine Corps Air Station Miramar

MCAS Miramar is home to the 3rd Marine Aircraft Wing and houses some 11,000 personnel. Located in San Diego, California, Miramar started military life as an army base, Camp Kearny, in 1917, during WORLD WAR I. The U.S. Navy took it over in 1932, as a base for dirigible operations, and during World War II, both the USN and USMC occupied Miramar. After the war, the base was redesignated Marine Corps Air Station Miramar, but in 1947 the marines moved to El Toro, near Los Angeles. Miramar was redesignated a Naval Auxiliary Air Station, but was revived during the VIETNAM WAR as the USN's "Top Gun" school and "Fightertown, USA." In 1993, Naval Air Station Miramar was redesignated as Marine Corps Air Station Miramar, the USN's Top Gun school moved, and, in 1996, personnel from MCAS El Toro and Marine Corps Air Facility Tustin were relocated to Miramar. On July 2, 1999, MCAS El Toro and MCAF Tustin were closed.

Miramar operates F/A-18 Hornets and KC-130 Hercules squadrons, as well as its CH-46E Sea Knight and CH-53E Super Stallion helicopters. The air station covers more than 23,000 acres.

Further reading: MCAS Miramar web site: www.miramar.usmc.mil.

Marine Corps Air Station New River

MCAS New River is located in New River, North Carolina, adjacent to Marine Corps Base Camp Lejeune and began operations in 1944, during World War II, as Peterfield Point, named after a Mr. Peter, on whose former tobacco field much of the station was built. The station was inactivated after the war, then reactivated as Marine Corps Air Facility Peterfield Point, Camp Lejeune, in October 1951, during the Korean War. In 1952, it was renamed Marine Corps Air Field New River and became home to Marine Air Group 26, a helicopter unit. Redesignated Marine Corps Air Station (Helicopter) New River during the Vietnam War in 1968, the station became a major operational airfield. In May 1972, Marine Aircraft Group 29 and supporting units were installed at the station, and in 1983, New River–based squadrons flew combat missions during the invasion of GRENADA. New River marines also fought in Operations Desert Shield and Desert Storm during the Persian Gulf War in 1990–91.

Currently, New River-based units provide direct helicopter support for Marine Forces, Atlantic, and the 2,600-acre facility is the USMC's premier helicopter air station.

Further reading: MCAS New River web site: www.newriver.usmc.mil.

Marine Corps Air Station Yuma

Located in Yuma, Arizona, MCAS Yuma is a major aviation training base. With access to 2.8 million acres of bombing and aviation training ranges, MCAS Yuma supports 80 percent of USMC air-to-ground aviation training. The station is home to Marine Aviation Weapons and Tactics Squadron 1, Marine Aircraft Group 13, Marine Wing Support Squadron 371, Marine Fighter Training Squadron 401, Marine Air Control Squadron 1, and Combat Service Support Detachment 16.

The origin of MCAS Yuma was as Fly Field, a U.S. Army facility established in 1928. In 1943, during World War II, it became Yuma Army Air Base, a training facility for USAAF pilots. Inactivated after the war, it was reactivated by the U.S. Air Force during the Korean War, on July 7, 1951, and was signed over to the USN on January 1, 1959. It became MCAS Yuma on July 20, 1962, and served primarily as a training base for pilots flying the F-4 Phantom, A-4 Skyhawk, and AV-8A Harrier. Today, MCAS Yuma is the busiest air station in the USMC, its primary mission to support aerial weapons training for the FLEET MARINE FORCE, Atlantic and Fleet Marine Force, Pacific, as well as for the USN. MCAS Yuma also serves as a base of operations for Marine Aviation Weapons and Tactics Squadron 1 and Marine Aircraft Group 13.

Further reading: MCAS Yuma web site: www.yuma.usmc.mil.

Marine Corps Base Camp Lejeune

MCB Camp Lejeune is located in Onslow County, North Carolina, and was established in September 1941 by the 1st Marine Division. Today, Camp Lejeune encompasses 246 square miles and is a base for active units as well as the USMC's largest training facility.

When it was established, the base was called Marine Barracks New River, North Carolina. It was given its present name toward the end of 1942, in honor of the 13th Commandant of the Marine Corps, Major General JOHN A. LEJEUNE. Camp Lejeune has not only trained thousands of marines, it was also the site of the development of USMC special operations; today it also serves for special training in riverine and urban operations.

Camp Lejeune includes satellite facilities at Camp Geiger, Camp Johnson, Stone Bay, and the Greater Sandy Run Training Area. Camp Johnson, today a key training base, was the first training facility for African-American Marines (when it was called Montford Point). Camp Geiger is devoted to marine combat training, and, during World War II, was home to the 1st Marine Division. The total population of Camp Lejeune is 150,000 people, including civilian employees.

Further reading: MCB Camp Lejeune web site: www.lejeune.usmc.mil.

Marine Corps Base Camp Pendleton

MCB Camp Pendleton is the USMC's major base in the west. Located north of San Diego, California,

it was established in March 1942 and named for General JOSEPH H. PENDLETON. During World War II, Camp Pendleton was headquarters for the USMC Training and Replacement Command.

Today, Camp Pendleton consists of 3,800 buildings and structures on 200 square miles. There are 14 family housing areas, six on-base public schools, and a 600-bed naval hospital. Each year more than 40,000 active-duty and 26,000 reserve military personnel from all services use Camp Pendleton's ranges and training facilities. Located here is the USMC's premier amphibious training base. The facility is also home to the First Marine Expeditionary Force and two of its major subordinate commands, the 1st Marine Division and 1st Force Service Support Group.

Further reading: MCB Camp Pendleton web site: www.pendleton.usmc.mil.

Marine Corps Base Camp Smedley D. Butler

Located on OKINAWA, at Camp Foster, MCB Camp Smedley D. Butler is responsible for the operation of all USMC facilities on the island, including Camps Schwab, Kinser, McTureous, Hansen, Courtney, and Foster, as well as Marine Corps Air Station Futenma. MCB Camp Smedley D. Butler is headquarters of the THIRD Marine Expeditionary Force and 3rd Division.

Further reading: MCB Camp Smedley D. Butler web site: www.mcbbutler.usmc.mil.

Marine Corps Base Hawaii

MCB Hawaii consists of 4,500 acres on the island of Oahu and includes Camp Smith, Kaneohe Bay, Marine Corps Training Area Bellows, Manana Family Housing Area, Pearl City Warehouse Annex, and Puuoloa Range Complex. MCB Hawaii maintains key operations, training, and support facilities. The mission of MCB Hawaii is to "support readiness and global projection" for the USMC. Its tenant units include U.S. Pacific Command; 3rd Marine Regiment; Commander Patrol and Reconnaissance Force Pacific; Fleet Marine Force, Pacific; Marine

Aircraft Group 24; Helicopter Antisubmarine Squadron Light 37; Special Operations Command, Pacific; Combat Service Support Group 3; Fleet Logistics Support Squadron 51; Joint Task Force–Full Accounting; First Radio Battalion; Fleet Aviation Specialized Operational Training Group Pacific Detachment Hawaii; Defense Logistics Agency–Pacific; USMC College of Continuing Education Satellite Campus; National Security Agency Central Security Service Pacific Headquarters; and 4th Force Reconnaissance Company.

Further reading: MCB Hawaii web site: www. mcbh.usmc.mil.

Marine Corps Base Quantico

Marine Corps Base Quantico, usually shortened to Quantico, stretches for five miles along the Potomac River in Virginia, occupying about 100 square miles. It is the major USMC base on the East Coast and is the location of the Development and Education Command, the principal educational arm of the USMC.

Quantico was established during World War I, in April 1917, when the expanding Marine Corps outgrew its two principal bases in Philadelphia and Washington, and was first occupied the following month by the 5th Marines. Between the world wars, Quantico became the site of the USMC schools. By 1944, during World War II, Quantico was almost exclusively used as a replacement training center. Today, although the Marine Barracks in Washington, D.C., remains the spiritual center of the USMC, Quantico is at the heart of day-to-day operations.

Further reading: MCB Quantico web site: www. quantico.usmc.mil.

Marine Corps Logistics Base Albany

Located in Albany, Georgia, MCLB Albany furnishes supplies for USMC forces east of the Mississippi River and to forces that are part of Fleet Marine Force, Atlantic. Marine Corps Logistics Base Barstow supplies USMC forces west of the Mississippi, in the Far East and Asia.

Further reading: MCLB Albany web site: www. ala.usmc.mil/base.

Marine Corps Logistics Base Barstow

Located in Barstow, California, MCLB Barstow was established as the Marine Corps Depot of Supplies during World War II, on December 28, 1942. In November 1978, the base received its present title of Marine Corps Logistics Base, reflecting its broad logistics support mission.

The Marine Corps Logistics Bases are comprised of three major components, Marine Corps Logistics Base Albany, Georgia; MCLB Barstow, California; and Blount Island Command, Jacksonville, Florida. MCLB Albany furnishes supplies for USMC forces east of the Mississippi and to Fleet Marine Force, Atlantic. MCLB Barstow supports USMC forces west of the Mississippi and in the Far East and Asia. Blount Island Command provides logistical support for the USMC Maritime Prepositioning Ships and the Norway Geo-Prepositioning programs (see MARITIME PREPOSITIONING SQUADRONS).

The Barstow base is comprised of three principal sites: Nebo, which encompasses 1,879 acres and functions as base headquarters; the Yermo Annex, encompassing 1,859 acres and serving as a storage and industrial complex; and a third site, of 2,438 acres, serving as a rifle and pistol range.

Further reading: MCLB Barstow web site: www. bam.usmc.mil.

Marine Corps Recruit Depots

Familiarly called "Boot Camp," MCRDs provide BASIC TRAINING for new marines. The USMC has two MCRDs, Marine Corps Recruit Depot Parris Island, South Carolina, and Marine Corps Recruit Depot San Diego, California. Male recruits from east of the Mississippi and all female recruits train at Parris Island, whereas male recruits from west of the Mississippi are sent to San Diego. Under special circumstances, training may also take place at the Marine Barracks, Washington, D.C., Marine Corps Base Camp Lejeune, or Marine Corps Base Quantico, Virginia.

Boot camp consists of 11 weeks of basic training, encompassing USMC history, close-order drill, the military Code of Conduct, and other USMC fundamentals. Recruits are conditioned physically, and they master a confidence course; they are trained in self defense, lifesaving, PUGIL STICK, individual combat training, and marksmanship.

See also DRILL INSTRUCTOR.

Marine Corps Recruit Depot Parris Island

"Parris Island" is one of the most famous places in the USMC. Located off the coast of South Carolina, it has served as "boot camp" for more than a million USMC recruits since 1915. Today, Parris Island delivers basic training to male recruits from the eastern United States and to all female USMC recruits, regardless of region.

Further reading: MCRD Parris Island web site: www.mcrdpi.usmc.mil.

Marine Corps Recruit Depot San Diego

MCRD San Diego has a twofold mission: recruiting marines from the Western Recruiting Region and delivering basic training to male recruits from the western United States. The depot is located in San Diego, California.

Further reading: MCRD San Diego web site: www.mcrdsd.usmc.mil.

basic training

Basic training, familiarly called "boot camp," is delivered at two locations, Marine Corps Recruit Depot Parris Island and Marine Corps Recruit Depot San Diego. Men who enlist west of the Mississippi are assigned to San Diego. Men who enlist east of the river are sent to Parris Island, as are female recruits, regardless of where they enlist.

USMC basic training consists of 12 weeks of training in addition to a week of processing. It begins with Receiving, which includes basic indoctrination in the Uniform Code of Military Justice, paperwork processing, getting the traditional "buzz" haircut, and receiving initial uniforms and field gear. During three to five days in Receiving, recruits are given the Initial Strength Test (IST). Failure to do two pull-ups, 35 sit-ups (in two minutes), and a 1.5-mile run in 13.5 minutes means assignment to the Physical Conditioning Platoon.

During week 1 of basic, the DRILL INSTRUCTOR commences the process of "forming" through "total immersion." This includes immersion in USMC vocabulary, military courtesy, and general discipline in addition to a Physical Training routine. Week 1 also includes an introduction to bayonet fighting and to the M16A2 rifle. Martial arts training was also added to the basic training program in 2000 and is introduced in week 1.

Week 2 continues the basics of close combat skills, including the use of the PUGIL STICK. Field first aid and academic classes on USMC values and

Trainees move to another stage of basic training on Parris Island.   *(U.S. Marine Corps)*

other subjects are also part of week 2, as is instruction on basic weapons handling.

Week 3 continues pugil stick exercise and other close combat training, more advanced classes on first aid and values, a 3-mile march (with packs), and the "Confidence Course"—an obstacle course.

Week 4 continues pugil stick and close combat training, as well as academic classes. Platoon drill is emphasized during this week as well.

Week 5 includes Combat Water Survival, a 5-mile hike, an examination on marine customs and courtesies, more first aid training and academics, and a major inspection.

Weeks 6 and 7 are devoted mainly to weapons training, including live-fire training with the M-16. In addition, recruits receive basic training in grenades and other types of weapons and, in week 7, take a 6-mile night march and run the Confidence Course a second time.

Week 8, called "Team Week," is devoted to various fatigue duties, such as work in the mess hall. It is followed during week 9 by training in the fundamentals of field firing and a 10-mile march.

Week 10 trains in the basics of patrolling, firing, setting up camp, and other field skills. Recruits are also given nuclear-biological-chemical training.

Week 11 begins with the Company Commander's Inspection and culminates in "The Crucible"—a 54-hour ordeal that includes food and sleep deprivation and some 40 miles of marching and problem solving as well as teamwork tests. When the Crucible is successfully completed, the DI presents each recruit with the USMC EMBLEM.

Week 12 is the final week and includes indoctrination in USMC history and other classes.

After basic training, graduates go on to further training at the SCHOOL OF INFANTRY. Those designated as infantry marines graduate from the school to their first permanent duty station, while non-infantry marines are assigned to the Marine Combat Training Battalion at the School of Infantry. MCT enhances combat skills and prepares marines for further training in the appropriate USMC "military occupation specialty" (MOS) school.

Basilone, John (1916–1945) *Marine Corps gunnery sergeant*

Born in Buffalo, New York, Basilone attended local parochial schools, then enlisted in the U.S. Army and served in the Philippines. In July 1940, he left the USA and enlisted in the USMC, serving in Cuba, at Marine Corps Base Quantico, and at Camp Lejeune before he was deployed with the 7th Marines to the South Pacific during WORLD WAR II.

In the Lunga area of Guadalcanal, on October 24, 1942, he took charge of two machine gun sections and was principally responsible for repulsing repeated Japanese attacks. Ultimately, his actions resulted in the destruction of an entire Japanese regiment. For this, Basilone was awarded the Medal of Honor.

While serving on Iwo Jima as a gunnery sergeant with the 27th Marines, Basilone single-handedly attacked and demolished a blockhouse under heavy fire. Although he succeeded in this mission, he was cut down by enemy fire. He was awarded the Navy Cross posthumously. A U.S. Navy destroyer was also named in Basilone's honor.

battalion   See ORGANIZATION BY UNITS.

beachhead

In an AMPHIBIOUS ASSAULT, the area of the enemy's shore where troops and equipment are landed. The first objective of the assault is to secure the beachhead, which then becomes the maneuver area from which the assault is pushed inland. During ongoing operations, the beachhead is the point at which supplies and reinforcements are landed. The beachhead serves as the main support base until a port or harbor is captured from the enemy. Supply operations into and out of the beachhead are the responsibility of a logistics officer known as the "beachmaster."

Belleau Wood

One of the great USMC triumphs of WORLD WAR I. The 4th Marine Brigade, attached to the army's

2nd Division, not only successfully repelled a German attack in this location on the Western Front (June 6, 1918), but also staged a determined counteroffensive at great cost (1,087 casualties) but with great effect. The marines repelled another counterattack and, on June 23, resumed the offensive, securing the entire woods by June 26. A grateful French commander renamed Belleau Wood *Bois de la Brigade de Marine,* and the Germans took to calling the marines "devil dogs" (after which the USMC adopted its English bulldog mascot).

bellhop

Derogatory term sailors sometimes apply to a marine, especially one serving aboard ship. Also called a "seagoing bellhop."

Biddle, William P. (1853–1923) *Marine Corps commandant*

The 11th COMMANDANT OF THE MARINE CORPS, Biddle received his officer's commission in 1875 and served in the SPANISH-AMERICAN WAR and the BOXER REBELLION. Subsequently, he was stationed in the Philippines and in PANAMA. He succeeded Commandant GEORGE F. ELLIOTT on February 3, 1911, and served until February 24, 1914, when he retired.

Bladensburg, Battle of

During the WAR OF 1812, this town in Maryland, five miles east of Washington, D.C., was the site of a one-sided skirmish, on August 24, 1814, between U.S. Army and raw militia troops on the one side and an invasion force of British regulars commanded by General Robert Ross on the other. Although Ross brushed aside the army and militia troops, who barely offered resistance, 400 U.S. Navy sailors and 103 marines used five pieces of naval artillery to block the road to Washington. Their position was ultimately hopeless, since they were vastly outnumbered, but they held the road long enough to give President James Madison and

the government sufficient time to evacuate the capital. The marines and sailors repulsed three full-on infantry charges before they were finally flanked and forced to withdraw.

Once in Washington, Ross and his men put most of the public buildings to the torch.

Boeing PW-9   See AIRCRAFT, FIXED-WING.

Boomer, Walter E. (1938–   ) *Marine Corps general*

Born in Rich Square, North Carolina, Boomer took a B.A. from Duke University in 1960 and completed USMC Basic School the following year. He served with the 2nd Division at Marine Corps Base Quantico and was promoted to captain in 1966. He served in Vietnam during the VIETNAM WAR as commanding officer of a company in the 4th Marines during 1966. After his tour, in 1967, he

General Walter E. Boomer   *(U.S. Marine Corps)*

attended the Amphibious Warfare School, then became aide-de-camp (with the rank of major), assigned to the deputy chief of staff for plans in Washington, D.C. After attending the Armed Forces Staff College and taking the Short Advisors Course in 1971, he returned to Vietnam as an adviser to a South Vietnamese marine infantry battalion.

Boomer returned to the United States, where he received an M.S. degree in management and technology from American University, then was assigned to the U.S. Naval Academy in 1974, where he was chairman of the Department of Management. In 1977, Boomer was assigned as executive officer of the 3rd Marines in Hawaii, and in 1980 became commander of the 2nd Battalion of the 3rd Marines.

Boomer attended the Naval War College in 1980–81, then was assigned to the 4th Corps district in Philadelphia. Promoted to colonel in 1983, Boomer became director of the 4th Corps district. He was given command of the Marine Security Guard at Quantico in 1985, promoted to brigadier general the following year, and named director of public affairs at Marine Headquarters, Washington.

Boomer was given command of 4th Division in March 1989 and promoted to major general. The next year came promotion to lieutenant general and an appointment as commander of the Marine Central Command and the First Expeditionary Force. These he led during the PERSIAN GULF WAR (Operations Desert Shield and Desert Storm) during 1990–91.

After the war, Boomer became commanding general of Corps Combat Development Command at Quantico. He was promoted to general and assigned, on September 1, 1992, as assistant commandant. Boomer retired in 1994.

boot camp   See BASIC TRAINING.

Bougainville, Battle of

One of the Solomon Islands, Bougainville was occupied by Japanese forces early in WORLD WAR II. Operation Cherry Blossom was conceived by U.S. Navy planners to take Bougainville and use it for an air base from which to stage operations against Rabaul and NEW BRITAIN. The main Japanese base on Bougainville was located on the southern end of the island. Instead of attacking here, the 3rd Marine Division was landed at Empress Augusta Bay, a third of the way up the west coast of Bougainville, on November 1, 1943. The landing was preceded by intense naval and aerial bombardment, which knocked out Japanese naval and air strength on the island. Since few troops were positioned near Empress Augusta Bay, the USMC landing was almost unopposed, and the marines quickly established a perimeter. The army's 37th Division landed on November 8 and positioned itself on the marines' right flank. From here, USMC and USA forces advanced on the main Japanese position. Even while this action was proceeding, a fighter airstrip was quickly scratched out, followed by a bomber field.

By the end of December, the U.S. Army's Americal Division relieved USMC forces on Bougainville. In March 1944, the army had to resist two substantial Japanese assaults. Later, the army units were relieved by Australian troops, who continued to fight Japanese resistance until the very end of the war. Although Bougainville was never completely secured, it served from the end of 1943 to the end of the war as a base for American fighters and bombers.

Boxer Rebellion

Antiforeign rebels, covertly supported by the Empress Dowager, de facto ruler of China, attacked Europeans and Americans, including diplomats, in Peking (Beijing) and Tientsin in 1900. The rebels called themselves the "Righteous Fists of Harmony," which prompted Westerners to refer to them as the Boxers and the ensuing conflict as the Boxer Rebellion.

A small coalition of European and American military forces was sent to relieve the besieged diplomatic legations in Peking, to restore order,

Painting by Sergeant John Clymer (USMC) shows marines fighting the Boxers outside the Peking Legation, 1900. *(National Archives and Records Administration)*

and to put down the uprising. On May 24, 1900, Captain John Myers led a contingent of 54 marines and 5 sailors on a march to Peking. They arrived, with European troops, at the end of the month. The marines successfully held a position at the southwest corner of Legation Square and even counterattacked with good effect. The arrival of a multinational relief column, the 1st Marine Regiment, on August 13 enabled the liberation of all the legation buildings by August 14. The relief of Peking ended the Boxer Rebellion. Although greatly outnumbered initially, USMC losses were 17 killed and wounded.

Boyington, Gregory "Pappy" (1912–1988)
Marine Corps aviator

Most famous USMC aviator of WORLD WAR II, Boyington commanded Squadron 214, consisting mostly of novice pilots and known as the "Black Sheep" squadron. At 31, Boyington was the old man of the bunch and thus merited the nickname "Pappy." Piloting his F4U Corsair, Boyington personally shot down 14 Japanese aircraft in 32 days during the first combat tour of the squadron. He fought at GUADALCANAL, New Georgia, New Britain, and Rabaul before he was shot down and made a prisoner of war on January 3, 1944. He was liberated on August 29, 1945. Boyington received the Medal of Honor and retired from the USMC, a colonel, in 1947. His exploits became the basis of a popular television series, *Black Sheep Squadron*.

brig

USMC and USN term for a prison or other place of punitive confinement, either aboard ship or on shore.

Colonel Gregory "Pappy" Boyington (USMC)   *(U.S. Marine Corps)*

brigade   See ORGANIZATION BY UNITS.

brigadier general   See RANKS AND GRADES.

burp
U.S. Army slang for a marine.

Burrows, William Ward (1758–1805)
   Marine Corps commandant
Burrows was the first commandant of the U.S. Marine Corps, appointed by President John Adams on July 12, 1798, the day after Congress passed legislation creating the Marine Corps; traditionally, however, the marines have regarded SAMUEL NICHOLAS, captain of the CONTINENTAL MARINES, as the first commandant of the Corps and Burrows as the second. Burrows served from 1798 until March 6, 1804, when ill health forced his retirement.

Born in Charleston, South Carolina, on January 16, 1758, Burrows served in the AMERICAN REVOLUTION with the state troops of South Carolina and was commissioned a major at the time of his appointment as marine commandant. His command consisted of 881 officers, noncommissioned officers, privates, and musicians.

Burrows organized the marines primarily for service aboard some 25 navy vessels during the undeclared naval conflict generally called the Franco-American Quasi-War (1798–1800). Major Burrows was promoted to lieutenant colonel on May 1, 1800, but, as the Quasi-War wound down, he found himself embattled with a parsimonious Congress, which stinted on funds for the Corps and ordered a reduction in its already modest size. This made it very difficult for the commandant to recruit the caliber of personnel he wanted in what he intended to become an elite organization. Nevertheless, Burrows demanded high standards of professional performance and personal conduct from the officers and enlisted personnel he did manage to recruit. These standards stood the Corps in good stead when hostilities escalated with the BARBARY PIRATES and Congress authorized the expansion of the marines. As Burrows had fought the earlier reduction, now he presided over the expansion.

Commandant Burrows established a number of marine institutions, including the MARINE BARRACKS that still stand at Eighth and I Streets in Washington, D.C., and the first U.S. MARINE BAND, which he partially financed by securing contributions from his officers. Most important, his insistence on the highest possible standards of professionalism and character established a rigorous tradition that became a Marine Corps hallmark.

Butler, Smedley D. (1881–1940) *Marine Corps general*
Smedley D. Butler, nicknamed "Ol' Gimlet Eye," was one of two marines in the history of the Corps to receive *two* Medals of Honor (see also DALY, DANIEL). Born on July 30, 1881, in West Chester, Pennsylvania, he secured a marine commission as a

second lieutenant on May 20, 1898, by lying about his age. Sent to Cuba during the SPANISH-AMERICAN WAR, he arrived too late to see any action and returned to Washington, D.C., for a brief period of instruction. He was next assigned to the Marine Battalion, North Atlantic Squadron, with which he served until February 11, 1899. He was honorably discharged a few days later, on February 16, 1899, but quickly returned to the Corps, reentering with a commission as first lieutenant on April 8, 1899.

Butler was immediately assigned to duty with the Marine Battalion at Manila, Philippine Islands; then, from June 14, 1900, to October of that year, he served in China, during the BOXER REBELLION. He was breveted to the rank of captain for his heroism in action near Tientsin, during which he was wounded on July 13, 1900.

Butler returned to the United States in January 1901 and served variously ashore and at sea before he was promoted to major in 1909 and, in Decem-

Major General Smedley D. Butler (USMC)   *(U.S. Marine Corps)*

ber of that year, assigned to command the 3rd Battalion, 1st Marine Regiment in PANAMA. He was detached to command an expeditionary battalion to NICARAGUA on August 11, 1912, and participated in the bombardment, assault, and capture of Coyotepe, during October 12 to 31. He returned to Panama in November 1912 and, in 1914, was deployed with marines to Veracruz, Mexico, where he commanded the force that landed and occupied the city. For action here during April 21–22, he received his first Medal of Honor, going on to claim his second the very next year, for his bravery and leadership as commanding officer of detachments of the marines and sailors who repulsed Caco resistance at Fort Rivière, HAITI, on November 17, 1915.

In August 1916, Butler was promoted to lieutenant colonel and, during WORLD WAR I, commanded the 13th Marine Regiment in France. He emerged from the Great War with the Army Distinguished Service Medal, the Navy Distinguished Service Medal, and the French Order of the Black Star. Promoted to the temporary rank of colonel on July 1, 1918, and to temporary brigadier general on October 7, he reverted to permanent colonel on March 9, 1919, but was soon promoted to the permanent rank of brigadier general and was appointed commanding general of the Marine Barracks, Quantico, Virginia, serving in this capacity from 1920 to January 1924. Butler was the youngest general officer in the history of the Corps.

In January 1924, Butler was granted a leave of absence to accept the post of director of public safety of the city of Philadelphia, but, two years later, in February 1926, he returned to active duty as commandant of Marine Corps Base San Diego, California. In March 1927, Butler returned to China with the 3rd Marine Brigade, then came back to the States later in the year to resume command at Quantico. Promoted to major general on July 5, 1929, Butler was passed over for the post of COMMANDANT OF THE MARINE CORPS and, in disappointment, retired on October 1, 1931.

Always a maverick, Butler probably should not have been surprised that he was not named commandant. In 1935, he published *War Is a Racket*, a shockingly candid memoir that characterized the role of the marines in China and Central America as hired thugs protecting the interests of American big business. In addition to publishing this scathing book, Butler also exposed what he identi-

fied as a fascist/corporate cabal to overthrow President Franklin Roosevelt immediately after his inauguration in 1933.

Butler died at the Naval Hospital, Philadelphia, on June 21, 1940, after a brief illness.

C

C-12 Huron   See AIRCRAFT, FIXED-WING.

camp

In contrast to a post—a permanent military installation—a camp is a temporary installation; however, note that some permanent USMC facilities include the word "camp" in their name, for example, Camp LeJeune.

See also BASES, CAMPS, AND OTHER INSTALLATIONS.

captain   See RANKS AND GRADES.

Carlson, Evans F. (1896–1947) *Marine Corps commando*

Carlson was a pioneer of the concept of an elite ranger or commando force, which he led to great effect in WORLD WAR II.

A native of Portland, Oregon, Carlson first joined the U.S. Army in 1912, and attained the rank of sergeant by the time he was discharged in 1916 after serving in Hawaii and the Philippines. He reenlisted and was part of General John J. Pershing's Punitive Expedition against Pancho Villa later in 1916. During World War I, he served in the Argonne campaign, in which he was wounded. Commissioned a second lieutenant in May 1917, he was promoted to captain and served in the army of occupation.

In 1922, Carlson enlisted in the USMC as a private, but was soon commissioned (in 1923), based on his army experience. He served at Marine Corps Base Quantico, Puerto Rico, Pensacola, and Shanghai, then fought against insurgents in Nicaragua. His action leading a small unit earned him the

Brigadier General Evans Fordyce Carlson (USMC)
(U.S. Marine Corps)

534

Navy Cross—and doubtless inspired his interest in developing small-unit tactics.

In 1933, Carlson was assigned to the U.S. legation in Peking (Beijing), China, and began to learn Chinese. After a brief return to the United States, he was sent back to China in 1937, this time as a military observer during the Sino-Japanese War. During 1937–38, he studied guerrilla tactics with Chinese communist forces and was so struck by the dangers of Japanese aggression that he briefly resigned from the USMC to devote himself to lecturing on the topic.

Carlson reentered the USMC in 1941, on the eve of WORLD WAR II, at the rank of major. He was given command of the 2nd Marine Raider Battalion and shaped this unit into an elite commando/guerrilla force. "Carlson's Raiders" fought on Makin Island (August 1942)—an action for which Carlson, now a lieutenant colonel, won his second Navy Cross—and on GUADALCANAL. Carlson led his Raiders in classic small-unit actions during this pivotal 1942 battle.

Carlson functioned as an observer of the TARAWA invasion and served as a vital liaison between the overall commander and the commander on the ground. Carlson also ensured logistical continuity during the Guadalcanal campaign; he kept supplies flowing to the advanced and isolated USMC units. After Guadalcanal, Carlson was named assistant operations officer of the 4th Marine Division, charged with assisting with plans for the invasion of the MARSHALL ISLANDS early in 1944. Wounded in action on SAIPAN in June 1944, Carlson was forced to retire in July 1946 as a brigadier general.

Cates, Clifton B. (1893–1970) *Marine Corps commandant*

The 19th COMMANDANT OF THE MARINE CORPS, Cates was born and raised in Tennessee, graduated with a law degree from the University of Tennessee in 1916, then served in the MARINE CORPS RESERVE. With America's entry into WORLD WAR I, Cates was sent to France in 1918 and led a platoon of the 6th Marines at BELLEAU WOOD and in other engagements. Wounded six times and gassed, Cates was decorated with the Navy Cross, the Silver Star, the Croix de Guerre, and the French Legion of Honor. He remained in the USMC after the war, serving on sea duty, then becoming a White House aide to the commandant of the Marine Corps. Later he served as aide-de-camp to the commander of the Pacific. Joining the 4th Marines at Shanghai in 1929, he served in China until 1932. Back in the States, he served in the War Plans section at USMC headquarters, then returned to China in command of a regiment. In 1940, he was given command of the USMC Basic School in Philadelphia.

During WORLD WAR II, Colonel Cates led the 1st Marines at GUADALCANAL, then returned to the United States in 1943 with the rank of brigadier general. He was given command of Marine Base Quantico, then returned to the Pacific front in 1944 as commander of the 4th Marine Division and led the successful attacks on TINIAN and then on IWO JIMA, in February 1945. Returning to the United States later in the year, he once again assumed command at Quantico.

Promoted to general in 1948, he was appointed commandant and immediately found himself obliged to fight for the future of the USMC, which was the victim of severe postwar cutbacks. Cates was highly successful in rallying congressional support for the USMC; this and the outbreak of the KOREAN WAR put an end to the cutbacks and prompted an expansion.

In 1952, at the conclusion of his four-year term as commandant, he requested continued active duty. To secure this, he accepted reversion to the rank of lieutenant general and took command at Quantico. When he finally retired on January 30, 1954, his four-star rank was reinstated.

CH-37 "Mojave"   See AIRCRAFT, ROTARY-WING.

CH-46 Sea Knight   See AIRCRAFT, ROTARY-WING.

CH-53D Sea Stallion   See AIRCRAFT, ROTARY-WING.

CH-53E Super Stallion   See AIRCRAFT, ROTARY-WING.

Chapman, Leonard F., Jr. (1913–   ) *Marine Corps commandant*

The 24th COMMANDANT OF THE MARINE CORPS, Chapman was raised in Florida and received an army commission after completing a University of Florida ROTC course; however, he entered the USMC in 1935, received artillery training, and served with the 10th Marines before he was sent to Hawaii in 1940. He was on sea duty during the early part of WORLD WAR II in the Pacific.

In 1942, Major Chapman was assigned as an artillery instructor at Marine Corps Base Quantico, and in 1944, as a lieutenant colonel, he took command of a battalion of the 11th Marines at PELELIEU. He continued as 4th Battalion commander at OKINAWA during April–July 1945.

After the war, Chapman served in the USMC Division of Plans, then in important positions at Quantico and Marine Corps Base Camp Pendleton. He took command of the 12th Marines in 1952, serving with them in Japan before going on to command Marine Barracks Yokosuka. After commanding the Force Troops of the FLEET MARINE FORCE Atlantic (1958–61), Chapman was promoted to brigadier general and was named deputy chief of staff at HEADQUARTERS MARINE CORPS, Washington, D.C. On January 1, 1968, as a major general, Chapman became assistant chief of staff. After WALLACE GREENE retired as commandant of the USMC, Chapman replaced him on January 1, 1968. Chapman was commandant during the first stages of U.S. troop withdrawal from Vietnam (see VIETNAM WAR). When he retired from the USMC on December 31, 1971, he was named director of the U.S. Immigration and Naturalization Service.

Chapultepec, Battle of

Chapultepec was a hilltop fortress two miles southwest of Belen Gate, one of the entrances to Mexico City. As General Winfield Scott's (USA) forces closed on the Mexican capital during the U.S.-MEXICAN WAR, Chapultepec was garrisoned by about 800 men and was heavily defended by artillery. The young students of an on-site military academy also participated in the defense of this position.

On September 13, 1847, a USMC battalion attached to the army's 2nd Brigade attacked Chapultepec from the south. Marines were part of a 40-man advance party that stormed the walls of Chapultepec during the initial assault. Simultaneously, marines captured Mexican artillery and neutralized it.

After Chapultepec fell, Mexico City followed, and marines were assigned mop-up operations on the day after the capital surrendered. USMC personnel raised the Stars and Stripes over the National Palace.

The USMC action at Chapultepec and Mexico City is commemorated in the "Halls of Montezuma" reference in the MARINE HYMN.

Château-Thierry

This French town, on the River Aisne, 60 miles northeast of Paris, was a principal objective of a German offensive late in WORLD WAR I. The 2nd Division took over defense of Château-Thierry from the battle-weary French on May 30, 1918. By June 6, the marines had stopped the German advance and commenced a counteroffensive at BELLEAU WOOD. With Belleau Wood, Château-Thierry demonstrated the extraordinary combat performance of the USMC.

Chemical Agent Monitor   See NUCLEAR-BIOLOGICAL-CHEMICAL EQUIPMENT.

chicken plate

Marine and army slang for a steel or ceramic insert worn inside a bullet-proof vest for added protection.

chief of naval operations (CNO)

The CNO is effectively the U.S. Navy's chief of staff. He or she commands the major USN headquarters and shore commands and activities as well as the operating forces of the USN. It is to the CNO (and the SECRETARY OF THE NAVY) that the COMMANDANT OF THE MARINE CORPS reports.

Choiseul Raid

Choiseul is one of the Solomon Islands in the Pacific, and in October 1943 during WORLD WAR II the little island became the target of a USMC paratroop landing. The battalion-strength raid was led by Colonel VICTOR KRULAK on October 27 and was intended to draw Japanese forces away from BOUGAINVILLE, the main objective of a combined USMC-USA assault. The marines knew they were greatly outnumbered—at least 4,300 Japanese occupied the island—but their objective was not to capture Choiseul, but merely to create a diversion.

This succeeded, although historians still dispute whether or not the raid was necessary, and many doubt that it caused the Japanese to modify their Bougainville positions. Nevertheless, the marines were successfully evacuated in November, and the operation is celebrated in USMC annals as an example of outstanding performance against a vastly superior enemy force—the kind of mission for which the USMC is specially trained and suited.

Chosin Reservoir, Battle of

On October 26, 1950, during the KOREAN WAR, the 1st Marine Division (attached to X Corps, USA) was transported to Wonson, on the east coast of the Korean Peninsula and assigned to attack the hydroelectric plant at Chosin. On November 2, while advancing along a rugged mountain road northwest of Hungnam, the 7th Marines made contact with Chinese forces. Nevertheless, by November 10, marines had reached the southern end of the

U.S. forces withdrew southward following the massive Chinese intervention in the Korean War. Shown here is Weapons Company, in line with Headquarters and Service Company, 2nd Battalion, 7th Marines, on November 27, 1950. *(Naval Historical Center)*

Chosin Reservoir. Elements of this force moved west to Yudam-ni, where, on November 26, they were joined by the 5th Marines. In the meantime, the 1st Marines were thinly distributed to the rear, assigned to hold open the lines of communication to the advance marine positions. Thus strung out along a zone of action approximately 300 miles long, the marines were expected to effect a pincers action to flank North Korean forces in the area. Two adversaries intervened, however. The weather plunged below zero, and the Communist Chinese crossed the border in great numbers in a massive incursion into the war.

The Chinese attacks halted the U.S. advance to the Yalu River, then turned it. The thinly distributed marines found themselves under heavy attack and, as the great Eighth Army retreated, they were forced, in small units, to fight for their survival. They succeeded to a remarkable degree, but Chosin Reservoir is recorded in USMC annals as perhaps the most bitter fight of the Korean War.

Close Quarters Battle/Direct Action Program

The Close Quarters Battle/Direct Action Program consists of the following components: Individual Assault Kit, Assault Breacher's Kit, HAZMAT Assault Mask, Assault Vest, and Assault Suit. It is intended for use by Force Reconnaissance Companies; Marine Corps Security Force Battalions, Fleet Anti-terrorist Security Team (FAST) Companies, Special Operations Training Groups (SOTGs), Marine Security Guard (MSG) Units, and Military and Police Special Reaction Teams (SRTs).

The function of the Close Quarters Battle/Direct Action Program is to provide standardized personal, protective, and load-bearing capability for select Special Operations personnel. The Individual Assault Kit contains items required by the individual marine for the Direct Action, including climbing/rappelling equipment, individual protective apparel, personnel restraining devices, and load-bearing and accessory equipment. The As-

sault Breacher's Kit includes tools and equipment (other than munitions) to conduct mechanical and explosive forced entries into enclosed buildings and structures. Its components consist of mechanical entry devices, hand tools, firing devices, and safety equipment. The HAZMAT Assault Mask provides protection from toxic fumes that may be encountered during DA operations. This advanced mask incorporates enhanced communications and an expanded field of view. The Assault Vest combines combat load-bearing capabilities with enhanced torso ballistic protection. The Assault Suit provides a functional, durable, fire-retardant, protective outerwear that combines the most desirable features of the combat vehicle crewman/aviator suits.

The Close Quarters Battle/Direct Action Program package was designed using the input of marines who have performed the DA mission. It is intended to ensure that those performing the mission will have state-of-the-art equipment and that no improvisation of equipment will be necessary.

code talkers See NAVAJO CODE TALKERS.

color sergeant of the U.S. Marine Corps

This noncommissioned officer commands the U.S. MARINE CORPS COLOR GUARD and also serves as the keeper of the Battle Color of the USMC—the official USMC flag. Special qualifications for the color sergeant include a height of at least 6 feet 4 inches and a White House security clearance. The color sergeant carries the National Ensign (U.S. flag) in ceremonies and the Presidential Color in all White House state functions and ceremonies. The color sergeant must use only one arm to carry the flag, whereas other military services permit both arms to be used.

Combat Rubber Raiding Craft See

LANDING CRAFT.

Combat Service Support Schools (MCCSS)

The Marine Corps CSSS conducts formal resident training for commissioned officers and noncommissioned officers in logistics, motor transport, personnel administration, supply, and fiscal accounting and disbursing. The schools also conduct instructional management and combat water survival swim training.

MCCSSS is located at Camp Johnson, adjacent to Marine Corps Base Camp Lejeune, North Carolina. The individual schools include:

Combat Water Survival Swimming School

The Combat Water Survival Swimming School trains marine combat water survival instructors. The school works closely with the navy and the American Red Cross in developing appropriate advanced training.

Further reading: Web site: www.lejeune.usmc.mil/mccsss/schools/cwsss/cwsss.shtml.

Financial Management School

The Financial Management School provides six formal courses of instruction to marines as well as to Department of Defense civilian personnel: Financial Management Officer Course—Finance; Financial Management Officer Course—Comptroller; Advanced Finance Course; Financial Management Career Course; Basic Finance Technician Course; and Fiscal Budget Technician Course.

Further reading: Web site: www.lejeune.usmc.mil/mccsss/schools/fms/fms.shtml.

Instructional Management School

The Instructional Management School trains and educates the personnel who train and educate marines. Three sets of courses are offered:

1. The Formal School Instructor Course covers basic communication skills, preparation techniques, and adult learning, employing various teaching methods and instructional aids.
2. The Curriculum Developer Course focuses on the design and development of instructional materials, including conducting a learning analysis, writing learning objectives, test items, selecting a delivery system (method/media), media development, and constructing of both instructor and student outlines.
3. The Administrator Course addresses the management and supervision of instruction using the Systems Approach to Training (SAT), specially developed for the marines.

Further reading: Web site: www.lejeune.usmc.mil/mccsss/schools/ims/ims.shtml.

Logistics Operations School

The Logistics Operations School trains marines in organizational and intermediate motor transport maintenance, logistics and motor transport operations, maintenance management, landing support operations, and embarkation.

Further reading: Web site: www.lejeune.usmc.mil/mccsss/schools/los/los.shtml.

Personnel Administration School

The Personnel Administration School provides basic, intermediate, and advanced, resident, formal school instruction to marine personnel administrators, with special emphasis on combat service support. The Administrative Clerk Course and the Personnel Clerk Course are the entry-level offerings. Career-level courses are the Adjutant Course, Personnel Officer Course, Advanced Personnel Administration Course, Senior Clerk Course, and Reserve Administration Course.

Further reading: Web site: www.lejeune.usmc.mil/mccsss/schools/pals/pals.shtml.

Supply School

The Supply School designs, develops, conducts, and evaluates entry-level, intermediate, and advanced resident, formal education and training for officers and enlisted personnel assigned to the marine corps supply occupational field. The school offers the following courses of study:

Ground Supply Officer Course
Noncommissioned Officer Supply Course
Ground Supply Chief Course
Enlisted Supply Independent Duty Course
Basic Preservation and Packaging Course
Enlisted Supply Basic Course
Enlisted Warehouse Basic Course
Functional System Administrator Course
Enlisted Supply Basic Course (Reserve)
Ground Supply Officer Course (Reserve)

Further reading: Web site: www.lejeune.usmc.mil/mccsss/schools/supplyschool.

combined arms team

A USMC and U.S. Army term for combat force in which two or more arms are represented; for example, aircraft providing close air support for an infantry assault may be said to constitute a combined arms team, as does (for instance) a team that combines infantry, engineers, and defense artillery.

commandant of the Marine Corps

The CMC reports to the SECRETARY OF THE NAVY and THE CHIEF OF NAVAL OPERATIONS and is responsible for the administration, discipline, organization, training, and readiness of the USMC. The CMC is a member of the Joint Chiefs of Staff.

communications equipment

Special communications equipment used by the marines includes:

AN/TTC-42 (V)
Automatic Telephone Central Office

The AN/TTC-42 (V) Automatic Telephone Central Office is an important component of USMC communications, providing automatic telephone switching and satellite telephone subscriber service. It is an S-280 shelterized telephone central office, which provides secure automatic switching service (loop-to-loop, loop-to-trunk, and trunk-to-trunk) as well as such subscriber service functions as loop and trunk hunting, precedence, and preemption. These services are available to the TRI-TAC family of 4-wire, digital subscribers and non-secure voice terminals (DSVTs and DNVTs) and to 4-wire digital trunks, including both single-channel and Time Division Multiplexed (TDM) groups. The AN/TTC-42 will also perform automatic switching for 4-wire analog loops and trunks. Sophisticated communication security used in the AN/TTC-42 includes the HGF-93, HGF-94, KG-82, KG-93, and KG-94 protocols. The USMC has 61 AN/TTC-42 (V) Automatic Telephone Central Offices—at a unit cost of $2 million—allocated as of late 2003.

General characteristics of the system include:

Contractor: ITT Aerospace/Communications Division
Length: 181 in
Width: 88.4 in
Height: 87 in
Weight: 5,525 lb
Displacement: 805.3 cu ft
Power: 115/230 volts, 50/60 hertz single-phase, 3 kilowatt; 30 ampere
Terminations: 280 circuits—180 via 7 mux groups and 100 single-channel terminations
Circuits: 152 switched (loops and trunks) and 144 sole user
Trunks: 90 (up to 24 analog)
Multiplexed groups: four
Signaling modes: analog 4-wire DTMF, 4-wire SF AC Supervised AUTOVON
Traffic (average): 650 calls/hr

SB-3865
Automatic Telephone Switchboard

The SB-3865 Automatic Telephone Switchboard is a team-transportable, tactical, digital switching system for voice and data communication across secure as well as non-secure telephone lines. It provides automatic switching service (loop-to-loop, loop-to-trunk, and trunk-to-trunk) and subscriber service functions such as loop and trunk hunting, precedence, and preemption. The USMC maintained 425 of the switchboards in its inventory as of 2004.

General characteristics of the SB-3865 Automatic Telephone Switchboard include:

Manufacturer: ITT Aerospace/Communications Division
Length, switch module: 20.7 in
Length, power module: 20.6 in
Width, switch module: 21.1 in
Width, power module: 17.8 in
Height, switch module: 19.6 in
Height, power module: 17.7 in
Weight, switch module: 99 lb
Weight, power module: 125 lb
Displacement, switch module: 3.5 cu ft
Displacement, power module: 3.5 cu ft
Power source: 120/208 VAC, 50/60 or 400 hertz single-phase, 480 watts, or 28 VDC, 304 watts
Terminations: 86 circuits per module (maximum of 96 per stack)
Circuits: 32 switched (loops and trunks) or 36 sole user
Trunks: 18 per module, 54 per stack maximum
Multiplexed groups: Three per module, nine per stack maximum
Signaling modes: analog 2-wire and 4-wire DTMF, 4-wire SF AC Supervised AUTOVON
Traffic: 130 calls/hr per module, 390 per stack maximum

Single-Channel Ground and Airborne Radio System (SINCGARS)

This USMC system provides the primary means of command, control, and communications (C^3) for the Ground Combat Element, Air Combat Element, and Combat Service Support Element of the MARINE AIR GROUND TASK FORCE (MAGTF). SINCGARS is capable of transmitting voice and analog or digital data up to 16 kilobytes per second. The system employs electronic counter-countermeasures to minimize vulnerability to enemy electronic warfare, and it provides secure communications with an integrated communications security (ICOM) device. This state-of-the-art system replaces the AN/PRC-77 and VRC-12 series radios to provide improved reliability, availability, and maintainability. As of 2004, 25,390 of these $6,500 units were in the USMC inventory.

General characteristics of the SINCGARS tactical communications radio include:

Manufacturer: ITT Aerospace/Communications Division
Length: 10 in
Width: 10.7 in
Height: 3.4 in
Weight: 15.4 lb

company See ORGANIZATION BY UNITS.

company clerk
In the USMC, a company clerk assists the master sergeant of the company. (In the army, he or she assists the first sergeant.) The company clerk is chiefly responsible for the day-to-day flow of paperwork and routine administrative procedures.

company grade officer See RANKS AND GRADES.

Continental Marines

On November 10, 1775, the Continental Congress commissioned Robert Mullan, proprietor of the Tun Tavern in Philadelphia, to raise two battalions of marines under the leadership of SAMUEL NICHOLAS. On November 28, Nicholas was formally commissioned captain of the new force, called the Continental Marines, and although never officially appointed as commandant, he assumed that role as a practical matter. Today, the Tun Tavern is still considered the birthplace of the United States Marine Corps.

The Continental Congress authorized two battalions of marines, specifying that those recruited be good seamen, "able to serve to advantage by sea." Nicholas was soon promoted to major and, in

March 1776, under the overall command of the navy's John Paul Jones, Nicholas led 200 marines (and 50 sailors) in the first marine amphibious assault, landing on New Providence Island in the Bahamas. In a 13-day operation, the marines secured two forts, occupied Nassau, seized control of Government House, and captured 88 guns, 16,535 rounds of ammunition, and other supplies.

Nicholas and the marines next saw action in December 1776, when three companies (80 men) accompanied Washington's army in the successful Battle of Trenton. The marine companies remained with Washington in winter quarters at Morristown, New Jersey, until February 1777. In the spring, Washington formally incorporated some marines into artillery units of his Continental army, while Nicholas returned to Philadelphia and his shore-based marines were assigned to defensive duty in Delaware.

A small number of marines were deployed to New Orleans in January 1778 to keep British traders out of the port, and in April of that year, 20 marines were attached to service with John Paul Jones to sail on the *Ranger,* which raided the English coast. The marines participated in two raids, the first on British soil in some seven centuries. A handful of marines also accompanied Jones on the *Bon Homme Richard* during August 1779.

Continental Marines participated in a valiant but failed attack on Fort George in the Penobscot River in July 1779; they also served escort duty, assigned to guard a caravan of ox carts conveying a million silver crowns, loaned by France, from Boston's harbor to Philadelphia. In January 1783, Continental Marines formed the boarding party that seized the British ship *Baille* in the West Indies. This was the last military operation performed by the force.

At the conclusion of the American Revolution, Congress acted swiftly to disband the Continental army and the Continental navy. The Continental Marines was officially dissolved in June 1785, and it was not until July 11, 1798, that President John Adams signed the bill creating its successor organization, the United States Marine Corps.

corporal   See RANKS AND GRADES.

corps   See ORGANIZATION BY UNITS.

corpsman

In the USMC and U.S. Navy, a corpsman is an enlisted medic. With the dark humor typical of the military, the corpsman is often called a "corpseman."

Cuban Rebellion

After the disputed presidential election of 1906, Cuba, independent from Spain following the SPANISH-AMERICAN WAR OF 1898, was on the brink of civil war. The outgoing Cuban president requested U.S. military aid. In response, 130 marines and sailors of the West Indies Squadron landed at Havana on September 13 to protect U.S. property. This force was followed by two USMC battalions to support a provisional government under the U.S. secretary of war, William Howard Taft. A second USMC regiment was landed on October 1. When units of the U.S. Army arrived later, the marine brigade was disbanded, save for the 1st Marine Regiment, which remained under army command and did not leave the island until 1909.

Marines returned in May 1912 to help quell a new rebellion. This provisional brigade consisted of two regiments. Once a new Cuban government regained control, the marines were withdrawn in late July.

Cushman, Robert E., Jr. (1914–1985) *Marine Corps commandant*

The 25th COMMANDANT OF THE MARINE CORPS, Cushman was born in St. Paul, Minnesota, and graduated from the U.S. Naval Academy in 1935. He attended Basic School, then was stationed with the 4th Marines in Shanghai in 1936. After serving in a number of stateside posts, Cushman was in command of the detachment aboard the battleship

Pennsylvania when it was attacked by the Japanese at Pearl Harbor on December 7, 1941.

During WORLD WAR II, Cushman, promoted to major, was assigned to the 9th Marines and, in May 1943, was given command of the 2nd Battalion. He led his command in combat on BOUGAINVILLE and GUAM, winning the Navy Cross for gallantry in repulsing a banzai charge on Guam.

Toward the end of the war, Cushman was stationed at Marine Corps Base Quantico and then was assigned to command the Amphibious War Branch, headquartered in Washington, D.C. He subsequently served on the staff of the commander of U.S. Naval Forces in the Atlantic and Mediterranean, then was assigned as director of plans and operations at the Armed Forces Staff College. In July 1956, Cushman was given command of the 2nd Marines at Marine Corps Base Camp Lejeune. During this period, he also served Vice President Richard M. Nixon as assistant for national security affairs.

In 1960, Cushman was appointed assistant commander of the 3rd Division, Okinawa, and in July 1962, now a major general, Cushman was named assistant chief of staff to the commandant of the USMC. Promoted to lieutenant general in 1967, Cushman became commander of III Marine Amphibious Force in Vietnam (see VIETNAM WAR).

During his two years as commander of III MAF, Cushman sharply disagreed with army general William Westmoreland, overall commander of U.S. forces in the theater, over the most effective use of the marines. Westmoreland wanted to use them as part of the so-called main force strategy, incorporating them in conventional massed assaults, whereas Cushman wanted to deploy the marines in separate hit-and-run raids and guerrilla-style actions and to have them work with South Vietnamese forces in furthering the so-called pacification of the rural villages.

Cushman left Vietnam and returned to the United States in 1969. He served as deputy director of the Central Intelligence Agency until he was appointed commandant on January 1, 1972. During his tenure, Cushman saw the last of the marines leave Vietnam and presided over the peacetime reduction of the Marine Corps to 194,000 marines. Although the Marine Corps was officially desegregated in 1949, de facto segregation persisted in some areas, especially in the Stewards Branch, which was all black. Cushman ordered an end to de facto and "voluntary" segregation throughout the corps.

Robert E. Cushman, Jr., retired as commandant in 1975 and died on January 2, 1985.

D

Daly, Daniel (1873–1937) *Marine Corps gunnery sergeant*

No less a figure than JOHN A. LEJEUNE, COMMANDANT OF THE MARINE CORPS, lauded Dan Daly as "the outstanding Marine of all time," and SMEDLEY D. BUTLER (with Daly, the only marine in history awarded *two* Medals of Honor) called him "the fightingest Marine I ever knew." Daly is perhaps best known for his rallying cry at WORLD WAR I's Battle of BELLEAU WOOD: "Come on, you sons of bitches, do you want to live forever?"

Born in Glen Cove, Long Island, New York, on November 11, 1873, the slightly built Daly (5 feet, 6 inches, 134 pounds) enlisted in the marines on January 10, 1899, eager to get in on the SPANISH-AMERICAN WAR. The fighting ended before he was out of boot camp, and he was deployed instead to shipboard service with the Asiatic Fleet. In 1900, he landed with the marines in China during the BOXER REBELLION and, in defense of the Tartar Wall, south of the American Legation, he held off a Boxer assault almost single-handedly. This action, on August 14, earned him his first Medal of Honor. His second Medal of Honor came 15 years later, when, on October 24, 1915, as a gunnery sergeant, he led a detachment of 35 marines against some 400 Caco insurgents in HAITI.

In addition to combat service in China and Haiti, Daly served in Panama, Cuba, Veracruz, Mexico, and Puerto Rico, in addition to various postings in the United States before the nation entered World War I. During this conflict, Daly served in France from November 4, 1917, to April 21, 1919, and saw combat in the Toulon Sector (March–May 1918), in the Aisne Operations (June 1918), and in the Château-Thierry Sector (June 1918). In this latter sector, he distinguished himself

Gunnery Sergeant Daniel Daly (USMC)   *(U.S. Marine Corps)*

at Belleau Wood, a battle in which a handful of marines successfully repulsed a major German offensive aimed directly at Paris. Daly went on to serve in the St. Mihiel Offensive (September 1918) and the Champagne Offensive (September–October 1918). He was wounded on June 21 and twice wounded on October 8, 1918.

Daly was the epitome of the marine noncommissioned officer. Repeatedly offered commissions, he turned them down, always expressing his desire to be an "outstanding sergeant" rather than a mediocre officer. Retired officially on February 6, 1929, with the rank of sergeant major, Daly spent the last years of his life as a Wall Street bank guard.

Dauntless bombers   See AIRCRAFT, FIXED-WING.

decorations and medals

Marines are eligible for decoration with the following medals and commendations. They are also eligible for many of the medals and decorations offered by the other services.

Marine Corps Expeditionary Medal

This medal is awarded to marines who have participated in operations against armed opposition on foreign territory. The medal, made of bronze, depicts a marine in full pack charging with bayonet through waves and onto the shore. The medal is suspended from a gold ribbon bearing three vertical red stripes, one at either end and in the middle.

Marine Corps Reserve Ribbon

The ribbon is presented to marines who have completed 10 years of service in the MARINE CORPS RESERVE. Ribbon is gold colored, with a narrow vertical stripe on each end.

Medal of Honor

The highest military honor in the United States, the Medal of Honor has been awarded 3,428 times in the nation's history and is presented by the president in the name of Congress to a person "who distinguishes himself or herself conspicuously by gallantry and intrepidity at the risk of his life or her life above and beyond the call of duty while engaged in an action against an enemy of the United States; while engaged in military operations involving conflict with an opposing foreign force; or while serving with friendly foreign forces engaged in an armed conflict against an opposing armed force in which the United States is not a belligerent party. The deed performed must have been one of personal bravery or self-sacrifice so conspicuous as to clearly distinguish the individual above his comrades and must have involved risk of life. Incontestable proof of the performance of the service will be exacted and each recommendation for the award of this decoration will be considered on the standard of extraordinary merit."

The marines have earned 295 Medals of Honor. The first was awarded to Corporal John F. Mackie for his actions on May 15, 1862, during the Civil War. The most recent was awarded to Lance Corporal James D. Howe for his actions in May 1970 at Quang Ngai, South Vietnam.

Marines are also eligible for the medals listed below, from the other services:

Combat Action Ribbon, Joint Meritorious Unit Award, Joint Service Achievement Medal, Meritorious Service Medal, Military Outstanding Volunteer Service Medal, National Defense Service Medal, NATO Medal–Former Republic of Yugoslavia, NATO Medal–Kosovo Operations, Navy Cross, Navy/Marine Corps Achievement Medal, Navy/Marine Corps Commendation Medal, Navy/Marine Corps Medal, Navy/Marine Corps Overseas Service Ribbon, Navy Occupation Service Medal, Philippine Defense Medal, Philippine Independence Medal, Philippine Liberation Medal, Philippine Presidential Unit Citation, Presidential Unit Citation, Prisoner of War Medal, Republic of Korea Presidential Unit Citation, Republic of Korea War Service Medal, Republic of Vietnam Campaign Medal, Republic of Vietnam Gallantry Cross with Palm, Southwest Asia Service Medal, United Nations Medal, United Nations Service Medal, Vietnam Service Medal, World War II Victory Medal.

Derna   See BARBARY PIRATES; O'BANNON,
PRESLEY.

Desert Shield and Desert Storm   See PER-
SIAN GULF WAR.

Devereux, James P. S. (1903–1988) *Marine
Corps general*
Devereux was the son of a military family and was
born on post in Cuba. After attending the Army
and Navy Preparatory School, Washington, D.C.,
he was sent to boarding school in Switzerland. He
joined the USMC in 1923 and received his commission as a second lieutenant in 1925. His first
overseas assignment was in NICARAGUA during
1926–27. After sea duty, he became an officer of the
legation guard in Peking (Beijing). During the
1930s, back in the United States, he was assigned to
Marine Corps Base Quantico and then to the Coast
Artillery School at the U.S. Army's Fort Monroe,
Virginia. During the later 1930s, he served as an
instructor at the Base Defense Weapons School,
Quantico.

After brief sea service and service at Marine
Corps Base San Diego, Devereux was posted to
Pearl Harbor, Hawaii, in January 1941, then was
sent to command the USMC detachment—449
marines—at WAKE ISLAND, little more than a way
station for commercial seaplane flights via the Pan
American Clipper.

After the outbreak of WORLD WAR II in the
Pacific, Wake Island was attacked by Japanese
forces on December 11, 1941. Major Devereux
commanded the remarkable, but ultimately hopeless, defense of the island. The marines surrendered
to overwhelming numbers on December 23, and
Devereux spent the rest of the war as a prisoner of
war.

After World War II, Devereux was promoted to
colonel, retroactive to November 1, 1942. He
served in Washington, D.C., Quantico, and Camp
Pendleton, retiring in August 1948 with the rank of
brigadier general. After leaving the Marine Corps,

Devereux gained election to the U.S. House of Rep-
resentatives.

Diver Propulsion Device (DPD)   See
PERSONAL AND MISCELLANEOUS EQUIPMENT.

division   See ORGANIZATION BY UNITS.

Dominican Republic
With the assassination of Dominican dictator
Leonidas Trujillo in May 1961, leftist political
groups threatened to topple the government.
USMC and USN forces were sent to the region in
1961 and 1963 to demonstrate support for what
was deemed an anticommunist government. On
each occasion, the show of force was sufficient to
restore order. In 1965, however, a civil war erupted,
and the government lost ground, including most of
the capital city, Santo Domingo. The president
hastily stepped down, and the United States feared
that the Dominican Republic would go the way of
Cuba. Accordingly, on April 28, 1965, 500 marines
were sent to reinforce loyalist Dominican troops to
secure landing areas for helicopters, so that U.S.
and other nationals could be evacuated. Before the
end of the month, three USMC battalions had been
landed, with a fourth battalion held in reserve on
board a waiting ship. When, on April 29, U.S. Army
forces (82nd Airborne) arrived, command passed
to an army general.

In light combat, nine marines died and 30 were
wounded, but the rebels quickly backed down, the
government forces retook Santo Domingo, an
inter-American peace-keeping force was created by
the Organization of American States, and a communist takeover of the nation was averted.

double trouble
Also known as "dual cool," the term describes a
marine specially qualified as a SCUBA diver and as
a paratrooper.

See also U.S. MARINE CORPS RECONNAISSANCE BATTALIONS.

Dragon Weapon System   See ANTIARMOR WEAPONS.

drill instructor

The DI is a noncommissioned officer who trains and oversees training of recruits during BASIC TRAINING. In the USMC, each recruit platoon is assigned three drill instructors, who are also called "Hats," after the distinctive campaign-style headgear the DI wears. Of the three drill instructors, one is senior and is distinguished by a black leather belt (so is called "Black Belt"; also, "Big Dad"). The senior DI is assisted by the "Second Hat"; together, they are in charge of instruction. The third DI ("Third Hat") deals with issues and matters of discipline.

The USMC DI is almost legendary for toughness; however, today's DI undergoes a rigorous 10-week training course and is forbidden from abusing recruits in any way. The term "drill sergeant," formerly interchangeable with "drill instructor," is now obsolete.

A drill instructor prepares his platoon for final drill competition.   *(U.S. Marine Corps)*

dual cool   See DOUBLE TROUBLE.

DUKW   See AMPHIBIOUS VEHICLES.

E

EA-6B Prowler   See AIRCRAFT, FIXED-WING.

Elliott, George F. (1846–1931) *Marine Corps commandant*

Tenth COMMANDANT OF THE MARINE CORPS, Elliott attended the U.S. Military Academy at West Point for two years before he was commissioned a second lieutenant in the USMC in 1870. After serving in a variety of posts, he commanded a company during the SPANISH-AMERICAN WAR in 1898. The following year, he commanded a battalion at Cavite in the Philippines. He was appointed commandant of the USMC in October 1903, with the rank of brigadier general.

The USMC commanded by Elliott consisted of a mere 7,800 men, but, as a result of his lobbying President Theodore Roosevelt and Roosevelt's successor, William Howard Taft, the USMC was expanded. Equally important, its duties, often vaguely specified in the past, were clarified. Elliott retired in 1910.

embarked marines

While marines have always served aboard U.S. Navy ships in security and other roles, most marines sail as "embarked marines"—troops being transported for amphibious landing in a combat area.

emblem, USMC

The "Globe and Anchor" or "Corps Badge" is the official insignia of the USMC and features a spread eagle atop the world globe (Western Hemisphere) crossed by a fouled anchor. The eagle holds in its beak a scroll bearing the inscription SEMPER FIDELIS. The elements of the emblem acknowledge the USMC as an American maritime force (the eagle and the anchor) capable of global deploy-

The USMC emblem   *(U.S. Marine Corps)*

ment (the globe). The current emblem was designed in 1868 by General JACOB ZEILIN.

Eniwetok Atoll, Battle of

Eniwetok is a circular atoll located in the Marshall Islands and was the site of an important USMC engagement during WORLD WAR II. The 22nd Marines were assigned to take Engebi, northernmost of the Eniwetok islands, while the army's 106th Regiment landed on Eniwetok Island, at the south end of the atoll. When Engebi and Eniwetok had been secured, the large island between them, Parry, would be taken and occupied. The entire operation was code-named Catchpole.

The marines began by taking two tiny islands near Engebi and placing artillery on these. Fire was directed from this land-based position, as well as from U.S. Navy ships, against Engebi to prepare it for the USMC landing, which took place on February 19, 1944. The battle here lasted only six hours. All but 16 of the island's 1,200-man garrison were killed.

Operation Catchpole had assumed that Engebi was the most heavily defended of the islands. In fact, Eniwetok proved far more heavily defended, and a USMC battalion was deployed to assist the army regiment heavily engaged there. On February 21, Eniwetok was secured.

Now it was time to take Parry Island. However, while USN intelligence had concluded that the island was undefended, it was, in fact, occupied by a 1,300-man garrison. Nevertheless, supported by naval bombardment, a pair of USMC battalions took the island by February 22.

Possession of the Eniwetok atoll gave U.S. forces a valuable fleet anchorage and an air base from which operations against the Mariana Islands could be efficiently and adequately supported.

expeditionary force

This general term for an armed force assembled to accomplish a specific mission in a foreign country is also often used specifically to describe the USMC, which is above all an "expeditionary force," deployed to foreign countries to carry out a specifically defined mission.

Extreme Cold Weather Tent (ECWT)   See

PERSONAL AND MISCELLANEOUS EQUIPMENT.

F

F2A Buffalo   See AIRCRAFT, FIXED-WING.

F2H Banshee   See AIRCRAFT, FIXED-WING.

F2T Black Widow   See AIRCRAFT, FIXED-WING.

F4B Phantom II   See AIRCRAFT, FIXED-WING.

F4D Skyray   See AIRCRAFT, FIXED-WING.

F4F Wildcat   See AIRCRAFT, FIXED-WING.

F4U Corsair   See AIRCRAFT, FIXED-WING.

F6F Hellcat   See AIRCRAFT, FIXED-WING.

F8 Crusader   See AIRCRAFT, FIXED-WING.

F8C-5 Helldiver   See AIRCRAFT, FIXED-WING.

F9F-8 Cougar   See AIRCRAFT, FIXED-WING.

F/A-18A/C/CN Hornet   See AIRCRAFT, FIXED-WING.

F/A-18D Hornet   See AIRCRAFT, FIXED-WING.

Field Pack, Large, with Internal Frame (FPLIF)   See PERSONAL AND MISCELLANEOUS EQUIPMENT.

FIM-92A Stinger   See AIR DEFENSE ARTILLERY.

Financial Management School   See COMBAT SERVICE SUPPORT SCHOOLS.

fire base
A field combat base staffed by a company or platoon and used as a base from which patrols are sent out. Fire bases are sometimes established to provide security in a given area.

fire support base
An FSB is set up near a combat area to supply field combat units with logistical and artillery support. The FSB is not placed in the forefront of the front lines.

first lieutenant See RANKS AND GRADES.

FJ1-FJ4 Fury See AIRCRAFT, FIXED-WING.

flame thrower See WEAPONS, INDIVIDUAL AND CREW-SERVED.

Fleet Marine Force

The FMF is the land assault component of the Navy Expeditionary Forces and consists primarily of marines. Currently, there are two principal FMFs: FMFLANT, assigned to the Atlantic and headquartered at Camp Lejeune, North Carolina, and FMFPAC, assigned to the Pacific and headquartered at Camp H. M. Smith, Hawaii.

Each FMF is organized into MARINE AIR-GROUND TASK FORCES (MAGTF) ranging in size from marine expeditionary units (MEU) of 1,000 to 4,000 marines, to marine expeditionary forces (MEF), comprising 30,000 to 60,000 marines. Currently, the total strength of each FMF is 89,000 marines.

forward observer

Artillery liaison officer attached to an infantry unit in the field for the purpose of directing artillery fire against the enemy.

Fuller, Ben H. (1870–1937) *Marine Corps commandant*

The 15th COMMANDANT OF THE MARINE CORPS, Fuller was born in Big Rapids, Michigan, and graduated from the U.S. Naval Academy at Annapolis in 1889. After a two-year cruise prior to his appointment as a USMC second lieutenant, Fuller served seven years at sea, then commanded a marine detachment aboard the *Columbia* in the West Indies during the SPANISH-AMERICAN WAR. He fought in the PHILIPPINE INSURRECTION, then in the BOXER REBELLION in 1900.

Major General Ben Hebard Fuller (USMC) *(U.S. Marine Corps)*

In 1904, Fuller was assigned to command the USMC base at Honolulu, Hawaii. After serving in various other posts, he attended the Naval War College and was assigned to command the marine barracks in Philadelphia. He fought in SANTO DOMINGO in 1918–19, then served on the faculty of the Naval War College during 1920–22 before taking command of Marine Corps Base Quantico.

Fuller commanded the 1st Brigade in HAITI during 1924–25, and in July 1925 was named assistant commandant of the USMC. Promoted to major general, he became commandant in 1930, retiring early in 1934.

Functions Paper, The

Sometimes referred to as the "Key West Agreement," *The Functions Paper* was drawn up and agreed to in 1948 among the armed services and is the principal interservice agreement that defines the functions of each service. According to *The Functions Paper,* the USMC is to perform the following functions:

To provide FLEET MARINE FORCES of combined arms for service with the Fleet in the seizure or defense of advanced naval bases for the conduct of land operations necessary to the prosecution of a naval campaign.

To provide detachments and organizations for service on armed navy vessels as well as security detachments for the protection of navy property, bases, and naval stations.

To collaborate with the other services in developing doctrine, equipment, and techniques for amphibious operations.

To train and equip marine forces for airborne operations.

To collaborate and coordinate with the other services in developing doctrines, procedures, and equipment for marine airborne operations.

G

Gale, Anthony (1782–1843) *Marine Corps commandant*

Fourth COMMANDANT OF THE MARINE CORPS, Gale was born in Dublin, Ireland, and immigrated to the United States late in the 18th century. He was infamous for his hot temper, and in 1801 he killed a U.S. Navy officer in a duel. Despite this, Gale became commandant in 1819, appointed by the secretary of the navy to replace ARCHIBALD HENDERSON, who became acting commandant after the death of FRANKLIN WHARTON in 1818. His appointment was by virtue of his seniority within the Marine Corps.

Gale was quarrelsome—quarreling even with the navy secretary—and was a notorious imbiber. Court-martialed for his drunkenness and generally disreputable behavior in 1820, he unsuccessfully pleaded temporary insanity. President James Monroe dismissed him from the USMC, but directed that his pension be continued for life.

Geiger, Roy S. (1885–1947) *Marine Corps general*

Geiger commanded amphibious assaults on key Pacific islands during WORLD WAR II. Born in Middleburg, Florida, he graduated from John B. Stetson University in 1907 and took a law degree, but practiced for just a few months before enlisting in the USMC in November 1907. After only two years in the Marine Corps, he was commissioned a sec-

ond lieutenant and in 1915 was promoted to first lieutenant, having served at sea and in the Caribbean, the Philippines, and China. Promoted to captain in 1917, Geiger become the fifth USMC officer to complete pilot training. He served during

General Roy Stanley Geiger (USMC)   *(U.S. Marine Corps)*

WORLD WAR I in France as a major in command of a squadron of the 1st Marine Aviation Force.

After the war, Geiger served in HAITI as commander of the 1st Aviation Group, 3rd Marine Brigade, from 1919 to 1921. Transferred to Marine Corps Base Quantico in 1921, he attended and graduated from the U.S. Army's Command and General Staff School in 1925. Four years later, he graduated from the Army War College, and from 1929 to 1931 he commanded Aircraft Squadrons, East Coast Expeditionary Force, stationed at Quantico. In 1931 he was appointed officer in charge of aviation at HEADQUARTERS MARINE CORPS, Washington, D.C., serving there from 1931 to 1935.

Promoted to lieutenant colonel in 1934, Geiger commanded Marine Air Group One, 1st Marine Brigade, from 1935 to 1939, and then was sent to the Naval War College. Graduating in 1941, he was promoted to brigadier general and given command of the 1st Marine Air Wing, Fleet Marine Force, in September. With the outbreak of World War II, Geiger took command of the air wing on GUADALCANAL as soon as the island was captured. He served on Guadalcanal from September 1942 to February 1943, was promoted to major general, and returned to Washington as director of the Marine Division of Aviation. In November 1943, he succeeded General ALEXANDER A. VANDEGRIFT as commander of I Amphibious Corps (later redesignated III Amphibious Corps), which he led in the invasion of GUAM during July 21–August 10, 1944. Geiger was also in charge of the bloody invasion of PELELIU from September 15 to November 25, 1944, then went on to participate in the landing on OKINAWA from April 1 to June 18, 1945. In the Okinawa campaign, his corps was part of the Tenth Army, commanded by General Simon B. Buckner. When Buckner was killed in battle, Geiger assumed command of the Tenth Army until the arrival of General Joseph W. Stilwell on June 23. Thus Geiger became the only USMC officer ever to command a field army.

In July 1945, Geiger was appointed to command Fleet Marine Force, Pacific. After the war, in November 1946, he was assigned to a post in Washington, but soon fell ill. He died before receiving promotion to general, which Congress conferred posthumously in July 1947.

general   See RANKS AND GRADES.

Gilbert Islands, USMC assaults on

Early in WORLD WAR II, the Gilbert Islands, a widespread chain of several Pacific islands and atolls that was then a British colony, were seized from the British and occupied by the Japanese. MAKIN Island, one of the islands in the chain, was the site of a key Japanese radio station, which fell to a USMC raid in August 1942. While this raid was valuable, it also prompted the Japanese to beef up their defenses in the area, especially on Betio Island. This became the objective of an assault by the 2nd Division, USMC, in November 1943. After a battle of three days, the island fell to the marines. Simultaneously U.S. Army forces occupied Makin.

The action in the Gilberts was important in the Pacific war because it represented the first significant breach in Japan's outer defenses. It was the first step in the "island hopping" campaign that would constitute the war in the Pacific.

Glenn, John H., Jr. (1921–   ) *Marine Corps aviator, astronaut, U.S. senator*

Glenn was a distinguished USMC aviator, who achieved his greatest fame as an astronaut, the first American to orbit the Earth. Elected to the U.S. Senate in 1974, he became the oldest human being in space, when he volunteered for a Space Shuttle flight in 1998.

Born in Cambridge, Ohio, Glenn enlisted in the MARINE CORPS RESERVE in 1942 during WORLD WAR II and was subsequently designated an aviation cadet. After completing his flight training in March 1943, he shipped out to the Pacific in February 1944 and flew 59 missions in the Marshalls and Marianas with Fighting Squadron 155. He was sent back to the United States in February 1945, then served in GUAM after the war and on the North China patrol.

Colonel John H. Glenn, Jr. (USMC) *(U.S. Marine Corps)*

After promotion to major in July 1952, Glenn took jet refresher training and, in February 1953, was ordered to Korea and assigned to Fighting Squadron 311. He flew 63 missions with that squadron and another 27 assigned to the USAF's 51st Fighter Wing. He shot down three MiGs.

On his return from Korea, Glenn went to the USN's Test Pilot School, completing his training in 1954 and working in advanced testing. His flight from Los Alamitos to New York in an F8U-1 Crusader on July 16, 1954, was the first coast-to-coast, nonstop supersonic flight in aviation history, which earned Glenn his fourth Distinguished Flying Cross.

Chosen as a Mercury astronaut in 1959, Glenn became the first American to achieve orbital spaceflight on February 20, 1962. Three years later, he retired from the USMC to enter business and to work as a civilian NASA consultant. Elected to the Senate from Ohio in 1974, he retired from the Senate in 1999, but in 1998 flew aboard Space Shuttle *Discovery* as "Payload Specialist 2" and the oldest person ever to fly in space.

Gray, Alfred M., Jr. (1928–) *Marine Corps commandant*

The 29th COMMANDANT OF THE MARINE CORPS, New Jersey-born Alfred M. Gray, Jr., enlisted in the USMC in 1950, served in the Pacific, then was commissioned a second lieutenant in 1952. He attended Basic School and the Army Field Artillery School before shipping out to the KOREAN WAR, where he served as an artillery officer with the 1st Division. He served a second Korean tour as an infantry officer with the 7th Marines before returning to the United States in December 1954.

From 1956 to 1961, Gray served in various stateside posts before moving to an assignment at GUANTÁNAMO BAY. He served in the VIETNAM WAR with the 12th Marines in 1965 and subsequently served in Vietnam with other outfits until his return to Washington in 1968 as a lieutenant colonel working on Department of Defense special projects. At Marine Corps Base Quantico, he helped to develop sensor technology.

In 1969, Gray returned to Vietnam for a second tour, specializing in surveillance and reconnaissance with I Corps. Subsequently, he served in intelligence and later attended the Command and General Staff School. In 1971, he commanded a battalion of the 2nd Division and was deployed to the Mediterranean. He was made commander of the 2nd Marines in April 1972 and then assistant chief of staff, G-3, 2nd Division.

After attending the U.S. Army War College in 1973, he was named to command the 4th Marines and simultaneously served as commander of Camp Hansen, Okinawa. In 1975, Gray returned to Vietnam, this time as deputy commander of the 33rd Amphibious Brigade, directing the U.S. evacuation of Southeast Asia.

Promoted to brigadier general in 1976, Gray commanded the 4th Amphibious Brigade and the Landing Force Training Command, Atlantic. In 1980, as a major general, he commanded 2nd

Division, Marine Corps Base Camp Lejeune. Promoted to lieutenant general in 1986, he commanded FLEET MARINE FORCE, Atlantic; Fleet Marine Force, Europe; and II Amphibious Force. On July 1, 1987, promoted to general, he was appointed commandant of the USMC.

Greene, Wallace M., Jr. (1907–2003)

Marine Corps commandant

The 23rd COMMANDANT OF THE MARINE CORPS, Wallace M. Greene, Jr., was born in Burlington, Vermont, and graduated from the U.S. Naval Academy in 1930. Commissioned a second lieutenant in the USMC, he served in a variety of shore and sea duties before being posted to GUAM and Shanghai. Shortly before WORLD WAR II, he was stationed at GUANTÁNAMO BAY, Cuba. In 1941, he served in England as a military observer and also attended British amphibious warfare and demolition schools.

Greene was promoted to major and assigned in February 1942 as assistant chief of staff of the 3rd Marine Brigade, with which he sailed to Samoa. Late in 1943, he was sent to Hawaii as assistant chief of staff of V Amphibious Corps and was instrumental in planning the Marshall Islands campaigns. Early in 1944, as operations officer for the 2nd Division, Greene served in the SAIPAN campaign and in operations against TINIAN. He returned to Washington in October 1944 as operations officer, Division of Plans, Marine Headquarters.

After the war, Greene served in numerous staff positions, then attended the National War College and, in September 1955, was promoted to brigadier general and named assistant commandant at Marine Corps Base Camp Lejeune. He became base commandant in 1957, then was transferred to Washington, where he served as assistant chief of staff to the commandant of the Marine Corps. Promoted to major general, he became deputy chief of staff in 1958, then chief of staff in 1960. Greene was appointed commandant of the Marine Corps in 1964.

Greene oversaw operations in the DOMINICAN REPUBLIC in 1965 and the first major marine build-up in the VIETNAM WAR, at Da Nang, also in 1965. Greene presided over the deployment of marine forces during the early years of the war, until his retirement at the end of 1967.

Grenada invasion

Grenada is a small island nation (population 110,100) at the southern end of the Windward Islands chain in the West Indies. In 1979, a Marxist-Leninist coup led by Maurice Bishop, head of the radical New Jewel movement, overthrew the government. Subsequently, his pro-Cuban regime built a 9,800-foot-long airstrip, apparently for military purposes. The administration of Bishop proved short-lived; he was killed in a 1983 coup, which left Deputy Prime Minister Bernard Coard and General Hudson Austin in charge of the government. Sir Paul Scoon, Grenada's governor-general, secretly communicated with the Organization of Eastern Caribbean States (OECS), requesting aid in restoring order to the troubled country. The OECS, in turn, asked for U.S. military intervention, to which President Ronald Reagan enthusiastically agreed, citing a need to protect the approximately 1,000 American citizens in Grenada —most of them students at a local medical school.

Operation Urgent Fury was launched and included a naval battle group centered on the aircraft carrier *Independence,* as well as the helicopter carrier *Guam,* two USMC amphibious units, two Army Ranger battalions, a brigade of the 82nd Airborne Division, and special operations units. These massive forces landed on Grenada on October 25, 1983, and found themselves facing no more than 500 to 600 Grenadan regulars, 2,000 to 2,500 poorly equipped and poorly organized militiamen, and about 800 Cuban military construction personnel. The invading force seized the airport and destroyed Radio Free Grenada, a key source of government communications. Next, the U.S. nationals were evacuated, and Grenada was declared to be under U.S. military control by October 28.

Eighteen U.S. personnel died in the assault on Grenada, and 116 were wounded. Grenadan forces lost 25 dead and 59 wounded, while Cuban casualties were 45 dead and 350 wounded.

grunt

In the USMC and army, a grunt is an enlisted infantryman.

Guadalcanal

In WORLD WAR II, this southwest Pacific island became the site of a turning-point battle after Japanese forces began construction of an airfield on the island at the end of May 1942. This base posed a grave threat to the Allied supply line to Australia and New Zealand; therefore, Major General ALEXANDER VANDEGRIFT was ordered to lead two USMC regiments against it. The marines landed on August 7, 1942, taking the Japanese by surprise and capturing the airfield (renamed Henderson Field), but suffering an intense counterattack in return. The marines of the 1st Division held the island alone until the arrival of the 7th Marines in mid-September and the U.S. Army American Division and 2nd Marines in November, followed soon by

On Guadalcanal, a casualty from the front-line fighting is transferred from a makeshift stretcher before being taken through the jungle and downriver to a nearby hospital. *(Library of Congress)*

the U.S. Army's 25th Division. By February 1943, the remaining Japanese forces had been evacuated from Guadalcanal. Combined with the U.S. victory in the naval battle of Midway, Guadalcanal was a turning point in the Pacific war, marking an Allied shift to offensive warfare in this theater.

Guam

During WORLD WAR II, this U.S. Pacific possession in the Mariana Islands was taken by the Japanese on December 8, 1941. It had been defended by a badly outnumbered garrison of 125 marines and 271 sailors.

Operation Forager, the reconquest of Guam, commenced on July 21, 1944, and was a combined USMC and army operation. The island was declared secure on August 10, after virtually the entire 18,000-man Japanese garrison had been killed. Combined marine and army casualties were 7,714 killed and wounded. Securing Guam gave the U.S. Army Air Forces a key base from which B-29s could raid the Japanese home islands.

Guantánamo Bay

The United States has maintained a major naval base, with a USMC contingent, at Guantánamo Bay, Cuba, since December 1903. The base is the oldest U.S. base overseas and the only one in a communist country. It was leased by the United States in December 1903 as a coaling station for warships. The lease was reaffirmed by a 1934 treaty, which stipulates that the lease can be terminated only by the mutual consent of the United States and Cuba.

Since 1961, when President Dwight D. Eisenhower severed diplomatic relations with Cuba after Fidel Castro instituted a communist government there, the primary duty of the USMC contingent at Guantánamo has been to secure the base and patrol its 17.4-mile fence line.

Existing in essentially hostile territory, Guantánamo is wholly self-sufficient, with a desalination plant to provide fresh water and a generating plant to produce more than 800,000 kilowatt hours of electricity daily. The base is divided in two by Guantánamo Bay, which is 2.5 miles wide. The airfield is located on the leeward side, the main base on the windward side.

In 1991, USMC personnel were assigned the additional task of accommodating some 34,000 refugees who fled Haiti after a violent coup there. In May 1994, USMC and U.S. Navy personnel participated in Operation Sea Signal in support of Joint Task Force 160, tasked with providing humanitarian assistance to thousands of Haitian and Cuban migrants. The last Haitian migrants departed the base in November 1995, and the last Cuban refugees left on January 31, 1996.

In January 2002, USMC personnel took charge of "Camp X-Ray" at Guantánamo, a hastily constructed temporary prison compound for Taliban fighters captured during military action in Afghanistan following the September 11, 2001, terrorist attacks on New York and Washington. Following Operation Iraqi Freedom in 2003, some prisoners captured in Iraq have also been housed at Camp X-Ray.

gung-ho

A thoroughly committed, highly aggressive, extremely motivated soldier—a hard charger. The term *gung-ho* originated during WORLD WAR II with the USMC, which borrowed it from the Mandarin Chinese word gōnghō, meaning "to work together," but *gung-ho* has also found its way into the other services and into the civilian realm as well.

Gungi Marine

A "Gungi Marine" is the ideal marine, possessed not only of boundless courage and initiative, but also of good sense, good humor, and supreme competence. The term is doubtless related to GUNG-HO.

gunnery sergeant See RANKS AND GRADES.

gyrene

Slang for a marine, this term is widely used but of unknown origin. Since it rhymes with *marine,* it is reasonable to assume that it is a play on the word *marine* and may well be a combination of *G.I.* and *marine.* It may also be a combination of JARHEAD and "marine." Some have suggested that the word derives from *gyrinus,* the Latin term for tadpole, a reference to the amphibious mission of the USMC; this etymology seems farfetched, to say the least.

H

Hagaru-ri, breakout from

After the massive Communist Chinese incursion into Korea during the KOREAN WAR, which drove the marines out of their positions at the CHOSIN RESERVOIR, USMC units retreated to the town of Hagaru-ri. Chinese forces positioned themselves to the north, on high ground, and set up blocking forces along the route of retreat to Koto-ri. To prevent the capture of the marines, the order was given for the 7th Marine Division to attack to the south while the 5th Marines held Hagaru-ri. Simultaneously, a reinforced company of the 1st Marines, aided by British Royal Marines, would push northward from Koto-ri. The idea was to attack the Chinese forces from two directions and provide the marines at Hagaru-ri with a retreat route.

Although the 1st Marines and the Royal Marines were badly cut up, they managed to fight their way through, and, on December 1, 1950, were relieved by elements of the 7th Marines. This allowed the 5th and 7th Marines to make their break from Hagaru-ri on December 6. In a remarkable running fight, the USMC successfully evacuated the town, bringing all personnel and equipment out and reaching the safety of Koto-ri by December 7.

The breakout from Hagaru-ri is recorded in USMC annals as a classic withdrawal operation under extremely unfavorable conditions. Although the marines lost 730 killed and more than 3,600 wounded, their withdrawal had mauled the vastly superior Chinese forces, which were rendered incapable of pursuing the evacuated forces. The marines had transformed a costly encirclement and strategic retreat into an even more costly tactical defeat for the enemy.

Haiti

USMC action in Haiti first came in December 1914, when a USMC detachment was landed to secure the Haitian treasury during an uprising. In March 1915, two USMC companies were landed and advanced on Port-au-Prince, the Haitian capital, to restore order there. More marines followed, and by late August the total number of marines in country was 2,000. They fought pitched battles, including hand-to-hand combat in an abandoned French fort atop a 4,000-foot mountain, against insurgents called the Cacos.

With the defeat of the Cacos, the United States backed a new government friendly to its interests and established an indigenous Haitian Constabulary, commanded and trained by marines. When the Cacos reemerged in strength in March 1919, 1,000 marines of the 1st Brigade were landed to support the constabulary. During the summer, two marines and a Haitian constable penetrated the camp of the Caco leader, Charlemagne Peralte. The three killed Peralte. A new Caco leader emerged, and the 1st Brigade, now reinforced by the 8th Marines, began a systematic campaign against the Cacos. The rebellion ended in May 1920, when the

Marines from Lima Company, 3rd Battalion, 8th Marine Regiment, offload chairs at a local school in Haiti on May 11, 2004. The marines handed out nearly 30 desks, more than 100 chairs, and several tables to Escole Eu Venesuala (Venezuela School) as part of the Multinational Interim Forces effort to help the struggling Caribbean nation. *(U.S. Marine Corps)*

new Caco leader was killed by a marine patrol. Marines remained in Haiti until 1934.

The USMC intervened in Haiti again after President Jean-Bertrand Aristide was overthrown in a military coup d'état. In 1994, marines were part of the U.S. military force that returned Aristide to office.

Han River Forts, Battle of the

Korea was long known as the "Hermit Kingdom" because of its intransigent, hostile posture toward any contact with foreigners. When a band of Koreans known as the Salee River pirates attacked and killed the crew of the shipwrecked USS *General Sherman,* the United States minister to China was sent to Seoul to negotiate a settlement. His escort consisted of an intimidating armada of five U.S. Navy warships, in advance of which a survey party was sent to chart the best passage up the Han River to Seoul. After the Koreans fired upon this party, the fleet commander, Admiral John Rodgers, demanded an apology. Receiving none, he sent a force of sailors and 109 marines under Captain McLane Tilton (USMC) to attack the ancient Han River Forts. The force landed near the first fort on June 10, 1871, and was bogged down in the mud. However, covered by naval bombardment, they assaulted the first fort, took it, and spiked its artillery. On June 11, the second fort fell, followed by the principal fort, known as the Citadel. Situated atop a 150-foot hill, the fort was a formidable objective for an assault, but the marines and sailors took it after a sharp hand-to-hand contest. Korean casualties were 243 killed; the marines lost two of their number.

The action at the Han River Forts made way for the U.S. minister, who negotiated at length with the Koreans, but failed to emerge with a treaty. Despite the absence of a document, the Koreans never attacked the Americans again.

Harpers Ferry

Harpers Ferry, Virginia (today, West Virginia), was, in 1859, the site of a federal arsenal. With 18 men, the radical abolitionist militant John Brown raided and captured the arsenal on October 16, 1859, with the object of arming slaves for a local slave revolt that, he hoped, would precipitate widespread slave revolts across the South.

Brown and his men, with hostages, holed up in a firehouse. No regular army detachment was available, so Lieutenant Israel Greene, with 86 marines, was ordered to Harpers Ferry from MARINE BARRACKS, Washington, D.C. On arrival, he was to turn over command to the senior army officer present, Colonel Robert E. Lee—who thus became the only U.S. Army officer ever to lead marines into combat.

On October 17, Lee deployed his marines in two storming parties, then sent his aide, Lieutenant J. E. B. Stuart, to parley with Brown in the hope of persuading him to surrender peacefully. When Brown refused, Lee ordered Lieutenant Greene to storm the firehouse. The battle lasted a mere three minutes. Greene wounded Brown, and his men killed all but four of Brown's followers. In the melee, four hostages, including the mayor of Harpers Ferry, were killed. One marine died.

Taken prisoner, Brown and his surviving followers were tried by the state of Virginia, which convicted them of murder and conspiracy to foment servile insurrection. They were hanged.

Harris, John (1793–1864) *Marine Corps commandant*

The sixth COMMANDANT OF THE MARINE CORPS, Harris was commissioned a second lieutenant in

Colonel John Harris (USMC) *(U.S. Marine Corps)*

the USMC in 1814, saw no significant action in the WAR OF 1812, then served sea duty for most of the next two decades. He fought in the SECOND SEMINOLE WAR during 1836–37 and was breveted a major. Harris led a battalion in the U.S.-MEXICAN WAR, but reached the front too late to see action. He did serve in Mexico in the occupying forces.

Promoted to colonel in 1855, Harris became commandant at that rank in January 1859. He was commandant when a USMC detachment was ordered to HARPERS FERRY to quash John Brown's raid. Harris also commanded the USMC during the Civil War, until his death on May 12, 1864. He was widely criticized as too old and lethargic to lead the USMC in this great conflict.

hash marks

Hash marks are service stripes worn on the lower left sleeve of the uniform of an enlisted marine. Each stripe (hash mark) stands for four years of service.

hasty defense

Also called a hasty perimeter, a hasty defense is a defensive perimeter quickly set up under enemy fire. The art of the hasty defense relies heavily on existing terrain features to provide ready-made cover, since, by definition, creating a hasty defense allows no time for preparing formal defensive works.

HAWK   See AIR DEFENSE ARTILLERY.

Headquarters Marine Corps (HQMC)

HQMC is nominally located in Washington, D.C., but is physically accommodated in the Pentagon, with some offices at Marine Corps Base Quantico; the Navy Annex, Arlington; and Clarendon Center, Rosslyn, Virginia. HQMC is the USMC executive and includes the office of the COMMANDANT OF THE MARINE CORPS and all executive departments.

Henderson, Archibald (1783–1859) *Marine Corps commandant*

Fifth COMMANDANT OF THE MARINE CORPS, Henderson was born in Colchester, Virginia, and was commissioned a second lieutenant in the USMC in 1806. Promoted to captain in 1811, he served at sea during the WAR OF 1812 on board the USS *Constitution*. For his service, he was breveted major. Henderson also served at the Battle of NEW ORLEANS as commander of the USMC contingent in that celebrated victory of December–January 1814–15.

Henderson became USMC commandant in 1820, a period of crisis for the Marine Corps, which had suffered under the incompetent leadership of Henderson's predecessor, ANTHONY GALE, such that President Andrew Jackson agitated for its dissolution. Henderson spearheaded the effort to save the USMC, and he also led its reorganization through Congress in 1834. This put the USMC under the secretary of the navy, not the secretary of war, and increased its size.

In 1836, Henderson led the USMC contingent participating in the SECOND SEMINOLE WAR and emerged a brevet brigadier general, the first marine to hold that rank. Henderson did not personally lead troops in the U.S.-MEXICAN WAR, but he did secure presidential approval to increase the size of the USMC again and dispatched two battalions for service in the conflict. Henderson died in office in 1859, having served as a dynamic commandant for 39 years.

Heywood, Charles (1839–1915) *Marine Corps commandant*

Ninth COMMANDANT OF THE MARINE CORPS, Heywood was a native of Maine and received his commission as second lieutenant in 1858. While serving aboard a number of ships during the Civil War, he participated in the capture of Fort Clark and Fort Hatteras and commanded guns aboard USS *Cumberland* when it was sunk by the Confederate ironclad *Virginia (ex-Merrimack)*.

After the war, Heywood continued to serve sea duty until he was given command of MARINE BARRACKS, Washington, D.C., in 1876. He commanded

Major General Charles Heywood (USMC)   *(U.S. Marine Corps)*

the USMC in PANAMA in 1885. In 1891, Heywood was appointed commandant and introduced important personnel reforms, requiring fitness reports and promotion examinations, and establishing the School of Application, a training facility for new USMC officers. Heywood was commandant during the SPANISH-AMERICAN WAR and during subsequent action in the PHILIPPINE INSURRECTION, NICARAGUA, and again in Panama. Promoted to major general in 1902, he was the first USMC officer to hold that rank. He retired the following year, having presided over the first great period of USMC expansion, from 3,300 men at the time of the Spanish-American War to 7,600 men upon his retirement.

HH-1H Iroquois   See AIRCRAFT, ROTARY-WING.

higher

USMC slang for an officer more interested in advancing to the next rank than in proper command and welfare of his marines.

High-Mobility Multipurpose Wheeled Vehicle (HUMVEE)   See WHEELED VEHICLES.

history, overview of USMC

American Revolution through War of 1812

The CONTINENTAL MARINES, precursor of the USMC, was established early in the AMERICAN REVOLUTION, on November 10, 1775, by resolution of the Continental Congress. Two battalions of marines were authorized for service as landing forces with the newly born Continental navy. The size of the Marine Corps was no more that 300 to 400 men, and it was disbanded, along with the Continental navy, after the Treaty of Paris ended the war in 1783.

By the end of the 18th century, U.S. relations with its revolutionary ally France had deteriorated to the point that, in 1798, an undeclared naval war, often called the Franco-American Quasi-War, began. Anticipating the development of a full-scale war, the Congress reestablished the USMC on July 11, 1798. Marines formed a contingent of U.S. warship crews, their duties being to keep order aboard ship, to help man the guns, and to serve as boarding and landing parties.

Although the Franco-American Quasi-War petered out by 1800, U.S. shipping, like that of other "Christian" nations, was preyed upon in the opening years of the 19th century by the BARBARY PIRATES, state-sanctioned seaborne raiders operating from the coast of North Africa, especially Tripoli. Marines were instrumental in operations against the pirates on what the MARINE HYMN commemorates as the "Shores of Tripoli."

During the WAR OF 1812, the USMC served mainly aboard U.S. Navy ships and therefore participated in a number of brilliant tactical naval victories. On land, a small USMC contingent was part of the defense of Washington at the disastrous Battle of BLADENSBURG (Maryland), in 1813. While army and militia forces crumbled before the British advance on the capital, marines and

An MCAS Miramar CH-53 Super Stallion from Marine Heavy Helicopter Squadron 466, the Wolfpack, makes a pass hitting its target, allowing the pilots to complete their requirements for California Department of Forestry Certification. Once certified, the pilots are authorized to provide air support to ground fire fighters as they fight wildfires.   *(U.S. Marine Corps)*

sailors held fast, until they were flanked and overwhelmed by vastly superior numbers. Far more successful was USMC participation in the Battle of NEW ORLEANS in 1814–15, when a small contingent formed the very center of Andrew Jackson's defensive line.

U.S.-Mexican War

The major USMC action after the War of 1812 was during the SECOND SEMINOLE WAR (1835–42), when the Corps was assigned to assist with the "removal" of the Seminoles from Florida and Georgia in accordance with the Indian Removal Act of 1830.

The next major conflict was the U.S.-MEXICAN WAR (1846–48), in which the USMC not only performed its traditional seaborne duties, but also served with General Winfield Scott (USA) in his advance on Mexico City in 1847. Marines successfully operated to seize Mexican seaports on both the Gulf and Pacific coasts before joining Scott's advance at Pueblo, Mexico. Their participation in the invasion of Mexico City is commemorated in the Marine Hymn reference to the "Halls of Montezuma."

Civil War

The USMC was involved in the earliest action commonly associated with the Civil War when, on October 18, 1859, under the command of Colonel Robert E. Lee (USA), a company of marines fought a three-minute battle to recover the U.S. arsenal at HARPERS FERRY, Virginia (present-day West Virginia), which had been seized by militant abolitionist John Brown and a handful of followers. During the war itself, marines served mainly at sea, with the Union navy, but a USMC battalion did fight at the First Battle of Bull Run (July 21, 1861). Other USMC units saw action while serving with naval blockading squadrons at Cape Hatteras, New Orleans, Charleston, and Fort Fisher.

Post–Civil War Years

The USMC was by no means idle after the Civil War, but was landed in small parties to protect U.S. lives and property worldwide, in Egypt, Colombia, Mexico, China, Cuba, Formosa, Uruguay, Argentina, Chile, Haiti, Alaska, NICARAGUA, Japan, Samoa, and PANAMA. The largest operation during this period was in Korea in 1871, against the so-called "Salee River pirates." In a "weekend war," marines captured 481 guns, 50 Korean battle standards, and neutralized the important Han River forts. Two marines were awarded the Medal of Honor, the first time this decoration had been presented to members of the service.

Spanish-American War and After

At the commencement of the SPANISH-AMERICAN WAR in 1898, the USMC consisted of fewer than 3,000 men. One of these men, Private William Anthony, serving as orderly to Charles D. Sigsbee, captain of the U.S. battleship *Maine,* rescued his skipper after the ship exploded in Havana Harbor. Thus, a U.S. marine was the very first hero of the war.

Marines attached to the U.S. Navy squadron commanded by Commodore George Dewey at Manila Bay landed to secure the Cavite Navy Yard and held this position for three months until the arrival of the U.S. Army.

As the USMC was the first to fight in the Philippines, so it was the first to land in Cuba. On June 10, 1898, a USMC battalion hit the beach at GUANTÁNAMO BAY and seized an advance base for the U.S. fleet. The Battle of Cuzco Well, four days later, was also a USMC victory.

After the war, marines fought in the PHILIPPINE INSURRECTION and the BOXER REBELLION. They also served elsewhere in China and in Nicaragua, Panama, the DOMINICAN REPUBLIC, Cuba, Mexico (in the 1914 U.S. landings at VERACRUZ), and HAITI.

World War I

By the time of U.S. entry into WORLD WAR I in April 1917, the USMC had already proven itself as a bold expeditionary force, especially effective in small-scale police actions. Army strategists, including the overall commander of the American Expeditionary Force, General John J. Pershing (USA), had strong doubts about the effectiveness and usefulness of the USMC in large-scale conventional warfare. These doubts were soon laid to rest by USMC performance in France, especially at BELLEAU WOOD, Soissons, SAINT-MIHIEL, Blanc Mont, and the Meuse-Argonne. USMC aviation also got its start in World War I, providing close air support for Allied troops.

Of the more than 309,000 marines who served in France, about one-third were either wounded or killed in action.

Interwar Period

Like the other services, the USMC suffered severe cutbacks after World War I. Yet, under Major General JOHN A. LEJEUNE, 13th COMMANDANT OF THE MARINE CORPS, the USMC became neither demoralized nor complacent. It was during the interwar years that the Corps pioneered and developed the doctrines of AMPHIBIOUS ASSAULT and AMPHIBIOUS OPERATION that would prove critical to victory in the Pacific campaign of the war to follow.

World War II

Although the USMC would fight almost exclusively in the Pacific theater of WORLD WAR II, the 1st Provisional Marine Brigade (4,000 marines) was assigned to occupy and garrison strategically important Iceland, landing in July 1941, six months before the United States entered the war.

After the United States entered the war, following the Japanese attack on Pearl Harbor, December 7, 1941, marines were caught in the early defeats—in the Philippines and at GUAM and WAKE ISLAND—but would be instrumental in the amphibious operations that retook the islands of the Pacific, one by one, during the course of the war. GUADALCANAL, BOUGAINVILLE, TARAWA, NEW BRITAIN, KWAJALEIN, ENIWETOK, SAIPAN, GUAM, TINIAN, PELELIU, IWO JIMA, and OKINAWA were all hard-won USMC victories.

USMC strength at the beginning of World War II was 70,425 men. By war's end, this CORPS had grown to its historical maximum strength of 471,905. Almost 87,000 marines were killed or wounded in action; 82 were awarded the Medal of Honor.

Korean War

As the USMC developed amphibious doctrine and tactics between World War I and World War II, the Corps focused, after World War II, on developing "vertical envelopment" capability using helicop-

ters. However, the first major USMC operation of the KOREAN WAR (1950–53) was amphibious, as marines played a key role in the brilliant landing at INCHON in September 1950. Following the recapture of Seoul, marines participated in the UN advance to the CHOSIN RESERVOIR, then participated in the retreat and recovery that followed the entry of the Chinese Communists into the war in October and November 1950. Although an armistice was concluded in 1953, USMC ground forces were not completely withdrawn until 1955. Some 25,000 marines were killed or wounded in Korea.

Cold War Conflicts

The Cold War era saw an explosion of so-called brush-fire wars, the kind of insurgent and guerrilla conflicts that had long been the Corps's specialty. Between 1955 and 1963, marines were sent to intervene in conflicts in the Tachen Islands (port of Zhejian Province, China), in Taiwan, Laos, and Thailand, as well as, early on, in South Vietnam. Marines evacuated U.S. nationals from Egypt during the Suez crisis of 1956, and in July 1958, at the request of the government of LEBANON, a brigade-size USMC force landed there to stave off a communist coup.

In April 1965, a USMC brigade was landed in the Dominican Republic to protect Americans and evacuate those who wished to leave after a leftist uprising.

Vietnam War

The USMC entered the VIETNAM WAR (which began as a conflict between French colonial forces and Vietnamese nationalists shortly after World War II) in 1962, flying helicopter missions, providing ground reconnaissance, and furnishing advisers to the Vietnamese Marine Corps. However, the landing of the 9th Marine Expeditionary Brigade at Da Nang in 1965 was the beginning of the Corps's large-scale presence in the war; by the summer of 1968, following the Tet Offensive (see KHE SANH), USMC strength in Vietnam rose to its maximum of about 85,000. The following year, USMC withdrawal began as part of the process and policy of

"Vietnamization," the transition of responsibility for the war to South Vietnamese forces.

The last major USMC ground forces left Vietnam in June 1971, but USMC units played critical roles in the desperate, dramatic, and highly successful evacuation of Saigon in 1975 and were, in true marine tradition, the "last out" of the zone of combat. The Vietnam War was the longest conflict in USMC history. Over almost 10 years, 13,000 marines were killed and 88,000 wounded.

After Vietnam

Marines continued to play a major role in defending U.S. interests worldwide after the Vietnam War. In July 1974, USMC forces evacuated U.S. and foreign nationals from Cyprus during unrest there; from mid-decade on, the Corps figured with increasing importance in Europe, defending the northern flank of NATO. With the other services, the USMC played a leading role in developing the Rapid Deployment Force, a multi-service unit designed to provide flexible and timely military response to any crisis in the world. It was also during the post-Vietnam era that the MARITIME PREPO-SITIONING SQUADRONS (MPSs) were developed to enhance rapid deployment capability.

In response to a growing number of terrorist attacks on U.S. embassies during the 1980s, marines landed in August 1982 at Beirut, Lebanon, as part of a multinational peacekeeping force. On October 23, 1983, a truck packed with 12,000 pounds of explosives crashed through the outer defenses of the USMC headquarters building at the Beirut airport, killing 241 marines and wounding 70 others. The tragic event was a demonstration of just how hazardous peacekeeping duty can be.

Grenada Invasion and Operation Just Cause

In October 1983, marines participated in a controversial but ultimately successful intervention in GRENADA, a mission to checkmate leftist forces there and to rescue some 1,000 U.S. nationals. Six years later, the marines were instrumental in Operation Just Cause, an invasion of Panama with the objective of taking into custody Panamanian dictator Manuel Noriega, who had been indicted on charges of international drug trafficking. The operation also supported the installation of a new Panamanian government.

Persian Gulf War

The invasion and annexation of Kuwait by Iraq in August 1990 triggered Operation Desert Shield and Operation Desert Storm—the PERSIAN GULF WAR. As part of a massive military force of a coalition of nations, including the United States, between August 1990 and January 1991, 24 USMC infantry battalions and 40 squadrons, more than 92,000 marines, deployed to the gulf.

Following an intensive air campaign beginning on January 16, 1991, the ground war commenced on February 24, and the 1st and 2nd Marine Divisions broke through Iraqi defenses to occupy Kuwait. Simultaneously, Marine Expeditionary Brigades pinned down Iraqi forces along the coast of Kuwait; by the morning of February 28, the Iraqi army had been effectively neutralized.

Somalia, Bosnia, and Rwanda

In December 1992, USMC forces landed in the African nation of SOMALIA, torn by war and famine, to participate in Operation Restore Hope, a humanitarian relief effort that often turned violent.

Simultaneously, half a world away, USMC aviators were participating in Operation Deny Flight, patrolling a no-fly zone over Bosnia-Herzegovina in an effort to control the outbreak of renewed violence there.

Two years later, in April 1994, USMC units were sent into Rwanda, Africa, to evacuate 142 U.S. nationals during intense civil unrest.

Recent Operations

Marines landed in Haiti in September 1994 as part of a U.S. force working to effect a peaceful transition of democratic government in that perpetually troubled nation. During the 1990s, marines also participated in domestic counternarcotics efforts, in battling an epidemic of wildfires in the American West, and in a variety of flood and hurricane relief operations.

Following the terrorist attacks on the United States on September 11, 2001, a contingent of marines was landed in southern Afghanistan, on November 26, becoming the first U.S. troops deployed on the ground in the "War on Terrorism," a campaign to kill or capture forces of the Taliban and al-Qaeda—both of them terrorist organizations—and to locate, capture, or kill Osama bin Laden, identified as the mastermind behind the attacks on the United States. As of 2005, USMC forces were continuing to serve in Afghanistan.

In 2003, marines participated in Operation Iraqi Freedom, the U.S. invasion of Iraq to remove Iraqi dictator Saddam Hussein from office. The fiercest marine action was the 21-day Battle of Fallujah, which cleared the city of insurgents and pro-Saddam loyalists.

General Thomas Holcomb (USMC)   *(U.S. Marine Corps)*

hit the deck!

In the marines, as in the navy, a command meaning "Get up and get out of bed."

Holcomb, Thomas (1879–1965) *Marine Corps commandant*

Seventeenth COMMANDANT OF THE MARINE CORPS, Holcomb was born in New Castle, Delaware, and was commissioned a second lieutenant in the USMC in 1900. He served at sea and then was assigned as part of the legation guard of the U.S. minister at Peking (Beijing). Promoted to major in 1916, he fought in all the major USMC actions during WORLD WAR I and was highly decorated by the United States and France. Promoted to lieutenant colonel in 1920, he was assigned to command the USMC detachment at GUANTÁNAMO BAY, Cuba; then, after attending Command and General Staff School, he was assigned to command the USMC detachment at Peking.

From 1930 to 1932, Holcomb attended the Naval War College and Army War College, then was assigned to the Office of Naval Operations.

Promoted to brigadier general in 1935, he was given command of Marine Corps Base Quantico and then made commandant in 1936. He was jumped in rank to major general.

Holcomb oversaw the massive expansion of the USMC during WORLD WAR II, from 15,000 to 305,000 men, and in 1942 was promoted to lieutenant general, the first USMC officer to achieve that rank. Holcomb retired as commandant in April 1944, with the rank of general, and was named U.S. ambassador to South Africa. He served for four years in that post.

Horse Marines

This unit was formed from the legation guard at Peking (Beijing) late in the 1920s, ostensibly to facilitate the protection of U.S. lives and property there; however, the unit's function was chiefly ceremonial. When formed, the Horse Marines, who were trained and equipped in the manner of U.S. Army cavalrymen, numbered only 20 individuals. By the mid-1930s, the unit had grown to 50 men.

HRP Rescuer ("Flying Banana")   See
AIRCRAFT, ROTARY-WING.

Hue, action in and around

Hue was the old capital of Vietnam and, during the VIETNAM WAR, remained a very important city. It was a frequent target of North Vietnamese and Vietcong attacks, and, during the infamous Tet Offensive that began on January 31, 1968, Hue fell to an overwhelming attack and was immediately occupied by North Vietnamese forces.

Marines were sent to reinforce the beleaguered South Vietnamese troops (ARVN) pinned down in the city. The 1st Battalion of the 1st Marines were the first to arrive and were soon reinforced by the 5th Battalion of the 5th Marines. Intense urban fighting ensued, house to house. It was February 9 before the southern area of the city and environs had been retaken.

On February 12, ARVN units joined the 1st Battalion, 5th Marines in an attack on the central city, approaching from the north. The battle raged for 10 more days, again largely house to house. Although the historical heart of the city was destroyed in four weeks of combat, the marines and ARVN forces retook it and dealt the North Vietnamese and the Vietcong a costly tactical defeat—one of many the communists suffered as a result of the Tet Offensive. Yet, although Tet was a tactical disaster for the North, it was for them a strategic victory in that it intensified the antiwar movement in the United States and essentially broke the will of the American people to continue prosecuting the war.

I

Improved ECWCS Fiberpile Shirt and Trousers   See PERSONAL AND MISCELLANEOUS EQUIPMENT.

Inchon

During the KOREAN WAR, Inchon, on the west coast of Korea near Seoul, was the site of a spectacular and daring amphibious landing of marines and army troops, the 1st Marine Division and the army's 7th Division. The challenge was to land on a strategically critical but geographically difficult inlet, subject to extreme tides. The marines made the initial landing at 6:30 A.M. on September 15, 1950, at the island of Wolmi-do. The marines secured this objective within two hours and set up blocking positions. Later in the day, additional USMC battalions landed on the western side of Seoul. Early the next day, September 16, all USMC elements linked up east of Inchon and readily defeated a North Korean counterattack. The army contingent landed on the 18th.

The Inchon landing put U.S. and UN forces in position to take the offensive against the invading North Koreans and drive them deep into their own territory.

indirect fire systems

The following indirect fire systems are either currently included in the USMC inventory or are of historical importance in the service.

Advanced Field Artillery Tactical Data System

AFATDS is a joint army–USMC automated fire-support command, control, and coordination system intended to control and coordinate all fire-support weapons in the field.

Built by Raytheon Systems, AFATDS replaces the army's TACFIRE command system, which was only partially automated. The fully automated AFATDS fire support system minimizes the sensor-to-shooter timeline and increases the hit ratio. The system provides fully automated support for planning, coordinating, and controlling mortars, field artillery cannon, rockets, guided missiles, close air support, attack helicopter, and naval gunfire.

AN/TPQ-36 Firefinder Radar

This mobile radar set is designed to locate—with first-round accuracy—hostile artillery and mortar fire. Secondarily, it can also be employed to register friendly fire. The principal features of the AN/TPQ-36 Firefinder Radar are its light weight, its compact size, and its high degree of mobility. The set can detect projectiles launched at any angle within selected 90-degree azimuth sectors over 360 degrees of coverage. This includes the capacity to locate simultaneous-fire weapons as well as weapons that fire in separate bursts or volleys. Additionally, the set can be used to register and adjust friendly fire. In this mode, the weapon location is computed and then used to direct counter-battery fires. The set can be used by the artillery battalions to locate hostile weapons, both mortars and short- to medium-range weapons.

The AN/TPQ-36 system consists of an operational control group, OK-398/TPQ-36, and an antenna transceiver group, OY-71/TPQ-36. The latest configuration, Version 8, developed by Toby Hanna Army Depot and Grumman Electronics, consists of a new Operations Control Group (OCG) using the army Lightweight Multipurpose Shelter (LMS) mounted on a M-1097 HMMWV. This vehicle tows the Antenna Transceiver Group (ATG) with the integrated Modular Azimuth Positioning System (MAPS) mounted on an M-116A2E1 trailer. The OCG is controlled by an operator located either within the shelter or at a remote location. The second M-1097 HMMWV carries a MEP-112A generator mounted on an M-116A2E1 trailer. Yet another vehicle carries the crew. As of late 2003, the USMC operated 22 AN/TPQ-36 Firefinder Radar units.

General characteristics of the system include:

Manufacturer: Hughes Aircraft Company
Length, shelter: 106 in
Length, antenna/transceiver: 181.1 in
Width, shelter: 82.7 in
Width, antenna/transceiver: 82.7 in
Height, shelter: 70.9 in
Height, antenna/transceiver (in operation): 145.7 in
Height, antenna/transceiver (in transit): 82.7 in
Weight, shelter: 2,400 lb
Weight, antenna/transceiver: 3,200 lb
Power requirements: 115/200 VAC, three-phase, four-wire, 400 hertz, 10 kilowatt
Support equipment required: two M923 five-ton trucks, two 10-kilowatt generators
Crew: nine enlisted marines

The radar sets are deployed with headquarters batteries in artillery regiments and in counter-battery radar platoons.

AN/USQ-70 Position Azimuth Determining System

The AN/USQ-70 Position Azimuth Determining System is an artillery inertial survey system designed to provide to firing elements rapid and accurate measurements in position, elevation, and azimuth. It is a highly mobile surveying system that uses an inertial measurement unit interfaced with a digital computer to provide an accurate means of performing artillery survey. The AN/USQ-70 consists of an inertial measurement unit, a control and display unit, the computer, the power supply, the installation kit, and the electrical cable set. Also required are the primary pallet, the battery box, and the transit case.

General characteristics of the AN/USQ-70 Position Azimuth Determining System include:

Manufacturer: Litton Industries
Weight: 539 lb, including primary pallet, battery box, and transit case
Transported by: Humvee or helicopter
Surveying accuracy, horizontal position error: 23 ft
Surveying accuracy, vertical position error: 9.8 ft
Surveying accuracy, azimuth: 0.4 mm
Power requirements: 961 watts, 40 amperes, 24 VDC

The system is used by Artillery Survey Sections in artillery regiments and battalions and by Unmanned Aerial Vehicle (UAV) units. Two crew members operate the system.

M-49 Telescope

The M-49 is a a 20-power observation telescope for daytime use. It is used for observing target areas and also for assessing the effectiveness of artillery fire. The telescope has no reticle, and is therefore not intended for use as a sighting device. The telescope is mounted on the M-15 Tripod and includes an objective assembly, body tube, prism housing assembly, and eyepiece assembly with focusing sleeve. The front end of the body tube, which extends three quarters of an inch beyond the objective, provides an integral and permanent sunshade.

The M-49 has long been used by the USMC, especially in scout or sniper sections of the infantry battalion. Marines use it to detect and identify targets.

General characteristics of the telescope include:

Manufacturer: IMO, VARO, and other vendors
Length: 13.5 in
Weight (without tripod): 2.75 lb
Magnification: 20x

M-90 Radar Chronograph

The M-90 Radar Chronograph measures the muzzle velocity of field artillery weapons by means of a Doppler radar system consisting of a radio-frequency antenna, transmitter-receiver, readout display, and mounting brackets semi-permanently mounted to each artillery weapon. The antenna and transmitter-receiver are mounted on a nonrecoiling part of the howitzer and are connected to the control and display unit by a 30-meter cable. The radar chronograph itself is powered by an external source of 18 to 30 volts DC. The M-90 provides muzzle velocity data to the Fire Direction Center (FDC), enabling it to compute accurate fire control solutions. Each artillery battery is assigned one M-90. The instrument's only limitation is that it is unable to measure muzzle velocities of rocket-assisted projectiles or basebleed projectiles (specially designed to reduce drag and thereby enhance in-flight velocity).

General characteristics of the M-90 Radar Chronograph include:

Length: 33 in
Width: 380 in
Height: 20 in
Weight (including transit case and accessories): 200 lb

M-94 Muzzle Velocity System (MVS)

The newly developed M-94 Muzzle Velocity System (MVS) is designed to replace the standard M-90 Radar Chronograph at the artillery battery level. Its function is to measure the muzzle velocity of field artillery weapons using Doppler radar in conjunction with digital signal processing. This will enable artillery batteries to eliminate gross range bias errors, a large contributing factor to artillery inaccuracies. This system will measure all types of field artillery rounds, including base-bleed and rocket-assisted projectiles—two types of rounds the M-90 cannot measure.

The system consists of an antenna, an antenna bracket assembly, remote display unit, antenna cable/cable reel, and a transport case. Its general characteristics include:

Velocity measuring range: 150–2,000 m/per second
Caliber range: 20 mm and up
Projectile types: conventional, base-bleed, sabot-discarding, rocket-assisted, tracer ammunition, deep cavity
Accuracy: Within 0.05 percent of the true muzzle velocity
Firing rate: 18 rounds/min
Power requirement: 18–33 VDC
Power consumption: 18 watts in standby mode, 30 watts in measure mode
Total weight: less than 100 lb

M-101A1 105-mm Light Howitzer, Towed

The M-101A1 105-mm Light Howitzer, Towed is a light, towed, general-purpose field artillery weapon used as a contingency weapon during MARINE AIR GROUND TASK FORCE (MAGTF) deployments that require greater mobility than the heavier and bigger M-198 155-mm howitzer can provide.

The M-101A1 consists of the 105-mm howitzer cannon, an M-2-series recoil mechanism, and carriage. The weapon can be used for direct or indirect fire. The cannon consists of a tube assembly, breech ring, and locking ring and is mounted on the recoil sleigh assembly. The firing mechanism is a continuous pull (self cocking) type activated by pulling a lanyard. Operation is single-load, air-cooled; ammunition is semi-fixed. The carriage is of the single axle and split trail type, with the trails divided at emplacement and drawn together (and locked) during travel. The howitzer is towed from an integral drawbar.

The M-101A1 carriage consists of an equilibrator, shield, elevating mechanism, cradle, gear, elevating arcs, traversing mechanism, top carriage, wheels, and trails. The recoil mechanism is a constant hydropneumatic-type shock absorber, which decreases the energy of the recoil gradually and so avoids violent movement of the cannon or carriage. It is installed in the cradle of the carriage. The USMC has 248 of these weapons.

Other general characteristics of this light howitzer include:

Manufacturer: Rock Island Arsenal
Length: 19.5 ft
Width: 7.25 ft
Height: 5.66 ft
Weight: 4,980 lb
Bore diameter: 105 mm
Maximum effective range: 6.99 miles
Rate of fire, maximum: 10 rounds/min
Rate of fire, sustained: 3 rounds/min

M-198 155-mm Medium Howitzer, Towed

The M-198 155-mm Medium Howitzer, Towed, provides field artillery fire support for all MARINE AIR GROUND TASK FORCE (MAGTF) units. The weapon is built of aluminum and steel, and is air transportable by CH-53E Super Stallion helicopter and KC-130 Hercules fixed-wing aircraft. The M-198 replaces the M-114A2, providing increased range, improved reliability, and enhanced maintainability. Moreover, the use of rocket-assisted projectiles greatly extends the range, lethality, and counterbattery fire of artillery battalions using this weapon. The M-198 fires all current and developmental 155 mm ammunition, and the USMC, as of late 2003, maintains an inventory of 541.

General characteristics of the M-198 155-mm Medium Howitzer, Towed, include:

Manufacturer: Rock Island Arsenal
Length, in tow: 40 ft, 6 in
Length, firing: 36 ft, 2 in
Width, in tow: 9 ft, 2 in

U.S. Marines cover their ears as a round is fired from an M-198 155-mm Medium Howitzer during exercise Rim of the Pacific '04 in the Hawaiian Islands, on July 14, 2004.   *(Department of Defense)*

Height, in tow: 9 ft, 6 in
Weight: 15,758 lb
Bore diameter: 155 mm
Maximum effective range with conventional ammunition: 13.92 miles
Maximum effective range with rocket-assisted projectile: 18.64 miles
Rate of fire, maximum: 4 rounds/min
Rate of fire, sustained: 2 rounds/min
Crew: nine marines

M-224 60-mm Lightweight Mortar

The M-224 60-mm Lightweight Mortar provides USMC company commanders with an indirect-fire weapon. The mortar is a smooth-bore, muzzle-loading, high-trajectory weapon. Its cannon assembly is made up of a barrel, combination base cap, and firing mechanism, and its mount consists of a bipod and a base plate, which is provided with screw-type elevating and traversing mechanisms. A supplementary short-range sight is attached to the base of the cannon tube for firing on the move and during assaults. The weapon is equipped with a spring-type shock absorber to absorb recoil.

The M-224 60-mm Lightweight Mortar is the modern replacement for the WORLD WAR II–era M-2 and M-19 60-mm mortars. Whereas these weapons had an effective range of little more than one mile, the new weapon can reach targets at 2.17 miles, using improved long-range ammunition. The M-224 is also backward-compatible with older ammunition.

General characteristics of the M-224 include:

Length: 40 in
Weight: 46.5 lb
Bore diameter: 60 mm
Maximum effective range: 2.17 mi
Rate of fire, maximum: 30 rounds/min
Rate of fire, sustained: 20 rounds/min

M-252 81-mm Medium Extended Range Mortar

The M-252 81-mm Medium Extended Range Mortar was adopted by the USMC in 1986 and is a modified version of the standard British 81 mm mortar developed in the 1970s. It is the USMC weapon assigned to the mortar platoon of an infantry battalion. This crew-served, medium weight weapon is highly accurate and capable of great range—15,000 to 18,500 feet—and impressive lethality. The cannon has a crew-removable breech plug and firing pin, and a short, tapered muzzle lead-in that acts as a blast attenuator. The finned breech end facilitates cooling. The M-252 uses the standard M-64 mortar sight that is compatible with the USMC's M-224 60-mm Lightweight Mortar.

General characteristics of the M-252 81-mm Medium Extended Range Mortar include:

Length: 56 in (142.24 cm)
Weight, mortar assembly: 35 lb
Weight, bipod: 26 lb
Weight, base plate: 25.5 lb
Weight, sight unit: 2.5 lb
Weight, total: 89 lb
Bore diameter: 81 mm
Maximum effective range: 18,700 ft
Rate of fire, maximum: 33 rounds/min
Rate of fire, sustained: 16 rounds/min
Elevation: 45 to 85 degrees

Pack Howitzer 1923-E2

This highly mobile 75-mm gun began replacing the USMC's imported French 75s in 1930. Because the Pack Howitzer was relatively light and could be easily broken down for transportation, it was ideally suited to use in rough terrain and mountains and in amphibious campaigning. Operation required a crew of five. The weapon fired a 16-pound shell 10,000 yards. The Pack Howitzer was very extensively used in the Pacific during World War II.

Individual Tactical Load-Bearing Vest

(ITLBV)   See PERSONAL AND MISCELLANEOUS EQUIPMENT.

Infantry Fighting Vehicle   See WHEELED

VEHICLES.

infantry shelter   See PERSONAL AND MISCELLAN-
EOUS EQUIPMENT.

inspector-instructor

The inspector-instructor is a regular USMC officer
assigned to MARINE CORPS RESERVE units to ensure
that each unit has the benefit of current and coordinated professional training. The "I&I" provides
training assistance as well as guidance to the
reserve unit. Additionally, the I&I ensures that the
unit is trained up to the standards set by the
USMC.

Instructional Management School   See
COMBAT SERVICE SUPPORT SCHOOLS.

Iran Hostage Crisis

In 1979, religious extremists backed a successful
coup d'état against the secular, U.S.-allied government of the shah of Iran. In February, the U.S.
embassy in the capital city of Tehran was stormed
by insurgents. Using tear gas and birdshot, the 19
marines of the legation guard fought the attackers
off, but, under repeated attack, were forced to surrender. Two marines were wounded, and one was
held by the guerrillas for a week. Ultimately, all
marines and embassy staff were released. However,
after this incident, the embassy staff was reduced—
as was the legation guard, to 13 marines. In the
meantime, the U.S. government had decided to
allow the deposed shah, a longtime ally, to undergo
cancer treatment in an American hospital. This
prompted a new attack on the embassy on November 4, 1979. USMC legation guards do not constitute a defensive force—their mission is to keep
order within the embassy—and the corporal in
charge of the guards ordered his men to hold fire.
He determined that an attempt to defend the
embassy was likely to cause more casualties. As a
result, 61 Americans were taken prisoner. In January 1980, five secretaries and five marines were
released. The rest of the prisoners became hostages
for 444 days.

On April 11, 1980, President Jimmy Carter
approved a plan to rescue the hostages. The plan
called for all of the armed services to participate in
the rescue force. This led to operational confusion,
which was compounded by a series of mechanical
failures with the helicopters, one of which crashed
into a C-130 transport plane on takeoff, killing
eight persons, including five marines. The rescue
mission was aborted, and, the element of surprise
having been lost, no further attempt was made.

Iwo Jima

This tiny Pacific island in the Bonin group
assumed critical strategic significance in WORLD
WAR II because of two Japanese airfields located
there. Possession of these was important to Japan,
but even more important to the United States; they
could be used as bases for B-29 fighter escorts over
Japan and as emergency landing fields for crippled
B-29s returning from missions.

In early 1945, the Japanese positions were
extremely well prepared on the island, with some
20,000 troops hunkered down in pillboxes,
bunkers, and blockhouses, as well as volcanic caves.
The V Amphibious Corps, consisting of the 3rd,
4th, and 5th Marine Divisions, landed on February
19, 1945, following extremely heavy USAAF and
USN bombardment. Despite this softening-up
operation, resistance to the invaders was very
heavy. While the USMC inflicted staggering casualties on the Japanese defenders, it also sustained
heavy losses. On February 22, a battalion of
marines attained the key objective of Mount Suribachi, highest point on the island, and raised a
small flag. Shortly afterward, a party raised a larger
flag, which was the subject of a Pulitzer Prize–winning photograph and the inspiration for the IWO
JIMA MEMORIAL in Washington, D.C., as well as
becoming an unofficial symbol of the USMC.

However, the taking of Mount Suribachi hardly
signaled the end of the battle. The major phase of
combat occurred on the flatlands, which were most
vigorously defended by the Japanese. Although a
flag-raising ceremony was held on March 13, fighting continued, and it was not until the Japanese

Sergeant Michael Strank, Corporal Harlon H. Block, Private First Class Franklin R. Sousley, Private First Class Rene A. Gagnon, Private First Class Ira Hayes, and Pharmacist's Mate Second Class John H. Bradley (USN) raise the American flag over Mount Suribachi, Iwo Jima, February 19, 1945. *(Arttoday)*

commander committed suicide (rather than surrender) on March 26 that the island was deemed
secure. USMC casualties were 6,821 killed and
19,207 wounded. Japanese casualties were virtually
total: nearly 20,000 defenders killed.

Iwo Jima Memorial

Officially the U.S. Marine Corps War Memorial,
this bronze sculpture group is located in Arlington,
Virginia, a short distance from Arlington National
Cemetery. The monument is based on the famous
Pulitzer Prize–winning photograph by combat
photographer Joe Rosenthal depicting five marines
and a U.S. Navy hospital corpsman (Sergeant
Michael Strank, Corporal Harlon H. Block, Private
First Class Franklin R. Sousley, Private First Class
Rene A. Gagnon, Private First Class Ira Hayes, and
Pharmacist's Mate Second Class John H. Bradley
[USN]) raising the Stars and Stripes on Mount
Suribachi, Iwo Jima, on February 19, 1945, during
the extremely costly battle to take this Pacific
island. It is intended to commemorate the sacri-
fices of all marines who have died in battle since
the founding of the USMC in 1775. The memorial
was completed in 1954 by artist Felix de Weldon
and was financed privately. Its flag flies 24 hours.

J

jarhead

Slang term for a marine. Presumably, the term is a reference to the buzz-like haircut marines typically wear, which gives the human head a somewhat jar-like appearance.

Javelin   See ANTIARMOR WEAPONS.

Joint Service Combat Shotgun   See WEAPONS, INDIVIDUAL AND CREW-SERVED.

Joint Service Lightweight Integrated Suit Technology   See NUCLEAR-BIOLOGICAL-CHEMICAL EQUIPMENT.

Jones, James L. (1943–   ) *Marine Corps commandant*

The 32nd COMMANDANT OF THE MARINE CORPS, Jones was born on December 19, 1943, in Kansas City, Missouri, and was raised in France, returning to the United States to attend the Georgetown University School of Foreign Service, from which he earned a bachelor of science degree in 1966. The next year he was commissioned a second lieutenant in the USMC, completed Basic School in October 1967, and was ordered to South Vietnam, where he served as a platoon and company commander with Company G, 2nd Battalion, 3rd Marines. While serving in the VIETNAM WAR, he was promoted to first lieutenant in June 1968.

On his return to the United States in December 1968, Jones was assigned to Marine Corps Base Camp Pendleton as a company commander until May 1970. He was then posted to MARINE BARRACKS, Washington, D.C., again as a company com-

General James L. Jones (USMC)   *(U.S. Marine Corps)*

mander, serving in this assignment until July 1973. Promoted to captain in December 1970, he studied at the Amphibious Warfare School, Quantico, Virginia, during 1973–74, and in November 1974 was ordered to the 3rd Marine Division, OKINAWA, where he served as the commander of Company H, 2nd Battalion, 9th Marines, until December 1975.

From January 1976 to August 1979, Jones served in the Officer Assignments Section at HEAD-QUARTERS MARINE CORPS, Washington, D.C., and was promoted to major in July 1977. He subsequently became Marine Corps Liaison Officer to the U.S. Senate, receiving promotion to lieutenant colonel in September 1982, and serving as liaison until July 1984. Selected to attend the National War College in Washington, D.C., Jones graduated in June 1985 and was assigned command of the 3rd Battalion, 9th Marines, 1st Marine Division, Camp Pendleton, from July 1985 to July 1987, returning in August 1987 to Headquarters Marine Corps as senior aide to the commandant of the Marine Corps.

Promoted to colonel in April 1988, Jones was named military secretary to the commandant in February 1989 and the following year was assigned as commanding officer, 24th Marine Expeditionary Unit at Marine Corps Base Camp Lejeune, North Carolina. During his tour as commander, he participated in Operation Provide Comfort in northern Iraq and Turkey and was promoted to brigadier general on April 23, 1992.

In July 1992, Jones was named deputy director, operations and training, U.S. European Command, Stuttgart, Germany, then was reassigned as chief of staff, Joint Task Force Provide Promise, for operations in Bosnia-Herzegovina and Macedonia. In 1994, on his return to the United States, Jones was advanced to major general and was assigned to command 2nd Marine Division, Marine Forces Atlantic, Camp Lejeune. During 1996, Jones served as director, Expeditionary Warfare Division, Office of the Chief of Naval Operations and was subsequently named deputy chief of staff for Plans, Policies and Operations, Headquarters Marine Corps, Washington, D.C., and promoted to lieutenant general. After his promotion, Jones was assigned as military assistant to the secretary of defense, and, on June 30, 1999, he was promoted to general. The following month, he assumed the post of commandant.

K

See AIRCRAFT, FIXED-WING.

KC-130 Hercules   See AIRCRAFT, FIXED-WING.

Kelley, Paul X. (1928–   ) *Marine Corps commandant*

The 28th COMMANDANT OF THE MARINE CORPS, Kelley was born in Boston and was commissioned a second lieutenant after graduating from Villanova University in 1950. After serving at Marine Corps Base Camp Lejeune and Marine Corps Base Camp Pendleton, he was ordered to sea duty with the Sixth Fleet, then was stationed in Japan, where he became aide-de-camp to the deputy commander of FLEET MARINE FORCE, Pacific. After training at the army's Airborne Pathfinder School, Fort Benning, Georgia, Kelley saw service with the British Royal Marines as an exchange officer. He served in Aden, Singapore, Malaya, and Borneo before he returned to the United States as commanding officer of the Marine Barracks Newport, Rhode Island.

Kelley served in Vietnam (see VIETNAM WAR) in 1964 with the 3rd Amphibious Force. Promoted to lieutenant colonel, he returned to the United States in 1966 as USMC representative at Fort Benning. After attending the Air War College, Kelley was appointed military assistant to the commandant of the Marine Corps in 1969. The following year, as colonel, he returned to Vietnam in command of the 1st Marines, then brought the regiment back to Camp Pendleton in 1971.

In 1971, Kelley was appointed assistant to the director of the Joint Staff in Plans and Policy. In 1974, promoted to brigadier general, he was given command of the 4th Division and, in 1975, became director of the Development Center at Marine Corps Base Quantico.

Kelley became deputy chief of staff at HEADQUARTERS MARINE CORPS, Washington, D.C., in 1978 and, in 1981, was appointed to command the Rapid Deployment Joint Task Force, headquartered at MacDill Air Force Base. At this time, Kelley was promoted to general and, in July of 1981, was made assistant commandant of the Marine Corps. He was named commandant in 1983 and served until June 30, 1987.

Khe Sanh

During the VIETNAM WAR this village in South Vietnam's Quang Tri Province, near the Demilitarized Zone (DMZ), was a major USMC strong point from which marines attempted to control infiltration of South Vietnam from the north. Khe Sanh came under siege in February 1968 as part of the Tet Offensive and was successfully defended, although the 77-day siege was not broken until April. The position assumed a political importance far in excess of its actual strategic significance, as both sides came to see possession of it as vital to victory.

KLR 250-D8 Marine Corps Motorcycle

See WHEELED VEHICLES.

Korean War

The Korean War began on June 25, 1950, when Soviet-trained and Soviet-equipped troops of the North Korean army crossed the 38th parallel to invade South Korea, quickly overrunning the modest forces of that country.

Pursuant to his administration's policy of "containment"—using limited military action to confront and contain the spread of communism wherever it appeared—President Harry S. Truman mobilized U.S. forces. The supremely difficult objective of United Nations–sanctioned intervention in Korea was to prevent the spread of communism into the south and even, perhaps, to unify the nation, north and south, under a democratic government, while avoiding direct confrontation with the People's Republic of China or the Soviet Union. Such a "limited war" made victory difficult, but the alternative, an all-out war, was too risky to contemplate in an era of atomic weapons.

The first U.S. strikes were from the air, followed by U.S. Army divisions brought in from Japan and the Central Pacific and fighting under the aegis and authority of the United Nations. Post–WORLD WAR II demobilization had greatly reduced the strength and readiness of U.S. forces, which, initially, were badly outnumbered and compelled to fight a desperate holding action in the south.

In contrast to past interventions, there were no initial plans to use USMC forces in Korea; nevertheless, all MARINE CORPS RESERVE units were put on active status, and on July 7, 1950, the 6,500-man 1st Provisional Brigade was formed at Marine Corps Base Camp Pendleton. It arrived in Korea on July 12. Marine Air Group 33, flying the F4U Corsair, was also deployed. Although the theater commander, General Douglas MacArthur (USA), planned to hold the 1st Provisional Brigade for use in his daring landing at INCHON, he deployed it early to help defend Pusan. Incurring heavy losses, the marines nevertheless drove the North Koreans back some five miles before the brigade was pulled back on September 5 preparatory to the Inchon operation.

The marines were a key part of the Inchon operation, which put UN forces in a position from which they drove the North Korean invaders back across the 38th parallel and, ultimately, deep into North Korean territory.

The UN counterattack was swift and successful. But warnings came from various military and political advisers that the action would surely provoke intervention from China as the counterattack neared the Yalu River and the Manchurian border. General MacArthur repeatedly dismissed the likelihood of such intervention, but it in fact occurred in October and November 1950. Marine units now functioned to protect the rear and flanks of the retreating army forces in what proved to be some of the hardest, most bitter fighting of the war. The enemy was not only the North Koreans and Chinese, but the northern winter, which dropped temperatures to some 20 degrees below zero.

Early in 1951, the retreat was halted south of the 38th parallel. By June 1951, peace talks were under way, and UN forces were used mainly in a defensive strategy, which proved costly to the communists, yet also frustrating to American military commanders, who believed that politicians and diplomats were denying them victory. Marine operations during the rest of the war, from June 1951 until the truce declared on July 27, 1953, focused on attacking and seizing certain strategic strong points in order to keep them from falling to the enemy. It was a heartbreaking and difficult mission.

When the shooting ceased on July 27, 1953, UN forces had achieved at least one of Truman's original policy objectives: Intervention had "contained" communism north of the 38th parallel. This did little to moderate the frustration of some U.S. military commanders, who felt that genuine victory had been withheld. Nevertheless, the intervention had succeeded in containing communism without triggering a third world war.

Krag-Jorgenson Rifle See WEAPONS, INDIVIDUAL AND CREW-SERVED.

Krulak, Charles C. (1942–) *Marine Corps commandant*

The 31st COMMANDANT OF THE MARINE CORPS, Krulak was born in Quantico, Virginia, and graduated from the U.S. Naval Academy at Annapolis in 1964. He graduated from the Amphibious Warfare School in 1968 and was awarded a master's degree from George Washington University in 1973. Krulak also graduated from the Army Command and General Staff College (1976) and from the National War College (1982). In addition, Krulak saw combat in the VIETNAM WAR and was commanding officer of the Special Training Branch at Marine Corps Recruiting Depot San Diego and commanded the Counter Guerrilla Warfare School at OKINAWA.

Krulak was company officer at the U.S. Naval Academy in 1970 and, from 1973 to 1976, commanded the Marine Barracks at the North Island USMC Air Station. From 1983 to 1985, Krulak was commanding officer of the 3rd Battalion, 3rd Marines, then served in various staff positions, before receiving appointment as plans officer in the FLEET MARINE FORCE in 1982. After serving as deputy director in the White House Military Office beginning in 1987, he was given command of the 10th Marine Expeditionary Brigade in 1989, then made assistant divisional commander of the 2nd Division. Named to command the 6th Marine Expeditionary Brigade in 1990, Krulak went on to assignment as assistant deputy chief of staff for manpower in August 1991. Promoted to major general in 1992, he was named commander of the Combat Development Command at Marine Corps Base Quantico in August 1992. As a lieutenant general, Krulak was appointed to command Fleet Marine Force, Pacific, in July 1994; promoted to general the following year, he was named commandant of the Marine Corps on June 30, 1995.

Krulak, Victor H. (1913–) *Marine Corps general*

A Denver native, Krulak graduated from the United States Naval Academy with a commission as a second lieutenant in the USMC in May 1934. In 1936, he was assigned to the 6th Marines at Marine Corps Base San Diego, then was stationed the next year at Shanghai with the 4th Marines. After his return to the United States, he attended the junior course at Marine Corps Base Quantico and was assigned to the 1st Brigade.

Krulak was appointed to the staff of the Amphibious Corps, Atlantic, in April 1941 and was promoted to captain. He was then transferred to the staff of Major General Holland "Howlin' Mad" Smith in September 1942, when the Amphibious Corps was moved to San Diego. After taking parachute training in February 1943, Krulak was shipped out to New Caledonia in the Pacific, where he assumed command of the 2nd Parachute Battalion. As a lieutenant colonel, Krulak led his unit in action at Vella Lavella (September) and on CHOISEUL Island (October). He was decorated with the Navy Cross for Choiseul, but had to return to the United States for treatment of wounds suffered during the assault.

After light duty at the Division of Plans in Washington, D.C., Krulak joined the 6th Division in October 1944 as assistant chief of staff for operations. In this capacity, he participated in planning and directing the invasion of OKINAWA. For his contribution to this invasion, Krulak received the Legion of Merit.

In the postwar USMC, Krulak was given command of the USMC Research Section and was appointed assistant director of the Senior School at Quantico. He assumed command of the 5th Marines at Marine Corps Base Camp Pendleton in June 1949, was promoted to colonel, and became assistant chief of staff for operations of the FLEET MARINE FORCE, Pacific. In 1951, he was named chief of staff, Fleet Marine Force, Pacific.

Promoted to brigadier general in 1956, Krulak was named assistant commander of the 3rd Divi-

Lieutenant General Victor H. Krulak (USMC)   *(U.S. Marine Corps)*

sion, stationed at Okinawa. He subsequently returned to Quantico as director of the Educational Center there and was promoted to major general in November 1959. Shortly after this, he was appointed to command Marine Corps Recruit Depot San Diego, then became, in 1962, special assistant to the director for counterinsurgency under the Joint Chiefs of Staff. This appointment made Krulak the obvious choice for chief of the Joint Staff Mission to Vietnam in January 1963. Krulak became an important figure in U.S. military policy with regard to Vietnam, and he favored a strategy of pacification rather than the all-out confrontation strategy advocated by the army.

Krulak's final command was as commander of Fleet Marine Force, Pacific; although he was a candidate for COMMANDANT OF THE MARINE CORPS, he retired in 1968 before any such appointment was made.

Kwajalein, Battle of

A large atoll among some 90 islands in the Marshall Islands, Kwajalein was the focus of an important U.S. assault and invasion during WORLD WAR II. The objective was Kwajalein, largest of the atoll islands, and the twin islands of ROI-NAMUR. On February 1, 1944, two regiments of the USMC 4th Division landed on Roi-Namur. Roi was quickly secured, but the marines met stubborn resistance on Namur, which was not taken until February 2.

While the marines defeated the Japanese on Roi-Namur, the army's 7th Division captured a number of small islands to put them in position to attack Kwajalein, which fell after a three-day battle.

Kwajalein Atoll provided ample anchorage for U.S. Navy ships mounting attacks against the Marianas, while Roi became the base for a bomber airfield.

L

lance corporal See RANKS AND GRADES.

landing craft

Strictly speaking, landing craft include any sea-going craft used in landing operations. This entry also includes the broader range of assault craft used by the marines.

Air-Cushion Vehicles

Air-cushion vehicles travel at high speeds over water, ground, or marshy surface on a cushion of air generated by the vehicle and trapped beneath it in a flexible-skirted chamber. The marines (as well as the navy and army) use these vehicles for amphibious assaults and, sometimes, to move troops and equipment from ship to shore.

The marines employ the following air-cushion vehicles:

Landing Craft, Air Cushion (LCAC)

LCACs transport weapons systems, equipment, cargo, and personnel of marine assault elements from ship to shore and across the beach. The LCAC is a high-speed, over-the-beach, fully amphibious landing craft capable of carrying a payload of 60–75 tons at speeds in excess of 40 knots. A hovercraft, the LCAC can operate in waters regardless of depth, underwater obstacles, shallows, or adverse tides. It can operate inland, clearing obstacles up to 4 feet, regardless of terrain or topography. The craft

A U.S. Navy Landing Craft, Air Cushion, more commonly known as LCAC, loaded with Marines and their equipment from 3rd Marine Regiment, heads toward the beach during amphibious assault training. *(Department of Defense)*

operates on mud flats, sand dunes, ditches, marsh-lands, riverbanks, wet snow, and slippery and icy shorelines.

Developed by the marines and navy during 1977–81, the LCAC was authorized for full production in 1987. The craft are operated by the navy for the landing of marines. General characteristics of the LCAC include:

Builder: Textron Marine and Land Systems; Lockheed Aircraft; Avondale Gulfport Marine
Power plant: four Avco-Lycoming gas turbines, 12,280 horsepower; two shrouded reversible-pitch propellers; four double-entry fans for lift
Length: 88 ft
Beam: 47 ft
Displacement, fully loaded: 200 tons
Capacity: 60 tons (75-ton overload)
Speed: 40+ knots, with payload
Armament: two 12.7-mm machine guns; gun mounts support a wide variety of weapons
Crew: five
Range: 200 miles at 40 knots, with payload; 300 miles at 35 knots, with payload
Personnel capacity: 24 marines

LACV-30

The LACV-30 is the most versatile hovercraft operated by the navy. It may be used in a variety of roles, including patrol of intercoastal, harbor, and inland waterways and for search and rescue, but the marines generally employ it for personnel and cargo transport in landing assault scenarios.

The LACV-30 maneuvers on snow, desert, ice, slush, marshes, river beds, and swamps. It can operate in rough seas. Payload is 30 tons, with more than 1,600 square feet of cargo deck. General characteristics include:

Length, overall: 76.5 ft
Beam, overall (on cushion): 36.9 ft
Height, overall (on cushion): 28.11 ft
Height, cargo deck (on cushion): 7.1 ft
Cargo deck: 51 ft by 32 ft
Cruise speed: 45 mph
Payload, maximum: 30 tons

Main propulsion: two Pratt and Whitney ST6-76 Twin Packs (gas turbines)
Propellers: two 9-foot-diameter variable-pitch propellers
Lift fans: two 7-foot-diameter centrifugal fixed-pitch fans
Fuel capacity: 2,240 gal

Before the advent of air-cushion craft, the marines used an array of conventional landing craft. Some are still in use.

Landing Craft, Personnel (LCP)

The LCP was developed by the USMC in conjunction with the Eureka Tugboat Company (New Orleans) in 1940. The original boats were 36 feet long and capable of carrying 36 fully equipped marines. Although some had gas engines, most were diesels, capable of making eight knots. Wood hulled and with plywood gunwales, the LCPs were not very durable and were replaced by a new generation of LCP, the LCP(R), in mid-1942. The most important innovation was a forward ramp for easier and faster troop unloading. Early in 1943, the LCP(R) was replaced by the landing craft, vehicle, personnel (LCVP) and the landing craft vehicle, tracked (LVT).

Landing Craft, Tank (LCT)

The LCT originated in England, and a U.S. version, LCT, Mk-5, entered service late in 1942. The ship was 112 feet long and could carry five 25-ton or four 40-ton tanks for an AMPHIBIOUS OPERATION and in an AMPHIBIOUS ASSAULT. An improved Mk-6 appeared in 1944. Although slow, making a top speed of only 7 knots, the ships were used extensively in the Pacific to transport and land tanks.

Landing Craft, Vehicle Personnel (LCVP)

The landing craft, vehicle personnel (LCVP) replaced the landing craft, personnel (LCP) in 1943 for amphibious assault. Like the earlier craft, it was 36 feet long and made of wood, but it was armored and had an armored ramp. Its 225-horsepower engine drove it at 9 knots, a knot better than the LCP. LCVPs were built in profusion—25,358 by the end of the war—and they were used by the USMC and USA, in both the Pacific and European theaters.

In addition to major landing craft, the marines employ a variety of specialized small craft for landing assault purposes. These include:

Combat Rubber Raiding Craft

The CRRC, or "Rubber Duck," is a raft used by the USMC as well as by army units (Green Berets and Rangers) and Navy SEALs for clandestine insertions and extractions. The raft is 15 feet long and 6 feet wide and can hold five troops with equipment. The CRRC is normally powered by a 55-horsepower outboard motor, which will move the raft at 20 knots over a range of 65 miles.

Riverine Assault Craft (RAC)

The USMC uses the Riverine Assault Craft (RAC) as an inland and coastal waterway patrol craft. Its assigned missions typically include armed escort; command, control, and communications; transport; armed reconnaissance; and pursuit and interception.

The Riverine Assault Craft is fast, very maneuverable, and highly survivable in the river environment, enabling it to direct fire support and to conduct command/control, armed escort, electronic warfare, pursuit/intercept, and scout/patrol missions. It can serve as an effective platform for a wide array of military and commercial communication and electronic systems as well as crew-served weapons systems.

The craft features an aluminum hull and is powered by twin inboard, 300-horsepower Cummins turbo diesels, which are connected to Hamilton water jets. Fore and aft gun tubs may mount either the M-2 50-caliber Heavy Machine Gun or the Mk-19 40-mm Grenade Machine Gun. Medium machine guns may also be mounted, on pintles that are fixed to the port and starboard gunwales.

The Riverine Assault Craft is crewed by four marines and can additionally transport as many as 15 combat-loaded marines. It has a very shallow draft, which enables it to operate in as little as 8 inches of water while on plane and 30 inches of water while moving slowly or stopped. The craft's transport trailer may be towed by a 5-ton cargo truck.

General characteristics of the Riverine Assault Craft (RAC) include:

Length: 35 ft
Beam: 9 ft, 2 in
Draft: 30 in (8 in on plane)
Displacement, empty: 13,600 lb
Displacement, full load: 16,400 lb
Speed, maximum: 43 mi per hr
Speed, cruise: 31 mi per hr
Acceleration from cruise to 40 miles per hour: 10 sec
Range: 400 mi
Fuel endurance: 8 hr
Power: twin 300-hp Cummins diesel engines driving Hamilton 271 waterjets
Crew: four to five
Troop lift capacity: a combat-loaded USMC rifle SQUAD, consisting of 10 to 15 marines
Communications: military HF/VHF/UHF RAY-90 Marine band transceiver
Navigation: R40X Radar; V820 Depth Finder; Raystar 920 GPS; RayNav 780 LORAN-C; Fluxgate Compass; Magnetic Compass
Armament: fore and aft gun tubs capable of mounting 7.62-mm, 50-caliber or 40-mm automatic weapons; port and starboard pintle mounts for 7.62-mm machine guns
Transportability: Amphibious Ship, CH-53E Super Stallion, KC-130 Hercules C-141 (or larger transport aircraft), 5-ton truck

Landing Operations Doctrine

Published by the U.S. Navy in 1938, *Landing Operations Doctrine* was a revision of a USMC document, *Tentative Manual for Landing Operations,* published in 1934. The original document and its revision embodied the amphibious warfare doctrine that would dominate U.S. assault operations in the Pacific during WORLD WAR II and put the USMC front and center as the service of choice for amphibious assault operations. The U.S. Army based its field manual, *Landing Operations on Hostile Shores,* on the USMC document and the USN revision of it.

Landing Vehicle, Tracked (LVT and LVT[A])
See AMPHIBIOUS VEHICLES.

Laser Rangefinder AN/GVS-5   See PERSONAL AND MISCELLANEOUS EQUIPMENT.

LAV-25   See AMPHIBIOUS VEHICLES.

leatherneck
This nickname for a marine is as old as the USMC itself and comes from the leather collar or stock prescribed in 1776 by the U.S. Navy as part of the marine uniform. The idea behind the leather stock was utilitarian—to ward off saber blows to the neck—but it was never practical for this purpose. Moreover, it was singularly uncomfortable. Despite its questionable utility and the discomfort it caused, the leather stock remained a part of the USMC uniform until after the CIVIL WAR. The nickname survived well beyond that period and was especially current during WORLD WAR II.

Lebanon
USMC forces were first dispatched to this small Middle Eastern nation in 1958 at the request of the Lebanese president, who was threatened by a Syrian-backed revolution. Three battalions were deployed, later reinforced by an army unit. The withdrawal of U.S. forces began after an election on July 31, 1958, restored stability. The withdrawal was completed in October.

In 1982, the U.S. deployed 800 marines of the 32nd Marine Amphibious Unit to operate with French and Italian troops as UN peacekeepers in Lebanon. The 32nd was relieved by the 24th on October 30, 1982. By this time, marines and other

UN forces were the frequent targets of warring factions contending for control of Lebanon, particularly in the capital city of Beirut. On October 23, 1983, a truck packed with 12,000 pounds of explosives crashed through the outer defenses of the USMC headquarters building at the Beirut airport. The suicide bomber detonated the explosives, killing 241 marines and wounding 70 others; simultaneously, another bomber attacked a building housing French paratroops, killing 58.

Despite this tragedy, the USMC presence was maintained in Lebanon until February 7, 1984, when President Ronald Reagan announced the withdrawal of all marines except for a small force charged with guarding the embassy.

Legation Guards   See U.S. MARINE CORPS SECURITY GUARD BATTALION.

Lejeune, John A. (1867–1942) *Marine Corps commandant*
The 13th COMMANDANT OF THE MARINE CORPS, Lejeune was a Cajun born and raised in Pointe Coupee Parish, Louisiana. He graduated from Louisiana State University and, subsequently, the U.S. Naval Academy (1888), cruised as a navy midshipman for two years, then was commissioned a second lieutenant in the USMC. During the SPANISH-AMERICAN WAR, Lejeune commanded the marine contingent serving aboard the USS *Cincinnati*. In November 1903, as a major, he landed at Colón, Panama, to protect the newly created Panamanian government, which the United States supported, largely to ensure the future construction of the Panama Canal.

Lejeune commanded 3,000 marines in the occupation of VERACRUZ, Mexico, to oppose the Huerta regime in 1913 and support the installation of Venustiano Carranza as president. Four years later, Lejeune commanded the 2nd Division during WORLD WAR I and participated at SAINT-MIHIEL and the Meuse-Argonne. On his return to the United States in 1919, Lejeune served as commandant of Marine Corps Base Quantico until, in Jan-

Lieutenant General John A. Lejeune (USMC)   *(U.S. Marine Corps)*

was promoted to lieutenant general on the retired list. Marine Corps Base Camp Lejeune, North Carolina, is named in his honor.

uary 1920, he was named commandant of the USMC. He served in this post for nine years, retiring in 1929 to become superintendent of the Virginia Military Academy. Shortly before he died, he

lieutenant colonel   See RANKS AND GRADES.

lieutenant general   See RANKS AND GRADES.

Light Armored Vehicle–Command and Control (LAV-C2)   See AMPHIBIOUS VEHICLES.

Light Armored Vehicle–Logistics (LAV-L)
See AMPHIBIOUS VEHICLES.

Light Armored Vehicle–Mortar (LAV-M)
See AMPHIBIOUS VEHICLES.

Light Armored Vehicle–Recovery (LAV-R)
See AMPHIBIOUS VEHICLES.

Logistics Operations School   See COMBAT SERVICE SUPPORT SCHOOLS.

M

M-1 .30-caliber Carbine   See WEAPONS, IN-DIVIDUAL AND CREW-SERVED.

M-1A1 Main Battle Tank   See TRACKED VEHICLES.

M-1 Mine-Clearing Blade System   See TRACKED VEHICLES.

M-2HB Browning Machine Gun   See WEAPONS, INDIVIDUAL AND CREW-SERVED.

M-3A1 Antitank Gun   See ANTIARMOR WEAPONS.

M-9 Armored Combat Earthmover (ACE)   See TRACKED VEHICLES.

M-9 Personal Defense Weapon   See WEAPONS, INDIVIDUAL AND CREW-SERVED.

M-16A2 Rifle   See WEAPONS, INDIVIDUAL AND CREW-SERVED.

M-17 Lightweight Decontamination System   See NUCLEAR-BIOLOGICAL-CHEMICAL EQUIPMENT.

M-21 Remote-Sensing Chemical Agent Automatic Alarm   See NUCLEAR-BIOLOGICAL-CHEMICAL EQUIPMENT.

M-40/42 Chemical/Biological Protective Masks   See NUCLEAR-BIOLOGICAL-CHEMICAL EQUIPMENT.

M-40A1 Sniper Rifle   See WEAPONS, INDIVIDUAL AND CREW-SERVED.

M-47 Dragon II   See ANTIARMOR WEAPONS.

M-49 Telescope   See INDIRECT FIRE SYSTEMS.

M-60 Machine Gun   See WEAPONS, INDIVIDUAL AND CREW-SERVED.

M-60A1 Armored Vehicle-Launched Bridge (M60A1 AVLB)   See TRACKED VEHICLES.

M-82 Special Application Scope Rifle (SASR)   See WEAPONS, INDIVIDUAL AND CREW-SERVED.

M-90 Radar Chronograph   See INDIRECT FIRE SYSTEMS.

M-94 Muzzle Velocity System (MVS)   See INDIRECT FIRE SYSTEMS.

M-101A1 105-mm Light Howitzer, Towed   See INDIRECT FIRE SYSTEMS.

M-151 TOW   See ANTIARMOR WEAPONS.

M-198 155-mm Medium Howitzer, Towed   See INDIRECT FIRE SYSTEMS.

M-203 40-mm Grenade Launcher   See WEAPONS, INDIVIDUAL AND CREW-SERVED.

M-224 60-mm Lightweight Mortar   See INDIRECT FIRE SYSTEMS.

M-240G machine gun   See WEAPONS, INDIVIDUAL AND CREW-SERVED.

M-249 SAW   See WEAPONS, INDIVIDUAL AND CREW-SERVED.

M-252 81-mm Medium Extended-Range Mortar   See INDIRECT FIRE SYSTEMS.

M-1911A1 .45-caliber Pistol   See WEAPONS, INDIVIDUAL AND CREW-SERVED.

M-1917A1 Browning Machine Gun   See WEAPONS, INDIVIDUAL AND CREW-SERVED.

M-1918 Browning Automatic Rifle (BAR)   See WEAPONS, INDIVIDUAL AND CREW-SERVED.

M-1919A4 Browning Machine Gun   See WEAPONS, INDIVIDUAL AND CREW-SERVED.

M-1919A6 Browning Machine Gun   See WEAPONS, INDIVIDUAL AND CREW-SERVED.

M-1921 and M1928A1 Thompson Submachine Gun   See WEAPONS, INDIVIDUAL AND CREW-SERVED.

M-1941 Johnson Light Machine Gun   See WEAPONS, INDIVIDUAL AND CREW-SERVED.

major   See RANKS AND GRADES.

major general   See RANKS AND GRADES.

Makin, Battle of

Located in the GILBERT ISLANDS, Makin Atoll was the site of a key Japanese radio station (on Butaritari Island) early in WORLD WAR II. Colonel EVANS CARLSON led his 2nd Raider Battalion against the island on October 17, 1942, destroying the radio station and wiping out the Japanese garrison there almost to a man.

While this early USMC triumph was most welcome—and elimination of the radio station an important tactical victory—the raid had an important but adverse strategic effect. It alerted the Japanese to the need for strengthening island defenses, and it made the situation in the Pacific that much more difficult for the navy, army, and Marine Corps.

Mameluke Sword

Worn by USMC officers, the Mameluke Sword copies the pattern of the swords used by Muslims in North Africa and Arabia at the time of the successful USMC assault on Tripoli in 1805 during the Tripolitan War. Lieutenant PRESLEY NEVILLE O'BANNON received a Muslim-style sword from the governor of Tripoli in token of the governor's surrender. (The engagement is commemorated in the MARINE HYMN as the "shores of Tripoli.") A cross hilt and

An original Mameluke Sword from the 1800s   *(U.S. Marine Corps)*

ivory grip distinguish the ceremonial weapon, which is carried on parade and, occasionally, to denote the officer of the day.

The Mameluke Sword is reserved for officers' wear. Staff noncommissioned officers wear an NCO Sword whenever dress blues are worn. Additionally, sergeants may wear the NCO Sword for drill with troops, parades, reviews, and ceremonies. While the Mameluke Sword is distinctive to the USMC, the NCO Sword is identical to the U.S. Army infantry officer's sword.

See also BARBARY PIRATES.

Mariana Islands Campaign

The Marianas are 14 islands some 1,500 miles east of the Philippines. Three of the islands in the group, SAIPAN, TINIAN, and Rota, had been administered by Japan since the end of WORLD WAR I. Guam, the largest of the Marianas, was a U.S. possession. Guam fell to Japanese invasion on December 8, 1941, and Saipan figured as the main Japanese base.

As a result of the U.S. "Island-hopping" campaign strategy in the Pacific, Saipan was isolated by mid-1944. Therefore, on June 15, 1944, the 2nd and 4th Marines combined with the army's 27th Division to land on Saipan, which was secured after very heavy fighting on July 9.

After Saipan was taken, the 3rd USMC Division and 1st USMC Brigade made an assault on Guam on July 21. This, too, proved a very hard fight, but with the aid of the army's 77th Division, the island was retaken on August 10.

The final Marianas objective was Tinian, which the United States wanted as a base for B-29 bomber operations against the Japanese mainland. Tinian was captured on August 1 by the USMC's 2nd and 4th Divisions.

Marine Aircraft Group 36

Marine Aircraft Group (Helicopter Transport) 36 was commissioned at Marine Corps Air Facility, Santa Ana, California on June 2, 1952. On March

16, 1959, "Helicopter Transport" was dropped from MAG 36's designation and, in August 1965, the unit was deployed to Vietnam during the VIET-NAM WAR, the first complete Marine Aircraft Group to arrive in the combat zone. Operating from an air facility at Ky Ha, MAG 36 provided resupply, troop lifts, air strikes, recon inserts and extracts, and medical evacuation for allied troops in the southern I Corps area. In the fall of 1967, MAG 36 moved to Phu Bai, and in early 1968, the unit was heavily involved in defending against the Tet Offensive. MAG 36 was redeployed from Vietnam to Marine Corps Air Station Futenma on November 4, 1969, and subsequently redeployed detachments to Thailand and Vietnam to provide combat air refueling for USMC fighter/attack aircraft.

In April 1975, MAG 36 participated in Operation Eagle Pull, the emergency evacuation of American civilians from Cambodia. Then, during April 29–30, the unit evacuated more than 7,000 people from Saigon, South Vietnam, during the general evacuation of the capital.

Since the Vietnam War, MAG 36 has supported USMC fleet operations in the Pacific Theater.

Marine Air Ground Task Force Training Command

Formerly the Marine Corps Air Ground Combat Center (MCAGCC), the command was redesignated Marine Air Ground Task Force Training Command (MAGTF) on October 1, 2000. MAGTF began on August 20, 1952, as Marine Corps Training Center at Twentynine Palms, California, for live-fire training. Originally, the center was used primarily for artillery training, then evolved into a combined-arms training facility, a kind of "combined-arms exercise college" for the USMC.

Today, MAGTF is operated under the Training and Education Command.

Marine Assault Climbers Kit See PERSONAL
AND MISCELLANEOUS EQUIPMENT.

Marines of the Second Reconnaissance Battalion practice their rappelling from a UH-1 Huey helicopter at the Marine Corps Air Ground Task Force Training Center, Twentynine Palms, California. *(Department of Defense)*

Marine Aviation Weapons and Tactics Squadron One

MAWTS-1 is part of the Training and Education Command and provides standardized advanced tactical training and certification of unit instructor qualifications in support of Marine aviation training and readiness. The squadron also provides assistance in the development and employment of aviation weapons and tactics for the USMC.

Special Weapons Training Units (SWTUs) were formed in the 1950s to provide training for USMC attack squadrons, which were assigned to carry special weapons. During the 1960s, conventional weapons delivery was added to the curriculum and the SWTUs were redesignated as Marine Air Weapons Training Units, MAWTULant at Cherry Point, North Carolina, and MAWTUPac at El Toro, California. In 1976, a USMC study group recommended establishment of the Weapons and Tactics Training Program (WTTP) for all of Marine aviation, including development of a graduate-level Weapons and Tactics Instructor (WTI) Course. Consolidated WTI courses were then conducted at Marine Corps Air Station Yuma, Arizona, by a combined MAWTU staff in May 1977 and February 1978. These proved so successful that Marine Aviation Weapons and Tactics Squadron One was commissioned at Yuma on June 1, 1978.

Since its commissioning, MAWTS-1 has conducted two WTI courses per year and now produces more than 300 WTI graduates annually. In June 1983, an Aviation Development, Tactics, and Evaluation Department (ADT&E) was established to coordinate the MAWTS efforts in developing and evaluating tactics and hardware in all functional areas of Marine Corps aviation. In 1988, a Ground Combat Department was added to encourage increased participation during the WTI course by infantry, artillery, and armor officers. Other MAWTS-1 courses embedded within WTI include the Intelligence Officers Course; Aviation Ground Support and Logistic Officers Course; the Rotary Wing Crew Chief Course; and KC-130 Navigator Course; KC-130 Loadmaster Course; KC-130 Flight Engineer Weapons Course; Tactics Instructor Course; and the MACCS Enlisted Weapons and Tactics courses. An advanced curriculum includes the Tactical Air Commanders Course, MEU/SPMAGTF ACE Commanders Course, and the MAWTS-1 Commanders Course. MAWTS-1 personnel conduct a Mobile Training curriculum consisting of the MEU ACE Training Course, the MAGTF Aviation Integration Course, and the Marine Division Tactics Course.

MAWTS-1 maintains liaison with the aviation and tactics schools of the USN, USA, and USAF, as well as the armed forces of certain Allied nations.

Marine Barracks

The term has two meanings. It may denote the ceremonial and special security unit assigned to Washington, D.C., and located at 8th and I Streets (often nicknamed "8th and Eye"). The oldest USMC post, it includes the residence of the COMMANDANT OF THE MARINE CORPS. It is considered the "spiritual home" of the USMC.

"Marine Barracks" also refers to a special guard unit assigned to ensure the internal security of major U.S. Navy shore stations, including the protection of USN nuclear weapons.

Marine Corps Air Ground Combat Center
See MARINE AIR GROUND TASK FORCE TRAINING COMMAND.

Marine Corps Air Station Beaufort   See
BASES, CAMPS, AND OTHER INSTALLATIONS.

Marine Corps Air Station Cherry Point
See BASES, CAMPS, AND OTHER INSTALLATIONS.

Marine Corps Air Station Futenma   See
BASES, CAMPS, AND OTHER INSTALLATIONS.

Marine Corps Air Station Iwakuni   See
BASES, CAMPS, AND OTHER INSTALLATIONS.

Marine Corps Air Station Miramar   See
BASES, CAMPS, AND OTHER INSTALLATIONS.

Marine Corps Air Station New River   See
BASES, CAMPS, AND OTHER INSTALLATIONS.

Marine Corps Air Station Yuma   See BASES,
CAMPS, AND OTHER INSTALLATIONS.

Marine Corps Base Camp Lejeune   See
BASES, CAMPS, AND OTHER INSTALLATIONS.

Marine Corps Base Camp Pendleton   See
BASES, CAMPS, AND OTHER INSTALLATIONS.

Marine Corps Base Camp Smedley D. Butler   See BASES, CAMPS, AND OTHER INSTALLATIONS.

Marine Corps Base Hawaii   See BASES,
CAMPS, AND OTHER INSTALLATIONS.

Marine Corps Base Quantico See BASES, CAMPS, AND OTHER INSTALLATIONS.

Marine Corps Combat Development Command

MCCDC had its origin in the MARINE CORPS SCHOOLS established at Marine Corps Base Camp Lejeune in 1920. The MCCDC is the intellectual core of the USMC and is the central agency responsible for training, concepts, and doctrine development for the USMC. In addition to the Marine Corps University and the Marine Corps Schools, MCCDC consists of 10 divisions: Requirements; Concepts and Plans; Warfighting Integration; Doctrine; Training and Education; Studies and Analysis; Coalition and Special Warfare; War Gaming and Combat Simulation; Marine Corps Presentation Team; and Science and Innovation.

Marine Corps Combat Identification Program (MCCIP)

Fratricide, death by friendly fire, has always been a major problem on the battlefield, and it has become even more pressing as the tactical nature of warfare grows more complex. Under the oversight of the Joint Combat Identification Office (JCIDO), the Marine Corps Combat Identification Program provides ground-to-ground and air-to-ground identification of friendly and unknown (hostile or neutral/noncombatant) forces in the battle space. The program uses an active millimeter wave (MMW) question and answer system for target interrogation, validation, and identification prior to engagement. In the ground-to-ground format, the system consists of an installation kit (A-kit) and the BCIS equipment set (B-kit). These kits consist of an Interrogator Antenna, Transponder Antenna, Ballistic Armor Housing, Comm Unit Display Interface, and the Display/Interface Mount. The narrow-beam, directional Interrogator Antenna is bore sighted to the main weapon system on long-range, direct-fire armored platforms. The omnidirectional Transponder Antenna is mounted on all high fratricide-risk armored platforms deployed forward of the battle area. The air-to-ground system consists of a BCIS pod mounted to the AIM-9 Sidewinder missiles fired from rotary-wing and fixed-wing aircraft. The Marine Corps Combat Identification Program (MCBIP) provides to platform gunners and commanders a visual and/or audio signal that identifies potential targets, day or night, and in all weather conditions. The object is to use currently available technologies to reduce or prevent fratricide. The advantage of the Marine Corps Combat Identification Program (MCBIP) is that the components can be assembled off the shelf and fielded immediately.

General characteristics of the Marine Corps Combat Identification Program (MCBIP) include:

Manufacturer: TRW/Magnavox
Probability of correct target identification: 90 percent under all battlefield conditions (99 percent objective)
Target engagement time: > 1 sec
Multiple interrogations/responses: ≥ 3 simultaneous
Maximum effective range (minimum-maximum), ground-to-ground: 500 ft–18,000 ft
Maximum effective range (minimum-maximum), air-to-ground: 500 ft–26,000 ft
Discrimination between targets: >+/– 22.5 mils in azimuth or > 800 ft in range
Reliability: 1,242 hr (threshold) to 2,760 hr (objective)

Marine Corps Expeditionary Medal See DECORATIONS AND MEDALS.

Marine Corps Intelligence

Marine Corps Intelligence, also called Marine Corps Intelligence Activity (MCIA), supports USMC acquisition policy and budget planning and programming, and provides pre-deployment training and force contingency planning for requirements that are not satisfied by theater, other service, or national capabilities. MCIA works in conjunction with Naval Intelligence and Coast Guard Intelligence at the National Maritime Intelligence Center in Washington, D.C., and at Marine Corps Base Quantico, Virginia.

Marine Corps Logistics Base Albany   See
BASES, CAMPS, AND OTHER INSTALLATIONS.

Marine Corps Logistics Base Barstow   See
BASES, CAMPS, AND OTHER INSTALLATIONS.

Marine Corps Recruit Depot Parris Island
See BASES, CAMPS, AND OTHER INSTALLATIONS.

Marine Corps Recruit Depots   See BASES,
CAMPS, AND OTHER INSTALLATIONS.

Marine Corps Recruit Depot San Diego
See BASES, CAMPS, AND OTHER INSTALLATIONS.

Marine Corps Reserve
The Marine Corps Reserve began in 1916 with three officers and 33 enlisted men, but did not commence in earnest until passage of the Naval Reserve Act of 1925 and the Naval Reserve Act of 1938. By the end of WORLD WAR II, when the USMC reached its historical maximum strength of 471,000, 70 percent of marines were reservists. Today, the USMCR, like other military reserve forces and the National Guard, is fully integrated in all military planning.

The USMCR is composed of three classes and one special category.

Fleet Marine Corps Reserve constitutes Class I and is composed of former regular enlisted marines with at least 20 years of service in the regular marines. This class may be employed as needed without further training. Class I reservists remain in this class until they have completed 30 years of combined regular and reserve service.

Selected Marine Corps Reserve constitutes Class II and, like Class I marines, can be instantly assimilated into regular service. Most Class II marines have six months of training with a six-year military obligation and attend semimonthly or monthly drills and annual training.

Individual Ready Reserve (Class III) consists of physically qualified marines who are not assigned to Class I or Class II. These personnel are available for mobilization in time of war or national emergency. They do not participate in the level of unit training engaged in by Class II members.

In addition to the three basic classes of reservists, a Limited Assignment (Overage) Category allows certain USMCR officers with special qualifications to serve as needed in special mobilization assignments.

Marine Corps Reserve Ribbon   See DECO-
RATIONS AND MEDALS.

Marine Corps Schools
Marine Corps Schools is headquartered at Marine Corps Base Quantico and is under the command of the president of Marine Corps University, who reports to the commanding general of MARINE CORPS COMBAT DEVELOPMENT COMMAND. The schools include:

- Marine Corps War College: a top-level school that annually convenes a class of 12 colonels, including peers from other services
- School of Advanced Warfighting: provides a year of advanced training for graduates of the Command and Staff College
- Command and Staff College: provides a nine-month course for majors and lieutenant colonels

- Amphibious Warfare School: provides career-level instruction for captains to prepare them for company-level command and battalion-level staff work
- Command and Control Systems Course: a specialized Amphibious Warfare School curriculum for communications and intelligence officers
- Basic Communications Officer Course: to qualify for the communications specialty
- Officer Candidate School: provides enlisted marines with basic officer training; graduates become commissioned USMC officers
- Staff Noncommissioned Officers' Academy: provides advanced NCO training
- Basic School: provides further training for newly commissioned officers and certain enlisted personnel

Marine Corps Supply

Marine Corps Supply services furnish logistics support for the USMC. The USMC maintains a central inventory control point (ICP) at Marine Corps Logistics Base Albany, Georgia, where all procurement is centralized. Processing of all requisitions goes through this ICP. Additionally, the inventory control point is responsible for cataloging all USMC items; for provisioning, which means providing necessary support, maintenance, and repair items for all USMC equipment and equipment systems; for providing technical services and support; and for providing publications necessary to supply functions.

In addition to the ICP, the USMC maintains remote storage activities. The two principal RSA are at Albany and at Marine Corps Logistics Base Barstow, California. The USMC also maintains numerous smaller RSAs to ensure that supply needs are met anywhere they occur.

Marine Expeditionary Brigade (MEB)   See

ORGANIZATION BY UNITS.

Marine Expeditionary Force (MEF)   See

ORGANIZATION BY UNITS.

Marine Expeditionary Unit (MEU)   See

ORGANIZATION BY UNITS.

Marine Forces

The USMC is currently deployed in seven "Forces," as follows:

- Marine Forces Atlantic (MARFORLANT), headquartered in Norfolk, Virginia
- Marine Forces Europe (COMMARFOREUR), headquartered in Stuttgart, Germany
- Marine Forces Korea (USMARFORK), headquartered in Seoul, South Korea
- Marine Forces Pacific (MARFORPAC), headquartered at Camp Smith, Hawaii
- Marine Forces Reserve (MFR), headquartered at Marine Corps Base Quantico, Virginia
- Marine Forces South (MARFORSOUTH), headquartered in Broward and Dade Counties, Florida
- Marine Forces Unitas (MARFORUNITAS), which works in cooperation with the military of various Latin American nations

Marine Helicopter Squadron One

Established in December 1947 as an experimental unit to test and evaluate helicopters and tactics, Marine Helicopter Squadron One (HMX-1) was subsequently also tasked with providing all helicopter transportation for the president of the United States overseas and within the United States. HMX-1 also provides helicopter transportation for the vice president, members of the cabinet, and foreign dignitaries, under the direction of the White House Military Office. In addition, HMX-1 provides emergency evacuation and other support as directed by the COMMANDANT OF THE MARINE CORPS.

MARINE ONE is the call sign used when the president is on board any HMX-1 helicopter; however, the primary presidential helicopter is the Sikorsky VH-3D Sea King.

Marine Hymn

The Marine Hymn is the anthem of the USMC and came into use shortly after the Civil War. Its melody is a close approximation of a marching song from Jacques Offenbach's (1819–80) opera *Genviève de Brabant* and its lyrics are anonymous.

*From the Halls of Montezuma
To the Shores of Tripoli,
We will fight our country's battles
In the air, on land and sea.
First to fight for right and freedom
And to keep our honor clean,
We are proud to claim the title
of United States Marine.*

*Our flag's unfurled to every breeze
From dawn to setting sun.
We have fought in ev'ry clime and place
Where we could take a gun.
In the snow of far-off Northern lands
And in sunny tropic scenes,
You will find us always on the job—
The United States Marines.*

*Here's health to you and to our Corps,
Which we are proud to serve.
In many a strife we've fought for life
And never lost our nerve.
If the Army and the Navy
Ever look on Heaven's scenes,
They will find the streets are guarded
By United States Marines.*

Marine One

The call sign used when the president of the United States is on board of one of the helicopters of MARINE HELICOPTER SQUADRON ONE. (Compare "Air Force One," the call sign of any USAF aircraft when the president is on board.)

President George H. W. Bush enters Marine One on the South Lawn of the White House. *(George H. W. Bush Library)*

Maritime Prepositioning Squadrons (MPSs)

The USMC maintains three permanent MPSs, on station in the eastern Atlantic; at Diego Garcia, in the Indian Ocean; and off the Mariana Islands in the Central Pacific. These floating squadrons stand at readiness to meet crises quickly. They consist of transport vessels preloaded with supplies, ready to receive marines for rapid deployment.

Marshall Islands Campaign

The Marshall group consists of atolls some 1,500 miles southeast of SAIPAN. Following WORLD WAR I, the League of Nations gave the Japanese a mandate over the principal atolls of Jaluit, Mili,

Maloelop, Majuro, Wotje, KWAJALEIN, and ENIWE-TOK. Well before WORLD WAR II, the Japanese exploited their mandate by building airfields on islands in these atolls, so that they were very well established in this strategic location.

The first U.S. strike against the Marshalls was at Kwajalein: a landing by the USMC's 4th Division on February 1, 1944, at ROI-NAMUR, while the army attacked Kwajalein Island. Engebi Island, in the Eniwetok Atoll, was struck next, on February 19, and on February 22, marines secured Parry Island, also a part of the Eniwetok Atoll.

The successful completion of the Marshall Islands Campaign put U.S. forces in an excellent position to press the next campaign, against the MARIANA ISLANDS.

mascot

The official mascot of the USMC is the English bulldog. The mascot dates from 1918 and World War I, when German soldiers, overwhelmed by the fighting prowess of the marines, called them *Teufelhunden,* or "devil dogs."

master gunnery sergeant   See RANKS AND GRADES.

master sergeant   See RANKS AND GRADES.

Mayaguez incident

On May 12, 1975, the *Mayaguez,* a U.S.-flagged container ship, was stopped by a Cambodian gunboat while en route from Hong Kong to Thailand. The ship was compelled to anchor off Koh Tang, a jungle island some 30 miles from the Cambodian port of Kampong Som, to which the 39 crew members were taken and temporarily held.

In response to the seizure of the *Mayaguez,* President Gerald Ford ordered a military operation to retake the vessel and free the crew. The U.S. Air Force, U.S. Navy, and USMC participated in the joint operation, in which marines boarded the abandoned *Mayaguez* on May 15, while the destroyer escort *Wilson* intercepted Cambodian boats transporting the prisoners from Kampong Som and freed them. In the meantime, more marines attacked Koh Tang, but were pinned down by heavy resistance and had to be evacuated on May 16.

Although the mission was a success—the *Mayaguez* recovered, the crew freed—it was costly: 11 marines, two sailors, and two airmen were killed; 41 marines, two sailors, and seven airmen were wounded. Three USAF helicopters were destroyed and another 11 damaged.

MC-5 Static Line/Free-Fall Ram Air Parachute System (SL/FF RAPS)   See PERSONAL AND MISCELLANEOUS EQUIPMENT.

McCawley, Charles G. (1827–1891) *Marine Corps commandant*

The eighth COMMANDANT OF THE MARINE CORPS, McCawley was born in Philadelphia and was commissioned in the USMC in 1847. Directly upon his commissioning, McCawley participated in the amphibious invasion of VERACRUZ during the U.S.-MEXICAN WAR, then went on to fight through to the invasion of Mexico City. He was breveted captain at the Battle of CHAPULTEPEC.

McCawley served in the Civil War, commanding a battalion that participated in the capture of Port Royal, South Carolina, and in the unsuccessful attempts to take the forts defending Charleston in 1863. As a result of his heroic actions in an unsuccessful assault on Fort Sumter on September 8, 1863, McCawley was breveted major.

After the war, McCawley served in Washington and was appointed commandant in 1876. He generally raised the standards for USMC enlistment and reformed the organization of the Marine Corps. In 1882, he managed to ensure that a certain number of U.S. Naval Academy graduates would be available for service as USMC officers, thereby greatly increasing the quality of the organization's officer corps. McCawley is also fondly remembered for assigning JOHN PHILIP SOUSA as leader of the U.S. MARINE BAND. McCawley retired, with the rank of colonel, on January 29, 1891.

Medal of Honor   See DECORATIONS AND MEDALS.

MEU (SOC) Pistol   See WEAPONS, INDIVIDUAL AND CREW-SERVED.

Midway, Battle of

Midway is a coral atoll lying 1,134 nautical miles to the northwest of Honolulu. A U.S. possession since 1867, Midway was garrisoned by three USMC units, the 6th Defense Battalion and two air squadrons, on the eve of WORLD WAR II. On June 4, 1942, Japanese forces began operations against Midway, intending to capture it. USMC pilots, vastly outnumbered, flew obsolescent F2A Buffalos and a few new F4F Wildcats against Zeros and got the worst of it. Aerial attacks on two Japanese aircraft carriers were to no avail. Nevertheless, the marines held their positions until the main U.S. Navy force was in position and the final phase of the Battle of Midway got under way on June 6. The great naval battle would be costly to both sides, but would prove the turning point of the war in the Pacific. After Midway, U.S. forces assumed the offensive and remained on the offensive through the end of the war.

Mitchell PBJ   See AIRCRAFT, FIXED-WING.

Mk-19 40-mm Machine Gun, MOD 3

See WEAPONS, INDIVIDUAL AND CREW-SERVED.

Mk-48 Power Unit and Mk-14 Container Transporter Rear Body Unit   See WHEELED VEHICLES.

Mk-48 Power Unit and Mk-15, Recovery/Wrecker Rear Body Unit   See WHEELED VEHICLES.

Mk-48 Power Unit and Mk-16, Fifth-Wheel Semi-trailer Adapter Rear Body Unit   See WHEELED VEHICLES.

Mk-48 Power Unit and Mk-18 Self-loading Container and Ribbon Bridge Transporter   See WHEELED VEHICLES.

Mk-155 Mine Clearance Launcher   See WHEELED VEHICLES.

Mobile/Unit Conduct of Fire Trainer (M/U-COFT)   See TRACKED VEHICLES.

Modular Sleeping Bag (MSB)   See PERSONAL AND MISCELLANEOUS EQUIPMENT.

MP-5N Heckler and Koch 9-mm Submachine Gun   See WEAPONS, INDIVIDUAL AND CREW-SERVED.

Mundy, Carl E., Jr. (1935–   ) *Marine Corps commandant*

The 30th COMMANDANT OF THE MARINE CORPS, Mundy was born in Atlanta, graduated from Auburn University in Alabama, and was commissioned a USMC second lieutenant in 1957. After service at sea and as a Basic School instructor, Mundy served in the VIETNAM WAR during 1966–67 as an operations officer and executive officer with the 3rd Battalion, 26th Marines and as intelligence officer in III Amphibious Force. After his return to the States, Mundy served in a variety of staff positions, culminating in a promotion to brigadier general and assignment as director of personnel at HEADQUARTERS MARINE CORPS in 1982.

Mundy subsequently commanded 4th Amphibious Brigade, then became director of operations for the USMC. Promoted to major general in 1986 and lieutenant general in 1988, he served as deputy chief of staff and deputy to the Joint Chiefs before assuming command of FLEET MARINE FORCE, Atlantic. After promotion to general in 1991, he was named commandant.

N

Navajo code talkers

The need for rapid but secure communications is always important in war and was especially urgent in the Pacific during WORLD WAR II, where rapid movement and surprise tactics were of critical value against the Japanese.

Philip Johnston, the son of a missionary to the Navajos and one of the very few non-Navajos who spoke the language, was a veteran of WORLD WAR I who knew that Native American languages, especially Choctaw, had been used during that war to encode messages. He believed that the Navajo language would be ideal for secure communications in World War II. The language is unwritten and extremely complex. Its syntax, qualities of intonation, and its dialectical variety render it wholly unintelligible to those who lack either lifelong exposure or extensive training. At the time of World War II, it was estimated that fewer than 30 non-Navajos—none of them Japanese—could understand Navajo.

With all of this in mind, Johnston met with Major General Clayton B. Vogel, commanding general of Amphibious Corps, Pacific Fleet, early in 1942 and presented his idea. Johnston agreed to conduct tests under simulated combat conditions. The tests demonstrated that Navajos could encrypt, transmit, and decrypt a three-line message in 20 seconds. Cipher machines of the period required a half-hour to perform the same task. Thoroughly impressed, Vogel recommended to the COMMANDANT OF THE MARINE CORPS that the USMC recruit 200 Navajos.

The first 29 Navajo recruits reported for BASIC TRAINING in May 1942. Working at Marine Corps

Two of the Navajo code talkers of World War II
(National Archives)

FLO

Base Camp Pendleton, this first contingent created the Navajo code, quickly accomplishing the task of developing a dictionary and inventing many words for military and technological terms. This dictionary, including all code words, had to be committed to memory during the training of the so-called code talkers. After completing that training, the code talker was sent to a USMC unit in the Pacific. His principal mission was to transmit orders and information relating to tactics and troop movements over field telephones and radios. Secondarily, the code talkers served as messengers. They participated in every assault and campaign the USMC conducted in the Pacific from 1942 to 1945, including GUADALCANAL, TARAWA, PELELIU, and IWO JIMA, and they served in all six USMC divisions as well as in USMC Raider battalions and parachute units. The Japanese never succeeded in breaking the code.

As of 1945, some 540 Navajos had enlisted in the USMC, of whom 375 to 420 were trained as code talkers. Their contribution went largely unheralded until September 17, 1992, when the code talkers were officially recognized by a special permanent exhibition at the Pentagon. A highly fictionalized account of the code talkers was presented in the 2002 film *Windtalkers.*

naval relations

While both the U.S. Navy and U.S. Marine Corps are regulated by and subordinate to the Department of the Navy, they are separate, although intimately partnered, services. Neither service is subordinate to the other.

Neville, Wendell C. (1870–1930) *Marine Corps commandant*

Nicknamed "Whispering Buck," Neville was born in Portsmouth, Virginia, and graduated from the U.S. Naval Academy in 1890. He cruised for two years as a navy midshipman, then was commissioned a second lieutenant in the USMC. He served with distinction in the SPANISH-AMERICAN WAR, receiving the Brevet Medal, at the time the highest decoration the USMC awarded. He next saw action in China, during the BOXER REBELLION, then served in the Philippines, Cuba, NICARAGUA, PANAMA, and Hawaii.

Neville, as lieutenant colonel, led the 2nd Marines during the U.S. invasion of VERACRUZ, Mexico, in 1914, and received the Medal of Honor for his actions. During WORLD WAR I, as colonel, Neville fought in major battles, including BELLEAU WOOD and Soissons. He was promoted to major general on his return to the United States in 1919 and assigned as assistant commandant, then as commander of the Department of the Pacific. Appointed commandant in 1929, he died in office a year later.

New Britain, Battle of

Located in the Bismarck chain in the Solomon Sea, opposite New Guinea, New Britain was occupied by the Japanese early in WORLD WAR II. With Rabaul, it figured as an important Japanese air base and harbor. In support of the campaign against Rabaul, the USMC's 1st Division landed on New Britain at Cape Gloucester on December 26, 1943. Landing on two beaches, the marines fought through the torrential rains of the monsoon, captured the airfield, then pursued the retreating Japanese, flushing them from the highlands to the coast, and then pushing them along the coast toward Rabaul.

Although Japanese resistance was tough, as it always was, the chief adversaries in the New Britain battle were the rugged terrain of the island's highland area and the relentless monsoon rains.

New Georgia, Battle of

Located northwest of GUADALCANAL, New Georgia Island had a Japanese airfield at a place called Munda, which, acting in concert with the army's 43rd Division, the USMC's 4th Raider Battalion secured in June 1944.

While the 43rd Division made the principal landing on New Georgia, the marine raiders, on June 21, landed separately on the north end of the island and took Viru Harbor. They advanced southward to secure the harbor at Bairoko with the purpose of sealing off the Japanese retreat from Munda. The marines were thwarted by Japanese resistance and rugged jungle terrain. In the meantime, the 43rd Division had to take up a position short of Munda, and two additional army divisions were called in to take the airfield.

Although the airfield was secured as an important U.S. base, much of the Japanese garrison evacuated to Kolombangara Island and thereby escaped annihilation.

new man rule

An unwritten rule in USMC procedure directing that replacements take the point, or advance position, in a ground operation.

new meat

A new replacement assigned to a USMC combat unit. He or she may be subject to the new man rule.

New Orleans, Battle of

The Battle of New Orleans, commanded on the American side by Andrew Jackson, is remembered as one of the few great American land victories of the WAR OF 1812, even though it took place after the signing of the Treaty of Ghent, which ended the war. (The slow pace of transatlantic communications in the early 19th century kept the news of peace from both sides.)

Jackson led a combination of regular army troops and miscellaneous militia forces in his successful defense of New Orleans against a veteran British force led by General Edward Pakenham. However, a force of 400 marines under the command of Major Daniel Carmick also played an important role in Jackson's victory. A portion of the USMC force was deployed in five gunboats, which challenged the British landing. Most of the force was positioned in the center of Jackson's line of defense.

The first British attack was a probe on December 28, 1814, which was aimed directly at the marines' sector. The marines held their ground and repelled the probe. Eleven days after this initial assault, Pakenham unleashed his main attack, a formed charge by 3,500 men. The action was as stupid as it was gallant, and 2,300 British troops were either wounded or killed. Pakenham was among the slain. As for Jackson, he was full of praise for the small USMC contingent, which had contributed significantly to the victory.

Nicaragua

The U.S. Marine Corps was first sent to intervene in Nicaragua in 1852 and then again in 1854, when three landings were made in the Bluefields area to protect U.S. lives and property during one of many uprisings that followed independence from Spain in 1821. A Conservative regime brought a modicum of peace to the nation from the 1860s until 1893, when José Zelaya, a Liberal militant, seized power. He maintained control until 1909, after a Conservative revolution erupted against his regime. A provisional USMC regiment of 750 was landed to aid the Conservatives; after the situation was stabilized, the marines were withdrawn in September 1910.

In 1912, Liberal forces reemerged and seized much of the southeastern portion of the country. Three hundred fifty marines were landed in May 1912 and were eventually reinforced by 780 more. Very rapidly, the marines seized the initiative and suppressed the rebels. They then withdrew, except for a contingent of 100 legation guards.

After an interval of about 10 years of relative stability, the Liberals rose in revolt yet again, in 1922, but a coalition government was formed by 1924 and the prospects for peace looked hopeful. Perhaps unwisely, the legation guards were withdrawn, which triggered renewed fighting in the Bluefields region. Marines were landed again in 1926 and more in January 1927. The United States also supplied arms to the government, and the entire 5th Marines arrived, reconstituting in-country the 2nd Brigade. The show of force reinstated the Conservatives. When the charismatic Liberal leader Augusto Sandino persisted in fighting the Conservative regime, the United States backed the formation of a Guardia Nacional, which collaborated with the marines in a campaign against the so-called Sandinistas during 1928. The marines continued to participate in combat against the Sandinistas until 1931, when President Herbert Hoover withdrew them. By this time, a Conservative government, friendly to the United States and under the dictatorship of Anastasio Somoza (head of the Guardia Nacional), had been installed. Somoza treacherously captured Sandino under the pretext of truce talks and ordered his execution in 1934.

Nicholas, Samuel (1744–1790) *Marine Corps commandant*

The Continental Congress commissioned Philadelphia-born Samuel Nicholas captain of the CONTINENTAL MARINES on November 28, 1775, a few days after this service was created. Although he was not

Major Samuel Nicholas (Continental Marines)
(U.S. Marine Corps)

officially called commandant, he served effectively in that capacity during the AMERICAN REVOLUTION and is generally honored by marines as the first COMMANDANT OF THE MARINE CORPS.

In the spring of 1776, Nicholas, promoted to major, led the first marine amphibious assault, landing 200 marines and 50 sailors at New Providence, Bahamas, where he captured important forts and appropriated much-needed supplies. He next led 80 marines (three companies) in George Washington's triumphant assault on Trenton on December 26, 1776.

Nicholas and his marines remained with Washington until early 1777, when Nicholas was sent to Philadelphia and the marines were used for defensive duty in Delaware. Nicholas was the senior marine commander throughout the American Revolution. With peace, however, the Continental Marines was disbanded, and Nicholas retired to civilian life.

nuclear-biological-chemical equipment

Nuclear, biological, and chemical weapons have become increasingly significant battlefield threats in recent years. The following equipment is included in the Marine Corps inventory.

Chemical Agent Monitor

The Chemical Agent Monitor is a handheld device for monitoring chemical agent contamination on personnel and equipment, primarily in a post-attack situation. The device is simple to operate, having only two controls, an on/off push-button switch and a mode-select push-button switch, which selects the blister or nerve-agent mode of operation.

The Chemical Agent Monitor detects vapors of chemical agents by sensing molecular ions of specific mobilities—time of flight—and uses advanced timing and microprocessor technologies to reject incorrect inferences. This enables the unit to detect and to discriminate between vapors of nerve or blister agents and also to display the relative concentration of either. The USMC instrument is also capable of detecting and discriminating among other agents.

General characteristics of the device include:

Length: 17 in
Width: 4 in
Height: 7 in
Weight: 5.5 lb
Agent concentration detectability: 0.1 mg/m^2
Response time: under 60 sec for 0.1 mg/m^2 of
  agent

In the modern battlefield environment, chemical agents have become an increasingly important threat, and monitors will become more and more common in the field.

M-17 Lightweight Decontamination System

NBC (Nuclear-Biological-Chemical) weapons are a heightened risk in the battlefield of the 21st century, making it critical that USMC field forces have rapid access to effective decontamination apparatus. The Lightweight Decontamination System is a compact, lightweight, entirely portable decontamination system consisting of a 7.3-horsepower engine, a self-priming pump for drawing and pressurizing water, a fan assembly to deliver combustion air to the heater, a water heater, a self-priming pump for the heater fuel system, and a small generator to supply electricity for ignition and safety control functions. The system is transportable by ¾-ton trailer, 1¼-ton cargo truck, cargo aircraft, and, as a sling load, by helicopter.

The system provides pressurized water at temperatures up to 248° Fahrenheit at a rate of up to 9 gallons per minute. It draws water from any natural source up to 30 feet away and 9 feet below pump level. The system incorporates an additional 3,000 gallon water-storage tank in case of a lack of natural water sources. The system is also saltwater resistant.

By 2004, the USMC had fielded almost 3,000 units. General characteristics of the M-17 Lightweight Decontamination System include:

Main unit dimensions—
Length: 40.2 in
Width: 23.2 in

Height: 33.9 in
Weight: 360 lb

Accessory kit dimensions—
Length: 41.8 in
Width: 20.5 in
Height: 15.4 in
Weight: 143 lb

Water bladder dimensions—
Height: 5.8 ft when full
Weight: 70 lb
Capacity: 1,580 gal
Water temperature: up to 248°F
Water delivery rate: 9 gal/min
Setup time: under 30 min

M-21 Remote-Sensing Chemical Agent Automatic Alarm

The USMC employs the Remote Sensing Chemical Agent Automatic Alarm as a two-man-portable, automatic scanning, passive infrared sensor to detect nerve and blister agent vapor clouds. The sensor measures changes in the infrared energy emitted from remote objects or from a cloud formed by the agent.

The M-21 Remote Sensing Chemical Agent Automatic Alarm is a stand-alone, tripod-mounted, chemical agent overwatch system intended for use in a defensive role. Components of the system include the detector, tripod, the M-42 remote alarm unit, transit case, power cable assembly, and a standard military power source. The unit may be used for reconnaissance and surveillance missions to search areas between friendly and enemy forces for chemical agent vapors and to provide advance detection and warning of chemical hazards. The most desirable use of the unit is deployment in pairs—two reconnaissance teams—so that one alarm can be used in the overwatch position while the other reconnaissance team is on the move.

The remote warning can be transmitted by two methods. A hardwire can be run to the M-42 alarm, or a digital signal can be transmitted from the M-21 via an RS-232 cable. This latter arrangement provides a capability to link with the Marine Corps Hazard Warning System/Network.

General characteristics of the M-21 Remote Sensing Chemical Agent Automatic Alarm include:

Length, operational configuration: 20 in
Width, operational configuration: 48 in
Height, operational configuration: 51.5 in
Weight, operational configuration: 66 lb
Length, storage/shipping configuration: 31 in
Width, storage/shipping configuration: 30 in
Height, storage/shipping configuration: 22 in
Weight, storage/shipping configuration: 117 lb
Power requirements: 120 watts at 21 to 30 volts
Chemical agent detection range: 1.86 to 3.1 mi
Instantaneous field of view, vertical: 1.5 degrees
Instantaneous field of view, horizontal: 60 degrees
Chemical agent spectral range: 800 to 1,200 cm^{-1}
Mean time between operational-mission failures: 277 hours

M-40/42 Chemical/Biological Protective Masks

The M-40/42 series of chemical/biological protective masks replaced three earlier models, the M-17 (general purpose), M-25 (vehicle crewman), and M-9 (heavy duty) masks, to provide respiratory, eye, and face protection against field concentrations of chemical and biological agents. The M-40/42 masks are effective against chemical and biological agent vapors, aerosols, toxins, and radiological fallout particles.

The masks consist of a silicone rubber face piece with an in-turned peripheral face seal and rigid binocular lens system. A face-mounted gas and aerosol filter canister may be mounted on either the left or the right cheek. Each filter is effective against a maximum of 15 nerve, choking, and blister agent attacks and against a maximum of two blood agent attacks. Biological agents do not degrade the filter.

The masks are available in small, medium, and large sizes to ensure a proper fit. They afford unobstructed and undistorted forward vision, and corrective lenses may be obtained and fitted into the mask. The mask also permits intelligible speech, does not interfere with hearing, and provides for a drinking capability while being worn. Microphone air adapters are provided for combat vehicle and aircraft applications. Because of all these features, the mask may be worn continuously for up to 12 hours.

The M-40/42 Chemical/Biological Protective Masks afford the following protection probabilities:

95 percent effective against 5,000 mg-min/m^3
75 percent effective against 20,000 mg-min/m^3
50 percent minimum probability of achieving no more than .002 percent penetration of *Bacillus globigii*

The breathing resistance of the mask is no greater than 55 millimeters of water at 85 liters per minute.

Portable Collective Protection System

The Portable Collective Protection System is an uncontaminated, positive-pressure shelter for use in a chemical/biological environment. The system consists of the protective shelter, a support kit, and a hermetically sealed filter canister. The shelter is a tent and fly. The tent floor and the fly are made of a Saranaex composite material. The tent is supported by an aluminum structure, and when overpressure is applied, the shelter provides protection from liquid and vapor chemical agent penetration as well as biological agent penetration. An integral airlock allows decontamination of entering personnel.

The system's support kit contains all the accessories required for deployment of the system, including the motor/blower assembly that supplies air to the system and the flexible ducts that guide the air to and through the hermetically sealed filter and then to the shelter. The filter canister consists of a hermetically sealed aluminum canister containing a gas filter and a particulate filter.

The system provides an uncontaminated, positive-pressure shelter for use as a command and control facility or as a rest and relief facility for up to 14 marines at a time. The tactical plan is to provide about four hours of rest and relief per day.

General characteristics of the Portable Collective Protection System include:

Operational configuration: 300 sq ft
Storage/shipping configuration, length: 9 ft
Storage/shipping configuration, width: 2.5 ft
Storage/shipping configuration, height: 3.4 ft
Storage/shipping configuration, weight: 673 lb
Air supply rate: supplies 200 cubic feet/min of clean air to the shelter
Temperature range: −25 to 120°F
Filter effectiveness: particulates, 0.3 microns or larger

Saratoga Chemical Protective Overgarment

The Saratoga suit was developed in the 1990s to replace the long-standard Overgarment 84 (OG-84) to provide improved and enhanced protection against chemical and biological agents. This protective outerwear is intended as part of a system to cover the entire body, feet, hands, and face. It is effective against chemical agent vapors, aerosols, and droplets, as well as all known biological agents.

The suit consists of a coat and trousers. The coat has a full-length zippered opening that is covered by a single protective flap. It also incorporates an integrated hood as well as hook and pile sleeve closures. The trousers may be adjusted by waist tabs. The trousers are held up by suspenders, and there are closures on the lower outside section of each leg. The suit can be worn over the duty uniform or undergarments and is wearable in all environments and conditions. It is not degraded by fresh or salt water, and it is fully launderable. The suit is intended to be used with appropriate gloves, boots, and mask.

The Saratoga suit uses spherical carbon technology to provide effective body protection from all known chemical/biological warfare agents while offering excellent flow conditions for body heat dissipation. This makes the Saratoga suit more comfortable than previous protective overgarments. The outside layer of material is cotton ripstop, which has been corpel treated. The suit comes in small, medium, large, and x-large sizes, and, as of 2004, the USMC had an inventory of 654,000 suits; however, the Saratoga suit is schedule to be replaced by the Joint Service Lightweight Integrated Suit Technology, which is already being acquired by the USMC.

General characteristics of the Saratoga Chemical Protective Overgarment include:

Protection period: 24 hours
Durability: 30 days continuous wear
Concentration resistance: 10mg/m^2 challenge for chemical agents and any challenge (battlefield) for biological agents
Length: size dependent
Width: size dependent
Height: size dependent
Weight: approximately 4.7 lb
Maximum effective temperature: 120°F
Storage life: 13 years

O

O'Bannon, Presley (1776–1850) *Marine Corps lieutenant*

O'Bannon was one of the first high-profile heroes of the USMC. Born in Fauquier County, Virginia, he was commissioned a second lieutenant in the USMC in 1801 and quickly rose to first lieutenant. In 1804, he was attached to the naval fleet that President Thomas Jefferson ordered to the Mediterranean to combat the BARBARY PIRATES. O'Bannon commanded a small USMC detachment, and led seven marines from this unit in company with a mixed force of European mercenaries and Arabs against the fortified town of Derna on April 27, 1805. O'Bannon's marines penetrated the enemy defenses, making way for the Arab troops to attack and defeat the soldiers of the bey of Tunis. This accomplished, O'Bannon raised the Stars and Stripes over the fort at Derna—the first time the American flag had been raised on foreign soil. The capture of Derna had little effect on the outcome of the war against the Barbary Pirates, since the bashaw of Tripoli had already agreed in principle to a favorable treaty with the United States; however, it was a dramatic vindication of the honor and effectiveness of the USMC.

O'Bannon's successful operation is alluded to in the MARINE HYMN—"the shores of Tripoli"—and is commemorated by the marine officer's MAMELUKE SWORD, a stylized replica of the ornate weapon reputedly presented to O'Bannon by the bey of Tripoli, Yusuf Hamet (who had been exiled by his brother, the bashaw).

Lieutenant Presley Neville O'Bannon (USMC)
(U.S. Marine Corps)

OE-1 Bird Dog   See AIRCRAFT, FIXED-WING.

Okinawa

Largest of the Ryukyu Islands, Okinawa was stubbornly defended by the Japanese during WORLD WAR II, largely because it was recognized that possession of the island would put the Americans in an ideal position from which to invade Japan itself.

The actual landing on Okinawa—by Tenth Army and the USMC III Amphibious Corps (consisting of the 1st and 6th Divisions)—was made on Easter Sunday, April 1, 1945, and met with only light opposition. Indeed, by April 21, resistance in the northern part of the island had been overcome; the main fighting took place in the south and consumed far more time than had been anticipated, ending only in late June. USMC casualties included some 2,938 killed (army and navy combined KIA were 12,500). Japanese losses were astronomical by comparison, 110,000 killed, 7,400 taken prisoner. An estimated 80,000 civilians on the well-populated island lost their lives. Capture of the island provided air bases for unremitting B-29 bombing raids against Japanese cities, as well as a staging area for a planned invasion that was made unnecessary by the dropping of two atomic bombs in August 1945.

Operation Just Cause   See PANAMA.

Operation Starlight

During the VIETNAM WAR, Operation Starlight was the first major U.S. operation against the Vietcong. The 7th Marines, the 3rd Marines, and a battalion of the 4th Marines attacked the 1st Vietcong regiment on the Van Tuong Peninsula. The USMC elements deployed both overland and amphibiously, supported by AD-4s as well as by naval bombardment, to envelop the Vietcong within a pincers movement.

The operation stepped off on August 19, 1965, and was a great success, resulting in the destruction of an entire enemy regiment.

organization, administrative and by major commands

As of 2004, the Marine Corps consisted of approximately 173,000 men and women, including 42,000 members of the MARINE CORPS RESERVE. In addition, the Corps employs approximately 18,000 civilian support workers.

The marines operate under the control of the Department of the Navy and secretary of the navy, to whom the COMMANDANT OF THE MARINE CORPS directly reports. The commandant presides over Operating Forces and a Supporting Establishment. The heart of the Corps, the Operating Forces consist of three elements: Marines Corps Security Forces, Marine Security Guard Battalion, and the Fleet Marine Forces. The Supporting Establishment, about 28,000 marines, is responsible for recruiting, for systems development and testing, and for developing doctrine, tactics, and techniques.

Within the Operating Forces, the U.S. MARINE CORPS SECURITY FORCE consists of about 5,000 marines and is responsible for shipboard security and for the security of onshore establishments. The Marine Corps Security Guard Battalion provides legation guards to 128 embassies worldwide. (see U.S. MARINE CORPS SECURITY GUARD BATTALION). Fleet Marine Forces are the major warfighting element of the Corps and are deployed as needed in Marine Air Ground Task Forces. These MAGTFs include Marine Expeditionary Forces (MEFs), Marine Expeditionary Units (MEUs), and Special Purpose MAGTFs, all of which vary in size as required for a particular mission.

organization by units

Operationally and tactically, the marines are organized into the following units, listed in order of ascending size and scope of responsibility:

Fire Team

A fire team is an informal tactical group, usually consisting of four marines and constituting one-third of a squad.

Squad

A marine squad is usually commanded by a sergeant or staff sergeant and composed of three fire teams, each fire team typically consisting of four men. The total strength of the Marine Corps squad is 13, including the commander.

Platoon

A low-level infantry unit, a marine platoon (beginning in the WORLD WAR II era) consists of three squads. There are three platoons to a company. The strength of a contemporary platoon is not fixed, but varies depending on the nature of the unit; however, a World War II marine rifle platoon generally consisted of 76 men.

Company

In the marines and in the army, a company is a unit of troops under the command of a captain and consists of a headquarters section and two or more platoons. A company consists of 140 or more personnel and is the basic element of a battalion. Conventionally, companies within the battalion are assigned alphabetic names (Company C, or Charlie Company, for example), although independent companies are assigned numerical names (3rd Communications Company).

Battalion

Until the expansion of the marines during WORLD WAR I, the battalion was the largest organizational unit in the service, varying in size from 150 men to 300. World War I introduced the brigade and regiment. Each brigade at this time consisted of 9,300 men and was divided into two regiments, each of which consisted of four battalions, with 1,160 men each. During World War II, the battalion was reduced to 881 men, which remains more or less the strength of this unit currently.

Regiment

A traditional unit term no longer officially used by the marines or the army (having been supplanted in both by the brigade), "regiment" is still used unofficially in deference to tradition.

Brigade

Brigades were unknown in the marines before a reorganization of the Corps in 1913, at which time a brigade consisted of two regiments. During World War I, a marine brigade was large, at 9,300 men. In World War II, the brigade was upgraded to divisional status, and in the VIETNAM WAR, the brigade concept was revised as the Marine Expeditionary Brigade, which consists of about 16,000 marines.

Marine Expeditionary Brigade (MEB)

The Marine Expeditionary Brigade (MEB) was a mainstay of marine deployment beginning in the 1950s and was employed in the KOREAN WAR, Vietnam War, and the PERSIAN GULF WAR. The MEB was eliminated throughout the Marine Corps during the early 1990s, but was reactivated, one MEB within each Marine Expeditionary Force (MEF), as of January 1, 2000. The MEB was seen as a force structure that had the capability of responding rapidly and with great flexibility to crises and trouble spots. The MEB supports such marine doctrines as Operational Maneuver From the Sea, which calls for strike capability 220 miles inland with fast-moving and sustainable forces, and also in urban combat; the marines believe that access by sea offers the best early-entry force into most urban areas.

The Amphibious MEB embarks aboard navy ships to destinations throughout the world, where it can make an amphibious assault, take a beachhead, and open a lane to project offensive combat power ashore.

The Amphibious MEB consists of more than 4,000 marines. A Maritime Prepositioning Force MEB can be much larger—greater than 16,000 marines—and large enough to project offensive combat power throughout its theater of operation. This would be used as a land-based force.

The Marine Expeditionary Brigade (MEB) is a Marine Air-Ground Task Force (MAGTF) built around a reinforced infantry regiment, an aircraft group, and a Brigade Service Support Group (BSSG). It is commanded by a brigadier general. As a marine expeditionary force, it is capable of rapid deployment via amphibious shipping or strategic airlift. The MEB deploys with 30 days of supplies, so that the MEB is intended as the forward echelon of the MEF.

The Ground Combat Element (GCE) of an MEB is normally an infantry regiment reinforced with selected division units. The Aviation Combat Element (ACE) is a task-organized marine aircraft group that includes varied aviation capabilities as well as antiair warfare capabilities, as required by the situation.

The Combat Service Support Element (CSSE) is a Brigade Service Support Group (BSSG) organized to provide maintenance support, front-line haul transportation, expeditionary vertical and horizontal construction, supply support, medical collecting and clearing, and landing support functions.

Division

The division was the largest marine unit at the beginning of World War II and consisted of two brigades for a total of 16,000 men per division. When the marines were reorganized during the 1980s into Marine Air Ground Task Force units, divisions operated within the larger units.

Marine Air Ground Task Force (MAGTF)

The MAGTF is a combined armed force consisting of a command element, a ground combat element, an aviation combat element, and a combat service (support) element. MAGTFs are established on an as-needed basis to accomplish specific missions, then disbanded on completion of the mission. There are currently four types of generic MAGTFs. The Marine Expeditionary Brigade (MEB) is explained above. The other three generic MAGTFs are the Marine Expeditionary Force (MEF), Marine Expeditionary Unit (MEU), and the Special Purpose Force (SPF). The strength of the MAGTFs is flexible; the largest, as in the Persian Gulf War, may contain up to 100,000 marines.

Marine Expeditionary Force (MEF)

The largest MAGTF, an MEF consists of 30,000 to 60,000 marines under the command of a lieutenant general. There may be one or more infantry divisions and an aircraft wing. The MEF is highly self-sustaining, capable of remaining in combat without resupply for 60 days.

Marine Expeditionary Unit (MEU)

The MEU is a MAGTF consisting of 1,000 to 4,000 marines, typically an infantry battalion and a composite aircraft squadron, under the command of a colonel. The MEU is the basic building-block unit of a MAGTF.

Special Purpose Force (SPF)

The smallest generic MAGTF, the SPF consists of 100 to 1,000 marines and/or navy SEALs. The SPF typically responds to crises in foreign locations, and they are often the first U.S. military personnel on the scene. Often, they are used in unconventional operations.

Corps

Spelled with a capital C, "The Corps" is a synonym for the United States Marine Corps. Spelled with a lowercase C, the corps is an organizational unit that was too large for the small USMC until the middle of World War II, when the first USMC corps was organized following the Battle of GUADALCANAL in 1943. By the end of the war, the marines fielded two amphibious corps. After the war, the term *corps* was not used, but the function of a corps was assumed first by the III Marine Amphibious Force (during the Vietnam War era) and then, during the 1970s and 1980s, by Marine Air Ground Task Forces.

Marine Corps Aviation

Marine Corps aviation units use two special organization terms. A *squadron* is the basic marine aviation unit, which generally consists of aircraft of a single type. The marine squadron consists of two or more *flights,* which are generally defined as a group of aircraft and crews assigned a common mission.

OV-10 Bronco   See AIRCRAFT, FIXED-WING.

Oxygen Transfer Pump System   See PERSONAL AND MISCELLANEOUS EQUIPMENT.

P

Pack Howitzer 1923-E2 See INDIRECT FIRE SYSTEMS.

Panama

In 1988, Panama's strongman dictator, Manuel Noriega, was indicted in absentia by a U.S. federal grand jury for drug trafficking. Pursuant to the indictment, Presidents Ronald Reagan and George H. W. Bush employed economic and diplomatic sanctions in an effort to pressure Noriega into resigning. After these attempts failed, and amid deteriorating U.S.-Panamanian relations, USMC and U.S. Army reinforcements were deployed to U.S. installations in Panama during the spring of 1989. This show of force did not prompt Noriega to step down; after a coup attempt against him failed in October 1989, Noriega issued a "declaration against the United States," which was followed by several incidents of harassment against U.S. nationals in Panama. The most severe incident was the shooting of an off-duty USA officer by Panamanian troops. This brought about, on December 19, 1989, the creation of a U.S.-sponsored alternative government for Panama, led by President Guillermo Endara. Early the next morning, December 20, Operation Just Cause was launched.

The operation began with an air assault (by then-new USAF F-117 Stealth fighters) against the barracks of the Panamanian Defense Force (PDF). U.S. Army Rangers were given responsibility for the main ground action, while marines guarded the entrances to the Panama Canal and other U.S. defense sites located in the Canal Zone. Rangers, reinforced by marines, advanced on the central Canal Zone, attacking en route the Commandancia, headquarters of Noriega and the PDF. Marines of the elite Task Force Semper Fi secured a six-mile area southwest of Panama City, encompassing the U.S. Naval Station, Howard Air Force Base, the Arraijan Tank Farm, and the Bridge of the Americas. Other units took and held Torrijos International Airport.

The fighting in Panama City was conducted house-to-house over a five-day period, as marines hunted down PDF troops and sought Noriega. In the meantime, a civil-affairs army Ranger battalion assisted President Endara in establishing order. The Rangers quickly created a new Panamanian police force, the Panama Public Force, to preserve civil order after U.S. troops withdrew. As for Noriega, he was not located until January 1990, when he was arrested and transported to the United States for trial. On April 10, 1992, Noriega was convicted on eight counts of cocaine trafficking, racketeering, and money laundering. He was sentenced to 40 years' imprisonment.

Casualties included 190 PDF soldiers killed and 124 wounded; 5,313 were taken prisoner. Nineteen American troops were killed and 303 wounded, including one marine killed and two wounded. The total number of marines deployed in Operation Just Cause was only 600 out of a total military force of 24,000.

Parachutist Individual Equipment Kit

(PIEK) See PERSONAL AND MISCELLANEOUS EQUIPMENT.

Parris Island See BASES, CAMPS, AND OTHER IN-STALLATIONS.

Pate, Randolph McCall (1898–1961) *Marine Corps commandant*

The 21st COMMANDANT OF THE MARINE CORPS, Pate was born in Port Royal, South Carolina, and saw his first military service in the U.S. Army, as an enlisted soldier during WORLD WAR I. After the war, he attended Virginia Military Institute, graduating in 1921 and receiving a commission as a second lieutenant in the MARINE CORPS RESERVE. Pate served in SANTO DOMINGO (1923–24) and China (1927–29), then was posted in the United States.

By the outbreak of World War II, Pate was a lieutenant colonel and took command as chief of logistics at GUADALCANAL. Later, he served as deputy chief of staff, FLEET MARINE FORCE, Pacific, and, after the war, became director of the Marine Corps Reserve and commandant of the Marine Corps Educational Center at Marine Corps Base Quantico.

As a major general, Pate commanded the 1st Marine Division during the KOREAN WAR in 1953, just before the armistice. He was appointed commandant in 1955 and personally commanded marines sent to Egypt during the Suez Crisis of 1956. Pate retired, a general, on December 31, 1959.

PBY-5A Catalina See AIRCRAFT, FIXED-WING.

Peleliu

An island in the Palau group of the western Carolines, Peleliu held important Japanese positions, which were attacked in September 1944 during WORLD WAR II. The 1st Marine Division, III Amphibious Corps, invaded, only to find that the number of Japanese defenders had been grossly underestimated. A 72-hour campaign had been envisioned; the assault actually lasted from September 15 to October 22 and exacted 1,300 USMC deaths. Army units, which were called in to reinforce the USMC invasion, suffered 827 casualties.

Although the Battle of Peleliu turned out to be one of the hardest fought in the Pacific war, the island proved of little strategic value.

Pendleton, Joseph H. ("Uncle Joe")

(1860–1942) *Marine Corps general*
A native of Rochester, Pennsylvania, Pendleton was a U.S. Naval Academy graduate (1882), served two years at sea, then was commissioned a second lieutenant in the USMC. He served in U.S. posts, at sea, and twice in Sitka, Alaska, before being posted to the Philippines. Promoted to major, he commanded the USMC base on Guam before assuming command of a USMC base at Bremerton, Washington, during 1906–09. After serving again in the Philippines, Pendleton assumed commands at Portsmouth, New Hampshire, and in NICARAGUA. In 1913, now a colonel, Pendleton led an expeditionary force at GUANTÁNAMO BAY.

Pendleton served in various U.S. commands until June 1916, when he led marines against rebels in SANTO DOMINGO. Promoted to brigadier general, he became acting military governor there until his return to the United States in October 1918, when he was appointed to command Marine Corps Recruit Depot Parris Island. In 1919, he assumed command of the advanced force base at San Diego, California, and in 1922 was appointed commanding general of the Department of the Pacific. He was promoted to major general in 1924 and retired later in the year, as commander of the 5th Brigade. Marine Corps Base Camp Pendleton, San Diego, is named for him.

Penobscot Bay Fiasco

During the AMERICAN REVOLUTION, 700 British troops and three Royal Navy men of war were deployed to Penobscot Bay at the mouth of the Penobscot River in Maine to build a fort and naval base from which operations could be directed against upper New England. A combined force of CONTINENTAL MARINES and Massachusetts State Marines was put at the head of a 900-man Patriot army to attack the British fort and drive out the garrison.

The marine elements of the Patriot force landed on July 28, 1779, easily neutralized the light opposition they encountered, and occupied the high ground before the still-incomplete British fort. At this point, however, the militia commander caught up with the marines, and a dispute over command ensued. This delayed the Patriot advance just 500 yards short of the fort. During this interval, a British frigate hove into sight, prompting the Patriot commander to order a general withdrawal against the vigorous objection of the marines. In this way, a magnificent opportunity was lost. The militia commander was subsequently convicted by a court-martial of dereliction of duty.

Persian Gulf War

On August 2, 1990, the Iraqi army, at the time the fourth largest ground force in the world, invaded Kuwait pursuant to a proclamation of annexation. Within a week, Kuwait had fallen to Iraq, and the United States worked through the United Nations to assemble a large coalition of nations to compel Iraq's dictator, Saddam Hussein, to withdraw from Kuwait.

U.S. military forces began a buildup in the Middle East on August 7, 1990, in response to a Saudi request for military aid to defend against possible Iraqi invasion. Dubbed Operation Desert Shield, the buildup included the 7th Marine Expeditionary Brigade, followed by the 4th Marine Expeditionary Brigade, and the 1st Marine Expeditionary Brigade, bringing USMC presence during Desert Shield to 30,000. A call-up of USMC RESERVES added another 31,000. The USMC presence included ground troops as well as the 1st and 2nd Air Wings. The total USMC presence was a small por-

tion of the 450,000 troops that would ultimately constitute the coalition forces arrayed against the Iraqi invaders.

Saddam Hussein defied a series of UN resolutions ordering his withdrawal from Kuwait. The UN set a withdrawal deadline of January 15, 1991. When this deadline elapsed, Operation Desert Shield became Operation Desert Storm—and the Persian Gulf War began on the morning of January 16 with a massive air campaign. The air war continued for five weeks and some 88,000 missions, which devastated Iraqi defenses. Then, on "G Day," February 24, 1991, the ground war was commenced with a marine attack from the extreme right of the coalition line. Two USMC divisions rapidly breached the Iraqi defenses, and by the end of that first day of the ground war, the marines had destroyed three Iraqi divisions.

At 4:30 in the morning of February 25, marines engaged in the largest tank battle in their history. Victory was total, and the Iraqi tanks completely destroyed. By the 27th, marines had liberated Kuwait City.

As spectacular as the USMC operations were, they represented a small part of the war. Coalition forces were on the verge of totally destroying the armed forces of Saddam Hussein when President George H. W. Bush, declaring that the objective of liberating Kuwait had been attained, announced that hostilities would cease at 8 A.M., February 28.

Despite his overwhelming military defeat, Saddam Hussein remained absolute dictator of Iraq. In 2003, as a result of the U.S. invasion of Iraq in Operation Iraqi Freedom, Saddam was driven from office, but marines and army forces were then faced with a long insurgency, which included resistance by Saddam loyalists.

personal and miscellaneous equipment

Important Marine Corps personal and miscellaneous equipment includes survival gear, parachute equipment, and equipment for operating in special environments. (Also see NUCLEAR-BIOLOGICAL-CHEMICAL EQUIPMENT.)

AN/PSN-11 Precision Lightweight GPS Receiver (PLGR)

The AN/PSN-11 Precision Lightweight GPS Receiver (PLGR) provides precise geopositioning and timing for USMC ground units. It is a small, handheld, Global Positioning System (GPS) receiver that incorporates selective availability/antispoofing (SA/A-S) and antijam capability. Like all GPS devices, it provides precise positioning and timing solutions based on signals received from GPS satellites. Five channels are available, and the unit is capable of Precision Code (P Code) and Y Code (encrypted P Code) reception. Positioning solutions may be displayed in latitude, longitude, military grid reference system, Universal Transverse Mercator, British National Grid, or Irish Transverse Mercator Grid coordinates. Containing 49 map datums, the PLGR can be programmed to support navigation.

Specifications of the unit include:

Length: 9.45 in
Width: 4.23 in
Weight: 2.75 lb

AN/PSS-12 Metallic Mine Detector

The AN/PSS-12 Metallic Mine Detector is employed to locate land mines during minefield breaching, road sweep, and follow-on clearance operations. It is a lightweight, handheld metallic mine detector capable of detecting very small metallic objects, including small firing pins in plastic and wooden mines. The detector can detect mines in fresh or salt water as well as mines and other metallic objects buried up to 20 inches in the ground.

The AN/PSS-12 is considered a state-of-the-art, world-class mine detector that is especially well suited to detecting the often very small amounts of metal used in the construction of modern land mines. As of 2004, the USMC had 547 of the units in its inventory, most of them deployed with combat engineer battalions, engineer support battalions, and Marine wing support squadrons.

General characteristics of the AN/PSS-12 Metallic Mine Detector include:

Manufacturer: Schiebel Instruments, Inc.
Power supply: 4 1.5-volt batteries
Operating time: 70 hr
Weight, in transport case: 13.7 lb
Mine detector alone: 8.5 lb
Materials: telescopic pole consists of an inner plastic tube and outer aluminum tube

Diver Propulsion Device (DPD)

Marine reconnaissance underwater combat divers currently engage in closed-circuit underwater diving, an expanded operational role that requires divers to use additional equipment to complete their missions. The DPD enhances the performance and survivability of the combat diver in amphibious reconnaissance operations by propelling the diver at a speed of 1 knot. Power is provided by rechargeable gel-cel lead oxide batteries connected to two drive motors, the batteries furnishing sufficient power to propel the diver about as long as his oxygen supply lasts. The DPD enables divers to conduct long-range "Over-The-Horizon" (OTH) operations. With the aid of the DPD, the diver can conserve his energy; moreover, the DPD also serves as a platform for real-time intelligence collection, while decreasing the possibility of detection by allowing the diver to stay submerged.

General characteristics of the Diver Propulsion Device (DPD) include:

Manufacturer: Coastal Systems Station
Weight: 165 lb
Speed: 1 knot
Endurance: 200 min

Field Pack, Large, with Internal Frame (FPLIF)

The field pack is a key piece of equipment for any infantry marine. The modern FPLIF is an internal frame pack that offers 6,800 cubic inches of storage space. It incorporates a detachable 2,500-cubic-inch patrol pack and an internal compartment for stowage of the sleeping bag. Water resistant, it is adjustable and is designed to complement the normal center of gravity to promote comfortable and efficient movement for the wearer.

The new FPLIF was designed to remedy the deficiencies of the large traditional "Alice Pack" by increasing storage capacity, enhancing comfort and mobility, and keeping all gear protected from the environment. The versatile pack can hold all additional gear needed in a cold weather environment.

General characteristics of the Field Pack, Large, with Internal Frame (FPLIF) include:

Length: 30 in
Width: 21 in
Weight: 8 lb
Area: 4.375 sq ft
Volume: 3.64 cu ft
Stowage: 3.64 cu ft
Color: woodland camouflage

Improved ECWCS Fiberpile Shirt and Trousers

The Improved ECWCS Fiberpile Shirt and Trousers were developed to provide marines with a flexible, comfortable means of staying warm in temperatures ranging from +40° to −25° Fahrenheit. The shirt is a front-opening jacket with long sleeves, hand-warming packets, two breast pockets, and a zip-up collar. The trousers are bib type, with built-in suspenders featuring quick-release fasteners and a full-length side zipper for easy donning and removal. Both the shirt and trousers are made of 100 percent polyester fleece. Models come in a variety of weights and insulation thicknesses.

The ECWCS was designed to reduce the uncomfortable bulk of traditional USMC extreme cold weather garments. Fleece is a commercially available fabric choice that is light in weight, water resistant, quick drying, and noted for its high level of comfort. The shirt and trousers together weigh only .6 pounds.

Extreme Cold Weather Tent (ECWT)

The Extreme Cold Weather Tent (ECWT) is a self-standing shelter capable of accommodating four marines to sleep, dry wet clothing, and prepare meals in extreme cold-weather environments. The ECWT is a domelike structure that incorporates a waterproof opaque fly sheet. It is especially designed for maximum stability in high winds and durability in generally harsh environmental conditions. The design includes a vestibule entrance area with sufficient space for two men to shed their packs and cold weather clothing before entering the tent body. Assembly can be accomplished by one person.

The Extreme Cold Weather Tent (ECWT) represents a major improvement over the previous tent used in extreme cold weather, which was constructed simply by putting five Norwegian tent sheets together. These tended to freeze when wet, becoming stiff and difficult to handle. To erect this type of tent, it was necessary to dig out the snow inside and tie the external liner to a tree. The self-standing dome-style tent is much more efficient in all respects.

General characteristics of the Extreme Cold Weather Tent (ECWT) include:

Length, erected: 102 in
Length, stored: 28.5 in
Width, erected: 110 in
Width, stored: 14.5 in
Height, erected: 55 in
Height, stored: 13 in
Storage volume: 3.1 cu ft
Weight: 20 lb

Individual Tactical Load-Bearing Vest (ITLBV)

The Individual Tactical Load Bearing Vest (ITLBV) was commissioned by the USMC to improve the fighting load's distribution of weight for the individual marine. Made of an 8-ounce nylon fabric, the vest weighs 1.8 pounds empty and has permanently attached ammunition and grenade pockets designed to carry six 30-round magazines and two grenades. The vest is intended for use with the standard cartridge belt. The shoulder pads have two attachment points for the cover of the field pack.

General characteristics of the Individual Tactical Load Bearing Vest (ITLBV) include:

Length: 16 in
Width: 8 in
Height: 3.5 in
Weight: 1.8 lb
Color: woodland camouflage

Infantry Shelter

The USMC Infantry Shelter provides cover and protection from the elements for two marines and their equipment. It is made of 1.9-ounce ripstop nylon and is a tent with an integrated waterproof floor and a waterproof, opaque, free-standing fly with vestibule. The tent provides protection from wind and rain, weighs less than 8 pounds, and, using telescoping aluminum poles, can be erected and struck rapidly.

The new Infantry Shelter replaces the traditional shelter half, which was not only time-consuming to erect and strike, but afforded inadequate protection from wind and rain and weighed too much.

The general characteristics of the Infantry Shelter include:

Storage, length: 22 in
Storage, diameter: 7 in
Sheltered area: 34 sq ft
Height: 45 in at apex
Weight: 8 lb

Laser Rangefinder AN/GVS-5

The AN/GVS-5 is a handheld, binocular-style laser rangefinder used by marines for observation and target acquisition. It consists of a panel assembly, optical assembly, and laser transmitter module and can use either battery or vehicle power. The rangefinder allows accurate determination of range to targets and includes 7 × 15 sighting optics, a multiple target indicator, and minimum range adjustment. The rangefinder can take one reading per second, up to 100 rangings per battery. The rangefinder provides a means of verifying the location of targets to be engaged by air or ground fire. The instrument is also useful in determining the adjustment of rounds on the target.

General characteristics of the Laser Rangefinder AN/GVS-5 include:

Length: 9 in
Width: 8 in
Height: 4 in
Weight: 5 lb with battery
Emission wavelength: 1.06 microns
Beam divergence: 1 milliradian
Range measurement limits: 650–3,277 ft
Range error: + or –32.8 ft
Power requirements: 24 volts

Marine Assault Climbers Kit

The Marine Assault Climbers Kit was developed to enable marines to safely negotiate obstacles up to a vertical distance of 300 feet. Fielded to infantry regiments, special operations training groups and reconnaissance units, the kit consists of equipment certified by the Union of International Alpinists Association and is intended for use on obstacles common to built-up areas, to complete operations over rivers and gorges, and to complete assaults on oil platforms or bridges. Each kit is sufficient to allow a 200-man company to negotiate a 300-foot vertical obstacle. The advantage of the Marine Assault Climbers Kit is that it is much lighter and more portable than previous mountaineering equipment. Moreover, traditional equipment is limited in function, difficult or impossible to remove, and leaves a trail signature. In contrast, the equipment in this kit is recoverable, reusable, quiet, need leave no trail signature, and represents the state-of-the-art in alpine gear.

MC-5 Static Line/Free-Fall Ram Air Parachute System (SL/FF RAPS)

The USMC has developed a state-of-the-art parachute system for insertion of reconnaissance and special operations forces. The highly versatile MC-5 Static Line/Free-Fall Ram Air Parachute System can be configured for static line or free-fall, depending on mission requirements. It uses identical main and reserve canopies, which reduces the logistics involved with separate canopies and eliminates the need for separate training and maintenance of two different canopies.

Manufactured by the Paraflite Company, the main and reserve parachutes are each 370 square feet, seven-celled, and are manufactured from 1.1 ounce F-111 nylon ripstop fabric. The parachute may be used at altitudes from 3,000 feet to 30,000 feet and achieves a forward speed of 15 to 25 miles per hour and a rate of descent of 14 to 18 feet per second, maximum. At 50 percent brakes, descent is from 8 feet to 14 feet per second. The MC-5 SL/FF RAPS is thus especially well suited to the high-altitude, high-opening (HAHO) parachute operations the USMC typically uses for insertion missions.

Modular Sleeping Bag (MSB)

In the mid-1990s, the USMC acquired an advanced-design modular sleeping bag to replace the heavier, water-absorbing, intermediate cold weather and extreme cold weather bags then in use. Not only are the new bags more comfortable, affording greater protection of wet and cold, they are also 7 pounds lighter than the traditional bags. The modular concept allows greater flexibility in adapting to a range of climate and weather.

The Modular Sleeping Bag system consists of two bags: a lightweight outer patrol bag (rated to 30°F) and an intermediate inner bag (rated to −10°F). The bags can be used independently or together to create the extreme cold weather bag, which is rated to −30°F. The bags are made from lightweight polyester fibers, which provide a very high degree of insulation. The bag is described as "hydrophobic" (water hating)—that is, highly waterproof. It is ultralight at under 7 pounds and is readily carried in its own compression stuff sack. The USMC maintains a large inventory of the MSB: 129,324 units for the active forces, and 42,848 for the MARINE CORPS RESERVE.

General characteristics of the MSB include:

Manufacturer: Tennier Industries, Inc.
Storage volume: 1,991 cu in
Weight: 4.5 lb

Oxygen Transfer Pump System

The USMC reconnaissance underwater combat diver and airborne-qualified marine must be able to undertake missions that include extended closed-circuit underwater diving and high-altitude parachute operations. These difficult and demanding missions require state-of-the-art oxygen breathing devices, which, in turn, must be safely and efficiently maintained in a ready status. The Oxygen Transfer Pump System is designed to maintain the equipment needed to perform closed-circuit diving and high altitude jumps in an environment that is oxygen safe.

The system is composed of a variety of oxygen-transferring times within a Marine Corps Expeditionary Shelter System. This equipment allows personnel to maintain all of their closed-circuit diving and military free-fall equipment on or off deployments. The system is designed for use in a variety of mission scenarios, ranging from expeditionary to shipboard. It is also operable in a range of climates, from extreme cold to extreme heat. As of 2004, the USMC maintained 14 Oxygen Transfer Pump Systems for its active forces and three for the Marine Corps Reserve.

General characteristics of the Oxygen Transfer Pump System include:

Length: 20 ft
Width: 96 in
Height: 96 in
Weight: 4,500 lb
Power Requirements: 120/208 volt AC, 3 phase, 60 hertz, 60 amperes max

Parachutist Individual Equipment Kit (PIEK)

The USMC uses the Parachutist Individual Equipment Kit (PIEK) to provide its parachutists with comprehensive protection from the environment. Manufactured by a variety of vendors—Intimar, Pennsylvania; Cabellas, California; Steve Snyder Enterprises, New Jersey; North American Aeronutronics, North Carolina; REI, Washington; and Television Associates, Inc., New York—the kit consists of a Goretex jumpsuit, a Polartec jumpsuit liner, a cotton ripstop jumpsuit, flyer's gloves, Goretex cold-weather gloves, overboots, an MA2-30 altimeter, helmet, flyer's helmet bag, and flyer's kitbag. The principal purpose of the kit is to combat the extreme cold encountered during high-altitude parachute operations.

Reverse Osmosis Water Purification Unit

USMC forces must be self-sufficient under the most difficult of environmental conditions. The Reverse Osmosis Water Purification Unit is a system designed to treat water from any available source and to render it potable. The unit performs a purification process that removes all nuclear-biological-chemical (NBC) contaminants from water, that produces potable water from brackish, shallow, and deep-well sources, and that also effectively produces freshwater from seawater sources.

Used by all U.S. armed forces, the Reverse Osmosis Water Purification Unit has performed especially well for the USMC. It was extensively employed during Operations Desert Shield/Desert Storm (the PERSIAN GULF WAR) and was shown to increase the expeditionary capability that is at the heart of USMC operational doctrine.

General characteristics of the unit include:

Transportation: the unit is transported in an 8 foot by 8 foot by 10 foot rigid frame
Production rate, seawater source: 600 gal/hr
Production rate, freshwater source: 1,800 gal/hr
Weight: 7,300 lb
Length: 120 in
Width: 96 in
Height: 96 in
Power source: 30-kilowatt generator

Second-Generation Extended Cold Weather Clothing System (ECWCS)

The second-generation Extended Cold Weather Clothing System (ECWCS) has been especially developed for the USMC to provide protection from wind, rain, and snow. The system consists of outer garments, including a parka and trousers. The parka features two hand-warming/cargo pockets, two side-access breast pockets, two upper-sleeve pockets, and a roll-and-stow hood, which fits into the collar. The parka also features water-shedding slide fasteners and zippered armpit vents. The trousers have suspender attachments, belt loops, two side-leg cargo pockets, and knee-high zippers for easy donning and doffing while wearing boots. Both garments are made of a tri-laminate using a waterproof, vapor-permeable membrane laminated between two nylon knits, and both are produced in a woodland camouflage pattern. The USMC inventory is planned to include 174,000 units for active forces and 45,203 for reserves.

General characteristics of the second-generation Extended Cold Weather Clothing System (ECWCS) include:

Weight, parka: 1.3 lb
Weight, trousers: 1 lb
Color: woodland camouflage

Single-Action Release Personal Equipment Lowering System (SARPELS)

Among the specialized equipment developed for USMC parachutists is the Single-Action Release Personal Equipment Lowering System (SARPELS), which is an integrated system for safely lowering a parachutist's combat equipment. Usable in both static line and free-fall parachute operations, the SARPELS allows parachutists to carry a variety of configurations of combat equipment. The system enables the parachutist to land with his equipment in a way that avoids injury: by lowering the equipment below the parachutist. Conventionally, separate types of equipment-lowering systems were required for static line and free-fall operations. The USMC SARPELS accommodates both. Moreover, it provides ready access to weapons and equipment after landing. Its single-action release makes for rapid and safe deployment of equipment, and this versatile system can be front or rear mounted on the parachutist.

The system consists of the SARPELS Cargo Carrier, horizontal and vertical cargo carrier securing straps, the single-action release handle, military free-fall equipment attaching strap, a 15-foot static lowering line, and an 8-foot military free-fall lowering line.

Tandem Offset
Resupply Delivery System (TORDS)

The Tandem Offset Resupply Delivery System (TORDS) is a parachute delivery system that the USMC uses to provide reconnaissance personnel with a parachute delivery system for supply and resupply of combat equipment or personnel. The system has a payload capacity of more than 500 pounds and consists of square main and reserve canopies, each manufactured from 1.1-ounce F-111 ripstop nylon fabric. The TORDS has a six-foot drogue parachute, which is deployed to reduce the terminal velocity of the tandem master and load (passenger/combat equipment) to approximately 120 miles per hour at opening altitude. The drogue, deployed by ripcord, also acts as a pilot chute and in turn deploys the main canopy.

USMC force reconnaissance teams often use highly maneuverable square parachutes for High Altitude High Opening (HAHO) parachute insertion operations. The Tandem Offset Resupply Delivery System is used in these operations to deliver an increased payload of combat-essential equipment or personnel.

Manufactured by Relative Workshop of Florida, TORDS consists of a main canopy with a surface area of 421 square feet arranged in nine cells, and a nine-cell reserve canopy of 360 square feet. The system can be deployed from 8,000 feet to 25,000 feet. Forward speed is 15 to 25 miles per hour, and rate of descent at full flight is 16 to 20 feet per second. At 50 percent brakes, rate of descent is 10 to 16 feet per second.

Woolly-pully

In the USMC, an olive-green rib-knit pullover sweater with reinforced shoulders, elbows, and forearms worn optionally during fall and winter. The name is derived from the manufacturer's trademarked name, Woolly-Pully.

Personnel Administration School

One of the USMC's COMBAT SERVICE SUPPORT SCHOOLS located at Camp Johnson, North Carolina, Personnel Administration School provides basic, intermediate, and advanced resident formal school instruction to USMC personnel administrators, with a special emphasis on combat service support. The Administrative Clerk Course and the Personnel Clerk Course are the entry-level offerings. Career-level courses are the Adjutant Course, Personnel Officer Course, Advanced Personnel Administration Course, Senior Clerk Course, and Reserve Administration Course.

Philippine Insurrection

Shortly after the SPANISH-AMERICAN WAR, the Filipino nationalist leader Emilio Aguinaldo, who had led guerrilla forces as an ally of the United States during the war with Spain, believed his nation had been betrayed because it won independence from Spain only to be annexed by the United States. Aguinaldo led an anti-U.S. insurrection, attacking Manila on February 4, 1899. Later in the year, two USMC battalions were sent to augment army efforts to pacify the rebels, but most were withdrawn in 1900 for service in China during the BOXER REBELLION. Returning later in the year, the marines operated mostly against the Moros, a Muslim people living on Samar and other southern Philippine islands. The Moros were adamant in their refusal to submit to U.S. control, and in October of 1900, a USMC battalion was placed under U.S. Army control to suppress Moro resistance. Within less than a month, most Moro resistance had been crushed, although no formal agreement to submit to U.S. authority was concluded.

platoon   See ORGANIZATION BY UNITS.

advancement while those who are least well suited are repeatedly passed over and eventually retire at a relatively low rank.

Entry-level USMC officers are commissioned as second lieutenants. A second lieutenant becomes eligible for promotion to first lieutenant after 24 months of service in grade. Promotion from first lieutenant to captain, all the way up through the ranks to major general, is by selection (merit) rather than seniority. However, years in service generally figure as a prerequisite for selection for promotion. Promotion to captain generally requires four years in service; to major, 10 years (9–11); to lieutenant colonel, 16 years (15–17); and to colonel 22 years (21–23). Failure to be promoted within the usual time span does not preclude promotion, as long as the candidate remains on active duty.

A regularly constituted selection board receives the names and files of officers eligible for consideration for promotion. The board begins with the most senior officer of the grade under consideration who has not previously failed to be selected. From here, the board works its way down through seniority in considering each candidate for promotion. Officers who are in the promotion zone (for example, captains with nine to 11 years in service and who are therefore eligible for promotion to major) but who fail to be selected are said to have been passed over. USMC regulations prescribe certain limits for service within each grade, beyond which retirement is mandatory.

The constitution of the selection board is very important. Generally, USMC boards consist of nine active or MARINE CORPS RESERVE officers. The board is convened by the SECRETARY OF THE NAVY annually. The members of the board are committed to recommend the best-fitted officers for promotion. They give equal weight to line duty as well as to administrative duty. They are not to consider as prejudicial the fact that a candidate for promotion may have been passed over previously, provided the candidate is within the allowable time-in-grade. They must make their promotions within the numerical limits set by the secretary of the navy.

A Marine Corps drill instructor screams instructions to a poolee.   *(U.S. Marine Corps)*

poolees

Unofficial but universally used name for USMC enlistees awaiting recruit training (boot camp). The time "in the pool" is typically three to 12 months.

private   See RANKS AND GRADES.

private first class   See RANKS AND GRADES.

promotion system

The modern USMC promotion system was instituted in 1915 and has been modified repeatedly since. The objective of the promotion system is to ensure that officers best suited are selected for

Selection for promotion does not automatically and immediately secure promotion. Selected officers are placed on a promotion list in order of seniority. As vacancies occur, the selected officers are promoted in order of seniority.

pugil stick

The pugil stick is a six-foot-long pole with padded ends used by the USMC in BASIC TRAINING to simulate bayonet combat.

Puller, Lewis B. "Chesty" (1898–1972)

Marine Corps general

Born in West Point, Virginia, Puller enlisted in the USMC during WORLD WAR I, in August 1918. He earned a reserve commission as second lieutenant in 1919, but was almost immediately inactivated when the USMC was reduced in size during the

Lieutenant General Lewis B. Puller (USMC)   *(U.S. Marine Corps)*

rush to demobilize following the Armistice. The very image of a GUNG-HO marine, Puller, undaunted, reenlisted as a noncommissioned officer. He served in HAITI with the ambiguous rank of USMC sergeant but as *captain* of the Haitian Gendarmerie. Puller served for five years in the turbulent island nation.

In 1924, Puller returned to the United States and received an officer's commission. After service at Norfolk and Marine Corps Base Quantico, Puller took flight training at Pensacola Naval Air Station in 1926. He shipped out to NICARAGUA in 1928 as an instructor assigned to train the U.S.-supported Nicaraguan Guardia Nacional in its fight against rebels led by Augusto Sandino. Puller fought in frequent engagements against the Sandinistas and was decorated with the Navy Cross.

After returning to the States in 1931, Puller attended a company officers' course, then returned to Nicaragua to continue leading the National Guard against the Sandinistas. During the course of this assignment, he won a second Navy Cross. From Nicaragua, Puller was assigned to the USMC legation detachment in Peking (Beijing) in 1933. After sea duty, Puller was made instructor at the basic school in Philadelphia (1936). Returning to sea duty in 1939, he was attached to the 4th Marines in 1940, and soon promoted to commanding officer of the unit.

At the outbreak of WORLD WAR II, Puller was given command of 1st Battalion, 7th Marines, which he led to Samoa and then in the assault on GUADALCANAL. Seriously wounded in this engagement, he refused evacuation until the defense of Henderson Field was complete. For this, he was given a third Navy Cross.

While recovering from his wounds, Puller toured U.S. posts, then rejoined the 7th Marines as executive officer of the division. He participated in the landings at Cape Gloucester and led a 1,000-man patrol on New Britain Island, earning his fourth Navy Cross. He led the marines in the invasion of PELELIU, his regiment sustaining 50 percent casualties.

Following World War II, Puller commanded the training regiment at Marine Corps Base Camp Lejeune, then was assigned as director of the 8th Reserve District. In 1950, he once again assumed command of the 1st Marines and led this regiment in the INCHON landing during the KOREAN WAR. His unit crossed the 38th parallel and advanced to the Yalu River, the border with Manchuria. When a massive Chinese counterattack drove Allied forces back, Puller was in charge of the covering operations that protected the vulnerable USMC flanks. Following this operation, Puller received a fifth Navy Cross, and in January 1951 was promoted to brigadier general and assigned as assistant division commander.

Back in the United States, Puller was given command of the 3rd Brigade and became assistant commander after the unit was upgraded to a division. Assigned to direct marine training at Coronado, California, Puller was promoted to major general in 1953 and was given command of the 2nd Division, headquartered at Camp Lejeune. He retired on November 1, 1955, with the rank of lieutenant general. "Chesty" Puller is celebrated as one of the great exemplary marines. His rise from enlisted man to general officer is regarded as the stuff of real-life legend.

Pusan, Defense of

As the biggest port in South Korea, Pusan was critically important to the defense of that nation. When the North Koreans invaded South Korea on June 25, 1950, starting the KOREAN WAR, the United Nations force, including elements of the U.S. Army, fell back on Pusan, forming a defensive perimeter with a radius of about 100 miles and centered on Pusan. The USMC's 1st Provisional Brigade, about 6,500 men, arrived at Pusan on August 2, 1950, and was put in at the extreme left of the Pusan perimeter, assigned to take the city of Sachon. This was accomplished on August 13. The brigade next moved 90 miles north to defend the Naktong Bridge, decisively repulsing the 4th North Korean Division and sending it into retreat across the Naktong River.

On September 3, the brigade supported the USA 2nd Division to blunt a major North Korean attack.

After the September action, the marines were withdrawn and held in reserve pending the arrival of the remainder of the 1st USMC Division. The entire division would play a key role in the daring INCHON landing.

Q

quad body
A marine qualified as a SCUBA diver and a paratrooper, and who has had Ranger training as well as exchange training with the British Royal Marines.

See also U.S. MARINE CORPS RECONNAISSANCE BATTALIONS.

R

R4D Skytrain   See AIRCRAFT, FIXED-WING.

ranks and grades

"Rank" refers to a person's official position within the military hierarchy. "Grade" is an alphanumeric symbol associated with rank, which is keyed to pay level (and is therefore often called "pay grade"). Officer grades range from O-1 to O-10 and enlisted grades from E-1 to E-9. Personnel of grades O-1 through O-3 are often termed "company grade officers."

USMC ranks and grades fall into two groups: commissioned officers and enlisted marines.

Commissioned Officers (in descending order)

General (O-10)

The highest-ranking officer in the USMC, the general wears a four-star insignia. There is no USMC equivalent to the army and air force's five-star generals, (general of the army and general of the air force). The equivalent USA and USAF rank is general, and the equivalent USN rank is admiral.

Lieutenant General (O-9)

The lieutenant general is, in the USMC, USA, and USAF, a general officer of grade O-9, outranking a major general and below a general. The insignia is three silver stars, and the U.S. Navy equivalent is vice admiral.

Major General (O-8)

In the USMC, USA, and USAF, the major general ranks below a lieutenant general and above a brigadier general. Two silver stars denote the rank of this officer, who typically commands a division. Equivalent navy rank is rear admiral.

Brigadier General (O-7)

The lowest-ranking general officer in the USMC, the brigadier ranks above a colonel and below a major general. Insignia is a single star in silver. The equivalent USA and USAF rank is brigadier general, and the equivalent USN rank is rear admiral, lower.

Colonel (O-6)

A field-grade officer in the USMC, USA, and USAF, colonel ranks above lieutenant colonel and below brigadier general. The equivalent USN rank is captain. Insignia is a silver eagle.

Lieutenant Colonel (O-5)

In the USMC, USA, and USAF, the lieutenant colonel ranks above a major and below a colonel. The insignia is a silver oak leaf, and the equivalent navy rank is commander.

Major (O-4)

This USMC, USA, or USAF officer ranks below a lieutenant colonel and above a captain. The insignia is a gold oak leaf, and the USN equivalent rank is lieutenant commander.

Captain (O-3)

In the USMC, as in the army and air force, a captain is a company-grade officer, ranking below a major and above a first lieutenant. This rank is equivalent to a navy lieutenant. The insignia of rank is two vertical silver bars.

First Lieutenant (O-2)

In the USMC, USA, and USAF, the first lieutenant is the second-lowest ranking commissioned officer, above a second lieutenant and below a captain. The insignia is a vertical single silver bar. Equivalent USN rank is lieutenant (j.g.).

Second Lieutenant (O-1)

The lowest-ranking commissioned officer in the USMC, USA, and USAF, the second lieutenant wears a single vertical gold bar and typically commands a platoon. Equivalent USN rank is ensign.

Enlisted Marines (in descending order)

Sergeant Major of the Marine Corps (E-9)

The SMMC is a noncommissioned officer of grade E-9, but outranks all other USMC noncommissioned officers. The appointment is unique and made directly by the COMMANDANT OF THE MARINE CORPS. The SMMC is the senior enlisted assistant and adviser to the commandant and is the USMC equivalent of the U.S. Army's sergeant major of the army, the U.S. Navy's master chief petty officer of the navy, and the U.S. Air Force's chief master sergeant of the air force.

Sergeant Major (E-9)

A senior noncommissioned officer, ranking below only the sergeant major of the Marine Corps, the sergeant major wears three chevrons above four rockers enclosing a star. Equivalent USA ranks are command sergeant major and staff sergeant major. USAF equivalent is chief master sergeant. Equivalent USN rank is master chief petty officer. The USMC sergeant major is the chief administrative assistant of a headquarters, with duties that are often of a support or technical nature.

First Sergeant (E-8)

In the USMC, this noncommissioned officer ranks above gunnery sergeant and below sergeant major.

A master sergeant is also an E-8, but, in the USMC, is junior to the first sergeant.

The first sergeant is the senior sergeant in a company and handles most administrative and personnel matters. Insignia is three chevrons over three rockers, enclosing a diamond device. The first sergeant is familiarly called a first shirt (or, if female, first skirt), first hog, first sleeve, first pig, top, topper, or top sergeant. Equivalent army rank is master sergeant; air force, senior master sergeant or first sergeant; navy, senior chief petty officer.

Master Sergeant (E-8)

A grade E-8 noncommissioned officer ranking above gunnery sergeant and below sergeant major and first sergeant, the master sergeant wears three chevrons above three rockers enclosing crossed rifles. The army equivalent rank is first sergeant. There are no exact air force or navy equivalents, although this rank is comparable to the air force master sergeant and navy senior chief petty officer.

Gunnery Sergeant (E-7)

The "gunny" typically functions as the senior NCO of a company or, in some cases, even a larger unit. Insignia is three chevrons over two "rockers" enclosing a crossed-rifles device. Gunnery sergeant is below first sergeant or master sergeant and above staff sergeant. The equivalent USAF rank is a first sergeant or master sergeant; USA rank, sergeant first class; USN, chief petty officer.

Staff Sergeant (E-6)

A USMC staff sergeant is equivalent to an army staff sergeant and an air force technical sergeant. The equivalent navy rank is petty officer first class.

Sergeant (E-5)

The USMC sergeant wears three chevrons above a crossed-rifle device and is equivalent in rank to the USA sergeant and the USAF staff sergeant. Equivalent USN rank is petty officer second class. In the USMC, sergeants are authorized to wear swords during ceremonies. In the other services, swords are reserved for commissioned officers exclusively.

Corporal (E-4)

In the USMC, the corporal is a noncommissioned officer ranking below a sergeant and above a lance corporal. Insignia is two chevrons, and the corporal usually functions as assistant squad leader. Equivalent USN rank is petty officer third class; USAF, airman first class or senior airman.

Lance Corporal (E-3)

An enlisted marine, the lance corporal ranks below a corporal and above a private first class. Insignia is a single chevron above a crossed-rifles device. This rank is equivalent to a private first class in the army, airman first class in the air force, and seaman in the navy. The lance corporal commands a fire team.

Private First Class (E-2)

Also called marine private first class, this marine ranks below lance corporal and above private. The rank is equivalent to a USA private and a USAF airman. The equivalent USN rank is seaman apprentice.

Private (E-1)

Private is the entry-level USMC rank and is equivalent to a USA private and a USAF airman basic. Equivalent USN rank is seaman recruit.

recruit

A newly enlisted marine, pay grade E-1, rank private.

recruiter

USMC recruiters are noncommissioned officers, from sergeant to gunnery sergeant (E-5 to E-7), responsible for recruiting personnel. The position is highly demanding, requiring great motivation and self-discipline. Moreover, recruiters generally live off base, among civilians. They are expected to meet a quota of acceptable recruits—generally three to four per month—and to manage POOLEES, enlistees who receive periodic training while awaiting boot camp. The recruiter's performance is evaluated not only on how well he or she meets a prescribed quota, but also on the retention rate among the recruits who actually enlist. The recruiter is therefore motivated to screen and evaluate candidates carefully.

regiment   See ORGANIZATION BY UNITS.

Reising Gun   See WEAPONS, INDIVIDUAL AND CREW-SERVED.

Reverse Osmosis Water Purification Unit

See PERSONAL AND MISCELLANEOUS EQUIPMENT.

revolver, .38-caliber   See WEAPONS, INDIVIDUAL AND CREW-SERVED.

rifle grenade   See WEAPONS, INDIVIDUAL AND CREW-SERVED.

Riverine Assault Craft (RAC)   See LANDING CRAFT.

Roi-Namur, Battle of

Twin islands in the Kwajalein atoll in the Marshall Islands, these were heavily fortified by the Japanese during WORLD WAR II. There was a garrison of 3,500 and, on Roi, an airfield with at least 150 planes.

In January 1944, Operation Flintlock targeted Roi-Namur. The campaign began on January 28 with bombing raids followed by naval bombardment. Next, three USMC battalions (25th Marines) occupied the small islands around Roi-Namur, set up howitzer positions on them, and shelled the main objective. Finally, on February 1, the 23rd and 24th Marines landed on Roi and Namur. Roi was lightly defended and fell within two hours of the landing. Namur, however, offered much more resistance, but the 24th Marines secured this island, too, by February 2. The Japanese garrison on both islands had been killed, virtually to a man.

Possession of Roi-Namur gave the U.S. forces a superb harbor and two airstrips, all positioned well forward and affording excellent staging areas for further penetration of Japan's defensive ring.

Russell, John H. (1872–1947) *Marine Corps commandant*

Sixteenth COMMANDANT OF THE MARINE CORPS, Russell was born on Mare Island, California, and graduated from the U.S. Naval Academy in 1892. After two years at sea as a midshipman, Russell was commissioned a second lieutenant in the USMC in 1894 and saw action during the SPANISH-AMERICAN WAR aboard the *Massachusetts* on blockade duty off Santiago, Cuba.

After the war, Russell was variously posted in the United States, Hawaii, and GUAM, then served on the faculty of the Naval War College. He led a battalion in the invasion of VERACRUZ in 1914 and, now as a lieutenant colonel, commanded 3rd Regiment in SANTO DOMINGO. Promoted to colonel, Russell commanded the 1st Marine Brigade in HAITI during 1919. Promoted to brigadier general in 1920, Russell served as U.S. high commissioner for Haiti, then returned to the States in 1930 as assistant commandant, becoming commandant in 1935 as a major general. Russell retired in 1937, having made two major operational contributions to the USMC: the transformation of the Expeditionary Force into the FLEET MARINE FORCE, and the creation of selection boards to govern the promotion of officers.

S

Saboted Light Armor Penetrator (SLAP) ammunition   See ANTIARMOR WEAPONS.

Saint-Mihiel

This French town in the department of the Meuse was the geographical focus of a German salient during WORLD WAR I, the reduction of which figured as a key Allied objective in the final months of the war. The American Expeditionary Force was given major responsibility for attacking the Saint-Mihiel salient, and the 4th, 5th, and 6th Marine Brigades commenced the attack early in September 1918. The operation was concluded successfully on September 15. The role of the USMC was less central at Saint-Mihiel than at BELLEAU WOOD, but all mission objectives were accomplished. USMC casualties were 703 killed and wounded.

Saipan

In the Pacific theater of WORLD WAR II, Saipan, a northerly island in the Marianas group, was a major Japanese base, manned by about 29,000 Japanese naval and air personnel. Twelve hundred miles from the Japanese home islands, Saipan was a key defensive point; moreover, possession of the island would give the Americans a base for B-29 bombing operations against Japan.

Operation Forager, as the invasion of the Marianas was called, began on June 15, 1944, with a USMC landing on Saipan, backed by the navy's Fifth Fleet in the largest assemblage of warships in the Pacific theater. Resistance was extremely heavy, and the 2nd and 4th Divisions suffered severe casualties, as did army reinforcing units. The Japanese defenders were dug into very well-prepared defenses, including natural caves.

The operation proceeded slowly, painfully, but successfully. A massive, last-ditch banzai charge on the night of July 7 inflicted severe casualties on Marine Corps and army units, but failed to dislodge them. Two days later, the island was declared secure, although mop-up operations during August killed almost 2,000 more Japanese soldiers. USMC casualties on Saipan totaled 3,119 killed and 10,992 wounded. As for the Japanese, the overwhelming number of Saipan's 29,000 defenders were killed; very few surrendered. Persuaded by Japanese propaganda that the American invaders would torture and rape them, large numbers of the island's civilian population committed suicide by leaping off the island's rocky cliffs.

Samar, USMC

One of the southern Philippines, Samar was a stronghold of the Moros, Philippine Muslims who fiercely resisted the U.S. occupation of the Philippine Islands during the PHILIPPINE INSURRECTION. In 1901, the USMC's 1st Regiment was deployed to Cavite to assist the U.S. Army in pacifying the

Moros. When, on September 16, Moros ambushed the army's 9th Infantry, the marines, 314 strong, retaliated with the terror tactics of total warfare, burning villages and summarily executing Moro prisoners. On November 15, the marines made a concerted strike against the village of Basey on Samar, wiping out the last of the organized resisters.

Following this action, on December 28, 1901, Major Littleton Waller (USMC) led 55 marines, native interpreters, and 30 Moro bearers on a mission to survey a telegraph route. The survey party was lost, and 10 marines died of disease and exposure. Waller assumed that his native interpreters and bearers had deliberately deceived him. He convened an ad hoc tribunal—a drumhead court—convicted 11 natives, and had them shot. When Waller returned to the naval base at Cavite, he was placed under arrest and tried for murder, but ultimately acquitted. The USMC and USA actions on Samar are a stain on the record of the U.S. administration of the islands.

Santo Domingo

When chronic political instability in this Caribbean nation (the eastern portion of the island of Hispaniola) rendered it vulnerable to European intervention at the start of the 20th century, the United States, invoking the Monroe Doctrine, assumed responsibility for Santo Domingo's finances. This did little to stabilize internal politics on a permanent basis, however, and on May 15, 1916, President Woodrow Wilson ordered two USMC companies (350 men) to the island. They were accompanied by 225 sailors. The marines and sailors occupied the capital city; two weeks later, additional marines were landed, bringing total USMC strength on Santo Domingo to 1,700, a regiment.

Under Colonel JOSEPH PENDLETON, the marines began a systematic campaign against rebel forces on all parts of the island, and, in July 1916, a U.S. military government was established. The USMC remained a presence on Santo Domingo for the next eight years, garrisoning towns and training the Guardia Nacional Dominicana, an indigenous police force.

In 1924, the USMC withdrew pursuant to a 1922 agreement with the nation, now renamed the Dominican Republic.

Saratoga Chemical Protective Overgarment

See NUCLEAR-BIOLOGICAL-CHEMICAL EQUIPMENT.

SB-3865 Automatic Telephone Switchboard　See COMMUNICATIONS EQUIPMENT.

School of Infantry

Located at Marine Corps Base Camp Lejeune, SOI provides infantry military occupational specialty (MOS) qualification to entry-level infantry marines, trains all noninfantry marines in the infantry skills essential to operate in a combat environment, and infantry NCOs and SNCOs with advanced infantry skills. Additionally, SOI supports "Marine Leader Training" courses. SOI is the next step after BASIC TRAINING.

Infantry marines are assigned to the Infantry Training Battalion, whose mission is to train and qualify trainees for MOS 0311 Rifleman, 0331 Machinegunner, 0341 Mortarman, 0351 Assaultman, or 0352 Anti-tank Guided Missileman. ITB consists of a 52-day training schedule. After completing ITB, marines are given their first duty assignment.

Noninfantry marines are assigned to Marine Combat Training Battalion, which provides training in the infantry skills essential to operate in a combat environment. After completing 22 days of MCTB, marines go on to specialized training at the appropriate MOS school.

Second-Generation Extended Cold Weather Clothing System (ECWCS)　See PERSONAL AND MISCELLANEOUS EQUIPMENT.

second lieutenant　See RANKS AND GRADES.

Second Seminole War

The Second Seminole War spanned 1835 to 1842 and was triggered by efforts of the government during the administration of Andrew Jackson to "remove" the Seminole and the closely related Creek (as well as other Indians east of the Mississippi) to "Indian Territory" (the region of modern Oklahoma and parts of neighboring states) pursuant to the Indian Removal Act of 1830. Two USMC battalions arrived in Georgia in June 1836 and quickly engaged the Creek, defeating them by early September. In Florida, ARCHIBALD HENDERSON led one of two brigades assigned to the area—although the men he commanded were a mixed unit of marines, army regulars, and volunteers. Henderson won a significant battle at Hatchee-Lustee in January 1837, which prompted a treaty in March.

Believing the war had ended, Henderson and most of the marines returned to Washington, leaving behind just two companies of marines. Despite the treaty, they were continually involved in combat with Seminole under the highly skilled war leader Osceola. Although that chief was captured in mid-1837, guerrilla action continued until the government withdrew the remaining marines and other troops in 1842. The war ended indecisively. Although some 4,000 Seminole and Creek had been "removed" to Indian Territory, many remained in the Everglades. It had become too costly, in men and money, to root them out.

secretary of the navy

Under Title 10 of the United States Code, SECNAV is responsible for the conduct of all the affairs of the Department of the Navy, including those of the department's two uniformed services, the U.S. Navy and the U.S. Marine Corps. Specific authority and responsibilities extend to the areas of recruiting, organizing, supplying, equipping, training, mobilizing, and demobilizing. SECNAV oversees the construction, outfitting, and repair of ships, equipment, and facilities and bears ultimate responsibility for the formulation and implementation of policies and programs consistent with the national security policies and objectives established by the president and the secretary of defense.

Semper Fidelis

Latin for "Always Faithful," Semper Fidelis has been the motto of the USMC since 1871, when it replaced "First to Fight." Marines, including retired veterans, may greet each other with a shortened version, "Semper Fi." "Semper Fidelis" is also the name of the march JOHN PHILIP SOUSA wrote for the USMC in 1888.

sergeant   See RANKS AND GRADES.

sergeant first class   See RANKS AND GRADES.

sergeant major   See RANKS AND GRADES.

sergeant major of the Marine Corps   See RANKS AND GRADES.

Sergeant Rock

The name of a comic book character, adopted by the USMC as a term for the ideal GUNG-HO marine, fearless and aggressive.

Shepherd, Lemuel C. (1896–1990) *Marine Corps commandant*

The 20th COMMANDANT OF THE MARINE CORPS, Shepherd was born in Norfolk, Virginia, attended Virginia Military Institute, and was commissioned a second lieutenant in the USMC in April 1917, shipping out for France during WORLD WAR I in June of that year. With the 5th Marines, he saw action at CHÂTEAU-THIERRY and at BELLEAU WOOD, where he was wounded twice. After recuperating, he participated in the SAINT-MIHIEL campaign and in the Argonne, where he was wounded for a third time. Shepherd was decorated with the Navy Cross, the Distinguished Service Cross, and the French Croix de Guerre.

Shepherd remained in Europe after the war as part of the army of occupation, then participated in mapping the areas of France in which the USMC fought. After this, he was appointed aide-de-camp to the commandant, served sea duty, then was assigned command of the Sea School, Norfolk. Shepherd served in China during 1927–29, then was posted to HAITI until 1934. In 1936, after graduating from the Naval War College, Shepherd, a lieutenant colonel, was assigned command of a FLEET MARINE FORCE, Atlantic battalion. After briefly serving as assistant commandant at Marine Corps Base Quantico, Shepherd was assigned in March 1942 to command of the 9th Marines. He led the unit to the Pacific under the 3rd Division. As brigadier general, he was assistant divisional commander during the Cape Gloucester campaign and was assigned command of the 1st Marine Provisional Brigade in May 1942. Shepherd led the brigade in operations on GUAM.

Early in 1945, Shepherd took command of the 6th Division and landed them in the assault against OKINAWA on April 1. By the end of the war, the 6th Division was occupying China at Tsingtao.

After WORLD WAR II, in December 1946, Shepherd was appointed assistant commandant. In 1950, now a lieutenant general, Shepherd participated in the INCHON landings during the KOREAN WAR. He became commandant on January 1, 1952, and introduced important organizational changes. He was also the first USMC commandant to enjoy coequal status with the Joint Chiefs whenever USMC-related matters were under consideration. Although he retired on January 1, 1956, Shepherd returned to duty for a time as chairman of the Inter-American Defense Board.

Shoulder-Launched Multipurpose Assault Weapon (SMAW)   See WEAPONS, INDIVIDUAL AND CREW-SERVED.

Shoup, David M. (1904–1983)   *Marine Corps commandant*

The 22nd COMMANDANT OF THE MARINE CORPS, Shoup was born in Battle Ground, Indiana, and graduated from Indiana's De Pauw University in 1926, having enrolled in the ROTC. After brief service as an army second lieutenant, Shoup was commissioned a USMC second lieutenant in July 1926 and saw service the following year at Tientsin, China. After completing basic school, he was posted variously in the United States, then served sea duty during 1929–31. During the 1930s, he served in various stateside posts, was an officer in the Civilian Conservation Corps, then shipped out to China, where he was posted at Shanghai and in Peking (Beijing). During the late 1930s, Shoup served as an instructor at Marine Corps Base Quantico.

In June 1940, Shoup was attached to the 6th Marines, with which he shipped out to Iceland in May 1941 and served as operations officer for the brigade. Early in WORLD WAR II, Shoup became operations officer for the 2nd Division, which he accompanied to New Zealand in October 1942. He was an observer with the 1st Division on GUADALCANAL and with the army's 43rd Division on NEW GEORGIA, suffering a wound during this campaign.

At TARAWA, Shoup, now a colonel, commanded the 2nd Marines. He was wounded at Tarawa and awarded the Medal of Honor. In December 1943, he was made chief of staff, 2nd Division, and took part in the invasions of SAIPAN and TINIAN before returning to the United States in October 1944. Shoup served at HEADQUARTERS MARINE CORPS in Washington, D.C., until 1947, when he was appointed commanding officer, Service Command, FLEET MARINE FORCE, Pacific. Two years after this, he was appointed chief of staff, 1st Division, then, in 1950, was assigned command of Basic School, Quantico.

Promoted to brigadier general, Shoup served as the USMC's first fiscal director. Promoted to major general, he commanded 1st Division in June 1957 and 3rd Division (on OKINAWA) in March 1958. Promoted to lieutenant general, he was assigned to headquarters in Washington and, on January 1, 1961, was appointed commandant by President Dwight D. Eisenhower in an action that jumped him over five seniors.

During Shoup's tour as commandant, the USMC took a leading position in the developing VIETNAM WAR; Shoup also built up the USMC presence at GUANTÁNAMO BAY to full regimental strength and oversaw deployment of the 5th Marine Expeditionary Brigade to the Caribbean in support of the quarantine imposed on Cuba during the Cuban missile crisis of October 1962. Shoup retired on December 31, 1964.

Single Action Release Personal Equipment Lowering System (SARPELS)   See PERSONAL AND MISCELLANEOUS EQUIPMENT.

Single Channel Ground and Airborne Radio System (SINCGARS)   See COMMUNICATIONS EQUIPMENT.

skinhead
USMC term for a recruit immediately after receiving the "high-and-tight" buzz-cut hairdo.
See also JARHEAD.

Smith, Oliver P. (1893–1977) *Marine Corps general*
A naive of Menard, Texas, Smith graduated from the University of California at Berkeley in 1916 and joined the USMC with a commission as second lieutenant in May 1917, the month after the United States entered WORLD WAR I. He served in Guam for the first two years of his USMC career, then, after sea duty and a posting in Washington, D.C., was dispatched to HAITI, where he served with the U.S.-controlled Gendarmerie on that troubled island.

Back in the United States, Smith attended the U.S. Army field officer's course at Fort Benning, Georgia, in 1931 and became an instructor and administrator at Marine Corps Base Quantico. Assigned to embassy duty in Paris in 1934, Smith attended the French Ecole de Guerre, then returned to the United States in 1936 as a Quantico instructor.

In 1939, Smith was transferred to the FLEET MARINE FORCE in San Diego and in 1940 was named to command a battalion of the 6th Marines. He served with this unit in Iceland in May 1941 during America's period of "armed neutrality" prior to its entry into WORLD WAR II.

Smith was working in the Division of Plans by May 1942, and in April 1943 took command of the 5th Marines, which he led in the NEW BRITAIN campaign. As assistant divisional commander of the 1st Division, Smith took part in the PELELIU campaign during September and October 1944. Next, Smith was appointed USMC deputy chief of staff of the Tenth Army and figured importantly in the OKINAWA campaign.

After the war, Smith commanded Quantico until he was named assistant COMMANDANT OF THE MARINE CORPS in April 1948. With the outbreak of the KOREAN WAR, Smith assumed command of the 1st Division in June 1950 and played a key role in the spectacular INCHON landing and the drive north. It was Smith who led the marines in their harrowing retreat from the CHOSIN RESERVOIR in November 1950 after the massive Communist Chinese incursion into Korea.

Smith was named commandant of Marine Corps Base Camp Pendleton in May 1951, then became commander of Fleet Marine Force, Atlantic in July 1953. He retired with the rank of general in September 1955.

sniper
A USMC specialist rifleman skilled at killing the enemy, from concealment and at great distance. The USMC trains not only marine snipers but also snipers in other agencies, including the FBI and CIA, and the Navy SEALs. Training takes place at Marine Corps Base Quantico, Virginia. Minimum sniper qualifications require an 80 percent on-target rate at 1,000 yards (stationary target) and 800 yards (moving target). Snipers must also demon-

Teamwork is an important part of being a scout sniper. While a sniper is firing, his partner, or spotter, tells him where his shots impact the target.   *(U.S. Marine Corps)*

strate mastery of camouflage and concealment tactics and techniques.

sniper team

In the USMC and USA, a two-person firing team, one who fires (SNIPER) and the other who spots targets (spotter), using binoculars or a 20x sniper scope. USMC sniper teams are typically equipped with the M-40A1 rifle and a 10x Unertl scope.

Soldiers of the Sea

Self-adopted nickname for the USMC.

Solomon Islands Campaign

The Solomons, located northeast of Australia, were occupied by the Japanese early in WORLD WAR II and were intended by them to serve both as a jump-

ing-off point for an invasion of Australia and as a base from which they could interdict U.S. and Allied supply lines to the South Pacific. Recognizing the danger posed by the Japanese presence in the Solomons, U.S. planners authorized the first American offensive of the Pacific war, the invasion of GUADAL-CANAL by the USMC's 1st Division. The operation stepped off in August 1942 and, in conjunction with the Battle of MIDWAY, represented a major turning point of the war. The Japanese were not only forced to evacuate Guadalcanal, they were also compelled to assume the defensive. From this point forward, the initiative was transferred to the U.S. forces.

The next major USMC-USA advance came at NEW GEORGIA in mid-1943, followed by a landing at BOUGAINVILLE in November. Bougainville became a major base and staging area from which army and Marine Corps units attacked and destroyed the principal Japanese base at Rabaul in the NEW BRITAIN campaign.

Somalia

This nation in northeast Africa on the Red Sea and Indian Ocean had been for years without real government, subject to civil warfare among various warlords. As part of a United Nations relief effort, the U.S. government sent military personnel primarily to provide protection to relief workers and to ensure that UN relief provisions did not fall into the hands of the warlords. The USN, USAF, and USA were given primary responsibility for the mission, but the first ground troops were mostly marines of the I Marine Expeditionary Force. Soon, some 9,000 marines were deployed, most of them in the capital city of Mogadishu.

From the beginning, the marines were put in an impossible situation, constrained by UN rules of engagement from disarming the warring clans. When disarming operations finally began, the warlords had gained a powerful hold on the populace, which turned against the marines and other UN forces. Judging the situation hopeless, President Bill Clinton ordered the withdrawal of most U.S. forces in May 1993. The last personnel were withdrawn in March 1995.

The popular view of the Somalia operation was that it failed and was, in fact, a military humiliation for the United States. While it is true that the U.S. military was withdrawn without significant resolution of the situation in Somalia, USMC and other

USMC amphibious vehicles land in Somalia.
(U.S. Marine Corps)

U.S. operations in the country did succeed in distributing relief supplies. To a significant degree, albeit for a limited period, the mission was a humanitarian success.

Sousa, John Philip (1854–1932) *composer*

The "March King," Sousa composed the most famous of all American marches, including "Washington Post March," "Stars and Stripes Forever," and "Semper Fidelis." Although he earned his fame and fortune as a civilian bandleader and composer, his musical career began in the United States Marine Corps.

Born in Washington, D.C., Sousa was the son of Antonio Sousa, a carpenter who worked on the commandant's quarters at the MARINE BARRACKS and also played in the U.S. MARINE BAND. Wishing to instill discipline in his willful son, the elder Sousa persuaded the commandant to allow the 13-year-old boy to enroll as a band apprentice. Sousa served in the USMC from 1867 until 1875, playing in the band during much of that period. After his discharge, he became a civilian bandleader, then, in 1880, was appointed leader of the U.S. Marine Band.

Sousa was a dynamic leader who transformed the band into a world-class musical organization. In 1891, he secured permission from President Benjamin Harrison to take the band on a national tour, which has since become an annual tradition.

The 1891 tour was Sousa's first and last. He left the USMC in 1892 to organize his own peerless band and to embark on his extraordinary career as a composer of marches as well as operettas and songs. Sousa also found time to write several popular novels.

Intensely patriotic, Sousa attempted to return to the USMC at the outbreak of the SPANISH-AMERICAN WAR in 1898, but the Corps had no bandmaster positions available. Sousa joined the army, but a bout of illness kept him from serving. During WORLD WAR I, however, he did join the USN and was commissioned a lieutenant commander, assigned as musical director of the Great Lakes Training Center north of Chicago. His concerts

John Philip Sousa   *(U.S. Marine Corps)*

with the Great Lakes band promoted the purchase of Liberty Bonds.

Discharged from the navy in 1919, Sousa resumed his civilian musical career. He returned to lead the U.S. Marine Band in 1932 at a Washington, D.C., celebration. He died a few days later, at Reading, Pennsylvania, the day before a scheduled band concert. Sousa was honored by the USMC, which allowed his body to lie in state at the Marine Barracks before interment.

Spanish-American War

When, in April 1898, the United States embarked upon war with Spain, ostensibly over the issue of Cuban independence, the nation was poorly prepared to fight a land war. Invasion plans were hastily prepared, and by the end of April the 2nd Marine Battalion was en route to Florida to reinforce the USMC detachments serving with the U.S. Navy fleet blockading the harbor at Santiago,

Cuba. Admiral William Sampson used the marines to capture Guantánamo BAY on June 10, 1898, which Sampson wanted to secure as a coaling station for his fleet. Although the landing was almost unopposed, the marines had to contend with sporadic sniper fire.

On June 14, two USMC companies were assigned to capture Cuzco Well, a major water source for the Guantánamo area. The marines were subject to friendly fire from USN ships, but nevertheless succeeded in defeating some 500 Spanish defenders of Cuzco Well.

All USMC forces were relieved in Cuba by the arrival of U.S. Army troops under General William Shafter later in the month. They saw no further action on Cuba; however, they would maintain a presence in the Philippines during the rest of the war and the PHILIPPINE INSURRECTION that followed. The marines had first been used in the Philippines on May 1, 1898, by Commodore George Dewey, who sent a marine detachment to seize the Spanish naval station at Cavite. Although successful in this mission, there was an insufficient number of marines to expand the action on land. Dewey blockaded Manila Bay until the arrival of army forces under General Wesley Merritt.

Special Purpose Force (SPF)   See ORGANIZATION BY UNITS.

squad   See ORGANIZATION BY UNITS.

squadron   See ORGANIZATION BY UNITS.

Stinger Weapons System: RMP and Basic
See AIR DEFENSE ARTILLERY.

Streeter, Ruth Cheney (1895–1990) *Marine Corps administrator*
Ruth Cheney Streeter was the first director of the U.S. MARINE CORPS WOMEN'S RESERVE, which was

activated on February 13, 1943. Streeter served as director until her retirement on December 7, 1945.

Born in Brookline, Massachusetts, Streeter was educated abroad and at Bryn Mawr College (Bryn Mawr, Pennsylvania), from which she graduated in 1918. During the 1930s, Streeter worked in public health and welfare, unemployment relief, and old-age assistance in New Jersey. Simultaneously, she pursued her passionate interest in aviation, completing a course in aeronautics at New York University and serving as adjutant of Group 221 of the Civil Air Patrol. Learning to fly in 1940, she became the only woman member of the Committee on Aviation of the New Jersey Defense Council the following year, also serving as chairperson of the Citizen's Committee for Army and Navy, Inc., based at Fort Dix, New Jersey. Streeter received a commercial pilot's license in April 1942.

After General THOMAS HOLCOMB approved the creation of a Women's Reserve, Streeter was selected to head the program and was commissioned a USMC major on January 29, 1943, the first woman to hold that rank in the service. She was promoted to lieutenant colonel on November 22, 1943, and to colonel on February 1, 1944. By the end of WORLD WAR II, Streeter commanded a force of 18,460 women, and on February 4, 1946, was recognized with the award of the Legion of Merit.

Colonel Ruth Cheney Streeter (USMC) *(U.S. Marine Corps)*

Supply School

One of the USMC's COMBAT SERVICE SUPPORT SCHOOLS located at Camp Johnson, North Carolina, the Supply School designs, develops, conducts, and evaluates entry-level, intermediate, and advanced formal resident education and training for officers and enlisted personnel assigned to the USMC supply occupational field. The school offers the following courses of study:

- Ground Supply Officer Course
- Noncommissioned Officer Supply Course
- Ground Supply Chief Course
- Enlisted Supply Independent Duty Course
- Basic Preservation and Packaging Course
- Enlisted Supply Basic Course
- Enlisted Warehouse Basic Course
- Functional System Administrator Course
- Enlisted Supply Basic Course (Reserve)
- Ground Supply Officer Course (Reserve)

Suribachi

This mountain on the Pacific island of IWO JIMA was made famous by the flag raising there on February 23, 1945, by members of the 28th Marines, 5th Division.

See also IWO JIMA MEMORIAL.

T

T-34C Turbo Mentor   See AIRCRAFT, FIXED-WING.

T-44 Pegasus   See AIRCRAFT, FIXED-WING.

T-45A Goshawk   See AIRCRAFT, FIXED-WING.

TA-4J Skyhawk   See AIRCRAFT, FIXED-WING.

Tactical Bulk Fuel-Delivery System, CH-53E (TBFDS, CH-53E)   See AIRCRAFT, ROTARY-WING.

Tactical Petroleum Laboratory, Medium (TPLM)

The USMC has developed a Tactical Fuel System to support Marine Air/Ground Task Forces and Marine Expeditionary Forces in receiving, dispensing, and testing Class III (A) and III (W) fuel products. The Tactical Petroleum Laboratory, Medium (TPLM) provides an organic quality control capability for bulk fuel operations in the field by affording facilities to monitor critical physical and chemical characteristics of aviation and ground fuels. The laboratory can test suspect deliveries for acceptability and suitability and permits captured fuels to be tested for suitability as well.

The Tactical Petroleum Laboratory provides the essential testing components integrated into a standard USMC 8 foot by 8 foot by 20 foot International Standard Organization shelter. The laboratory is capable of monitoring the critical physical and chemical characteristics of aviation and ground fuels, including JP-4, JP-5, JP-8, diesel, and their commercial grade equivalents. The USMC maintains 14 such laboratories.

General characteristics of the Tactical Petroleum Laboratory, Medium (TPLM) include:

> **Manufacturer:** Lexington-Bluegrass Army Depot (GOCO)
> **Length:** 20 ft
> **Width:** 8 ft
> **Height:** 8 ft
> **Weight:** 9,960 lb

Tandem Offset Resupply Delivery System (TORDS)   See PERSONAL AND MISCELLANEOUS EQUIPMENT.

Tarawa

The principal island of this Gilbert Islands atoll is a mere three miles long and 800 yards wide at its widest, but in mid-1943, during WORLD WAR II, the Japanese created a strong defensive position here, in effect a fortress garrisoned by 4,800

Marines assault a Japanese position on Tarawa.
(Arttoday)

elite troops, and it was seen as necessary to capture the island and its small airfield. The 2nd Division was tasked with the mission on November 20, 1943.

The mission was made especially difficult by a restriction imposed on prelanding bombardment and air support. It was feared that such an attack would bring on an offensive from the Japanese navy. Although the USMC landings went reasonably well, the marines encountered severe resistance from well-defended positions. Betio, the principal island, was taken after 70 hours of combat, in which 980 marines and 29 sailors were killed. Japanese losses were almost total: 4,690 killed. Throughout the rest of the war, marines referred to the costly victory as "terrible Tarawa."

"Tell It to the Marines!"

A popular, somewhat dated expression used to indicate contemptuous disbelief. The phrase did not originate with the USMC, but with the British Royal Marines, probably during the 18th century. Sailors considered the marines gullible landlubbers who would believe anything told to them about ships and sea matters.

Tinian

A nearly unpopulated Pacific island in the Marianas, three miles south of the large island of SAIPAN, Tinian was the objective of a superbly conducted USMC operation during WORLD WAR II. The 4th Division landed on the northwest coast on July 24, 1944, while the 2nd Division distracted the 6,000-man Japanese garrison near the island's only settlement, Tinian Town. The extremely efficient capture of the island was completed on August 1, 1944, with the loss of 317 marines.

Guarded by a USMC garrison (8th Marines), U.S. forces built a large airfield to accommodate B-29s, and Tinian became a key base from which the Japanese homeland was bombed. It was the base from which the two aircraft that released atomic bombs on Hiroshima and Nagasaki, *Enola Gay* and *Bock's Car,* were launched in August 1945.

tracked vehicles

The following tracked vehicles are either currently included in the marine inventory or are of historical importance in the service.

M-1A1 Main Battle Tank

The Marine Corp's M-1A1 Main Battle Tank is an improved version of the M-1 Main Battle Tank (MBT), which includes a 120-mm smoothbore main gun, an NBC (nuclear-biological-chemical) overpressure protection system, an improved armor package, a Deep Water Fording Kit (DWFK), a Position Location Reporting System (PLRS), enhanced ship tiedowns, a Digital Electronic Control Unit (DECU, which allows significant fuel savings), and Battlefield Override. The tank proved itself in battle during Operation Desert Storm (PERSIAN GULF WAR), when it successfully engaged enemy armor at ranges of nearly 13,000 feet.

The M-1A1 Main Battle Tank is fully compatible with all navy amphibious ships and craft, including navy Maritime Prepositioning Ships. The M-1A1 replaces the now obsolescent M-60A1 Rise/Passive tank, which cannot be expected to survive, let alone defeat, the threats of the modern

Marines of the 2nd Marine Division's 2nd Tank Battalion maneuver their M-1A1 main battle tanks during a combined arms exercise at the Marine Corps Air Ground Combat Center, Twentynine Palms, California. *(Department of Defense)*

battlefield. The marines collaborated with the army on the design of the M-1A1 (called the Abrams, in the army) to ensure mutual supportability as well as interoperability. As of 2004, the marines fielded 403 of the M-1A1 tanks. The tank was introduced into the marine inventory in 1990.

General characteristics of the M-1A1 Main Battle Tank include:

Manufacturer: General Dynamics (Land Systems Division)
Power plant: AGT-1500 turbine engine
Power train: hydrokinetic, fully automatic, with four forward and two reverse gear ratios
Propulsion: 1,500-horsepower gas (multifuel) turbine engine
Length, gun forward: 385 in
Width: 144 in
Height: 114 in
Weight, fully armed: 67.7 tons

Main gun: 120-mm M256
Commander's weapon: M-2 .50-caliber machine gun
Loader's Weapon: 7.62-mm M-240 machine gun
Coaxial Weapon: 7.62-mm M-240 machine gun
Cruising Range: 289 miles without NBC system; 279 miles with NBC system
Sight radius: 8 degrees at 8x power
Speed, maximum: 42 mph
Speed, cross-country: 30 mph
Ground clearance: 19 in
Obstacle crossing, vertical: 42 in
Obstacle crossing, trench: 9 ft wide
Slope: 60 degrees at 4.5 mph
Crew: four, including driver, loader, gunner, and tank commander
Warheads: capable of delivering both kinetic energy (sabot) and chemical energy (heat) rounds

Sensors: the 120-mm M256 main gun has a cant sensor, wind speed sensor, and automatic lead and ammunition temperature inputs to its ballistic fire control solution

M-1 Mine-Clearing Blade System

The M-1 Mine-Clearing Blade System is used on the M-1A1 Main Battle Tank to counteract and neutralize land mines. Electrically operated, the M-1 is capable of clearing surface or buried mines up to 6 feet in front of the path of the tank without additional equipment or the aid of supporting forces. (The M-1 was also used with the older Marine Corps M-60A1 Rise/Passive Tank, some of which are still maintained in the USMC inventory.) The Marine Corps has 71 M-1 systems in its inventory.

General characteristics of the M-1 Mine-Clearing Blade System include:

Manufacturer: Israel Military Industries
Weight: 4.5 tons
Length: 9.6 ft
Width: 14.9 ft
Height: 2.5 ft
Area: 143 sq ft
Volume: 346 cu ft

Four M-1 units are deployed per each USMC tank company.

M-9 Armored Combat Earthmover (ACE)

The M-9 Armored Combat Earthmover is a full-tracked, air transportable armored earthmover, which can be employed in a great many engineering tasks, including the clearing of obstacles, preparation of defilade and survivability positions, and myriad engineering construction tasks such as dozing, scraping, grading, hauling, towing, and winching. The M-9 ACE combines cross-country mobility with a high degree of armored protection. This versatility enables it to perform offensive as well as defensive operations in forward battle areas. The vehicle has a 200-mile range, is fully air transportable, and is amphibious. The M-9 ACE was first fielded with the USMC in 1995. As of 2004, the USMC inventory includes 87 of the vehicles.

General characteristics of the M-9 Armored Combat Earthmover (ACE) include:

Manufacturer: United Defense LP, York, Pennsylvania
Net weight: 36,000 lb
Ballasted weight: 54,000 lb
Length: 246 in
Height: 105 in
Width: 126 in
Speed, land: 30 mph
Speed, water: 3 mph
Cruising range: 200 mi

M-60A1 Armored Vehicle Launched Bridge (M-60A1 AVLB)

M-60A1 Armored Vehicle Launched Bridge is an armored vehicle modified to launch and retrieve a 60-foot scissors-type bridge. The vehicle consists of three major components: the launcher, the hull, and the bridge. The launcher is an integral part of the vehicle chassis, and the bridge, when emplaced, is capable of supporting tracked as well as wheeled vehicles with a military load bearing capacity up to Class 60. The roadway width is 12 feet, 6 inches. Once emplaced, the bridge can be retrieved from either end, so that the M-60A1 AVLB can emplace its bridge, cross it, then retrieve it and proceed to the next mission. Bridge emplacement normally takes no more than two to five minutes. Retrieval requires about 10 minutes and is generally performed under armor protection.

The vehicle was introduced in 1987, and, as of 2004, the USMC maintained an inventory of 55 bridges and 37 launchers. General characteristics of the M-60A1 Armored Vehicle Launched Bridge (M-60A1 AVLB) include:

Manufacturer: General Dynamics (Land Systems Division)
Contractor: Anniston Army Depot
Power plant: 12-cylinder diesel engine, AVOS-1790-20
Power train: CD-850-6A, 2 speed forward, 1 reverse

M-60A1 Tank Chassis—
Weight, combat loaded: 56.6 tons
Ground clearance: 18 in
Length: 31 ft
Width: 12 ft
Maximum speed (governed): 30 mph
Cross-country speed: 8–12 mph
Trench crossing: 8.5 ft wide
Range: 290 mi
Fuel capacity: 375 gal

Bridge—
Length, extended: 63 ft
Length, folded: 32 ft
Effective bridge span: 60 ft
Width, overall: 13.1 ft
Width, roadway: 12.5 ft
Width, treadway: 5.75 ft
Height, unfolded: 3.1 ft
Weight: 14.65 tons
Crew requirement: two

Mobile/Unit Conduct of Fire Trainer (M/U-COFT)

The Mobile/Unit Conduct of Fire Trainer (M/U-COFT) provides training in critical tasks performed by M-1A1 Main Battle Tank gunners and tank commanders in a simulated battlefield environment. The U-COFT gunnery trainer is housed at the unit level in transportable shelters mounted on concrete pads, whereas the mobile M-COFT is mounted on a trailer to be used by company-size elements of the MARINE CORPS RESERVE. Both configurations use the same basic hardware and software.

The COFT crew compartment replicates the turret interior of an M-1A1 tank, and the computer-generated scenes viewed through the fire control optics react to manipulation of the controls in a realistic fashion, thereby providing training in target acquisition, identification, and engagement with the main gun, coaxial machine gun, and the tank commander's weapons station. The COFT also includes an Instructor/Operator (I/O) Station, which provides the capability of monitoring both the gunner's and the commander's fire control equipment; selects from several hundred increasingly difficult scenarios to test crew members' judgments and reactions; and provides an automatic scoring and feedback system for evaluating individual and crew performance.

As of 2004, the USMC has four U-COFT and two M-COFT units. Before these were developed, tank gunnery training was restricted to annual periods of main gun firing and qualification. Not only did this limit training, it also greatly increased training costs. The COFT units provide initial and subsequent gunnery sustainment training and significantly improve crew proficiency in all aspects of tank gunnery. However, the USMC has not abandoned live-fire training, which is still required for combat training and qualification.

General characteristics of the Mobile/Unit Conduct of Fire Trainer (M/U-COFT) include:

Mobile Conduct of Fire Trainer
Builder: Elbit Computers
Length: 45 ft
Width: 8 ft
Height: 13 ft
Volume: 4,680 cu ft

Unit Conduct of Fire Trainer
Builder: Elbit Computers
Length: 33.5 ft
Width: 24.75 ft

Training and Education Command

Part of the U.S. MARINE CORPS COMBAT DEVELOPMENT COMMAND, based at Marine Corps Base Quantico, the Training and Education Command develops, coordinates, resources, executes, and evaluates training and education concepts, policies, plans, and programs to prepare marines "to meet the challenges of present and future operational environments." The command consists of the following schools:

Combat Service Support School
Communication and Electronics School
Field Medical Service School–Lejeune
Field Medical Service School–Pendleton

Instructional Management School
Mountain Warfare Training Center
School of Infantry–Lejeune
School of Infantry–Pendleton
Weapons Training Battalion

triple threat

A marine qualified as a SCUBA diver and a paratrooper, and who has also had Ranger training.

See also U.S. MARINE CORPS RECONNAISSANCE BATTALIONS.

Tube-Launched, Optically Tracked, Wire-Guided (TOW) Missile Weapon System

See ANTIARMOR WEAPONS.

U

★

UH-34/VH-34 Seahorse   See AIRCRAFT,
ROTARY-WING.

unconventional warfare (UW)

Unconventional warfare is a general and somewhat
imprecise term used to describe military operations conducted in enemy-controlled territory or
in politically sensitive places. UW is typically clandestine and makes extensive use of local resources
and local personnel. UW may include guerrilla
warfare, sabotage, and escape and evasion. The
USMC excels at UW. Its MARINE CORPS RECONNAIS-
SANCE BATTALIONS are typically deployed on such
missions, often in conjunction with Navy SEALs
and/or U.S. Army Special Forces.

uniforms

The first marine uniform was authorized for the
CONTINENTAL MARINES in September 1776 and consisted of white trousers and a white-faced green coat.
Headgear was a round hat with an upturned brim
featuring a cockade. Most distinctive was the leather
collar, or neck stock, a measure intended to ward off
sword blows, but always uncomfortable and much
despised by marines until 1875, when it was finally
dispensed with. The leather collar gave marines their
most enduring nickname, LEATHERNECKS, which
gained its greatest currency during WORLD WAR II,
long after the collar had been eliminated.

The USMC was disbanded after the conclusion
of the AMERICAN REVOLUTION, and when it was
reconstituted in 1798, it was issued surplus uniforms
from the army of General Anthony "Mad Anthony"
Wayne. The coat was blue with red facings—the first
"dress blues" of the service. As earlier, the hat was
round with an upturned brim. In 1804, this uniform
was updated in a lighter shade of blue with scarlet
facings, and the round hat was replaced by a high
shako featuring a brass eagle emblem.

In 1834, pursuant to orders of President
Andrew Jackson, the USMC uniform was toned
down. The coat was gray green with buff facings.
Trousers were gray. When it was found that the
gray green rapidly faded, a more reliable blue was
reintroduced in 1841: a coat of dark blue and
trousers of light blue. The undress uniform featured a dark blue cap with leather visor; the dress
uniform retained the high shako with a new device,
a brass anchor encircled by a wreath. In 1859, new
headgear, modeled after the French kepi (also used
by the U.S. Army), was adopted for fatigue wear.

After the Civil War, in 1869, the USMC adopted
a blue-black jacket with standing "choke" collar
and light blue trousers. Officers wore the MAME-
LUKE SWORD. This uniform became the dress blues
still worn today; however, field uniforms continued
to evolve more radically. During the 1890s, the coat
was abandoned for field use and was replaced by a
blue flannel shirt. Marines were issued tall leggings,
and a broad-brimmed white hat replaced the kepi.

It bore the now-familiar USMC EMBLEM. For dress parades, a spiked helmet, like those worn by the Prussian army, was adopted.

The SPANISH-AMERICAN WAR demonstrated the need for a tropical-weight field uniform. Khaki became standard. More than a decade later, in 1912, a service uniform of forest green was adopted, which included the "carbonized" (dull) brass buttons that are still part of the Class A service uniform. The Prussian helmet was discarded in favor of a visored hat. In the field, the high-crowned campaign hat was worn—the same headgear that still distinguishes USMC DRILL INSTRUCTORS today.

The pressing demands of WORLD WAR I forced the USMC to adopt what was in essence the uniform of the U.S. Army for field service, and, for the first time, a steel helmet (the British "washbasin"-style used by the U.S. Army) was worn. Between the wars, marines were distinguished by a roll-collar coat and khaki shirt with a green tie for service uniforms. WORLD WAR II saw the introduction of a lightweight fatigue and combat uniform as well as the redesigned helmet also worn by the U.S. Army. The combat uniform changed little until the era of the VIETNAM WAR, when combat uniforms were made even lighter in weight and in camouflage color schemes. After Vietnam, the most significant changes have been those made in the combat uniform, which include an array of new camouflage schemes and the adoption of a lightweight but very durable Kevlar helmet. Body armor, also based on Kevlar, is also often worn.

unmanned aerial vehicle (UAV)

Unmanned aerial vehicles are remotely piloted aircraft typically used for reconnaissance, but sometimes used as weapons platforms. The USMC uses close-range UAVs, aircraft that are small and lightweight, typically about 200 pounds, with a minimum flight radius of 18 miles. The purpose of these aircraft is strictly tactical, to provide an "over-the-hill" view of enemy disposition and activity.

For missions requiring somewhat longer range, the USMC uses short-range UAVs, which are heavier than the close-range aircraft, weighing in at about 1,000 pounds. Range is up to 186 miles, and flight endurance is an impressive 8 to 12 hours, so that these aircraft can be flown over a target and made to "loiter" for an extended period.

unmanned ground vehicle (UGV)

Unmanned ground vehicles are robot vehicles used to perform remote reconnaissance with a wide variety of sensors. In addition to assessing enemy disposition and activity, UGVs can be used to detect and even to clear obstacles and to detect chemical and biological warfare agents. UGVs can also be used to disarm unexploded ordinance, booby traps, and mines.

urban warfare

Urban warfare is any combat within urban areas. Traditionally, military battles have been fought in the open, usually on rural battlefields. Recently,

A marine from Charlie Company rushes to his objective at the Military Operations in Urban Terrain facility at Camp Lejeune, North Carolina. *(Department of Defense)*

wars and conflicts have been fought increasingly in the streets. Marine training now includes extensive experience with urban warfare scenarios.

U.S.-French Quasi-War

Shortly after the conclusion of the AMERICAN REVOLUTION, the Franco-American alliance that had prevailed during that war broke down. Subsequently, as the French government perceived that U.S. policy increasingly favored British interests over those of France, relations deteriorated further. When President John Adams authorized the U.S. minister to France, Charles Cotesworthy Pinckney, to call on the French Directory (successor government after the Reign of Terror) in an effort to repair relations, the Directory refused to receive the American minister. At this, Adams dispatched a commission consisting of Pinckney, John Marshall, and Elbridge Gerry to Paris in 1797. Three agents greeted the commissioners, conveying to them the startling message that before a new Franco-American treaty could be discussed, the United States would have to "loan" France $12,000,000 and pay Prime Minister Talleyrand a personal bribe of $250,000. Exposure of this diplomatic outrage resulted in the XYZ Affair (the French agents were designated not by name, but as X, Y, and Z), and, with French naval operations against the British in the West Indies already disrupting U.S. shipping, Congress launched an undeclared war in the spring of 1798.

In May 1799, a USMC detachment was put aboard the newly completed frigate *Constitution* and sailed with it for operations in the Caribbean. Ninety marines were put aboard a captured French sloop early in 1800 and sailed into Puerto Plata, Santo Domingo. There they captured a 14-gun French ship, after which they took the harbor fort, whose cannon they spiked.

This, the first USMC amphibious operation, was a modest but complete success. When Napoleon began his general withdrawal from the Caribbean, in order to concentrate on his European wars, harassment of U.S. shipping ceased, as did the Quasi-War.

U.S. Marine Band

Nicknamed the "President's Own," the Marine Band currently consists of 143 musicians led by five officers; their sole mission is to provide music for the president of the United States. The band's musicians are the only marines exempted from boot camp; however, they do receive a course in military etiquette and in marching, both administered at the MARINE BARRACKS in Washington, D.C., which is also where the band is quartered. Musicians hold the rank of staff sergeant.

The U.S. Marine Band was the first symphonic military band established in the United States, created by act of Congress on July 11, 1798. Although the band can march, it is primarily a concert orchestra. The schedule for the President's Own is crowded—about 600 engagements each year, including, every four years, the inauguration ceremonies.

The uniforms of the President's Own feature a scarlet blouse. The drum major sports a bearskin busby, wears a baldric sash listing the USMC's battle honors, and, although an enlisted man, wears an officer's belt buckle, emblazoned with the USMC emblem; he or she carries a mace surmounted by the U.S. Capitol dome and embellished with the seal of the president, battle honors, the USMC emblem, and a likeness of JOHN PHILIP SOUSA, the 17th and by far the most famous director of the U.S. Marine Band.

U.S. Marine Corps Air-Ground Task Force Expeditionary Training Center

Located at the U.S. Marine Corps Air-Ground Combat Center in Twentynine Palms, California, the training center was created on October 1, 1993, to oversee and integrate the resources of the Air-Ground Combat Center, the U.S. MARINE CORPS MOUNTAIN WARFARE TRAINING CENTER, and MARINE AVIATION WEAPONS AND TACTICS SQUADRON ONE.

U.S. Marine Corps Code

"Unit, Corps, God, Country." This is known in the USMC simply as "The Code," and it constitutes the individual marine's creed.

U.S. Marine Corps Color Guard

The Color Guard performs for parades, ceremonies, and official functions in the United States and elsewhere. The unit is assigned to Company A, MARINE BARRACKS, Washington, D.C., and consists of 13 members. In any given ceremony, the color guard consists of four members, two color bearers flanked by two riflemen. The USMC Color Guard is under the command of the color sergeant of the U.S. Marine Corps.

U.S. Marine Corps Combat Development Command (MCCDC)

MCCDC, based at Marine Corps Base Quantico, is the USMC agency responsible for education and development. The command's mission is to develop USMC warfighting concepts and to determine associated required capabilities in the areas of doctrine, organization, training and education, equipment, and support facilities to enable the USMC to field combat-ready forces.

U.S. Marine Corps Development Center

Built in 1994, the center is a 100,000-square-foot building at Marine Corps Base Quantico, which houses the Warfighting Development Integration Division, Requirements Division, Doctrine Division, Concepts and Plans Division, Studies and Analysis Division, Coalition and Special Warfare Division, and the MARINE CORPS INTELLIGENCE Center. The incorporation of these units and functions in a single facility is intended to facilitate the USMC's ability to assess its capabilities and resources in order to provide optimum support for FLEET MARINE FORCES.

U.S. Marine Corps Mountain Warfare Training Center (MWTC)

MWTC, nicknamed Pickle Meadows, is located at Bridgeport, California, and was established as part of the U.S. commitment to NATO to train marines in mountain and cold-weather combat. In this

A U.S. Marine on snowshoes patrols up a snowy slope with his squad from Kilo company at the Mountain Warfare Training Center, Bridgeport, California. *(Department of Defense)*

Sierra-based camp, marines are taught winter warfare and mountain warfare tactics, including fighting on skis. High-altitude climbing is taught during the summer months, both by day and by night.

U.S. Marine Corps Reconnaissance Battalions

"Scoop 'n Poop" teams are USMC units specially trained to infiltrate behind enemy lines, gather intelligence, and return or conduct clandestine search-and-destroy missions. The battalions specialize in infiltration and exfiltration without detection. The first recon battalions were trained in

WORLD WAR II, and the concept of commando training was brought into the USMC during the 1950s, inspired by units of Britain's Royal Marines. The first teams were formally established in 1961 and were widely deployed in the VIETNAM WAR.

Currently, the USMC has two recon battalions, one stationed at Marine Corps Base Camp Pendleton, California, and the other at Marine Corps Base Camp Lejeune, North Carolina. Membership in the battalions is voluntary and subject to stringent and demanding training.

See also DOUBLE TROUBLE; QUAD BODY; TRIPLE THREAT.

U.S. Marine Corps Research Center (MCRC)

The MCRC was put into operation at Marine Corps Base Quantico on May 6, 1993, and is the USMC's principal research facility, housing three libraries, the Marine Corps University archives, and conference facilities. The center is an adjunct and complement to the U.S. MARINE CORPS COMBAT DEVELOPMENT COMMAND.

U.S. Marine Corps Security Force (MCSF)

The MCSF is tasked with providing security force detachments for service on board U.S. Navy vessels, including aircraft carriers, submarine tenders, and guided missile cruisers, and at ammunition storage depots and other key military sites. Specially trained marines safeguard the security of nuclear weaponry, classified documents, and other sensitive material. On board ship, MCSF personnel also serve as a landing force and operate certain gun systems. In this, the MCSF performs the historical marine function, combining shipboard security with landing force and gun duty.

All MCSF detachments are under the control of a headquarters at Norfolk, Virginia. In 1993, this central command replaced the Atlantic Battalion (Norfolk) and the Pacific Battalion (Mare Island, California).

The Fleet Anti-Terrorism Security Team (FAST) is a contingent of the MCSF trained and equipped to respond worldwide to crisis situations that threaten military bases, nuclear ammunition or fuel facilities, and so on. FAST companies consist of 200 marines. Regular shipboard MCSF detachments are smaller; for instance, the detachment onboard an aircraft carrier consists of 64 enlisted marines and two officers.

U.S. Marine Corps Security Guard Battalion

Pursuant to the Foreign Service Act of 1946, marines of this battalion are responsible for providing security for U.S. embassies, consulates, and legations in foreign countries. Marine Embassy Guards were put into place beginning in 1949, replacing civilian guards in these installations.

The Security Guard Battalion currently consists of 140 State Department security detachments, ranging in size from six-marine units to 36-marine units. Each detachment is under the command of a noncommissioned officer—the only U.S. Marine Corps instance in which an NCO has independent command of a unit; however, with each diplomatic mission, the marine detachment is under operational command of an Embassy Security Officer and the ambassador. The guard detachment is responsible for safeguarding classified material and protecting embassy staff. Outside of the embassy proper, security is the responsibility of the host nation.

The Security Guard Battalion is staffed by more than 1,000 marines, carefully selected volunteers who are given six weeks of specialized training at the Marine Security Guard School (Department of State), located at Marine Base Quantico.

U.S. Marine Corps Women's Reserve

The USMC, with some reluctance, established the Women's Reserve during WORLD WAR II pursuant to a plan approved in November 1942. It was the last of the services to create a women's force.

Initial authorized strength was 1,000 officers and 18,000 enlisted women. The Reserve was commanded by Major RUTH STREETER. The first recruits were trained at Hunter College, New York City, and officers were trained at Mount Holyoke College (South Hadley, Massachusetts). Within months, however, all training was transferred to facilities at Marine Corps Base Camp Lejeune. The Women Reservists were not combat marines, but were assigned as clerks and stenographers. By the beginning of 1944, 85 percent of enlisted personnel at MARINE HEADQUARTERS in Washington were Women Reservists.

The organization had been formed on the understanding that it would be disbanded after the war and all personnel discharged; however, a small cadre of Women Reservists were retained, and in June 1948, the SECRETARY OF THE NAVY ordered the integration of women into the regular USMC.

Shortly after being commissioned at Mount Holyoke in South Hadley, Massachusetts, the new lieutenants pin on their bars. *(Mount Holyoke War Archives)*

U.S. Marine Drum and Bugle Corps

Known as the "Commandant's Own," the Drum and Bugle Corps was created in 1934 and is stationed at the MARINE BARRACKS, Washington D.C., with field units in Georgia and California. The main unit, at the Marine Barracks, consists of 75 musicians. In contrast to the U.S. MARINE BAND, Drum and Bugle Corps musicians are trained like other marines. After completing BASIC TRAINING, they are trained at the Navy School of Music (U.S. Naval Base Little Creek, Virginia).

The Drum and Bugle Corps performs 11 months out of the year, touring the United States and abroad.

U.S.-Mexican War

Texas had won independence from Mexico in 1836 and existed as a republic until the U.S. Congress voted to annex it in 1845, even though Mexico warned that to do so would mean war. On April 25, 1846, Mexican forces crossed the Rio Grande and attacked U.S. dragoons. The army fought two major battles, at Palo Alto on May 8 and at Resaca de la Palma on May 9, emerging victorious from both. Initially, the USMC presence was restricted to the complements aboard the navy's Gulf Squadron. However, these detachments were formed into a battalion and staged raids on Frontera and Tampico, playing a key role in the capture of Tampico in November 1846.

During March 1847, marines were involved in the troop landings at VERACRUZ. The principal USMC role was to secure gulf ports that remained under Mexican control after the Veracruz operation.

Marines also participated in General Winfield Scott's (USA) assault on Mexico City. An advance battalion of a newly formed marine regiment joined Scott's army at Puebla in August 1847, as the general prepared the final assault. While the army advanced on the gates of Mexico City, the marines were assigned to guard baggage trains; however, marines did participate in the taking of Chapultepec Castle in September. After this operation, marines were part of the force that stormed

San Cosme Gate on September 13, and it was a U.S. marine who cut down the Mexican flag and ran up the U.S. flag over the Palacio Nacional after Mexican commander Santa Anna evacuated the city.

In addition to participating in the invasion of Mexico proper, marines were also involved in the Bear Flag Rebellion, which quickly became the California theater of the U.S.-Mexican War. A USMC "California Battalion" was formed and participated in battles at San Diego and San Pascual, as well as the occupation of Los Angeles in January 1847.

USMC amphibious forces attacked Mexican west coast ports during 1847, occupying Guaymas, San Blas, and San Jose. Mazatlán fell to a combined USMC-USN force of some 700 on November 10, 1847. Captain JACOB ZEILIN (USMC) served as military governor at Mazatlán until the Treaty of Guadalupe Hidalgo, ending the war, was concluded on February 2, 1848.

V

V

V-22 Osprey   See AIRCRAFT, ROTARY-WING.

Vandegrift, Alexander (1887–1973) *Marine Corps commandant*

Born in Charlottesville, Virginia, Vandegrift became the 18th COMMANDANT OF THE MARINE CORPS. He attended the University of Virginia for two years before entering the USMC as a second lieutenant in 1909. During 1912–23, he served in the Caribbean and Central America and took part in action in NICARAGUA, in the invasion and occupation of VERACRUZ, Mexico, in 1914, and, in 1915, the pacification of HAITI.

As a major, Vandegrift commanded a USMC battalion at Marine Corps Base Quantico, Virginia, from 1923 to 1926. In 1926, he was appointed assistant chief of staff at Marine Corps Base San Diego, then shipped out to China in 1927–28. He then served in Washington, D.C., and again at Quantico. Promoted to lieutenant colonel in 1934, Vandegrift returned to China the following year and was promoted to colonel in 1936. He was stationed at HEADQUARTERS MARINE CORPS during 1937–41, was promoted to brigadier general in 1940 and became assistant commander of 1st Marine Division in 1941. Early in 1942, he was made commanding general of the division.

Major General Vandegrift led the division to the South Pacific in May 1942 and commanded it during the GUADALCANAL campaign (August–December 1942), for which he received the Medal of Honor. Promoted to lieutenant general, Vandegrift commanded the First Marine Amphibious Corps during the opening of the BOUGAINVILLE campaign, returning to the United States late in 1943 to become commandant of the Marine Corps (January 1, 1944).

As commandant, Vandegrift presided over the continued wartime expansion of the USMC, then directed its orderly contraction after the war, fighting a strenuous battle to prevent its complete dissolution. Promoted to general in March 1945, Vandegrift was the first USMC officer to attain that rank while on active duty. Vandegrift stepped down as commandant on January 1, 1948, and retired from the USMC the following year.

Veracruz

A major Mexican seaport on the Bay of Campeche, Veracruz figured in two USMC operations. The first, during the U.S.-MEXICAN WAR, was a landing by the 1st Marine Battalion in August 1847, which followed landings by the U.S. Army. The second came in 1914, when President Woodrow Wilson ordered the seizure of the city following a diplomatic incident. The Wilson administration refused to recognize the government of General Victoriano Huerta, and, amid bad feelings between the dictatorial Huerta regime and the United States, some U.S. sailors were imprisoned briefly. The admiral commanding the U.S. Gulf Squadron demanded an apology and a 21-gun salute to the U.S. flag. The incident might have stopped with that had not the Wilson administration discovered that a German ship was bound for Veracruz with arms for Huerta. Following this discovery, the 2nd Marine Regiment landed on April 21, 1914. Light resistance met the landing, but the city itself was more heavily defended. The 2nd Marine Regiment was accordingly reinforced by the USMC's Panama Battalion and a brigade of sailors to a strength of 7,000 (3,100 were marines). After street fighting, the Mexican garrison surrendered on April 24.

The Veracruz operation proved highly effective. With the city in U.S. hands and the port blockaded, Huerta stepped down as head of state on July 15, 1914.

VH-3D Sea King   See AIRCRAFT, ROTARY-WING.

VH-60A Black Hawk   See AIRCRAFT, ROTARY-WING.

VH-60N Seahawk   See AIRCRAFT, ROTARY-WING.

Vietnam War

During the administrations of Harry S. Truman and Dwight D. Eisenhower, the United States began sending increasing amounts of military aid, mainly in the form of financing, to the French, who were struggling to maintain their hold on French Indochina, or Vietnam. In 1954, however, following an ignominious defeat at Dien Bien Phu at the hands of the Viet Minh, the communist nationalists of Vietnam, the French agreed to leave. Vietnam was then partitioned along the 17th parallel, the communists to the north, the democratic Republic of Vietnam to the south.

Pursuant to the U.S. cold war policy of "containing" communism to prevent its spread without provoking a third world war, the United States supported the government of Ngo Dinh Diem in the south until he proved corrupt and incapable of holding his embattled nation together. With the covert cooperation of the CIA, Diem was overthrown and ultimately murdered by the South Vietnamese military. The U.S. desperately sought to bolster a succession of leaders and, under President John F. Kennedy, sent increasing numbers of military "advisers" to assist the South Vietnamese forces in prosecuting the war against the communists. On August 7, 1964, after North Vietnamese ships allegedly attacked two American destroyers (this "Tonkin Gulf incident" was later revealed to have been partially fabricated), the U.S. Congress passed the "Gulf of Tonkin Resolution," giving President Lyndon B. Johnson extensive war-making authority. From this point on, U.S. involvement in the Vietnam War escalated steadily. By 1969, more than a half-million American military personnel would be engaged in combat operations.

The USMC made its first appearance in Vietnam in April 1962, when a helicopter squadron arrived in the delta south of Saigon and was subsequently headquartered at Da Nang, second largest city in Vietnam. USMC helicopter pilots transported South Vietnamese Army (ARVN) troops into battle. By 1965, half of the USMC's helicopter squadrons were serving in Vietnam.

The first USMC advisers arrived in Vietnam in 1964, and in 1965, after an attack on the American outpost at Pleiku in early February, the 9th Expeditionary Brigade was landed at Da Nang. It was the first major U.S. ground combat force in country. The marines were assigned to protect the Da Nang airfield. By the end of summer 1965, the USMC had four ground regiments in Vietnam, plus four air groups.

The first major ground operation was Operation Starlight, which cleared Vietcong troops operating on the Von Tuong Peninsula south of Chu Lai. In another operation, the 9th Marines cleared the coastal areas as far as Hoi An. The objective of such operations was "pacification," flushing the Vietcong out of villages, then providing security and other benefits for the villagers, so that they would not be tempted to support the Vietcong again. Pacification—winning the "hearts and minds" of the people—was strongly advocated by the USMC, but higher military command increasingly adopted a strategy of search-and-destroy, abandoning the campaign to win the loyalty of the people. Throughout the war, this became a subject of bitter controversy between the USMC and the U.S. Army. Indeed, the USMC became largely subordinated to the USA, and its special skills as an expeditionary force were underutilized.

By June 1966, the rest of the 1st Division arrived in Vietnam and was deployed to Chu Lai. The III Marine Amphibious Force, under the command of Lieutenant General Lewis Walt, would consist of two divisions and would fight in Vietnam for nearly six years. In 1966, the USMC mission focused principally on defending three bases in the area of I Corps: Chu Lai, Phu Bai (near the ancient city of Hue), and Da Nang. Additionally, the USMC was assigned to guard the Demilitarized Zone (DMZ) in Quang Tri Province, effectively the buffer zone between North and South. Additionally, the USMC coordinated with the ARVN in several offensives. Near the DMZ, the marines enjoyed considerable success with combined arms assaults, the close coordination of ground troops, helicopter units, and close support from fixed-wing attack aircraft. However, because U.S. policy was to fight a strictly limited war, the marines were not permitted to penetrate into North Vietnam, so, even when defeated, the communist forces could retreat to safe haven.

The year 1967 brought 14 major battles, prosecuted mainly by the army, with the USMC providing support on the DMZ and along major transportation routes. In April, the 3rd Marines were successful in clearing the enemy from Khe Sanh, which became a key USMC outpost.

The Vietcong made two massive attacks on the 26th Marines at Khe Sanh as part of the Tet Offensive, an all-out communist push on virtually all fronts. Supported by tactical and strategic air strikes, the marines survived a 77-day siege at Khe Sanh and defeated the North Vietnamese, who had hoped to achieve against the United States what they had achieved against the French in 1954 at Dien Bien Phu.

By far the heaviest fighting during the Tet offensive occurred in the ancient capital of Hue, which involved marines (and the ARVN) in difficult house-to-house combat during February. The city was declared secure on March 2.

Marine, U.S. Army, and ARVN forces had scored a major tactical victory in repelling, on all fronts, the Tet Offensive. However, the rules of engagement precluded exploiting this triumph by pursuing a general offensive with the object of final victory. Indeed, in the United States, amid burgeoning popular opposition to the war, Tet was grossly misperceived as a communist victory. It was nevertheless true that Tet demonstrated the incredible resolve of the communist forces, which showed themselves willing to absorb catastrophic losses and keep fighting.

Tet signaled a new direction in the war. U.S. operations were greatly reduced in scale as American political leaders desperately groped for an exit strategy. The USMC was called on less to conduct offensive operations and instead focused on the ongoing defense of Da Nang and the region near the Laotian border, through which the communists often infiltrated the South. In November 1968, six marine battalions destroyed more than 1,200 North Vietnamese troops along the border region, and early in 1969, parts of the 1st Division operated in the hill country west of Da Nang, while, to the north, the 3rd Division, operating in Quang Tri Province, cleaned out enemy bases in the Da Krong Valley (Operation Dewey Canyon).

When President Richard M. Nixon entered the White House in 1969, he began a program to withdraw U.S. ground forces in Vietnam and turn over more responsibility for the war to the South Vietnamese. The 9th Marines and elements of the 1st Air Wing were relieved in 1969; the 1st Division was sent late in the year to the Que Son Valley to replace army units, which had been withdrawn.

In September 1969, the 3rd Division was withdrawn and stationed in OKINAWA and at Marine

Corps Base Camp Pendleton, and in March 1970, the army took over the defense of Da Nang, while III Marine Amphibious Force—reduced essentially to the 1st Division—defended Quang Nam Province. Small-scale offensives were conducted, even during the period of withdrawal, with the marines acting mainly to support ARVN forces, which were expected to shoulder most of the burden. By February 1971, the 1st Marines was the only USMC presence left in Vietnam. Soon even this was reduced to a single amphibious brigade. Before the year was over, only some 500 marines remained in Vietnam, serving as legation guards and as advisers to ARVN forces. However, the North Vietnamese Easter offensive of 1972, in which some 120,000 communists invaded the northern provinces of South Vietnam brought additional USMC air units into the country on a short-term basis.

When the final North Vietnamese offensive began in March 1975, the 9th Amphibious Brigade, during April, effected the evacuation of U.S. citizens. USMC legation guards, reinforced by elements of the 9th Marines, guarded the U.S. Embassy in Saigon as helicopters evacuated remaining U.S. personnel and certain Vietnamese and foreign citizens. The last marines were themselves airlifted from the embassy on the morning of April 30, 1975.

The largest USMC complement to serve in Vietnam was nearly 86,000 men. USMC casualties were 12,926 men killed in action and 88,582 wounded.

W

Wake Island

Despite its name in the singular, Wake Island is a group of three remote coral islets in the Pacific 2,300 miles west of Hawaii. Claimed by the United States after the SPANISH-AMERICAN WAR, Wake Island was defended by 449 marines of the 1st Defense Battalion at the outbreak of WORLD WAR II. There were also a dozen F4F Wildcat fighter aircraft based on Wake.

The Japanese first attacked the island on December 11, 1941, but were repulsed by the small USMC garrison. Firing five-inch guns, marines sank two destroyers, damaged a third, and also damaged two Japanese cruisers. On December 22, the Japanese returned in force and, with 2,000 men, overwhelmed the USMC garrison. In addition to the cost in warships, the Japanese suffered 1,500 infantry killed in the taking of this outpost.

War of 1812

The War of 1812, between the United States and Britain, involved substantial action at sea. Most of the USMC, which numbered fewer than 500 men in 1812, served aboard U.S. Navy ships and participated in such celebrated naval battles as that between USS *Constitution* and HMS *Guerrière*, USS *Wasp* versus HMS *Frolic*, *Constitution* versus *Java*, and *United States* versus *Macedonian*. In contrast to most of the land battles, which U.S. federal and militia forces often lost to the British, the fledgling navy and Marine Corps performed with extraordinary skill and success against the Royal Navy, most powerful seagoing force in the world.

In addition to oceangoing service, marines served with Commodore Oliver Hazard Perry (USN) in the spectacular U.S. triumph on Lake Erie.

On land, marines participated in the disastrously failed defense of Washington, D.C., against the advance of British general Robert Ross. On August 24, 1813, Ross defeated U.S. Army and militia forces, augmented by 400 sailors and 103 marines, at Bladensburg, Maryland, just five miles outside of Washington, D.C. After crossing the Anacostia River, Ross quickly routed the remaining militia. The sailors and marines, however, held a line across the main road, using five naval guns to repulse several British attacks. However, with overwhelming strength, the British were able to flank this force and send it into retreat. Once the USN-USMC line had collapsed, Ross marched into Washington and burned most of the public buildings.

The Battle of New Orleans, fought at the end of 1814 and beginning of 1815, had a much happier outcome. Three hundred marines participated in the battle and played a key role in the very center of General Andrew Jackson's defenses. The main British attack was launched on January 8, 1815, and was repulsed within 20 minutes. Of 3,500 British troops involved, 2,300 were killed or wounded. Edward Pakenham, the British commander, was among the dead. That the battle was fought some two weeks after the Treaty of Ghent had formally ended the War of 1812 (neither Jackson nor Pakenham had received word of this) did not diminish the positive impact of the victory on the American public. It made a costly war, which gained the United States virtually nothing, seem like a brilliant triumph.

weapons, individual and crew-served

The following individual and crew-served weapons and auxiliary equipment are either currently included in the USMC inventory or are of historical importance in the service.

AN/PAQ-3 Modular Universal Laser Equipment (MULE)

The AN/PAQ-3 Modular Universal Laser Equipment, or MULE, is a man-portable, tripod-mounted or shoulder-fired unit that incorporates a laser rangefinder/target designator compatible with all laser-guided weapons now under development. This target locator and guide for laser-guided projectiles can track moving targets and can combine range, azimuth, and elevation into a digital message that is sent to the tactical fire control center. The MULE consists of the Laser Designator/Rangefinder Module and the Stabilized Tracking Tripod Module. Additionally, the North Finding Module assists in orientation of the equipment. The system can be run on 24-volt rechargeable batteries or from 24-volt vehicle-supplied power. The MULE effectively ranges a moving target to almost 10,000 feet and a stationary target to 16,400 feet. Drawbacks to the MULE include its weight and bulk (108 pounds when configured with the night sight) and technical limitations of its sight. Nevertheless, the MULE has enjoyed a significant degree of acceptance by marines in the field.

General characteristics of the AN/PAQ-3 Modular Universal Laser Equipment (MULE) include:

Manufacturer: Hughes Aircraft
Weight, daylight operations: 42 lb

Weight, night operations: 108 lb
Weight in shipping cases: 220 lb
Laser designator/rangefinder module field of view: 4 degrees
Laser designator/rangefinder module magnification: 10x
Stabilized tracking tripod module field of rotation: 360 degrees
Stabilized tracking tripod module elevation: up 16.9 degrees, down 22.5 degrees
Terrain capability: 0–15 degrees
Power requirements, rechargeable batteries: 24 volts, nickel-cadmium
Run time: 10 min for each 7-hour recharge

Unit may also be run on vehicle-supplied power.

AN/PAQ-4A/4C Infrared Aiming Light

The AN/PAQ-4A Infrared Aiming Light is a lightweight, battery-powered, pulsating, infrared-emitting target-marking beam. Invisible to the unaided eye, the AN/PAQ-4A's beam allows the user to engage targets at night while wearing night-vision goggles. The aiming light is adapted for use with the M-16A2 rifle and can also be adapted for use on the M-60 Machine Gun, the M2-HB Browning Machine Gun, and the M-249 SAW.

The AN/PAQ-4A uses a Class I laser (helium-neon) to generate the aiming point, marking targets out to a minimum of 325 feet and a maximum of 650 to nearly 1,000 feet, depending on the ambient light available. The system can be powered by one standard lithium battery, which will operate the aiming light for about 40 hours continuously. If necessary, two standard AA batteries can also be used. Once the beam is boresighted to the weapon, the firer simply places the pulsating beam on the target and shoots. The AN/PAQ-4A is intended for use in conjunction with AN/PVS-7B Night Vision Goggles. The AN/PAQ-4C is an improved version of the AN/PAQ-4A. General characteristics of both versions include:

Manufacturer: Insight Technology, Manchester, New Hampshire

Length: 6.1 in
Width: 1.7 in (4.32 cm)
Weight, with batteries: 9 oz
Range: 325 ft min
Beam divergence: less than 2 milliradians
Power source: 1 BA-5567 or 2 AA batteries (BA-3058)

AN/PVS-4 Individual Weapon Night Sight

The USMC employs the AN/PVS-4 Individual Weapon Night Sight as a night vision device for passive night vision and aiming fire of individual weapons using ambient light—moonlight, starlight, or skyglow—for illumination. This advanced instrument, portable and battery operated, amplifies reflected light to enhance night vision. The device is entirely passive and does not emit visible or infrared light, which can be detected by the enemy.

The AN/PVS-4 Individual Weapon Night Sight can be used with the M-16 Rifle, M-249 Machine Gun, and M-60 Machine Gun, as well as the 83 mm Mk-183 Mod 1 (SMAW) Rocket. The AN/PVS-4 comes furnished with mounting brackets for the M-16 and M-60; reticules and mounting brackets for use with other weapons are separately requisitioned.

General characteristics of the night sight include:

Manufacturer: IMO Industries, Garland, Texas
Length: 12 in
Width: 4 in
Height: 4.5 in
Weight: 4 lb
Magnification: 3.6x
Range (man-sized target), starlight: 400 yd
Range (man-sized target), moonlight: 600 yd
Field of view: 14.5 degrees, circular
Power source: 2.7-volt mercury battery

AN/PVS-5 Night Vision Goggles (NVG)

The AN/PVS-5 Night Vision Goggles (NVG) are a self-contained, passive, image intensifying, night-vision viewing system worn on the head either with or without the standard battle helmet or aviator helmet. They are a second-generation binocular system that magnifies starlight or moonlight for enhanced night vision. Although the system is passive, it incorporates a built-in infrared light source for added illumination to aid in performing such close-up tasks as map reading. The goggles are equipped with a headstrap for "hands-free" operation and demist shields to prevent fogging of the eyepiece. The USMC has some 8,200 AN/PVS-5s in its inventory.

The AN/PVS-5 Night Vision Goggles (NVG) were first acquired by the USMC in the early 1980s and, since that time, have been used by vehicle drivers, riflemen, and unit leaders.

General characteristics of the AN/PVS-5 Night Vision Goggles (NVG) include:

Manufacturer: IMO Industries, Garland, Texas; ITT, Roanoke, Virginia; Litton, Tempe, Arizona
Length: 6.5 in
Width: 6.8 in
Height: 4.7 in
Weight: 30 oz
Magnification: 1x
Range (man-sized target), starlight: 164 ft
Range (man-sized target), moonlight: 500 ft
Field of view: 40 degrees (circular)
Power source: 2.7-volt mercury battery

AN/PVS-7B Night Vision Goggle (NVG)

The AN/PVS-7B is a single-tube night vision goggle system, which employs a Generation III image intensifier using prisms and lenses to provide the user with simulated binocular vision. The device incorporates a high light-level protection circuit in a passive, self-contained image intensifier device, which amplifies existing ambient light—starlight, moonlight, skyglow—to enhance night vision for night operations. A demist shield prevents fogging of the eyepiece.

The AN/PVS-7B augments the earlier AN/PVS-5 Night Vision Goggles (NVG) and will eventually replace it entirely. It is a state-of-the-art instrument.

General characteristics of the AN/PVS-7B Night Vision Goggle (NVG) include:

Manufacturer: ITT, Roanoke, Virginia; Litton, Tempe, Arizona
Length: 5.9 in
Width: 6.1 in
Height: 3.9 in
Weight: 24 oz
Magnification: 1x
Range, starlight, man-sized target: 325 ft
Range, starlight, vehicle-sized target: 1,640 ft
Range, moonlight, man-sized target: 1,000 ft
Field of view: 40 degrees (circular)
Power source: mercury, nickel-cadmium, or lithium battery
Operation time: 12 hours on one 2.7-volt battery

AN/TVS-5 Crew-Served Weapon Night Sight

The AN/TVS-5 Night Sight is a portable, battery operated, electro-optical instrument used for observation and aimed fire of weapons at night. Entirely passive, it emits no light of its own, but works by amplifying reflected ambient light from such sources as moonlight, starlight, and sky glow. An eye guard ensures that no visible and/or infrared light will escape from the eyepiece to alert enemy forces.

The AN/TVS-5 is currently the standard USMC night sight for the M-2 50-caliber machine gun and the 40-mm Mk-19 machine gun; however, the sight can also be used as a stand-alone instrument, mounted on a tripod or even hand-held for surveillance.

The AN/TVS-5 was designed in the 1970s and was acquired by the USMC in the 1980s. Its general characteristics include:

Manufacturer: IMO Industries, Garland, Texas, and various other vendors
Length: 15 in
Width: 6 in
Height: 6 in
Weight: 8 lb
Magnification: 6.5x
Range (vehicle-sized target), starlight: 1,000 yd
Range (vehicle-sized target), moonlight: 1,200 yd
Field of view: 9 degrees (circular)
Power source: 2.7-volt mercury battery

Flamethrower

A weapon that may be mounted on a tank or carried by an individual marine and that propels a burning stream of gelled gasoline. Marines made extensive use of flamethrowers during the Pacific Campaign in WORLD WAR II, in which Japanese troops were often hunkered down in extremely inaccessible positions, especially in caves on coral islands.

Joint Service Combat Shotgun

The USMC, like other services, plans to adopt a semiautomatic, repeating 12-gauge shotgun to replace the 12-gauge shotgun models in current use. The Joint Service Combat Shotgun is planned as a compact, lightweight, semiautomatic weapon configured with a standard magazine with a minimum capacity of six 2.75-inch cartridges. It will be capable of firing 12-gauge 3.0-inch magnum ammunition and will be interoperable with standard 2.75-inch ammunition without adjustment to the operating system. Construction will be of lightweight polymer materials and corrosion-resistant metal components. It will be equipped with such modular components as modular stocks in various configurations and modular barrels of various lengths. The new weapon is intended for use by USMC units in the execution of security and selected Special Operations missions.

General characteristics of the weapon include:

Length: 41.75 in or less
Weight: 6–8.5 lb
Bore diameter: 12 gauge
Maximum effective range: 130–165 ft with "00" buckshot load

Krag-Jorgenson Rifle

This .30-caliber rifle was adopted by the USA and USMC in 1894, modified from a Danish-made bolt-action design. The side-mounted magazine gate of this rifle held five cartridges packed with 40 grains of smokeless powder, which produced a muzzle velocity far superior to the black powder cartridges used in earlier rifles. The Krag-Jorgenson was replaced in 1903 by the Springfield 1903 model.

M-1 .30-caliber Carbine

This Winchester weapon was adopted early in World War II by all the services to replace both submachine guns and the .45-caliber automatic pistol. Although the USMC used the weapon, preference was given to the heavier M-1 Garand, which had heftier striking power. Nevertheless, the weapon was used by USMC forces through the KOREAN WAR and well into the 1950s.

M-2-HB Browning Machine Gun

This weapon was issued during World War II to the USMC and other services and was a heavy—.50-caliber—air-cooled machine gun weighing 125 pounds. It could be mounted in a four-gun configuration (the "quad 50"), which made it highly effective against nonarmored vehicles. Range was 1,000 yards. The weapon was defensive in nature, and its effect against attacking personnel was devastating.

M-9 Personal Defense Weapon

A Beretta 9-mm semiautomatic, double-action pistol that is used in the USMC and throughout the Department of Defense. The weapon was first fielded in 1985 and replaced the M-1911A1 .45-caliber pistol and the .38-caliber revolver formerly used by officers. However, the M-1911A1 is still used by USMC Maritime Special Purpose Forces (MSPF).

M-14 7.62-mm Rifle

The M-14 7.62-mm magazine-fed, gas-operated rifle is designed primarily for semiautomatic fire and was the standard USMC service rifle until it was replaced in the late 1960s by the 5.56-mm M-16A1 rifle, which, in turn, has been replaced by the M-16A2 rifle. Although the M-14 is no longer standard issue for the USMC, it is still used in the Competition in Arms program and for drill and ceremonial purposes.

General characteristics of the M-14 7.62-mm rifle include:

Length: 44.14 in
Length of barrel: 22 in
Weight, empty magazine: 8.7 lb
Weight, full magazine and sling: 11.0 lb
Bore diameter: 7.62 mm
Maximum effective range: 1,509.26 ft
Muzzle velocity: 2,800 ft/sec
Cyclic rate of fire: 750 rounds/min
Magazine capacity: 20 rounds

M-16A2 Rifle

The standard 5.56-mm semiautomatic combat rifle issued to marines and U.S. Army troops. Air cooled and gas operated, the M-16A2 is a low-impulse rifle weighing less than 9 pounds and carrying a 20- to 30-round magazine. The shooter can select three-burst or semiautomatic mode, firing at the rate of 90 rounds per minute in three-burst mode and 45 rounds per minute in semiautomatic mode. The standard M-16A2 load is a steel penetrator inside a lead and copper jacket, which pierces lightly armored vehicles and body armor. Muzzle velocity is 3,250 feet per second.

The M-16A2 represents a substantial improvement on accuracy over the M-16A1, thanks to redesigned rifling. The M-16A1 was never a favorite with the USMC.

M-40A1 Sniper Rifle

This modification of the Remington 700 bolt-action rifle is used by the USMC as its principal scout and sniper rifle. Weighing 14.5 pounds, the 7.62-mm rifle is equipped with a 10x sight and has an effective range of 3,250 feet. The integral magazine holds five rounds.

M-60 Machine Gun

Based on World War II German designs, the M-60 replaced the M-1919A4 Browning Machine Gun during the VIETNAM WAR. It was widely adopted by the army and Marine Corps and is gas operated, bipod equipped, and can fire 550 rounds per minute or can be used as a single-shot weapon.

M-82 Special Application Scope Rifle (SASR)

The SASR is a semiautomatic .50-caliber rifle used by marine (and army and navy) snipers. The weapon is manufactured by Barrett, is 5 feet long, and weighs almost 30 pounds. It delivers a muzzle velocity of 2,732 feet per second and has a great range, in excess of a mile. Two M-82 SASRs are assigned to USMC surveillance and target-acquisition (STA) platoons.

M-203 40-mm Grenade Launcher

The USMC employs the M-203 40-mm Grenade Launcher as an attachment to the M-16A2 Rifle to create a lightweight, compact, breech-loading, pump-action, single-shot launcher. Basic components of the launcher include a hand guard and sight assembly with a folding, adjustable, short-range blade sight assembly and an aluminum receiver assembly, which houses the barrel latch, barrel stop, and firing mechanism. The launcher also has a quadrant sight, which may be attached to the M-16A2 carrying handle. This sight is used to increase precision out to the maximum effective range of the weapon. The launcher fires a variety of low-velocity 40-mm ammunition and was designed as a replacement for the M-79 grenade launcher of the Vietnam War era. The USMC inventory holds 10,500 of the weapons as of 2004.

General characteristics of the M-203 40-mm Grenade Launcher include:

Weight, launcher: 3 lb (1.36 kgs)
Weight, M-16A2 rifle: 8.79 lb
Weight, total (including 30 rounds): 11.79 lb
Bore diameter: 40 mm
Maximum effective range, area target: 1,148.35 ft
Maximum effective range, point target: 492.15 ft
Maximum range: 1,312.4 ft
Minimum safe range, training: 426.53 ft
Minimum safe range, combat: 101.71 ft

M-240G Machine Gun

A gas-operated, air-cooled, belt-fed 7.62-mm machine gun with cyclical rate of fire of 600 rounds per minute and a sustained rate of 100 rounds per minute. The weapon is typically mounted on a LAV-25 vehicle.

M-249 SAW

"SAW" stands for Squad Automatic Weapon. The M-249 is a gas-operated, air-cooled weapon with a cyclical rate of fire of 750 rounds per minute and a sustained 85-round-per-minute rate. The weapon is highly portable at a little over 16 pounds and has an effective range of more than 3,000 feet. Nine SAWs are assigned to each USMC platoon.

M-1911A1 .45-caliber Pistol

The .45-caliber semiautomatic pistol M-1911A1 was the standard handgun of the USMC for many years. A magazine-fed semiautomatic weapon, it fires one round each time the trigger is squeezed once the hammer is cocked by prior action of the slide or thumb. The thumb safety may be activated only after the pistol is cocked, and the hammer remains in the fully cocked position once the safety is activated. This is the old "single-action only" design; modern pistols are "double action" designs, which allow the hammer to move forward to an uncocked position when the thumb safety is activated.

The longevity of the M-1911A1 was in large part due to its reliability and lethality. However, its single-action design proved a significant liability in that it required the user to be highly trained and experienced when carrying the pistol in the ready-to-fire mode. Because of the potential hazard, M-1911A1s were often ordered to be carried without a round in the chamber, which, of course, compromised their usefulness as a ready weapon. Moreover, even with this restriction, the pistol was involved in many unintentional discharges. By the 1980s, it was replaced by the modern M-9 Personal Defense Weapon; however, a modified version of the weapon, the MEU (SOC) Pistol, is still used as a backup weapon for USMC units armed with the MP-5N Heckler and Koch 9-mm Submachine Gun.

General characteristics of the venerable M-1911A1 .45-caliber Pistol include:

Length: 8.625 in
Length of barrel: 5.03 in
Weight, magazine empty: 2.5 lb
Weight, magazine loaded: 3.0 lb
Bore diameter: .45 cal
Maximum effective range: 82.02 ft
Muzzle velocity: 830 ft/sec
Magazine capacity: 7 rounds

M-1917A1 Browning Machine Gun

This heavy (93 pounds) .30-caliber water-cooled machine gun was introduced in WORLD WAR I and saw use throughout World War II and even in the Korean War. During World War I and at the beginning of World War II, it was fed by a 250-round fabric belt, which, later in World War II, was replaced by a disintegrating link belt. The weapon could fire 450 to 600 rounds per minute. Its weight ensured that the M-1917A1 would function in a defense rather than assault role.

M-1918 Browning Automatic Rifle (BAR)

The BAR was a relatively lightweight weapon (16 pounds), capable of firing in semiautomatic and automatic mode and firing a 30.06 cartridge at the (automatic) rate of 500 pounds per minute. It was used in World War I, World War II, and, modified as the M-1918A2, in the Korean War and Vietnam War. It was replaced by the M-60 Machine Gun and the M-249 SAW.

M-1919A4 Browning Machine Gun

This .30-caliber air-cooled machine gun was designed during World War I, but was not adopted by the USMC until after the war. Its great advantage was its light weight of 31 pounds, compared to 93 pounds for the M-1917A1 Browning Machine Gun. The M-1919A4 saw extensive service in World War II as a marine weapon and continued to be used throughout the Korean War until it was replaced by the M-60 Machine Gun.

M-1919A6 Browning Machine Gun

This was an improvement on the M-1919A4 Browning Machine Gun. Its redesigned mount and butt rest made it faster to set up. Moreover, unlike the A4, it required no tripod, but had a detachable shoulder stock and a self-contained folding bipod. More than 43,000 of these weapons were produced during World War II, and many A4 models were converted to A6s. The USMC used the weapon in the Korean War as well as in the early stages of the Vietnam War.

M-1921 and M-1928A1 Thompson Submachine Gun

This weapon was made famous—or infamous—by its widespread use among American gangsters during the late 1920s and 1930s. As a military weapon, it was invented by a retired USA colonel, John Thompson, and proved highly valuable in raider-type operations. The weapon fired .45-caliber ball ammunition from a 50-round drum or a 20-round magazine at the very high rate of 800 rounds per minute.

The weapon was not officially adopted by the USMC before World War II, but was nevertheless used in marine action in NICARAGUA. The M-1928 models were produced and purchased in quantity during World War II. Even after it was officially replaced by the M-1 Carbine during the war, USMC raider units continued to favor the Thompson. The weapon continued to see limited use by the USMC after World War II, both in the Korean War and in the Vietnam War.

M-1941 Johnson Light Machine Gun

The USMC adopted this weapon in World War II when it could not obtain sufficient numbers of the older and more desirable M-1918 Browning Automatic Rifle (BAR). At 12.3 pounds, the Johnson was lighter than the BAR, making it ideal for use by raiders and other forward troops. It could fire between 300 and 900 30.06 mm rounds per minute. The Johnson became popular with marines during the war, but it was not an adequate replacement for the BAR.

MEU (SOC) Pistol

This weapon is a modification of the M-1911A1 .45-caliber Pistol that was long-standard USMC issue before it was replaced by the M-9 Personal Defense Weapon. The MEU (SOC) Pistol is a "near match" or "combat accuratized" version of the M-1911A1 and is the designated backup weapon of USMC units armed with the MP-5N Heckler and Koch 9 mm Submachine Gun. These units chose the M-1911A1 because of its reliability and lethality. The MEU (SOC) modifications make the venerable design safer and generally more user friendly. These modifications include the incorporation of a commercial/competition-grade ambidextrous safety, a precision barrel, precise trigger, rubber-coated grips, rounded hammer spur, high-profile combat sights, and an extra-wide grip safety for increased comfort and controllability—aiding in a quick follow-up second shot. The standard-issue magazines are replaced with stainless-steel competition-grade magazines that include a rounded plastic follower and extended floor plate. The USMC maintains an inventory of 500 of the modified weapons.

Designed in 1986, the modifications that produced the MEU (SOC) Pistol are hand crafted by specially trained armorers at the USMC's Rifle Team Equipment (RTE) shop in Quantico, Virginia.

General characteristics of the MEU (SOC) Pistol include:

Length: 8.625 in
Length of barrel: 5.03 in
Weight, magazine empty: 2.5 lb
Weight, magazine loaded: 3.0 lb
Bore diameter: .45-caliber
Maximum effective range: 164 ft
Muzzle velocity: 830 ft/sec
Magazine capacity: 7 rounds

Mk-19 40-mm Machine Gun, MOD 3

The Mk-19 40-mm machine gun, MOD 3 is a fully automatic weapon, air-cooled, fed by disintegrating metallic link-belt ammunition, and blowback operated. With limited amounts of ammunition, the weapon is crew transportable over short distances.

The Mk-19 can fire a variety of 40-mm grenades, including the M-430 HEDP 40 mm grenade, which will pierce armor up to 2 inches thick and will produce fragments lethally effective against personnel within 16 feet of the point of impact and will wound personnel within 50 feet of the point of impact.

The machine gun is usually mounted on the Mk-64 Cradle Mount, MOD 5, or the M-3 Tripod Mount. It may also be mounted in the up-gunned weapons station of the LVTP-7A1.

Originally developed for the USN as a riverine patrol weapon in the Vietnam War, the weapon was subject to a product improvement program in the late 1970s, which produced the Mk-19 Mod 3 that was subsequently adopted by the USMC. General characteristics include:

Manufacturer: Saco Defense Industries
Length: 43.1 in
Weight, gun: 72.5 lb
Weight, cradle (Mk-64 Mod 5): 21.0 lb
Weight, tripod: 44.0 lb
Weight, total: 137.5 lb
Muzzle velocity: 790 ft/sec
Bore diameter: 40 mm
Maximum range: 7,200 ft
Maximum effective range: 5,250 ft
Rate of fire, cyclic: 325–375 rounds/min
Rate of fire, rapid: 60 rounds/min
Rate of fire, sustained: 40 rounds/min

MP-5N Heckler and Koch 9-mm Submachine Gun

The USMC employs the MP-5N Heckler and Koch 9-mm Submachine Gun as its main weapon in the close-quarters battle (CQB) environment. The weapon fires from a closed and locked bolt in either the automatic or semiautomatic modes. Recoil operated, the weapon incorporates a unique, delayed roller, locked bolt system, a retractable butt stock, a removable suppressor, and an illuminating flashlight that is integral to the forward handguard. The flashlight is operated by a pressure switch fitted to the pistol grip. The USMC inventory includes both suppressed and nonsuppressed versions of the

MP-5 weapon, which is the same basic weapon used by the FBI's Hostage Rescue Team and other counterterrorist organizations. Force Reconnaissance companies and Marine Security Force battalions are the principal USMC users of the weapon.

General characteristics of the MP-5N Heckler and Koch 9 mm Submachine Gun include:

Manufacturer: Heckler and Koch, Sterling, Virginia
Length, collapsed stock: 19.29 in
Length, extended stock: 25.98 in
Weight (with 30-round magazine): 7.44 lb
Bore diameter: 9 mm
Maximum effective range: 328.1 ft
Rate of fire: 800 rounds/min

Reising Gun

A submachine gun developed in 1940 on the eve of World War II by Eugen Reising, the gun was produced in a Model 50 and a Model 55. Model 50 had a wooden stock and was intended for standard infantry use; weighing just 6 pounds, it fired .45-caliber ammunition. It had a muzzle-mounted compensator to reduce climbing during fire. Model 55 was equipped with a folding metal stock, a shorter barrel, and lacked the compensator. This more compact, lighter weapon was intended for paratroop use.

The Reising Gun was, at best, an expedient used by the USMC early in the war, through 1942. The weapon tended to malfunction in humid conditions—precisely the conditions found in the Pacific, where it was most extensively used. It jammed frequently, and it had a dangerously faulty safety mechanism.

Revolver, .38-caliber

The USMC has used .38-caliber revolvers, manufactured by Colt and by Smith & Wesson, since World War II. During the 1970s, Ruger-made weapons entered USMC service; however, during the mid-1980s, the revolvers were largely replaced by the M-9 Personal Defense Weapon.

The .38-caliber revolver is a pistol with a rotating cylinder that presents six loaded chambers to the barrel for discharge in succession. The USMC has used several models with 2-inch and 4-inch barrels, manufactured variously by Colt, Ruger, and Smith & Wesson. Criminal Investigation Division and counterintelligence personnel still sometimes use the 2-inch barrel revolvers, while USMC aviators formerly used the 4-inch barrel weapons, which have been more common in the USMC.

All revolvers are cylinder-loaded, exposed-hammer, selective double-action hand weapons. The action of cocking the hammer causes the cylinder to rotate and align the next chamber with the barrel. At the full cocked position, the revolver is ready to fire in the single action mode by a relatively light squeeze on the trigger. If the hammer is not in the full cocked position, the revolver may still be fired, but in "double action," requiring a longer and heavier squeeze on the trigger.

General characteristics of the 4-inch-barrel weapon include:

Length: 9.25 in
Barrel length: 4 in
Weight: 1.9 lb
Bore diameter: .38-caliber
Maximum effective range: 82.02 ft
Rate of fire: 12–18 rounds/min

Rifle Grenade

A grenade designed to be fired from a rifle instead of thrown by hand. Rifle grenades may be fired using an M-203 Grenade Launcher, an attachment designed for the M-16A1 rifle; however, the standard weapon currently in use is the Mk-19-3 40-mm Automatic Grenade Launcher, a machine-gunlike weapon that fires 325 to 375 grenades per minute.

Shoulder-Launched Multipurpose Assault Weapon (SMAW)

The Shoulder-Launched Multipurpose Assault Weapon (SMAW) is primarily a portable antiarmor rocket launcher capable of using a dual-mode rocket to destroy bunkers and other fortifications during assault operations. With an HEAA rocket, the SMAW can be used against main battle tanks.

As its name suggests, the Shoulder-Launched Multipurpose Assault Weapon is man-portable. It is an 83 mm weapon system consisting of the Mk-153 Mod 0 launcher, the Mk-3 Mod 0-encased HEDP rocket, the Mk-6 Mod 0-encased HEAA rocket, and the Mk-217 Mod 0 spotting rifle cartridge. The launcher component consists of a fiberglass launch tube, a 9 mm spotting rifle, an electro-mechanical firing mechanism, open battle sights, and a mount for the Mk-42 Mod 0 optical sight and the AN/PVS-4 night sight.

For use against bunkers, masonry and concrete walls, and light armor, the High Explosive, Dual Purpose (HEDP) rocket is employed. The High Explosive Antiarmor (HEAA) rocket is used against modern tanks and is effective, provided that they do not have additional armor. The 9 mm spotting rounds are ballistically matched to the rockets and significantly increase the gunner's first-round hit probability.

The SMAW Mk-153 Mod 0 launcher is based on an Israeli design, the B-300, and consists of the launch tube, the spotting rifle, the firing mechanism, and mounting brackets. The launch tube is constructed of fiberglass/epoxy with a gel coat on the bore. The spotting rifle is a British design and is mounted on the right side of the launch tube. The firing mechanism mechanically fires the spotting rifle and uses a magneto to fire the rocket. The encased rockets are loaded at the rear of the launcher.

The complete SMAW system was initially fielded in 1984 and was unique to the USMC. The Mk-6 Mod 0 encased HEAA rocket is a relatively new addition to the system. During Operation Desert Storm (PERSIAN GULF WAR), the USMC provided 150 launchers and 5,000 rockets to the U.S. Army, which has adopted it in limited use.

General characteristics of the Shoulder-Launched Multipurpose Assault Weapon (SMAW) include:

Length, carrying: 29.9 in
Length, ready-to-fire: 54 in
Weight, carrying: 16.6 lb
Weight, ready-to-fire (with HEDP missile): 29.5 lb
Weight, ready-to-fire (with HEAA missile): 30.5 lb
Bore diameter: 83 mm
Maximum effective range, 1 × 2 m target: 820 ft
Maximum effective range, tank-sized target: 1,650 ft

12-gauge Shotgun

The 12-gauge shotgun is a manually operated (pump) repeating shotgun, with a seven-round tubular magazine, a modified choke barrel, and ghost ring sights. The USMC version is equipped with a bayonet attachment, sling swivels, and a standard-length military stock. Some models have folding stocks. USMC infantry units use the 12-gauge as a special-purpose individual weapon for such missions as guard duty, prisoner supervision, local security, riot control, and any other situation requiring the use of armed personnel with limited range and ammunition penetration.

The USMC has used shotguns since 1901 and currently has four different 12-gauge models in its inventory: the Remington 870, Winchester 1200, Mossberg 500, and Mossberg 590. Maximum effective range of all of these weapons is about 50 yards using a "00" buckshot load.

Wharton, Franklin (1767–1818) *Marine Corps commandant*

The third COMMANDANT OF THE MARINE CORPS, Wharton was born in Philadelphia and commissioned a USMC captain on August 3, 1798. He served during the U.S.-FRENCH QUASI-WAR aboard the frigate *United States* until 1801, then was assigned to command the Philadelphia garrison until March 7, 1804, when, as a lieutenant colonel, he was named commandant.

Wharton oversaw development of the MARINE BARRACKS at 8th and I Streets in Washington, D.C., and was in command of the Corps during the war with the BARBARY PIRATES and the WAR OF 1812. With 400 sailors, his 103 marines were the only U.S. military personnel to resist the British march to Washington after the invaders dispersed the U.S. militia at the Battle of Bladensburg, Maryland, on

August 24, 1814. Wharton, however, was court-martialed in 1817 for having failed to attempt a defense of the capital (he fled with President James Madison and others). The court-martial exonerated him, and Wharton continued to serve as commandant until his death.

wheeled vehicles

The following wheeled vehicles are either currently included in the marine inventory or are of historical importance in the service.

High-Mobility Multipurpose Wheeled Vehicle

The HMMWV—or Humvee—has generally replaced the Jeep as the USMC's principal light, four-wheel-drive tactical vehicle. Diesel powered, the HMMWV is used variously as a light personnel transport, an ambulance, a light cargo transport, and as a vehicle to tow light artillery and missile systems. The HMMWV is manufactured by Hummer, a General Motors company.

Infantry Fighting Vehicle

The IFV is a lightly armored combat vehicle for transporting marines and for conducting mounted warfare. The marine IFV is the LAV-25, an eight-wheeled Light Assault Vehicle, also used as a personnel carrier.

See also AMPHIBIOUS VEHICLES.

M-113 Armored Personnel Carrier

The "Battle Taxi" is a lightly armored vehicle designed to carry marines into combat. At 16 feet long and almost 9 feet wide, the M-113 carries a crew of two and 11 combat marines. Its six-cylinder turbocharged engine propels the 24,000-pound

A Humvee from the Combined Antiarmor Team of the 1st Battalion, 6th Marines   (U.S. Marine Corps)

vehicle to a top speed of 42 miles per hour on land and 3.6 miles per hour in water. Range is 300 miles. The vehicle's thin aluminum armor is supplemented by bolt-on exterior armor panels and interior Kevlar liners.

The M-113 is a venerable vehicle, having been introduced in 1964. The LAV-25 vehicle has replaced it in many combat roles, but it is still used in such roles as maintenance support, engineer squad transport, and as an armored ambulance. It is also suitable for use as a command vehicle.

KLR 250-D8 Marine Corps Motorcycle

The marines use motorcycles as an alternate means of transporting messages, documents, and light cargo, and also for conducting some reconnaissance. The KLR 250-D8 Marine Corps Motorcycle is a lightweight and rugged cross-country motorcycle modified from commercial production for military use. In addition to transporting messages, documents, and light cargo between units, the motorcycle is also used to transport forward observers, military police, and reconnaissance personnel. The motorcycle is equipped with a pair of detachable document carrying cases. The 1991 model KLR 250-D8 replaces the 1984 KLR 250 and is the second generation of marine motorcycles. Field commanders have learned to rely on it as a backup and alternate means of communication, and its commercial design ensures the ready availability of repair parts and ordinary commercial service facilities.

General characteristics of the KLR 250-D8 Marine Corps Motorcycle include:

Length: 7 ft
Weight: 258 lb
Estimated range: 210 mi (highway)

Mk-48 Power Unit and Mk-14 Container Transporter Rear Body Unit

The marines introduced this heavy tactical vehicle system during the mid-1980s. The key component of the system is the Logistics Vehicle System (LVS), a modular system that consists of an Mk-48 front power unit and interchangeable rear body units

(RBU). The front power unit and rear body units are joined by a hydraulically powered articulated joint, which assists in steering the vehicle and allows a significant degree of independent movement between the front and rear units for enhanced mobility. The articulated joint transfers automotive power to the rear body unit axles and also provides hydraulic power for any hydraulically operated equipment in the RBU.

Complete LVS units are 8 × 8 vehicles, four powered wheels in front and four in the rear, with two front steering axles. Each LVS has an off-road payload of 12.5 tons and an on-road payload of 22.5 tons.

The Mk-48 Front Power Unit incorporates an enclosed cab, a diesel engine, and an automatic transmission. By itself, it is a 4 × 4 vehicle, which provides all automotive and hydraulic power for the various LVS combinations.

The Mk-14 Container Transporter Rear Body Unit is a flatbed trailer designed for transporting bulk cargo as well as standardized cargo containers. It is equipped with ISO (International Standards Organization) lock points for securing 20-foot standard containers, as well as Marine Corps Field Logistics System (FLS) bulk liquid tanks and pump units (SIXCONS). The Mk-14 is also capable of transporting the entire standard Marine Corps Expeditionary Shelter System (MCESS).

The Mk-14 Container Transporter Rear Body Unit can be equipped with a tow bar adapter kit, which allows it to be tandem towed as an un-powered trailer behind another Mk-48/Mk-14 combination. However, the tandem tow is limited to the 12.5 ton off-road payload in all environments.

Mk-48 Power Unit and Mk-15, Recovery/Wrecker Rear Body Unit

For Logistics Vehicle System (LVS) background and a description of the Mk-48 Power Unit, see Mk-48 Power Unit and Mk-14 Container Transporter Rear Body Unit.

The Mk-15 Recovery/Wrecker Rear Body Unit is a component of the USMC's Logistics Vehicle System (LVS) and provides a lift and tow capability and an ability to recover disabled heavy vehicles.

Mk-48 Power Unit and Mk-16, Fifth-Wheel Semi-trailer Adapter Rear Body Unit

The Mk-16 Fifth-Wheel Semi-trailer Adapter Rear Body Unit is designed for use in the USMC's Logistics Vehicle System (LVS) to move semi-trailers with loads up to 70 tons.

Mk-48 Power Unit and Mk-18 Self-loading Container and Ribbon Bridge Transporter

The Mk-18 Self-loading Container and Ribbon Bridge Transporter is intended for use as a component of the USMC's Logistics Vehicle System (LVS). The USMC inventory includes 325 Mk-18 Self-loading Container and Ribbon Bridge Transporters. These units are capable of self-loading and off-loading fully loaded 20-foot standard containers as well as the ribbon bridge interior and ramp bays and the standard bridge boat.

In addition to the Mk-18, the USMC has developed 164 Mk-18A1 units, which feature an improved loading and off-loading mechanism.

Mk-155 Mine Clearance Launcher

The function of the USMC's Mk-155 Mine Clearance Launcher is to clear a lane through a minefield during breaching operations. The Mk-155 is part of the Mark 2 Mine Clearance System, which also includes one M58A3/A4 Linear Demolition Charge (LDC) and one Mk-22 Mod 3/4 Rocket. Mounted on an M353 Trailer Chassis, the Mk-155 is towed by an assault amphibious vehicle. The LDC is fired, clearing a lane 328 feet long by 52 feet wide. This is normally the initial minefield breaching asset employed; however, because the LDC is effective only against single impulse, non-blast-resistant, pressure fused mines, its use must be supplemented by a mechanical proofing device, which is used in the lane that has been breached explosively.

The Mk-155 is a hydraulic system, with all of the hydraulics self-contained. A hand pump is operated to store hydraulic pressure in an accumulator. A lanyard, running from the accumulator to inside the towing vehicle, is pulled, thereby raising the launch rail to firing position. A power cable is fed from the launcher to the towing vehicle, from which the launch equipment for the Mk-22 rocket is operated.

As of 2004, the USMC had 271 Mk-155 LMC kits, most of which were deployed with combat engineer battalions and engineer support battalions. The Mk-155 was developed during the 1960s and was used in the VIETNAM WAR.

General characteristics of the Mk-155 Mine Clearance Launcher include:

> **Host vehicle:** M353 General Purpose, 3.5-ton, 2-wheeled, Trailer Chassis
> **Weight (including trailer and launch rail):** 3,775 lb
> **Weight, fully loaded (including one Linear Demolition Charge and one rocket):** 6,405 lb
> **Shipping height:** 74 in

Wilson, Louis H., Jr. (1920–   ) *Marine Corps commandant*

The 26th COMMANDANT OF THE MARINE CORPS, Wilson was born in Brandon, Mississippi, and enlisted in the MARINE CORPS RESERVE in May 1941. He was tapped for active duty in June. After attending Officer Candidate School, he was commissioned a second lieutenant in November and assigned to Marine Corps Base San Diego with the 2nd Division. He was commissioned in the regular USMC in April 1942 and in February 1943 served at GUADALCANAL with the 9th Marines, 3rd Division.

Promoted to captain, Wilson landed on BOUGAINVILLE and GUAM, where he was wounded while resisting one of numerous banzai attacks on the 9th Marines. For his leadership during a 10-hour defense of his unit's position, Wilson received the Medal of Honor.

The wounded Wilson was evacuated to the United States, where he served in Washington for the rest of WORLD WAR II. After the war, he served as aide-de-camp to the commander of FLEET MARINE FORCE, Pacific, then returned to the United States in 1949 as officer in charge of the

New York USMC recruiting station. After serving at Marine Corps Base Quantico from 1951 to 1954, Wilson was assigned to the 1st Division in Korea and, the following year, was given command of a battalion of the 5th Marines. Back in the States in 1958, he commanded the Basic School at Quantico, then, in 1962, was assigned to the Plans and Programs section of HEADQUARTERS MARINE CORPS, Washington.

In the 1960s Wilson served a tour in Vietnam during the VIETNAM WAR and was promoted to major general. He served as commander of Fleet Marine Force, Pacific, before becoming commandant on July 1, 1975. He served in that post until July 1, 1979, a period of great pressure on the USMC in the aftermath of the Vietnam War.

women in the Marines   See U.S. MARINE CORPS WOMEN'S RESERVE.

woolly-pully   See PERSONAL AND MISCELLANEOUS EQUIPMENT.

World War I

For the nations of Europe, World War I was triggered by the assassination, on June 28, 1914, of the heir to the thrones of Austria-Hungary, Archduke Francis Ferdinand and his wife, the Grand Duchess Sophie, in Sarajevo, Bosnia-Herzegovina. By the end of July, a tangle of treaties and alliances, some of them secret, had doomed virtually all of Europe to a war of unparalleled devastation. President Woodrow Wilson navigated a course of strict neutrality for the United States, but the actions of Germany made this increasingly difficult. That nation's policy of unrestricted submarine warfare resulted in the sinking of the British liner *Lusitania* on May 7, 1915, with the loss of American lives. Although Wilson negotiated the suspension of unrestricted submarine warfare, other vessels were subsequently lost, and, on January 31, 1917, Germany resumed unrestricted submarine war-

fare. On February 3, 1917, the United States severed diplomatic relations with Germany. Then, on March 1, in this climate of crisis, the American government published the infamous Zimmerman Telegram, a German proposal of an alliance with Mexico against the United States. On April 6, the Congress voted a declaration of war against Germany.

The United States entered the war with a military that was minuscule by comparison with the massive armies of the European belligerents. Nevertheless, the National Defense Act of 1916 authorized the expansion of the USMC from 10,000 to 15,500 men, and by May 1917, voluntary enlistment raised this number to 31,000. (The strength of the U.S. Army was raised far more precipitously by means of conscription.) Military planners had never given much consideration to deploying U.S. land forces to a European war. It was generally assumed that the USMC would serve, as usual, aboard ships and in defense of bases at home, with occasional small-force forays abroad. But USMC commanders instantly lobbied for a role in the American Expeditionary Force (AEF), and in June 1917 the 5th Regiment embarked for France, where it was assigned to guard duty at Saint-Nazaire, an Atlantic port city. Early in 1918, a new regiment, the 6th, was formed, along with a machine gun battalion. Together, these units constituted the 4th Brigade, which joined with the U.S. Army's 3rd Brigade to make up the 2nd Division. The first major action the 2nd Division—and the marines—saw was at BELLEAU WOOD during June 4–July 10, 1918. On June 6, with the 4th Brigade in the lead, the 2nd Division attacked German positions, beginning a brutal 20-day battle for the sector. The 4th Brigade suffered 55 percent casualties, the highest casualty rate any U.S. brigade would incur during the war. However, the Germans were repulsed, and their last-ditch drive into Paris was halted. The performance of the USMC was celebrated by the French, who renamed Belleau Wood "Bois de la Brigade de Marine." And the Germans paid perhaps an even higher compliment, cursing the marines as "Devil Dogs."

Marines in France, on their way to the front *(Arttoday)*

Driven by the conviction that American numbers would soon increase along the front, Erich Ludendorff, the principal German commander, swallowed the defeat and mounted yet another offensive on July 15, hoping to score a victory before additional U.S. forces were in place. He hurled at the Allies no fewer than 52 divisions. The U.S. 2nd Division was moved up to the Forêt de Retz, where it coordinated a counterattack with the French XX Corps near Soissons. On July 18, the marines attacked, overrunning the German front-line positions before being withdrawn to rest at Nancy.

At this point, Brigadier General JOHN LEJEUNE assumed command of the 2nd Division, and, on September 12, USMC forces coordinated with the army's 3rd Brigade in an assault on the Saint-Mihiel salient, long a key enemy incursion into the Allies' front. Defeat at Saint-Mihiel spelled the end of the final Ludendorff offensive, and the Allies

began a major advance on all fronts. The 2nd Division was attached to the French Fourth Army, with which it coordinated action in the Meuse-Argonne offensive. When the French advance was arrested at the end of September in the Champagne sector, the 2nd Division was assigned to take the key German strong point at Blanc Mont, a position the enemy had held since 1914.

On October 2, the USMC brigade attacked Blanc Mont head-on, while the army's 3rd Infantry hit the right flank and the French attacked another position, the so-called Essen Hook. The 6th Marines secured Blanc Mont, but the French drive stalled, and the 5th Marines simply passed through the French lines to achieve what the French could not. After driving the Germans from the Essen Hook, the marines pressed on with the attack, repulsed German counterattacks, and secured Saint-Etienne on October 6. After this action, 2nd Division was reassigned to the American V Corps, and France awarded the two USMC regiments the Croix de Guerre streamer.

As reassigned, 2nd Division was deployed along a narrow front in the center of the First U.S. Army line. The division advanced on November 1 and broke through the German defenses, forcing the Germans to withdraw across the Meuse. Stubbornly, however, the Germans continued to hold in the Argonne, and on November 10, the 5th Marines crossed the Meuse and attacked here. A battle was in progress when the Armistice was announced at 11 A.M. on November 11, 1918.

More than 32,000 marines served in France. Of this number, 2,459 were killed in action and 8,900 wounded. USMC performance was uniformly outstanding. Marines received 12 Medals of Honor, 34 Distinguished Service Medals, and 393 Navy Crosses. The brigade remained in Europe as part of the army of occupation until the fall of 1919.

World War II

World War II began in Europe when Germany invaded Poland on September 1, 1939. Within a year, Britain was the last remaining, major Western European democracy, fighting a desperate battle for survival. Although President Franklin D. Roosevelt clearly sided with Britain in the West and, after it was invaded by Hitler, the Soviet Union in the East, the United States ostensibly maintained a state of "armed neutrality," although it supplied Britain with arms. It was not until Germany's Pacific ally, Japan, attacked Pearl Harbor on December 7, 1941, that the United States entered the war as a combatant. For the United States, it would be chiefly a two-theater war, fought in Europe (after the Allied reconquest of North Africa) and the Pacific. For the USMC, it was overwhelmingly a one-theater war: Marines fought almost exclusively in the Pacific.

For the first six months of the Pacific war, the Japanese made stunning advances, taking Malaya, Singapore, Burma, the East Indies, and the Philippines. From the beginning, USMC garrisons confronted the onslaught. The 4th Marines surrendered with U.S. Army and Filipino forces at Corregidor, Philippines, in May 1942. A marine garrison, overwhelmed, surrendered at GUAM and, after a remarkable defense, surrendered at WAKE ISLAND as well. However, the naval battles of the Coral Sea (May 1942) and Midway (June 1942) began to turn the tide of the Pacific War.

The Midway engagement was critical. The island served the United States as a forward air base. If the Japanese took it, the Americans would relinquish a major staging area for attacks on Hawaii and the West Coast. While a small USMC defense battalion held the island—suffering the loss of most of its obsolescent fighters—the U.S. Navy, at great cost, won the naval battle, sinking four Japanese aircraft carriers and destroying many Japanese aircraft. The Imperial Navy never recovered from these losses and, from Midway on, was unable to resume the offensive in the Pacific.

After Midway, it was the Americans' turn to seize the initiative. A strategy of "island hopping" was formulated, the object being to attack and occupy key Japanese-held islands, while hopping over others, which would, in effect, be cut off by the conquest of the targeted islands. In this way, relatively rapid progress could be made in the Pacific. The marines played the lead role in the extensive amphibious island hopping campaign, almost always making the initial landings and, in many cases, taking sole responsibility for the conquest of a particular island.

GUADALCANAL was the first objective. It was the site of a Japanese base and airfield that threatened the shipping lanes to Australia and New Zealand. In August 1942, the 1st Marine Division was landed and managed to hold off a sustained Japanese counterattack through December. Finally reinforced by the 2nd Division and U.S. Army units, the island was taken on February 8, 1943. Along with Midway, victory at Guadalcanal definitively changed the course of the war.

Beginning in mid-1943, the Allies advanced up the north coast of New Guinea, a strategy that culminated in the invasion of the Philippines late in 1944. In this southwestern Pacific campaign, the

1st Division coordinated with army forces. The marines played a more important role in the South Pacific, invading and securing the central and northern Solomon Islands. In November 1943, the 3rd Division invaded BOUGAINVILLE, which aided in neutralizing the major Japanese air and supply base at Rabaul. In the Central Pacific, the 2nd Division coordinated with the army in taking the TARAWA atoll in November 1943, after which the V Amphibious Corps, composed of the USMC 4th Division and the USA 7th Division, took the islands of ROI-NAMUR and KWAJALEIN in the Marshall chain during January 1944. Next to fall were the islands of Engebi and Parry, to a regiment of the 4th Division early in 1944.

Marines were next landed in the Marianas. The most important of these islands was SAIPAN, just 1,500 miles from Tokyo. Secure this, and the Americans would have a base from which B-29 bombing operations could be launched against the Japanese homeland on a continuous basis. The 2nd and 4th Divisions were landed on Saipan on June 15, 1944, and, supported by the army's 27th Division, advanced across the island in an extremely hard-fought and costly campaign. By July 9, Japanese forces were confined to the northern corner of Saipan. While virtually all 30,000 men of the Japanese garrison had been killed, USMC casualties, killed and wounded, amounted to a staggering 13,000.

After Saipan had been secured, the 2nd and 4th Divisions invaded TINIAN, taking it within two weeks, thereby securing another island from which B-29s could bomb Japan, and from which two aircraft in particular, *Enola Gay* and *Bock's Car*, would drop the atomic bombs that ended the Pacific war.

The campaign to retake Guam, lost in the first great Japanese onslaught of the war, commenced on July 21, 1944, as the 3rd Division and 1st Brigade, supported by the army's 77th Division, landed on the eastern shore of the island. Guam was retaken by August 10.

If American planners had been eager to retake Guam, they were even more committed to the reconquest of the Philippines. Army forces landed on Leyte in October 1944, provoking desperate action from the Japanese fleet, including the widespread deployment of kamikaze suicide attacks. To protect the eastern flank of Leyte operations, USMC ground and air forces attacked the Palau group of islands. The 1st Division landed on PELELIU on September 15 and encountered resistance extraordinary even for the Japanese. The division suffered nearly 50 percent casualties. The island did not fall until November 27.

Early in 1945, the Allied offensive in the southwest Pacific converged with that in the Central Pacific, as the Philippines became the major Pacific campaign focus. Here would be established the Allied bases from which the final invasion of Japan itself would be launched. However, an important tactical objective was to provide emergency landing bases for B-29s damaged in raids over Japan. Moreover, establishing air bases close to Japan would enable relatively short-range fighters to accompany the B-29s all the way into Japan. Thus IWO JIMA, a minuscule island strategically located, was targeted for the next USMC operation. The Japanese garrison, more than 23,000 strong, was housed in virtually impregnable caves and blockhouses. Taking Iwo Jima would prove the costliest USMC action of the war. The V Amphibious Corps, composed of the 4th and 5th Divisions, landed on February 19, 1945, and took the high ground, Mt. Suribachi, on February 23 (see IWO JIMA MEMORIAL). The fighting, however, was hardly over, and the island was not declared secure until March 26. USMC casualties topped 26,000.

In addition to major invasion bases in the Philippines, Allied commanders chose OKINAWA, a mere 850 miles from Tokyo, as the necessary forward base of operations. Some 100,000 Japanese troops garrisoned the island. Although U.S. Army forces were given primary responsibility for the campaign to take Okinawa, three USMC divisions participated as well—81,000 of the 182,000-man force that executed the campaign. Landings began on April 1, 1945, but the principal Japanese resistance was not encountered until USA and USMC forces had moved well inland. On June 18, when General Simon Buckner, commander of Tenth Army, was killed, overall command was temporarily assumed by Lieutenant General ROY GEIGER (USMC), who became the only marine ever to command an army. The island was secured by June 21.

Now, along with USA and USN forces, the USMC girded for the invasion of Japan itself, which, they knew, would be the costliest action of the entire war. But the invasion proved unneces-

sary. Atomic attacks were launched against Hiroshima and Nagasaki on August 6 and 9, 1945, and, on August 10, Emperor Hirohito announced his acceptance of the Allies' Potsdam Declaration, a call for unconditional surrender. The surrender was formalized on September 2, 1945, in a ceremony on board the battleship *Missouri* in Tokyo Bay. USMC World War II casualties were 86,940 killed and wounded.

Z

Zeilin, Jacob (1806–1880) *Marine Corps commandant*

The sixth COMMANDANT OF THE MARINE CORPS, Zeilin was born in Philadelphia and commissioned a second lieutenant in the USMC on October 1, 1831. He served at sea until the U.S.-MEXICAN WAR, when he commanded a detachment that captured San Pedro, California, then served with the legendary Kit Carson as part of a reinforcement column for Stephen Kearny at San Bernardino in December 1846. Zeilin, promoted to captain, led a USMC landing at Mazatlán, Mexico, on November 10, 1847, and served there as military governor until June 1848.

In 1853, Major Zeilin commanded the 200-man USMC contingent attached to Commodore Matthew Perry's momentous diplomatic mission to Japan and China, and at the outbreak of the Civil War Zeilin commanded a company at the First Battle of Bull Run. He was wounded in the engagement and did not return to active service until August 1863, when he led 300 marines in reinforcing army and USMC forces attempting to take Charleston, South Carolina. He was appointed commandant on June 9, 1864, and promoted to colonel. He served in this post for a dozen years.

U.S. Marine Corps Abbreviations and Acronyms

★

AAV   Assault Amphibious Vehicle

APC   Armored Personnel Carrier

BAR   Browning Automatic Rifle

COMMARFOREUR   Commander, Marine Forces Europe

CP   Command Post

DMZ   Demilitarized Zone

FMF   Fleet Marine Force

HMX-1   Marine Helicopter Squadron One

KIA   Killed in Action

LCP   Landing Craft, Personnel

LCT   Landing Craft, Tank

LCVP   Landing Craft, Vehicle Personnel

LST   Landing Ship, Tank

LVT   Landing Vehicle, Tracked

LVTP   Landing Vehicle, Tracked Personnel

MACV   Marine Amphibious Corps Vietnam

MAF   Marine Amphibious Force

MAG   Marine Air Group

MAGTF   Marine Air-Ground Task Force

MarDiv   Marine Division

MARFORLANT   Marine Forces Atlantic

MARFORPAC   Marine Forces Pacific

MARFORSOUTH   Marine Forces South

MARFORUNITAS   Marine Forces Unitas. Cooperative program with several South American armed forces.

MARINE (as acronym)   "My Ass Rides In Navy Equipment." Denotes the USMC's position within the Department of the Navy.

MAWTS-1   Marine Aviation Weapons and Tactics Squadron One

MBT   Main Battle Tank

MCRD   Marine Corps Recruit Depot

MEB   Marine Expeditionary Brigade

MEF   Marine Expeditionary Force

MEU   Marine Expeditionary Unit

MFR   Marine Forces Reserve

MIA   Missing in Action

MPF   Marine Prepositioning Force

MPS   Maritime Prepositioning Squadron

RAP   Rocket-Assisted Projectile

RCT   Regimental Combat Team

SOP   Standing Operating Procedure

SPF   Special Purpose Force

SWTU   Special Weapons Training Unit

USMARFORK   U.S. Marine Forces Korea

USMCR   United States Marine Corps Reserve

VMA   USMC unit designation for an attack squadron. A VMA flies the AV-8B Harrier "jump jet," of which the typical VMA squadron carries 20.

See also VMA(AW); VMFA; VMFA (AW).

VMA (AW) USMC unit designation for an Attack (All Weather) squadron. These units flew the A-6E Intruder. With the phaseout of this aircraft and the transition to the F/A-18D Hornet, the units are being redesignated VMFA(AW).

VMAQ USMC unit designation for an Electronic Warfare Squadron. These squadrons fly the EA-6B Prowler. Each VMAQ squadron flies five Prowlers.

VMFA USMC unit designation for Fighter Attack Squadron. Currently, these squadrons fly the F/A-18 Hornet strike fighter. Each VMFA flies 12 F/A-18s. See also VMFA (AW).

VMFA (AW) USMC unit designation for a Fighter Attack (All Weather) Squadron. These squadrons fly the F/A-18D Hornet in a reconnaissance role.

VMGR USMC unit designation for a Refueler-Transport Squadron. These squadrons fly the KC-130/F/R/Hercules tanker. One VMGR squadron is tasked to support the U.S. Navy's famed Blue Angels Flight Demonstration Squadron, which tours widely.

VMO USMC unit designation for an Observation Squadron. These squadrons formerly flew the OV-10A/D Bronco, an STOL aircraft used for counterinsurgency, reconnaissance, and escort until it was removed from operational service in 1994. The last active VMO was disestablished on July 31, 1993.

V/STOL (Vertical/Short Takeoff and Landing) Aircraft capable of vertical takeoff and landing (without requiring runway movement) and of short takeoff and landing (requiring very limited runway movement). The most common USMC V/STOL examples are the AV-8 Harrier "jump jet" and the V-22 Osprey. See also VTOL.

VTOL (Vertical Takeoff and Landing) Designation applied to aircraft capable of vertical takeoff and landing, without requiring movement on a runway. The most common USMC VTOL aircraft is the helicopter; however, the AV-8 Harrier "jump jet" and the V-22 Osprey are also VTOL-capable aircraft, which may also be classified as V/STOL (Vertical/Short Takeoff and Landing) aircraft.

WIA Wounded in Action

United States Navy

ENTRIES A–Z

A

Acme **Class (MSO 508)** See MINESWEEPERS.

Acoustic Research Ship (T-AG) See RE-
SEARCH SHIPS.

admiral See RANKS AND GRADES.

**Advanced Auxiliary Dry Cargo Ships
(T-AKE)** See CARGO, FUEL, AND REPLENISHMENT
SHIPS.

**Advanced Medium-Range Air-to-Air
Missile (AMRAAM)** See MISSILES.

Aegis Weapons System See MISSILES.

Afloat Prepositioning See COMBAT PREPOSI-
TIONING SHIPS; LOGISTICS PREPOSITIONING SHIPS;
MARITIME PREPOSITIONING SHIPS; PREPOSITIONING
PROGRAM.

Afloat Training Group, Atlantic
Afloat Training Group, Atlantic, is made up of
three regional commands—in Norfolk, Virginia;

Mayport, Florida; and Ingleside, Texas—and provides afloat training to USN and USCG sailors,
with emphasis on training ships' training teams
and watch teams to improve combat readiness.
ATG also conducts shakedown training for newly
commissioned ships and for post-overhaul AIR-
CRAFT CARRIERS. In addition to training designated
USCG units, ATG trains some foreign navy units.

Afloat Training Group, Pacific
ATG Pacific includes Afloat Training Group, Middle Pacific (Pearl Harbor, Hawaii); Afloat Training
Group, Western Pacific (Yokosuka, Japan); and
Afloat Training Group, Pacific Detachment (Everett, Washington). It provides unit-level training
aboard ship with the primary goal of training the
ship's crew to train themselves. ATG Pacific conducts the following training assessments and qualifications: Logistic Management Assessment (LMA),
Cruise Missile Tactical Qualification (CMTQ),
Explosive Handling Personnel Qualification and
Certification Program (EHOP/CP), Dental Readiness Assessment (DRA), Medical Readiness Assessment (MRA), and Aviation Readiness Evaluation
(ARE).

African Americans in the U.S. Navy
A small number of African-American sailors
served in the Continental navy during the AMERI-

CAN REVOLUTION and, beginning in 1798, when the USN was formally created, blacks were accepted for service. It is believed that, during the WAR OF 1812, some 16 percent of all enlisted sailors were African Americans. A significant proportion of these were fugitive slaves who hoped to obtain their freedom by service. No records exist as to the numbers who were actually freed.

With the outbreak of the CIVIL WAR, the Union army at first excluded blacks, and their eventual, hard-won acceptance into segregated service was accomplished by free black activists (such as Frederick Douglass) and white abolitionists and reformers. The USN, which had never entirely excluded blacks, was, from the beginning of the war, far more open to their enlistment. By the end of the Civil War, African Americans had served on virtually every one of the Union's nearly 700 warships. Although there were no black navy officers during the war, and most of the black sailors were assigned to menial and labor duties, six African-American sailors were awarded the Medal of Honor for gallantry in combat.

Among the many changes brought by the Civil War was the beginning of the transformation of the U.S. Navy from wood and sail to iron and steam. Without sails to haul and set, the demand for "hands" aboard each vessel diminished, and the recruitment of African Americans sharply decreased. Those blacks who did join the USN were principally assigned to service positions, typically as "mess boys," stewards, and orderlies serving white officers. Segregation was enforced aboard ship in eating and sleeping areas. By the beginning of the 20th century, after the United States had gained control of the Philippines, black mess, steward, and orderly personnel were increasingly replaced by Filipinos, so that, by America's entry into WORLD WAR I in 1917, Filipinos outnumbered African Americans in the navy.

Beginning about 1932, enlistment of Filipino volunteers declined and African-American enlistment rose; however, black personnel were still confined to mess and steward positions, and segregation was enforced on board ships as well as in shore accommodations. In 1940, Walter White

of the National Association for the Advancement of Colored People (NAACP), together with black labor leader A. Phillip Randolph and activist T. Arnold Hill, wrote a letter to President Franklin D. Roosevelt protesting the strictures on black employment in the USN. In response, the president approved a plan in support of "fair treatment," but the USN failed to implement it, arguing that morale would suffer if blacks were assigned to nonservice positions. It was not until WORLD WAR II was fully under way that the NAACP again appealed to the administration, this time to Secretary of the Navy FRANK KNOX, to accept African Americans in nonservice USN positions. When Knox declined to act, the NAACP again appealed directly to the president, who, in June 1942, personally prevailed on USN officials to adopt an expanded assignment policy. The new guidelines admitted African-American sailors to service in construction battalions, supply depots, air stations, shore stations, section bases, and yard craft. Most of these new positions were labor assignments rather than combat postings.

In December 1942, President Roosevelt issued an executive order calling for African Americans to make up 10 percent of all personnel drafted for the services. This created a dramatic increase in USN enlistment of blacks, so that, by July 1943, 12,000 blacks were being inducted monthly. As of December 1943, 101,573 African Americans had enlisted in the USN. Of this number, 37,981 (37 percent) served in the Stewards Branch. The others served as boatswains, carpenters, painters, metalsmiths, hospital apprentices, firemen, aviation maintenance, and in SHORE PATROL (police security) positions. Again, opportunities for direct combat service were severely limited. In many cases, even those who had trained for specialized duty and skilled positions were actually assigned to labor details and service positions. Relatively few were assigned any sea duty.

At last, late in 1943, largely in a move to improve morale among African-American sailors, the navy decided to commission a small number of black officers. The men selected were divided into line and staff officers. In January 1944, the line officers began segregated 10-week training at Naval Training Center Great Lakes. This program produced 12 commissioned officers and one warrant officer, the first African-American officers in USN history, christened the "Golden Thirteen." They were assigned to recruit training programs and small patrol craft and USN tugs.

Those selected for commissioning as staff officers received their training in the summer of 1944 and graduated as ensigns or lieutenants junior grade. Two of the first group of staff graduates were assigned to the Chaplain Corps, two to the Dental Corps, two to the Civil Engineer Corps, three to the Medical Corps, and three to the Supply Corps. During the entire span of World War II, a mere 58 of 160,000 African-American sailors were commissioned as officers. By the end of the war, only a single officer was promoted to lieutenant.

Among enlisted personnel during the war, reform began during 1944. After Secretary Knox died in April of that year, JAMES FORRESTAL was named secretary of the navy. A political liberal and a civil rights activist, Forrestal was persuaded that racial integration of the USN was not only the right thing to do, it was also necessary to alleviate growing racial tensions within the service. He launched a trial program in which black personnel were assigned to general sea duty positions. To discourage segregation aboard ship, the African-American sailors were placed exclusively on large auxiliary vessels (such as cargo craft and tankers) and were limited to constituting no more than 10 percent of the crew of any one ship. Twenty-five ships were thus integrated, and none reported significant race-relation problems. The success of the pilot program prompted Forrestal to assign African-American general service personnel to all auxiliary ships of the fleet. Even more significantly, the special training program for African-American recruits was terminated, and they were now assigned to the same training centers as whites.

Following World War II, in 1948, President Harry S. Truman issued Executive Order 9981 ordering an end to racial discrimination and segregation in all the armed services. It took the personnel demands of the KOREAN WAR beginning in 1950 to motivate implementation of the order in a significant way. During that conflict, in all the services, blacks and whites lived and fought in fully integrated units. This notwithstanding, the USN officer corps remained overwhelmingly white. In 1952, 1 percent of navy officers were African American. (This was also true of the air force and Marine Corps; the U.S. Army officer corps was 3 percent black at this time.) Among the Korean War–era black officers was Ensign Wesley A. Brown, the first black graduate of the UNITED STATES NAVAL ACADEMY. Brown also became the first African-American naval aviator; he was killed in action during the war.

During the 1960s, with the rise of the civil rights movement, the USN actively encouraged African-American recruitment and the commissioning of black officers. In 1971, Samuel L. Gravely, Jr., was promoted to rear admiral, the first black man to hold flag rank. (He retired in 1980 as vice admiral.) As of 1983, after a full decade of operating as an "all volunteer force" (the military draft ended in 1973), the USN had a force that was 12 percent African American, compared with 14 percent for the USAF, 22 percent for the USMC, and 33 percent for the USA. However, the USN black officer corps was still very small, 3 percent, compared with 5 percent in the USAF, 4 percent in the USMC, and nearly 10 percent in the USA. Significantly, black women made up a sizable proportion of African Americans in the USN by 1983: 18 percent of black enlisted personnel and 5 percent of the black officer corps.

As of February 1, 2001, there were eight African-American male admirals and one woman admiral, and as of December 31, 2000, there were 115 male captains and 22 female captains. Two hundred sixty-eight black men had achieved the highest USN noncommissioned rank of master chief petty officer by the end of 2000, as had 15 black women.

African Slave Trade Patrol

After 1820, U.S. Navy vessels were dispatched to an area off the west coast of Africa to participate in the suppression of the African slave trade. Although the United States pledged to maintain 80 guns in the patrol area, the actual presence was rarely this great. Moreover, in 1823, some ships had to be redeployed to suppress West Indian pirates.

The USN was not highly successful in the suppression of the slave trade. Not only was its presence slight, but also stationing the vessels at the Cape Verde Islands or at Madeira put them too far from the patrol area to be truly effective. Between 1845 and 1850, only 10 slavers were interdicted and captured.

Aggressive Class (MSO 422)   See MINE-SWEEPERS.

aircraft carriers (CV, CVN)

In today's U.S. Navy, aircraft carriers provide a credible, sustainable, independent forward presence and conventional deterrence. During times of crisis, they operate as the central element of joint and allied maritime expeditionary forces. In war, the aircraft carrier operates and supports aircraft attacks, protects friendly forces, and engages in sustained independent operations.

Today's aircraft carriers are the largest warships afloat and are nothing less than seagoing military airbases. The USN deploys the vessels worldwide, and they are typically the first responders in crisis situations.

At present, the USN CV (non-nuclear-powered) and CVN (nuclear-powered) fleet consists of:

USS *Enterprise*
USS *John F. Kennedy*
Kitty Hawk–class carriers (two operational)
Nimitz-class carriers (nine operational and one under construction)

USS *Enterprise* (CVN 65)

Deployed on November 25, 1961, USS *Enterprise* (CVN 65) was the USN's first nuclear-powered aircraft carrier. Still operational, *Enterprise* is the only ship of its class. Its general characteristics include:

Builders: Newport News Shipbuilding Co., Newport News, Virginia
Power plant: eight nuclear reactors, four shafts
Length, overall: 1,101 ft 2 in
Flight deck width: 252 ft
Beam: 133 ft
Displacement: 89,600 tons full load
Speed: 30+ knots
Aircraft: 85
Crew: ship's company, 3,350; air wing, 2,480
Armament: two Sea Sparrow missile launchers, three Phalanx 20-mm CIWS mounts

John F. Kennedy (CV 67)

Christened in May 1967 by Caroline Kennedy, daughter of the slain president for whom the vessel was named, *John F. Kennedy* (CV 67) is the last conventionally powered super carrier built for the USN. Designed as an attack aircraft carrier, the *John F. Kennedy* actually performs a broader mission, which includes supporting antisubmarine warfare aircraft in addition to fighter and strike aircraft.

In September 1995, the *John F. Kennedy* became the first carrier assigned to the NAVAL RESERVE. The ship is homeported at Naval Station Mayport, Florida, and is used primarily to provide surge

USS *Constellation* (CV 64) returns to its home port, Naval Station San Diego, after operating in the Persian Gulf, 2002–03. *(U.S. Navy)*

capability during contingency operations and to support USN training activities. As a Naval Reserve vessel, the *John F. Kennedy* is maintained at all times in a mission-ready status. She fought in the PERSIAN GULF WAR, launching 114 strikes and 2,895 sorties, which delivered more than 3.5 million pounds of ordnance.

The *John F. Kennedy* is the only ship of its class. Its general specifications include:

Power plant: Eight boilers, four shafts, 280,000 total shaft horsepower

Length: 1,052 ft

Flight deck width: 252 ft

Beam: 130 ft

Displacement: 82,000 tons full load

Speed: 30+ knots

Aircraft: approximately 85

Crew: ship's company, 3,117; air wing, 2,480

Armament: Sea Sparrow missiles; three Phalanx CIWS 20-mm mounts

Combat systems: SPS-43; SPS-48C; three Mk-91 Fire Control; SLQ-29 EW; WLR-1 ESM; and WLR-11 ESM

Kitty Hawk Class (CV 63)

USS *Kitty Hawk* and the two other ships of its class, *Constellation* and *America,* are conventionally powered, post–WORLD WAR II USN aircraft carriers. *Kitty Hawk,* the lead ship of the class, carries the F-14 Tomcat Fighter, F/A-18 Hornet Strike Fighter, F/A-18 Super Hornet, E-2C Hawkeye Early Warning and Control Aircraft, EA-6B Prowler Electronic Warfare Aircraft, S-3B Viking, and SH-60 Sea Hawk Helicopter. These enable the ship to bring a multidimensional response to air, surface, and subsurface threats.

Commissioned on September 29, 1961, *Kitty Hawk* has undergone two major overhauls at the Bremerton, Washington, Naval Shipyard during 1977 and 1982, as well as extensive modification in the Service Life Extension Program (SLEP) in the Philadelphia Naval Shipyard from 1987 through 1991. This added 20 years to the planned 30-year life of the ship, transforming it into a fully modern

An EA-6B Prowler prepares to take off from the deck of the USS *Nimitz* in the Arabian Gulf. *(U.S. Navy)*

super carrier. Another major overhaul took place in 1998. *Kitty Hawk* (CV 63) is now forward deployed at Yokosuka, Japan.

The second carrier of the *Kitty Hawk* class is USS *Constellation,* commissioned in 1961. The ship has seen service in the VIETNAM WAR and in the Indian Ocean. It was massively overhauled in the Service Life Extension Program (SLEP), completed at the Philadelphia Naval Shipyard in March 1993, which installed, among many other systems, an advanced Combat Systems Suite, including SPS-48E three-dimensional fire control, TAS missile targeting, and SPS-49 long-range air search radar systems. Operating together, these allow the vessel's tactical action officer to gather and assess all hostile contacts. The systems are linked to worldwide satellite communications. Other advanced systems include the Aircraft Carrier Data system, Super High Frequency communications, Automatic Identification and Tracking, Joint Tactical Identification, and Positive Identification, Friend or Foe. *Constellation* was decommissioned in 2003.

The last ship of the *Kitty Hawk* class is USS *America* (CV-66), a modified variant of the *Constellation.* Launched in 1965, it was decommissioned on August 9, 1996, after a short active career. As of 2005, the vessel is in inactive reserve at the Naval Inactive Ship Maintenance Facility (NISMF), Philadelphia. Its last deployment was in 1995–96, launching combat missions in the skies of Bosnia and Herzegovina. During 1990–91, *America* participated in Operation Desert Storm (Persian Gulf War) and was the only aircraft carrier to launch strikes against Iraqi targets from both sides of the Arabian Peninsula—the Red Sea as well as the Persian Gulf.

General specifications of the *Kitty Hawk* class include:

Power plant: eight boilers, four geared steam turbines, four shafts, 280,000 shaft horsepower
Length: 1,062.5 ft
Flight deck width: 252 ft
Beam: 130 ft
Displacement: 80,800 tons full load
Speed: 30+ knots
Aircraft: 85
Crew: ship's company; 3,150; air wing: 2,480
Armament: Sea Sparrow missiles; three Phalanx CIWS 20-mm mounts;
Combat systems: SPS-48C; SPS-49; SPS-10f or SPS-67; three Mk-91 Fire Control; SLQ-29 EW; WLR-1 ESM; and WLR-11 ESM

The ships of the class include *Kitty Hawk* (CV 63), *Constellation* (CV 64), and *America* (CV 66).

Nimitz Class

The USN's CVN (nuclear-powered aircraft carrier) fleet includes 10 *Nimitz*-class vessels, nine operational and one under construction. The largest warships in the world, the *Nimitz* class has the following general characteristics:

Builder: Newport News Shipbuilding Co., Newport News, Virginia
Power plant: two nuclear reactors, four shafts
Length, overall: 1,092 ft
Flight deck width: 252 ft
Beam: 134 ft
Displacement: approximately 97,000 tons full load
Speed: 30+ knots
Aircraft: 85
Cost: about $4.5 billion each
Crew: ship's company, 3,200; air wing, 2,480

Armament: two or three (depending on modification) NATO Sea Sparrow launchers, 20-mm Phalanx CIWS mounts (three on *Nimitz* and *Dwight D. Eisenhower*, four on *Carl Vinson* and later vessels of the class)

The first ship of this class, USS *Nimitz* (CVN 68) was deployed on May 3, 1975, and the class currently includes: USS *Nimitz* (CVN 68), homeport: San Diego, Calif.; USS *Dwight D. Eisenhower* (CVN 69), homeport: Newport News, Va.; USS *Carl Vinson* (CVN 70), homeport: Bremerton, Wash.; USS *Theodore Roosevelt* (CVN 71), homeport: Norfolk, Va.; USS *Abraham Lincoln* (CVN 72), homeport: Everett, Wash.; USS *George Washington* (CVN 73), homeport: Norfolk, Va.; USS *John C. Stennis* (CVN 74), homeport: San Diego, Calif.; USS *Harry S. Truman* (CVN 75), homeport: Norfolk, Va.; USS *Ronald Reagan* (CVN 76); and USS *George H. W. Bush* (CVN 77), under construction and scheduled to be launched in 2009.

Important Historical Aircraft Carriers

The following vessels and classes are of special historical interest.

See also WARSHIPS: WORLD WAR II.

Essex Class

This important class of aircraft carriers was developed during World War II and saw navy service for nearly half a century. During this period, the *Essex* class was at the core of the U.S. Navy's World War II and postwar fleets. The ships lent themselves to extensive modification, and many were fitted out with such features as a reinforced angled flight deck and a mirror landing system to accommodate jet aircraft.

The USS *Essex* (CV 9) itself was put out of commission and in reserve on January 9, 1947. Its sister ship, the USS *Oriskany* (CV 34), became the very first of the World War II carriers to undergo modernization, including a new flight deck and a streamlined island superstructure. The *Essex* and other carriers of its class were modernized to enable them to handle aircraft up to 40,000 pounds. Also essential was the installation of two

USS *Essex* (CV 9) underway in May 1943. Among planes on deck are SBDs, F6Fs, and TBMs. *(Naval Historical Foundation)*

H-8 catapults and clearing the flight deck of guns. Elevator capacity was also significantly increased, and jet blast deflectors installed. *Essex* followed and was recommissioned on January 16, 1951. On August 23, she entered combat in the KOREAN WAR and became the first USN aircraft carrier to launch F2H Banshee twinjet fighters on combat missions.

Another especially noteworthy *Essex*-class aircraft carrier was the USS *Lexington*, commissioned on February 17, 1943, and compiling a World War II record that included the destruction of some one million tons of enemy shipping and more than a thousand aircraft. After the war, the Lexington served with the SEVENTH FLEET, was on standby duty during the Laotian crisis of 1959, and served as an attack carrier during the CUBAN MISSILE CRISIS of 1963. After this, *Lexington* was homeported at Naval Air Station, Pensacola, where it began service as an aviation training carrier designated AVT 16. It was the navy's only aircraft carrier used exclusively for training before it was decommissioned on November 8, 1991. Today it is preserved as a naval museum in Corpus Christi, Texas.

General specifications of the *Essex* class include:

Displacement: 27,100 tons as built; 41,200 tons full load, with postwar modification
Length: 872 ft; 910 ft as modified

Beam: 147 ft 6 in
Draft: 28 ft 7 in
Speed: 33 knots
Crew: 2,631–3,448

Ships of the class include: *Essex* (CV 9), *Yorktown* (CV 10), *Intrepid* (CV 11), *Hornet* (CV 12), *Franklin* (CV 13), *Ticonderoga* (CV 14), *Randolph* (CV 15), *Lexington* (CV 16), *Bunker Hill* (CV 17), *Wasp* (CV 18), *Hancock* (CV 19), *Bennington* (CV 20), *Boxer* (CV 21), *Bon Homme Richard* (CV 31), *Leyte* (CV 32), *Kearsage* (CV 33), *Oriskany* (CV 34), *Reprisal* (CV 35), *Antietam* (CV 36), *Princeton* (CV 37), *Shangri-La* (CV 38), *Lake Champlain* (CV 39), *Tarawa* (CV 40), *Valley Forge* (CV 45), *Iwo Jima* (CV 46), and *Philippine Sea* (CV 47).

Forrestal Class

Forrestal, named for Secretary of the Navy and Secretary of Defense JAMES V. FORRESTAL, was the navy's first super carrier, and it was the first aircraft carrier expressly designed to operate jet aircraft. It also introduced, as part of its original design, an angled deck, which permitted simultaneous takeoffs and landings. This set the pattern for all U.S. aircraft carriers that followed, though the flight deck of *Forrestal* had a somewhat different layout than later designs, with the island superstructure located nearer to the bow and a starboard elevator configuration—one forward, two aft—and portside configuration—number four elevator forward of the two waist catapults—different from later ships. Today's carriers put the port elevator aft of the waist catapults.

Yet *Forrestal* is remembered less for its epoch-making innovations than for the catastrophic accident it suffered on July 29, 1967, while operating off the coast of Vietnam during the Vietnam War. A Zuni rocket accidentally fired from an F-4 Phantom, hitting a parked and armed A-4 Skyhawk. This caused the belly fuel tank and a 1,000-pound bomb on the Skyhawk to fall off, disgorging JP5 jet fuel onto the flight deck, which quickly ignited. To compound the disaster, the bomb boiled off, exploding and thereby initiating a massive chain reaction of explosions fed by fuel and bombs from

other aircraft. Fuel and bombs also spilled into the holes blown into the flight deck, igniting even deadlier fires on the lower decks. In the single worst loss of life on a navy vessel since the USS *Franklin* (CV 13) was bombed in World War II, 134 died and 64 were severely injured.

The *Forrestal* recovered from this accident and was not decommissioned until 1993. The ship had 21 successful operational deployments, including support for Operation Provide Comfort. In February 1992, the *Forrestal* moved her homeport from Naval Station Mayport, Florida, to Naval Station Pensacola, Florida, becoming the navy's training carrier for naval aviators and aviation support personnel. *Forrestal* was decommissioned on September 11, 1993, at the Philadelphia Naval Shipyard. As of the end of 2003, she is still moored there, awaiting final disposition and made available by the navy for donation as a museum and historical center.

Other important ships of this class include *Saratoga,* launched on October 8, 1955. *Saratoga* was part of the task force that patrolled off the coast of Cuba near Guantánamo Bay during the Cuban missile crisis. The ship was also stationed off the coast of Lebanon during the Arab-Israeli Six-Day War. During the Vietnam War, she fought in Tonkin Gulf, and, during the Persian Gulf War, in the Red Sea. *Saratoga*'s final deployment was in support of UN and NATO operations over Bosnia and Herzegovina in 1994. The ship was decommissioned on August 20, 1994.

USS *Independence* was commissioned at the Brooklyn Naval Shipyard, New York, on January 10, 1959, and was overhauled in the Service Life Extension Program (SLEP) at the Philadelphia Naval Shipyard in 1988. Deployed to Yokosuka, Japan, in 1991, she was the USN's only forward-deployed aircraft carrier. On June 30, 1995, *Independence* also earned the distinction, at age 36, of being the oldest ship in the USN's active fleet. She was decommissioned in 1998.

The USN planned a total of eight ships of the *Forrestal* class, but improvements incorporated in the last four were so significant that these ships were redesignated as the separate *Kitty Hawk* Class.

General specifications of the *Forrestal* class include:

Displacement: 75,900 to 79,300 tons full load
Length: 1,063 to 1,086 ft
Beam: 129 ft
Flight deck width: 252 ft
Speed: 30 knots +
Power plant: eight boilers, four geared steam turbines, four shafts, 260,000 shaft horsepower for *Forrestal,* 280,000 for others in the class
Aircraft: approximately 75
Armament: Sea Sparrow missiles; three Phalanx CIWS 20-mm mounts (installed during SLEP)
Combat systems: SPS-48C 3-D Air Search Radar; SPS-49 Air Search Radar; SPS-67; three Mk-91 Fire Control; SLQ-29 EW; WLR-1 ESM; WLR-3 ESM; WLR-11 ESM
Crew: 3,019 ship's company; 2,480 in air wing

Ships of the *Forrestal* class include: *Forrestal* (CV 59), *Saratoga* (CV 60), *Ranger* (CV 61), and *Independence* (CV 62).

Midway Class

The carriers of the *Midway* class were all of late World War II vintage, but none was launched before the end of the war. They were the largest aircraft carriers of their time—in any nation's navy. Ships of the class displaced more than 67,000 tons fully loaded, carried a crew of 4,500, and held as many as 70 aircraft. The vessels pushed the envelope of diesel technology, burning about 100,000 gallons of fuel oil each day.

Commissioned on September 10, 1945, days after the end of World War II in the Pacific, the lead carrier of the class was named for the turning-point Battle of Midway and was the first of a total of three ships completed in her class (two planned vessels were cancelled). *Midway* sailed for 47 years, serving during the Vietnam War and the Persian Gulf War before decommissioning in April of 1992.

It was another ship of the *Midway* class, USS *Franklin D. Roosevelt* (CVB 42), that first demonstrated the long-range attack capabilities of the modern carrier and its modern aircraft. A P2V-3C Neptune took off from the carrier near Jacksonville, Florida, on February 7, 1950, and landed in San Francisco, having made a flight of 5,060 miles—the longest ever made from a carrier deck.

Although designed during World War II, the ships of the *Midway* class proved highly capable of adapting to new technologies, systems, platforms, and operational needs. *Midway* was designed with piston-powered aircraft in mind, but, during the Persian Gulf War, flew the U.S. Navy's most modern jet fighters. Originally launched with an axial-deck design, *Midway* was modified to an angled-deck layout, her original hydraulic catapults were replaced with more powerful steam catapults, and the electronics thoroughly upgraded. In its final service, *Midway* carried an air wing consisting of four squadrons of F/A-18 Hornets and two squadrons of A-6 Intruders—68 attack aircraft in all.

Midway is currently in mothballs at Bremerton, Washington, and has been offered by the USN for use as a non-moving museum or memorial.

General specifications of the *Midway* class include:

Displacement: 62,000 tons full load
Length: 979 ft
Beam: 121 ft
Flight Deck Width: 238 ft
Speed: 30 knots+
Power plant: 12 boilers, four geared steam turbines, four shafts, 212,000 shaft horsepower
Aircraft: 65+
Armament: Sea Sparrow missiles; three Phalanx CIWS 20-mm mounts
Combat systems: SPS-48C 3-D Air Search Radar; SPS-49 Air Search Radar; SPS-65 Navigation Radar; two Mk-115 Fire Control
Crew: 2,533 ship's company; 2,239 in air wing

Ships of the *Midway* class include: CV 41 *Midway,* CV 42 *Franklin D. Roosevelt,* CV 43 *Coral Sea.*

United States (CVA 58)

The aircraft carrier *United States* may well be the most famous ship the navy never built. It was authorized, after many years of planning, on July 29, 1948, as the first of a new class of "supercarriers" and was to be, in fact, the first of the USN's post–World War II carriers.

The ship was laid down in April 1949, planned as a 65,000-ton, flush-deck carrier capable of launching and recovering very large aircraft— 100,000 pounds—that could deliver nuclear weapons. The *United States* ship was to be more than a thousand feet long and feature a radical new design: the absence of an island superstructure. Projected cost was $190 million, and it was planned as the nucleus of a 39-ship task force, which was to be built at a total cost of $1.265 billion. The planned purpose of the *United States* was to provide both nuclear (strategic) strike capability as well as tactical air support for air and amphibious forces.

It was the nuclear capability of the *United States* that proved the ship's undoing. The newly independent U.S. Air Force saw the ship as a challenge to its monopoly on strategic nuclear weapons delivery. The USAF's concern was that this duplication or usurpation of its role would stifle the growth of the new service, and, indeed, most of the Joint Chiefs of Staff agreed. Acting on opposition by both the army and USAF and faced with postwar budgetary constraints, Secretary of Defense Louis Johnson announced on April 23, 1949, the cancellation of construction of the vessel. This prompted Secretary of the Navy John Sullivan to resign summarily, and it triggered a general assault on USN funding, especially in naval aviation. Simultaneously with the reduction of USN funding, the USAF advocated creating a 70-group bomber force. This ignited the infamous "Revolt of the Admirals," a general protest at the highest levels of the U.S. Navy. More importantly, the controversy retarded the development of the aircraft carrier as a versatile platform for projecting U.S. military power worldwide.

General specifications of the unbuilt *United States* include:

Displacement: 75,900–79,300 tons full load
Length: 1,090 ft
Beam: 130 ft
Flight deck width: 190 ft
Speed: 33 knots
Power plant: eight boilers, four geared steam turbines, four shafts, 280,000 shaft horsepower
Aircraft: 12 nuclear-capable bombers; 45 XF2H Banshee fighters
Armament: eight 5-inch guns; six 3-inch guns
Crew: 3,019 ship's company; 2,480 in air wing

aircraft: Korean War

The major U.S. Navy aircraft of the KOREAN WAR period include:

Bell HTL. This helicopter was introduced into the USN inventory in 1947 and could cruise at 70 miles per hour (top speed, 100 mph) over a range of 250 miles. The aircraft could accommodate a pilot and two passengers and was used for utility and training purposes.

Douglas AD Skyraider. This large single-seat attack bomber was the last such propeller-driven, carrier-based aircraft used by the USN. A 2,700-horsepower engine drove the large plane to a top speed of 321 miles per hour at 18,300 feet. Range was 915 miles, and armament consisted of two 20-mm guns. The aircraft carried a wide array of ordnance and was highly adept at close air support. The Skyraider was introduced in 1945, too late for use in WORLD WAR II, but in time for Korea. It was also used extensively early in the VIETNAM WAR, albeit more by the USMC than the USN.

Douglas F3D Skyknight. Introduced in 1951, the Skyknight was an all-weather carrier-based fighter equipped with two 3,400-pound jets, which drove it to 600 miles per hour at 20,000 feet. Cruising range was 1,200 miles. The pilot and radar observer sat side by side, the observer operating four forward-firing 20-mm guns. The Skyknight was used in Korea as well as in the Vietnam War.

Douglas F4D Skyray. The navy's first delta-wing jet, the Skyray was introduced in 1956, too late to serve in the Korean War; it was discontinued by 1958 and therefore saw no service in Vietnam. A single 9,700-pound or 10,500-pound turbojet pushed the Skyray to 695 miles per hour at 55,000 feet over 1,200 miles. Four cannon and 4,000 pounds of ordnance constituted armament. The Naval Reserve flew the jet after 1962.

Grumman F9F-2/5 Panther. A straight-wing jet, the Panther was delivered to the navy in 1949. A 6,250-pound thrust jet made a cruising speed of 481 miles per hour. Service ceiling was 42,800 feet, and range was 1,300 miles. Armament consisted of four 20-mm guns. The Panther was the first jet used in Korea.

Grumman F11F Tiger. Introduced after the war, in 1957, the Tiger did not last long and was phased out beginning in 1959. It was used briefly by the Blue Angels. Four 20-mm guns fired forward, and four Sidewinders were mounted under the swept wings. A 7,450-pound thrust engine made for a 577 miles per hour cruising speed.

Grumman S-2 Tracker. Acquired by the navy in 1954, just after the Korean War, the Tracker was a carrier-launched antisubmarine aircraft manned by a crew of four. The twin-engine plane had a cruising speed of 149 miles per hour and service ceiling of 22,000 feet. It could carry a full complement of depth charges, torpedoes, rockets, and sonobuoys.

Lockheed P2V Neptune. The twin-engine (two 3,200-horsepower engines) patrol and antisubmarine warfare aircraft was introduced in 1947 and served until 1962. Maximum speed was 337 miles per hour at 13,000 feet over 3,930 miles. Ordnance included mines, torpedoes, and depth charges.

Lockheed TO, TV, and T2V Seastar. This jet trainer was introduced into the navy inventory in 1949. Top speed from the 6,100-pound thrust engine was 580 miles per hour at 35,000 feet. Pilot and instructor were seated in tandem.

Lockheed WV, R7V, and C-121 Constellation "Warning Star." The Constellation, a popular commercial transport, was also built in numerous military configurations for the USAAF, USAF, and USN. Beginning in 1945, the USN used it for cargo and personnel transport, then also for airborne early-warning patrol as well as weather duty. In 1954, the aircraft was outfitted with state-of-the-art radar for radar early warning service. The Con-

stellation was powered by four 3,400-horsepower engines and reached a maximum speed of 368 miles per hour at 20,000 feet.

Martin P5M Marlin. The last of the navy's flying boats, the Marlin was operational from 1952 to 1966 and was a development of the PBM Mariner from World War II (see AIRCRAFT: WORLD WAR II). Its two engines each delivered 3,450 horsepower for a maximum speed of 251 miles per hour. Range was 2,050 miles. The plane was capable of carrying four torpedoes or four 2,000-pound bombs or as much as 8,000 pounds of smaller munitions.

McDonnell F2H Banshee. The Banshee was a single-seat jet fighter, carrier launched, and equipped with two 3,250-pound thrust turbojets. Introduced in 1949, the Banshee could make 532 miles per hour at 10,000 feet. Range was 1,475 miles, and armament included four 20-mm guns and 2,500 pounds of ordnance.

McDonnell FD/FH Phantom. Introduced in 1947, the FD/FH Phantom was the navy's first jet fighter. However, it was superseded before it became fully operational. A pair of 1,600-pound thrust turbojets made 479 miles per hour. Ceiling was 41,100 feet, and range was 980 miles. Four .50-inch guns were mounted in the nose.

North American FJ-1 Fury. A single-seat carrier-launched fighter, the Fury entered the navy inventory in 1948–49 and was the first fully operational carrier-based jet. Top speed was 547 miles per hour (driven by a 4,000-pound thrust turbojet) and range was 1,500 miles. Six forward-firing .50-inch guns constituted the FJ-1's armament.

North American FJ-2/4 Fury. The successor to the FJ-1, this was the navy version of the USAF's epoch-making F-86 Sabrejet. A 7,700-pound turbojet moved the craft to a top speed of 680 miles per hour. Ceiling was 46,800 feet, and range was 2,020 miles. The FJ-2/4 was fitted with four 20-mm guns and four wing pylons for a 3,000-pound load of bombs or four Sidewinder missiles.

North American T-28 Trojan. This basic trainer never achieved the popularity of the earlier Texan (see AIRCRAFT: WORLD WAR II), with 489 delivered to the navy compared with over 16,000 of the Texan. The aircraft came on line in 1952 and carried a pilot and instructor, seated in tandem. A 1,425-horsepower engine made a maximum speed of 343 miles per hour. Service ceiling was 35,500 feet, range 1,060 miles.

Sikorsky HO4S and HRS. Also known as the Sikorsky S-55, the helicopter was designed as a general-purpose transport but was used by the USN during the 1950s chiefly for antisubmarine operations. A single 550-horsepower engine made 101 miles per hour. Service ceiling was 10,500 feet. The helicopter could carry eight passengers in addition to the pilot. By 1962, the aircraft served only utility functions.

Sikorsky HR2S-1. Also designated Sikorsky S-56, this large helicopter had two 1,190-horsepower engines mounted on subwings off the fuselage. It

A CH-46 Sea Knight conducts an emergency personnel transfer hoist training exercise with a USN submarine in Apra Harbor, Guam. *(U.S. Navy)*

carried two pilots and up to 20 troops (or 24 litter patients). While the marines used it for transport during the Korean War, the navy adopted it in 1957 mainly as an early-warning radar craft.

Sikorsky HSS Seabat. Acquired by the navy just after the Korean War, this hunter-killer helicopter had a single 1,525-horsepower engine that achieved 123 miles per hour. It was used for antisubmarine warfare.

H-3H Sea King helicopter. This twin-engine, all-weather helicopter is variously configured for a variety of missions. The Naval Reserve uses the SH-3H model to detect, classify, track, and destroy enemy submarines. (In the navy, the Sea King has been replaced by the SH-60F Sea Hawk for the antisubmarine mission.) The SH-60F variant also provides logistical support and search-and-rescue capability. The UH-3H utility model is configured especially for logistical support and search and rescue, while the VH-3D is used for executive transport.

Vought F7U Cutlass. The carrier-based Cutlass featured a distinctive and highly unconventional design: wings sharply swept back (38 degrees), with pitch and roll controls combined in elevons on the wings and twin fins and rudders that were also wing mounted. Two 4,600-pound thrust turbojets drove the Cutlass to a top speed of 680 miles per hour. Service ceiling was 40,000 feet. Four 20-mm guns fired forward, and the aircraft could carry four Sparrow missiles. Delivered in the early 1950s, production ceased in 1955.

aircraft: pre–World War II

The major U.S. Navy aircraft of the pre–World War II period include:

Aeromarine 39A and 39B. This training biplane was introduced in 1921. The 39B version made the first USN landing on an aircraft carrier, the USS *Langley,* on October 26, 1922. The aircraft had a small, 100-horsepower engine and a top speed of 100 miles per hour.

Boeing FB. Built in the 1920s as a shore-based fighter, the aircraft was later modified for AIRCRAFT CARRIER flight. A biplane, its 435-horsepower engine drove the FB to a maximum of 159 miles per hour over a range of 390 miles. The plane was armed with 30-inch and 1.50-inch guns.

Boeing F2B. Built in 1928, the F2B was designed for carrier flight. Its 425-horsepower engine pulled it to a top speed of 158 miles per hour over a 317-mile range. Its armament was identical to that of the FB.

Boeing F3B. A more sophisticated version of the F2B, the F3B had the same top speed and carried the same armament as its predecessor, but could fly 340 miles. It first appeared later in 1928 but in the same year than the F2B.

Curtiss CR. This race plane was built after WORLD WAR I for the USN for speed research. Top speed was 194 miles per hour, ceiling was 19,200 feet, and range 522 miles. The CR captured two race trophies for USN fliers, in 1921 and in 1922.

Curtiss F59C Sparrowhawk. This tiny biplane fighter was designed to be carried by airships and launched and recovered by them. Wingspan was a mere 25.5 feet, length 20 feet 7 inches. A large airship could accommodate eight. The aircraft were first deployed in 1932.

Curtiss F6C Hawk. A carrier-launched single-seat biplane fighter, the Hawk had a top speed of 155 miles per hour and a service ceiling of 22,900 feet over a range of 360 miles. The aircraft was in service from 1925 to 1930.

Curtiss JN. The "Jenny" was the ubiquitous American military aircraft of the World War I era. Hopelessly inferior to European combat aircraft of the period, it was used by the army and navy exclusively as a trainer. Of 4,000 built, the USN acquired 216. Top speed was a poky 93 miles per hour and service ceiling was 10,525 feet.

Curtiss Pusher. The Pusher design first entered the USN inventory in 1911 and was used in early experiments with ship-launched flight. In 1910, a Pusher flew from the cruiser *Birmingham* and in 1911 from the battleship *Pennsylvania.* Top speed from the 75-horsepower motor was only 60 miles per hour.

Douglas DT. This biplane torpedo bomber was in service with the USN from 1922 to 1926 and was available in a land and seaplane version. A World War I–vintage Liberty engine made only 99 miles

per hour over a range of 274 miles, but the large plane was carrier launchable.

Great Lakes BG-1. This carrier-based biplane dive bomber was in service from 1934 to 1938. Manned by a pilot and an observer/gunner, the plane had a 750-horsepower engine that made only 188 miles per hour with a range of 549 miles and a service ceiling of 20,100 feet. Two guns, both .30-inch, one forward firing, one rear, constituted the armament.

Grumman FF and SF. Introduced in 1933, this biplane carrier-based scout and fighter was withdrawn three years later. A single 700-horsepower engine made for a maximum speed of just over 200 miles per hour; range was 921 miles. The FF and SF were the first USN aircraft with retractable landing gear.

Grumman TBF and TBM Avenger. The most widely used USN torpedo bomber in World War II, the Avenger carried a pilot, gunner, and radar operator, cruised at 145 miles per hour (1,700-horsepower engine) over 1,215 miles. Nearly 10,000 TBMs were produced during the war. The Avenger remained in service after the war, until 1954.

Naval Aircraft Factory N3N. This biplane primary trainer accommodated a pilot and an instructor and could make ground or water landings. A 235-horsepower engine achieved a maximum speed of 126 miles per hour. Service ceiling was 15,200 feet, and range was 470 miles. The USN used the N3N from 1936 to 1961, and it was the last U.S. military biplane.

Naval Aircraft Factory TS. This single-seat biplane fighter could be used as a floatplane, a land aircraft, or a carrier-based plane. The aircraft could also be carried by destroyers, cruisers, and battleships, then launched as a floatplane. In service during the 1920s, it had a single 200-horsepower motor that made a top speed of 123 miles per hour. Ceiling was 16,250 feet and range 482 miles.

Shenandoah (Airship ZR-1). Built in 1923, the *Shenandoah* was the USN's first rigid airship. It measured 680 feet in length with a maximum diameter of 79 feet and a gas volume of 2,115,000 cubic feet. Six 300-horsepower engines propelled the craft to a top speed of 60 miles per hour. The *Shenandoah* was lost in a storm over Ohio on September 3, 1925. Fourteen of 43 crew on board during this flight were killed.

Stearman NS and N2S Kaydet. Introduced in 1935, the Kaydet was a biplane trainer accommodating an instructor and pilot in tandem. Top speed was 124 miles per hour, driven by a 220-horsepower engine. Both the USN and USA used it extensively for primary training.

Vought FU-1. This seaplane fighter was designed for catapult launch off cruisers and battleships. A single 220-horsepower engine made 122 miles per hour. Service ceiling was 26,500 feet. Armament consisted of a pair of forward-firing .30-inch guns. Introduced during the 1920s, the FU-1 was in service with the USN through the early 1930s.

Vought O2U Corsair. Designed as an observation craft, the biplane Corsair had a single 450-horsepower engine and could reach a top speed of 150 miles per hour. Service ceiling was 18,700 feet. It was equipped with a fixed .30-inch gun as well as two ring-mounted 30-inch guns. Introduced in 1927, the Corsair featured an all-steel fuselage in a modern tube configuration. It was equipped with wheels as well as floats.

Vought O3U and SU Corsair. Introduced in 1930, the O3U superseded the O2U and offered a bigger engine (550 to 600 horsepower) and greater speed (167 miles per hour with the 600-horsepower engine). Service ceiling was 18,600 feet with the 600-horsepower engine. The O3U Corsair was still in service at the outbreak of World War II, but was removed from operational units by the end of 1941.

Vought SBU. Introduced in 1935 and in service up to the outbreak of World War II, the SBU was a biplane scout bomber, carrier based and crewed by two. Its 700-horsepower engine topped out at 205 miles per hour, and service ceiling was 23,700 feet. One .30-inch gun fired forward, and one flexibly mounted gun fired toward the rear.

Vought UO. The UO entered the USN inventory during the 1920s and served through the early 1930s. It could be launched from land or from a ship-mounted catapult and was crewed by a pilot and observer. A single 200-horsepower engine pro-

pelled this biplane to a top speed of 124 miles per hour and a service ceiling of 18,800 feet. It replaced the earlier VE-7 and VE-9.

Vought VE-7 and VE-9. Built in the early 1920s, these aircraft served as observation planes as well as fighters and trainers. Top speed of the VE-7 was only 117 miles per hour with a 15,000-foot service ceiling. The Vought UO brought a performance improvement over the VE-7 and VE-9.

ZR-2 and ZR-3 (aka, *Los Angeles*). The USN acquired ZR-2 from the German firm of Zeppelin as part of reparations for World War I; however, it broke up before delivery, apparently sabotaged by the German construction crew that had built it. The ZR-3 *Los Angeles* was built expressly for the U.S. Navy as a replacement for the destroyed ship. It had five 400-horsepower engines, which propelled the 658-foot-long *Los Angeles* to a top speed of 76 miles per hour. Diameter was 90 feet 6 inches, and gas volume was 2,472,000 cubic feet. Commissioned in 1924, it was retired in 1932 and scrapped in 1939.

ZRS-4 (Akron). Built by Goodyear-Zeppelin (Akron, Ohio), the *Akron* was commissioned in 1931. Eight 560-horsepower engines attained 84 miles per hour. The ship was 785 feet long and had a diameter of 132 feet 9 inches. Gas volume was 6,500,000 cubic feet. The behemoth was lost in a storm off the New Jersey coast on April 3–4, 1933. All but three crew members were killed. Among the dead was Admiral WILLIAM A. MOFFETT.

ZRS-5 (Macon). Sister ship of the *Akron,* the *Macon* was lost on February 11, 1935, off the coast of California. All but two crew members were rescued. The loss of the *Macon* ended the U.S. Navy's rigid airship program.

See also AIRSHIPS.

aircraft: Vietnam War and after

Major USN aircraft of the VIETNAM WAR era and later include:

Bell UH-1 Iroquois. One of the most successful helicopter designs ever built, the UH-1 was widely used by the army for general utility work and by the navy mainly for local base rescue and support, especially in the Antarctic region. The aircraft's powerful 1,250-horsepower engine drove a turboshaft that enabled the UH-1 to make 127 miles per hour while carrying a 4,000-pound load over 286 miles. Up to 14 passengers could be accommodated in addition to the pilot.

Bell-Boeing V-22A Osprey tiltrotor aircraft. The V-22 is a joint service aircraft with vertical takeoff and landing (VTOL) capability. Its wing-mounted tiltrotors enable the aircraft to operate as a helicopter for takeoff and landing; once airborne, the tiltrotor nacelles rotate forward 90 degrees for horizontal flight as a high-speed turboprop airplane.

The first flight of the Osprey took place in March 1989. The Marine Corps is the major user of the aircraft (360 units are planned); the navy will take 48, and the air force 50. After extensive testing because of a number of mishaps, some fatal, the aircraft was finally accepted for service in 2004.

The marine version, MV-22A, is intended as an assault troop transport, and the air force version, CV-22A, will be assigned long-range special forces missions. The navy's HV-22A is planned to provide combat search and rescue, delivery and retrieval of special warfare teams, and fleet logistic support transport.

Powered by two pivoting Rolls-Royce/Allison AE1107C engines, the Osprey has a ceiling of 25,000 feet and a top speed of about 300 miles per hour. It is armed with two .50-caliber cabin guns.

Bell Helicopter Textron TH-57 Sea Ranger. The TH-57 is the navy version of the civilian Bell Jet Ranger 206. Its primary mission is advanced IFR (instrument flight rules) training, but the aircraft is also used for photo, chase, and utility missions. It is propelled by an Allison 250-C20BJ turbofan engine and has a range of 368 nautical miles. Ceiling is 18,900 feet, and top speed is 138 miles per hour. Crew consists of one pilot and four students. The aircraft was first deployed in 1968.

Boeing C-9 Skytrain logistics aircraft. The navy and Marine Corps employ the C-9 for cargo and passenger transportation as well as forward deployment logistics support, whereas the air force uses it for medical evacuation, passenger transportation, and special missions. The aircraft is the military version of the McDonnell Douglas DC-9, long a mainstay of commercial airlines.

Built by Boeing Aircraft Corporation, the aircraft is propelled by two Pratt and Whitney JT8D-9A turbofan engines and has a range of more than 2,000 miles. Ceiling is 37,000 feet and top speed 565 miles per hour. Crew consists of two pilots plus cabin attendants. The aircraft was first deployed in August 1968.

Boeing C-40A Clipper logistics aircraft. The military version of the Boeing 737-700 airliner, the C-40A provides logistics support to the navy and is intended to replace the USN's aging C-9 Skytrains for passenger transport, cargo transport, or combination passenger and cargo transport.

The U.S. NAVAL RESERVE operates and maintains the C-40A fleet and provides all of the navy's in-theater medium and heavy airlift. Propulsion is provided by two CFM56-7 SLST engines. Cruising speed is 585 to 615 miles per hour and ceiling is 41,000 feet. Range is 3,000 nautical miles with 121 passengers or 40,000 pounds of cargo. The aircraft is crewed by four.

Boeing E-6A Mercury airborne command post. The E-6A is a communications relay and strategic airborne command post aircraft, which provides airborne command, control, and communications between the National Command Authority (NCA) and U.S. strategic and nonstrategic forces. Both E-6A and a subsequent version, the E-6B, may be used to provide communications relay for fleet ballistic missile submarines. The E-6B is a modification of the E-6A, incorporating battle-staff positions and other specialized equipment to enable its use as a true strategic airborne command post; it is operated primarily by the air force, but also serves as an airborne command post for U.S. strategic forces.

Delivered to the navy in 1989, the E-6A is based on the Boeing 707 commercial airliner. The aircraft incorporates a very low frequency (VLF) communication system with dual trailing wire antennas. This system is capable of communicating with the submarine fleet and the National Command Authority.

The E-6A is driven by four CFM-56-2A-2 high-bypass turbofans and has a ceiling of more than 40,000 feet. Top speed is about 600 miles per hour and range is 6,600 nautical miles. The aircraft is crewed by 14.

Boeing T-45A Goshawk training aircraft. This tandem-seat, carrier-capable jet trainer is used for the intermediate and advanced portions of the training program for jet carrier aviation and tactical strike missions. The aircraft is a version of the British Aerospace Hawk and has replaced the T-2 Buckeye trainer and the TA-4 trainer. The T-45A, which became operational in 1991, contains an analog-design cockpit; the new T-45C, which began delivery in 1997, features a digital "glass cockpit." The aircraft is powered by a Rolls-Royce F405-RR-401 turbofan engine and has a top speed of 645 miles per hour. Ceiling is 42,500 feet, range 700 nautical miles. Crew consists of an instructor pilot and a student pilot.

Boeing Vertol CH-46 Sea Knight. In its CH-46D version, this medium-lift assault helicopter is used primarily by the navy for shipboard delivery of cargo and personnel. The CH-46E model is used by the marines for all-weather, day-or-night assault transport of combat troops, supplies, and equipment. The helicopters may be used for search and rescue, support for forward refueling and rearming points, aeromedical evacuation of casualties from the field, and recovery of aircraft and personnel.

The marines began taking delivery of the CH-46 in 1964 to meet the medium-lift requirements of the Corps, and the navy acquired the helicopters in 1978. The navy's CH-46 fleet is slated for replacement during 2004 by the MH-60S Knighthawk.

The Sea Knight is powered by two GE-T58-16 engines, making 1,770 horsepower. Maximum takeoff weight is 24,300 pounds, and range is 132 nautical miles. Top speed is 166.75 miles per hour, ceiling more than 10,000 feet. The aircraft is crewed by four (pilot, copilot, crew chief, and mechanic) and can deliver a combat payload of 22 troops and two aerial gunners; an evacuation pay-

load of 15 litters and two attendants; and a cargo payload of 5,000 pounds.

Douglas A3D Skywarrior. Introduced in 1956, the Skywarrior was an attack bomber, carrier-based and carrying a three-man crew, originally designed for strategic warfare, but used extensively in the difficult tactical theater Vietnam presented. Two 12,400-pound turbojets propelled the aircraft to a top speed of 610 miles per hour at 10,000 feet over 1,050 miles. Two 20-mm guns were mounted in a radar-controlled rear turret for defense, and ordnance capacity was 12,000 pounds. The aircraft was also modified for photo-reconnaissance.

Grumman A-6 Intruder. More than 700 of these highly versatile and enduring planes were delivered to the U.S. Navy beginning in 1963. A two-seat all-weather attack jet, the Intruder was widely used in Vietnam and, driven by two 9,300-pound turbojets, made a top speed of 644 miles per hour. Equipped with advanced sensors and avionics, the Intruder carried 18,000 pounds of ordnance, including an array of bombs and air-to-ground missiles. In addition to service in Vietnam, the A-6 has seen much use during the cold war era.

Grumman Aerospace C-2A Greyhound logistics aircraft. The C-2A is a twin-engine cargo aircraft designed to land on aircraft carriers for carrier on-board delivery, its primary mission. Secondarily, its cabin is readily convertible to accommodate passengers or a mixed load of passengers and cargo. The aircraft can also accept litter patients in medical evacuation missions.

A specially designed cage system or transport stand restrains cargo during carrier launch and landing. The plane is equipped with a large cargo ramp and door aft, which enables fast turnaround as well as airdrop of supplies and personnel, when required.

The C-2 Greyhound derives from the E-2 Hawkeye; it was prototyped in 1964 and began production in 1965. The original C-2A aircraft were overhauled in 1973; in 1984, the USN contracted for 39 new C-2As, with improved airframes and avionics. The last of these new models was delivered in 1990.

The C-2 is powered by two Allison T-56-A-425 turboprop engines and has a cruising speed of 345 miles per hour and a ceiling of 30,000 feet. Range is 1,300 nautical miles. It is crewed by four.

Grumman E-2 Hawkeye. The E-2C Hawkeye is a carrier-based, tactical warning and control system aircraft, which provides all-weather airborne early warning and command and control functions for the carrier battle group. In addition, the E-2C can perform surface surveillance coordination, strike and interceptor control, search-and-rescue guidance, and communications relay.

The E-2, which became operational in 1964, replaces the Grumman E-1 Tracer (a variant of the S-2 Tracker antisubmarine aircraft), which served from 1954 to 1964. The aircraft is powered by two Allison T-56-A427 turboprop engines (5,000 shaft horsepower each) and has a top speed of about 345 miles per hour.

Grumman F9F-6/8 Cougar. The swept-wing successor to the straight-wing Grumman F9F-2/5 Panther used in the KOREAN WAR (see AIRCRAFT: KOREAN WAR), the Cougar was introduced into the USN inventory in 1953. The 7,250-pound-thrust turbojet engine made a top speed of 690 miles per hour. Service ceiling was 50,000 feet. Four 20-mm guns fired forward, and ordnance capacity was two 1,000-pound underwing bombs. A most durable aircraft, the Panther was used well into the 1970s.

An E-2C Hawkeye, wings about to unfold, prepares to take off from the USS *Nimitz* in the Arabian Gulf, May 20, 2003.   *(U.S. Navy)*

Grumman F-14 Tomcat fighter. The F-14 Tomcat is a supersonic, twin-engine, variable-sweep-wing, carrier-based two-place strike fighter. Primary missions are air superiority, fleet air defense, and precision ground strike. The aircraft is designed to deliver Phoenix and Sparrow missiles and is also equipped with an M-61 gun and Sidewinder missiles for air-to-air combat. Fitted with night-vision LANTIRN (Low Altitude Navigation and Targeting Infrared) targeting, the F-14 can deliver laser-guided bombs for precision air-to-ground strikes. When equipped with Tactical Air Reconnaissance Pod System (TARPS), the F-14 may be used as a manned tactical reconnaissance platform.

The F-14 entered service with the navy in 1973, replacing the F-4 Phantom II. The F-14B, introduced in November 1987, incorporated new General Electric F-110 engines. The F-14D, delivered in 1990, brought F-110 engines, an APG-71 radar system, Airborne Self Protection Jammer (ASPJ), Joint Tactical Information Distribution System (JTIDS), and Infrared Search and Track (IRST).

F-14A engines are two Pratt and Whitney TF-30P-414A turbofan engines with afterburners; F-14B and F-14D versions have two General Electric F110-GE-400 turbofan engines with afterburners. The aircraft is capable of speeds in excess of Mach 2 and has a ceiling of 50,000 feet. Armament, up to 13,000 pounds, includes AIM-54 Phoenix missile, AIM-7 Sparrow missile, AIM-9 Sidewinder missile, air-to-ground precision strike ordnance, and one M61A1/A2 Vulcan 20-mm cannon. The aircraft is crewed by two.

Gulfstream C-20 logistics aircraft. The C-20D is a Gulfstream III executive aircraft, which the navy uses to provide airlift for senior leadership and dignitaries; the C-20G is a Gulfstream IV, which provides long-range, medium airlift logistics support for fleet battle groups. The C-20D is an all-weather, long-range, high-speed aircraft powered by two Rolls-Royce Spey Mk-511-8 turbofan engines with thrust reversers. The aircraft's executive compartment accommodates five passengers, and its staff compartment accommodates eight. The 157-cubic-foot walk-in baggage area is fully pressurized and accessible in flight from the cabin. The

C-20G, powered by two Rolls-Royce Tay Mk-611-8 turbofans, may be configured for cargo operations, passenger operations, or combinations. As a passenger aircraft, it accommodates 26 and a crew of four. Top speed is Mach 0.75, and range is 3,700 nautical miles in the C-20D configuration and 5,130 nautical miles in the C-20G configuration.

Kaman HU2K/H-2 Seasprite. This antisubmarine helicopter was powered by a pair of 1,350-horsepower engines and could reach a top speed of 168 miles per hour. It was delivered to the USN in 1962 and performed search and rescue and other duties during the Vietnam War. Attack versions were equipped with cutting-edge strike electronics.

Lockheed C-130 Hercules logistics aircraft. The four-engine turboprop C-130 is used by all the military services for personnel and cargo transport and has proved such a flexible platform that it is also used as a gunship, weather plane, in-flight tanker, firefighter, and medical evacuation aircraft. There are more than 40 versions of the Hercules, and it is widely used by more than 50 nations. The C-130A commenced delivery to the U.S. armed services in December 1956, and the aircraft has been frequently improved. The current version is the C-130H.

The great advantage of this large global airlift plane is its ability to take off and land on poor runways, such as those found in front-line situations. The aircraft thus combines high-capacity payload with extreme practicality in the field.

Power plant is four Allison T56-A-15 turboprops, and top speed is 374 miles per hour. Ceiling is 33,000 feet with a 100,000-pound payload, and range is 2,050 nautical miles with maximum payload. Crewed by five (two pilots, navigator, flight engineer, and loadmaster) the Hercules can carry 92 troops, 64 paratroops, or 74 litter patients, or five standard freight pallets.

Lockheed Martin P-3C Orion long-range ASW aircraft. The P-3C is a land-based, long-range, antisubmarine warfare (ASW) patrol aircraft incorporating advanced submarine detection sensors, including directional frequency and ranging (DIFAR) sonobuoys and magnetic anomaly detection (MAD) equipment. The P-3C is equipped with highly advanced avionics, which are integrated by a computer supporting all tactical displays that monitor and automatically launch ordnance, providing flight information to the pilots. Additionally, the P-3C can carry a mixed payload of weapons both internally and on wing pylons.

Development of the *Orion* began in February 1959, when the USN awarded Lockheed a contract to develop a replacement for the P2V Neptune. The P3V Orion was derived from the L188 Electra commercial airliner and entered the USN inventory in July 1962. Today, it is still the USN's only land-based antisubmarine warfare aircraft. The current P-3C is the only version of the aircraft in active service, the last one having been produced in April 1990.

Propulsion is provided by four Allison T-56-A-14 turboprop engines, and maximum speed is 466 miles per hour. Ceiling is 28,300 feet, with a maximum mission range of 2,380 nautical miles. The *Orion* is crewed by 11. It carries 20,000 pounds of ordnance, including Harpoon (AGM-84D) cruise missiles, SLAM (AGM-84E) missiles, Maverick (AGM-65) air-to-ground missiles, Mk-46/50 torpedoes, rockets, mines, depth bombs, and special weapons.

Lockheed Martin EP-3E Aries II signals intelligence reconnaissance aircraft. A modified version of the P-3C Orion long-range ASW aircraft, this four-engine turboprop functions as a signals intelligence (SIGINT) reconnaissance aircraft using the Airborne Reconnaissance Integrated Electronic System II. The 11 EP-3Es in the USN inventory provide fleet and theater commanders worldwide with near real-time tactical SIGINT, monitoring a wide range of electronic emissions from deep within targeted territory.

Driven by four Allison T-56-A-14 turboprop engines (4,900 shaft horsepower each), the aircraft has a top speed of 466 miles per hour and a ceiling of 28,300 feet. Effective range is 2,380 nautical miles. The aircraft accommodates a specialist crew of 22 or more.

A P-3C Orion flies near Naval Air Station Sigonella, Sicily.   *(U.S. Navy)*

Lockheed Martin Joint Strike Fighter. The JSF, to be designated the F-35, is being developed by Lockheed Martin Aeronautics Company for the air force, marines, and navy, and for the United Kingdom's Royal Navy. Three variants of this stealthy, supersonic multirole fighter are being built: a conventional takeoff and landing aircraft (CTOL) for the USAF, a short takeoff and vertical landing (STOVL) aircraft for the USMC and Royal Navy, and a carrier-based variant (CV) for the USN, which intends its variant, the F-35C, to serve as a first-day-of-war strike fighter to replace F/A-18B/C Hornet and A-6 Intruder and to complement the F/A-18E/F.

The JSF incorporates advanced stealth design features. Weapons are carried in two parallel bays located in front of the landing gear and can accommodate a very large array of ordnance. Targeting will employ an electro-optical targeting system (EOTS) for long-range detection and precision targeting, along with a distributed aperture system thermal-imaging system. An advanced electronically scanned array (AESA) multifunction radar is being specially developed for the F-35. Early production lots of all three variants will be powered by the Pratt and Whitney afterburning turbofan F-135 engine, which may be replaced after production by the F-136 turbofan.

It is planned that the F-35A will begin replacing USAF F-16s and A-10s by 2010 and that the USMC and USN will begin acquiring their F-35Bs and F-35Cs by 2011.

Lockheed Martin S-3B Viking. The S-3B Viking is an all-weather, carrier-based jet aircraft tasked with providing protection against hostile surface ships. The S-3B also functions as the primary overhead/mission tanker for carrier battle groups. Indeed, this highly versatile aircraft is equipped for such missions as day/night surveillance, electronic countermeasures, command/control/communications warfare, and search and rescue.

The Viking uses a high-speed computer system to process information generated by its targeting-sensor systems, including inverse/synthetic aperture radar (ISAR/SAR), infrared (IR) sensor, and electronic support (ESM) system. Viking carries the AGM-84 Harpoon Anti-Ship Missile, AGM-65 Maverick IR missile, and an array of bombs and torpedoes. Upgraded Vikings will also launch the SLAM-ER missile (AGM 84 Standoff Land Attack Missile–Extended Range).

The S-3B was originally developed from the S-3A as an antisubmarine aircraft, but evolved during the 1990s as a surveillance and precision-targeting platform. Propulsion is provided by two General Electric TF-34-GE-400B turbofan engines. Top speed is 518 miles per hour, and ceiling is 40,000 feet. Maximum range exceeds 2,300 nautical miles. The aircraft is armed, at up to 3,958 pounds, with the AGM-84 Harpoon, AGM-65 Maverick, or AGM-84 SLAM missiles, in addition to torpedoes, rockets, and bombs. Crew consists of two to four, depending on the mission. The S-3A version was deployed in 1975.

LTV A-7A Corsair II. First received by the USN in 1966, this single-seat carrier-based attack bomber was propelled by a single 14,250-pound thrust turbofan jet to a top speed of nearly 700 miles per hour. It was capable of delivering 15,000 pounds of ordnance and was used extensively in Vietnam for close air support.

LTV F-8 Crusader. Introduced in 1957, this carrier-based fighter was not phased out until 1976. Its single turbojet delivered 10,700 pounds of thrust for a cruising speed of 560 miles per hour at 40,000 feet. Service ceiling was 58,000 feet, and range was 1,100 miles. Armament consisted of four 20-mm cannon, and ordnance loads ranged from four Sidewinders to 5,000 pounds of bombs.

McDonnell F3H Demon. Delivered to the USN from 1951 to 1965, the Demon saw some action in Korea and more in the early phases of Vietnam. A single-seat carrier-launched jet, the Demon had a 9,700-pound-thrust engine and was capable of a maximum speed of 647 miles per hour. Range was 1,370 miles. Four 20-mm guns and underwing hardpoints for bombs and rockets constituted armament.

McDonnell Douglas A-4 Skyhawk. Introduced in 1956, the delta-wing A-4 was very widely deployed in Vietnam and, indeed, was continuously delivered to the USN until 1979, by which time some 3,000 had been produced. A single 11,200-pound thrust turbojet made 670 miles per hour. The aircraft could carry 4,000 pounds of bombs or 9,155 pounds of other ordnance. Two fixed cannon faced forward.

McDonnell Douglas F-4 Phantom II. One of the most important of all modern naval aircraft, the F-4 was developed for the USN, but was also adopted by the USMC and USAF. Carrier launched (USN version), it featured a swept delta wing and was a multirole fighter, crewed by a pilot and radar intercept officer. Two 10,900-pound-thrust turbojets drove the aircraft to approximately Mach 2 at 48,000 feet (ceiling 62,000). It could carry six Sea Sparrow or four Sidewinder missiles. Some 5,200 F-4s had been produced by 1980, and more than half of these were still in service, with reserve units, during the 1990s. The F-4 saw extensive Vietnam War service.

McDonnell Douglas F/A-18 Hornet strike fighter. The single-seat F/A-18 Hornet was designed as a strike fighter, capable of performing such strike applications as interdiction and close air support without compromising its capabilities as a fighter aircraft. The F/A-18 supplements the F-14 Tomcat in performing the fleet air defense mission. F/A-18s are deployed to 37 tactical squadrons at air stations worldwide and to 10 aircraft carriers. The BLUE ANGELS currently fly the aircraft in their demonstrations.

The F/A-18 A and C versions are single-seat aircraft; the F/A-18B and D versions are dual-seaters. The B model is used primarily for training, and the D model is used in attack, tactical air control, forward air control, and reconnaissance squadrons.

An F/A-18C Hornet prepares to launch from the USS *Theodore Roosevelt,* deployed to the Arabian Gulf. *(U.S. Navy)*

The newest models are the E and F, rolled out in 1995 (see F/A-18 Super Hornet, below). The E is a single-seat aircraft, the F a two-seater.

C and D models are equipped with two F404-GE-402 enhanced-performance turbofan engines. Combat range is 1,089 nautical miles, ceiling better than 50,000 feet, and top speed in excess of Mach 1.7. These aircraft are armed with one M61A1/A2 Vulcan 20-mm cannon, and can accommodate AIM-9 Sidewinder, AIM-7 Sparrow, AIM-120 AMRAAM, Harpoon, Harm, SLAM, SLAM-ER, Maverick missiles, the Joint Stand-Off Weapon (JSOW), and Joint Direct Attack Munition (JDAM). Additionally, the aircraft can deliver a variety of general-purpose bombs, mines, and rockets.

The aircraft became operational in October 1983 (A/B models) and September 1987 (C/D models).

McDonnell Douglas F/A-18 Super Hornet. The F/A-18E/F Super Hornet is the newest iteration of the F/A-18 Hornet Strike Fighter and was first seen at Patuxent River Naval Air Station in September 1995. The aircraft performs air-to-air and air-to-ground combat missions, including air superiority, day/night strike with precision-guided weapons, fighter-escort, close air support, sup-

pression of enemy air defenses, reconnaissance, and forward air control and refueling. Compared with the Hornet, the Super Hornet has greater range (flies 40 percent farther) and endurance (remains on station 80 percent longer), a greater payload capacity, and enhanced survivability. It is also designed to incorporate future systems and technologies.

The E and F models are equipped with two F414-GE-400 turbofan engines and have a combat range of 1,275 nautical miles. Ceiling is greater than 50,000 feet and top speed exceeds Mach 1.8. The aircraft is armed with one M-61A1/A2 Vulcan 20-mm cannon and can accommodate the AIM-9 Sidewinder, AIM-7 Sparrow, AIM-120 AMRAAM, Harpoon, HARM, SLAM, SLAM-ER, and Maverick missiles, as well as the Joint Stand-Off Weapon (JSOW) and Joint Direct Attack Munition. Additionally, the aircraft can deploy the Paveway laser-guided bomb and a variety of general purpose bombs, mines, and rockets.

North American A-5 Vigilante. Designed as a carrier-based, two-place (accommodating pilot and electronic warfare officer) electronic and visual reconnaissance plane, the A-5 was equipped with two 10,800-pound-thrust turbojets that made

Mach 2.1. Ceiling was 48,400 feet and combat radius 1,500 miles. The A-5 was fitted with a bomb bay capable of carrying nuclear ordnance. The A-5 entered the USN inventory in 1961.

Northrup Grumman EA-6B Prowler electronic warfare aircraft. The mission of the EA-6B is to provide protection for strike aircraft, ground troops, and ships by jamming enemy radar, electronic data links, and communications. Secondarily, the EA-6B uses electronic surveillance equipment to obtain tactical electronic intelligence within a combat area.

The aircraft, used by the navy and marines, is a modification of the A-6 Intruder and is designed for carrier and advanced base operations. Propelled by two Pratt and Whitney J52-P408 engines (10,400 pounds thrust each), the EA-6B has a top speed of 575 mph, a range greater than 1,000 nautical miles, and a ceiling of 37,600 feet. It is crewed by four, a pilot and three electronic countermeasures officers, and is armed with AGM-88B or C HARM missiles. The aircraft first flew on May 25, 1968, and became operational in July 1971.

Pioneer UAV RQ-2A System. The RQ-2A is an unmanned aerial vehicle (UAV) used by the navy to perform a wide variety of reconnaissance, surveillance, target acquisition, and battle damage assessment missions. First deployed as a land-based system in 1986, the RQ-2A provides tactical commanders with real-time images of the battlefield or target. Currently, the RQ-2A is configured to operate from AMPHIBIOUS TRANSPORT DOCK (LPD) SHIPS. During the PERSIAN GULF WAR, the RQ-2A was deployed from battleships.

The aircraft is driven by a 2-stroke, 2-cylinder 26-horsepower gasoline engine. The airframe consists of a 14-foot fuselage and wings with a span of 16.9 feet. Maximum gross takeoff weight is only 416 pounds. Top speed is 109.37 miles per hour and ceiling is 15,000 feet. Range exceeds 100 nautical miles.

Raytheon C-12F Huron logistics aircraft. The C-12F Huron provides logistics support between naval air stations. Powered by two PT-6A-42 turboprops, the C-12F can deliver a total payload of up to 4,215 pounds, its cabin accommodating cargo, passengers, or both. The aircraft can be equipped to accept litter patients in medical evacuation missions.

Built by Raytheon Aircraft Company (formally Beech Aircraft), the C-12F is powered by two Pratt and Whitney PT-6A-42 turboprop engines. Cruising speed is 334 miles per hour and ceiling 35,000 feet. Range is 1,974 nautical miles. The aircraft is crewed by two and was first deployed by the navy in 1994.

Raytheon T-6A Texan II turboprop trainer. The T-6A Texan II is a tandem-seat, turboprop flight trainer and a component of the Joint Primary Aircraft Training System (JPATS), a program of the USN and USAF. Built by Raytheon Aircraft Company, the T-6A derives from the Swiss Pilatus PC-9 aircraft with a Pratt and Whitney PT-6A-68 engine, digital cockpit, Martin-Baker ejection seats, cockpit pressurization, and an onboard oxygen-generating system. The T-6A entered into full production in 2001.

Propulsion is provided by one Pratt and Whitney Canada PT-6A-68 turboprop engine, and top speed is about 300 miles per hour, ceiling 31,000 feet. Maximum range is 850 nautical miles. The aircraft is crewed by an instructor pilot and a student pilot. It became operational with the navy on November 1, 2002.

Raytheon T-34C Turbomentor training aircraft. This unpressurized, two-seat, tandem-cockpit turboprop trainer is used to provide primary flight training for navy and marine pilots. The plane is derived from the civilian Beechcraft Bonanza and is powered by a single Model PT6A-25 turboprop engine from Pratt and Whitney Aircraft of Canada. Top speed is 322 miles per hour and range about 600 nautical miles. Ceiling is 25,000 feet. It is crewed by a student pilot and an instructor. The aircraft was first deployed in 1977.

Rockwell International T-2C Buckeye jet trainer. This tandem-seat, carrier-capable, all-purpose jet trainer is used for intermediate and advanced training of USN and USMC pilots and naval flight officers in jet carrier aviation and tactical strike missions.

The design is based on the FJ-1 Fury, a USN jet fighter from the 1950s. For armament training, the aircraft is fitted with underwing strongpoints to carry bombs, rockets, or gun pods, and it has an arresting hook for carrier landings. Although originally designed with a single engine, the T-2C variant has two. Most T-2Cs have been replaced by the T-45 Goshawk.

Propulsion is provided by two General Electric 085-GE-4 turbojets, and top speed is 521 miles per hour. Ceiling is 44,400 feet, maximum range 910 miles. The aircraft may be armed with guns, bombs, or rockets under the wings. It is crewed by an instructor pilot and student pilot.

The first flight was January 1958, and the aircraft became operational in July 1959. The T-2C variant first flew in April 1968.

Rockwell T-39N/G Sabreliner training aircraft. This multipurpose low-wing, twin-jet trainer is used to train navy and marine flight officers. The N version is used for training in radar navigation and airborne radar intercept procedures, and the G version for nonradar training. The aircraft is powered by two Pratt and Whitney J-60-P-3 jet engines and has a maximum speed of 499.44 mph. Ceiling is 42,000 feet, and range 1,476 nautical miles. The aircraft accommodates two flight crew and seven students.

Sikorsky H-3H Sea King. This twin-engine, all-weather helicopter is variously configured for a variety of missions. The Naval Reserve uses the SH-3H model to detect, classify, track, and destroy enemy submarines. (In the navy, the Sea King has been replaced by the SH-60F Sea Hawk for the antisubmarine mission.) The SH-60F variant also provides logistical support and search-and-rescue capability. The UH-3H utility model is configured especially for logistical support and search and rescue, while the VH-3D is used for executive transport.

The powerplant consists of two General Electric T58-GE-402 turboshaft engines; maximum takeoff weight is 21,000 pounds, and range is 542 nautical miles. Ceiling is 14,700 feet and cruising speed 217.6 miles per hour. The helicopter is armed with a pair of Mk-46 torpedoes and is crewed by four. First flight of the Sea King took place in March 1959, and the aircraft became operational with the navy by June 1961.

Sikorsky H-53 Sea Stallion. This was principally a USA and USMC aircraft, but the USN acquired 15 in 1971 for mine countermeasure operations. A pair of 3,925-horsepower turbines achieved 196 miles per hour and a service ceiling of 21,000 feet.

Sikorsky MH-53E Sea Dragon. The MH-53E is based on aircraft carriers and other warships and is an upgrade modification of the CH-53E Super Stallion, offering more power and endurance than the Super Stallion. The MH-53E can carry 55 troops. It can carry a 16-ton payload for a distance of 50 nautical miles or a 10-ton payload for a distance of 500 nautical miles. Additionally, the aircraft can tow a variety of mine-sweeping countermeasures systems.

The MH-53E Sea Dragon first flew in 1982 and is the largest helicopter in the West. It is propelled by three General Electric T64-GE-416 turboshaft engines and has a range of 1,120 nautical miles. Ceiling is 27,900 feet, top speed, 172 miles per hour. It is crewed by two pilots and one to six crewmen, depending on mission.

Sikorsky MH-60S Knighthawk. The MH-60S will replace the H-3H Sea King helicopter in the navy inventory. The MH-60S combines the U.S. Army UH-60 Blackhawk fuselage and U.S. Navy SH-60 Seahawk dynamic components, including engines, rotor system, folding tail pylon, improved durability gearbox, rotor brake, and automatic flight control computer.

Primary missions of the Knighthawk will include day and night amphibious search and rescue (SAR), vertical onboard delivery, and airhead operations. Secondary missions will include combat search and rescue (CSAR), special warfare support (SWS), recovery of torpedoes, drones, unmanned aerial vehicles, and unmanned undersea vehicles, noncombatant evacuation operations, aeromedical evacuations, humanitarian assistance, executive transport, and disaster relief.

The first demonstration Knighthawk flew in October 1997 and delivery began in 2000. Driven by two GE T700-GE-401C turboshaft engines, the helicopter has a top speed of 206 miles per hour.

Sikorsky SH-60 Sea Hawk. The SH-60 is the navy version of a twin-engine, medium-lift, utility or assault helicopter that is also used by the army (UH-60 Black Hawk), air force (MH-60G Pave Hawk), and U.S. Coast Guard (HH-60J Jayhawk). The navy uses the helicopter for antisubmarine warfare, search and rescue, drug interdiction, anti-ship warfare, cargo lift, and special operations. It is operated from CRUISERS, DESTROYERS, and FRIGATES as well as from AIRCRAFT CARRIERS.

The UH-60 Black Hawk was deployed by the army in 1979, and the Seahawk by the navy in 1983. An upgraded SH-60F version was deployed in 1988. The power plant consists of two General Electric T700-GE-700 or T700-GE-701C engines. Top speed is about 200 miles per hour and range about 380 nautical miles. Usual armament includes two 7.62-mm machine guns mounted in the windows, but the helicopter may also be equipped with AGM-114 Hellfire or AGM-119 Penguin missiles, three Mk-46 torpedoes or Mk-50 torpedoes, or additional .50-caliber machine guns mounted in the doors. Crew consists of three or four.

aircraft: World War II

The major U.S. Navy aircraft used during the WORLD WAR II period include:

Beech JRB Expeditor. This light transport aircraft was crewed by two and could carry six passengers. Its twin engines made 450 horsepower each, for a top speed of 225 miles per hour. Range was 1,250 miles. The Expeditor proved highly durable and was still in use during the 1960s, mainly for light transport and training.

Brewster F2A Buffalo. First produced in 1939, this single-seat carrier-based aircraft was the first USN monoplane fighter. It saw service early in World War II, but was not a successful design and proved far inferior to its Japanese adversaries. The Buffalo's 1,200-horsepower engine propelled it to a top speed of 320 miles per hour at 16,500 feet. Armament consisted of two .50-inch guns in the upper cowling and two more in the wings.

Consolidated PB4Y Liberator. This shore-based patrol bomber was used against surface ships and submarines. The bomber had four engines, 1,200 to 1,350 horsepower each, which drove the plane at 279 miles per hour at 26,500 feet. Range was nearly 3,000 miles. Like its USAAF counterpart, also called the Liberator, the USN version bristled with eight to 12 .50-inch guns. Ordnance capacity was eight 1,600-pound bombs. The aircraft remained in USN service after the war, until 1952.

Consolidated PBY Catalina. The most famous large plane in the navy's World War II inventory, the Catalina was introduced in 1937. Equipped with two engines and a parasol-mounted overhead wing, the PBY was a versatile amphibious flying boat, which could be used for search and rescue, transport, and bombing. It was an especially effective antisubmarine weapon. Crewed by seven to nine, the Catalina lumbered along at a top speed of 189 miles per hour over a range of nearly 3,000 miles. It could carry four 1,000-pound bombs, four depth charges, or two torpedoes, all underwing mounted.

Curtiss SBC Helldiver. Delivered to the USN in 1937, the Helldiver was the last combat biplane produced for the U.S. military. Designed as a scout-bomber, the airplane was crewed by a pilot and an observer/gunner. Its 950-horsepower engine propelled the Helldiver to 237 miles per hour at 15,200 feet. Range was 590 miles with a 500-pound bomb load.

Curtiss SC-1 Seahawk. Designed for antisubmarine warfare, the Seahawk was a single-seat aircraft that could be launched from battleships as well as operated from aircraft carriers. With a single 1,250-horsepower engine, it made a top speed of 313 miles per hour at 28,600 feet, although its cruising speed was a leisurely 125 miles per hour. Few Seahawks were deployed during World War II.

Curtiss SOC Seagull. Produced between 1935 and 1938, the Seagull was a biplane and quite obsolescent by World War II, but was used nevertheless for some scouting and observation work. Its 600-horsepower engine was capable of no more than 165 miles per hour over 675 miles. Armament was a single .30-inch gun mounted in the rear cockpit. The plane could be used as a seaplane or for carrier takeoff and landing, depending on the undercarriage fitted.

Curtiss SOC3 Seamew. This aircraft replaced the Seagull for use on battleships and aircraft carriers. Top speed was up to 172 miles per hour, and range was increased from 675 miles to 1,150. The aircraft was produced from 1942 to 1944.

Douglas SBD Dauntless. The Dauntless was a widely used dive bomber, capable of 245 miles per hour at 15,800 feet. Range was 1,100 miles. Two .50-inch guns faced forward, and two .30-inch guns were mounted dorsally. Sixteen hundred pounds of ordnance could be carried under the fuselage, and two 325-pound bombs under the wings. More than 5,300 Dauntlesses were built for the USN during the war.

Douglas TBD Devastator. The Devastator was a carrier-launched torpedo bomber delivered to the USN in 1937 and used early in the war. Proving inadequate against superior Japanese aircraft, it was withdrawn after the Battle of Midway. A 900-horsepower engine propelled the Devastator to a top speed of 206 miles per hour at 8,000 feet. Range was 716 miles carrying 1,000 pounds of ordnance. A .30-inch gun fired forward, and another was mounted dorsally.

Grumman F2F and F3F Flying Barrel. Introduced in 1935, these biplanes were the USN's first closed-canopy single-seat carrier-based fighters. They saw brief service at the beginning of World War II. A 950-horsepower engine made a top speed of 264 miles per hour. Range was under 1,000 miles.

Grumman F4F Wildcat. This was the only carrier-based monoplane fighter in the USN inventory during the first two full years of World War II. It cruised at 155 miles per hour over a range of 770 miles and was heavily armed with six .50-inch guns.

Grumman F6F Hellcat. Introduced in 1943, the Hellcat replaced the Wildcat, providing better range (945 miles), speed (168 miles per hour, cruising), and ceiling (37,300 feet versus 34,900). The Hellcat could be armed identically to the Wildcat or equipped with two 20-mm and four .50-inch guns. A spectacular 12,275 Hellcats were built for the USN. A few saw service during the KOREAN WAR.

Grumman F8F Bearcat. Successor to the Hellcat, the Bearcat was an interceptor with a 2,000-horsepower engine and a cruising speed of 163 miles per hour. Its range was better than 1,100 miles. Introduced at the end of the war, it continued in production until 1949.

Grumman JF and J2F Duck. This amphibious biplane was introduced into the USN inventory in 1934 and proved durable enough to serve throughout World War II. Its 1,850-horsepower engine made for a cruising speed of 150 miles per hour. Service ceiling was 27,000 feet and range 780 miles. A large float was mounted under the fuselage, into which wheels retracted.

Martin AM Mauler. Ordered during the war, the first Maulers were not delivered until 1948 and were soon relegated to NAVAL RESERVE use. A single-seat carrier-based aircraft capable of carrying 4,500 pounds of varied ordnance, the Mauler made 367 miles per hour with its 2,975-horsepower engine. Range was 1,800 miles.

Martin PBM Mariner. With the Consolidated PBY Catalina, the Mariner was used by the USN as a flying patrol boat. Twin 1,700-horsepower engines made 198 miles per hour. Range was 2,137 miles. Armament consisted of two .50-inch guns in the nose and another two in a dorsal turret. Ordnance load was 2,000 pounds of bombs or depth charges.

North American NJ and SNJ Texan. The USN version of the basic trainer popular with the U.S. Army Air Forces and, later, U.S. Air Force, the Texan accommodated a pilot and instructor in tandem. Its 500-horsepower engine made 167 miles per hour. Service ceiling was 24,900 feet, range 944 miles. Later versions achieved somewhat higher performance. Used during the war and into the 1950s, the USN acquired more than 16,000 Texans.

SNB Kansan. A military version of the civil aviation Beech 18, the Kansan was used by the USSAF, USAF, USMC, and USN for instrument and gunnery training. It was equipped with a .30-inch gun mounted in a dorsal turret, and it could carry 10 100-pound bombs. Twin 450-horsepower engines attained a maximum speed of 209 miles per hour. The USN used it from 1942 well into the 1960s.

Vought OS2U Kingfisher. Delivered to the USN during 1941–42 in a quantity of more than 1,000, this observation/scout airplane carried a pilot and observer/gunner and had a top speed of only 164 miles per hour. Service ceiling was 13,000 feet. Defense consisted of a .30-inch fixed gun and a flexible-mounted .30-inch gun. It was produced in floatplane and land plane versions.

Vought SB2U Vindicator. A carrier-based scout/dive bomber, the Vindicator carried a pilot and observer/gunner seated in tandem. A single 825-horsepower engine made 243 miles per hour at 9,500 feet. One .50-inch gun fired forward and another, flexible, .50-inch gun fired toward the rear. The Vindicator was the first USN monoplane scout-bomber. A mediocre performer, it was out of service by 1943.

airships

The U.S. Navy operated both nonrigid and rigid airships. The service began acquiring nonrigid airships (blimps) during the late 1920s, including the metal-clad ZMC-2, delivered to the USN in 1929 by the Aircraft Development Corporation. It remained in service for 12 years.

During the 1930s, the USN called on the Goodyear Tire and Rubber Company to build a new fleet of nonrigid airships. The prototype, designated K-1, burned a propane-like fuel, which could be contained in cells within the airship envelope because its density was about the same as that of air. Testing

of the K-1 began on October 7, 1931, and the ship was used until September 1940.

After successful testing of the K-1, the USN acquired a series of G-type airships from Goodyear. The first, the *Defender,* was delivered in 1935. The G series was replaced by L-type airships beginning in 1937.

Running parallel with its nonrigid airship program, the USN acquired rigid airships, beginning in 1923 with the ZR-1 (*Shenandoah*), which broke up during a storm over Ohio on September 3, 1925, killing 14 of its 43 crewmen. In 1924, Goodyear acquired U.S. patent rights to build zeppelins. Two giants built for the USN, the *Akron* and *Macon,* crashed. The *Akron* was destroyed in a storm in 1933, and the *Macon* was lost in the Pacific Ocean in 1935. Although subsequent USN investigations authorized continued use of rigid airships, no new aircraft were constructed, and, in the years leading up to World War II, resources were devoted exclusively to nonrigid airships.

In 1937, the USN took over sole control of the U.S. airship program from the U.S. Army Air Corps. Naval Air Station Lakehurst, New Jersey, became the center of USN airship operations. The following year, the service expanded its fleet with the K-type airship. The prototype, K-2, was delivered on December 16, 1938. It was the largest nonrigid airship in the USN inventory, with a capacity of 404,000 cubic feet.

Early in World War II, Congress authorized construction of 200 airships, of which Goodyear delivered 168 before the end of the war. These K-type craft were somewhat larger that the K-2 prototype, with a gas capacity of 416,000 to 425,000 cubic feet. They were 253 feet long and 60 feet in diameter. Propulsion came from two 425-horsepower engines, which gave the ships a maximum speed of 50 miles per hour. Endurance was high: A K-ship could stay aloft for up to 60 hours.

During the war, the USN used airships for minesweeping, search and rescue, photographic reconnaissance, scouting, escorting convoys, and antisubmarine patrols. They patrolled an area of over three million square miles and operated over the Atlantic, Pacific, and Mediterranean. Only a single airship, the K-74, was lost to enemy action.

The USN was the only American military service to use airships during World War II. After the war, the ships continued to be employed for anti-submarine warfare, intermediate search missions, and early warning missions. For the latter application, some airships were equipped with very large airborne radar equipment.

The largest postwar airships were the ZPG-2 (324 feet long, with a capacity of 875,000 cubic feet) and the ZPG-3 (403 feet long, with a capacity of 1,516,000 cubic feet). This was the largest non-rigid airship ever built and was capable of remaining aloft in excess of 200 hours.

Despite an impressive war record, the U.S. Navy discontinued its airship operations on August 31, 1962. Although the service began reconsidering the use of the craft during the 1980s, funding for the blimp program was terminated in 1989.

American Revolution

Responding to a succession of taxes imposed by Britain's Parliament, in which the North American colonies had no direct representation, an independence movement gained support in the 13 colonies below Canada. A revolution broke out in 1775, and, in 1776, a formal Declaration of Independence was issued.

On paper, the Royal Navy was a formidable force, but, in fact, it was languishing at a low point during the 1770s, having been drastically reduced following the end of the French and Indian War (in Europe called the Seven Years' War). Vice Admiral Samuel Graves, stationed in Boston, had at his disposal a mere 29 ships to blockade and patrol the long coast of America. Nevertheless, the new "United States" had virtually nothing with which to oppose the Royal Navy. A Continental navy was quickly authorized, and many of the colonies—now called states—maintained their own small naval forces. The Continental Congress relied

A painting by V. Zveg of the Second Battle of the Chesapeake (Battle of the Virginia Capes), September 5, 1781 (*Naval Historical Foundation*)

Engagement between the *Bonhomme Richard* and the *Serapis,* September 23, 1779   (*Naval Historical Foundation*)

heavily on privateers, American merchant sailors commissioned to raid British shipping; they were compensated by the award of any "prizes" they captured.

Prior to the creation of the Continental navy on October 13, 1775, Jeremiah O'Brien, a merchant sailor, managed to capture the Royal Navy schooner *Margaretta* (June 1775), while an ad hoc force assembled by George Washington conducted minor engagements of little consequence. Esek Hopkins was appointed commander in chief of a fleet of eight ships acquired by the end of 1775, the largest of which were *Alfred* and *Columbus,* merchant ships hastily armed and converted into frigates of 24 and 20 guns. The other six vessels were considerably smaller. The Continental navy put to sea on February 17, 1776, with congressional orders to clear the Chesapeake of British ships, then sail to the Carolinas, clear British shipping

there, and, finally, drive the Royal Navy from Rhode Island. Needless to say, this was an unrealistic assignment. At this point, the Royal Navy had been augmented so that it had 78 ships in theater. Recognizing the impossibility of the mission, Hopkins interpreted his orders very broadly and decided instead to sail to Nassau, in the Bahamas, which he captured during March 3–4, 1776. After this, he captured a British schooner and a brig. However, after the *Alfred* suffered ignominious defeat by HMS *Glasgow* on April 6, Esek and the fleet returned to Providence, Rhode Island, where Esek was relieved of command.

JOHN PAUL JONES, who had sailed under Esek, was given command of the 12-gun *Providence,* which, during the second half of 1776, he used to capture or sink five transport vessels, two warships, six schooners, seven brigantines, a sloop, and a 16-gun privateer. Jones emerged as the USN's first hero and, indeed, one of the world's great combat sailors.

Jones went on in 1778 to score even more remarkable victories against British shipping, but his greatest triumph came on September 23, 1779, when, sailing the *Bonhomme Richard,* he defeated HMS *Serapis,* a 44-gun Royal Navy man o' war.

The Continental and various state navies never commissioned more than 100 ships during the war, whereas the British ultimately brought 468 into the North American theater, of which 174 mounted at least 60 guns or more. While the Royal Navy unquestionably achieved naval supremacy, using its vessels to blockade American ports and to transport troops and supplies, it maintained this supremacy at a surprising and staggering cost. Despite the disparity in numbers, Continental navy and state navy frigates sank or captured nearly 200 British vessels. Privateers claimed another 600 British ships, mostly commercial transports. For all its resources, the Royal Navy was very poorly led during this period. Nevertheless, the achievement of the fledgling American federal and state navies was astounding.

ammunition ships (T-AE)   See CARGO, FUEL, AND REPLENISHMENT SHIPS.

amphibious assault ships (LHA/LHD/LPH)

Navy LHAs, LHDs, and LPHs are primary landing ships, which resemble small AIRCRAFT CARRIERS. Their mission is to land troops on hostile shores, and they are used as primary landing ships for assault operations of USMC expeditionary units. The ships launch and recover LANDING CRAFT, AIR CUSHIONED (LCAC), conventional landing craft, and helicopters to land assault forces. Secondarily, these vessels deploy AV-8B Harrier jets and antisubmarine warfare helicopters.

Tarawa Class

The five ships of the *Tarawa* class, commissioned between 1976 and 1980, have the primary warfighting mission of landing and sustaining USMC forces during hostilities. These amphibious assault ships are the core of a multiship Amphibious Readiness Group (ARG). The *Tarawa*-class vessels are designed to enable landing forces to maintain tactical integrity, that is, to ensure that a balanced force arrives at the same place at the same time. Therefore, each LHA is equipped to carry a complete USMC battalion, along with all the weapons, vehicles, supplies, and equipment needed in an assault. Each assault element and component is landed either by helicopter or by amphibious craft launched from the LHA.

The ability to launch both an airborne and an amphibious assault makes the *Tarawa*-class ships highly versatile. This versatility extends to the capability of the *Tarawa* class to operate independently or as a unit of a force, either as a flagship or as an individual ship unit. The design of the *Tarawa* class incorporates the best design features and capabilities of several conventional amphibious assault ships, such as the AMPHIBIOUS TRANSPORT DOCK SHIPS (LPD) and DOCK LANDING SHIPS (LSD).

The ships of the *Tarawa* class also serve as small aircraft carriers and can accommodate a 35-aircraft complement, including AV-8B Harriers, AH-1 helicopter gunships, CH-53E Super Sea Stallion helicopters, and CH-46D/E Sea Knight helicopters. As an amphibious assault launching platform, the ships are capable of deploying a variety of surface assault craft, including the landing craft, air cushioned (LCAC), and LANDING CRAFT, MECHANIZED AND UTILITY (LCM, LCU), as well as an assortment of amphibious assault vehicles.

Tarawa-class ships can be configured as hospital ships, with a capacity of 17 ICU beds, four operating rooms, 300 beds, a 1,000-unit blood bank, full dental facilities, and orthopedics, trauma, general surgery, and X-ray capabilities. They can also be configured as complete Command, Control, Communication, Computer, and Intelligence (C^4I) ships, incorporating SHF and EHF satellite communications capability. Finally, the *Tarawa* class serves as an assault provisions carrier, with the capacity to sustain embarked forces with fuel, ammunition, and other necessary supplies. Each ship is capable of embarking 3,000 marines when deployed.

General specifications of the *Tarawa* class include:

Power plant: two boilers, two geared steam turbines, two shafts, 70,000 total shaft horsepower

Length, waterline: 778 ft

Length, overall: 820 ft

Beam, extreme: 106 ft

Beam, waterline: 106 ft

Maximum navigational draft: 26 ft

Draft limit: 27 ft

Displacement: 39,925 tons full load

Dead weight: 13,670 tons

Speed: 24 knots

Aircraft, depending on mission: six AV-8B Harrier attack planes; four AH-1W Super-Cobra attack helicopters; 12 CH-46 Sea Knight helicopters; nine CH-53 Sea Stallion helicopters; four UH-1N Huey helicopters

Boats: two LCU; one LCAC; four LCPL

Elevators: one deck-edge (40,000-pound capacity); one stern (80,000-pound capacity)

Crew: ship's company, 82 officers, 882 enlisted; USMC Detachment, 1,900+

Armament: two 21-Cell Rolling Airframe Missile (RAM); four 25-mm Mk-38 gun mounts; two 20-mm Close-In Weapons System Block 1; five 50-caliber mounts; two SLQ-25 NIXIE; six Mk-36 Super Rapid-Blooming Off Board Chaff System (SRBOC)

Sensors: Mk-23 Target Acquisition System (TAS) Mod 5; SPS-67 surface search radar; SPS-40E air search radar; SPS-48E 3-D air search radar; SPS-64 navigation radar; SPN-35A aircraft control/approach radar; SPN-43C aircraft control/approach radar; SLQ-32(V)3 electronic warfare suite; URN-25 TACAN Furuno navigation radar

Ships of the *Tarawa* class include: *Tarawa* (LHA-1), *Saipan* (LHA-2), *Belleau Wood* (ex-*Philippine Sea*) (LHA-3), *Nassau* (ex-*Leyte Gulf*) (LHA-4), and *Peleliu* (ex-*Da Nang*, ex-*Khe Sanh*) (LHA-5).

Wasp Class

The largest amphibious ships in the world, the *Wasp*-class LHD represents the next step beyond the five-ship *Tarawa*-class LHA. The *Wasp* class shares with the *Tarawa* class the same basic hull and engineering plant, but the LHD ships have enhanced well decks, which enable them to carry three landing craft, air cushioned (LCAC), whereas the *Tarawa* vessels could carry only one. Also upgraded are the flight deck and elevators. The new ships carry two more helicopters than the *Tarawa* predecessor vessels. *Wasp*-class ships are also the first expressly designed to accommodate the AV-8B Harrier "jump jet." In all, each *Wasp*-class vessel can carry all the helicopters, conventional landing craft, and amphibious assault vehicles to support a Marine Expeditionary Unit (MEU) of 2,000 marines.

The ships of this class are each 844 feet long with a beam of 106 feet. They are powered by a pair of steam propulsion plants, the largest used in the USN, which develop 70,000 shaft horsepower for each of the two propulsion shafts, pushing the ship to speeds greater than 20 knots. Each of the ships accommodates 3,000 marines and crew members and includes six fully equipped operating rooms and a 600-bed hospital. Except for designated hospital ships, these facilities are far and away the largest at sea.

The mission of the *Wasp*-class ships is to conduct prompt, sustained combat operations at sea, providing the means to deliver, command, and support all elements of a USMC landing force in an assault by air and amphibious craft. To accomplish this, the ships can use various combinations of helicopters, Harrier II (AV-8B) "Jump Jets," and air cushioned landing craft (LCAC), in addition to conventional landing craft and assault vehicles. The ships transport and land not only troops but also the tanks, trucks, jeeps, other vehicles, artillery, ammunition, and various supplies necessary to support the amphibious assault mission. Six-hundred-foot-per-minute monorail trains transport cargo and supplies from storage and staging areas throughout the ship to a 13,600-square-foot well deck, which opens to the sea through giant gates in the ship's stern. From here, the cargo, troops, and vehicles are loaded aboard landing craft for transit to the beach. Whereas air-cushioned landing craft can "fly" out of the dry well deck, the deck can be ballasted down and flooded for conventional craft to float out to the assault area.

General specifications of the *Wasp* class include:

Power plant: two boilers (600 psi), two geared steam turbines, two shafts, 70,000 shaft horsepower

Length: 844 ft

Beam, at waterline: 106 ft

Beam, with flight deck elevators extended: 200 ft

Draft, fully loaded: 27 ft

Draft, ballasted: 36 ft at the stern

Displacement: 40,500 tons full load

Speed: 20+ knots

Aircraft, depending on mission: six AV-8B Harrier attack planes; four AH-1W Super-Cobra attack helicopters; 12 CH-46 Sea Knight helicopters; nine CH-53 Sea Stallion helicopters; four UH-1N Huey helicopters. Or: six AV-8B Harrier attack planes; 12 CH-46 Sea Knight helicopters; nine CH-53 Sea Stallion helicopters. Or, if configured for assault: 42 CH-46 Sea Knight helicopters. Or, if configured for sea control: 20 AV-8B Harrier attack planes; six ASW helicopters

Landing craft: two LCU landing craft, utility; or three LCAC landing craft, air cushioned; or six LCM-8 landing craft, mechanized; or 40 AAV amphibious assault vehicles (normal); or 61 AAV amphibious assault vehicles (stowed)

armament: two Mk-29 launchers for NATO Sea Sparrow; three Mk-15 20-mm Phalanx CIWS mounts; eight Mk-33 .50-caliber machine guns

Combat and control systems: AN/SLQ-49 Chaff Buoys; AN/SLQ-25 NIXIE Towed Torpedo Countermeasures; AN/SLQ-32(V)3 Electronic Warfare (EW) system; one AN/ SPS-48 radar; one AN/SPS-49(V)7 radar; one AN/SPS-64 radar; one AN/SPS-67 radar; AN/SYS-2 Detection/Tracking System; one Mk-23 Target Acquisition System (TAS); one Mk-36 Chaff Launcher; Mk-91 fire control system

Crew: ship's company, 104 officers, 1,004 enlisted; USMC detachment: 1,894

Shipboard departments: Aircraft Maintenance; Air; Combat Systems; Combat Cargo; Communications; Deck; Dental; Engineering; Executive; Medical; Navigation; Operations; Safety; Supply

Ships of the *Wasp* class include: *Wasp* (LHD-1), *Essex* (LHD-2), *Kearsarge* (LHD-3), *Boxer* (LHD-4), *Bataan* (LHD-5), *Bonhomme Richard* (LHD-6), and *Iwo Jima* (LHD-7).

LPH Ships

The navy operated two amphibious assault ship classes designated LPH, the *Iwo Jima* class and the single-ship *Thetis Bay* class.

Iwo Jima Class (LPH)

The navy operated seven *Iwo Jima*–class amphibious assault ships, each designed to transport more than 1,700 fully equipped U.S. Marine Corps assault troops into combat areas, landing them by helicopter at the designated inland points for the vertical envelopment mission. Each ship supports a Marine Battalion Landing Team, together with its armament, vehicles, equipment, and a reinforced squadron of transport helicopters, including support personnel.

Ships of this class also supported mine-sweeping operations using Helicopter Mine Countermeasure Squadrons, and they were also assigned to provide humanitarian assistance and noncombatant evacuations of American embassy personnel and of citizens caught in civil conflict overseas. The ships of this class were commissioned between 1958 and 1964 and all except *Inchon* were decommissioned during the 1990s.

The *Iwo Jima* was deployed to the Persian Gulf during the Persian Gulf War. A catastrophic high-pressure steam leak on October 30, 1990, killed 10 crew members, but the ship was subsequently repaired. *Iwo Jima* was scrapped in 1996.

USS *Inchon* saw service with the U.S. Naval Amphibious Forces from 1970 to 1994 in both the ATLANTIC FLEET and the PACIFIC FLEET. This ship was converted from amphibious assault ship to a dedicated command, control, and support ship for mine countermeasures operations in 1996. The converted vessel is the only member of this class still in service (see MINESWEEPERS, COASTAL MINEHUNTERS, AND MINE COUNTERMEASURES SHIPS).

General specifications of the *Iwo Jima* class include:

Power plant: two boilers, one geared steam turbine, one shaft, 22,000 shaft horsepower
Length: 598 ft
Waterline length: 556 ft
Flight deck width: 104 ft
Beam: 84 ft
Maximum navigational draft: 29 ft
Draft limit: 30 ft
Displacement: 19,395 tons full load
Dead weight: 5,930 tons
Speed: 23 knots
Aircraft, depending on mission: 11 CH-53 Sea Stallion helicopters; 20 CH-46 Sea Knight helicopters; one UH-1 or SH-3 for search and rescue; three UH-1 USMC helicopters; three AH-1 USMC helicopters
Crew: ship's company, 80 officers, 638 enlisted; USMC detachment, 1,750
Armament: two 20-mm Phalanx CIWS

Ships of the *Iwo Jima* class included: *Iwo Jima* (LPH 2), *Okinawa* (LPH 3), *Guadalcanal* (LPH 7), *Guam* (LPH 9), *Tripoli* (LPH 10), *New Orleans* (LPH 11), and *Inchon* (LPH 12).

USS *Thetis Bay* (LPH 6)

Originally, USS *Thetis Bay* was a WORLD WAR II *Casablanca* class escort aircraft carrier, launched on December 22, 1944. Decommissioned on August 7, 1946, she was placed in the Pacific Reserve Fleet at Bremerton, Washington, then, in May 1955, was towed to the San Francisco Naval Shipyard for conversion to the navy's first assault helicopter aircraft carrier. On July 1, 1955, her designation was changed from CVE 90 to CVHA 1, and on May 28, 1959, she became LPH 6. She was finally decommissioned on March 1, 1964, and, in December, scrapped.

General characteristics of *Thetis Bay* included:

Builder: Kaiser Shipbuilding Co., Vancouver, Washington
Propulsion system: four boilers
Propellers: two
Length: 512.5 ft
Flight deck width: 108 ft
Beam: 65 ft
Draft: 22.6 ft
Displacement: 10,400 tons full load
Speed: 19 knots
Catapults: one as CVE, none as LPH
Aircraft: 28 planes as CVE, numerous helicopters as LPH
Armament: 16 40-mm guns as LPH
Crew: 860

amphibious cargo ships (LKA)

LKAs were designed to carry troops, heavy equipment, and supplies in support of amphibious assaults. The five ships made up a single class, the *Charleston* class.

Charleston class (LKA)

Commissioned between 1968 and 1970 and decommissioned during 1992–94, the five ships of the *Charleston* class were the first class of ship that was designed specifically to carry troops, heavy equipment, and supplies in support of amphibious assaults. These ships were also among the first to be fitted with a fully automated main propulsion plant.

General specifications of the *Charleston* class included:

Overall length: 576 ft
Waterline length: 550 ft
Extreme beam: 82 ft
Waterline beam: 82 ft

Maximum navigational draft: 26 ft
Draft limit: 28 ft
Displacement: 18,589 tons full load
Dead weight: 8,373 tons
Crew: officers, 34; enlisted, 375

Ships of the class included *Charleston* (LKA-113), *Durham* (LKA-114), *Mobile* (LKA-115), *St. Louis* (LKA-116), and *El Paso* (LKA-117).

amphibious command ships (LCC)

The two USN amphibious command ships are of the *Blue Ridge* class, commissioned in 1970 to provide command and control for fleet commanders. Prior to these vessels, amphibious command ships were incapable of keeping up with a 20-knot amphibious force.

Blue Ridge Class (LCC 19)

The USS *Blue Ridge* (LCC-19) and the USS *Mount Whitney* (LCC-20) make up the *Blue Ridge* class of the amphibious command ship category. These vessels provide command and control for fleet commanders and are the only navy ships originally designed for the amphibious command ship role. USS *Blue Ridge* became the SEVENTH FLEET command ship in 1979, and USS *Mount Whitney* became the SECOND FLEET command ship in 1981.

The *Blue Ridge* was built by the Philadelphia Naval Shipyard in 1967 and commissioned on November 14, 1970. Conceived from the beginning as a platform for the mission of command and control coordination, the *Blue Ridge* was designed to provide facilities for directing and managing every phase of command and control operations. Among its suite of electronics, the *Blue Ridge* incorporates the Joint Maritime Command Information System (JMCIS), which consists of a number of powerful computers distributed throughout the ship from which information and data from worldwide sources are entered into a central database. The database concentrates the available information into a complete tactical picture of air, surface, and subsurface contacts, enabling the fleet commander to assess and address any situation

that presents itself. Coordinated with the data processing systems is a state-of-the-art communications system. Finally, the 23-knot speed of the *Blue Ridge* ensures that she can more than keep up with the forces she is assigned to coordinate.

USS *Blue Ridge* is homeported in Yokosuka, Japan, and USS *Mount Whitney* is homeported in Norfolk, Virginia. General specifications of the *Blue Ridge* include:

Power plant: two boilers, one geared turbine, one shaft; 22,000 shaft horsepower
Length: 634 ft
Beam, extreme: 108 ft
Displacement: 18,874 tons full load
Speed: 23 knots
Aircraft: all helicopters except the CH-53 Sea Stallion can be carried
Crew: 52 officers, 790 enlisted in addition to flag staff

Ships of the *Blue Ridge* class include USS *Blue Ridge* (LCC-19) and USS *Mount Whitney* (LCC-20).

amphibious transport dock ships (LPD)

LPDs embark, transport, and land elements of a landing force for a variety of expeditionary warfare missions. These vessels are used to transport and land air-cushioned or conventional landing craft or amphibious vehicles, augmented by helicopters or vertical takeoff and landing (VTOL) aircraft. Currently, operational navy LPDs are of two classes, the *San Antonio* class and the *Austin* class. Both classes perform the mission of amphibious transports, amphibious cargo ships, and the older LPDs by incorporating both a flight deck and a well deck, which can be ballasted and deballasted to support landing craft or amphibious vehicles. When completed, the vessels of the *San Antonio* class will replace the *Austin* class, providing increased vehicle and cargo carrying capacity.

Austin Class (LPD-4)

Although designated amphibious transport dock (LPD) ships, the vessels of the *Austin* class actually combine the functions of three different categories of ships—the landing ship dock (LSD), the landing ship, tank (LST), and the attack cargo ship (LKA)—in addition to the amphibious transport dock. The *Austin* class replaces the earlier, less versatile *Raleigh* class (LPD-1) and is used to transport and land marines, with their equipment and supplies, using embarked landing craft or amphibious vehicles augmented by helicopters in the amphibious assault mission. As the *Austin* class replaced the *Raleigh* class, so the new *Whidbey Island* class (LSD-41) has capabilities superior to those of the *Austin*-class ships. However, the *Austin* class vessels, built between 1965 and 1971, have continued to operate through the first half of the first decade of the 21st century. They are being replaced by the *Whidbey Island* class and by the *San Antonio* Class (LPD-17).

The *Austin*-class ships are configured as flagships and are equipped to provide extensive command, control, and communications facilities to support an amphibious task force commander and landing force commander. During an amphibious assault, a ship of this class functions as the primary control ship, which coordinates boat waves and vectors landing craft to the beach. The *Austin* class has as its secondary mission evacuation and civilian disaster relief. The ships can be loaded with hundreds of tons of relief supplies, which can be delivered ashore at great speed. On board, the ships' medical and dental facilities, intended to support landing assault forces, can be used to provide a limited degree of hospitalization care for hundreds of sick or injured.

All ships of this class incorporate a large flight deck for helicopter operations and a well deck, which carries amphibious landing vehicles. Each ship can carry one landing craft air-cushioned (LCAC) or one utility landing craft (LCU) boat or four mechanized landing craft (LCU), and six CH-46 amphibious transport helicopters or three CH-53 helicopters. Troop capacity is in excess of 800, with equipment and supplies up to 2,000 tons. The ship's company consists of an additional 400 officers and enlisted men.

The helicopter platform on the *Austin* class is built over a well deck in the aft portion of the vessel. This allows troops, their combat equipment, and supplies to be lifted on the same ship. The well decks are upper and lower vehicle storage areas and hold most of the troops' heavy combat equipment, including tanks, tracked amphibious landing vehicles (AAV), and trucks. To facilitate the docking and loading of landing craft of various sizes, the ship can be ballasted down, flooding the well deck with enough water to enable the landing craft to enter the well deck through the stern gate door. Once docked inside the well deck, troops, supplies, and combat equipment can be loaded or unloaded. Simultaneously with these operations, troops and equipment can be transported by helicopter from the flight deck.

General specifications of the *Austin* class include:

Power plant: two boilers, two steam turbines, two shafts, 24,000 shaft horsepower
Overall length: 569 ft
Waterline length: 548 ft
Extreme beam: 105 ft
Waterline beam: 84 ft
Maximum navigational draft: 22 ft
Draft limit: 23 ft
Ballasted draft: 34 ft
Displacement: 16,914 tons full load
Dead weight: 7,713 tons
Speed: 21 knots
Aircraft: up to six CH-46 Sea Knight helicopters
Well deck capacity: one Landing Craft, Air Cushioned (LCAC), or one Landing Craft, Utility (LCU), or four LCM-8 Landing Craft, Mechanized (LCM), or nine LCM-6 Landing Craft, Mechanized (LCM), or 24 AAV Amphibious Assault Vehicles
Crew: ship's company: 420 (24 officers, 396 enlisted); marine detachment: 900
Combat systems: SPS-40 Air Search Radar; SPS-60 Surface Search Radar; SPS-64 Navigational Radar; Furuno Navigational Radar

Armament: two 25-mm Mk-38 guns; two Phalanx CIWS; eight .50-caliber machine guns

Ships of the class include: *Austin* (LPD-4), *Ogden* (LPD-5), *Duluth* (LPD-6), *Cleveland* (LPD-7), *Dubuque* (LPD-8), *Denver* (LPD-9), *Juneau* (LPD-10), *Coronado* (configured as a command ship, AGF-11), *Nashville* (LPD-13), *Trenton* (LPD-14), and *Ponce* (LPD-15).

San Antonio Class

The *San Antonio* class is the latest of the navy's amphibious transport dock (LPD) ships and is designed for 21st-century amphibious warfare. As of 2004, two ships of this class, the *San Antonio* and the *New Orleans,* had been commissioned, with another 10 craft planned for commissioning by 2008. The ships are the first that have been designed, from the keel up, to execute Operational Maneuver From The Sea (OMFTS) and Ship to Objective Maneuver—that is, to support embarking, transporting, and landing elements of a USMC landing force in an assault by helicopters, landing craft, and amphibious vehicles.

While the ship's mission is to transport and land the marines, vehicles, and equipment embarked, much of the success of the mission depends on state-of-the-art electronics, radar, navigation, and communications. Installed is the SPS-73 system, a commercial surface search radar that replaced the SPS-67 and SPS-64 radars. More reliable than the earlier radars, the SPS-73 consolidates training requirements, reduces maintenance, and is less expensive. The Advanced Enclosed Mast/Sensor (AEM/S) system is an octagonal, detachable structure that enables modular upgrade of future combat sensors and Command, Control, Communications, Computer, and Intelligence (C^4I) systems. The AEM/S system mast is a 93-foot-high hexagonal structure 35 feet in diameter. It is constructed of a multilayer, frequency-selective composite material designed to allow passage of own-ship sensor frequencies with very low loss while reflecting other frequencies. Additionally, the mast's shape is designed to provide a smooth silhouette and thus a degree of stealth capability by reducing radar cross section.

General specifications of the *San Antonio* class include:

Length, overall: 684 ft

Beam, extreme: 105 ft

Draft: 23 ft full load

Displacement: approximately 25,000 tons full load

Sustained speed: about 22 knots

Accommodations, officers: 115; CPO/SNCO: 82; enlisted: 1,005

Vehicles/cargo: three vehicle decks (2,500 sq ft); two cargo/ammo magazines (25,000 cu ft); cargo fuel, JP-5 (42,000 cu ft); cargo fuel, MOGAS (1,300 cu ft); two LCACs Medical: two operating rooms; 24-person hospital ward; 100 casualty overflow capacity

Aviation facilities, hangar: "O"-level maintenance facilities for: one CH-53E, or two CH-46s, or one MV-22, or three UH/AH-1s

Aviation facilities, landing: two CH-53s, or four AH/UH-1s, or four CH-46s, or two MV-22s, or one AV-8B Harrier

Main propulsion: four medium-speed turbocharged marine diesels; two shafts; two single reversing reduction gears; two inboard rotating (top) fixed-pitch propellers

Electric plant: five 2,500 kilowatt ship service marine diesel generators

Auxiliaries: seven 700 kilowatt non-cfc air conditioning plants; five reverse osmosis desalination plants; 10 navy standard firepumps; five air compressors; three deballast air compressors

Navigation: Digital Flux Gate Magnetic Compass; AN/WSN-7(V)1 Inertial Navigation System; AN/WQN-2 Doppler Sonar Velocity Log System; AN/UQN-4A Sonar Sounding Set; Dead Reckoning System; Navigation Telex System; AN/SSN-6 NAVSSI

Ship's weapons: one Mk-41, 16 Cell VLS (space and weight); two Mk-31 Mod 0 RAM launchers; two Mk-46 Mod 1 30-mm machine guns; two Mk-26 Mod 17 .50-caliber machine guns

Command and control: AN/SPQ-12(V) Radar Display Distribution System; Mk-2 SSDS; AN/USQ-119C(V)27 JMCIS; AN/KSQ-1 Amphibious Assault Direction System; Mk-91, two-channel MFCS; AN/USG-2 CEC Radar Systems AN/SPS-48E; AN/SPQ-9B; AN/SPS-73; EW and Decoy Systems AN/SLQ-25A NIXIE; AN/SLQ-32Q(V)2; Mk-36 SRBOC; Mk-53/NULKA; TISS

As of 2004, ships of the class included *San Antonio* (LPD-17) and *New Orleans* (LPD-18).

Raleigh Class

The *Raleigh*-class LPDs were designed to transport and land marines, with their equipment and supplies, using embarked landing craft or amphibious vehicles augmented by helicopters in the amphibious assault mission. The LPDs replaced amphibious transports (APA), amphibious cargo ships (AKA), and the older LSDs. However, the *Raleigh* class has itself been replaced by the more versatile *Austin* class (LPD-4) and the *Whidbey Island* class (LSD-41). The lead ship of the class, *Raleigh*, was disposed of on December 4, 1994, as a target in Ship Shock Test/Trials.

The *Raleigh* class consisted of two ships built as amphibious transport dock (LPD) vessels, commissioned in 1962 and 1963 and decommissioned in 1991 and 1992, and one ship, the *La Salle* (LPD-3), which was completed as AGF-3, a COMMAND SHIP (AGF).

General specifications of the *Raleigh* class include:

Power plant: two boilers, two steam turbines, two shafts, 24,000 shaft horsepower
Overall length: 522 ft
Waterline length: 500 ft
Extreme beam: 100 ft
Waterline beam: 84 ft
Maximum navigational draft: 23 ft
Draft limit: 23 ft
Displacement: 14,113 tons full load

Dead weight: 5,463 tons
Armament: six Mk-33 three-inch .50-caliber guns; two 20-mm Phalanx CIWS
Speed: 21 knots
Crew, ship's company: 429; embarked marines, 930

Ships of the class included *Raleigh* (LPD-1), *Vancouver* (LPD-2), and *La Salle* (LPD-3), which was completed as AGF-3, a command ship.

Anderson, George W., Jr. (1906–1992) *chief of naval operations*

Sixteenth CHIEF OF NAVAL OPERATIONS, Anderson was a UNITED STATES NAVAL ACADEMY graduate (1927) and served in the Pacific theater during WORLD WAR II. He rose to command of SIXTH FLEET during 1959–61 and was appointed CNO in 1961. Because of sharp disagreements with Secretary of Defense Robert McNamara, Anderson served only a single term as CNO, retiring from the navy in 1963. He later served as ambassador to Portugal and was chairman of the president's Foreign Intelligence Advisory Board.

Arleigh Burke Class (DDG-51)   See DESTROYERS.

Atlantic Fleet

The Atlantic Fleet supports United States and NATO commanders in the North Atlantic Ocean, the Adriatic, and part of the Mediterranean with more than 118,000 sailors and marines, 186 ships, and 1,300 aircraft. Eighteen major shore stations provide training, maintenance, and logistics support. The fleet's area of responsibility encompasses the Atlantic Ocean from the North Pole to 28 degrees north latitude, and from the Adriatic Sea to the Arabian Gulf. In addition, it covers the Norwegian, Greenland, and Barents Seas. SECOND FLEET is the operational fleet of the Atlantic Fleet, responsible for operational tasking as well as training carrier battle groups and amphibious ready groups for forward deployments. The Atlantic Fleet is headquartered in Norfolk, Virginia, with regional commanders loacated in New London, Connecticut, and Jacksonville, Florida, in addition to Norfolk.

The Atlantic Fleet was established in 1906 by President Theodore Roosevelt.

Atlantic Undersea Test and Evaluation Center (AUTEC)

AUTEC supports undersea warfare by providing accurate three-dimensional tracking, performance measurement, and data collection resources to satisfy research, development, test and evaluation requirements, and for assessment of fleet training and tactical and material readiness. The center's administrative and technical support offices are located in West Palm Beach, Florida, and test programs are conducted at facilities on Andros Island. A range support facility on the island houses torpedo test and analysis facilities and an extensive technical laboratory.

attack submarines (SSN)   See SUBMARINES.

auxiliary crane ships (T-ACS)   See CARGO, FUEL, AND REPLENISHMENT SHIPS.

***Avenger* Class (MCM-1)**   See MINESWEEPERS.

aviation logistic ships (T-AVB)   See CARGO, FUEL, AND REPLENISHMENT SHIPS.

B

Bainbridge, William (1774–1833) *naval officer*

New Jersey native William Bainbridge joined the U.S. Navy in 1798 and commanded, in succession, *Retaliation, Norfolk,* and *George Washington.* During the BARBARY WARS, he was in command of USS

Captain William Bainbridge, with USS *Constitution* and HMS *Java* in the background   *(Naval Historical Foundation)*

Philadelphia, which was captured on October 31, 1803, after it ran aground off Tripoli. Although STEPHEN DECATUR led a daring and successful raid to burn *Philadelphia* and thereby prevent the bey of Tripoli from using it, Bainbridge and his crew remained prisoners until 1805.

After Bainbridge returned to the United States, he was named to command Charleston Naval Yard, then was given command of USS CONSTITUTION, in which he defeated HMS *Java* off the coast of Brazil on November 29, 1812, during the WAR OF 1812. Subsequently, Bainbridge was assigned command of USS *Independence,* then created a school for naval officers in 1817. From 1832 until his death, Bainbridge was president of the Board of Navy Commissioners.

Bainbridge Class (CGN 25)   See FRIGATES.

ballistic missile submarines (SSBN)   See SUBMARINES.

Bancroft, George (1800–1899) *secretary of the navy*

The first major American historian, Bancroft was the founder of the UNITED STATES NAVAL ACADEMY, which he established during his term as SECRETARY OF THE NAVY under President James K. Polk

716

(1844–46). He was subsequently appointed ambassador to the Court of St. James's (Great Britain), Prussia, and Germany.

Barbary Wars

"Barbary Wars" is a collective name for two naval conflicts, the Tripolitan War of 1800–05 and the Algerine War of 1815. Both were USN actions against the state-sanctioned piracy of Muslim mariners operating out of the "Barbary states" (present-day Morocco, Algeria, Tunisia, and Libya) on the coast of North Africa. Such piracy had been directed against the shipping of Christian (i.e., non-Muslim) nations since the 17th century, and governments became accustomed to paying extor-

tionate tribute money to the Barbary states for protection against the pirates. Beginning in the administration of Thomas Jefferson, however, U.S. policy would no longer brook extortion, which was seen as a threat to sovereignty.

The origin of the Tripolitan War may be traced to 1785, when Great Britain encouraged Algiers to capture two American vessels. At the time, Jefferson was American minister plenipotentiary to France; from this post, he attempted to draw Portugal, Naples, Sardinia, Russia, and France into an anti-Algerian alliance. A French refusal to cooperate brought the collapse of the alliance, and Britain incited Algeria to an even more vigorous piracy, in which a dozen American ships were captured and more than 100 American sailors

Battle of Tripoli involving Commodore Edward Preble's U.S. squadron, August 3, 1804   *(Naval Historical Foundation)*

imprisoned. The U.S. government negotiated a treaty with the bey of Algiers in 1795, pledging tribute to secure release of the captives and to ensure freedom of navigation. Additional treaties were concluded with Tunis and Tripoli. The United States, however, delayed sending the tribute money, which, shortly after the inauguration of President Jefferson in 1801, moved Pasha Yusuf Qaramanli, Tripoli's ruler, to declare war, albeit informally.

Jefferson responded by creating a coalition with Sweden, Sicily, Malta, Portugal, and Morocco against Tripoli, forcing Qaramanli to back down. From 1801 to 1803, one USN frigate and several smaller USN vessels patrolled the Tripolitan coast. In October 1803, USS *Philadelphia* ran aground and was captured; 300 American sailors were imprisoned in Tripoli. In February 1804, however, Lieutenant STEPHEN DECATUR led a daring raid on Tripoli harbor and burned *Philadelphia,* thereby denying the prize to the bey. Following this, Commodore Edward Preble increased an ongoing bombardment of Tripoli while the American consul at Tunis, William Eaton, proposed an alliance with Ahmed Qaramanli, the brother Yusuf had deposed in 1795. At the same time, Eaton recruited a force of Arabs and Greeks who joined a contingent of U.S. Marines to support the restoration of Ahmed. In coordination with the USN bombardment, Eaton's force captured Derna in 1805. Eaton had never secured the authorization of the Jefferson government, however, and the president concluded a treaty of peace with Yusuf Qaramanli on June 4, 1805. Although the treaty stipulated a $60,000 ransom to be paid for the release of the American prisoners, it also ended the practice of annual tribute payment, establishing unhindered commerce between the United States and Tripoli. Americans hailed the war as a triumph of U.S. seapower.

Despite the Treaty of Tripoli, Barbary piracy soon revived, especially during the WAR OF 1812, when U.S. Navy vessels that had been patrolling the Barbary waters had to be withdrawn for service closer to home. The bey of Algiers exploited the absence of patrolling vessels to resume piracy. After expelling the U.S. consul and imprisoning or enslaving American nationals, the bey formally declared war in 1815. His timing, however, was bad. With the War of 1812 ended, Commodore Stephen Decatur was able to lead a 10-ship squadron into the Mediterranean and, between March 3 and June 30, 1815, capture two Algerian warships. He then sailed into the harbor of Algiers, where, at the mouth of his cannon, he demanded an end to tribute and the release of all prisoners without ransom. The bey acquiesced, concluding on June 30, 1815, a treaty ending state-sanctioned piracy. Decatur continued on to Tunis and Tripoli, where he also coerced treaties and even secured compensation for American vessels that had been seized by those states (at British prompting) during the War of 1812.

Like the Tripolitan War, the briefer Algerine War was a triumph for the U.S. Navy as an instrument of American international policy. Nevertheless, despite the treaty of 1815 and another concluded in 1816, Algerian piracy remained a threat—although at a significantly reduced level—until France captured Algiers in 1830.

Barney, Joshua (1759–1818) *navy captain*

Baltimore-born Joshua Barney joined the Continental navy in 1775 and fought in the AMERICAN REVOLUTION. He was instrumental in the capture of New Providence, Bahamas, in 1776, then was given command of *Hyder Ally,* in which he captured HMS *General Monk* in 1782.

Barney served for a short time in the French navy, then returned to the United States and rejoined the U.S. Navy in time to command a GUNBOAT flotilla on Chesapeake Bay during the WAR OF 1812. He distinguished himself during the otherwise disastrous Battle of Bladensburg on August 24, 1814. While U.S. militia forces crumbled before the British advance on Washington, D.C., Barney stood firm with a mixed force of 500 sailors and marines. Wounded, he was taken prisoner. On his release, he retired from the navy.

bases, stations, and other installations

With the exception of Naval Base Ventura County and its three major submarine bases, major modern USN installations are generally called stations. Ship-related installations are, of course, located near major waterways, but a number of the U.S. Navy's naval air stations are located well inland.

Naval Air Station Atlanta, Georgia

Located outside of Atlanta proper, in Marietta, Georgia, NAS Atlanta is home to more than 900 active-duty military and civilian personnel associated with Marine Air Group (MAG) 42, Carrier Air Group (CAG) 20, three USN squadrons (flying the F/A-18 Hornet, E-2, and C-9 aircraft), two USMC squadrons (flying the F/A-18 aircraft, and AH-1W and UH-1 helicopters), and other commands.

NAS Atlanta was established when Fort Gordon was converted to a Naval Reserve aviation base on March 22, 1941, with primary responsibility for training USN and USMC aviators. In January 1943, the base was officially designated U.S. Naval Air Station Atlanta. After the war, a NAVAL AIR RESERVE FORCE training program was activated at NAS Atlanta. In 1959, NAS Atlanta moved to the large military reservation it now jointly occupies with Dobbins Air Force Base and the Lockheed-Martin Company.

Further reading: NAS Atlanta web site: "Naval Air Station, Atlanta," at www.nasatlanta.navy.mil.

Naval Air Station Brunswick, Maine

NAS Brunswick is currently the only active-duty Department of Defense airfield in the Northeast. It is home to five active-duty and two reserve squadrons. The active-duty squadrons fly Lockheed P-3 Orion long-range maritime patrol aircraft. In addition, NAS Brunswick has 29 tenant commands, including a Reserve P-3 squadron and a Reserve Fleet logistics support squadron flying C-130 Hercules transports.

Further reading: NAS Brunswick web site: www.nasb.navy.mil.

Naval Air Station Fallon, Nevada

NAS Fallon provides integrated air warfare training support to carrier air wings, USMC air groups, tenant commands, and individual units participating in training events, which include joint and multinational exercises. The facility is home to four major commands:

The Naval Strike and Air Warfare Center (NSAWC), a center for naval aviation training and tactics development, consists of more than 130 officers, 250 enlisted, and 500 contract personnel, and flies and maintains F/A-18 Hornets, F-14 Tomcats, and SH-60F Seahawk helicopters.

Strike Fighter Wing Detachment Fallon provides maintenance for F/A-18 aircraft.

Fighter Squadron Composite 13 (VFC-13), the "Fighting Saints," flies the F-5E/F Tiger II.

Construction Battalion Unit 416 (CBU-416) is a SEABEES unit consisting of one officer and 39 enlisted personnel.

Further reading: NAS Fallon web site: www.fallon.navy.mil.

Naval Air Station Jacksonville, Florida

NAS Jacksonville is home to Sea Control Wing Atlantic, Patrol and Reconnaissance Wing 11, Helicopter Antisubmarine Wing Atlantic, a Naval Air Reserve unit, Patrol Squadron 30, and NAS Operations C-12. In all, this multimission base hosts more than 100 tenant commands and is home to P-3C Orion long-range antisubmarine reconnaissance and maritime patrol aircraft, SH-60F Seahawk antisubmarine warfare helicopters, and S-3B Viking sea control planes.

NAS Jacksonville occupies 3,896 acres along St. Johns River and employs more than 23,000 active-duty and civilian personnel. Support facilities include an airfield for pilot training, a maintenance depot employing more than 150 different trade skills capable of performing maintenance as basic as changing a tire, or as specialized as micro-electronics or total engine disassembly. The station also includes a naval hospital, a fleet industrial supply center, a navy family service center, and recreational facilities for the single sailor or the entire family.

Further reading: NAS Jacksonville web site: www.nasjax.navy.mil.

Naval Air Station
Joint Reserve Base Fort Worth, Texas

NAS JRB Fort Worth, located at the site of the former Carswell Air Force Base, was officially established on October 1, 1994, as the first joint service reserve base. Relocated here are Naval Air Station Dallas and its tenant commands, as well as tenant commands from other services.

Further reading: NAS JRB Fort Worth web site: http://nasftw.cnrf.nola.navy.mil.

Naval Air Station Joint Reserve Base
Willow Grove, Pennsylvania

Naval Air Station Willow Grove was commissioned in January 1943. After WORLD WAR II, it was designated a Naval Air Reserve training station, and in 1994, the facility's name was again changed, to Naval Air Station Joint Reserve Base (NAS JRB) Willow Grove, to reflect the joint composition and mission of the reservists serving there. NAS JRB Willow Grove is shared by USN, USMC, USAF, and USA reservists, as well as the Pennsylvania Air National Guard.

Further reading: NAS JRB Willow Grove web site: www.nasjrbwillowgrove.navy.mil.

Naval Air Station Lemoore, California

The Pacific Strike Fighter Wing with its supporting facilities is home-ported at NAS Lemoore. The wing flies the F/A-18 Hornet and consists of 18 squadrons and the Strike Fighter Weapons School. In addition, five carrier air wings are based here, along with several tenant commands.

Further reading: NAS Lemoore web site: www. lemoore.navy.mil.

Naval Air Station Meridian, Mississippi

NAS Meridian is home to Training Air Wing One, the Navy Technical Training Center, a naval reserve center, the Regional Counterdrug Training Academy, a Marine Aviation training support squadron, and other tenant commands.

Further reading: NAS Meridian web site: www. cnet.navy.mil/meridian.

Naval Air Station North Island,
San Diego, California

NASNI is part of the largest aerospace-industrial complex in the U.S. Navy, the 57,000-acre Naval Base Coronado. The commanding officer of North Island also commands Naval Base Coronado, as well as Naval Amphibious Base Coronado, Outlying Field Imperial Beach, Navy Radio Receiving Facility, Mountain Training Facility LaPosta, Warner Springs Training Area, and Naval Air Landing Facility, San Clemente Island. NASNI hosts 23 squadrons and 80 additional tenant commands and activities, including the headquarters for the Naval Special Warfare Command (see SEALS).

NASNI's airfield has over 230 aircraft and it is homeport to three AIRCRAFT CARRIERS: USS *Constellation* (CV-64), USS *John C. Stennis* (CVN-74), and USS *Nimitz* (CVN-68). The USN's two Deep Submergence Rescue Vehicles, *Mystic* (DSRV-1) and *Avalon* (DSRV-2), are homeported here. Four major military flag staffs are housed at NASNI: Commander Naval Air Force, U.S. PACIFIC FLEET, responsible for maintenance and training of all naval aircraft and aircraft carriers in the Pacific Fleet; Commander Carrier Group One; Commander Carrier Group Seven; and Commander Cruiser Destroyer Group One. The population of the station is nearly 35,000, including active duty and reserve military personnel as well as civilians.

Further reading: NAS North Island web site: www.nasni.navy.mil.

Naval Air Station Oceana,
Virginia Beach, Virginia

NAS Oceana supports Pacific and Atlantic aircraft carriers and USCG, USA, USAF, and National Guard forces in maintaining optimum combat readiness. The station covers some 6,000 acres and is home to more than 9,700 U.S. Navy personnel and about 12,300 of their dependents. The station employs 2,273 civilians. Nine F-14 Tomcat fighter squadrons and 11 F/A-18 Hornet squadrons assigned to the ATLANTIC FLEET and Pacific Fleet are based here, and three of the squadrons that train air crews and maintenance personnel are permanently stationed at NAS Oceana. The station also has a Search and Rescue (SAR) unit flying the UH-3H Sea King helicopter. One hundred twelve Tomcats, 170 Hornets, six T-34 Mentors, and two H-3 Sea Kings are operated out of the station.

Further reading: NAS Oceana web site: www. nasoceana.navy.mil.

Naval Air Station Patuxent River, Maryland
NAS Patuxent River supports operations of the NAVAL AIR WARFARE CENTER Aircraft Division and other activities and units. The station was commissioned in 1943, during WORLD WAR II, and currently hosts acquisition management, research and development capabilities, air and ground test and evaluation, and aircraft logistics and maintenance management operations. The station complex includes the Webster Field Annex and Bloodsworth Island. About 19,100 people work at "Pax."

Further reading: NAS Patuxent River web site: http://nas.nawcad.navy.mil/cs/nas.

Naval Air Station Pensacola, Florida
Naval Air Station Pensacola has long been known as the "Cradle of Naval Aviation." Every naval aviator, naval flight officer (NFO), and enlisted aircrewman begins his or her career here, and some 15,000 USN aviation personnel annually receive training here in the technical aeronautical phases of naval operations.

NAS Pensacola's primary flying organization is Training Wing Six (TRAWING 6); it includes three jointly manned (USAF and USN personnel) USN training squadrons, VT-4, VT-10, and VT-86. These units have the mission of training USN naval flight officers and navigators as well as those of other services. The training squadrons fly such aircraft as the T-2C Buckeye Jet Trainer, T-6A Texan II

Turboprop Trainer, T-34C Turbomentor Training Aircraft, T-39N/G Sabreliner Training Aircraft, and T-45A Goshawk Training Aircraft. NAS Pensacola also serves as the home station and primary practice site for the USN's famed BLUE ANGELS. In 1971, NAS Pensacola was selected as the headquarters site for CHIEF OF NAVAL EDUCATION AND TRAINING (CNET), which exercises combined direction and control over all USN education and training programs and activities. The Naval Air Basic Training Command was absorbed by the Naval Air Training Command, which moved to Corpus Christi. Today, the Pensacola Naval Complex in Escambia and Santa Rosa counties employs more than 9,600 military and 6,800 civilian personnel. The training aircraft carrier USS *Lexington* (AVT-16) operated out of Pensacola as the USN's only training carrier for two decades, until November 8, 1991.

The USN presence in Pensacola began in 1825, when construction of a naval base and naval yard were authorized. Both were destroyed by Confederate forces during the CIVIL WAR in 1862. Rebuilt after the war, much of the base was again destroyed in 1906, this time by the forces of nature: a hurricane and tidal wave. Reconstruction of the base took place during the early years of the development of aviation and of naval aviation in particular. In 1913, a naval aviation training station was authorized for Pensacola, and the following year the USN established the United States Naval Aeronautical Station there. When the United States entered WORLD WAR I in 1917, Pensacola was the only USN naval air station and was occupied by a mere 38 naval aviators, 163 enlisted men trained in aviation, and held 54 airplanes in its inventory. By the end of the war in November 1918, the air station had trained a thousand naval aviators.

During the years following the war, aviation training slowed drastically. An average of 100 aviators were graduating yearly. A formal cadet training program was inaugurated in 1935, signaling the beginning of a long period of expansion at NAS Pensacola. In World War II, Pensacola was the hub of USN aviation, and in the KOREAN WAR, it became a vital center for the development of jet aviation technology, tactics, and training. It continues to serve as the USN's premier training facility and a center for the development of advanced naval aviation technology and tactics.

Further reading: NAS Pensacola information, GlobalSecurity.Org, "Naval Air Station Pensacola": www.globalsecurity.org/military/facility/pensacola.htm.

Naval Air Station Sigonella, Italy

NAS Sigonella, Sicily, is nicknamed the "Hub of the Med" and is the primary logistical support element for U.S. SIXTH FLEET operations. Naval Air Facility Sigonella was established on June 15, 1959, and was redesignated as a naval air station during the 1980s.

Further reading: NAS Sigonella web site: www.sicily.navy.mil.

Naval Air Station Whidbey Island, Washington

NAS Whidbey Island was commissioned during World War II on September 21, 1942, principally as a seaplane base for navy PBY Catalinas. Soon, it accommodated Wildcat and Hellcat fighters as well. Today, NAS Whidbey Island is home to most of the USN's EA-6B Prowler electronic warfare aircraft squadrons. The P-3C Orion and EP-3E Aries II are also flown out of NAS Whidbey, and a Search and Rescue Unit flies UH-3H Sea King helicopters, as well as two C-12 King Airs for fleet logistic support. In all, there are 19 active-duty squadrons currently based here, as well as Naval Air Reserve Force operations. More than 50 tenant commands are based at NAS Whidbey, providing training, medical and dental, and other support services, including a Marine Aviation training support group for Whidbey's marines.

Further reading: NAS Whidbey Island web site: www.naswi.navy.mil.

Naval Air Station Whiting Field, Florida

Located in Milton, Florida, NAS Whiting Field is the busiest naval air station in the world, responsi-

ble for more than 10 percent of USN and USMC total flight time. More than 1,200 personnel complete flight training here yearly, and its current mission is to train student naval aviators in the primary and intermediate phases of fixed-wing aviation and in the advanced phases of helicopter training. NAS Whiting Field hosts Training Wing Five.

Further reading: NAS Whiting Field information: www.globalsecurity.org/military/facility/whiting-field.htm.

Naval Air Terminal Norfolk

Located at Naval Station Norfolk, Virginia, the terminal moves passengers, mail, and cargo by air to service areas that include destinations in the European, Mediterranean, Southwest Asian, and Caribbean regions, as well as the U.S. East Coast, Texas, California, and Washington State. The terminal is staffed by 200 civilians and 20 military personnel and handles, on average, 9,000 passengers, 18,000 cargo pieces, and 500 aircraft per month.

Further reading: NAT Norfolk web site: www.airtermnorva.navy.mil.

Naval Base Ventura County

Located in southern California, Naval Base Ventura County includes a 4,490-acre site at Point Mugu, about 65 miles northwest of downtown Los Angeles, on the Oxnard Plain, and the Port of Hueneme, the only USN deep water port between San Diego and Seattle. Hueneme provides training, administrative, and logistic support for Seabees worldwide. A 36,000-square-mile, fully instrumented and integrated sea test range for test and evaluation of weapons and aircraft systems is also administered by the base.

More than 60 tenant commands are homeported at Naval Base Ventura, including:

◆ 1st Naval Construction Regiment
◆ 31st Naval Construction Regiment Headquarters (NCR)

- Construction Battalion Center (CBC)
- Defense Automation & Production Service (DAPS)
- Detachment 1, 345th TRS USAF
- Engineering Duty Officers School (EDO)
- Mobile Utilities Support Equipment (MUSE)
- Navy Cargo Handling Battalion 14
- U.S. Naval School, Civil Engineer Corps Officers (CECOS)
- Naval Construction Force Support Unit Two
- Naval Construction Training Center (NCTC)
- Naval Facilities Acquisition Center for Training (NFACT)
- Naval Facilities Engineering Service Center (NFESC)
- Naval Reserve Center
- Naval Reserve COMNAVFORKOREA HQ
- Port Hueneme Division, Naval Surface Warfare Center (NSWC)
- Underwater Construction Team (UCT) TW
- Air National Guard
- Naval Air Reserve, Point Mugu, California
- Commander, Carrier Airborne Early Warning Wing, US PACFLT
- Naval Air Warfare Center (NAWC)
- Naval Pacific Meteorology and Oceanography Detachment
- Naval Weapons Test Squadron (NWTS)

Further reading: NBVC web site: www.nbvc.navy. mil.

Naval Station Everett, Washington

The USN's newest facility, Naval Station Everett was opened in 1994. Currently, the station is homeport to three DESTROYERS, three FRIGATES, and one nuclear-powered aircraft carrier.

Some 6,000 sailors and civil service personnel are assigned to commands located at Everett, while the station itself has a complement of about 450 sailors and civilians. The station is home to C-HET Everett (Combatant Homeport Engineering Team Everett); Cruiser-Destroyer Group 3; Destroyer Squadron 9; Naval Surface Group, Pacific Northwest; Naval Reserve Readiness Command North-west; Naval Reserve Center, Everett; Naval Intermediate Maintenance Facility Detachment Everett; Fleet Industrial Supply Center, Detachment Everett; Construction Battalion Unit 421 (CBU 421); Personnel Support Activity West; Naval Radio Station (T) Jim Creek; Branch Medical Clinic, Everett; Branch Dental Clinic, Everett; Navy Legal Service Office, Branch Office Everett; Trial Service Office, Detachment Everett; Afloat Training Group Pacific, Northwest; Fleet Technical Support Center Pacific, Detachment Everett; Supervisor of Shipbuilding, Conversion and Repair, Puget Sound; Mobile Inshore Undersea Warfare Unit 101; and Naval Criminal Investigative Service Resident Agent, Everett.

Further reading: NAS Everett web site: www. everett.navy.mil.

Naval Station Mayport, Florida

Commissioned in December 1942, Naval Station Mayport is now the third largest fleet concentration area in the United States. The 3,400-acre station encompasses a harbor capable of accommodating 34 ships and an 8,000-foot runway capable of handling any U.S. military aircraft. More than 70 tenant commands are resident here, including the aircraft carrier USS *John F. Kennedy* (CV-67), 21 other USN ships, and six Light Airborne Multi-purpose System (LAMPS) Mark III helicopter squadrons. NS Mayport is also the operational and training headquarters for the SH-60B Seahawk Lamps Mk-III (primary mission, antisubmarine warfare).

Further reading: NS Mayport web site: www. nsmayport.navy.mil.

Naval Station Newport, Rhode Island

Although Newport, Rhode Island, has figured in U.S. Navy operations since the AMERICAN REVOLUTION, its official status was not established until 1869, when the secretary of war authorized construction of an experimental torpedo station on Goat Island. A precursor to the NAVAL UNDERSEA WARFARE CENTER, the torpedo station developed

The aircraft carrier USS *John F. Kennedy* (CV-67) undergoes "extended service" repairs at Naval Station Mayport, Florida.   *(U.S. Navy)*

torpedoes, torpedo equipment, explosives, and electrical equipment. It was active for 80 years, until its disestablishment in 1951. The station was an important center of naval ordnance development and in experimentation with shipboard electricity. Over the years, the torpedo station grew, as general research and development became an increasingly higher priority for the USN.

In 1884, the NAVAL WAR COLLEGE was founded at Newport, and the area became increasingly important as a training center. In 1887, a recruit training station was added to the local facilities, which expanded even more rapidly after the United States entered World War I in 1917. World War II brought even greater growth, including the introduction of Naval Air Station Quonset Point in July 1941.

The postwar years saw reductions in Newport's activities, but new projects were introduced begin-

ning in the 1960s, and by the 1980s, the Naval Underwater Systems Center became the largest command at Newport. In the 1990s, the Naval Undersea Warfare Center assumed an increasing presence at Newport, with an array of laboratories to provide research, development, testing, and evaluation, as well as engineering and fleet support, for submarines and underwater systems.

Further reading: NS Newport web site: www.nsnpt.navy.mil.

Naval Station Norfolk, Virginia

The mission of the 4,300-acre Naval Station Norfolk at Sewells Point, Hampton Roads, Virginia, is to support and improve the personnel and logistics readiness of the U.S. Atlantic Fleet. Not only is NS Norfolk the world's largest naval station, it is the largest military installation in the world. Seventy-six ships (including combatant as well as MILITARY SEALIFT COMMAND logistics craft) and 138 aircraft are homeported here. Fourteen piers are available, as are 15 aircraft hangars. Vessels homeported include aircraft carriers, CRUISERS, destroyers, large amphibious ships, SUBMARINES, supply and logistics ships, and C-2, C-9, C-12, and E-2 fixed-wing aircraft, and H-3, H-46, H-53, and H-60 helicopters. More than 3,100 ship movements are controlled annually in and out of NS Norfolk facilities, and Norfolk Air Operations conducts more than 100,000 flight operations yearly, about 275 flights per day. The station serves as the hub for USN logistics going to the European and Central Command theaters as well as to the Caribbean.

Property for the station was purchased in 1917, immediately after the United States entered World War I. Construction proceeded rapidly, and the station was in use within a month. More land was acquired as the station expanded, and by 1939, it was the biggest naval installation on the Atlantic coast. It expanded vastly during World War II. Known officially as Naval Operating Base Norfolk until December 31, 1952, the name was officially changed to Naval Station Norfolk on January 1, 1953. For years, NS Norfolk and Naval Air Station Norfolk operated separately; on February 5, 1999, the two were consolidated as NS Norfolk.

Further reading: NS Norfolk web site: www.navstanorva.navy.mil.

Naval Station Pascagoula, Mississippi

NS Pascagoula is located on 187 acres of Singing River Island, on the mainland side of Mississippi Sound in the Gulf of Mexico. Opened in 1992, NS Pascagoula is a strategic homeport of *Perry*-class guided-missile frigates and *Ticonderoga*-class guided-missile cruisers. The station also supports precommissioning crews of surface combatant ships built at the nearby Ingalls Shipbuilding.

Further reading: NS Pascagoula information: www.globalsecurity.org/military/facility/pascagoula. htm.

Naval Station Pearl Harbor, Hawaii

Since the Japanese attack of December 7, 1941, the "day of infamy" that brought the United States into World War II, Pearl Harbor has been the most famous of all USN installations. Not only does it contain a moving memorial to the Pearl Harbor attack, the shrine built over the wreckage of the battleship *Arizona,* NS Pearl Harbor is also a major active facility of the U.S. Pacific Fleet. The Pearl Harbor Naval Shipyard, a vast repair facility, is located here, and the station is homeport to a large number of submarines and surface ships.

See also PEARL HARBOR, JAPANESE ATTACK ON.

Further reading: NS Pearl Harbor web site: www.pearlharbor.navy.mil.

Naval Station Roosevelt Roads, Puerto Rico

NS Roosevelt Roads is located on 8,600 acres on the eastern edge of Puerto Rico. It was built by order of President Franklin Roosevelt beginning in 1940 and completed in 1943. During World War II, it served as a training facility and a base for USN ships and aircraft. During the postwar years, the station was periodically closed, but became in 1955 the site of the Atlantic Fleet Guided Missile Training Center (today's Atlantic Fleet Weapons Training Facility). Nearby Vieques has been used for maneuvers and training since 1947; however, after a civilian death on the Vieques target range in April 1999, the future of the Vieques facility was cast into doubt.

Naval Station Rota, Spain

NS Rota is located in southwestern Spain on the Atlantic coast, halfway between Gibraltar and the border with Portugal. This strategically important location enables the station to provide support to both the Sixth Fleet and to USAF Air Mobility Command units transiting into or through the theater. The station is located within the boundaries of the 6,100-acre Spanish Base Naval de Rota; per the Agreement for Defense Cooperation, the USN and Spanish navy work together here, sharing many facilities.

NS Rota supports both USN and NATO ships, as well as the movement of USN and USAF flights and passengers. It also provides cargo, fuel, and ammunition to units in the region.

More than 6,000 U.S. service members are housed at NS Rota, and the commanding officer of the station also serves as commander, U.S. Naval Activities (COMNAVACTS) Spain, coordinating all USN activities in Spain and Portugal. The base was developed beginning in the early 1950s.

Further reading: NS Rota web site: www.rota. navy.mil.

Naval Station San Diego

NSSD is homeport for some 60 USN ships and home base to 50 commands. About 48,000 military and civilian personnel work at the station, and 3,000 are resident on base.

Major shore commands at NSSD include Fleet Training Center, Naval Dental Center, Naval Legal Services Office, Naval School of Dental Assisting and Technology, Shore Intermediate Maintenance Activity, Navy Public Works Center, Supervisor of Shipbuilding, Conversion and Repair, Naval Education and Training Support Center, Naval Electronics Systems Engineering Center, Fleet Industrial Supply Center, and Naval Investigative Service.

Fleet support is the principal mission of NSSD, a mission that extends to all 98 ships homeported in the area. This support includes providing tugs and pilots and pier space for homeported ships, for all Pacific Fleet ships undergoing refresher training or shakedown, for four MILITARY SEALIFT COMMAND ships, and for all foreign navy ships visiting San Diego. Some 3,500 ship movements are performed annually.

Further reading: NS San Diego web site: www. navstasd.navy.mil.

Naval Submarine Base Bangor, Washington

Located on Washington's Puget Sound, SUBASE Bangor hosts more than 54 tenant commands, most of which support the Trident missile program. Facilities at the base provide for administration and personnel support, including base security, berthing, messing, and recreational services as well as logistics support.

In 1942, the site of SUBASE Bangor was used for shipping ammunition to the Pacific theater during World War II. The U.S. Naval Magazine was established there on June 5, 1944, and through January 1973, Bangor served as a U.S. ammunition depot responsible for shipping conventional weapons abroad. Later in 1973, the USN announced the selection of Bangor as homeport for the first squadron of Trident submarines, and on February 1, 1977, SUBASE Bangor was officially activated.

Further reading: SUBASE Bangor web site: www. bangor.navy.mil/nsb_homepage.htm.

Naval Submarine Base Kings Bay, Georgia

SUBASE Kings Bay supports the USN's submarine-launched ballistic missile program and is the only East Coast naval base capable of supporting the Trident II D-5 ballistic missile. The base is home to Submarine Squadron 20 and Submarine Squadron 16, under the guidance of Submarine Group 10. Four submarines are attached to each squadron. The base supports the submarines with its Trident Refit Facility, Trident Training Facility, and Strategic Weapons Facility Atlantic.

Naval Submarine Support Base Kings Bay was commissioned in July 1978 primarily as the forward refit site for Submarine Squadron 16, then operating out of Naval Station Rota, Spain. In May 1980, SUBASE Kings Bay became the Atlantic Fleet homeport of the Trident (*Ohio*-class) SSBNs and was expanded with facilities for crew training, weapons handling and storage, submarine maintenance and repair, and personnel support. The base was redesignated Naval Submarine Base Kings Bay in April 1982.

The base includes some 16,000 acres and employs more than 9,000 military and civilian personnel.

Further reading: SUBASE Kings Bay web site: www.subasekb.navy.mil.

Naval Submarine Base
New London, Connecticut

The 750-acre SUBASE NLON is homeport to 16 attack submarines and the nuclear research deep submersible NR-1 and is adjacent to a major submarine construction yard. In addition, the base supports more than 55 tenant commands and the housing and support facilities for more than 19,000 civilian workers, and for active-duty service members and their families.

SUBASE NLON, the USN's first submarine base, received its first four submarines, together with the monitor *Ozark,* a submarine tender, on October 13, 1915. After World War I, schools and training facilities were established at the base.

Further reading: SUBASE New London web site: www.subasenlon.navy.mil.

Navy Support Facility Diego Garcia

Diego Garcia is a British territorial island strategically located in the middle of the Indian Ocean and largely occupied by U.S. military installations, including Navy Support Facility Diego Garcia as well as USAF, USA, and U.S. merchant marine facilities and the United Kingdom military. It has been described as a British colony colonized by the U.S. military establishment. Some 1,700 U.S. military personnel and 1,500 U.S. civilian contractors are stationed here, along with about 50 British troops. The USN has the largest contingent on the island. A narrow jungle reef about 1,000 miles south of the southern India coast, Diego Garcia has been called a "stationary aircraft carrier," covering just 6,720 acres.

The USN presence on Diego Garcia began in January 1971, when the island was surveyed for possible military use. In March, construction began on Naval Communication Facility Diego Garcia, the first USN facility built on the island. Facilities were greatly expanded in 1975 and 1976, to provide minimal logistics support for U.S. task groups in the Indian Ocean. In 1979 and 1980, support for several prepositioned ships, loaded with critical supplies, was added, and by the mid-1980s, Diego Garcia became a major fleet and U.S. armed forces support base.

Navy Support Facility Diego Garcia was established on October 1, 1977, and supports U.S. military units operating in the Indian Ocean and Arabian Gulf. Major USN activities include a naval computer and telecommunications station, maritime prepositioning ships anchored in the lagoon, and Military Sealift Command.

battleships See WARSHIPS: WORLD WAR I; WARSHIPS: WORLD WAR II.

***Belknap* Class (CG-26)** See CRUISERS.

***Benjamin Franklin* Class** See SUBMARINES.

Biddle, James (1783–1848) *navy commodore*
Born in Philadelphia, Biddle had a long and distinguished U.S. Navy career. He served in the BARBARY WARS and was held prisoner for a year. Subsequently, in command of a GUNBOAT, he hunted pirates on the South Atlantic coast. After an interval in the merchant marine, Biddle returned to the USN during the WAR OF 1812 and was an officer aboard USS *Wasp* when it captured HMS *Frolic.*

Biddle served in the peacetime USN variously, then, as commodore of the East India Squadron, negotiated the first U.S.-China treaty in 1846. Returning to the United States, he served in the U.S.-MEXICAN WAR on the Pacific coast.

Blue Angels (Navy Flight Demonstration Squadron)

The Blue Angels are the USN's flight demonstration squadron, their mission to enhance USN and USMC recruiting and to represent the USN and USMC to the U.S. civilian community, the elected leadership, and foreign nations.

Currently, the Blue Angels fly F/A-18 aircraft, modified only by removal of the nose cannon and installation of a smoke-oil tank for smoke effects during aerobatics. The Blue Angels fly six F/A-18s in their demonstrations, which consist of highly choreographed refinements of USN-trained flying skills, including the four-plane Diamond Formation counterpointed to the maneuvers of two solo pilots, and the celebrated six-jet Delta Formation.

During the show season, the Blue Angels are stationed at Forrest Sherman Field, Naval Air Station Pensacola, Florida; in winter (nonshow) season, the squadron trains at Naval Air Facility El Centro, California.

The Blue Angels were formed at the end of WORLD WAR II by order of Chief of Naval Operations Admiral CHESTER W. NIMITZ and gave their first show in June 1946, flying Grumman F6F Hellcats. Two months later, the squadron transitioned to the Grumman F8F Bearcat, and in 1947 the Blue Angels' trademark diamond formation was introduced. By 1949, the squadron was flying its first jet aircraft, the Grumman F9F-2 Panther.

Beginning in 1950, the KOREAN WAR prompted the reassignment of the Blue Angels to the aircraft carrier USS *Princeton* (CV-37) as part of a combat squadron, VF-191, "Satan's Kittens." However, the squadron was reconstituted as the Blue Angels in 1951 and began flying the F9F-5, the faster version of the Panther. In 1954, the Blue Angels began fly-

ing the swept-wing Grumman F9F-8 Cougar, in 1957 the Grumman F11F-1 Tiger, and in 1969 the dual-engine McDonnell Douglas F-4J Phantom II. The Blue Angels began flying the Douglas A-4F Skyhawk II in 1974 and, in 1986, the F/A-18 Hornet. Since they began flying in 1946, the Blue Angels have flown for more than 337 million spectators. Twenty-three pilots have been killed in air shows or training.

Boorda, Jeremy Michael (1938–1996) *chief of naval operations*

Sixteen-year-old Boorda enlisted in the USN in 1954, gaining entrance by lying about his age. In 1962, he entered officer candidate school and rose steadily, becoming commander of NATO Forces, Southern Europe, in 1991 and CHIEF OF NAVAL OPERATIONS in 1994. He was the first CNO to rise from the enlisted ranks.

Borie, Adolph E. (1809–1880) *secretary of the navy*

Philadelphian Adolph Borie made his living in international trade and, in 1843, was appointed U.S. consul to Belgium. With the outbreak of the CIVIL WAR, he organized a regiment and became acquainted with Ulysses S. Grant. In 1869, when Grant was elected president, Borie was appointed the 25th SECRETARY OF THE NAVY. He resigned later in the year, over a dispute with Admiral DAVID DIXON PORTER.

Boxer Rebellion   See CHINA RELIEF EXPEDITION.

Bronstein Class (FF 1037)   See FRIGATES.

Bureau of Aeronautics

The USN established this bureau on August 10, 1921, as air power became increasingly important

The Blue Angels make a low pass in tight formation.   *(U.S. Navy)*

to the service. The first commander of the bureau was Rear Admiral WILLIAM A. MOFFETT.

Bureau of Medicine and Surgery (BUMED)

BUMED was created on August 31, 1842, when Congress enacted a USN appropriations bill that created five bureaus to replace the notoriously inefficient "Board of Navy Commissioners: Yards and Docks; Construction, Equipment, and Repair; Provisions and Clothing; Ordnance and Hydrography; and Medicine and Surgery." Since that time, BUMED has been charged with providing health care to USN and USMC personnel. Today, it provides these services to some 700,000 active-duty sailors and marines and to about 2.6 million retired personnel and the family members of active duty and retired personnel. In addition, the bureau is responsible for administering naval medicine during contingency operations as well as in humanitarian and joint operations worldwide. BUMED is headquartered at the UNITED STATES NAVAL OBSERVATORY, Washington, D.C.

Bureau of Naval Personnel (BUPERS)

BUPERS is the U.S. Navy's human resources arm. It supports the needs of the USN by "providing the fleet with the right person in the right place at the right time." Additionally, the bureau serves individual sailors by striving "to [help them] satisfy [their] personal goals and improve their quality of life."

Originally, all USN personnel matters were handled by the secretary of war and then by the DEPARTMENT OF THE NAVY, after it was established by Congress on April 30, 1798. In 1815, the SECRETARY OF THE NAVY assumed direct control of personnel matters. An Office of Detail was created in 1861 to administer the detailing of officers and the appointment and instruction of volunteer officers; additionally, the office handled matters relating to the purchase of ships. At the same time, a Bureau of Equipment and Recruiting was established to administer enlisted recruiting and the maintenance of service records. In 1862, the Bureau of Naviga-

tion was established, and in 1865 the Office of Detail was placed under it. The Bureau of Equipment and Recruiting transferred its enlisted personnel responsibilities to the Bureau of Navigation in 1889. This command became the Bureau of Naval Personnel on May 13, 1942, and, in 1982, the Naval Military Personnel Command. In 1991, the name reverted to Bureau of Naval Personnel, more commonly called "BUPERS." The command is led by the chief of naval personnel.

Burke, Arleigh A. (1901–1996) *chief of naval operations*

Burke was the 15th CHIEF OF NAVAL OPERATIONS, appointed in 1955 over 92 senior admirals. Born in Boulder, Colorado, he graduated from the UNITED STATES NAVAL ACADEMY in 1923 and served in the Pacific through 1928. After earning a master's degree in engineering from the University of Michigan, he was assigned to the Bureau of Ordnance during the 1930s, although he also served at sea during this period.

Promoted to captain in 1943, he commanded a destroyer squadron in the South Pacific and earned renown as "Thirty-One-Knot Burke" after high-speed operations in key battles. Appointed chief of staff to Admiral MARC MITSCHER in 1945, he then was named to command Task Force 58 and, in 1947, became chief of staff to the ATLANTIC FLEET. That same year, he was assigned to the USN's nuclear weapons development program.

At the outbreak of the KOREAN WAR, Burke commanded Cruiser Division 5, then, from 1952 to 1954, was director of the Strategic Plans Division of the DEPARTMENT OF THE NAVY. Shortly before his appointment as CNO, he commanded cruisers.

Burke served three terms as CNO, retiring in 1966. He championed the development of the Polaris submarine missile program.

Bushnell, David (1742–1824) *army engineer*

Bushnell was the inventor of a one-man submarine, called the *Turtle,* which he built in 1775 and

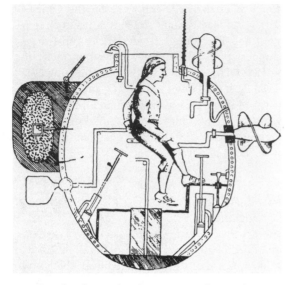

David Bushnell's *Turtle* submarine   *(Library of Congress)*

which he intended for use by the Continental navy during the AMERICAN REVOLUTION. The submarine was propelled and maneuvered by its occupant. It featured, on the outside, a detachable powder magazine rigged with a clock mechanism. The idea was to use the submarine to place this magazine below the waterline of an enemy ship, allow it to detonate, and thereby sink the ship. Although the submarine functioned—that is, it submerged, maneuvered, and resurfaced—it never succeeded as a practical weapon during the period 1776–77, when it was operational.

Bushnell served as an engineer in the Continental army from 1779 to 1783, then went on to command the Army Corps of Engineers at West Point. He lived for a time in France, returning to the United States in 1795, where he became a teacher and a physician in Georgia.

C

cable repair ship (T-ARC)

USNS *Zeus* (T-ARC 7) is currently the only ship of the *Zeus* class and is a multimission cable ship specially designed by the U.S. Navy. The ship has two main missions: oceanographic survey and the installation and maintenance of submarine cable systems.

Zeus is tasked with performing maintenance on the Sound Surveillance System (SOSUS), a network of strategically placed sonar sensors that provides early warning of enemy submarines. *Zeus* is capable of laying and retrieving deep-water acoustic cables. The vessel may also be used to support oceanographic research.

Not only is *Zeus* the navy's only active cable repair ship, it is also the first multimission cable ship designed and built by the navy specifically as a cable repair vessel. Its design includes advanced propulsion features, centralized integrated displays for monitoring ship and cable machinery parameters and functions, passive flume stabilization, improved maneuverability and cable handling capabilities at both bow and stern, and survey equipment that combines high performance and versatility with a minimal maintenance requirement.

Main propulsion is diesel-electric (five GM diesels) and rated horsepower is 10,000. Bow- and stern-mounted tunnel thrusters provide the precise track-keeping and position-holding capabilities absolutely necessary for cable laying and repair, array laying operations, projector towing, acoustic surveys, and other missions. Special application of roll damping techniques enables *Zeus* to provide a highly stable platform for safe cable operations at slow speeds.

Zeus is operated by the MILITARY SEALIFT COMMAND and is manned by civilian crews and under the command of a civilian master. It is fitted with a wide array of cable handling equipment, including five cable tanks, cable transporters, DO-HB tension machines, self fleeting cable drums, overboarding sheaves, and dynamometer cable fairleader. In addition to its cable laying and repair primary mission, *Zeus* serves secondarily as an Oceanographic Survey vessel. For this mission, it makes use of its single-beam and multi-beam (SIMRAD EM 121) sonars for bottom profiling, and can also deploy towed sidescan sonars and camera sleds.

General specifications of the *Zeus* vessel include:

Shipbuilder: National Steel and Shipbuilding
Launched: 1984, San Diego, California
Length: 513 ft 2 in
Beam: 73 ft
Draft, maximum: 25 ft 11.75 in
Navigational draft: 27 ft 9.75 in
Displacement, full load: 14,335 tons
Maximum height above keel: 112 ft
Maximum speed: 15 knots
Endurance: 10,000 nautical mi
Crew: 88 civilian, six USN, and 30 technicians

California Class (CGN 36)   See CRUISERS.

captain   See RANKS AND GRADES.

cargo, fuel, and replenishment ships

The navy operates, either directly or under lease and contract agreements with civilian operators, a very wide array of cargo, fuel, and replenishment ships. The major types and classes include:

Advanced Auxiliary Dry Cargo Ships (T-AKE)

The T-AKE is a Combat Logistics Force UNDERWAY REPLENISHMENT ship that replaces the *Kilauea*-class (T-AE 26) ammunition ship, *Mars*-class (T-AFS 1) combat stores ship, and, in concert with a *Henry J. Kaiser*-class (T-AO 187) oiler, the *Sacramento*-class (AOE 1) fast combat support ship. As planned, the T-AKE program will consist of 12 ships.

The primary role of the T-AKE is to provide logistics lift from such sources of supply as friendly ports, or at sea from specially equipped merchant ships; the T-AKE will transfer cargo at sea to station ships. Secondarily, working with a *Henry J. Kaiser*-class (T-AO 187) oiler, the T-AKE provides direct logistics support to the ships within a carrier battle group.

Ammunition Ships (T-AE)

The mission of ammunition ships is to deliver munitions to warships at sea via slings on ship-to-ship cables and by helicopters. All of the USN's T-AE ships are of the *Kilauea* class.

Kilauea Class (T-AE 26)

Kilauea-class ammunition ships (AE) transport and deliver bombs, bullets, missiles, mines, projectiles, powder, torpedoes, and other explosive devices and incendiaries and associated ordnance cargo to USN ships while under way. Secondarily, ships of this class also provide limited quantities of fuel, water, and combat store products, as well as some basic ship repair and maintenance services. Underway Replenishment is carried out via connected replenishment as well as by ship-to-ship

helicopter, where appropriate. The *Kilauea* class represents the state of the art in ammunition ships, featuring facilities for the very rapid transfer of ammunition and other cargo. Each ship of the class has four cargo holds, which break down into 14 magazines. The holds are serviced by six high-speed cargo weapons elevators. Also, all ships have certified helicopter flight decks, seven cargo transfer stations, and one fuel delivery station. Four cargo booms allow shore or barge transfer. The ships of this class are outfitted with an advanced fleet satellite communication system.

General specifications of the class include:

Builders: General Dynamics; Quincy and Ingalls Shipbuilding
Power plant: three Foster-Wheeler boilers, 600 psi; one turbine, 22,000 horsepower; one shaft, 22,000 shaft horsepower; one six-bladed fixed-pitch propeller
Overall length: 564 ft
Waterline length: 540 ft
Extreme beam: 81 ft
Waterline beam: 81 ft
Maximum navigational draft: 31 ft
Draft limit: 28 ft
Displacement, full load: 20,169 tons
Dead weight: 8,254 tons
Speed: 20 knots
Aircraft: two UH-46E Sea Knight helicopters
Hangar: two
Helicopter deck: aft helicopter flight deck
Crew: 125 civilian mariners, in addition to 55 USN personnel, including a helicopter detachment
Armament: none
Cargo hold: 60,000 cubic feet with a capacity of 6,000 tons of munitions
Refrigerators for ship's stores: two
Fuel storage: seven 100,000-gallon fuel tanks—2,500 tons

Ships of the class include *Kilauea* (T-AE 26), *Butte* (T-AE 27), *Santa Barbara* (T-AE 28), *Mount Hood* (T-AE 29), *Flint* (T-AE 32), *Shasta* (T-AE 33), *Mount Baker* (T-AE 34), and *Kiska* (T-AE 35).

Auxiliary Crane Ships (T-ACS)

T-ACS are ships of the MILITARY SEALIFT COM-MAND's READY RESERVE FORCE available to support military sea transportation needs. The ships are used in ports that have limited, damaged, or undeveloped port facilities. T-ACS are converted container ships featuring three twin-boom pedestal cranes, which can lift containers or other cargo from themselves or adjacent vessels and deposit it ashore. All 10 of the U.S. Navy's T-ACS are of the *Keystone State* class, a conversion program spanning 1984 to 1997.

Keystone Class (T-ACS)

The T-ACS vessels are USNS *Keystone State* (T-ACS 1), converted from SS *President Harrison;* USNS *Gem State* (T-ACS 2), converted from SS *President Monroe;* USNS *Grand Canyon State* (T-ACS 3), converted from SS *President Polk;* USNS *Gopher State* (T-ACS 4), converted from *Export Leader;* USNS *Flickertail State* (T-ACS 5), converted from *Export Lightning;* USNS *Cornhusker State* (T-ACS 6), converted from *Staghound;* USNS *Diamond State* (T-ACS 7), converted from *President Truman;* USNS *Equality State* (T-ACS 8), converted from *American Banker;* USNS *Green Mountain State* (T-ACS 9), converted from *American Altair;* and USNS *Beaver State* (T-ACS 10), converted from *American Draco.*

Keystone class T-ACS share the following general characteristics:

Power plant: two boilers; two GE turbines; 19,250 horsepower; one shaft
Length: 668.6 ft
Beam: 76.1 ft
Displacement: 31,500 tons full load
Cargo capacity: 300+ standard containers
Speed: 20 knots
Crew: 89 civilians

Aviation Logistic Ships (T-AVB)

Two T-AVBs are assigned to the Military Sealift Command's Maritime Prepositioning Program to carry aviation maintenance equipment in support of USMC fixed- and rotary-wing aircraft. The *Wright* and *Curtiss* incorporate a stern ramp and side ports, as well as roll-on/roll-off decking, so that the ships can readily service aircraft while anchored offshore. Together they constitute the *Wright* class.

Wright Class (T-AVB 3)

The two ships of the *Wright* class, *Wright* (T-AVB 3) and *Curtiss* (T-AVB 4), are tasked with providing a rapid, dedicated means of providing intermediate maintenance capability for forward-deployed aircraft. Operated by the Military Sealift Command, the ships provide sealift for a specially tailored aviation Intermediate Maintenance Activity to support deployment of USMC fixed- and rotary-wing aircraft. Most of the necessary intermediate maintenance activity equipment and supplies can be transported on the *Wright*-class ships. Use of the T-AVB takes the place of some 140 C-141 airlifts.

Both vessels are conversions from civilian cargo ships, the *Wright* (T-AVB 3) converted from SS *Young America* by Todd Shipyards of Galveston, Texas, in 1986, and the *Curtiss* (T-AVB 4) by the same shipyard from SS *Great Republic* in 1987.

Both the USNS *Wright* and USNS *Curtiss* have roll-on/roll-off capability. They are, in fact, Seabridge class, commercial combination container, roll-on/roll-off (RO/RO) and lift-on/lift-off (LO/LO) cargo vessels. The *Wright* is berthed at Baltimore, Maryland, and the *Curtiss* at Port Hueneme, California. Curtiss is assigned to support the 2nd Marine Aircraft Wing, MCAS Cherry Point, North Carolina, and the *Wright* supports the 3rd Marine Aircraft Wing, MCAS EL Toro, California. Both vessels are maintained in a five-day Reduced Operating Status (ROS-5) by the Maritime Administration (MARAD). This means that each ship can be elevated to full operating status within 120 hours. A U.S. Merchant Marine crew is stationed aboard each ship at all times, and when activated, the ships are operated by the Military Sealift Command, also with civilian mariners.

Each of the vessels of this class carries berthing for 41 crew members and 300 embarked troops, plus an additional 25 berthing spaces for officers and senior noncommissioned officers. Material handling equipment on board includes: 11 ship booms—10 30-ton and one 70-ton—one diesel-powered front-loading forklift (15,500 pound maximum capacity), one diesel-powered side-loading forklift (16,500 pound maximum capacity), and three 6,000-pound-capacity electric forklifts. A helicopter platform is available, capable of landing the CH-53E helicopter for the transfer of personnel and cargo.

General specifications of the *Wright* class include:

Displacement, full load: 23,800 long tons
Length, overall: 602 ft
Length, waterline: 560 ft
Beam: 90 ft
Draft, scantling: 34 ft
Draft, full load: 29.8 ft
Ship crew: 41
Embarked troops: 300
Officer/SNCO: 25
Total accommodations: 366
Speed at 80 percent power: 18 knots
Ship weight, light: 14,000 long tons
Containers: 608 TEUs in transport mode, using 8-foot by 8-foot by 20-foot containers

Cape RO/RO Ships (T-AKR)

The Military Sealift Command operates three types of *Cape* roll-on/roll-off ships for the Army Preposition Afloat program.

The MV *Cape* D ships are the MV *Cape Decision* and MV *Cape Douglas,* each of which can carry up to 554 standard (8 foot by 8 foot by 20 foot) ISO containers. These vessels are not equipped with shipboard cranes and so require either pier cranes or an auxiliary crane ship to unload them. They have a fixed 65-ton-capacity vehicle ramp on the starboard stern quarter, which allows roll-on/roll-off operations to the starboard side or aft only. The ships of this class can carry up to 170,000 square feet of cargo.

The MV *Cape* H ships are three in number: MV *Cape Henry,* MV *Cape Horn,* and MV *Cape Hudson.* Their capacity is 6,766 standard ISO containers distributed over four holds. These vessels are

equipped with a 39-ton crane for unloading the containers, and they also have a fixed, 63.9-ton-capacity vehicle ramp on the starboard stern quarter, which allows roll-on/roll-off operations to the starboard side or aft only. Ships of this class can carry 180,000 square feet of cargo.

The MV *Cape* W ships, *Cape Washington* and *Cape Wrath,* each have a container capacity of 1,203 and carry one twin-boom shipboard crane with a capacity of 5 tons for self-unloading of vehicles. Each vessel has a fixed vehicle ramp on the starboard stern quarter and a vehicle ramp on the starboard side, amidships. The side ramp allows roll-on/roll-off operations to starboard, while the stern ramp allows such operations to the starboard side or aft. These ships can carry 190,000 square feet of cargo.

Combat Stores Ships (T-AFS)

The USN's Military Sealift Command currently operates six combat stores ships to provide supplies to navy combatant ships at sea for extended periods of time. Transfer of such supplies as repair parts, fresh food, clothing, and mail are made by tensioned cargo rigs as well as UH-46 versions of the CH-46 Sea Knight helicopter.

T-AFS ships are of two classes, *Mars* and *Sirius.*

Mars Class (T-AFS-1)

The vessels of the *Mars* class are combat stores ships (AFS), which have as their mission the underway replenishment of operating forces with refrigerated stores, dry provisions, technical spares, general stores, and fleet freight, mail, and personnel. The ships employ either alongside or vertical replenishment means.

General specifications of the class include:

Builder: National Steel and Shipbuilding
Displacement, full load: 17,381 tons
Dead weight: 7,529 tons
Overall length: 581 ft
Waterline length: 530 ft
Extreme beam: 79 ft
Waterline beam: 79 ft
Maximum navigational draft: 27 ft

Draft limit: 28 ft
Speed: 20 knots
Power plant: three boilers, steam turbines, one shaft, 22,000-shaft horsepower
Aircraft: two UH-46 Sea Knight helicopters
Armament: four three-inch .50-caliber guns; two Phalanx close-in weapons systems
Crew: 42 officers, 445 enlisted

Ships of the class include: *Mars* (AFS 1, decommissioned 1993), *Sylvania* (AFS 2; decommissioned 1995), *Niagara Falls* (T-AFS 3), *White Plains* (AFS 4; decommissioned 1995), *Concord* (T-AFS 5), *San Diego* (AFS 6; decommissioned 1993), and *San Jose* (T-AFS 7).

Sirius Class (T-AFS 8)
The *Sirius* class is the navy's newest class of combat stores ship (AFS), which have as their mission the underway replenishment of operating forces by providing refrigerated stores, dry provisions, technical and aviation spares, general stores, fleet freight, mail, personnel, and other items. Each ship has five alongside transfer stations and a flight deck from which two H-46 helicopters can be operated for vertical replenishment.

All ships of this class were formerly Royal Navy replenishment ships of the British *Lyness* class, built in England in 1965 and 1966. When acquired by the USN in 1981–83, they were extensively modernized with improved communications and underway-replacement facilities.

General specifications of the class include:

Builder: Swan Hunter and Wigham Richardson Ltd., Wallsend-on-Tyne, United Kingdom
Displacement full load: 16,680 tons
Dead weight: 6,475 tons
Overall length: 523 ft
Waterline length: 498 ft
Extreme beam: 72 ft
Waterline beam: 72 ft
Maximum navigational draft: 26 ft
Draft limit: 26 ft
Speed: 18 knots
Power plant: one diesel, 11,520-brake horsepower

Aircraft: two UH-46 Sea Knight helicopters
Complement: 123 civilian mariners, 47 USN personnel, including helicopter detachment

Ships of the class include *Sirius* (T-AFS 8), *Spica* (T-AFS 9), and *Saturn* (T-AFS 10).

Container Ships (T-AK)
Container ships are operated by the Military Sealift Command as part of its PREPOSITIONING PROGRAM. There are four ships, MV *Captain Steven L. Bennett* and MV *Major Bernard F. Fisher,* both prepositioned in the western Mediterranean Sea and assigned by the MSC to carry U.S. Air Force cargo, and MV *LTC Calvin P. Titus* and MV *SP5 Eric G. Gibson,* located in Saipan and assigned to carry support equipment and supplies for the U.S. Army. All three vessels are "self-sustaining"; that is, they incorporate cranes that allow them to load and off-load even at ports with undeveloped or battle-damaged harbors. The ships are all owned and operated by civilian companies and are chartered to Military Sealift Command.

Captain Steven L. Bennett Class
The two ships of the *Captain Steven L. Bennett* class are operated by the Military Sealift Command as USAF ammunition prepositioning ships and are deployed in the Mediterranean Sea. Like most other MARITIME PREPOSITIONING SHIPS, the two vessels are operated under charter and manned by civilian mariners. Both ships are converted commercial container ships. Cranes installed aboard the vessels make them self-sustaining for loading and off-loading cargo.

General specifications for the *Captain Steven L. Bennett* class include:

Length: T-AK 4296, 687 feet; T-AK 4396, 652 ft
Beam: T-AK 4296, 100 ft; T-AK 4396, 105 ft
Draft: T-AK 4296, 38 ft; T-AK 4396, 34 ft
Displacement: T-AK 4296, 52,878 long tons full load; T-AK 4396, 48,000 long tons full load
Speed: 19.0 knots

Ships of the class include *Captain Steven L. Bennett* (T-AK 4296) and *Major Bernard F. Fisher* (T-AK 4396).

LTC Calvin P. Titus Class

General characteristics of the *LTC Calvin P. Titus* class include:

Builder: Odense Steel Shipyard, Odense, Denmark
Power plant: 23,030 shaft horsepower Sulzer, Model 7RTA76; one shaft
Length: 652 ft
Beam: 105 ft
Displacement: 48,000 long tons full load
Speed: 19 knots (maximum speed)
Crew: 25 civilians

The ships are MV *LTC Calvin P. Titus* (T-AK 5089) and MV *SP5 Eric G. Gibson* (T-AK 5091).

Fast Combat Support Ships (AOE)

These high-speed ships function as oilers and ammunition and supply vessels. The largest combat logistics ships in the U.S. Navy, the AOEs are sufficiently fast and sufficiently well-armed to keep up with carrier battle groups. Each ship can carry in excess of 177,000 barrels of oil, 2,150 tons of ammunition, 500 tons of dry stores, and 250 tons of refrigerated stores. The AOE takes on petroleum products, ammunition, and stores from shuttle ships, then redistributes them to the ships of the carrier battle group. The object is to minimize the vulnerability of serviced ships by reducing alongside time. The two classes are the *Sacramento* class and *Supply* class.

Sacramento Class (AOE-1)

The ships of this class are fast combat support ships (AOE), the navy's largest combat logistics vessels. Ships of this class are capable of the speed, and are equipped with the armament, to keep up with AIRCRAFT CARRIER battle groups. They rapidly replenish USN task forces, and each ship carries in excess of 177,000 barrels of oil, 2,150 tons of ammunition, 500 tons of dry stores, and 250 tons of refrigerated stores. The fast combat support ship takes on petroleum products, ammunition, and stores from shuttle ships, then redistributes this cargo simultaneously to the ships of the carrier battle group. This significantly reduces the vulner-

ability of serviced ships by restricting alongside time.

The ships of the *Sacramento* class are multi-commodity. Their advanced replenishment facilities and sophisticated cargo-handling equipment achieves speed and efficiency. Moreover, the ships also perform limited ship repair and maintenance services.

All ships of this class are equipped with the Standard Tensioned Replenishment Alongside Method (STREAM) to provide rapid transfer of materials. Fuel is delivered through four double and two single hose fuel lines, which are fed by large turbine-driven cargo fuel pumps that supply fuel at 40 to 120 pounds per square inch at a maximum flow rate of 3,000 gallons per minute per pump used. Cargo, ammunition, and other supplies are moved vertically over seven decks by seven different elevators. Elevators one through six service the four ammunition holds, and number seven elevator and a package conveyor service the provisions hold. The supplies are then moved horizontally by a fleet of 33 forklift trucks. The cargo is transferred by four heavy-lift and three standard-lift STREAM cargo stations or by a detachment of two CH-46 helicopters.

The crew of the *Sacramento* class represent a wide range of technical skills to maintain and operate all shipboard equipment. There are seven on-board departments: Deck, Engineering, Operations, Supply, Medical, Air, and Administration.

General specifications of this class include:

Propulsion plant: two turbines, producing 50,000 horsepower at 4,829 rpm
Boilers: four at 600 psi
Main reduction gear diameter: 14 ft 4 in
Propellers: two 23 feet in diameter propellers with six blades
Overall length: 795 ft
Waterline length: 770 ft
Extreme beam: 107 ft
Waterline beam: 107 ft
Maximum navigational draft: 39 ft
Draft limit: 41 ft
Displacement: 53,000 tons full load

Dead weight: 31,820 tons
Speed: 26 knots
Cargo capacity, liquid: 8,219,387 gallons
Cargo capacity, ordnance: 3,000 tons
Cargo capacity, provisions: 675 tons
Aircraft: two CH-46E Sea Knight helicopters
Boats: two 26-foot motor whale boats; two 33-foot personnel boats
Cranes: one 15-ton
Armament: NATO Sea Sparrow missiles; two Phalanx close-in weapon systems
Crew: 24 officers, 576 enlisted

Ships of the class include *Sacramento* (AOE 1), *Camden* (AOE 2), *Seattle* (AOE 3), and *Detroit* (AOE 4).

Supply Class (AOE 6)

The navy's newest fast combat support ships (AOE) are the vessels of the *Supply* class, all commissioned during 1994–98. The AOE ships are the USN's largest combat logistics ships, capable of the speed, and fitted with the armament, necessary to keep up with aircraft carrier battle groups. The ships of this class rapidly replenish task forces. They carry in excess of 177,000 barrels of oil, 2,150 tons of ammunition, 500 tons of dry stores, and 250 tons of refrigerated stores. They take on petroleum products, ammunition, and stores from shuttle ships, then, in turn, redistribute them to the ships of the battle group.

The *Supply*-class ships are unique in that they are built to extremely rigid shock, noise, and vibration standards. They have very robust survivability features against shock, blast, and so on. The ships of the class are the world's largest gas turbine ships, ships powered by what is essentially a jet engine.

Supply-class ships replenish the ships of the battle group by two methods, alongside transfer —Connected Replenishment (CONREP)—and helicopter delivery, or Vertical Replenishment (VERTREP). Each ship of the class can replenish up to four warships simultaneously, even while conducting self-defense, electronic surveillance, and battle group command and communication functions.

General specifications of the class include:

Propulsion: four LM-2500 gas turbine engines (100,000 shaft horsepower), two reversing reduction gears (RRGs), four reversing converter couplings (RRCs), and two shafts with 23-foot fixed-pitch propellers
Speed: 25 knots
Length: 754 ft
Beam: 107 ft
Displacement: 48,800 tons full load
Cargo capacity, diesel fuel marine: 1,965,600 gal
cargo capacity, JP-5 fuel: 2,620,800 gal
Cargo capacity, DFM/JP-5 convertible: 1,965,600 gal
Cargo capacity, lube oil: 500 55-gallon drums
Cargo capacity, bottled gas: 800 gallons
Cargo capacity, ordnance stowage: 1,800 long tons
Cargo capacity, chill and freeze stowage: 400 long tons
Cargo capacity, water: 20,000 gal (emergency transfer)
Underway replenishment systems: six Stream stations (3 port/3 starboard); one Receive-Only Sliding Padeye; four 10-ton cargo booms; three Double-Probe Stream Fueling Stations; two Single-Probe Stream Fueling Stations
Aircraft: three CH-46E Sea Knight helicopters
Command, control, and communications: AN/SPS-67 Surface Search Radar; AN/SPS-64(V)9 Navigation Radar; Mk-23 Target Acquisition System; WRN-6 NAVSTAR GPS Satellite Navigation Receiver; OMEGA Navigation Receiver; Mk-22 AIMS IFF; Full Communications Suite
Armament: one NATO Sea Sparrow Missile System (NSSMS); two Close-In-Weapons System (CIWS); two 25-mm machine guns; four .50-caliber machine guns; one AN/SLQ-32(V)3 Electronic Warfare System; four decoy launchers; one NIXIE (Torpedo Decoy System)

Crew: 40 officers, 36 chief petty officers, 591 enlisted

Ships of the class include: *Supply* (AOE 6), *Rainer* (AOE 7), *Arctic* (AOE 8), and *Bridge* (AOE 10).

Congressional funding of USS *Supply* (AOE 6), lead ship of the *Supply* class, was appropriated in 1987. *Supply* and its sister ship USS *Arctic* were decommissioned in 2001 and 2002, respectively, then transferred to Military Sealift Command and placed back into service as United States Naval Ships (USNS). The currently active USN *Supply*-class ships are USS *Rainer* (AOE 7) and USS *Bridge* (AOE 10), both homeported at Bremerton, Washington.

Fast Sealift Ships (T-AKR)

T-AKRs are the fastest cargo ships in the world, capable of making 33 knots for the rapid delivery of military equipment in a crisis. The ships have roll-on/roll-off and lift-on/lift-off capability and are equipped with onboard cranes and self-contained ramps to enable off-loading where shore cargo facilities are unavailable. The ships are primarily vehicle transport vessels. All eight T-AKRs are of the *Algol* class. Using all eight, 98 percent of a U.S. Army mechanized division can be sealifted.

Algol Class (T-AKR 287)

The eight ships of the *Algol* class, designed to transport vehicles, are nearly the length of an aircraft carrier. Appropriately, they are all named after supergiant stars, and they are the fastest cargo ships in the world, capable of making 33 knots, which means that they have the ability to sail from the East Coast of the United States to Europe in six days, or to the Persian Gulf (via the Suez Canal) in 18 days. Their speed ensured the rapid delivery of military equipment in response to crisis. Together, the eight Fast Sealift Ships have the capacity to transport nearly all of the equipment required to outfit a full U.S. Army mechanized division.

The ships of this class all have roll-on/roll-off and lift-on/lift-off capability. Their on-board cranes and self-contained ramps enable them to off-load onto lighterage while anchored at sea or in ports without equipment unloading facilities. The intended cargo for these vessels includes tanks, large wheeled vehicles, and helicopters.

The ships of *Algol* class were all converted from container ships built for and operated by Sea-Land Services, Inc., out of Port Elizabeth, New Jersey. Because these fast giants consume vast quantities of fuel, they did not prove cost-effective as merchant ships. Military Sealift Command acquired six in 1981 and another two the following year. The purchase price included 4,000 containers and 800 container chassis for use in container ship configuration. Conversion of the vessels to Fast Sealift Ships was completed in 1986. Besides adding roll-on/roll-off features, the conversion reconfigured the cargo holds into a series of decks connected by ramps so that vehicles could be driven into and out of storage areas for rapid loading and unloading. Four cranes were also installed, to give the ships the ability to discharge in stream or in unimproved or damaged ports. When paired, the aft cranes can lift 100 tons. Midship cargo cranes have a 70-ton capacity. There is sufficient area between the forward and after superstructures to permit emergency high-hover helicopter lifts.

Together, the eight ships of this class can transport 93 percent of an army mechanized division. Indeed, seven of these ships transported 13 percent of all the cargo sent from the United States to Saudi Arabia during and following the PERSIAN GULF WAR.

General specifications of the *Algol* class (T-AKR 287) include:

Builders: T-AKR 287, 289, 293, Rotterdamsche D.D.Mij N.V., Rotterdam, Netherlands; T-AKR 288, 291, Rheinstahl Nordseewerke, Emden, West Germany; T-AKR 290, 292, A.G. Weser, Bremen, West Germany

Conversions: T-AKR 287, 288, 292, National Steel and Shipbuilding, San Diego, California; T-AKR 289, 293, Pennsylvania Shipbuilding, Chester, Pennsylvania; T-AKR 290, 291, Avondale Shipyards, New Orleans, Louisiana

Power plant: two Foster-Wheeler boilers, 875 psi; two GE MST-19 steam turbines, 120,000 horsepower; two shafts, 60,000 shaft horsepower each

Length, overall: 946.2 ft

Length, waterline: 893 ft

Beam: 106 ft

Displacement: 55,350 tons full load

Dead Weight: 32,295 tons

Speed: 33 knots

Crew: 42 civilian mariners when fully operational; 24 civilian mariners (USCG minimum); 18 civilian mariners (reduced operating status)

Ships of the class include *Algol* (T-AKR 287), *Bellatrix* (T-AKR 288), *Denebola* (T-AKR 289), *Pollux* (T-AKR 290), *Altair* (T-AKR 291), *Regulus* (T-AKR 292), *Capella* (T-AKR 293), and *Antares* (T-AKR 294).

Float-On/Float-Off Type Cargo Ships (T-AKF)

Currently, the Military Sealift Command operates one T-AKF vessel, the *MV American Cormorant*, stationed at Navy Support Facility Diego Garcia as part of the navy's Prepositioning Program. The ship carries port-opening lighterage and small watercraft for the U.S. Army and is operated under contract by Osprey-Acomarit.

T-AKF ships are semisubmersible and carry all the equipment needed to establish a working port. The *American Cormorant*'s cargo deck can be submerged 26 feet below the surface of the water by ballasting the ship to a draft of 66 feet. This allows barges and other embarked water craft to be floated off directly into the water. The barges contain the material-handling equipment required to move containers and other cargo and equipment ashore. Also embarked aboard the *American Cormorant* are three tug boats, two LCM 8s, a ROWPU barge, and a floating 100-ton crane barge. These constitute the complete army water craft package.

During a contingency, after the navy has completed conducting the initial assault landings, the army is responsible for all subsequent sustainment operations, including moving equipment, troops, and supplies ashore, opening and operating ports, and sustaining main water supply routes. Although most of the USA's water craft have the capacity to self-deploy across great distances, this consumes a great deal of time and exposes crews to danger. *American Cormorant* allows the army to project its force in about a third of the time.

American Cormorant was built as *Ferncarrier* in 1974 by Eriksbergs Mekaniska Verkstads AB in 1982, then converted as *American Cormorant* and acquired in 1985 for time charter by Military Sealift Command. The ship's general characteristics include:

Power plant: one Eriksberg/Burmeister and Wain 10K8EF diesel, 19,900 horsepower, one shaft; two thrusters, 3,000 horsepower

Length: 738 ft

Beam: 135 ft

Displacement: 69,555 tons full load

Speed: 14 knots

Crew: 21 civilians

Large, Medium-Speed Roll-On/Roll-Off Ships (T-AKR)

LMSR ships are the Military Sealift Command's newest category of vessels. Nineteen *Gordon*-class, *Shughart*-class, *Bob Hope*–class, and *Watson*-class LMSRs have been converted or built. With a capacity of 380,000 square feet, these ships can carry an entire U.S. Army task force, including 58 tanks, 48 other tracked vehicles, and more than 900 trucks and other wheeled vehicles. The slewing stern ramp and removable ramp for service to side ports enable vehicles to be driven on and off (roll on, roll off) the ship. Within the vessel, interior ramps between decks expedite traffic flow once cargo is loaded aboard ship. The LMSRs are also fitted with two 110-ton single-pedestal twin cranes for loading and unloading from and to undeveloped ports. A commercial helicopter deck accommodates emergency landings.

Gordon Class (T-AKR 296)

The two Military Sealift Command ships of the *Gordon* class (T-AKR 296) are large, medium-speed, roll-on/roll-off ships, the command's newest class of ships, which were acquired in response to a post–Persian Gulf War study by the Joint Chiefs of Staff calling for vastly increased sealift capacity for U.S. forces. Each of these vessels has roll-on/roll-off capability, and each is capable of transporting an entire USA task force, consisting of 58 tanks, 48 other tracked vehicles, in addition to more than 900 trucks and other wheeled vehicles. These vessels are equipped with a slewing stern ramp as well as a removable ramp that services two side ports. Thus, it is an easy matter to drive vehicles on and off the ship; moreover, a system of interior ramps between decks facilitates traffic flow once cargo is loaded aboard ship. The ships of this class are equipped with two 110-ton single-pedestal twin cranes, which enable the loading and unloading of cargo where shoreside infrastructure is limited, damaged, or nonexistent. A commercial helicopter deck is available for emergency landing in the daytime.

General specifications of the *Gordon* class include:

Builder: built in Denmark in 1972 and lengthened by Hyundai in 1984, with the conversion completed by Newport News Shipbuilding.

Power plant: one Burmeister and Wain 12K84EF diesel, 26,000 horsepower; two Burmeister and Wain 9K84EF diesels, 39,000 horsepower; three shafts and bow thruster

Length: 956 ft

Beam: 105.9 ft

Displacement: 55,422 tons full load

Cargo capacity: 284,064 sq ft, plus 49,991 sq ft deck cargo

Speed: 24 knots

Crew: 26–45 civilian mariner crew and up to 50 USN personnel

Ships of the class include *Gordon* (ex-*Jutlandia*) (T-AKR 296) and *Gilliland* (ex-*Selandia*) (TAKR 298).

Shughart Class (T-AKR 295)

The three ships of the *Shughart* class (T-AKR 295) are large, medium-speed, roll-on/roll-off ships and constitute the newest class of ships operated by the Military Sealift Command. These vessels provide afloat prepositioning of an army heavy brigade's equipment and a corps's combat support. They also furnish surge capability for lift of a heavy division's equipment from the United States. The ships were acquired after the Persian Gulf War, which, according to a study by the Joint Chiefs of Staff, revealed a pressing need for increased sealift capacity to transport military equipment and supplies during wartime and other national contingencies. These ships were then acquired through the Strategic Sealift Acquisition Program.

Each *Shughart*-class ship can carry an entire USA task force, consisting of 58 tanks and 48 other tracked vehicles in addition to more than 900 trucks and other wheeled vehicles. Such cargo can be used to support humanitarian missions as well as combat missions. Each has a cargo carrying capacity of more than 380,000 square feet, the equivalent of nearly eight football fields. The ships are equipped with a slewing stern ramp and a removable ramp, which services two side ports to facilitate driving vehicles on and off the ship. There are also interior ramps between decks to ease traffic flow once cargo is loaded aboard ship. On deck are two 110-ton single-pedestal twin cranes, which make it possible to load and unload cargo from unimproved or damaged ports. A commercial helicopter deck may be used for emergency, daytime landing.

General specifications of the *Shughart* class include:

Builder: built in Denmark in 1981, the ships were lengthened by Hyundai in 1987 and conversion was completed by National Steel and Shipbuilding Company.

Power plant: one Burmeister and Wain 12L90 GFCA diesel, 46,653 horsepower; one shaft; bow and stern thrusters

Length: 906.75 ft

Beam: 105.5 ft

Displacement: 55,298 tons full load

Cargo capacity, enclosed fixed decks: 228,331 sq ft

Cargo capacity, enclosed hoistable decks: 32,448 sq ft

Cargo capacity, weather decks: 51,682 sq ft

Total cargo capacity: 312,461 sq ft

Speed: 24 knots

Endurance: 12,200 nautical miles at 24 knots

Helicopter facility: day and emergency only for CH-47D and CH-53E helicopters

Crew: 26–45 civilian mariners, in addition to as many as 50 USN crew members

Ships of the class include *Shughart* (ex-*Laura Maersk*) (TAKR 295), *Yano* (ex-*Leise Maersk*) (TAKR 297), and *Soderman* (ex-*Lica Maersk*) (TAKR 299).

Bob Hope and *Watson* Class (T-AKR)

These large, medium-speed, roll-on/roll-off ships constitute the newest category of Military Sealift Command ships. In contrast to LMSRs of the *Gordon* class (T-AKR 296) and *Shughart* class (T-AKR 295), which consist of vessels converted from commercial cargo ships, the ships of the *Bob Hope* class are all newly constructed. They are intended to provide the army with the ability to preposition afloat all of a heavy brigade's equipment and a corps' combat support. They also furnish surge capability for the lift of a heavy division's equipment from the United States. Each vessel can carry an entire USA task force, consisting of 58 tanks, 48 other tracked vehicles, and more than 900 trucks and other wheeled vehicles. With a cargo carrying capacity of more than 380,000 square feet, the new ships have a slewing stern ramp and a removable ramp that services two side ports. This facilitates driving vehicles on and off the ship. In addition, interior ramps between decks facilitate traffic flow once cargo is loaded. A pair of 110-ton single-pedestal twin cranes enables the ship to load and unload cargo even in the absence of adequate shoreside infrastructure. The ships are provided with a commercial helicopter deck for emergency, daytime landing.

The lead ship of the class *Bob Hope,* named for the great American comic actor who devoted much of his career to entertaining U.S. sailors, soldiers, airmen, and marines, was launched on March 15, 1997. Ships of this class are closely related to those of the *Watson* class, the lead ship of which was launched in 1998. Other vessels in both classes have followed through 2001.

General specifications of the *Bob Hope* class include:

Builder: Avondale Industries

Power plant: four Colt Pielstick 10 PC4.2 V diesels, 65,160 horsepower; two shafts

Length: 951.4 ft

Beam: 106 ft

Displacement: 62,069 tons full load

Cargo capacity: 380,000 sq ft

Speed: 24 knots

Crew: 26–45 civilian mariners plus up to 50 USN personnel

General specifications of the *Watson* class include:

Builder: National Steel and Shipbuilding

Power plant: two GE Marine LM gas turbines, 64,000 horsepower, two shafts

Length: 951.4 ft

Beam: 106 ft

Displacement: 62,968 tons full load

Cargo capacity: 393,000 sq ft

Speed: 24 knots

Crew: 26–45 civilian mariners plus up to 50 USN personnel

Ships of the *Bob Hope* class include: *Bob Hope* (T-AKR 300), *Fisher* (T-AKR 301), *Seay* (T-AKR 302), *Mendonca* (T-AKR 303), *Pililaau* (T-AKR 304), *Brittin* (T-AKR 305), and *Benavidez* (T-AKR 306). Ships of the *Watson* class include: *Watson* (T-AKR 310), *Sisler* (T-AKR 311), *Dahl* (T-AKR 312), *Red Cloud* (T-AKR 313), *Charlton* (T-AKR 314), *Watkins* (T-AKR 315), and *Pomeroy* (T-AKR 316).

LASH Type: Cargo Ships, Barge (T-AK)

LASH stands for "lighterage aboard ships" and designates self-contained cargo vessels capable of unloading themselves in areas without developed harbor infrastructure. The Military Sealift Command's Prepositioning Program operates four LASH vessels under charter, SS *Green Valley,* SS

Green Harbour, SS *Austral Rainbow,* and MV *Jeb Stuart,* all of which are capable of carrying both barges and containers. All are stationed at Navy Support Facility Diego Garcia in the Indian Ocean.

Green Valley Class (T-AK 2049)

The three ships of this class are maritime prepositioning ships with the mission of quick-response delivery of army equipment for ground troops. LASH vessels *Green Valley* and its sister ships carry their own lighter barges for loading and off-loading cargo in places where no lighterage facilities are available. The *Green Valley* class ships carry up to 88 cargo lighter barges, but may carry a reduced number to make more room for containers and pusher boats (to manage the barges).

Each lighter carried aboard these ships weighs between 82 and 86 long tons and may discharge either pierside or in stream. *Green Valley* has two gantry-style cranes, one 30-long-ton crane (forward) for moving containers, and one 465.18-long-ton gantry for moving lighters. The larger gantry can move along almost the entire length of the ship to discharge pusher boats, lighters, and hatch covers. LASH vessels also carry a 3-long-ton general cargo crane to help load the ship's own stores.

Specifications for the *Green Valley* class include:

Length: 892 ft
Beam: 100 ft
Draft: 40 ft
Displacement: 62,314 tons full load

In addition to *Green Valley,* the class includes SS *Austral Rainbow* (T-AK 1005) and SS *Green Harbour* (T-AK 2064).

MV *Jeb Stuart* (T-AKB 9204)

This vessel constitutes a single-ship class. She was originally built as the *Atlantic Forest* by Sumitomo Shipbuilding. Specifications include:

Power plant: one Sulzer 9RND90 diesel; 26,000 horsepower; one shaft
Length: 857 ft
Beam: 106 ft
Displacement: 66,629 tons full load

Cargo capacity: 1,191,683 cu ft
Speed: 16 knots
Crew: 24 civilians

Modular Cargo Delivery System Vessel

Cape Jacob (T-AK 5029)

The *Cape Jacob* (T-AK 5029) is the Military Sealift Command's first modular cargo delivery system (MCDS) vessel. A maritime prepositioning ship, the *Cape Jacob* is used for USN prepositioning, primarily to carry USN ordnance and to operate, when necessary, as a shuttle replenishment ship for naval battle groups. The vessel is prepositioned at Naval Support Facility Diego Garcia.

The Modular Cargo Delivery System (MCDS) used on this ship is a fully mechanized cargo transfer unit, which works as a combination elevator and winch. It hoists pallets of cargo into the air, then across wire lines run between two ships sailing side-by-side. MCDS units have been installed on the Ready Reserve Force ships SS *Cape Johnson,* SS *Cape Alexander,* SS *Cape Gibson,* SS *Cape Girardeau,* SS *Cape John,* SS *Cape Juby,* and SS *Cape Jacob.* This means that the *Cape Jacob* can transfer cargo to and from these ships at sea.

General specifications of the *Cape Jacob* (T-AK 5029) include:

Length: 565 ft
Beam: 76 ft
Draft: 31 ft
Displacement: 22,929 long tons full load
Speed: 17 knots
Crew: 38 civilians

Multi-Purpose Tween Decker (T-AK)

MV *Green Ridge* Class

The Military Sealift Command operates MV *Green Ridge* from Navy Support Facility Diego Garcia as a maritime prepositioning ship carrying a 500-bed fleet hospital in support of USMC forces deployed ashore. The MV *Green Ridge* is a multipurpose tween decker, which means that it can be readily configured to accommodate breakbulk, container, and wheeled and tracked vehicle cargo. The ship is equipped with three sets of twin 21-metric-ton-capacity cranes, which give it full self-sustaining capability. Its ice-strengthened hull enables it to deliver supplies to polar regions.

MV *Green Ridge* is owned and operated by Central Gulf Lines and chartered by MSC. Its general characteristics include:

Builders: HDW, Kiel, Germany
Power plant: single-engine diesel with 10,000 shaft horsepower
Length: 507.2 ft
Beam: 69.5 ft
Displacement: 18,178 tons full load
Cargo capacity: 749,032 cu ft
Speed: 16 knots
Crew: 20 civilians

Roll-On/Roll-Off Container Ships (T-AK)

Buffalo Soldier Class
Currently, this type of vessel consists of one single-ship class, the *Buffalo Soldier* class. MV *Buffalo Soldier* (T-AK 9881) was converted from the civilian container vessel CGM *Monet* and stationed at Navy Support Facility Diego Garcia and used by the Military Sealift Command as a prepositioning ship for USAF cargo. *Buffalo Soldier* is a reflagged French Government Line ship owned by RR and VO Partnership and operated by Red River Shipping.

A self-sustaining ship, the *Buffalo Soldier* can unload itself, enabling it to operate in harbors with little or no infrastructure. Its 120-ton-capacity roll-on/roll-off ramp accommodates tracked and wheeled vehicles. General characteristics of the *Buffalo Soldier* class include:

Builder: Chanters Navigation de la Ciotat
Power plant: two SEMT-Pielstick 18 PC2.5 V diesels; 23,400 horsepower; one shaft; bow thruster
Length: 670 ft
Beam: 87 ft
Displacement: 40,357 tons full load
Speed: 16 knots
Crew: 19 civilians

Roll-On/Roll-Off Heavy Lift Ships (T-AK)

Strong Virginian (T-AKR 9025) Class
Currently, the *Strong Virginian* class consists of a single ship, MV *Strong Virginian,* stationed out of Navy Support Facility Diego Garcia and loaded with U.S. Army lighterage and associated port-opening equipment. The vessel is a reflagged Antigua/Barbuda vessel owned by Kaoampanttv Corporation and operated by Van Ommeren Shipping for the Military Sealift Command and the maritime prepositioning mission.

A self-sustaining, heavy-lift ship, *Strong Virginian* requires no shoreside facilities to conduct cargo operations. The ship is fitted with an 800-long-ton-capacity cargo boom and gantry crane, which enable very heavy lifts.

General characteristics of the *Strong Virginian* class include:

Builder: Bremer-Vegesach, Germany
Power plant: two MAK 6M601 diesels; 16,320 horsepower; two shafts; bow thruster
Length: 512 ft
Beam: 105 ft
Displacement: 31,390 tons full load
Cargo capacity: 855,859 cu ft
Speed: 14.5 knots
Crew: 23 civilians

Transport Oilers/Tankers (T-AOT)

American Osprey Class
The *American Osprey* class consists of two ships configured as offshore petroleum discharge tankers. Each has a 235,000-barrel capacity and can serve the fuel needs of USMC onshore forces or, if necessary, army and air force forces.

General specifications of the class include:

Length: *American Osprey,* 661 ft; *Petersburg,* 736 ft
Beam: *American Osprey,* 89 ft, 11 in; *Petersburg,* 102 ft
Draft, both ships: 36 ft, 1 in
Displacement: *American Osprey,* 34,723 long tons full load; *Petersburg,* 48,993 long tons full load

Speed: *American Osprey,* 14.8 knots; *Petersburg,* 14.5 knots

The two ships of the class are *American Osprey* (T-AOT 5074) and *Petersburg* (T-AOT 5075). The *American Osprey* is homeported in Beaumont, Texas, whereas the *Petersburg* is forward deployed in Guam.

Ashtabula Class

The ships of the *Ashtabula* class were all commissioned during WORLD WAR II as fleet oilers for the underway replenishment of bulk petroleum and lubricants either to battle group station ships or directly to combatant ships and support forces. Delivery could be made by alongside as well as vertical replenishment means. All ships of this class have been decommissioned.

General specifications of the class include:

Displacement: 34,750 tons full load
Dead weight: 23,903 tons
Overall length: 644 ft
Waterline length: 616 ft
Extreme beam: 75 ft
Waterline beam: 75 ft
Draft: 35 ft
Speed: 18 knots
Power plant: steam turbine, four boilers, two shafts, 13,500 shaft horsepower
Armament: two 3-inch .50-caliber antiaircraft weapons
Aircraft: none, but a small area for vertical replenishment is provided
Crew: 22 officers, 362 enlisted

Ships of the class included: *Ashtabula* (AO 51), *Caliente* (AO 53), *Chikaskia* (AO 54), *Aucilla* (AO 56), *Marias* (AO 57), *Nantahala* (AO 60), *Severn* (AO 61), *Taluga* (AO 62), *Chipola* (AO 63), *Tolovana* (AO 64), *Allagash* (AO 97), *Caloosahatchee* (AO 98), and *Canisteo* (AO 99).

Champion Class

These vessels are used by the Military Sealift Command to transport fuel for the Department of Defense. All five T-AOTs are *Champion*-class tankers, also known as T5s. Their double hulls and ice-strengthened construction protect against possible environmental damage due to leaks or other mishaps.

Military Sealift Command charters the tankers from Ocean Product Tankers of Houston, Texas. The vessels are MV *Gus W. Darnell,* MV *Paul Buck,* and MV *Samuel L. Cobb,* which entered service with MSC in 1985, and MV *Richard G. Matthiesen* and MV *Lawrence H. Gianella,* which entered service the following year.

General characteristics of the *Champion* class include:

Builder: American Ship Building Co., Tampa, Florida
Power plant: one Sulzer 5RTA 76 diesel; 18,400 horsepower sustained; one shaft
Length: 615 ft
Beam: 90 ft
Displacement: 39,624 tons full load
Cargo capacity: 237,766 barrels of fuel oil
Speed: 16 knots
Crew: 23 civilians

Potomac (T-AOT 181)

Operated by Military Sealift Command, *Potomac* is an offshore petroleum discharge system (OPDS) tanker. It has the capability of supporting any logistics over-the-shore operation with 173,000 barrels of JP-5 (jet) fuel delivered through its integral OPDS system. The tanker is prepositioned at Naval Support Facility Diego Garcia.

Potomac was built in 1957 by Sun Shipbuilding and was assigned to the Afloat Prepositioning Force in 1991. It is operated by a civilian company, Bay Ship Management, and owned by MARAD.

General specifications of the *Potomac* (T-AOT 181) include:

Power plant: steam turbine; one propeller
Length, overall: 620 ft
Length, waterline: 600 ft
Beam, extreme: 84 ft
Beam, waterline: 84 ft
Maximum navigational draft: 35 ft
Draft limit: 35 ft
Displacement: 34,800 tons full load

Dead weight: 27,467 tons
Speed: 15 knots

Underway Replenishment Oilers (T-AO)

Cimarron Class

The *Cimarron* class are fleet oilers, which perform underway replenishment of petroleum products as well as bringing ordnance to the fleet at sea. The vessels of this class transport bulk petroleum and lubricants from depots to the ships of the battle group. Additionally, they transport and deliver limited fleet freight, mail, and personnel to combatants and support ships. All ships of this class are capable of providing three double-probe fuel rigs to port, and two single-probe fuel rigs to starboard, simultaneously, to deliver a maximum of 900,000 gallons per hour of marine diesel fuel. The ships can sustain 20 knots while carrying a load of 150,000 barrels of fuel and 625 tons of ordnance. Transfer of liquid cargo is provided by STREAM (Standard Tensioned Replenishment Alongside Method) double-hose stations located on both the port and starboard sides. For receiving fuel, there are double receivers, also at the port as well as starboard sides. An Automated Liquid Cargo Control System regulates fuel delivery.

General specifications of the class include:

Builder: Avondale Shipyards
Power plant: two 600 pounds per square inch boilers (automated steam), 24,000 shaft horsepower via a single shaft and propeller
Waterline length: 661 ft
Extreme beam: 88 ft
Waterline beam: 86 ft
Maximum navigational draft: 32 ft
Draft limit: 35 ft
Displacement: 36,977 tons full load
Dead weight: 25,332 tons
Speed: 20 knots
Cargo capacity, oil: 75,000 barrels
Cargo capacity, JP-5: 45,000 barrels
Cargo capacity, convertible: 30,000 barrels
Cargo capacity, total: 150,000 barrels
Capacity, ordnance: 625 tons

Capacity, provisions, dry fleet freight: 360 tons
Capacity, provisions, reefer: 60 tons
Capacity, provisions, lube oil: 125 55-gallon drums
Capacity, provisions, bottled gas: 584 cylinders
Capacity, provisions, ISO containers: 21
Armament: two Phalanx close-in weapons systems; two 25-mm Mk-38 machine guns; four .50-caliber machine guns

Ships of the class include *Cimarron* (AO 177; decommissioned 1998), *Monongahela* (AO 178), *Merrimack* (AO 179; decommissioned 1998), *Willamette* (AO 180), and *Platte* (AO 186).

Henry J. Kaiser Class

The *Henry J. Kaiser* is the lead ship of this new class of underway replenishment oilers (T-AO). All 18 ships of the class were delivered between 1982 and 1989; four of these were decommissioned during 1996–98. The ships are operated by the Military Sealift Command.

Oilers of this class are fitted with starboard and port stations for underway replenishment of fuel and stores. From five fueling stations, they can replenish two ships at a time, pumping up to 900,000 gallons of diesel fuel and 540,000 gallons of jet fuel per hour. Additionally, the ships can deliver small quantities of fresh and frozen provisions, stores, and other materials. Dry cargo carrying capacity is 7,400 square feet, and refrigerated deck vans can hold up to 128 pallets of chilled food. They deliver fleet cargo, mail, and provisions via CONREP (connected replenishment) from two dry cargo rigs or via VERTREP (vertical replenishment) on the helicopter deck. The ships of this class are crewed primarily by civilian mariners.

General specifications of the class include:

Builder: Avondale Shipyards, New Orleans, Louisiana
Power plant: two Colt-Pielstick 10 PC4.2 V 570 diesels, 34,442 horsepower sustained, two shafts
Overall length: 677 ft
Waterline length: 650 ft
Extreme beam: 97 ft

Waterline beam: 97 ft
Maximum navigational draft: 35 ft
Draft limit: 35 ft
Displacement: 42,000 tons full load
Capacity: 180,000 barrels of fuel oil or aviation fuel
Speed: 20 knots
Crew: 82 civilian mariners, 21 USN personnel, plus 21 spare personnel
Aircraft: helicopter platform-equipped

Ships of the class include: *Henry J. Kaiser* (T-AO 187), *Joshua Humphreys* (T-AO 188; decommissioned 1996), *John Lenthall* (T-AO 189), *Andrew J. Higgins* (T-AO 190; decommissioned 1996), *Benjamin Isherwood* (T-AO 191; decommissioned 1997), *Henry Eckford* (T-AO 192; decommissioned 1998), *Walter S. Diehl* (T-AO 193), *John Ericsson* (T-AO 194), *Leroy Grumman* (T-AO 195), *Kanawha* (T-AO 196), *Pecos* (T-AO 197), *Big Horn* (T-AO 198), *Tippecanoe* (T-AO 199), *Guadalupe* (T-AO 200), *Patuxent* (T-AO 201), *Yukon* (T-AO 202), *Laramie* (T-AO 203), and *Rappahannock* (T-AO 204).

USMC and USAF
Maritime Prepositioning Ships

Cpl. Louis J. Hauge Jr. Class

The *Cpl. Louis J. Hauge Jr.* class consists of five maritime prepositioning ships that carry the complete range of U.S. Marine Corps cargo, equipment, and supplies sufficient to support a Marine Air Ground Task Force (17,000 marines) for 30 days. Each ship of this class has lift-on/lift-off capabilities, as well as roll-on/roll-off capabilities. USN lighterage carried onboard consists of causeways, both powered and unpowered, and small boats to move them around. The ships are also certified to land USMC CH-53E helicopters. Container and breakbulk cargo capacity are also available. All ships of this class are prepositioned at Naval Support Facility Diego Garcia, and each can discharge cargo either pierside or while anchored offshore using the lighterage carried aboard. This gives the USMC the flexibility it needs to deploy wherever required.

General specifications of the *Cpl. Louis J. Hauge Jr.* class include:

Builder: Odense Stalskibsvaerft, Lindo, Denmark; converted by Bethlehem Steel
Power plant: one diesel, 16,800 horsepower, one shaft
Length: 755.5 ft
Beam: 90 ft
Draft: 32 ft
Displacement: 46,484 tons full load
Capacity: 120,080 sq ft; 1,283,000 gallons of fuel; 65,000 gallons of water; 332 TEU containers
Speed: 17.5 knots
Aircraft: CH-53E helicopter platform

Ships of the class include: *Cpl. L. Hauge Jr.* (T-AK 3000), *PFC William B. Baugh* (T-AK 3001), *PFC J. Anderson Jr.* (T-AK 3002), *1st Lt. A. Bonnyman* (T-AK 3003), and *Pvt. Franklin J. Phillips* (T-AK 3004).

1st Lt. Harry L. Martin Class

The three maritime prepositioning ships of the *1st Lt. Harry L. Martin* class were designed to accommodate new and upgraded combat equipment for USMC forces and constitute the Maritime Prepositioning Force (Enhanced), or MPF(E). Unlike other Maritime Prepositioning Ships, which are chartered by the U.S. Navy from civilian owners, the enhanced ships are owned by the USN. Each of the enhanced ships includes capacity to perform simultaneous roll-on, roll-off and lift-on, lift-off operations both pierside and in stream. Like most other prepositioning ships, those of the *1st Lt. Harry L. Martin* class have a flight deck for helicopter operations, but do not carry operational aircraft.

1st Lt. Harry L. Martin was converted from the MV *Tarago* and officially renamed on June 1, 2000. The two other ships were converted and commissioned later in the year. General specifications of the class include:

Power plant: T-AK 3015, one diesel, one shaft, 25,704 base horsepower; T-AK 3016 and T-AK 3017, two gas turbines, two shafts, 50,000 shaft horsepower

Length: T-AK 3015, 754 ft; T-AK 3016, 864 ft; T-AK 3017, 885 ft, 4 in

Beam: T-AK 3015, 106 ft; T-AK 3016, 98 ft; T-AK 3017, 105 ft, 7 in

Draft: T-AK 3015, 36 ft; T-AK 3016, 35 ft; T-AK 3017, 34 ft, 4 in

Displacement: T-AK 3015, 48,000 tons full load; T-AK 3016, 50,059 tons full load; T-AK 3017, 54,298 tons full load

Capacity: 128,000 sq ft vehicle; 1,017 TEU containers

Speed: T-AK 3015, 21 knots; T-AK 3016, 22 knots; T-AK 3017, 24.0 knots

Crew: T-AK 3015 and T-AK 3016, 24; T-AK 3017, 26

Aircraft: CH-53E helicopter platform

Ships of the class include *1st Lt. Harry L. Martin* (T-AK 3015), *LCpl. Roy Wheat* (T-AK 3016), and *Gysgt. Fred W. Stockham* (TAK 3017).

2nd Lt. John P. Bobo Class

The five maritime prepositioning ships of the *2nd Lt. John P. Bobo* class are operated by the Military Sealift Command and assigned to carry USMC cargo, enough to support a Marine Air Ground Task Force for 30 days. These ships are suited to operate in places without improved port facilities, and all five have lift-on/lift-off capabilities as well as roll-on/roll-off capabilities. They are LASH vessels—lighterage aboard ship—and carry causeways, both powered and unpowered, as well as small boats to move the causeways around as required. The vessels are all certified to land CH-53E helicopters. Normally, four of the ships are prepositioned in Guam and Saipan. The lead ship of the class, *2nd Lt. John P. Bobo,* is based in Europe.

The vessels of this class have all been designed to deliver USMC vehicles and gear. Onboard accommodations include facilities for about 130 marines as well as an operating crew of 25. The powerplants of these ships, housing a pair of Stork Werkspoor medium-speed propulsion engines, were designed to conserve space in order to maximize available cargo capacity. Each ship is equipped with five deck cranes, which give the ship the ability to unload its own cargo in remote locations that lack improved port facilities.

General specifications of the *2nd Lt. John P. Bobo* class include:

Power plant: two diesels, 26,400 horsepower; single shaft

Length: 673 ft

Beam: 105 ft

Draft: 29 ft

Displacement: 40,846 tons full load

Capacity: 162,500 sq ft vehicle; 1,605,000 gallons of petroleum; 81,700 gallons of water; 522 TEU containers

Crew: 7 USN officers, 30 civilian mariners, 25 civilian maintenance personnel

Aircraft: helicopter platform only

Ships of the class include *2nd Lt. John P. Bobo* (T-AK 3008), *PFC D.T. Williams* (T-AK 3009), *1st Lt. B. Lopez* (T-AK 3010), *1st Lt. Jack Lummus* (T-AK 3011), and *Sgt. W.R. Button* (T-AK 3012).

Sgt. Matej Kocak Class

Three maritime prepositioning ships of the Military Sealift Command make up the *Sgt. Matej Kocak* class. All are assigned to Maritime Prepositioning Ship Squadron One, which has responsibility for the operation of the Military Sealift Command Prepositioning Program in the eastern Atlantic Ocean and Mediterranean Sea. The three vessels are chartered from a civilian firm and are manned by USN officers and civilian mariners. Their mission is to carry prepositioned military cargo for the USMC and USAF.

General specifications of the *Sgt. Matej Kocak* class (T-AK 3005) include:

Power plant: steam turbines, two boilers, one shaft, 30,000 shaft horsepower

Length: 821 ft

Beam: 105.5 ft

Draft: 32 ft

Displacement: 48,754 tons full load
Capacity: 152,524 sq ft vehicle; 1,544,000 gallons petroleum; 94,780 gallons water; 540 TEU containers
Speed: 20 knots
Crew: seven USN officers, 29 civilian mariners, 25 civilian maintenance personnel
Aircraft: helicopter platform only

Ships of the class include *Sgt. Matej Kocak* (T-AK 3005), *PFC E.A. Obregon* (T-AK 3006), and *Maj. S.W. Pless* (T-AK 3007).

See also COMBAT PREPOSITIONING SHIPS; LOGISTICS PREPOSITIONING SHIPS.

Carney, Robert B. (1895–1990) *chief of naval operations*

Robert Carney graduated from the UNITED STATES NAVAL ACADEMY in 1916 and served on DESTROYERS during most of his navy career, which included tours in the Atlantic and Pacific during WORLD WAR II. On August 17, 1953, he was named 14th CHIEF OF NAVAL OPERATIONS and served until August 17, 1955, when he was relieved of command because of unauthorized and insubordinate remarks regarding the desirability of war with Communist China. After his retirement from the USN, he pursued a career in industry.

CH-46 Sea Knight helicopter   See AIRCRAFT: VIETNAM WAR AND AFTER.

Charles F. Adams Class (DDG-2)   See DESTROYERS.

chief of naval education and training (CNET)

CNET is responsible to the CHIEF OF NAVAL OPERATIONS (CNO) for the education and training of USN and USMC officers and enlisted personnel through a network of training and education programs. CNET is staffed by more than 22,000 military and civilian personnel and is administered through 167+ subordinate activities and detachments located throughout the country and in Japan. On any given day, some 48,000 students are enrolled in more than 3,600 different courses. In addition to training USN and USMC personnel, CNET oversees 57 NAVAL ROTC commands at colleges and universities throughout the United States, five departments of naval sciences, and 490 Naval Junior ROTC units at high schools in the United States, Guam, Italy, and Japan. Training is conducted through these major organizations: chief of naval air training (CNATRA), and Naval Air Station Corpus Christi, Texas, with responsibility for training aviators, flight officers, and enlisted aircrew at five naval air stations in Mississippi, Texas, and Florida. Naval Aviation Schools Command, the BLUE ANGELS, and the National Museum of Naval Aviation also report to CNATRA.

chief of naval operations (CNO)

The CNO is the senior active duty officer of the U.S. Navy. Appointed by the president of the United States, he or she serves as the navy member of the Joint Chiefs of Staff.

chief of navy chaplains

The Chaplain Corps is as old as the USN. The second article of *Navy Regulations,* adopted on November 28, 1775, specifies that "the Commanders of the ships of the thirteen United Colonies are to take care that divine services be performed twice a day on board and a sermon preached on Sundays, unless bad weather or other extraordinary accidents prevent." Reverend Benjamin Balch, who was the first USN chaplain, served in the Continental navy in 1778. *Naval Regulations* of 1802 was the first USN document to specify the duties of chaplain, which included, in addition to divine services, performing as "schoolmaster instructing the midshipmen and volunteers in writing, arithmetic, navigation and whatever else they might need to make them proficient." It was not until the early 20th century that USN chaplains steered away from the teaching function. In October 1906, a board of chaplains was established, along with a chief of navy chaplains.

The chief of navy chaplains commands all USN chaplains and is headquartered at the Office of the Chief of Chaplains (N097), Washington, D.C.

chief petty officer   See RANKS AND GRADES.

China Relief Expedition (Boxer Rebellion)

After the 1895 Sino-Japanese War, a number of European powers extorted territorial and commercial concessions from China. Their actions served to exacerbate the popular, already-growing antiforeign sentiment in the nation. A centuries' old secret society, the Yihequan (I Ho Ch'uan; Righteous Harmonious Fists), revived during this period and assumed militant leadership of the antiforeign movement. Westerners referred to members of the group as "Boxers," and by the end of the 19th century the Boxers had perpetrated a series of antiforeign acts, including burning the homes and businesses of Chinese Christians. On December 30, 1899, Boxers waylaid and murdered a British missionary. When Western governments protested to Dowager Empress Cixi (Tzu Hsi), she responded on January 11, 1900, that the Boxers legitimately represented a portion of Chinese society and were not to be branded as criminal. Increasingly, she lent her outright support to the Boxers. On May 30, the foreign ministers in the capital, Peking (Beijing), requested troops to protect their legations. Four hundred and thirty sailors and marines from eight countries arrived at the legations on May 31 and June 4. This first contingent included 56 U.S. sailors and marines from USS *Oregon* and USS *Newark*. On June 9, the Boxers attacked foreign property in Peking, prompting Great Britain's Sir Claude MacDonald, senior foreign minister stationed in China, to request a larger military relief force.

On June 10, 2,100 troops—mostly sailors and marines—from Great Britain, Germany, Russia,

France, Japan, Italy, and Austria as well as the United States marched from Tientsin but were forced to retreat on June 22. Realizing that a larger force was required, the Euro-American allies assembled 20,000 men, including 2,000 Americans (among them 500 sailors and marines), who set off from Tientsin on August 5, 1900. Two significant battles were fought and won, after which, on August 14, the relief force secured the endangered Peking legations.

Throughout the rest of the year, the relief forces, which included units from Europe, the United States, and Japan, seized full control of Peking, then fanned out into the rest of northern China, attacking any remaining pockets of Boxer resistance. At last, on February 1, 1901, Chinese authorities formally agreed to outlaw and abolish the I Ho Ch'uan. On September 7, the government of China signed the Peace Protocol of Peking, thereby ending the Boxer Rebellion.

China Service

"China Service" is the general name for U.S. Navy actions in and about China during 1937–39 and 1945–57. In 1937, Japanese aggression in China (ongoing since 1931) suddenly became a full-scale invasion, and ships of the U.S. Asiatic Fleet, commanded by Admiral Harry E. Yarnell, were dispatched to see to the evacuation of American nationals. The USN also resisted Japanese attacks on U.S. commercial shipping. The crisis reached its most intense point on December 12, 1937, when Japanese naval aircraft sank the river gunboat USS *Panay*. Despite the "Panay Incident," war did not immediately break out between Japan and the United States, although relations steadily deteriorated, ultimately eventuating in the December 7, 1941, attack on Pearl Harbor.

In 1945, as WORLD WAR II ended in Asia and the Pacific, the USN was again sent to China, this time to facilitate the repatriation of Japanese soldiers and to aid the Chinese central government in enforcing the surrender terms. In addition, SEVENTH FLEET ships furnished transport for Chinese

Nationalist troops and carried urgently needed food supplies from Shanghai up the Yangtze River in an effort to relieve widespread postwar famine.

China Service Medal   See DECORATIONS AND MEDALS.

Civil War

Although the Civil War was primarily a conflict fought on land, the U.S. Navy played an important role in it. Indeed, the USN was the key to the Union's strategy as set out by the first general-in-chief of the Union army, Winfield Scott. He proposed to use the USN to blockade some 3,500 miles of Confederate coast, from Virginia to Texas, in an effort to strangle the Southern economy and discourage any foreign interventions or alliances. The blockade—derisively dubbed "Scott's Anaconda"

by a skeptical Northern press—was also intended to buy time for the North to build up its army and naval forces for offensive action. Yet, at the beginning of the war in April 1861, the USN had only 42 active warships. This was almost 42 more than the "Confederate navy" managed to muster at the outset of hostilities, but it was hardly a sufficient force to blockade a vast coastline. Nevertheless, what the North did possess was the economic and industrial capacity to build many more ships and to recruit the sailors to man them. By the end of the first year of the conflict, the USN had grown to 250 vessels (including gunboats and other relatively small craft) and had 1,200 officers and 21,000 enlisted personnel. By this same time, the Confederate navy had a mere dozen or so miscellaneous craft, while only 321 USN officers had resigned their commissions to become officers of the Confederate navy.

Outmanned, outshipped, and outgunned, the Confederate navy assiduously avoided outright

Engagement between the CSS *Alabama* and the USS *Kearsage,* June 19, 1864; painting by Xanthus R. Smith *(Naval Historical Center)*

Flag Officer Andrew H. Foote's gunboats attack Fort Henry, February 6, 1862.   *(Library of Congress)*

combat with USN vessels. Instead, the Confederate government purchased (mostly from Britain) commerce raiders, fast ships designed not to fight USN combatant ships, but to prey upon Northern commercial vessels. These ships, paramountly the CSS *Alabama* commanded by RAPHAEL SEMMES, inflicted substantial losses against the loyal merchant marine, not only disrupting shipping but also inflating insurance costs and significantly adding to the North's economic war burden. *Alabama* was finally sunk by USS *Kearsarge* on June 19, 1864, off the French coast.

In addition to commerce raiding, Southern mariners concentrated on blockade running, using speed and stealth to evade the ever-growing "Anaconda" of Union blockaders. Although many of the blockade runners were daring, their success decreased as the North added more and more ships to the blockading force. Moreover, Southern logisticians failed to work closely with the blockade runners, who often dealt in high-profit luxury goods rather than such bulkier but far more necessary basics as food, building materials, and weapons.

The USN blockade of the South was never entirely passive or static. No fewer than 89 Confederate ports were seized quite early in the war. Such seizures not only deprived the South of the use of these ports, they also provided bases of operations for Union army and amphibious forces. Confederate planners continually looked for ways to break the blockade. On March 8, 1862, CSS *Virginia*, an ironclad vessel rebuilt from the captured USS *Merrimack*, steamed into Hampton Roads. The ironclad did significant damage to the Union blockaders in the area, and it incited great panic. However, the Union responded with the newly launched USS *Monitor*, a radical design plated with five layers of inch-thick iron over a wooden backing. The *Monitor* featured an epoch-making innovation, a gun mounted in a rotating armored turret. The "duel of the ironclads" took place in Hampton Roads on

March 9. It ended in a tactical draw but a strategic triumph for the Union, since the *Virginia* was forced to retreat and never figured in combat again. The Union produced many more *Monitor*-class ships, and the nature of naval warfare was changed forever.

On April 25, 1862, Flag Officer DAVID FARRAGUT captured, in a daring sea operation, New Orleans. The city and its port remained in Union hands throughout the rest of the war, depriving the Confederacy of navigation of the Mississippi River and thereby greatly impeding the movement of supplies to the South and its armies. Moreover, New Orleans provided a base for Union operations on and along the lower Mississippi. Gradually, Union land forces, supported by USN riverboats, severed the eastern portion of the Confederacy from the western. Control of the Mississippi, Cumberland, and Tennessee rivers extended the "Anaconda" blockade inward from the coast, into the very vitals of the South.

Most of the land battles of 1861 and 1862 went badly for the North. Despite superior numbers and resources, the Union army was repeatedly outgeneraled. The major turning of the tide in favor of the Union did not come until July 1863 with victory at Gettysburg, Pennsylvania, and the taking of Vicksburg, Mississippi. The capture of that fortress-city by General Ulysses S. Grant on July 4, 1863, after a long siege, put the Mississippi River wholly in Union hands. Vital to Grant's victory was coordination with riverborne naval forces under DAVID DIXON PORTER, whose gunboats successfully ran the gauntlet of Vicksburg's formidable river defenses, enabling Grant to cross the Mississippi from the west and conduct offensive operations from the south.

Deprived of its major ports and inland water courses, the Confederacy could ill afford to lose Mobile Bay, on the Gulf Coast, which nevertheless fell to Farragut on August 5, 1864. By this time,

Flag Officer Farragut's squadron passes the forts on the Mississippi, April 24, 1862, while the Union frigate *Mississippi* destroys the rebel ram *Manassas*. Lithograph by Currier and Ives   *(Library of Congress)*

"Scott's Anaconda," which had seemed so fanciful in 1861, had become a highly effective reality. At the beginning of 1865, the USN numbered more than 700 warships (among them no fewer than 65 of the *Monitor* class) and a complement of 60,000 officers and men. The combination of attrition—created mainly by USN actions—and an increasingly adept ground war waged by the North doomed the Confederate cause. The Civil War was effectively over by mid-April 1865.

Clark, Vern (1941–   ) *chief of naval operations*

Vern Clark became the 27th CHIEF OF NAVAL OPERATIONS (CNO) on July 21, 2000. Born in Sioux City, Iowa, he graduated from Evangel College and holds an MBA from the University of Arkansas. After attending Officer Candidate School, he received his commission in August 1968. Clark served aboard the DESTROYERS USS *John W. Weeks* (DD 701) and USS *Gearing* (DD 710). With the rank of lieutenant, he commanded USS *Grand Rapids* (PG 98). Subsequent commands included USS *McCloy* (FF 1038), USS *Spruance* (DD 963), the ATLANTIC FLEET's Anti-Submarine Warfare Training Center, Destroyer Squadron Seventeen, and Destroyer Squadron Five. As an admiral, Clark commanded the *Carl Vinson* Battle Group/Cruiser Destroyer Group Three, the SECOND FLEET, and the U.S. Atlantic Fleet.

Clark's shore assignments included service as special assistant to the director of the Systems Analysis Division in the Office of the Chief of Naval Operations, then as administrative assistant to the deputy chief of naval operations (surface warfare), and as the administrative aide to the vice chief of naval operations. Clark was also head of the Cruiser-Destroyer Combat Systems Requirements Section and Force Anti-Submarine Warfare officer for the commander, Naval Surface Force, U.S. Atlantic Fleet. During the PERSIAN GULF WAR, he directed the Joint Staff's Crisis Action Team for Desert Shield and Desert Storm.

After promotion to admiral, Clark became director of both Plans and Policy (J5) and Financial Management and Analysis (J8) at the U.S. Transportation Command. As commander of the *Carl Vinson* Battle Group, he was deployed to the Arabian Gulf and then served as deputy commander, Joint Task Force Southwest Asia. He also saw service as the deputy and chief of staff, U.S. Atlantic Fleet, and as director of operations (J3) and then director of the Joint Staff.

Combat Action Ribbon   See DECORATIONS AND MEDALS.

combat prepositioning ships

Combat prepositioning ships are, in effect, floating warehouses that provide afloat prepositioning for equipment, munitions, and supplies in support of U.S. Army combat units that deploy to potential contingency sites. The Combat Prepositioning Force calls for at-sea prepositioning of complete combat equipment for one heavy armored brigade and the 6th Brigade Afloat aboard eight large, medium-speed, roll-on/roll-off ships (LMSRs). In addition, other combat prepositioning ships carry cargo that supports and sustains the brigade, including water purification units, food, and initial combat support equipment.

commander   See RANKS AND GRADES.

commander in chief, Allied Forces, Southern Europe (AFSOUTH)

Allied Forces Southern Europe (AFSOUTH) is one of the two regional commands of NATO's Allied Command Europe (ACE). Pursuant to an order by Secretary of Defense Donald Rumsfeld reserving the title of commander in chief solely for the president of the United States, the title of the commander of AFSOUTH was changed from commander in chief Allied Forces, Southern Europe, to commander Allied Forces, Southern Europe, on October 14, 2002. The commander is a USN admiral, whose AFSOUTH area of responsibility includes Greece, Hungary, Italy, Spain, and Turkey, as well as the Black

Sea, the Sea of Azov, the whole of the Mediterranean, and the Atlantic approaches to the Strait of Gibraltar, east of longitude 7°23'48" W, and an area around the Canary Islands and its associated airspace.

commander in chief, U.S. Atlantic Fleet (CINCLANTFLT)

The mission of CINCLANTFLT is to ensure that the ATLANTIC FLEET provides fully trained, combat ready forces to support U.S. and NATO commanders in regions of conflict throughout the world. CINCLANTFLT responsibility extends from the Adriatic Sea to the Arabian Gulf and, in the Atlantic Ocean, from the North Pole to 28 degrees north latitude, and the Norwegian, Greenland, and Barents Seas. Currently the Atlantic Fleet consists of more than 118,000 sailors and marines, 186 ships, and 1,300 aircraft. The Atlantic Fleet includes 18 major shore stations to provide training, maintenance, and logistics support. The operational fleet in the Atlantic Fleet is SECOND FLEET.

The Atlantic Fleet was established under a single command in 1906 by President Theodore Roosevelt. The title "Commander in Chief, Atlantic Fleet" was used from 1906 to 1923 and again from 1941 to 2002. In October 2002, Secretary of Defense Donald Rumsfeld directed that the title of commander in chief be reserved solely for the president of the United States. Effective October 14, 2002, the title was changed to commander, U.S. Atlantic Fleet.

commander in chief, U.S. Naval Forces Europe (CINCUSNAVEUR)

The position of commander in chief, U.S. Naval Forces, Europe (CINCUSNAVEUR), was established in 1942, during WORLD WAR II. The name was changed on October 14, 2002, to commander, U.S. Naval Forces, Europe, pursuant to an order by Secretary of Defense Donald Rumsfeld, which reserved the title of commander in chief solely for the president of the United States.

Commander, U.S. Naval Forces, Europe plans, conducts, and supports naval operations in the European theater and Middle East. The command is not a NATO command, but it does ensure that ready forces are available for NATO if the need arises. The geographical area of responsibility includes all of Navy Region Europe, consisting of Naval Station Rota, Spain; Naval Support Activity Naples, Italy; Naval Air Station Sigonella, Sicily; Naval Support Activity Gaeta, Italy; Naval Support Activity La Maddalena, Sardinia; and Naval Support Activity Souda Bay, Crete. The forward-deployed submarine tender USS *Emory S. Land* (AS 39) is homeported in La Maddalena, Sardinia, and Helicopter Support Squadron Four is based at NAS Sigonella, Sicily. Fleet Air Reconnaissance Squadron Two is stationed in Rota, Spain. Most of the command's forces are concentrated in the Mediterranean, but its area of responsibility extends from the North Cape in Norway to the Cape of Good Hope in South Africa and includes the Adriatic, Baltic, and Black Seas, as well as the Mediterranean. In all, the area of responsibility encompasses 89 countries.

commander in chief, U.S. Pacific Fleet (CINCPACFLT)

Pursuant to an order by Secretary of Defense Donald Rumsfeld reserving the title of commander in chief solely for the president of the United States, the title of the commander of the U.S. PACIFIC FLEET was changed from commander in chief, U.S. Pacific Fleet (CINCPACFLT), to commander, U.S. Pacific Fleet (CINCPACFLT), on October 14, 2002.

The commander supports the U.S. Pacific Command's theater strategy and provides naval forces in an area of responsibility that covers more than half of the Earth's surface, some 100 million square miles. The Pacific Fleet includes about 200 ships, 2,000 aircraft, and more than 239,000 sailors, marines, and civilian employees. Pacific Fleet ships sail the Pacific, Indian, and Arctic Oceans, from the west coast of the United States to the Arabian Gulf.

Command Leadership School

Located in Newport, Rhode Island, the Command Leadership School offers courses to prepare USN officers for command. In addition to the basic Command Officers Course, the school offers an Executive Officers Course, as well as a "Spouse Course" for the spouses of command and executive officers.

command ships (AGF)

AGFs serve as the flagships for the commander, THIRD FLEET, and commander, SIXTH FLEET. The ships provide communications and accommodations for fleet commanders and staff. They are equipped with air and surface radars, helicopter, chaff launchers, and an electronic warfare suite. The two classes of AGF, *Coronado* and *La Salle,* each include one ship, each converted from amphibious warfare ships.

Coronado Class

The USS *Coronado* (AGF 11), homeported at San Diego, California, is the THIRD FLEET flagship. Like other command ships, it provides communications and accommodations for fleet commanders and staff. It is equipped with an advanced suite of air and surface radars and electronic warfare equipment. It can accommodate helicopters and has chaff launchers for defensive countermeasures.

The *Coronado* was built by Lockheed Shipbuilding and Construction Company in Seattle and launched on July 30, 1966, as an LPD. Refitted as an AGF command ship, it was so designated in 1980. To the original LPD design, additional superstructure was added to accommodate command ship duties. Over the years, the ship has been continuously updated, especially in the area of her Command, Control, Communications, Computers, and Intelligence (C^4I) capabilities.

Coronado was initially assigned to the U.S. ATLANTIC FLEET in the 1970s, when she conducted extensive operations and was deployed on numerous occasions to northern Europe and the Caribbean and Mediterranean Seas. In 1980, *Coronado* relieved the USS *LaSalle* (AGF 3) as the command ship for commander, U.S. Middle East Force, stationed in the Persian Gulf. Reassigned in October 1985, *Coronado* next relieved USS *Puget Sound*

(AD 38) as the command ship of commander, SIXTH FLEET, then was assigned to Third Fleet in 1986.

Continual modernization is intended to make *Coronado* a state-of-the-art Joint Task Force command ship. Not only can it embark a helicopter squadron during at-sea periods, her flight deck can also launch and recover the AV-8 Harrier "Jump Jet." General specifications include:

> **Power plant:** two Foster-Wheeler boilers, geared turbines, twin shafts, 24,000 shaft horsepower
> **Length:** 570 ft
> **Beam:** 100 ft
> **Displacement:** 16,912 tons full load
> **Speed:** 21 knots
> **Fuel capacity:** 750,000 gal
> **Aviation fuel:** 350,000 gal
> **Flight deck length:** 200 ft
> **Flight deck area:** 16,000 sq ft
> **Aircraft:** two light helicopters
> **Crew:** ship's company, 516; flag staff, 120

La Salle Class

The USS *La Salle* (AGF 3), forward deployed to Gaeta, Italy, is the Sixth Fleet's flagship. *La Salle* assumed the flagship role on November 8, 1994. By offering the accommodations and facilities necessary to embark a Joint Task Force, the ship increased the flexibility of the U.S. Sixth Fleet commander and his staff. Like all command ships, the *La Salle* is fitted out with a cutting-edge suite of communication, command, and control electronic equipment. This enables the ship to control any operation or exercise that involves sea, air, land, and amphibious forces. This can be carried out either while at sea or in port. Centralizing the command and control function makes the fleet more responsive in a contingency.

Following commissioning on February 22, 1964, USS *La Salle* served as the flagship for Atlantic Fleet Amphibious Forces during the Dominican crisis. In 1969, the ship served as the test platform for the prototype AV-8 Harrier "Jump Jet."

In 1972, *La Salle* was designated a "Miscellaneous Command Ship (AGF)" and assigned as the flagship for commander, Middle East Force, in which capacity it was forward-deployed to Bahrain. Painted white to reflect the Middle East sun, the ship was informally called the "Great White Ghost of the Arabian Coast." *La Salle* was responsible for control and coordination of the Maritime Intercept Force during the PERSIAN GULF WAR and became, on March 12, 1991, the first USN warship to enter the liberated port of Ash Shuaybay, Kuwait.

General specifications of the USS *La Salle* include:

Length: 521 ft
Beam: 84 ft
Draft: 21 ft
Displacement: 13,900 tons full load
Main propulsion system: De Laval steam turbines, twin shafts, two propellers; combined 24,000 shaft hp
Boilers: two Babcock and Wilcox, 600 psi
Speed: 20 knots, sustained; 21.6 knots, maximum
Armament: two 20-mm Mk-16 Phalanx Close-in Weapons Systems
Crew: ship's companys, 420 enlisted and 25 officers; staff, 90 enlisted and 48 officers

container ships (T-AK)   See CARGO, FUEL, AND REPLENISHMENT SHIPS.

counter-drug operations ships (T-AGOS)

The USNS *Stalwart* (T-AGOS 1), USNS *Indomitable* (T-AGOS 7), and USNS *Capable* (T-AGOS 16), monohull ocean surveillance ships originally designed to gather underwater acoustical data, make up the *Stalwart* class, vessels modified for drug interdiction.

Stalwart Class

The ships were converted from cold war–era vessels intended to hunt for Soviet submarines. All vessels of the *Stalwart* class were modified from their original design by the removal of their underwater acoustic arrays and the installation of an air-search radar, integrated display system, and special communications equipment, all intended to detect and monitor suspected drug traffickers. General characteristics of the class include:

Builder: Tacoma Boatbuilding, Tacoma, Washington
Power plant: diesel-electric; four Caterpillar D 3988 diesel generators, 3,200 horsepower, two motors, 1,600 horsepower; two shafts; bow thruster; 550 horsepower
Length: 224 ft
Beam: 43 ft
Displacement: 2,262 tons full load
Speed: 11 knots (12.65 mph)
Crew: 20 USN personnel and 18 civilians

cruisers (CG)

The modern U.S. Navy cruiser is a large combat vessel capable of addressing multiple targets. Typically, today's operational cruisers are called "guided missile cruisers," and their primary missions are antiair warfare (AAW), antisubmarine warfare (ASW), and antisurface warfare (ASUW).

The USN designates Guided Missile Heavy Cruisers as CAG; Guided Missile Light Cruisers and Guided Missile Cruisers as CG; Guided Missile Light Cruisers (Nuclear) and Guided Missile Cruisers (Nuclear) as CGN. However, all CGNs have been decommissioned, due to either old age or excessive refueling and overhaul costs. The *Long Beach,* a large guided missile cruiser launched in 1959, was the world's first nuclear-powered surface warship and the first USN guided missile cruiser designed and built as such. It was decommissioned in 1995. Currently, the only operational class of guided missile cruisers is the *Ticonderoga* class, which includes the following general characteristics:

Builders: Ingalls Shipbuilding (CG 47–50, 52–57, 59, 62, 65–66, 68–69, 71–73); Bath Iron Works (CG 51, 58, 60–61, 63–64, 67, 70)

Guided missile cruiser USS *Valley Forge* (CG-50) is assisted toward the pier at Naval Station San Diego by tugs. (*U.S. Navy*)

Power plant: 4 General Electric LM 2500 gas turbine engines; two shafts, 80,000 shaft horsepower total

Length: 567 ft

Beam: 55 ft

Displacement: 9,600 tons full load

Speed: 30+ knots

Aircraft: two SH-2 Seasprite (LAMPS) in CG 47–48; two SH-60 Sea Hawk (LAMPS III)

Crew: 24 officers, 340 enlisted

Armament: Mk-26 missile launcher (CG 47 thru CG 51); standard missile MR or Mk-41 vertical launching system (CG 52 thru CG 73); additionally, standard missile (MR), vertical launch ASROC (VLA) missile, Tomahawk cruise missile, six Mk-46 torpedoes (from 2 triple mounts), two Mk-45 5-inch/.54-caliber lightweight guns, and two Phalanx close-in weapons systems

Cost: about $1 billion each

The current ships of the class are USS *Ticonderoga* (CG 47), homeport: Pascagoula, Miss.; USS *Yorktown* (CG 48), homeport: Pascagoula, Miss.; USS *Vincennes* (CG 49), homeport: Yokosuka, Japan; USS *Valley Forge* (CG 50), homeport: San Diego, Calif.; USS *Thomas S. Gates* (CG 51), homeport: Pascagoula, Miss.; USS *Bunker Hill* (CG 52), homeport: San Diego, Calif.; USS *Mobile Bay* (CG 53), homeport: San Diego, Calif.; USS *Antietam* (CG 54), homeport: San Diego, Calif.; USS *Leyte Gulf* (CG 55), homeport: Norfolk, Va.; USS *San Jacinto* (CG 56), homeport: Norfolk, Va.; USS *Lake Champlain* (CG 57), homeport: San Diego, Calif.;

USS *Philippine Sea* (CG 58), homeport: Mayport, Fla.; USS *Princeton* (CG 59), homeport: San Diego, Calif.; USS *Normandy* (CG 60), homeport: Norfolk, Va.; USS *Monterey* (CG 61), homeport: Norfolk, Va.; USS *Chancellorsville* (CG 62), homeport: Yokosuka, Japan; USS *Cowpens* (CG 63), homeport: Yokosuka, Japan; USS *Gettysburg* (CG 64), homeport: Mayport, Fla.; USS *Chosin* (CG 65), homeport: Pearl Harbor, Hawaii; USS *Hue City* (CG 66), homeport: Mayport, Fla.; USS *Shiloh* (CG 67), homeport: San Diego, Calif.; USS *Anzio* (CG 68), homeport: Norfolk, Va.; USS *Vicksburg* (CG 69), homeport: Mayport, Fla.; USS *Lake Erie* (CG 70), homeport: Pearl Harbor, Hawaii; USS *Cape St. George* (CG 71), homeport: Norfolk, Va.; USS *Vella Gulf* (CG 72), homeport: Norfolk, Va.; and USS *Port Royal* (CG 73), homeport: Pearl Harbor, Hawaii. The lead ship of the class, *Ticonderoga*, was deployed on January 22, 1983.

Cuban missile crisis

In October 1962, United States U-2 "spy plane" surveillance revealed Soviet nuclear missile bases

A U.S. Navy aviator made this low-altitude surveillance photograph of a missile launching site in San Cristóbal, Cuba.   *(U.S. Navy)*

under construction in Cuba. On October 22, 1962, President John Fitzgerald Kennedy made a special television broadcast to the nation, announcing that, contrary to all assurances, the Soviet Union had been building bomber and missile bases on the island. In response, the president demanded the immediate withdrawal of the missiles and the dismantling of the bases. He declared a naval "quarantine," in effect a blockade, in order to prevent additional missiles, military supplies, and materiel from reaching the island.

The quarantine was intended as an alternative to outright assault or invasion, either of which was almost certain to trigger thermonuclear war between the United States and the Soviet Union. Because of the nature of the response, the U.S. Navy was called on to play the key role in the Cuban missile crisis.

USN forces under the U.S. Atlantic Command, headed by Admiral Robert L. Dennison (CINCLANT), deployed and set up the quarantine, intercepting merchant shipping en route to Cuba as well as Soviet submarines operating in the area. The quarantine proved highly effective. On October 28, Soviet premier Nikita Khrushchev agreed to remove the missiles under United Nations supervision. President Kennedy suspended the quarantine on the following day, and by November 2 the missile bases were, in fact, being dismantled. Although the quarantine had been lifted, USN DESTROYERS and FRIGATES were kept on station, maintained by UNDERWAY REPLENISHMENT, for a month. The ships were supported by USN fighter and airborne early warning aircraft.

D

Dahlgren, John A. (1809–1870) *navy engineer*

Dahlgren is best remembered as the inventor of the Dahlgren gun, which was widely used on U.S. Navy vessels during the CIVIL WAR. Its characteristic bottle shape allowed for the use of a very large powder charge, which improved range, accuracy, and destructive force.

Dahlgren joined the USN in 1826 and, after he patented a percussion lock in 1847, was appointed chief of the USN's Bureau of Ordnance. He served in this post from 1847 to 1863 and again from 1868

Eleven-inch Dahlgren aft pivot gun on the USS *Kearsage*   *(Naval Historical Foundation)*

to 1869. During the Civil War, Dahlgren created the USN's ordnance system and established the Navy Ordnance Yard.

Dahlgren was more effective as an ordnance designer and an administrator than as a seagoing commander. His performance at the siege of Charleston in 1863 did not enhance his reputation. Nevertheless, as rear admiral, Dahlgren served as professor of gunnery at the UNITED STATES NAVAL ACADEMY and, during the final two years of his life, he commanded the WASHINGTON NAVY YARD.

Decatur, Stephen (1779–1820) *navy commander*

The son of a privateer and USN captain during the QUASI-WAR WITH FRANCE, Decatur served as a midshipman in 1798 aboard the USS *United States*. His first command was the *Enterprise* during the BARBARY WARS. Operating from this vessel, Decatur led a small band of men into Tripoli harbor to burn the USS *Philadelphia,* which had been captured after it ran aground. This extraordinary exploit not only kept the ship out of Barbary hands, but also earned Decatur a reputation for daring.

During the WAR OF 1812, Decatur, promoted to captain, commanded the USS *United States,* in which he captured HMS *Macedonian*. After the war, Decatur returned to Barbary waters as commander of a small squadron, which intimidated the pirates into ending their depredations against U.S. shipping. Decatur personally secured treaties from the bey of Algiers and others.

Decatur served on the Board of Navy Commissioners after he returned to the United States, but in 1820 he was killed in a duel with James Barron, a navy officer over whose court-martial he had presided a decade earlier.

decorations and medals

USN sailors, noncommissioned officers, and commissioned officers are eligible for decoration with the following medals and commendations, the majority of which may also be awarded to members of the other services and, on occasion, to members of foreign armed services.

Battle "E" Ribbon

The Battle "E" Ribbon was established during WORLD WAR II to recognize the permanent-duty crew members of a ship that had been cited for battle efficiency. In 1976, Secretary of the Navy J. William Middendorf established the Navy "E" Ribbon to replace the earlier decoration.

China Service Medal

Originally, the China Service Medal was issued to commemorate services performed by USN and USMC personnel during operations in China from July 7, 1937, to September 7, 1939. Award of the medal was subsequently extended to include services performed by USN, USMC, and USCG personnel during operations in China subsequent to September 2, 1945.

See also CHINA SERVICE.

Combat Action Ribbon

The Combat Action Ribbon is awarded for active participation in ground or surface combat after March 1, 1961, while in the grade of captain or junior thereto. A gold star affixed to the ribbon denotes subsequent awards, and a silver star is affixed in lieu of five gold stars. The ribbon features narrow red, white, and blue bands in the center flanked by two broad gold bands, with a broad blue band on the left and a broad red band on the right.

Fleet Marine Force Ribbon

The USN Fleet Marine Force Ribbon was established on September 1, 1984, by Secretary of the Navy John F. Lehman, Jr. The ribbon is awarded to those who have acquired specific professional skills, knowledge, and military experience above what is normally required of USN personnel serving with the Fleet Marine Force (FMF). The ribbon is dark blue with a red central stripe edged by yellow and green stripes.

Naval Reserve Medal

The Naval Reserve Medal was established by Secretary of the Navy James K. Paulding on September 12, 1938. It was awarded for qualifying service between September 12, 1938, and September 12, 1958, and is now obsolete. The medal was awarded to members of the NAVAL RESERVE after completion of 10 years service in the Naval Reserve Force, National Naval Volunteers, or in any federally recognized naval militia force. The medal has been replaced by the Armed Forces Reserve Medal.

Naval Reserve Meritorious Service Medal

The Naval Reserve Meritorious Service Medal was authorized as a ribbon by Secretary of the Navy Fred A. Korth on June 25, 1962, and as a medal by Secretary of the Navy Paul H. Nitze on June 22, 1964. It is awarded selectively to USN reservists who, during any three consecutive years subsequent to January 1, 1958, fulfill with distinction the obligations of inactive reserve. The medal's obverse shows, in the center of a bronze medallion, a fouled anchor with a scroll around its shank. The scroll bears the words "MERITORIOUS SERVICE." Encircling the anchor are the words "UNITED STATES NAVAL RESERVE." The reverse is blank. The ribbon consists of a center band of blue flanked by broad red bands, each of which is edged by a thin gold line and a blue band.

Naval Reserve Sea Service Ribbon

The Naval Reserve Sea Service Ribbon was established by Secretary of the Navy John Lehman on May 28, 1986, for active duty, Selected Reserve, or any combination of active or Selected Reserve service after August 15, 1974, aboard a Naval Reserve ship or its Reserve unit or an embarked active or Reserve staff, for a cumulative total of 24 months.

Navy Arctic Service Ribbon

The Navy Arctic Service Ribbon was established on May 8, 1986, by Secretary of the Navy John F. Lehman, Jr. It is awarded to USN and USMC personnel as well as to civilian citizens, nationals, or resident aliens of the United States for 28 days of service above the Arctic Circle.

Navy Cross

The Navy Cross was established on February 4, 1919, and is awarded to any person serving in any capacity with the USN or USMC who distinguishes himself with extraordinary heroism not justifying the award of the Medal of Honor. The relevant incident must have taken place while engaged in an action against an enemy of the United States, while engaged in military operations involving conflict with an opposing foreign force, or while serving with friendly foreign forces engaged in an armed conflict against an opposing armed force in which the United States is not a belligerent party. The Navy Cross is awarded for an action that involves risk of life so extraordinary as to set this person apart from his contemporaries.

Navy Expeditionary Medal

The Navy Expeditionary Medal was established on August 15, 1936, by the DEPARTMENT OF THE NAVY and is awarded to USN personnel who have landed on foreign territory and have engaged in operations against armed opposition or who have operated under circumstances deemed to merit special recognition and for which no other campaign medal has been awarded.

In the center of a bronze medallion a sailor is shown beaching a boat containing three men in uniform; at the rear of the boat is an American flag, and in the upper quarter of the medal, following the contour of its rim, is the word "EXPEDITIONS." The reverse shows, in the center of the medallion, an eagle perched on an anchor. The eagle grasps sprigs of laurel. Above the eagle are the words "UNITED STATES NAVY," and above the laurel on the left is the word "FOR," and over the laurel on the right, "SERVICE." The ribbon to the Navy Expeditionary Medal consists of a blue background with a wide yellow stripe inside each edge.

Navy/Marine Corps Achievement Medal

Established on May 1, 1961, the medal is awarded to USN and USMC members in the grades of lieutenant commander or major and below for meritorious service or achievement in combat or noncombat based on sustained performance or specific achievement of a superlative nature, but not involving aerial flight.

Navy/Marine Corps Commendation Medal

The medal, established on November 1, 1943, as the Navy Commendation Ribbon, is awarded to any service member who, while serving in any capacity with the USN or USMC, distinguishes himself or herself by heroism, outstanding achievement, or meritorious service.

Navy/Marine Corps Medal

Established on August 7, 1942, the medal is awarded to service members who, while serving in any capacity with the USN or USMC, distinguish themselves by heroism not involving actual conflict with an enemy.

Navy/Marine Corps Overseas Service Ribbon

This dark blue ribbon, with a yellow-edged red central stripe and pale blue and yellow edge stripes, was created on September 17, 1968, for award to service members who complete 12 months of duty at overseas shore-based duty stations.

Navy Occupation Service Medal

The medal recognizes the services performed by USN, USMC, and USCG personnel in the occupation of the territories of the enemies of the United States during World War II and subsequent to the surrender of the enemies in that conflict. The medal was also awarded to USN personnel serving 90 consecutive days or more on permanent or temporary duty while assigned or attached to a unit participating in direct support of the Berlin Airlift between June 26, 1948, and September 30, 1949.

Navy Recruiting Service Ribbon

This ribbon, yellow with a black central stripe and bright green and blue edge stripes, was established on June 1, 1989, for award to USN personnel who have successfully completed a tour of recruiting duty.

Navy Unit Commendation

Established by order of the SECRETARY OF THE NAVY on December 18, 1944, this commendation is awarded to any ship, aircraft, detachment, or other USN unit that has, subsequent to December 6, 1941, distinguished itself by outstanding heroism in action against the enemy, but not sufficient to justify award of the Presidential Unit Citation. Individual personnel wear a ribbon, with a green center stripe flanked by red, yellow, and blue stripes.

Pistol Marksmanship Medal

The award is presented to members of the USN and NAVAL RESERVE who qualify as Expert with a military pistol on a prescribed military course. Worn without devices, the award signifies a Marksman qualification. The addition of a bronze "S" device denotes Sharpshooter, a bronze "E" denotes a first and second Expert qualification, and a silver "E" denotes a third (and final) Expert qualification.

Rifle Marksmanship Ribbon

This ribbon was established on October 14, 1969, by Secretary of the Navy John H. Chafee and recognizes those who score at the Marksman, Sharpshooter, or Expert level of qualification on a prescribed course of fire for the rifle.

Qualification at the Marksman level entitles the individual to wear the ribbon without device. Qualification at the Sharpshooter level is indicated by a silver letter "S," and qualification at the Expert level merits a silver "E" on the ribbon.

Sea Service Deployment Ribbon

This ribbon, pale blue with a yellow-edged dark blue central stripe and red edge stripes, was authorized on May 28, 1986, to recognize active duty, Selected Reserve, or any combination of active or Selected Reserve service after August 15, 1974, aboard a Naval Reserve ship or with a Naval Reserve unit for a cumulative total of 24 months.

Deep Drone 7200 Remotely Operated Vehicle   See RESCUE AND SALVAGE SHIPS.

Deep Submergence Craft (NR-1)   See RE-SEARCH SHIPS.

Deep Submergence Rescue Vehicles (DSRV)   See RESCUE AND SALVAGE SHIPS.

Department of the Navy

The Department of the Navy is the executive office of both the USN and USMC. By law, its head, the SECRETARY OF THE NAVY, is a civilian appointed by the president of the United States with the advice and consent of the Senate. Although the secretary of the navy, through the Department of the Navy, exercises full and final authority over all naval matters, both the secretary and the department are subordinate to the secretary of defense and the Department of Defense.

Department of the Navy Alternative Dispute Resolution (ADR) Program

Pursuant to a 1986 DEPARTMENT OF THE NAVY policy statement on alternative dispute resolution, an ADR program was first developed. On December 11, 1996, the Department of the Navy issued the current policy on ADR, SECNAVINST 5800.13, which mandates the use of alternative dispute resolution to avoid litigation "to the maximum extent practicable." ADR is administered by a dispute resolution specialist and a deputy dispute resolution specialist.

Department of the Navy Civilian Personnel/Equal Employment Opportunity

The USN is a major employer of civilians and, as such, maintains a policy of equal employment opportunity. Implementation of this policy is administered by the Office of the Deputy Assistant Secretary of the Navy for Civilian Personnel and Equal Opportunity, which has produced the *Department of the Navy Civilian Human Resources Manual.*

Department of the Navy Environmental Program

The Department of the Navy Environmental Program was created to ensure that USN shore facilities, ships, and all activities are operated or conducted in an environmentally responsible manner. The program addresses the full range of environmental concerns, from occupational health and safety, discharge from ships, pollution prevention, hazardous materials handling, alternative energy sources, and recycling, to supervising environmental impact studies for proposed construction and activities.

Department of the Navy Research, Development, and Acquisition

Under the direction of the assistant secretary of the navy for research, development, and acquisition, this department works with private industry to research, develop, and acquire defense technology for the USN, USMC, and, in joint programs, for the other services.

The assistant secretary of the navy for research, development, and acquisition is responsible for all acquisition functions and programs and manages USN research, development, and acquisition activities. The department consists of a staff reporting directly to the assistant secretary; program executive officers (PEOs); direct reporting program managers (DRPMs); and the Naval Systems Commands and their field activities. The PEOs and DRPMs are responsible for the actual development and acquisition of naval systems.

destroyers

Currently operational navy destroyers are fast warships that provide multimission offensive and defensive capabilities operating independently or

The guided missile destroyer USS *Cole* was damaged by a terrorist bomb detonated in the port of Aden, Yemen, on October 12, 2000, killing 17 sailors. *(U.S. Navy)*

as part of carrier battle groups, surface action groups, amphibious ready groups, and UNDERWAY REPLENISHMENT groups. Destroyers designated DD primarily perform antisubmarine warfare duty while guided missile destroyers (DDG) engage in antiair warfare (AAW), antisubmarine warfare (ASW), and antisurface warfare (ASUW).

Today's operational destroyers are of two classes, the *Arleigh Burke* class and the *Spruance* class.

Arleigh Burke Class (DDG)

The *Arleigh Burke* class of AEGIS-equipped guided missile destroyers represents the state of the art in destroyer design and has replaced or is replacing navy destroyers of other classes. As of 2004, the class consists of 42 ships, with more slated to be built at least through 2008. The navy regards the ships of the *Arleigh Burke* class to be the most capable and survivable surface combatant in any navy. In addition to incorporating an array of advanced electronics and weapons systems, the lead ship of the class, *Arleigh Burke* (DDG 51), was the first navy vessel designed to incorporate stealth or shap-

ing techniques that reduce the ship's radar cross-section. This decreases the ship's radar detectability. The ships of the class were also designed to defend against multiple threats, including aircraft, cruise missiles, and attack submarines. These destroyers can also be employed in strike operations against shore-based targets.

The ships of the *Arleigh Burke* class were constructed in "flights," which allowed for the incorporation of technological advances during construction. Flight I ships were commissioned between 1991 and 1997. Flight II ships, commissioned between 1998 and 1999, incorporate improvements to the SPY radar and the Standard missile, as well as to active electronic countermeasures and communications systems. Flight IIA, with ships commissioned beginning in 2000, added a helicopter hangar to accommodate an antisubmarine helicopter and an armed attack helicopter.

The ships of all three flights are equipped with the Aegis air defense system, incorporating the SPY phased-array radar. They are also armed with a 90-cell Vertical Launching System capable of storing and rapidly firing Standard, Tomahawk, and Vertically Launched ASROC (VLA) missiles. These may be used for air defense, strike warfare, or antisubmarine warfare missions. Additional armament includes the Harpoon antiship cruise missile, the 5-inch .54-caliber gun (with improvements integrating it with the Aegis weapon system), and the Phalanx Close-in Weapon System for self-defense.

The *Arleigh Burke* ships also carry the navy's newest antisurface warfare combat systems. Land-attack cruise missile capability is provided by Tomahawk missiles, launched from the Mk-41 Vertical Launching System (VLS), a multiwarfare missile launching system capable of firing a mix of missiles against airborne and surface threats. The 5-inch, .54-caliber gun is used in conjunction with the Mk-34 Gun Weapon System as an antiship weapon. It is also used for close-in air contacts or to support forces ashore in strike missions.

For the antisubmarine mission, the AN/SQQ-89 integrated ASW Suite is the most advanced antisubmarine warfare system in the world. The AN/SQR-19 Tactical Towed Array SONAR (TAC-

A guided missile destroyer fires a Tomahawk cruise missile.   *(Department of Defense)*

TAS) provides extremely long-range passive detection of enemy submarines, and the AN/SQS-53C Hull-Mounted SONAR is used to actively and passively detect and locate submarine contacts. The ships also have the capability to land the SH-60B LAMPS Mark III Helicopter, which greatly extends the anti-submarine role.

In terms of sea handling, the ships of the class feature a large, innovative waterplane-area hull form, which significantly improves seakeeping (the motions and related qualities of a ship at sea), allowing the ships to sail at high speed even in high seas. The seakeeping hull has a characteristic shape: pronounced flare and a "V" shape appearance at the waterline.

Engineering of the power plant was also fully revised in the *Arleigh Burke* class. The gas turbines are derived from aircraft designs and provide both propulsion and ship service electrical power generation. The power plant is highly automated for maximum efficiency and reliability. Four General Electric LM2500 gas turbine engines (GTEs) provide propulsion.

Arleigh Burke–class ships, which replace the older *Charles F. Adams*–class and *Farragut*-class guided missile destroyers, incorporate the following general characteristics:

Builders: Bath Iron Works and Ingalls Shipbuilding

Power plant: four General Electric LM 2500-30 gas turbines; two shafts, 100,000 total shaft horsepower

Length: Flights I and II (DDG 51–78), 505 ft; Flight IIA (DDG 79–98), 509.5 ft

Beam: 59 ft

Displacement: hulls 51 through 71, 8,315 tons full load; hulls 72 through 78, 8,400 tons full load; hulls 79 and on, 9,200 tons full load

Speed: 30+ knots

Aircraft: none

Crew: 23 officers, 300 enlisted

Armament: Standard missile; Harpoon; Vertical Launch ASROC (VLA) missiles; Tomahawk missiles; six Mk-46 torpedoes (from two triple tube mounts); one 5-inch/.54-

caliber Mk-45 lightweight gun; two 20-mm Phalanx CIWS

The USS *Arleigh Burke* (DDG 51) was deployed on July 4, 1991, and is homeported at Norfolk, Virginia. Other ships of the class are USS *Barry* (DDG 52), homeport: Norfolk, Va.; USS *John Paul Jones* (DDG 53), homeport: San Diego, Calif.; USS *Curtis Wilbur* (DDG 54), homeport: Yokosuka, Japan; USS *Stout* (DDG 55), homeport: Norfolk, Va.; USS *John S. McCain* (DDG 56), homeport: Yokosuka, Japan; USS *Mitscher* (DDG 57), homeport: Norfolk, Va.; USS *Laboon* (DDG 58), homeport: Norfolk, Va.; USS *Russell* (DDG 59), homeport: Pearl Harbor, Hawaii; USS *Paul Hamilton* (DDG 60), homeport: Pearl Harbor, Hawaii.; USS *Ramage* (DDG 61), homeport: Norfolk, Va.; USS *Fitzgerald* (DDG 62), homeport: San Diego, Calif.; USS *Stethem* (DDG 63), homeport: San Diego, Calif.; USS *Carney* (DDG 64), homeport: Mayport, Fla.; USS *Benfold* (DDG 65), homeport: San Diego, Calif.; USS *Gonzalez* (DDG 66), homeport: Norfolk, Va.; USS *Cole* (DDG 67), homeport: Norfolk, Va.; USS *The Sullivans* (DDG 68), homeport: Mayport, Fla.; USS *Milius* (DDG 69), homeport: San Diego, Calif.; USS *Hopper* (DDG 70), homeport: Pearl Harbor, Hawaii.; USS *Ross* (DDG 71), homeport: Norfolk, Va.; USS *Mahan* (DDG 72), homeport: Norfolk, Va.; USS *Decatur* (DDG 73), homeport: San Diego, Calif.; USS *McFaul* (DDG 74), homeport: Norfolk, Va.; USS *Donald Cook* (DDG 75), homeport: Norfolk, Va.; USS *Higgins* (DDG 76), homeport: San Diego, Calif.; USS *O'Kane* (DDG 77), homeport: Pearl Harbor, Hawaii; USS *Porter* (DDG 78), homeport: Norfolk, Va.; USS *Oscar Austin* (DDG 79), homeport: Norfolk, Va.; USS *Roosevelt* (DDG 80), homeport: Mayport, Fla.; USS *Winston S. Churchill* (DDG 81), homeport: Norfolk, Va.; USS *Lassen* (DDG 82), homeport: San Diego, Calif.; USS *Howard* (DDG 83), homeport: San Diego, Calif.; USS *Bulkeley* (DDG 84), homeport: Norfolk, Va.; USS *McCampbell* (DDG 85), homeport: San Diego, Calif.; USS *Shoup* (DDG 86), homeport: Everett, Wash.; USS *Mason* (DDG 87), under construction; USS *Preble* (DDG 88), homeport: San Diego, Calif.; USS *Mustin* (DDG 89), under construction; USS *Chafee* (DDG 90), under construction; USS *Pinckney* (DDG 91), under construction; USS *Momsen* (DDG 92), under construction; USS *Chung-Hoon* (DDG 93), under construction; USS *Nitze* (DDG 94), under construction; USS *James E. Williams* (DDG 95), under construction; USS *Bainbridge* (DDG 96), under construction; USS *Halsey* (DDG 97), under construction; USS *Forrest Sherman* (DDG 98), under construction; and USS *Farragut* (DDG 99), under construction.

Spruance Class (DD)

Thirty-one *Spruance*-class destroyers were commissioned between 1975 and 1983 with the primary mission of antisubmarine warfare, including operations as part of attack AIRCRAFT CARRIER forces. The destroyers of the *Spruance* class are a far cry from the destroyers of WORLD WAR II. More than twice the size of the earlier vessels, they are as large as a World War II CRUISER. Indeed, the Spruance hull was adapted for use in the *Ticonderoga* class cruisers. Not only are the *Spruance*-class destroyers much larger than the World War II ships, they have evolved into platforms for the most advanced antisubmarine weapons used by any navy. Their electronics suite and advanced weapons systems are also effective against surface ships and aircraft, as well as shore targets. This class of destroyers can support USMC amphibious operations by providing fire against shore-based enemies.

The *Spruance* ships were designed on a modular model, to facilitate future upgrades of entire subsystems within the ship. The ships were designed in anticipation of a continuous development of sensor, electronics, and weapons systems, and space as well as power reservations were provided for these. For example, 24 *Spruance*-class ships were expanded from their original antisubmarine (ASW) role by the addition of a 61-cell Vertical Launch System (VLS) capable of launching Tomahawk and Harpoon missiles. The *Spruance*-class destroyer is also a superb platform for surveillance operations. Endurance and response from the ship's four gas turbine engines make it possible to conduct such operations with minimal notice and with fewer fuel logistics concerns. Excellent command and control capabilities assure a thorough, carefully controlled effort.

The antisubmarine warfare capabilities of the *Spruance* class include an advanced sonar suite and a state-of-the-art fire control system. ASW weapons on board include two triple-barrel Mk-32 torpedo tubes and the Vertical Launch ASROC missile. The ships can also embark two SH-60B LAMPS Mk-III helicopters to extend the range of the ship's weapons and sensors in the ASW role.

As for antisurface warfare capability, the *Spruance* class was the first destroyer class to be retrofitted with the Mk-41 Vertical Launching System (VLS), capable of firing the Tomahawk cruise missile. This enables these vessel to engage shore-based as well as seagoing surface targets at long range. *Spruance*-class destroyers fired 112 Tomahawks into Iraq during the PERSIAN GULF WAR.

Finally, air defense capabilities of these ships include the NATO Sea Sparrow surface-to-air missile system, two 20-mm Close-in-Weapon Systems, and the SLQ-32 Electronic Counter Measures System.

General specifications of the *Spruance* class include:

Power plant: four LM 2500 General Electric gas turbines, two shafts, 80,000 shaft horsepower
Length: 563 ft
Beam: 55 ft
Displacement: 9,100 tons full load
Speed: 33 knots
Range: 6,000 nautical miles at 20 knots
Aircraft: two SH-60 Seahawk LAMPS III helicopters
Crew: 382 (30 officers, 352 enlisted)
Armament: two Mk-143 Armored Box Launchers for Tomahawk SLCM or one Mk-41 Vertical Launch System for Tomahawk SLCM; two Mk-141 quad launchers with eight Harpoon missiles; Mk-29 launchers for NATO Sea Sparrow Missile System; two Mk-15 20-mm Phalanx CIWS Close-In Weapon Systems; two 5-inch/.54-caliber Mk-45 light-weight guns; two Mk-32 triple tube mounts with six Mk-46 torpedoes; Mk-112 launcher for ASROC
Combat systems: SPS-40E air search radar; SPS-55 surface search radar; SPG-60 gun fire control radar; SPQ-9A gun fire control radar; SQS-53B sonar; SQR-19 tactical towed array sonar; SLQ-32 (V)3 OUTBOARD II

Ships of the class include: *Spruance* (DD 963), *Paul F. Foster* (DD 964), *Kinkaid* (DD 965), *Hewitt* (DD 966), *Elliot* (DD 967), *Arthur W. Radford* (DD 968), *Peterson* (DD 969), *Caron* (DD 970), *David R. Ray* (DD 971), *Oldendorf* (DD 972), *John Young* (DD 973), *Comte de Grasse* (DD 974), *O'Brien* (DD 975), *Merrill* (DD 976), *Briscoe* (DD 977), *Stump* (DD 978), *Connolly* (DD 979), *Moosbrugger* (DD 980), *John Hancock* (DD 981), *Nicholson* (DD 982), *John Rodgers* (DD 983), *Leftwich* (DD 984), *Cushing* (DD 985), *Harry W. Hill* (DD 986), *O'Bannon* (DD 987), *Thorn* (DD 988), *Deyo* (DD 989), *Ingersoll* (DD 990), *Fife* (DD 991), *Fletcher* (DD 992), and *Hayler* (DD 997). *Comte de Grasse, Merrill, Connolly, John Rodgers, Leftwich, Harry W. Hill,* and *Ingersoll* were decommissioned in 1998 and scrapped.

Charles F. Adams Class (DDG)

Built during the late 1950s, the guided missile destroyers of the *Charles F. Adams* class were important fixtures of the cold war–era fleet. In the late 1980s, they were judged to be obsolescent and did not undergo modernization with the navy's New Threat Upgrade (NTU) package. Instead, all were retired and decommissioned between 1989 and 1993. The multimission, Aegis-missile equipped *Arleigh Burke* class replaced these ships.

General specifications of the *Charles F. Adams* class included:

Builders: DDG 2-3, 10–11, Bath Iron Works; DDG 4–6, 15–17, New York Shipbuilding; DDG 7–8, 12–13, Defoe Shipbuilding; DDG 9, 14, 23–24, Todd Shipyards; DDG 18–19, Avondale Shipyards; DDG 20–22, Puget Sound Bridge and Drydock

Displacement: 4,500 tons full load
Length: 437 ft
Beam: 47 ft
Speed: 30 knots
Power plant: four 1,200 psi boilers; two geared turbines, two shafts, 70,000 shaft horsepower
Armament: Standard missiles (MR); Harpoon missiles (from Standard launcher); ASROC (from Mk-16 launcher); two Mk-32 triple tube mounts with six Mk-46 torpedoes; two 5-inch/.54-caliber Mk-42 guns
Crew: 383 (20 officers, 363 enlisted)

Ships of the class included: *Charles F. Adams* (DDG 2), *John King* (DDG 3), *Lawrence* (DDG 4), *Claude V. Ricketts* (Ex-Biddle) (DDG 5), *Barney* (DDG 6), *Henry B. Wilson* (DDG 7), *Lynde McCormick* (DDG 8), *Towers* (DDG 9), *Sampson* (DDG 10), *Sellers* (DDG 11), *Robison* (DDG 12), *Hoel* (DDG 13), *Buchanan* (DDG 14), *Berkeley* (DDG 15), *Joseph Strauss* (DDG 16), *Conyngham* (DDG 17), *Semmes* (DDG 18), *Tattnall* (DDG 19), *Goldsborough* (DDG 20), *Cochrane* (DDG 21), *Benjamin Stoddert* (DDG 22), *Richard E. Byrd* (DDG 23), and *Waddell* (DDG 24).

Farragut (DDG) *Coontz* (DDG) Class

The *Farragut*-class guided missile destroyers were built and commissioned during the late 1950s and early 1960s. These ships were also known as the *Coontz* class, since *Coontz* (DDG 40) was the first of the class actually designed and built as a guided missile destroyer. The three earlier ships of the class were designed as all-gun hunter-killer destroyers—designated DK rather than DDG. Only later were they converted to carry the Terrier surface-to-air missile.

The ships of the class were larger than previous destroyers, so the designation FRIGATE was reactivated to describe them. For a time, the class was called Destroyer Leader (DL), then reclassified as Guided Missile Frigate (DLG) in 1956. In 1975, the ships were reclassified yet again as Guided Missile Destroyers (DDG) and assigned new DDG hull numbers. The ships were periodically modernized, but were all finally retired and decommissioned

between 1989 and 1993, when they were replaced by the multimission, Aegis-equipped *Arleigh Burke* class.

General specifications of the *Farragut* (DDG 37) or *Coontz* (DDG 40) class included:

Displacement: 5,800 tons full load
Length: 512 ft
Beam: 52 ft
Speed: 33 knots
Power plant: four 1,200 psi boilers, two geared turbines, two shafts, 85,000 shaft horsepower
Armament: 40 Standard missiles (MR) from Mk-10 twin-arm launcher; eight Harpoon missiles (from two quad launchers); eight ASROCs (from Mk-16 launcher); two Mk-32 triple tube mounts with six Mk-46 torpedoes; two 5-inch/.54-caliber Mk-42 guns
Crew: 400 (25 officers, 375 enlisted)

Ships of the class included *Farragut* (DDG 37), *Luce* (DDG 38), *MacDonough* (DDG 39), *Coontz* (DDG 40), *King* (DDG 41), *Mahan* (DDG 42), *Dahlgren* (DDG 43), *William V. Pratt* (DDG 44), *Dewey* (DDG 45), and *Preble* (DDG 46).

Kidd Class (DDG)

Commissioned during 1981–82, the four ships of the *Kidd* class were the most powerful multipurpose destroyers in the fleet until they were decommissioned during 1998–99. All four ships were originally ordered and designed for sale to the navy of Iran, at the time a U.S. ally. After the Islamic revolution in Iran and the hostile actions of the regime, including the hostage crisis of 1979–80, the ships were accepted by the navy and were informally referred to as the "Ayatollah class," a reference to Iran's revolutionary leader, Ayatollah Khomeini. They combined the combat systems of *Virginia*-class CRUISERS with the antisubmarine warfare technologies and weaponry of *Spruance*-class destroyers. The result were ships that resembled the *Spruance* class, but had greater displacement (though they share the *Spruance* hull) and superior combat systems.

Designed expressly for action in the Persian Gulf, the *Kidd*-class ships were tailored less for antisubmarine warfare (the strong suit of the *Spruance* class) than for general purpose operations. The ship design incorporated advanced air-intake and filtration systems to cope with the prevalent dust and sand of the Persian Gulf, and they all featured augmented air conditioning capacity. The *Kidd*-class destroyers could fire surface-to-air missiles in support of Aegis guided missile cruisers. These larger ships could also, if necessary, assume direct control of the destroyer's missiles.

Kidd-class armaments included an advanced antiair warfare (AAW) system and two Mk-26 launchers for Standard surface-to-air missiles. The ships were outfitted with SQS-58 hull-mounted active sonar, ASROC, eight Harpoon surface-to-surface missiles, two five-inch guns, and hangar facilities for a single LAPMS Mk-1 helicopter. In sum, the *Kidd* class was the most formidable warship of her size.

General specifications of the *Kidd* class included:

Power plant: four LM 2500 General Electric gas turbines, 80,000 shaft horsepower, two shafts
Length: 563 ft
Beam: 55 ft
Displacement: 9,783 tons full load
Dead weight: 2,494 tons
Speed: 33 knots
Aircraft: one SH-3 helicopter or two SH-2 Seasprite LAMPS helicopters
Armament: two Mk-26 launchers for Standard missile; two Mk-141 quad launchers with eight Harpoon missiles; two Mk-15 20-mm Phalanx CIWS Close-In Weapon Systems; two 5-inch/.54-caliber Mk-45 lightweight guns; two Mk-32 triple tube mounts with six Mk-46 torpedoes; Mk-112 launcher for ASROC
Combat systems: SPS-48E air search radar; SPG-60 gun fire control radar; SPS-55 surface search radar; SPQ-9A gun fire control radar; SQS-53 sonar; SLQ-32 (V)3 OUTBOARD II

Ships of the class included *Kidd* (DDG 993), *Callaghan* (DDG 994), *Scott* (DDG 995), and *Chandler* (DDG 996).

Zumwalt Class (DD)

The *Zumwalt*-class Land Attack destroyer is scheduled to replace *Spruance*-class destroyers and *Oliver Hazard Perry*–class frigates in the navy fleet. The lead ship of the class, *Zumwalt* (DD 21), is scheduled for commission in 2008, and, as of 2004, a total of 33 ships of the class are planned, with commissioning out to the year 2020.

It is planned that the *Zumwalt* ships will provide an advanced level of land attack capability to support ground campaigns and contribute to naval, joint, and combined battlespace dominance in littoral (near-shore) operations. Although the primary mission of the *Zumwalt* class will be land attack, the ships of the class are intended to be true fleet destroyers, capable of taking on any mission, including antiaircraft warfare and antisubmarine warfare, as well as presence missions ("showing the flag"), noncombatant evacuations, escort, and diplomatic missions—the roles that have long been associated with navy destroyers.

The emerging class of ships will be armed with 5-inch/.62-caliber extended-range guided munitions and 155-mm howitzers. These will allow the ship to provide naval gunfire support up to 100 miles inland. Added to this, a land-attack missile system will extend support out to 200 miles. Tactical Tomahawk missiles can reach targets from a distance of 200 to 1,600 nautical miles.

In addition to the greatly enhanced land attack capability, the *Zumwalt* class will incorporate the most advanced undersea warfare combat systems ever installed on surface combatants. A hangar will be provided for attack helicopters as well as unmanned aerial vehicles (UAV). These will be used not only for antisubmarine warfare but also for surveillance and to assist in establishing and maintaining local air superiority.

In addition to providing greatly improved offensive and defensive capabilities, the advanced design of the *Zumwalt* ships will emphasize reduced maintenance requirements and significantly reduced manpower requirements. Other design characteristics will include submarine-like survivability and a drastically reduced radar signature, achieved through the incorporation of stealth-like design features, including a fully integrated topside design. The ship design will also include radical composite construction materials, radar absorbing materials, and optimized hull shaping both above and below the waterline. While such elements will reduce the radar signal, attention will also be given to acoustic quieting and degaussing. The integrated power system is expected to provide substantial quieting capability.

Not only will all these design features improve self-defense, they will also make the *Zumwalt* class far more effective as an offensive weapon by allowing the ship to operate closer to shore, regardless of threat conditions.

Additional innovations to be incorporated into the new ships will include a shock-resistant hull, an especially robust electrical power distribution system, and an integrated magazine protection system. To promote survivability in a reduced-manning environment, the ships will incorporate advanced automation, sensors and control, and systems such as robotic fire-fighting. Automated systems will be used to preconfigure and reconfigure systems for combat, to monitor equipment status, and to detect and counter smoke, fire, and flooding.

destroyer tenders (AD)

So-called destroyer tenders were ships that serviced not only DESTROYERS but also other surface ships, providing battle damage repair, maintenance, and logistics support to ships at anchor or moored to a pier while operating in a wartime environment. The ships were crewed primarily by technicians and repair personnel and consisted of two classes, *Samuel Gompers* and *Yellowstone*.

Samuel Gompers Class

The two ships of the *Samuel Gompers* class were commissioned in 1967 and 1968 and were decommissioned in 1995 and 1996. They were fitted with a helicopter platform and hangar, as well as two 30-ton and two 6-ton cranes. One ship of the class could provide simultaneous services to as many as five ships moored alongside.

General specifications of the class included:

Power plant: steam turbines
Overall length: 645 ft
Waterline length: 620 ft
Extreme beam: 85 ft
Waterline beam: 85 ft
Maximum navigational draft: 28 ft
Draft limit: 30 ft
Displacement: 20,132 tons full load
Dead weight: 6,674 tons
Crew: 136 officers, 1,671 enlisted personnel

Ships of the class included *Samuel Gompers* (AD 37) and *Puget Sound* (AD 38).

Yellowstone Class

The four ships of the *Yellowstone* class were commissioned during 1975–79 and decommissioned between 1994 and 1996. Like the vessels of the *Samuel Gompers* class, they serviced a wide variety of surface ships, including destroyers, and they offered approximately the same resources.

General specifications of the class included:

Builder: National Steel and Shipbuilding
Power plant: two boilers, steam turbines, one shaft, 20,000 shaft horsepower
Overall length: 642 ft
Waterline length: 620 ft
Extreme beam: 85 ft
Waterline beam: 67 ft
Maximum navigational draft: 27 ft
Draft limit: 25 ft
Displacement: 20,263 tons full load
Dead weight: 6,948 tons
Speed: 20 knots
Crew: 1,400

Ships of the class included *Yellowstone* (AD 41), *Acadia* (AD 42), *Cape Cod* (AD 43), and *Shenandoah* (AD 44).

Dewey, George (1837–1917) *Navy admiral*

Dewey is best remembered as the officer who led the U.S. fleet to total victory against the Spanish fleet at Manila Bay, the Philippines, during the

Admiral George Dewey at Manila Bay, Philippines, during the Spanish-American War   *(National Archives)*

SPANISH-AMERICAN WAR. He was born in Montpelier, Vermont, and attended Norwich University before enrolling in the UNITED STATES NAVAL ACADEMY, from which he graduated in 1858. After seeing service during the CIVIL WAR under DAVID FARRAGUT at the Battle of New Orleans (April 24–25, 1862) and at Port Hudson (March 14, 1863), he served with the North Atlantic Blockading Squadron and participated in the bombardment of Fort Fisher (December 23–27, 1864, and January 13–15, 1865).

During the postwar years, Dewey rose steadily, becoming captain in September 1884 and gaining appointment as chief of the Bureau of Equipment in 1889 and president of the Board of Inspection and Survey in 1895. From these posts, Dewey became a powerful advocate of modern battleship technology and was a prime mover behind the modernization of the USN.

Promoted to commodore in 1896, he was named commander of the Asiatic Squadron (November 1897) and was in Hong Kong when the Spanish-American War broke out on April 25, 1898. He took his squadron to the Spanish-held Philippines, where, on May 1, he destroyed the Spanish fleet there. Promoted to rear admiral on May 10, Dewey provided naval support to army troops, which took Manila on August 13.

In recognition of his achievements, Dewey was promoted to admiral of the navy on March 3, 1899, a unique rank (equivalent to the more modern fleet admiral) created especially for him. He served as president of the Navy General Board until his death.

dock landing ships (LSD)

LSDs support amphibious operations, including landings using LANDING CRAFT, AIR-CUSHIONED (LCAC), conventional landing craft, and helicopters. Currently, the USN operates three classes of LSD, the *Anchorage* class, *Harpers Ferry* class, and the *Whidbey Island* class.

Anchorage Class

The *Anchorage* class currently consists of four dock landing ships (LSD); the *Fort Fisher* (LSD-40), a fifth ship of the class, was decommissioned in 1998. These vessels support amphibious operations, including landings via landing craft, air-cushioned (LCAC), conventional landing craft, and helicopters. Ships of this class include both a well deck for the deployment of landing craft and a flight deck, for helicopter operations. The two modes, sea and air landing, can be operated simultaneously; however, these ships are designed primarily to transport preloaded heavy landing craft and discharge them rapidly. The *Anchorage* class ships are also furnished with machine shops and other facilities to provide dry docking and repairs to the landing craft as necessary.

The well deck of the *Anchorage*-class ships works by means of a ballasting system that fills the deck with sea water to a depth necessary for loading landing craft such as the LCU and LCAC. The ships have also been modified to handle landing craft, air cushioned (LCAC).

The *Anchorage* class features facilities for the berthing, messing, and cargo transportation of approximately 300 fully equipped combat troops in addition to the 360 members of the ship's company. A sophisticated suite of electronic equipment is on board, including air, navigation, and surface search radars, a complete communications suite, and an Electronic Emitter Detection System to support the ship's amphibious mission.

General specifications of the *Anchorage* class include:

Power plant: two 600 psi boilers, two geared steam turbines, two shafts, 24,000 total shaft horsepower
Length: 553 ft
Beam: 85 ft
Displacement: 14,000 tons full load
Speed: 22 knots
Landing craft: three LCAC
Crew: ship's company, 18 officers, 340 enlisted; Marine detachment: 330
Departments: Deck; Engineering; Navigation; Operations; Supply
Armament: four 3-inch/.50-caliber twin-barrel guns; two 25-mm Mk-38 machine guns; two 20-mm Phalanx CIWS

Ships of the class include: *Anchorage* (LSD-36), *Portland* (LSD 37), *Pensacola* (LSD 38), *Mount Vernon* (LSD 39), *Fort Fisher* (LSD 40, decommissioned in 1998).

Harpers Ferry Class

The ships of the *Harpers Ferry* class are modifications of the *Whidbey Island* class of dock landing ship (LSD) vessels. They dock, transport, and launch LANDING CRAFT, AIR-CUSHIONED (LCAC), and other amphibious craft and vehicles, loaded with crews and marines. The ships of the *Harpers Ferry* class can also operate as primary control ships during an amphibious assault. The only significant difference between the *Harpers Ferry* and *Whidbey*

Island classes is that the well decks of the *Harpers Ferry* ships are shortened to accommodate added vehicle stowage and cargo storage areas. This reduces the number of LCACs carried in the well deck from four to two.

Wheeled vehicles can be embarked and debarked from the *Harpers Ferry* ships by three methods: pier crane, ship's crane, or the well deck. Vehicles may be onloaded and offloaded by way of the well deck, either by using landing craft while the ship is ballasted down and the well deck flooded or by dropping the stern gate and backing up to a quay wall. The stern gate can support the weight of two AAVP-7A1 amphibian vehicles, an M-60A1 or M-1A1 main battle tank, or two M-923 5-ton trucks simultaneously.

Loaded LCACs can be launched while the LSD is under way when the ship is ballasted at 0 to 6 inches at the well-deck sill. Lighting, visual landing aids, and flight deck facilities are provided to allow launching and landing of helicopters as large as the CH-53E.

General specifications of the *Harpers Ferry* class include:

Overall length: 610 ft
Waterline length: 580 ft
Extreme beam: 84 ft
Waterline beam: 84 ft
Height: 177 ft, 2 in
Maximum navigational draft: 20 ft
Draft limit: 21 ft
Draft limit, ballasted (without cargo): 21.48 ft forward, 34 ft aft
Draft limit, ballasted (with cargo): 22.76 ft forward, 36.11 ft aft
Displacement: 16,400 tons full load
Dead weight: 4,853 tons
Compartments/Spaces: 733
Propulsion: four 16-cylinder Colt-Pielstick diesel engines, 33,000 combined shaft horsepower at 520 rpm; two propellers, 13.5-foot controllable-pitch blades
Speed: 20+ knots
Well deck capacity: two landing craft, air-cushioned (LCAC), or one landing craft, utility

(LCU), or four LCM-8 landing craft, mechanized (LCM), or nine LCM-6 landing craft, mechanized (LCM), or 15 AAV amphibious assault vehicles

Weapons: six Mk-36 Super Rapid Blooming Outboard Chaff (SRBOC); six .50-caliber machine guns; two Mk-38 25-mm machine guns; two Mk-15 MOD 12 BK 1 Close-In Weapon Systems Mounts

Crew: ship's company, 24 officers, 328 enlisted; landing force, 504 marines, including 102 surge troops

Ships of the class include *Harpers Ferry* (LSD 49), *Carter Hall* (LSD 50), *Oak Hill* (LSD 51), and *Pearl Harbor* (LSD 52).

Whidbey Island Class

The *Whidbey Island* class is the USN's newest class of dock landing ships (LSD). As of 2004, the class consists of eight ships, commissioned between 1985 and 1992 and scheduled to remain in service well into the 21st century. The *Whidbey Island*–class ships support amphibious operations, which include landings using LANDING CRAFT, AIR-CUSHIONED (LCAC), as well as conventional landing craft and helicopters. The *Whidbey* class is an advanced modification of the earlier *Anchorage* class and incorporates facilities to transport and launch loaded amphibious craft and vehicles with their crews and embarked personnel in amphibious assault operations. Each of the new ships has a 440-foot well deck, with a capacity of four LCACs, and a flight deck capable of landing and launching up to two Marine Corps CH-53E helicopters. The ships also incorporate the navy's most advanced diesel propulsion and engineering technology, and they include extensive repair facilities for landing craft. In addition, there are complete medical and dental facilities, as well as troop berthing accommodations for up to 627 embarked marines.

The *Whidbey Island*–class ships are all fitted with highly advanced electronics, with systems linked via a fiber-optic local area network (LAN). A wireless internal communications system (WICS) provides communications for command and control of combat systems, damage control, security, beach guard, sea and anchor detail, administration, and integrated team training.

General specifications of the *Whidbey Island* class include:

Propulsion: four Colt Industries 16-cylinder diesels, two shafts, 33,000 shaft horsepower; two five-blade controllable pitch propellers

Overall length: 610 ft

Waterline length: 580 ft

Extreme beam: 84 ft

Waterline beam: 84 ft

Maximum navigational draft: 21 ft

Draft limit: 21 ft

Displacement: 16,360 tons full load

Dead weight: 4,889 tons

Well deck: 440 ft long, 50 ft wide; floodable to 10 ft aft, 6 ft forward

Water barrier: 12 ft 3 in high, 50 ft long; divides well deck into forward (dry) and aft (wet) compartments

Helicopter deck: two spots, 212 ft long, 83 ft wide

Speed: 20+ knots

Landing craft: four LCACs

Combat systems: AN/SPS-49 Air Search Radar; AN/SPS-67 Surface Search Radar; AN/SPS-64 Navigation Radar; AN/SLQ-32 Electronic Counter Measures set; Mk-36, MOD-6 SRBOC; AN/SLQ-25 (NIXIE); Torpedo Counter Measures system

Armament: two 25-mm Mk-38 machine guns; two 20-mm Mk-15 Phalanx CIWS mounts; two .50-caliber machine guns

Generators: four Fairbanks-Morse 12-cylinder ship service diesel generators, each capable of producing 1,300 kw

Ship's boats: one Mk-6 50-foot utility boat; two Mk-12 36-foot LCP (L)s; one 14-foot punt

Cranes: one 15-ton gantry crane; one 20-ton fixed kingpost crane; one 60-ton fixed kingpost crane

dolphins (USN Marine Mammal Program)

The USN initiated the Marine Mammal Program in 1959 at Marineland of the Pacific. Navy scientists were interested in studying the hydrodynamics of the dolphin with the object of improving torpedo, ship, and submarine designs. It soon became apparent that dolphins offered more than a model of locomotion through water. The animals use sonar and are capable of making repeated deep dives without experiencing the bends (decompression sickness). These two characteristics, together with their intelligence and apparent affection for human beings, suggested that dolphins could be trained as assistants to USN divers. Accordingly, in 1962, a marine mammal facility was established at Point Mugu near Los Angeles, and, in 1965, as part of the SeaLab II program, a dolphin was successfully trained to work in the open ocean, bringing tools and equipment from the sea surface to divers working 200 feet below. Other studies were conducted on acoustics, diving physiology, anatomy, and medicine. Most recently, in 2003, during operations against the regime of Saddam Hussein in Iraq ("Operation Iraqi Freedom"), dolphins have been used to help detect mines in Iraqi harbors and waterways.

E

E-2C Hawkeye Early Warning and Control Aircraft   See AIRCRAFT: VIETNAM WAR AND AFTER.

EA-6B Prowler Electronic Warfare Aircraft   See AIRCRAFT: VIETNAM WAR AND AFTER.

Eberle, Edward W. (1864–1929) *chief of naval operations*
After graduating from the UNITED STATES NAVAL ACADEMY in 1885, Eberle served on the USS *Oregon*, saw action in the SPANISH-AMERICAN WAR and, in 1899, in the Philippine Insurrection as well. Eberle wrote the first modern ordnance manual for the USN and, in 1915, was appointed commandant of the Naval Academy. He returned to sea duty in 1919 and was named the third CHIEF OF NAVAL OPERATIONS in 1923. He stepped down in 1927 to serve on the Navy General Board, retiring in 1928.

ensign   See RANKS AND GRADES.

EP-3E ARIES II Signals Intelligence Reconnaissance Aircraft   See AIRCRAFT: VIETNAM WAR AND AFTER.

Ericsson, John (1803–1889) *navy engineer*
During the CIVIL WAR, Ericsson designed and built the USS *Monitor*, first of a new generation of steam-driven iron warships, which presaged the end of the era of wood and sail. Equally important, Ericsson installed on *Monitor* an armored, rotating

John Ericsson in 1862   *(Naval Historical Foundation)*

gun turret of his own design, the first truly modern naval gun. In addition, Ericsson was a pioneer in screw ship propulsion, a technology that quickly replaced the side or aft paddlewheel in steam craft.

Ericsson was a native of Sweden and saw service in the Swedish army before moving to London in 1826. There he designed and built the world's first screw-driven commercial vessel. He traveled to New York in 1839 on commission to build the screw steamer USS *Princeton* for the USN. Additionally, he designed a new 12-inch wrought-iron gun for the ship. The virtues of Ericsson's artillery design were proved dramatically when a conventional 12-incher exploded during a demonstration. Secretary of the Navy Thomas W. Gilmer and Secretary of State (and former secretary of the navy) ABEL P. UPSHUR were killed in the mishap.

During the Civil War, the USN commissioned Ericsson to build the *Monitor,* which he did, including all design work, in a mere 100 days. The vessel was the first of the *Monitor* class, popularly called "ironclads," although, in contrast to the Confederate CSS *Alabama,* which was a wooden ship (the former USS *Merrimack*) overlaid with iron plates, the *Monitor* and *Monitor*-class ships were not clad in iron, but built of it. During and after the war, Ericsson continued to design and build warships. He also engaged in other scientific work and, for the USN, continued to work in naval technology.

Essex Class (CV-9)   See AIRCRAFT CARRIERS.

Ethan Allen Class (SSBN-608)   See SUBMARINES.

Explosive Ordnance Disposal

The USN established the U.S. Naval Mine Disposal School at the Naval Gun Factory, Washington, D.C., in May 1941. In January 1942, the Bomb Disposal School was established on the campus of American University, also in Washington. During WORLD WAR II, graduates of these schools formed into Mine and Bomb Disposal teams, which were deployed to England, Normandy, North Africa, Panama, Alaska, Hawaii, Australia, Guadalcanal, and New Guinea. To ships' crews, team members furnished detailed information on Japanese torpedoes, data gleaned from unexploded torpedoes recovered at Pearl Harbor and elsewhere. The teams either recovered or countermined depth charges and mines. USN Mine and Bomb Disposal teams were always among the first military personnel to land on European and Pacific beaches, charged with clearing channels, harbors, and fields of mines, booby traps, and unexploded ordnance.

After World War II, the USN consolidated mine disposal units into a single Explosive Ordnance Disposal (EOD) Program, and, in 1953, two operational EOD units were formed to provide EOD services to the fleet. The development of nuclear weapons and increasingly sophisticated conventional ordnance prompted expansion of the EOD community, which is now extensive and can be quickly deployed anywhere in the world as needed. Today, EOD Group One is assigned to the Pacific area of responsibility, and EOD Group Two is assigned to the Atlantic.

F

F-14 Tomcat Fighter   See AIRCRAFT: VIETNAM WAR AND AFTER.

F/A-18 Hornet Strike Fighter   See AIRCRAFT: VIETNAM WAR AND AFTER.

F/A-18 Super Hornet   See AIRCRAFT: VIETNAM WAR AND AFTER.

Farragut, David Glasgow (1801–1870) *navy admiral*

One of the heroes of the U.S. Navy, Farragut was the most important Union naval commander during the CIVIL WAR. He was born near Knoxville, Tennessee, as James G. Farragut, the son of a naval officer. In 1810, three years after his father moved the family to New Orleans, Farragut's mother died and the boy was adopted by U.S. naval officer DAVID DIXON PORTER. Farragut joined the USN as a midshipman in December 1810 and served under his foster father aboard USS *Essex*. During the WAR OF 1812, he distinguished himself while serving on this vessel, and, after the war ended, he changed his first name from James to David to honor his foster father and commander.

After his War of 1812 service, Farragut obtained further education and also served aboard a number of USN ships during 1814–22. He became master

of the Arabic, French, and Italian languages, and in 1823, promoted to lieutenant, served in a campaign against Caribbean pirates, again under Porter (February 1823–December 1824). Farragut was promoted to commander in 1841 and, the following year, was assigned command of the sloop *Decatur* and was also stationed in Brazil. From 1854 to

David Glasgow Farragut   *(Arttoday)*

1858, he served in California, where he established the Mare Island Navy Yard, the USN's first permanent Pacific facility.

At the start of the Civil War, Farragut commanded the West Gulf Blockade Squadron. Using assets of the squadron, he assaulted rebel-held New Orleans in a brilliant campaign that captured the city on April 25, 1862, and forced the surrender of Mississippi River forts St. Philip and Jackson three days later. After this triumph, Farragut conducted operations upriver, successfully running past the formidable Vicksburg (Mississippi) batteries on June 28. On July 16, he was promoted to rear admiral, becoming the first USN officer to hold an admiral's rank.

Returning to New Orleans after Porter's arrival there on May 4, Farragut supported General Nathaniel Banks at the successful siege of Port Hudson during May 27–July 8, 1863. Next ordered to capture the defenses of Mobile, Alabama, he commanded a squadron of four *Monitor*-class vessels and 14 conventional wooden ships. After the monitor *Tecumseh* struck a torpedo mine and sank, Farragut, who had lashed himself to his flagship's rigging, shouted to his flag captain one of the most famous orders in USN history: "Damn the torpedoes! Full speed ahead, Drayton!" Farragut defeated the Confederate ironclad *Tennessee,* bringing about the surrender of Forts Gaines and Morgan at the mouth of Mobile Bay. This victory earned Farragut promotion to vice admiral on December 23, 1864. However, at this time, ill health forced Farragut's withdrawal from active service. Nevertheless, on July 25, 1866, after the war had ended, he was promoted to admiral.

Farragut (DDG-37) or *Coontz* (DDG-40) Class   See DESTROYERS.

Fast Combat Support Ships (AOE)   See CARGO, FUEL, AND REPLENISHMENT SHIPS.

Fast Sealift Ships (T-AKR)   See CARGO, FUEL, AND REPLENISHMENT SHIPS.

Fifth Fleet
Fifth Fleet supports all USN operations in the U.S. Central Command area of responsibility, which encompasses some 7.5 million square miles and includes the Arabian Gulf, Red Sea, Gulf of Oman, and parts of the Indian Ocean—25 countries, including Bahrain, Saudi Arabia, the United Arab Emirates, Iran, Iraq, Pakistan, and Somalia. The fleet usually operates more than 20 ships, with about 1,000 people stationed ashore and 15,000 afloat. Fleet elements include a carrier battle group, amphibious ready group, combat aircraft, and various support units and ships.

The Fifth Fleet was created during WORLD WAR II, on March 15, 1943, to operate under the PACIFIC FLEET. It was disestablished after the war, in 1947, and was reestablished on July 1, 1995.

fleet admiral   See RANKS AND GRADES.

Fleet Information Warfare Center
Located at Little Creek Amphibious Base, Virginia Beach, Virginia, FIWC provides computer incident response, vulnerability analysis and assistance, and incident measurement services to fleet and shore establishments. The center provides facilities, equipment, and personnel for directing the defensive information warfare program, including detecting and responding to computer attacks. The center became operational on October 1, 1995.

Fleet Marine Force Ribbon   See DECORATIONS AND MEDALS.

Fleet Numerical Meteorology and Oceanography Center
The mission of the center is to "combine innovative technology with the best available science in order to provide the best weather and oceanographic products, data and services to the operating and support forces of the DoD anywhere, anytime." The

center uses numerical meteorology techniques for the analysis and prediction of weather and climate, providing data for every region of the globe and "from the edge of space to the bottom of the sea."

fleet ocean tugs (T-ATF)

The MILITARY SEALIFT COMMAND operates seven oceangoing tugs to provide towing service and to assist in the recovery of downed aircraft and sunken ships. All T-ATFs are of the *Powhatan* class.

Powhatan Class

The seven ships of the *Powhatan* class are the navy's newest tugs. Their primary mission is to provide towing services; secondarily, they can be used as dive support vessels to assist in the recovery of downed aircraft as well as ships that have sunk.

Each *Powhatan*-class vessel is equipped with a 10-ton crane and a bollard pull of at least 54 tons. Fitted aft is a deck grid, which contains 1-inch bolt receptacles spaced 24 inches apart to allow for bolting down a wide variety of portable equipment. On board at all times are two GPH fire pumps supplying three fire monitors with up to 2,200 gallons of foam per minute. For naval diving team support, each ship can be fitted with a deep module. In addition to salvage towing, fleet tugs are used to tow cargo barges and gunnery targets.

General specifications of this class include:

Builder: Marinette Marine Corporation, Marinette, Wisconsin
Power plant: two GM EMD 20-645F7B diesels; 5.73 MW sustained; two shafts; Kort nozzles (except on *Powhatan*); bow thruster, 300 horsepower
Overall length: 226 ft
Waterline length: 204 ft
Extreme beam: 42 ft
Waterline beam: 42 ft
Maximum navigational draft: 15 ft
Draft limit: 15 ft
Displacement: 2,000 tons full load
Dead weight: 613 tons

Speed: 14.5 knots
Crew: 16 civilian mariners and four naval communications technicians

Ships of the class include *Powhatan* (T-ATF 166), *Narragansett* (T-ATF 167), *Catawba* (T-ATF 168), *Navajo* (T-ATF 169), *Mohawk* (T-ATF 170), *Sioux* (T-ATF 171), and *Apache* (T-ATF 172).

Fleet Surveillance Support Command

Fleet Surveillance Support Command provides tactically significant wide-area air surveillance information to military and law enforcement agencies. The command was created in July 1987 to operate the USN's Relocatable Over-the-Horizon Radar (ROTHR), a system originally designed to provide battle group commanders with tactical warning of air and surface threats at an extended range, allowing time for responsive engagement. The prototype system was installed on Amchitka, an island in Alaska's Aleutian chain. The ROTHR surveilled the western coastline of the Pacific Rim from April 1991 to March 1993, when it was dismantled and reinstalled at Chesapeake, Virginia. At present, in addition to the Virginia facility, the command operates ROTHR sites in Texas and Puerto.

Fleet Technical Support Center, Atlantic (FTSCLANT)

FTSCLANT provides direct support to commanders in matters of waterfront technical assistance, maintenance training, and logistics services associated with the installation, operation, maintenance, and readiness of shipboard equipment and systems. FTSCLANT's area of responsibility is the Atlantic; the Pacific area of responsibility is handled by Fleet Technical Support Center, Pacific (FTSCPAC).

Fleet Technical Support Center, Pacific (FTSCPAC)   See FLEET TECHNICAL SUPPORT CENTER, ATLANTIC.

Fleet Training Center Mayport, Florida

See FLEET TRAINING CENTER NORFOLK, VIRGINIA.

Fleet Training Center Norfolk, Virginia

FTC Norfolk provides operational and maintenance training in aspects of ashore and afloat operations and functions that are not normally taught aboard ship. The center provides training in advanced or specialized skills, and also provides reactivation and precommissioning training.

FTC Norfolk was established in 1946 and originally consisted of schools devoted to combat information, antisubmarine warfare, firefighting, and communications. Damage control and atomic, biological, and chemical defense courses were added in 1947. A Storekeeper School was established in 1956. Two years later a Gunnery School was added, and in 1959 the Leadership School was established. Ship Serviceman and Barber Schools opened in 1973, and during the 1990s courses in specialized technical fields were developed.

Similar centers are located at Mayport, Florida, and San Diego, California.

Fleet Training Center San Diego   See FLEET TRAINING CENTER NORFOLK, VIRGINIA.

Float-on/Float-off type cargo ships (T-AKF)

See CARGO, FUEL, AND REPLENISHMENT SHIPS.

Foote, Andrew Hull (1806–1863) *navy admiral*

Foote served with great distinction during the CIVIL WAR and was instrumental in gaining control of the Mississippi River for the Union. He was born in New Haven, Connecticut, and was appointed to West Point, but soon decided instead to accept an appointment as a navy midshipman in December 1822. From that year through 1843, Foote served in the Caribbean, Pacific, and Mediterranean, as well as at the Philadelphia Navy Yard. He was a zealous moral reformer, who organized a temperance society aboard the USS *Cumberland,* which grew into a movement that brought about the end of the grog ration aboard USN ships.

During 1849–51, Foote commanded USS *Perry* off the African coast, where he was active in suppressing the slave trade. This duty confirmed him as an abolitionist, and, in 1854, he published an antislavery tract, *Africa and the American Flag.*

Foote served in various shore posts from 1851 to 1856, when he was promoted to commander and assigned command of the sloop *Portsmouth.* While observing British operations against Canton during the Opium War, he came under attack from Chinese shore batteries, returned fire, and succeeded in destroying four barrier forts during November 20–22, 1856.

Returned to the United States, Foote assumed command of the Brooklyn Navy Yard in 1858. At the start of the Civil War, he commanded naval forces on the upper Mississippi (August 1861) and supervised the crash construction of a fleet of GUNBOATS and mortar craft. With these, he captured Confederate-held Fort Henry. A few days later, on February 14, Foote was wounded when his attack on Fort Donelson was repulsed. He returned to duty next month and supported General John Pope in taking the Confederate-held fortress of Island No. 10 during March 1–April 7. The collapse of this key position brought Memphis and the lower Mississippi into Union hands. However, Foote failed to recover fully from his wounds and was forced to retire from combat command in June. In July, he was promoted to rear admiral and appointed chief of the Bureau of Equipment and Recruiting. Eager to return to sea duty, he accepted a command in the North Atlantic Blockading Squadron, but died before he shipped out.

Forrestal, James V. (1892–1949) *secretary of the navy*

Forrestal was a prominent businessman who served as a naval airman during WORLD WAR I, returned to business, then was appointed undersecretary of the navy by President Franklin D. Roosevelt in 1940. He was elevated to the post of SECRETARY OF THE NAVY during WORLD WAR II in May 1944, after the death of FRANK KNOX. In 1947, Forrestal left the DEPARTMENT OF THE NAVY to become the nation's first secretary of defense. After suffering a mental breakdown, he resigned that office in March 1949 and, in May, died by his own hand.

Forrestal Class (CV-59)   See AIRCRAFT CARRIERS.

frigates (FFG)

Frigates perform protection of shipping (POS) and antisubmarine warfare (ASW) missions, and guided missile frigates (FFG) add antiair warfare (AAW) capability. Essentially, the U.S. Navy frigate was designed as a cost-effective surface combatant. This required a sacrifice of the multimission capability of modern guided missile CRUISERS and DESTROYERS. However, current U.S. Navy doctrine calls for ships with greater mission flexibility, so no additional frigates are planned for the fleet. The currently operational frigates are all of the *Oliver Hazard Perry* class.

Oliver Hazard Perry Class

The *Oliver Hazard Perry* class is primarily dedicated to antisubmarine warfare (ASW). The ships carry a LAMPS-III helicopter onboard for the ASW mission, while a Mk-13 Mod 4 missile launcher furnishes secondary antiaircraft warfare capability. Navy personnel rarely refer to this class by name, but refer to the ships as "FIG-7s," after the lead ship, *Oliver Hazard Perry* (FFG-7).

The *Perry*-class ships include most of the only frigates still active in the navy. Because recent navy doctrine considers the specialized ASW role assigned to the frigate as too narrow, no new frigates are being developed, and the guided missile destroyer is taking over the ASW role. Nevertheless, the ships of the *Perry* class still perform the protection of shipping (POS) mission as antisubmarine

warfare (ASW) combatants for amphibious expeditionary forces, UNDERWAY REPLENISHMENT groups, and merchant convoys.

Ships of the class were produced in two variants, known as short hull and long hull, which is eight feet longer than the short-hull version. The long-hull ships (FFGs 8, 28, 29, 32, 33, and 36–61) carry the SH-60B LAMPS III helicopter, whereas the short-hull units carry the less-capable SH-2G. These short-hull ships were decommissioned in the 1990s. Despite the limitations of the frigates, they are a hardy platform and highly survivable. Most of the "long" *Oliver Hazard Perry*–class ships will remain active well into the 21st century. A total of 55 *Oliver Hazard Perry*–class ships were built, 51 for the U.S. Navy and four for the Royal Australian Navy.

General specifications of the *Oliver Hazard Perry* class include:

Power plant: two General Electric LM 2500 gas turbine engines, one shaft, 41,000 shaft horsepower, total
Length, short: 445 ft
Length, long: 453 ft, with LAMPS III modification
Beam: 45 ft
Displacement: 4,100 tons full load
Speed: 29+ knots (33.4+ mph)
Aircraft, long: two SH-60 (LAMPS III) in FFGs 8, 28, 29, 32, 33, and 36–61
Aircraft, short: one SH-2F (Lamps Mk-I) in FFGs 9–27, 30, 31, 34
Armament: Standard missile (MR); Harpoon missile (from Standard missile launcher); six Mk-46 torpedoes (from two Mk-32 SVTT triple mounts); one 76-mm (3-inch) .62-caliber Mk-75 rapid-fire gun; one Phalanx close-in weapon system
Combat systems: AN/SPS-49 air search radar; AN/SPS-55 surface search sadar; Mk-92 fire control system; AN/SLQ-32 electronics warfare system; AN/SQS-56 sonar; Mk-36 SRBOC decoy system; AN/SQR-19 towed array sonar system; AN/SQQ-89 ASW integration system
Crew: 13 officers, 287 enlisted

Short-hull ships of the class—now decommissioned—included: *Oliver Hazard Perry* (FFG-7), *Wadsworth* (FFG-9), *Duncan* (FFG-10), *Clark* (FFG-11), *George Philip* (FFG-12), *Samuel Eliot Morison* (FFG-13), *Sides* (FFG-14), *Estocin* (FFG-15), *Clifton Sprague* (FFG-16), FFG-17 and FFG-18 to Australia, *John A. Moore* (FFG-19), *Antrim* (FFG-20), *Flatley* (FFG-21), *Fahrion* (FFG-22), *Lewis B. Puller* (FFG-23), *Jack Williams* (FFG-24), *Copeland* (FFG-25), *Gallery* (FFG-26), *Mahlon S. Tisdale* (FFG-27), *Reid* (FFG-30), *Stark* (FFG-31), *Aubrey Fitch* (FFG-34), FFG-35 and FFG-44 to Australia.

Long-hull ships of the class include: *McInerney* (FFG-8), *Boone* (FFG-28), *Stephen W. Groves* (FFG-29), *John L. Hall* (FFG-32), *Jarrett* (FFG-33), *Underwood* (FFG-36), *Crommelin* (FFG-37), *Curts* (FFG-38), *Doyle* (FFG-39), *Halyburton* (FFG-40), *McClusky* (FFG-41), *Klakring* (FFG-42), *Thach* (FFG-43), *Dewert* (FFG-45), *Rentz* (FFG-46), *Nicholas* (FFG-47), *Vandegrift* (FFG-48), *Robert G. Bradley* (FFG-49), *Taylor* (FFG-50), *Gary* (FFG-51), *Carr* (FFG-52), *Hawes* (FFG-53), *Ford* (FFG-54), *Elrod* (FFG-55), *Simpson* (FFG-56), *Reuben James* (FFG-57), *Samuel B. Roberts* (FFG-58), *Kauffman* (FFG-59), *Rodney M. Davis* (FFG-60), and *Ingraham* (FFG-61).

Oliver Hazard Perry, lead ship of the class (now decommissioned) was deployed on December 17, 1977.

Bronstein Class (FF)

The two ships of the *Bronstein* class were frigates, tasked with carrying out the Protection of Shipping (POS) mission, primarily as antisubmarine warfare (ASW) combatants for amphibious expeditionary forces, underway replenishment groups, and merchant convoys. Both ships were commissioned in 1963 and decommissioned in 1990. Generally, the USN has come to regard the ASW role of frigates as too narrow and has phased these ships out in favor of guided missile destroyers.

General specifications of the *Bronstein* class included:

Displacement: 2,650 tons full load
Length: 371 ft

Beam: 40 ft
Speed: 26 knots
Power plant: two 600 psi boilers, one geared turbine, one shaft, 20,000 shaft horsepower
Armament: eight ASROC (from Mk-16 launcher); two Mk-32 triple tube mounts with six Mk-46 torpedoes; two 3-inch/.50-caliber Mk-33 guns (one enclosed twin-gun mount)
Crew: 217 (16 officers, 201 enlisted)

Ships of the class included the *Bronstein* (FF-1037) and the *McCloy* (FF-1038).

Knox Class (FF)

All 45 ships of the *Knox* class, commissioned between 1969 and 1974, were decommissioned during 1991–94. These fast frigates carried out the protection of shipping (POS) mission as antisubmarine warfare (ASW) combatants for amphibious expeditionary forces, underway replenishment groups, and merchant convoys.

General specifications of the *Knox* class included:

Builders: FFs 1052–1054, 1062, 1066, 1070–1071, Todd Shipyards, Seattle; FFs 1055, 1058, 1060, 1067, 1074, 1076, Todd Shipyards, San Pedro; FFs 1057, 1063, 1065, 1069, 1073, Lockheed Shipbuilding; FFs 1056, 1059, 1061, 1072, 1068, 1075, 1077–1091, 1092–1097, Avondale Shipyards
Displacement: 4,200 tons full load
Length: 438 ft
Beam: 47 ft
Speed: 27 knots
Power plant: two 1200 psi boilers, one geared turbine, one shaft, 35,000 shaft horsepower
Aircraft: one SH-2F (LAMPS) helicopter
Armament: eight ASROCs (from Mk-16 launcher); eight Harpoon missiles (from Mk-16 box launcher); four Mk-46 torpedoes (from single tube launchers); one 5-inch/.54-caliber Mk-42 gun; one 20-mm Phalanx close-in weapon system; eight Sea Sparrow missiles (on some ships only)

Combat systems: AN/SPS-40 air search radar; AN/SPS-67 surface search radar; AN/SLQ-32 electronics warfare system; AN/SQS-26 sonar; AN/SQS-35 IVDS sonar (on some ships only); AN/SQR-18 towed array sonar system; Mk-68 gun fire control system; Mk-114 ASW fire control system; Mk-115 missile fire control system

Crew: 285 (18 officers, 267 enlisted)

Ships of the class included: *Knox* (FF-1052), *Roark* (FF-1053), *Gray* (FF-1054), *Hepburn* (FF-1055), *Connole* (FF-1056), *Rathburne* (FF-1057), *Meyerkord* (FF-1058), *W.S. Sims* (FF-1059), *Lang* (FF-1060), *Patterson* (FF-1061), *Whipple* (FF-1062), *Reasoner* (FF-1063), *Lockwood* (FF-1064), *Stein* (FF-1065), *Marvin Shields* (FF-1066), *Francis Hammond* (FF-1067), *Vreeland* (FF-1068), *Bagley* (FF-1069), *Downes* (FF-1070), *Badger* (FF-1071), *Blakely* (FF-1072), *Robert E. Perry* (FF-1073), *Harold E. Holt* (FF-1074), *Trippe* (FF-1075), *Fanning* (FF-1076), *Ouellet* (FF-1077), *Joseph Hewes* (FF-1078), *Bowen* (FF-1079), *Paul* (FF-1080), *Aylwin* (FF-1081), *Elmer Montgomery* (FF-1082), *Cook* (FF-1083), *McCandless* (FF-1084), *Donald B. Beary* (FF-1085), *Brewton* (FF-1086), *Kirk* (FF-1087), *Barbey* (FF-1088), *Jesse L. Brown* (FF-1089), *Ainsworth* (FF-1090), *Miller* (FF-1091), *Thomas C. Hart* (FF-1092), *Capodanno* (FF-1093), *Pharris* (FF-1094), *Truett* (FF-1095), *Valdez* (FF-1096), and *Moinester* (FF-1097).

G

Gates, Thomas S., Jr. (1906–1983) *secretary of the navy*

Thomas Gates began his career as a businessman but entered the NAVAL RESERVE during WORLD WAR II and participated in the invasion of North Africa (Operation Torch) and various Pacific-theater operations. He retired from the Reserve as a captain, and in 1953 was appointed undersecretary of the navy by President Dwight D. Eisenhower, who elevated him to SECRETARY OF THE NAVY in 1957. He was named deputy secretary of defense in 1959 and, shortly afterward, secretary of defense. With the end of the Eisenhower administration, Gates returned to the private sector. In 1976, he served as head of the U.S. Liaison Office to the People's Republic of China.

George Washington Class (SSBN-598)

See SUBMARINES.

Gravely, Samuel L., Jr. (1922–) *navy admiral*

Gravely was the first African-American ensign commissioned in WORLD WAR II. He took up his interrupted college education after the war, but returned to the navy during the KOREAN WAR. In 1961, he became the first African American to command a navy ship, and in 1971 became the first black rear admiral. He commanded THIRD FLEET from 1976 to 1978 and retired in 1980 as a vice admiral, the first African American to attain this rank.

See also AFRICAN AMERICANS IN THE U.S. NAVY.

Grenada operations

In 1979, a Marxist-Leninist coup led by Maurice Bishop and his New Jewel movement overthrew the government of Grenada, one of the smallest independent nations in the Western Hemisphere (population 110,000) and one of the southernmost Caribbean islands in the Windward chain. The new pro-Cuban regime built a 9,800-foot-long airstrip, clearly for military purposes, a fact that worried the administration of President Ronald Reagan. However, the Bishop government was short-lived. A 1983 coup killed Bishop and others, leaving Deputy Prime Minister Bernard Coard and General Hudson Austin in charge of the government. Sir Paul Scoon, Grenada's governor-general, secretly communicated with the Organization of Eastern Caribbean States (OECS) to request aid in restoring order. It was the OECS that, in turn, asked for U.S. military intervention.

Operation Urgent Fury included a USN battle group centered on the aircraft carrier *Independence,* as well as the helicopter carrier *Guam,* two USMC amphibious units, two USA Ranger battalions, a brigade of the 82nd Airborne Division, and special operations units. These impressive assets landed on Grenada on October 25, 1983, and found themselves facing no more than 500 to 600 Grenadan regulars, 2,000 to 2,500 poorly equipped and poorly organized militiamen, and about 800 Cuban military construction personnel. The invaders seized the airport and destroyed Radio Free Grenada, the major source of government communications. About 1,000 U.S. citizens, mostly students at a local medical school, were safely evacuated, and Grenada was under U.S. military control by October 28. Eighteen U.S. personnel died in the assault on Grenada, and 116 were wounded. Grenadan forces lost 25 dead and 59 wounded, while Cuban casualties were 45 dead and 350 wounded.

guided missile submarines (SSGN)   See
SUBMARINES.

gunboats

No longer used by the USN, gunboats were common in the navy during the 19th and early 20th century. Gunboats came in many varieties and variations, but all were small, well-armed vessels of shallow draft. They were used along coasts and on rivers for patrol and some escort duty. In contrast to the smaller PT BOAT of WORLD WAR II, gunboats were capable of moderate rather than fast speeds.

In the 1960s, the gunboat was reincarnated as the PGM, or patrol gunboat, for use in the various limited-warfare scenarios presented by the cold war and the VIETNAM WAR. The smallest of the USN's ocean-going craft (length was about 100 feet, beam about 24 feet), the PGMs were often difficult to manage on the open sea. By the 1970s, they were being phased out; all PGMs had been stricken, transferred, or scrapped by 1984.

See also SWIFT BOATS.

Halsey, William Frederick, Jr. (1882–1959)
navy admiral

One of the most famous of WORLD WAR II USN commanders, "Bull" Halsey was a champion of the supremacy of the AIRCRAFT CARRIER, which he employed in execution of his policy of the all-out offensive: "hit hard, hit fast, and hit often."

He was born in Elizabeth, New Jersey, and graduated from the UNITED STATES NAVAL ACADEMY in 1904. He served with Admiral GEORGE DEWEY on the world cruise of the Great White Fleet from August 1907 to February 1909, then served aboard several DESTROYERS and torpedo boats. He commanded USS *Flusser* (DD-20) and USS *Jervis* (DD-38) during 1912–15, then served in the Executive Department at the Naval Academy from 1915 to 1917 and was promoted to lieutenant commander. During WORLD WAR I, he commanded USS *Duncan* (DD-46) and USS *Benham* (DD-49), performing convoy escort duty from a base in Queenstown, Ireland. Following the war, Halsey commanded destroyers in the Atlantic and Pacific during 1918–21, when he was assigned to the Office of Naval Intelligence. He moved in the following year to the post of naval attaché in Berlin, also acting as attaché in Norway, Denmark, and Sweden. He served in these posts until 1924, when he returned to sea duty aboard destroyers in the Atlantic. During 1926–27, he was executive officer aboard the battleship USS *Wyoming* (BB-32). Promoted to captain in February 1927, he was

assigned command of the USS *Reina Mercedes* (IX-25), the Naval Academy training ship, which had been captured from Spain during the SPANISH-AMERICAN WAR.

In 1930, Halsey assumed command of Destroyer Squadron 14, leaving this command in 1932 to attend the NAVAL WAR COLLEGE (graduated 1933) and the Army War College (graduated 1934). At age 52, in May 1935, Halsey completed flight training at Pensacola, Florida, and took command of the aircraft carrier *Saratoga* (CV-3) in July. Two

Admiral William F. Halsey on the bridge of battleship *New Jersey,* December 1944 *(Naval Historical Foundation)*

years later, he was named to command of Naval Air Station Pensacola. Promoted to rear admiral in March 1938, he was assigned command of Carrier Division 2 (1938–39), followed by Carrier Division 1 (1939–40), then was promoted to vice admiral in June 1940 and took command of Aircraft Battle Force as well as Carrier Division 2.

Halsey was at sea with the carriers *Enterprise* (CV-6) and *Yorktown* (CV-5) during the Japanese attack on PEARL HARBOR on December 7, 1941. He made use of these carriers in the months that followed to raid outlying Japanese islands in the Central Pacific (January–May 1942) and enthusiastically collaborated with Colonel James H. Doolittle (USAAF) in carrying out a highly unconventional bombing raid on Tokyo, using B-25 bombers launched from the carrier *Hornet*. However, late in May 1942, Halsey fell ill and turned over command to RAYMOND AMES SPRUANCE, who led the fleet to triumph in the turning-point Battle of Midway (June 1942).

Halsey returned to active duty in October and replaced Admiral Robert L. Ghormley as commander of South Pacific Force and Area. He was, however, narrowly defeated at Santa Cruz during October 26–28, but managed to attain a strategic advantage by holding fast off Guadalcanal as U.S. land forces invaded. During November 12–15, 1942, Halsey defeated the Japanese at sea off Guadalcanal, then led naval support efforts of the amphibious campaign to retake the rest of the Solomon Islands during June–October 1943.

Halsey was named commander of THIRD FLEET in June 1944 and took the battleship USS *New Jersey* (BB-62) as his flagship in August. He directed landings at Leyte in the Philippines during October 17–20, 1944, but blundered by pursuing the remnant of the Japanese carrier force off Luzon on October 25, 1944, leaving the San Bernardino Strait covered only by a weak force of escort carriers and destroyers, which fell under attack by Admiral Takeo Kurita's superior Central Force. Astoundingly, the Americans repulsed Kurita's attack in the Battle of Samar (October 25) and, in "Bull's Run," Halsey raced to reinforce the small

American force. Although defeat was averted, the incident stained Halsey's reputation, which suffered another blow when his Third Fleet was struck by a typhoon that sank three destroyer escorts in December. Undaunted, Halsey went on to sweep through the South China Sea, destroying massive amounts of Japanese tonnage during January 10–20, 1945.

In January 1945, Halsey turned over command to Spruance, but returned to sea command during the last stages of the Okinawa campaign during May and June and the raids against the Japanese home islands during July and August. Japan's official surrender took place aboard his new flagship, USS *Missouri* (BB-64), in Tokyo Bay on September 2. In November, Halsey turned over command of Third Fleet to Admiral Howard Kingman and was promoted to fleet admiral in December. He retired in April 1947, enjoyed a prosperous career in business, but found himself frequently defending his sometimes rash policy of continual attack. Military critics notwithstanding, Halsey was always highly popular with the American public.

Hancock, Joy Bright (1898–1986) *navy admiral*

Born Joy Bright in Wildwood, New Jersey, Hancock became director of the WOMEN ACCEPTED FOR VOLUNTEER EMERGENCY SERVICE (WAVES) and was instrumental in integrating women into the regular USN. She enlisted in the USN as a yeoman (F) during WORLD WAR I and married Lieutenant Charles Gray Little after the war. He was killed in the crash of the USN airship ZR-2 in 1921, after which Joy Little worked for the USN's BUREAU OF AERONAUTICS as editor of the newsletter that became the magazine *Naval Aviation News*. In 1924, she married Lieutenant Commander Lewis Hancock, Jr., who died in the crash of USS *Shenandoah* (ZR-1) in September 1925. After the death of her second husband, Joy Bright Hancock returned to the Bureau of Aeronautics, having obtained a pilot's license herself. She directed the bureau's public affairs program until October 1942, when she was commissioned a lieutenant in the WAVES. By the end of the war, Hancock held the rank of commander, and, in February 1946, became assistant director (Plans) of the Women's Reserve. In July 1946, she was promoted to director of the WAVES, with the rank of captain, and worked to integrate women into the regular navy.

She retired in June 1953 as a rear admiral, married Vice Admiral Ralph A. Ofstie in 1954, and accompanied him on his 1955–56 tour as commander, SIXTH FLEET.

Hayward, Thomas R. (1924–   ) *chief of naval operations*

After graduating from the UNITED STATES NAVAL ACADEMY in 1947, Thomas Hayward became a naval aviator and commanded an air wing during the VIETNAM WAR. In 1969, he commanded the AIRCRAFT CARRIER USS *America* (CV-66) and, during 1970–71, was commander of the Hawaiian Sea Frontier, the 14th Naval District, and Fleet Air Hawaii. From 1976 to 1978, he was commander in chief of the PACIFIC FLEET, then served as CHIEF OF NAVAL OPERATIONS from 1978 to 1982.

Holland, John Philip (1840–1914) *navy engineer*

Holland designed and built the first submarine accepted by the USN, the *Holland* (SS-1), in 1898. He was born in County Clare, Ireland, and immigrated to the United States in 1873. He founded the J. P. Holland Torpedo Boat Company, which secured the USN submarine contract in 1895. *Plunger,* his first attempt to fulfill the contract, was rejected, but *Holland* was accepted. It was commissioned on October 12, 1900, and was powered by a gasoline engine on the surface and an electric engine when submerged.

In 1904, Electric Boat Company assumed all of Holland's major patents and became the principal builder of submarines for the USN. Holland is also noted for inventing a device to allow sailors to escape from disabled submerged submarines.

Hopkins, Esek (1718–1802) *Continental navy commander*

Hopkins was the first "commander in chief" of the Continental navy during the AMERICAN REVOLUTION. A native of Providence, Rhode Island, he skippered a privateer during the French and Indian War (1754–63) and, at the outbreak of the Revolution, was named brigadier general of the Rhode Island militia and charged with coastal defense. Hopkins was given command of the squadron of eight armed merchant vessels chartered as the first ships of the Continental navy. With these, he was ordered to patrol the coast of Virginia and the Carolinas, but instead sailed to the Bahamas, where he captured British-held Nassau in 1776. Despite this audacious act, Hopkins proved ineffective in resisting the attack of the frigate HMS *Glasgow* off Block Island. After the encounter with *Glasgow,* the squadron never sailed again, and, on August 16, 1776, Hopkins was formally censured by the U.S. Congress. This, added to complaints from his subordinates, prompted his dismissal from command in May 1777 and his dismissal from naval service altogether on January 2, 1778.

Horton, Mildred Helen McAfee (1900– 1994) *navy commander*

Mildred Helen McAfee became the USN's first female line officer when she was promoted to lieutenant commander on August 3, 1942, and named first director of the WOMEN ACCEPTED FOR VOLUNTEER EMERGENCY SERVICE (WAVES). A native of Parkville, Missouri, she graduated from Vassar College in 1920 and received a master's degree from the University of Chicago in 1928. In 1936, McAfee became president of Wellesley College. During WORLD WAR II, she took a leave of absence from her duties at Wellesley and secured a commission as a lieutenant commander in the NAVAL RESERVE. At this time she was also appointed director of the newly established Women's Reserve of the USN. In November 1943, she was promoted to captain.

As the first director of the WAVES, McAfee brought this force to its greatest wartime strength

Lieutenant Commander Mildred H. McAfee, ca. 1942–43   *(Naval Historical Foundation)*

of more 80,000. After her marriage to the Reverend Dr. Douglas Horton in August 1945, she took the name of her husband and, as Captain Horton, continued on active duty until February 1946, when she returned to Wellesley.

hospital ships (T-AH)

MILITARY SEALIFT COMMAND currently operates two hospital ships to provide emergency on-site care for U.S. combatant forces deployed in war or other operations. The *Mercy* class consists of two ships, USNS *Mercy* (T-AH 19) and USNS *Comfort* (T-AH 20). They were converted from *San Clemente*–class super tankers, the *Mercy* delivered in 1986 and *Comfort* the following year. In peacetime, the ships are kept in a reduced operating status at Baltimore and at San Diego. On five days' notice, the ships can be fully activated and crewed.

Mercy Class

Navy hospital ships have two missions. First, they provide a mobile, flexible, rapidly responsive afloat medical capability for acute medical and surgical care in support of amphibious task forces, marine,

army, and air force elements, as well as forward-deployed navy elements of the fleet and fleet activities located in areas where hostilities may be imminent. Second, they provide a full-service hospital for use by other government agencies involved in the support of disaster relief and humanitarian operations worldwide. The hospital ships work to minimize the effects of wounds, injuries, and disease on unit effectiveness, readiness, and morale. Secondarily, the mission includes returning patients to duty as quickly as possible and as far forward in the theater as possible.

Mercy and her sister ship, *Comfort*, offer inpatient capabilities that are comparable to major medical facilities ashore. Each of the ships has 12 fully equipped operating rooms, a thousand-bed hospital, full radiological services, a fully equipped medical laboratory, a pharmacy, an optometry lab, CAT scan equipment, and two oxygen-producing plants. Both vessels incorporate a helicopter deck capable of landing large military helicopters, as well as side ports to take on patients at sea.

Normally, both ships are maintained in a five-day reduced operating status (ROS) at East and West Coast berths—Baltimore, Maryland, and San Diego, California. During this ROS period, the ships are maintained by a reduced crew of civilian mariners and active duty navy medical and support personnel at a level of readiness that will permit activation for primary mission employment in five days.

Mercy served in the Philippines in 1987 on a humanitarian mission, and both it and *Comfort* were deployed to the Middle East during the PERSIAN GULF WAR.

Specifications of USNS *Mercy* include:

Builder: National Steel and Shipbuilding Co., San Diego, California
Power plant: two GE turbines; two boilers; one shaft; 24,500 shaft horsepower
Length: 894 ft
Extreme beam: 106 ft
Waterline beam: 106 ft
Draft: 33 ft

Displacement: 69,360 tons full load
Dead weight: 44,648 tons
Speed: 17.5 knots
Crew: 63 civilian mariners; 956 naval medical staff; 258 USN support staff

Multi-Purpose Tween Decker (T-AK)

While the *Mercy* and *Comfort* are currently the navy's only designated hospital ships, the Military Sealift Command also operates MV *Green Ridge* from Navy Support Facility Diego Garcia as a MAR-ITIME PREPOSITIONING SHIP that carries a 500-bed fleet hospital in support of U.S. Marine forces deployed ashore. This complete hospital is off-loaded and set up ashore, then reloaded when it is no longer needed.

The MV *Green Ridge* is a multi-purpose tween decker, which means that it can be readily config-ured to accommodate breakbulk, container, and wheeled and tracked vehicle cargo. The ship is equipped with three sets of twin, 21-metric-ton-capacity cranes, which give it full self-sustaining capability. Its ice-strengthened hull enables it to deliver supplies to polar regions.

MV *Green Ridge* is owned and operated by Central Gulf Lines and chartered by MSC. Its gen-eral characteristics include:

Builders: HDW, Kiel, Germany
Power plant: single-engine diesel with 10,000 shaft horsepower
Length: 507.2 ft
Beam: 69.5 ft
Displacement: 18,178 tons full load
Cargo capacity: 749,032 cu ft
Speed: 16 knots
Crew: 20 civilians

Humphreys, Joshua (1751–1838) *ship builder*

Humphreys was the major outfitter of ships for the CONTINENTAL NAVY during the AMERICAN REVOLU-TION. After the war, in 1794, Congress commis-sioned him to build six frigates, which included the great ships *United States,* USS CONSTITUTION, *Chesapeake, Constellation, President,* and *Congress.* Humphreys created masterpieces of warship design. His frigates rode low in the water and were exceptionally broad. This made them sturdy and stable without any sacrifice in maneuverability.

hydrofoils (PHM)

Between 1977 and 1982, the U.S. Navy commis-sioned six hydrofoil boats, which make up the *Pegasus* class. At 40 knots, they were the fastest ships in the fleet, intended to operate offensively against hostile surface combatants and other sur-face craft, and also to conduct surveillance, screen-ing, and special operations. The six hydrofoils of the class formed a single squadron, which operated from Key West, Florida.

Pegasus Class (PHM)

The *Pegasus*-class vessels were capable of operating in a hullborne mode, at about 12 knots, or on hydrofoils to attain the full 40-knot foilborne speed. Foilborne propulsion came from a single gas turbine, and hullborne propulsion from a pair of diesel engines. These gave the ships good range, and the gas turbines were reserved for occasions when hydrofoil speeds were called for. The vessels often participated in the national drug interdiction program.

Despite their successes, all six of the *Pegasus*-class vessels were retired and decommissioned on July 30, 1993.

General specifications of the *Pegasus* class included:

Builder: Boeing Marine Systems
Power plant, foilborne: one gas turbine, 18,000 shaft horsepower, waterjet propulsion units
Power plant, hullborne: two diesels, 1,600 brake horsepower, waterjet propulsion units
Length, foils extended: 133 ft
Length, foils retracted: 145 ft
Beam: 28 ft
Displacement: 255 tons full load

Armament: eight Harpoon missiles and one 76-mm gun
Speed, foilborne: 40+ knots
Speed, hullborne: 12 knots
Crew: 25

Ships of the class included: *Pegasus* (PHM-1), *Hercules* (PHM-2), *Taurus* (PHM-3), *Aquila* (PHM-4), *Aries* (PHM-5), and *Gemini* (PHM-6).

I

Iceland Defense Force

Iceland Defense Force (IDF), Keflavik, Iceland, is a unified command consisting of USA, USAF, and USN personnel as well as Icelandic civilians. IDF was created in 1951 at the request of NATO to provide for the defense of Iceland and the North Atlantic. IDF is commanded by a navy rear admiral, who also commands Fleet Air Keflavik (tasked with coordinating maritime patrol operations of P-3 Orion aircraft) and Iceland Sector Anti-Submarine Warfare Group. The USAF's 85th Group is responsible for deterring aggression in the North Atlantic and protecting Iceland's airspace; ground defense of Iceland is provided by U.S. Army Iceland (ARICE).

INSURV (Board of Inspection and Survey)

INSURV conducts acceptance trials and inspections of ships and service craft to determine quality of construction and compliance with USN specifications and requirements. INSURV makes recommendations as to acceptance. Additionally, INSURV conducts material inspections of all USN ships at least once every three years. The board also makes recommendations concerning the disposition of ships and service craft considered beyond economical repair or obsolescent beyond economical modernization.

INSURV, the Board of Inspection and Survey, was established by Congress in 1868 and was first commanded by Admiral DAVID GLASGOW FARRAGUT. On August 5, 1882, Congress enacted legislation to establish the Board of Inspection and Survey under statutory authority.

J

John F. Kennedy **(CV-67)** See AIRCRAFT CARRIERS.

Joint Direct Attack Munition (JDAM)

JDAM is not in itself a weapon, but an advanced guidance kit that converts existing "dumb" bombs into precision-guided "smart" munitions. The tail section of the JDAM contains an inertial navigational system (INS) and a global positioning system (GPS). JDAM-modified munitions can be launched from any fighter or fighter-attack aircraft in the USN inventory. Either 2,000-pound Mk-84 or 1,000-pound Mk-83 warheads are used as JDAM payloads. Once released from the aircraft, the JDAM independently navigates to the target. Target coordinates can be loaded into the aircraft before takeoff or they may be inputted by the pilot or weapons officer immediately before weapon release. When GPS data is available, the JDAM guides munitions to within less than 13 meters of the target.

The first JDAMs were delivered in 1997, and operational testing was conducted during 1998–99. General characteristics of JDAM include:

Contractor: Boeing Corporation
Length with warhead: GBU-31 (v) 1/B, 152.7 in; GBU-31 (v) 3/B, 148.6 in; GBU-32 (v) 1/B, 119.5 in
Weight with warhead: GBU-31 (v) 1/B, 2,036 lb; GBU-31 (v) 3/B, 2,115 lb; GBU-32 (v) 1/B, 1,013 lb

Wingspan: GBU-31, 25 in; GBU-32, 19.6 in
Range: up to 15 mi
Ceiling: 45,000+ ft
Guidance system: GPS-aided inertial navigation system (INS)

Jones, John Paul (1747–1792) *Continental navy captain*

Jones is the most famous naval hero of the AMERICAN REVOLUTION and is almost certainly the most famous man ever to sail under the American flag.

He was born John Paul near Kirkbean, Kirkcudbrightshire, on Solway Firth, Scotland, the son of a gardener. He went to sea as a cabin boy aboard a merchant vessel, then, in 1766, became chief mate on a Jamaican slaver. Disgusted by the slave trade, he quit in 1768 and sailed for Scotland. When the captain and first mate died en route, Jones assumed command and took the ship safely home. The owners responded by giving Jones command of the merchantman *John,* out of Dumfries, Scotland; however, during a voyage to Tobago, West Indies, Jones ordered the flogging of a sailor, who subsequently jumped ship and died. On his return to Scotland in November, Jones was arrested for murder, but released on bail to obtain exculpatory evidence. Incredibly, en route to Tobago in December 1773, he unintentionally killed a mutinous sailor. Fearing the consequences of a trial, John Paul appended "*Jones*" to the end of his name and fled to America.

Portrait of John Paul Jones by Charles Willson Peale
(United States Senate)

With the outbreak of the American Revolution, Congress hired Jones to fit out the 20-gun *Alfred,* the first ship purchased for the Continental navy. After raising the new nation's banner over the ship, on December 3, 1775, Jones was commissioned senior lieutenant in the Continental navy four days later. He sailed with the fleet (under ESEK HOPKINS) to the Bahamas, where he participated in the capture of New Providence during March 1776. On April 6, commanding *Alfred*'s main battery, he distinguished himself against HMS *Glasgow* and, two days later, was promoted to captain, with command of the 12-gun *Providence.*

Ordered to conduct raiding operations, Jones sank eight ships and captured eight others from the Bahamas to Nova Scotia during August 21–October 7, 1776. Returning to take command of the *Alfred,* he sailed in company with the *Providence* for Nova Scotia in November and captured a merchant ship as well as a military transport off Louisbourg. He also raided the coast of Nova Scotia, burning an oil warehouse and a ship, then capturing three vessels off Cape Breton.

Jones returned to Boston with his prize ships in December and was commissioned captain of the *Ranger* on June 14, 1777. He sailed it to France on November 1 to acquire the new frigate *Indien,* and, while in European waters, raided two forts at Whitehaven, England, though he failed in an attempt to kidnap Lord Selkirk at St. Mary's Island in Galway Firth on April 23. Nevertheless, he captured the 20-gun *Drake* off Carrickfergus, Ireland, on April 24, then put in at Brest on May 8. From Brest, he was assigned command of a U.S.-French expedition out of L'Orient on August 14, 1779. Jones sailed in the *Bon Homme Richard* (of 42 guns), with a flotilla that included the U.S. vessel *Alliance* (36 guns), and two French ships, the *Pallas* (32 guns) and the *Vengeance* (12 guns). When they encountered a British merchant fleet off Flamborough Head, Jones attacked and defeated the escort, *Serapis,* in a spectacular night battle on September 23. Following this, Jones took command of the *Alliance,* but this time enjoyed no success and was ignominiously marooned ashore when the vessel was seized by its former captain on June 1780.

In 1781, Jones returned to the United States aboard the *Ariel* and on April 14 received the Thanks of Congress. He was assigned command of the 74-gun *America,* which was subsequently given to France. Eager to remain in command of the vessel, Jones volunteered to serve in the French fleet, which sailed to the West Indies in December 1782.

After the Revolution, Jones went to France as a prize agent in November 1783, then returned to the United States, where Congress presented him with a gold medal on October 16, 1787. The following year, he accepted an appointment in the Russian navy as a rear admiral and, in this capacity, defeated the Turks at the Battle of Liman in the Black Sea during June 17–27. With his health failing, he retired to Paris in 1789 and lived there for the rest of his life. His Parisian grave was not identified until 1905; in 1913, his remains were returned to the United States for entombment at the UNITED STATES NAVAL ACADEMY.

Judge Advocate General, Office of the (OJAG)

The mission of the JAG Corps or Office of the Judge Advocate General (OJAG) is twofold. Its primary role is to support the judge advocate general (JAG) in providing legal and policy advice to the SECRETARY OF THE NAVY. Secondarily, OJAG supports JAG in advising and assisting the CHIEF OF NAVAL OPERATIONS in formulating and implementing policies and initiatives pertaining to the provision of legal services within the USN.

The origin of OJAG reaches back to 1775, when the Continental Congress enacted Articles of Conduct governing the ships and men of the Continental navy. When Congress authorized the first six ships of the USN in 1797, it also enacted the Rules for Regulation of the Navy, which were followed in 1800 by a more sophisticated and comprehensive code adapted from the British Naval Code of 1749. These early codes were sufficiently straightforward as to allow little or no legalistic interpretation and, therefore, the services of lawyers were not required. However, during the CIVIL WAR, Secretary of the Navy GIDEON WELLES found it necessary to appoint an assistant U.S. attorney as solicitor of the Navy Department to handle complex court-martial cases. It was not until late in the war, on March 2, 1865, that Congress authorized "the President to appoint, by and with the advice and consent of the Senate, for service during the rebellion and one year thereafter, an officer of the Navy Department to be called the 'Solicitor and Naval Judge Advocate General.'"

The first uniformed chief legal officer of the USN was Colonel William Butler Remey (USMC), who in 1878 persuaded the Congress that the DEPARTMENT OF THE NAVY needed a permanent, uniformed judge advocate general. The law was enacted in 1880, and in 1918 the Naval Appropriations Act elevated the billets of navy bureau chiefs and judge advocate general to rear admiral. In 1947, the USN created a "law specialist" program to allow line officers restricted duty in order to perform legal services. An act of May 5, 1950, mandated that the judge advocate general be a lawyer and specified a minimum degree of legal experience. That act also established the first Uniform Code of Military Justice. In 1967, the Judge Advocate General's Corps was established by law within the Department of the Navy, thereby ensuring the navy lawyer's status as a member of a professional group within the service and on a par with physicians and chaplains.

Currently, the USN judge advocate general commands an organization of more than 730 judge advocates, 30 limited duty officers (law), 630 enlisted personnel, and 275 civilian employees.

Kidd **Class (DDG-993)**   See DESTROYERS.

Kimmel, Husband Edward (1882–1968)
navy admiral

With his army counterpart, General Walter Campbell Short, Kimmel, as USN commander of naval facilities at Pearl Harbor, bore the brunt of blame for the military unpreparedness that made the installation vulnerable to Japan's attack on December 7, 1941.

Kimmel was born in Henderson, Kentucky, and graduated from the UNITED STATES NAVAL ACADEMY in 1904. He served on battleships in the Caribbean during 1906–07 and sailed with the Great White Fleet around the world from December 16, 1907 to February 22, 1909. Kimmel participated in the U.S. occupation of Veracruz, Mexico, in April 1914 and was wounded in that action.

In 1915, Kimmel was appointed aide to Assistant Secretary of the Navy Franklin D. Roosevelt, then was detached to an adviser post with the British Grand Fleet, where he taught British officers new gunnery techniques during WORLD WAR I. Recalled to U.S. service when the nation entered the war, he served as squadron gunnery officer with the U.S. Sixth Battle Squadron from 1917 to 1918. He was executive officer aboard USS *Arkansas* (BB-33) from 1918 to 1920, then served ashore at the Naval Gun Factory in Washington, D.C., from 1920 to 1923. During 1923–25, he commanded the Cavite

navy yard in the Philippines and was also assigned command of Destroyer Divisions 45 and 38.

After attending the NAVAL WAR COLLEGE in 1926, Kimmel was promoted to captain and assigned to the office of the CHIEF OF NAVAL OPERATIONS from 1926 to 1928. He then assumed

Commander of the Pacific Fleet, Admiral Husband E. Kimmel, December 1941   *(Naval Hitorical Foundation)*

command of Destroyer Squadron 12 in the Battle Fleet from 1928 to 1930, then returned to the office of the CNO in 1930. In 1933, he was assigned command of USS *New York* (BB-34). Two years later, he returned to a shore assignment at the Navy Budget Office and was promoted to rear admiral in November 1937. The following year he was made commander of Cruiser Division 7 and, later, commander of Battle Force Cruisers and of Cruiser Division 9.

As war loomed, Kimmel was jumped over 46 more senior admirals and named CINCPAC (commander in charge of the Pacific), with his flag aboard USS *Pennsylvania* (BB-38) in Pearl Harbor, Territory of Hawaii. In February 1941, he was promoted to admiral and diligently prepared for an anticipated war. Tragically, of course, the single contingency for which he had not adequately prepared was a preemptive attack on Pearl Harbor itself. And when the devastating attack came on December 7, 1941, it was Kimmel and his army counterpart, General Short, who shouldered the blame. On December 17, Kimmel was relieved of his Pearl Harbor command and sent to Washington to testify in the initial inquiries. Unlike Short, Kimmel was not officially blamed for Pearl Harbor. Nevertheless, his naval career was destroyed, and he retired on March 1, 1942. Through 1946, he was from time to time summoned to additional Pearl Harbor inquiries. He worked for an engineering firm during 1946–47, then retired, later publishing *Admiral Kimmel's Story* as a vindication of his actions.

See also PEARL HARBOR, JAPANESE ATTACK ON.

King, Ernest Joseph (1878–1956) *chief of naval operations*

An irascible and indispensable WORLD WAR II commander, King was one the USN's most innovative strategists. He was born in Lorain, Ohio, and served as a midshipman during the SPANISH-AMERICAN WAR. He returned to the UNITED STATES NAVAL ACADEMY after the war and graduated near the top of the class of 1901. Serving as an ensign aboard USS *Cincinnati,* he was an observer of naval action during the Russo-Japanese War (February 1904–

September 1905). After promotion to lieutenant in June 1906, King became an ordnance instructor at the academy. In 1909, he sailed with battleships of the Atlantic Fleet. Promoted to lieutenant commander in July 1913, he served ashore with the Engineering Experimental Station at Annapolis, then, in 1914, was given command of the DESTROYER USS *Terry* (DD-25) off Veracruz during the April–November Mexican crisis.

King was promoted to commander in 1917 with America's entry into WORLD WAR I. In September 1918, he was promoted to the temporary rank of captain and served in the Atlantic Fleet. After the Armistice, he headed the postgraduate department at the Naval Academy until 1921, when he chose sea duty again, as commander of a refrigerator ship operating off the East Coast. The following year, he enrolled in submarine training at New London, Connecticut, then assumed command of Submarine Division II through 1923.

Fleet Admiral Ernest J. King   *(Naval Historical Foundation)*

After a stint as commandant of the submarine base at New London, he was appointed senior aide to Captain H. E. Yarnell, commander of Aircraft Squadrons, Scouting Fleet (1926–27). At this time, King enrolled in aviator training and received his pilot's wings at the age of 48 in May 1927. His proficiency in naval aviation gained King an appointment as assistant chief of the Bureau of Aeronautics (1928–29) and as commander of the naval air base at Hampton Roads, Virginia. From 1930 to 1932, he was captain of the aircraft carrier *Lexington* (CV-3). After graduating from the Naval War College senior course in 1933, King was promoted to rear admiral and appointed chief of the Bureau of Aeronautics, a post he held until 1936, when he assumed command of the Aircraft Scouting Force.

In 1938, following promotion to vice admiral, King took command of the five-carrier Aircraft Battle Force, leaving this post the next year to join the General Board and then, in 1940, to assume command of the Fleet Patrol Force in the Atlantic. Promoted on February 1, 1941, to admiral and named commander in chief of the Atlantic Fleet, he directed the undeclared antisubmarine war against Germany off the U.S. East Coast prior to America's entry into World War II.

Following Pearl Harbor, King was named CHIEF OF NAVAL OPERATIONS (December 1941) and then commander in chief of the United States Fleet (March 13, 1942). He played a critical role in formulating Allied strategy and was a participant in all of the major Allied conferences. Promoted to fleet admiral on December 17, 1944, he served through the rest of the war, retiring from active service in December 1945, but continuing as adviser to the SECRETARY OF THE NAVY and the secretary of defense. He also reported directly to President Harry S. Truman, who relished his abrasive and frank style.

Kinkaid, Thomas Cassin (1888–1972) *Navy admiral*

Kinkaid was one of the most important USN leaders of WORLD WAR II, whose brilliance was demonstrated in his management of coordinated collaborative effort among the services. A native of Hanover, New Hampshire, Kinkaid graduated from the UNITED STATES NAVAL ACADEMY in 1908 and sailed with the Great White Fleet during 1908–11. Achieving expertise in naval gunnery, he attended the ordnance course at the Naval Postgraduate School in Annapolis in 1913 and was promoted to lieutenant junior grade in June 1916. Promoted to lieutenant in November 1917, after America's entry into WORLD WAR I, he was sent overseas as gunnery officer of USS *Arizona* (BB-39) in April 1918. After the war, Kinkaid was assigned as an officer in the Bureau of Ordnance, where he served until 1922 when he was promoted to lieutenant commander and became an aide to Admiral Mark Bristol.

Kinkaid received his first sea command, of the destroyer USS *Isherwood* (DD-284), in 1924, then returned to shore duty the following year as an officer at the Naval Gun Factory in Washington, D.C. From 1927 to 1929, he was a gunnery officer with the U.S. Fleet. From 1933 to 1934, Kinkaid was executive officer on the battleship USS *Colorado* (BB-45), then directed the Bureau of Navigation's Officer Detail Section from 1934 to 1937. Promoted to captain, he was assigned to command the cruiser *Indianapolis* (CA-35). He left this assignment in 1938 to become naval attaché and naval air attaché in Rome (November 1938) and naval attaché in Belgrade, Yugoslavia. He returned to the United States in March 1941 and was promoted to rear admiral.

On the eve of Pearl Harbor, Kinkaid assumed command of Cruiser Division 6. After the attack, his force was deployed to support raids against Rabaul and New Guinea (March 1942). Kinkaid fought in the Battle of the Coral Sea (May 4–8) and at Midway, during June 2–5. He assumed command of Task Force 16, built around the aircraft carrier *Enterprise* (CV-6), supported the landings on Guadalcanal (August 7), and fought in the great carrier battles of the Eastern Solomons during August 22–25 and off the Santa Cruz Islands (October 25–28). During November 12–15, he fought Japanese surface ships in the vicinity of Guadalcanal.

Appointed commander of the North Pacific Task Force, Kinkaid directed the recapture of the Aleutian Islands during February–May 1943, landing troops unopposed at Kiska on August 15. After promotion to vice admiral in June 1943, Kinkaid was transferred to command of Allied Naval Forces in the Southwest Pacific Area and, on November 26, was also assigned command of the U.S. SEVENTH FLEET. He coordinated with General Douglas MacArthur a massive amphibious advance along the New Guinea coast toward the Philippines. Also in coordination with Admiral WILLIAM F. HALSEY's THIRD FLEET, he covered the American landings on Leyte (October 20, 1944) and subsequently directed additional amphibious operations against Mindoro (December 15) and at Lingayen Gulf on Luzon (January 9, 1945).

After promotion to admiral in April 1945, Kinkaid directed the landing of American occupation forces in China and Korea during September, then left the Seventh Fleet to take command of the Eastern Sea Frontier at New York from January to June 1946. He was named commander of the Atlantic Reserve Fleet in January 1947, in which post he served until he retired on May 1, 1950.

Kitty Hawk Class (CV 63)   See AIRCRAFT CARRIERS.

Knox, Frank (1874–1944)   *secretary of the navy*

Boston-born Knox left college in his senior year to fight in the SPANISH-AMERICAN WAR with Theodore Roosevelt's celebrated Rough Riders. After a career in journalism, he served in the U.S. Army during WORLD WAR I, then, while remaining in the reserves, he resumed his newspaper career, purchasing the *Chicago Daily News* in 1931. In 1936, he unsuccessfully sought the Republican presidential nomination, but, despite his Republican affiliation, he was a committed supporter of President

Franklin D. Roosevelt, who appointed him the nation's 47th SECRETARY OF THE NAVY on July 11, 1940. Knox died in office on April 28, 1944.

Knox Class (FF 1052)   See FRIGATES.

Korean War

The Korean War began on June 25, 1950, when an army of about 110,000 North Koreans invaded South Korea, rolling up the Army of the Republic of South Korea, seizing Seoul, and advancing southward. The United States took the lead in United Nations–sanctioned operations against the invasion.

The Korean War presented grave challenges to the United States. President Harry S. Truman resolved to act according to his administration's policy of "containing" communist aggression wherever it occurred, yet he was also keenly aware that the intervention of the Soviet Union and/or Communist China could easily touch off World War III. Moreover, in the rush to demobilize after WORLD WAR II, the American military had become a greatly diminished force. Assets immediately available to General Douglas MacArthur, the overall U.S. military commander in the East, were not impressive.

President Truman's most immediate concern was not Korea, however, but Taiwan, the island to which the noncommunist Nationalist Chinese government had withdrawn after losing to the forces of Mao Zedong (Mao Tse-tung) in the Chinese Revolution. Truman ordered the USN's SEVENTH FLEET into the Formosa Strait to preempt any Communist Chinese attack on Taiwan—and, for that matter, to forestall a Nationalist attack on the Communists. The president's object was to contain both communist aggression and the expansion of the war.

Although, pursuant to UN sanctions, 19 nations joined the United States in fighting the Korean War, it was the United States that bore the brunt of combat. U.S. Navy operations began in support of land operations in South Korea. Surface ships bombarded communist positions, and carrier-launched aircraft provided most of the air cover for U.S. and other ground forces.

On July 5, 1950, the navy commenced a blockade of the Korean coast to prevent reinforcement of North Korean forces by sea. From early in the war, the USN's tripartite mission was clear: support ground operations with gunfire as well as air coverage, blockade the coast, and furnish transport and logistical support. In addition, during the opening weeks of the war, it was USN aviators who effectively neutralized the North Korean air force, destroying most of it on the ground.

The success of MacArthur's daring and brilliant landing at Inchon on September 15, 1950, was due in no small measure to USN components. Strategically, Inchon was a superb place for an amphibious invasion. By landing here, MacArthur put his forces in a position to envelop the enemy from the north and the south. Moreover, Inchon was poorly defended—and with good reason. The treacherous 29- to 36-foot tides there, coupled with dangerous currents, made Inchon an apparently impossible place for a landing. The USN accepted the risks and, operating with some 230 vessels, successfully landed marines at Inchon. They coordinated their attack with that of the Eighth Army, and MacArthur was thus able to lead a spectacular counterattack against the invaders, who were pushed not only out of South Korea (that is, across the 38th parallel), but also all the way to the Manchurian border along the Yalu River. However, this provoked the much-feared intervention of the Chinese, some 300,000 of whom poured into North Korea from Manchuria beginning on October 27, 1950.

In the face of the Chinese counterattack, the USN mission became one of supplying air cover for retreating UN forces and supplying ships for the evacuation of 105,000 U.S. and R.O.K. troops as well as 91,000 Korean civilians.

Over the next several months, UN/U.S. forces stabilized the front at the 38th parallel. Because President Truman was unwilling to risk a world war, the conflict was stalemated in this region. Peace talks began, but they stretched out over two years before an armistice was concluded on July 27, 1953.

L

Lafayette **Class (SSBN-616)**   See SUBMARINES.

landing craft, air-cushioned (LCAC)

LCACs are air-cushioned craft used for transporting—ship-to-shore and across the beach—the personnel, weapons, equipment, and cargo of a marine air-ground task force. These high-speed fully amphibious landing craft can carry up to 75 tons of weapon systems, equipment, cargo, and personnel. The air cushion feature allows the LCAC to negotiate more than 70 percent of the world's coastlines, whereas conventional landing craft can reach only 15 percent. General characteristics of LCACs include:

Builder: Textron Marine and Land Systems/Avondale Gulfport Marine

Power plant: four Avco-Lycoming TF-40B gas turbines, two for propulsion and two for lift; 16,000 horsepower sustained; two shrouded reversible-pitch airscrews; four double-entry fans, centrifugal or mixed flow (for lift)

Length: 87 ft 11 in

Beam: 47 ft

Displacement: 170–182 tons full load

Range: 200 miles at 40 knots with payload or 300 miles at 35 knots with payload

Speed: 40+ knots with full load

Load capacity: 60 tons nominal, 75 tons overload

Military lift: 24 troops

Armament: two 12.7-mm machine gun mounts to support M-2HB .50-caliber machine gun; Mk-19 Mod3 40-mm grenade launcher; M-60 machine gun

Crew: five

landing craft, mechanized and utility (LCM, LCU)

These landing craft transport vehicles and troops from amphibious assault ships to beachheads or piers. LCMs use a bow ramp for onloading and offloading, while LCUs have both bow and stern ramps, so that onloading and offloading can be carried out at either end.

Landing Craft, Mechanized (LCM)

The LCM is used to transport cargo or personnel from ship to ship or from ship to shore. LCMs have twin screws and are of welded-steel construction, with a forward cargo well and a bow ramp. The boat is designed to be transported aboard larger vessels and launched from them. It is powered by two 12V-71 diesel engines, the twin screws and rudders controlled from the pilothouse. These boats are manned by a four-man crew, including a boatswain's mate petty officer, engineman petty officer, a nonrated fireman, and a seaman.

The current LCM is designated LCM-8 and includes the following general specifications:

Overall length: 73.7 ft
Beam: 21 ft
Draft: 4 ft 3 in full load
Hoisting weight, maximum: 69,600 lb
Displacement: 105 tons full load
Fuel capacity: 768 gal
Cargo capacity: 68,800 pounds, or 80 troops and one M60 tank, or 200 troops
Propulsion: two Detroit 12V-71 diesel engines, 600 shaft horsepower per engine at 2,300 rpm; 680 horsepower sustained; twin shafts
Speed: 12 knots
Range: 190 miles at 9 knots, full loaded
Crew: four

Landing Craft Utility (LCU)

LCUs are capable of transporting tracked or wheeled vehicles as well as troops from amphibious assault ships to beachheads or piers. The boats are carried aboard the amphibious assault ships and launched when the objective area is reached. The LCU lands as well as retrieves personnel and equipment, typically after the initial assault waves of an amphibious operation. Each LCU can operate at sea for approximately seven days. The boats include their own galleys and berthing spaces.

The LCU 1610, LCU 1627, and LCU 1646 classes were built in the 1970s and are 135 feet long, with a crew of 11. The newer LANDING CRAFT, AIR-CUSHIONED (LCAC) 2,000 have supplanted the LCUs in some missions, but the older boats are capable of transporting heavier loads: 180 tons of equipment or 400 combat-equipped marines. The 1970s generation of LCUs was based on WORLD WAR II designs. The crew includes a radioman, engineman, electricians, mess management specialist, quartermasters, boatswain mate, and a chief or first class craftmaster, who is responsible for the craft and crew.

The LCU 2000 craft moves containers and general and vehicular cargo and is used for unit deployment and relocation. The vessel incorporates a bow ramp for roll-on/roll-off cargo, and is equipped with a bow thruster to aid in beaching and beach extraction. Like other LCU craft, the LCU 2000 carries cargo from deep-draft ships to shore ports or areas too shallow for larger ships. The boat is capable of receiving cargo from a ship anchored in a stream and transporting that cargo to shore for discharge over the bow ramp.

General specifications of the LCU 2000 include:

Overall length: 174 ft
Beam: 42 ft
Draft: 9 ft full load
Displacement: 1,087 long tons full load
Deck area: 2,500 sq ft, sufficient for five M-1 main battle tanks or 12 (24 double-stacked) 20-foot ISO containers
Payload: 350 tons
Propulsion: diesel
Range, light: 10,000 nautical miles at 12 knots
Range: 6,500 nautical miles at 10 knots, full load
Crew: 13

landing ship, tank (LST)

LSTs were widely used for amphibious operations during WORLD WAR II. They were capable of landing troops and tanks. In the modern navy, LSTs have been almost completely replaced by the larger DOCK LANDING SHIPS (LSD); however, the navy still operates one class of LSTs.

Newport Class

The *Newport*-class tank landing ships are larger and faster than World War II–vintage LSTs, and they replace the conventional bow doors with a 40-ton bow ramp, which is supported by two distinctive derrick arms. The ships also include a stern gate, which allows off-loading of amphibious vehicles directly into the water. This design allows for the construction of a hull shape compatible with the 20-knot speeds necessary to keep pace with contemporary amphibious squadrons. The flat-bottom hull of the World War II–type LST was redesigned as a DESTROYER-type bow, which enables the ships to attain speeds in excess of 20 knots.

Newport-Class ships load and transport cargo, vehicles, and marines to a combat area. Amphibious vehicles can be launched through the stern gate, while land vehicles can be off-loaded directly to a beach or causeway via the ship's bow ramp. The LST can also accommodate helicopter operations, providing yet another means of landing troops and equipment. Additionally, a pair of 10-ton booms off-load cargo to boats or a pier.

Total lift capacity is 29 tanks and more than 350 troops, with their equipment.

As of 2004, all but two of the *Newport*-class ships have been decommissioned. *Frederick* (LST-1184) and *La Moure County* (LST-1194) are currently assigned to the NAVAL RESERVE as the only remaining ships of what had been a 20-ship class.

General specifications of the *Newport* class include:

Displacement: 8,792 tons full load
Dead weight: 3,602 tons
Overall length: 522 ft
Waterline length: 500 ft
Extreme beam: 70 ft
Waterline beam: 70 ft
Maximum navigational draft: 19 ft
Draft limit: 19 ft
Speed: 20 knots
Power plant: six diesels, 16,000 brake horsepower, two shafts, twin controllable pitch screws; bow thruster: single screw, controllable pitch
Armament: four three-inch .50-caliber guns; Phalanx close-in weapon system
Vehicle stowage: 19,000 sq ft; lift capacity includes 29 tanks
Crew, ship's company: 14 officers, 210 enlisted; marine contingent, 360–400 troops

Ships of the class include *Newport* (LST-1179), *Manitowoc* (LST-1180), *Sumter* (LST-1181), *Fresno* (LST-1182), *Peoria* (LST-1183), *Frederick* (LST-1184), *Schenectady* (LST-1185), *Cayuga* (LST-1186), *Tuscaloosa* (LST-1187), *Saginaw* (LST-1188), *San Bernardino* (LST-1189), *Boulder County* (LST-1190), *Racine* (LST-1191), *Spartanburg County* (LST-1192), *Fairfax County* (LST-1193), *La Moure County* (LST-1194), *Barbour County* (LST-1195), *Harlan County* (LST-1196), *Barnstable County* (LST-1197), and *Bristol County* (LST-1198).

Large, Medium-speed Roll-on/Roll-off Ships (T-AKR)   See CARGO, FUEL, AND REPLENISHMENT SHIPS.

Large Scale Vehicle (LSV 2)

The *Cutthroat* (LSV 2), the world's largest unmanned autonomous submarine, was christened on November 15, 2000. The purpose of this test vehicle is to provide submarine-design engineers with a platform to test advanced submarine technologies, especially in the areas of stealth, hydrodynamics, hydroacoustics, and propulsion. The LSV 2 operates on Lake Pend Oreille at the Acoustic Research Detachment in Bayview, Idaho, the USN laboratory for demonstrating submarine stealth technology. Appropriately, the vessel is named after a native Idaho trout.

General characteristics of *Cutthroat* include:

Contractor: Newport News Shipbuilding and General Dynamics Electric Boat
Propulsion: electric drive (3,000 shaft horsepower plant coupled with electric motor controller, expandable to 6,000 shaft horsepower with additional motor-controlled modules)
Length: 111 ft
Diameter: 10 ft
Weight: 205 tons
Armament: none
Crew: none

LASH Type: Cargo Ships, Barge (T-AK)

See CARGO, FUEL, AND REPLENISHMENT SHIPS.

Lawrence, James (1781–1813) *navy captain*

Hero of the WAR OF 1812, Lawrence is best remembered for his dying words, "Don't give up the ship!" He was born in Burlington, New Jersey, and joined the USN as a midshipman on September 4, 1798. Promoted to lieutenant on April 6, 1802, he sailed in the Mediterranean aboard USS *Enterprise* the following year to fight the Barbary pirates. He was second-in-command under Lieutenant STEPHEN DECATUR during the daring raid on Tripoli harbor to burn the captured frigate *Philadelphia* on February 16, 1804.

Lawrence remained in service in Mediterranean waters until 1808, when he served aboard a number of vessels. On November 3, 1810, he was promoted to master commandant and given command of the 18-gun sloop *Hornet*. During the War of 1812, he sunk the British sloop *Peacock* off British Guiana on February 24, 1813, then returned to the United States to receive his promotion to captain on March 4. Given command of the USS *Chesapeake*, a 38-gun frigate, on June 1, he sailed out of Boston and, against orders, attacked HMS *Shannon* on June 4. *Shannon* quickly defeated *Chesapeake*, and Lawrence himself fell mortally wounded. As he was taken below decks, he pronounced the words that have entered history: "Don't give up the ship!"

Despite his great courage, Lawrence's daring verged on recklessness. Nevertheless, his fighting spirit continues to be celebrated by the U.S. Navy.

Leahy Class (CG-16)   See CRUISERS.

Lend-Lease

WORLD WAR II began in Europe on September 1, 1939, with the Nazi invasion of Poland. The United States did not enter the war until December 8, 1941, the day after the attack on Pearl Harbor (see PEARL HARBOR, JAPANESE ATTACK ON), and Germany and Italy did not declare war on the United States until December 11. While nominally maintaining American neutrality, President Franklin D. Roosevelt had committed the nation to aiding the powers opposed to Hitler and Mussolini. The first legislation required Britain, initial recipient of material aid, to pay cash for all arms purchased from the United States. In response to a request from Prime Minister Winston Churchill, who pleaded a shortage of cash, President Roosevelt proposed the concept of Lend-Lease as an alternative to cash for arms. The resulting legislation, *An Act to Promote the Defense of the United States,* signed March 11, 1941, gave the president the authority to aid any nation whose defense he deemed critical to that of the United States and further authorized the acceptance of repayment "in kind or property, or any other direct or indirect benefit which the President deems satisfactory." Under Lend-Lease, many WORLD WAR I–era U.S. DESTROYERS were transferred to the Royal Navy.

logistics prepositioning ships

These 10 ships are loaded with USAF ammunition, USN ammunition, and Defense Logistics Agency petroleum products. Two ships are designated aviation logistics support ships and serve as intermediate maintenance facilities for USMC fixed- and rotary-wing aircraft. One ship provides contract transport services to the USMC Third Expeditionary Force.

The ships that carry USAF munitions are MV *Capt. Steven L. Bennett* (T-AK 4296); MV *Major Bernard F. Fisher* (T-AK 4396); MV *Merlin* (AK 323); and MV *A1C William H Pitsenbarger* (T-AK 4638). Ships assigned to carry USN munitions are SS *Cape Gibson* (T-AK 5051); SS *Cape Jacob* (T-AK 5029); SS *Cape John* (T-AK 5022); and SS *Cape Johnson* (T-AK 5075). Ships that carry Defense Logistics Agency petroleum products are the SS *Chesapeake* (T-AOT 5084) and SS *Petersburg* (T-AOT 9101). Ships that provide USMC aviation logistics support are the SS *Curtiss* (T-AVB 4) and the SS *Wright* (T-AVB 3). The HSV *Westpac Express* (HSV 4676) is operated under contract to support the Third Marine Expeditionary Force.

Los Angeles–class submarines   See SUBMARINES.

M

MH-53E Sea Dragon helicopter See AIR-
CRAFT: VIETNAM WAR AND AFTER.

MH-60S Knighthawk See AIRCRAFT: VIETNAM
WAR AND AFTER.

MacDonough, Thomas (1783–1825) *navy
captain*

MacDonough won one of the most important
victories in the WAR OF 1812 at the Battle of Lake
Champlain. A native of New Castle County,
Delaware, he joined the USN as a midshipman
in 1800 after his brother returned from sea having
lost a leg in the QUASI-WAR WITH FRANCE. Mac-
Donough shipped out on a corvette bound for the
West Indies and participated in the capture of
three French vessels during May–September. After
the Quasi-War, MacDonough served on the 38-
gun frigate *Constellation* in 1801 and, from 1801
to 1803, participated in naval action against
Tripoli. He served on the frigate *Philadelphia*
in 1803 and then on the 12-gun sloop *Enterprise,*
skippered by Lieutenant STEPHEN DECATUR. With
Decatur, he took part in the daring raid on
Tripoli harbor to burn the *Philadelphia* on February 16, 1804. In recognition of his performance
on this raid, MacDonough was promoted to lieutenant and assigned to the 16-gun schooner
Syren.

During 1807–08, MacDonough commanded
the 18-gun *Wasp,* which he sailed on patrol duty to
enforce the Jefferson embargo. After an interval as
a merchant sailor during 1810–12, MacDonough
returned to active duty at the outbreak of the WAR
OF 1812 and took command of GUNBOATS defending Portland, Maine. He next assumed command
of naval forces on Lake Champlain in October. In
July 1813, MacDonough was promoted to master
commandant and readied a small flotilla of sloops
and gunboats for action against the British, driving
them from U.S. waters by the fall. When the British
pushed into New York in 1814, MacDonough exer-
cised ingenuity and masterful seamanship to defeat
a superior British fleet on Lake Champlain, a victory for which he received the Thanks of Congress
and a promotion to captain. However, stricken
with advanced tuberculosis, he accepted a shore
assignment as commander of the Portsmouth
Navy Yard on July 1, 1815. Three years later he
returned to sea as captain of the captured British
warship *Guerrière.* Next, he took command of the
74-gun frigate USS *Ohio* and then of the USS *CON-
STITUTION.* He fell ill on a cruise to the Mediterranean in 1824 and died at Gibraltar.

maritime prepositioning ships

Maritime prepositioning ships are the key components of the Afloat Prepositioning element of the
MILITARY SEALIFT COMMAND'S PREPOSITIONING PRO-

GRAM. The Prepositioning Program enables the rapid deployment of large U.S. military forces anywhere in the world, and "Afloat Prepositioning" puts into place in key ocean areas military equipment and supplies ready for use when needed. The Prepositioning Program supports USA, USAF, and USMC operations, with maritime prepositioning ships loaded with USMC equipment and operating within a short sailing time of potential contingency sites.

The maritime prepositioning ships operate in three forward-deployed squadrons: Maritime Prepositioning Ship Squadron One has five ships located in the Mediterranean, Maritime Prepositioning Ship Squadron Two has six ships that are stationed in the Indian Ocean, and Maritime Prepositioning Ship Squadron Three has four ships in the Western Pacific near Guam and Saipan.

Each squadron can provide all the equipment and supplies to support a USMC Expeditionary Brigade of about 17,000 personnel for 30 days.

Mark 38 gun

The Mk-38 is a 25-mm heavy machine gun, single barrel, air-cooled, semi- and fully-automatic, machine gun system with an effective range of 2,700 yards. First deployed in 1986, the Mk-38 is used on a variety of combatant and auxiliary ships and patrol craft. Its general characteristics include:

> **Contractor:** designed and assembled by Crane Division, Naval Surface Warfare Center, from components procured from various contractors
> **Range:** 2,700 yd (2,457 m)
> **Guidance system:** manually trained and elevated
> **Fire:** single shot or 175 rounds/min in automatic mode
> **Caliber:** 25 mm (1 in)

Mark 75 gun

This lightweight, rapid-fire, three-inch gun is designed to be mounted on small combat vessels. Currently, one Mk-75 is mounted on some USN FRIGATES and hydrofoils. The gun was first deployed in August 1978. Its general characteristics include:

> **Contractor:** designed by OTO Melara, Italy; manufactured by FMC Naval Systems Division and OTO Melara
> **Range:** 10 nautical mi
> **Guidance system:** remotely controlled
> **Fire:** 80 rounds/min automatic
> **Caliber:** 76 mm (3 in)

Mark V Special Operations Craft

The Mark V carries Special Operations Forces (SOF), typically SEALs, into and out of operations. The boats are also used for some coastal patrol and for the interdiction of enemy activities. Mark V craft are organized into detachments of two boats, crews, and a deployment support package mounted on such cargo transporters as C-5 aircraft or a variety of surface ships. General characteristics of the Mark V include:

> **Length:** 82 ft
> **Beam:** 17 ft 6 in
> **Weight:** 57 tons
> **Speed:** 50 knots

master chief petty officer   See RANKS AND GRADES.

master chief petty officer of the navy

See RANKS AND GRADES.

McDonald, David L. (1906–   ) chief of naval operations

McDonald was a UNITED STATES NAVAL ACADEMY graduate (1928) who entered naval aviation. He was head of a navy training command in WORLD WAR II and also served aboard aircraft carriers. In 1961, he was given command of SIXTH FLEET. From August 1, 1963, to August 1, 1967, he served as CHIEF OF NAVAL OPERATIONS.

Midway **Class (CV-41)**   See AIRCRAFT CARRIERS.

Military Sealift Command

Military Sealift Command provides ocean transportation of equipment, fuel, supplies, and ammunition to sustain U.S. forces worldwide during peacetime and in war. MSC is headquartered in Washington, D.C., with area commands in Norfolk, Virginia; San Diego, California; Naples, Italy; Yokohama, Japan; and Manama, Bahrain. The command employs about 7,500 people worldwide: approximately 4,700 employees are federal government civil service; 1,100 are military personnel; and 1,700 are civilians employed by MSC contractors. In contrast to other USN ships, MSC vessels are crewed by civilians, although some also have small military departments assigned to them. MSC is one of three component commands reporting to the joint-service U.S. Transportation Command, USTRANSCOM, which is headquartered at Scott Air Force Base, Illinois.

The history of MSC may be traced to the Military Sea Transportation Service created in 1949 as the single managing agency for the ocean transportation needs of the Department of Defense. The service was renamed Military Sealift Command in 1970.

minesweepers, coastal minehunters, and mine countermeasures ships

Minesweepers (MSO)

Minesweepers were the first specialized category of antimine ship. The most recent class was the *Aggressive,* ships commissioned during the KOREAN WAR to counter heavy North Korean mining. All of the vessels were decommissioned in the 1970s or early 1990s.

Aggressive Class

Some of this large class of oceangoing minesweepers were used as recently as the PERSIAN GULF WAR to clear many hundreds of mines in international waters. The ships of this class used AN/SQQ-14

MCM sonar to detect bottom and moored mines, and employed mechanical minesweeping gear to cut mine cables.

General specifications of the class include:

Builders: various, including Colberg Boatworks, Higgins Incorporated, J.M. Martinac Shipbuilding Corporation, Martinolich Shipbuilding Company, Wilmington Boat Works
Displacement: 853 tons full load
Length: 172 ft
Beam: 35 ft
Maximum speed: 15 knots
Power plant: four aluminum block diesels, two shafts, 2,400 base horsepower
Armament: two .50-caliber twin machine guns
Crew, active: 77, including seven officers and 70 enlisted men
Crew, Naval Reserve Force: 57, including five officers and 52 enlisted men, in addition to 25 Reserve crew members

Ships of the class included: *Agile* (MSO-421), *Aggressive* (MSO-422), *Bold* (MSO-424), *Bulwark* (MSO-425), *Conflict* (MSO-426), *Constant* (MSO-427), *Dash* (MSO-428), *Detector* (MSO-429), *Direct* (MSO-430), *Dominant* (MSO-431), *Dynamic* (MSO-432), *Engage* (MSO-433), *Embattle* (MSO-434), *Endurance* (MSO-435), *Energy* (MSO-436), *Enhance* (MSO-437), *Excel* (MSO-439), *Exploit* (MSO-440), *Exultant* (MSO-441), *Fearless* (MSO-442), *Fidelity* (MSO-443), *Firm* (MSO-444), *Force* (MSO-445), *Fortify* (MSO-446), *Guide* (MSO-447), *Illusive* (MSO-448), *Impervious* (MSO-449), *Implicit* (MSO-455), *Inflict* (MSO-456), *Loyalty* (MSO-457), *Lucid* (MSO-458), *Nimble* (MSO-459), *Observer* (MSO-461), *Pinnacle* (MSO-462), *Pivot* (MSO-463), *Pluck* (MSO-464), *Prime* (MSO-466), *Reaper* (MSO-467), *Skill* (MSO-471), *Vigor* (MSO-473), *Vital* (MSO-474), *Conquest* (MSO-488), *Gallant* (MSO-489), *Leader* (MSO-490), *Persistent* (MSO-491), *Pledge* (MSO-492), *Sturdy* (MSO-494), *Swerve* (MSO-495), and *Venture* (MSO-496).

Acme Class

This small class of oceangoing minesweepers represented an improvement over the larger *Aggressive* class. Like the earlier class, the *Acme* ships have been decommissioned.

Specifications of the class include:

Builder: Frank L. Sample, Jr., Boothbay Harbor, Maine
Displacement: 818 tons full load
Length: 173 ft
Beam: 36 ft
Maximum speed: 14 knots
Power plant: four aluminum block diesels, two shafts, 2,800 base horsepower
Armament: two .50-caliber twin machine guns
Crew: 57, including five officers, 52 enlisted men, and 25 reserves

Ships of the class include: *Acme* (MSO-508), *Adroit* (MSO-509; decommissioned 1992), *Advance* (MSO-510), and *Affray* (MSO-511; decommissioned 1992).

Coastal Minehunters (MHC)

In the early 1980s, the navy commenced development of the *Osprey*-class mine hunter-killers, designed to find, classify, and destroy moored and bottom mines. They are equipped with advanced sonar and video systems, cable cutters, and a mine detonating device that can be released and detonated by remote control. Additionally, the ships function as conventional minesweepers. Because many mines are detonated magnetically, the new ships have hulls made of glass-reinforced plastic (GRP) fiberglass, using a design based on the Italian navy's Lerici class.

Osprey Class

The class consists of 12 ships commissioned between 1987 and 1993. Each *Osprey*-class ship has a 15-day endurance and depends on a support ship or shore-based facilities for resupply.

General specifications of the *Osprey* class include:

Builders: MHC 53, 54, 56, 57, Avondale Industries Inc., Gulfport, Mississippi; MHC 51, 52, 55, 58, 59, 60, 61, and 62, Intermarine USA, Savannah, Georgia

Power plant: two diesels, 800 shaft horsepower each, two Voith-Schneider (cycloidal) propulsion systems
Length: 188 ft
Beam: 36 ft
Navigational draft: 12 ft 1 in
Displacement: 893 tons full load
Speed: 10 knots
Crew: five officers, 46 enlisted
Combat systems: AN/SLQ-48 mine neutralization equipment; AN/SQQ-32 minehunting sonar; AN/SYQ-13 navigation/command and control; AN/SSQ-94 onboard trainer
Armament: two .50-caliber machine guns

Ships of the class include: *Osprey* (MHC-51), *Heron* (MHC-52), *Pelican* (MHC-53), *Robin* (MHC-54), *Oriole* (MHC-55), *Kingfisher* (MHC-56), *Cormorant* (MHC-57), *Black Hawk* (MHC-58), *Falcon* (MHC-59), *Cardinal* (MHC-60), *Raven* (MHC-61), and *Shrike* (MHC-62).

Mine Countermeasures Ships (MCM)

MCMs clear mines from waterways. Currently, all navy MCMs are of the *Avenger* class and are designed to find, classify, and destroy moored and bottom mines. The ships use sonar and video systems, cable cutters, and a remote-control mine detonating device. The ships are constructed of fiberglass-sheathed wooden hulls.

Avenger Class

The *Avenger* class is the navy's newest class of MCM and the largest minesweepers the navy has ever commissioned. The ships of this class are designed as mine hunter-killers, which are capable of finding, classifying, and destroying moored and bottom mines. They perform precise navigation to clear minefields by sweeping moored, magnetic, and acoustic influence mines. The ships also conduct coordinated MCM operations with airborne and other mine countermeasure forces. *Avenger*-class ships use advanced sonar and video systems and are equipped with cable cutters and a mine detonating device, which can be deployed and detonated by remote control. In addition, the ships are capable of all conventional sweeping techniques.

The ships are constructed not with steel hulls, which can detonate magnetic mines, but of wood covered with glass-reinforced plastic (GRP) sheathing.

General specifications of the *Avenger* class include:

Builders: Peterson Shipbuilders, Sturgeon Bay, Wisconsin, and Marinette Marine, Marinette, Wisconsin

Power plant: four diesels, 600 shaft horsepower each, two shafts with controllable-pitch propellers

Length: 224 ft

Beam: 39 ft

Draft, navigational: 15 ft

Displacement: 1,312 tons full load

Speed: 14 knots

Crew: eight officers, 76 enlisted

Combat systems: AN/SLQ-37 magnetic/acoustic sweep system; AN/SLQ-38 mechanical sweep system; AN/SLQ-48 mine neutralization equipment; AN/SQQ-32 minehunting sonar; AN/SQQ-30 variable depth minehunting sonar; AN/SSN-2 navigation/command and control; AN/SSQ-94 onboard trainer

Armament: two .50-caliber machine guns

Ships of the class include: *Avenger* (MCM-1), *Defender* (MCM-2), *Sentry* (MCM-3), *Champion* (MCM-4), *Guardian* (MCM-5), *Devastator* (MCM-6), *Patriot* (MCM-7), *Scout* (MCM-8), *Pioneer* (MCM-9), *Warrior* (MCM-10), *Gladiator* (MCM-11), *Ardent* (MCM-12), *Dextrous* (MCM-13), and *Chief* (MCM-14).

The lead ship, *Avenger,* was deployed on September 12, 1987.

Inchon (MCS-12)

Commissioned as an AMPHIBIOUS ASSAULT SHIP (LHA/LHD) in 1970, *Inchon* was converted in 1994 to a mine countermeasures ship (MCS) after experience in the Persian Gulf War pointed up the need for a dedicated command, control, and support ship to support mine countermeasures operations. As part of the conversion, major changes were made to the Command, Control, Communications, Computers and Intelligence (C⁴I) system, including upgrades to the Phalanx close-in weapon system and an array of radars. The ship supports an embarked composite helicopter squadron of eight CH-53E and two SAR/spotter helicopters, and provides alongside support and services for up to four MCM/MHC ships. It can also support and accommodate four EXPLOSIVE ORDNANCE DISPOSAL (EOD) groups, including their equipment.

General specifications for the *Inchon* include:

Conversion builder: Ingalls Shipbuilding, Pascagoula, Mississippi

Power plant: 600-pound steam plant, one shaft, 22,000 shaft horsepower

Displacement: 19,468 tons full load

Dead weight: 5,587 tons

Overall length: 598 ft

Waterline length: 556 ft

Extreme beam: 84 ft

Waterline beam: 84 ft

Maximum navigational draft: 29 ft

Draft limit: 30 ft

Speed: 21 knots

Aircraft: two UH-46D Sea Knight helicopters; eight MH-53E Sea Stallion helicopters

Armament: four 50-caliber machine guns; four 25-mm Mk-38 machine guns; two Mk-15 Phalanx CIWS; Stinger missiles

Crew: 122 officers, 1,321 enlisted

mini remotely operated vehicles

The USN operates two shallow-water survey and light salvage vehicles, ROVs, rated to 1,000-foot depths. They are air transportable and operate with minimum support from surface vessels, piers, or shorelines. Remotely controlled, the vehicles use electric propulsion, carry high-resolution target-locating sonar, and have a manipulator capable of working with simple tools. A 35-mm still camera and a color television camera produce high-quality visual images.

General characteristics of the Standard Vehicle (MR-1) include:

Length: 4 ft 8 in
Width: 2 ft 3 in
Height: 2 ft 1 in
Propulsion: electrical
Maximum operating depth: 1,000 ft
Payload: 22 lb
Speed: 3 knots

The general characteristics of the Open Frame Vehicle (MR-2) include:

Length: 4 ft 2 in
Width: 2 ft 4 in
Height: 2 ft 4 in
Propulsion: electrical
Maximum operating depth: 1,000 ft
Payload: 90 lb
Speed: 3 knots

missile-range instrumentation ships (T-AGM)

The USN operates one missile-range instrumentation ship, the USNS *Observation Island,* which monitors compliance with strategic arms treaties and supports U.S. military weapons test programs. The ship, which carries a U.S. Air Force phased-array radar system for collection of data on missile tests, is operated by MILITARY SEALIFT COMMAND for the USAF Technical Applications Center at Patrick Air Force Base, Florida.

Observation Island (T-AGM-23)

Observation Island currently carries the AN/SPQ-11 Cobra Judy shipborne phased-array radar system. Operating out of Naval Station Pearl Harbor, *Observation Island* and the Cobra Judy radar detect, track, and collect intelligence data on United States, Russian, and other strategic ballistic missile tests over the Pacific Ocean. The Cobra Judy radar is designed to detect and track ICBMs launched by Russia in its west-to-east missile range. Operating in the 2900-3100 megaherz band, Cobra Judy uses an octagonal S-band array, composed of twelve 288-antenna elements arranged in a large octagonal structure approximately 23 feet in diameter. This array is integrated into a mechani-

cally rotated steel turret. The entire system is massive, weighing in at about 250 tons, and it towers more than 40 feet high.

Observation Island operates worldwide, monitoring foreign missile tests for the Air Force Intelligence Command. The ship has participated in several important firsts, including the first launching of a Polaris test missile at sea in September 1959 and the first A2 Polaris missile in 1961.

USNS *Observation Island* was built as a *Mariner*-class merchant vessel (SS *Empire State Mariner*), which was launched on August 15, 1953. The navy acquired her on September 10, 1956, for use as a fleet ballistic missile test ship. Placed in reserve in September 1972, the ship was reacquired by the navy on August 18, 1977. Her general specifications include:

Builder: New York Shipbuilding
Conversion: Maryland Shipbuilding and Drydock Company
Power plant: two boilers, geared turbines, single shaft, 19,250 shaft horsepower
Length: 564 ft
Beam: 76 ft
Displacement: 17,015 tons full load
Speed: 20 knots
Crew: 143 civilians

missiles

Modern navy missiles include weapons launched from ships and weapons launched from aircraft, as well as the latest generation of Trident ICBM, a strategic (nuclear) submarine-launched weapon.

Air-Launched Missiles

Advanced Medium-Range Air-to-Air Missile (AMRAAM)

The AIM-120 Advanced Medium-Range, Air-to-Air Missile, or AMRAAM, is an all-weather air-to-air missile with beyond-visual-range capability. The weapon is a follow-on to the AIM-7 Sparrow (see Sea Sparrow missile below) and is faster, smaller, and lighter than that weapon. It also is more effective against low-altitude targets.

The AMRAAM incorporates an active radar in conjunction with an inertial reference unit and micro-computer system to make the missile less dependent on the fire-control system of the launching aircraft. As the missile closes on its target, the internal active radar guides it to intercept. In this way, the pilot can aim and fire several missiles simultaneously at multiple targets while performing evasive defensive maneuvers as the missiles guide themselves to their targets.

HARM

The AGM-88 High-Speed Anti-Radiation Missile (HARM) is an air-to-surface missile that seeks out and destroys radar-equipped air defense systems. The weapon's proportional guidance system homes in on enemy radar emissions and destroys the source. The missile went into production in March 1983. Its general characteristics include:

Contractor: Raytheon
Power plant: Thiokol dual-thrust, solid propellant, rocket motor
Length: 13 ft 8 in
Launch weight: 800 lb
Diameter: 10 in
Wing span: 3 ft 8 in
Range: 80+ mi
Speed: 760+ mph
Guidance: radar homing
Warhead: blast fragmentation; warhead weight, 150 lb

Hellfire

The AGM-114B is a laser-guided air-to-ground subsonic missile used primarily against tanks, structures, and bunkers. Secondarily, the Hellfire can be used as an air-to-air weapon against helicopters or slow-moving fixed-wing aircraft. The missile can be guided to the target either from inside the aircraft or by lasers from outside the aircraft.

General characteristics of the missile include:

Contractors: Boeing, Lockheed Martin
Power plant: solid propellant rocket
Length: 5.33 ft
Launch weight: 98 to 107 lb

Diameter: 7 in
Wingspan: 28 in
Speed: subsonic
Warhead: shaped charge and blast fragmentation

The navy version of the Hellfire is launched from the SH-60B/HH-60H Seahawk helicopter.

Maverick

The AGM-65 Maverick is an air-to-surface missile designed for close air support, interdiction, and defense suppression. It may be used against armor, air defenses, ships, ground transportation, fuel storage facilities, and similar targets. The USN uses the AGM-65F (infrared targeting) variant, which has a larger (300 pound) penetrating warhead than the 125-pound shaped charge used by the USMC and USAF. The infrared guidance system for the USN variant is optimized for ship tracking. General characteristics of the missile include:

Contractors: Hughes Aircraft Company and Raytheon Company
Power plant: Thiokol TX-481 two-stage, solid propellant rocket motor
Length: 8 ft 2 in
Launch weight: 462 lb to 670 lb, depending on model and warhead weight
Diameter: 12 in
Wingspan: 2 ft 4 in
Range: 17+ mi
Speed: classified
Guidance: electro-optical in A and B models; infrared imaging in D and G models; laser guided in E models; infrared homing in the F models used by the USN
Warhead: contact fuse, 300 lb or delayed fuse penetrator, heavyweight, 300 lb

The missile was first deployed in August 1972.

Penguin

A helicopter-launched antiship missile, Penguin has an indirect flight path to target and is operated in "fire-and-forget" mode to allow multiple target acquisition. The missile was originally developed by and for the Norwegian navy, becoming operational on Norwegian fast attack boats in 1972. Its general characteristics include:

Contractor: Kongsberg Vaapenfabrikk (Norway)
Power plant: solid propellant rocket motor and solid propellant booster
Length: 120.48 in
Launch weight: 847 lb
Diameter: 11.2 in
Wing Span: 39 in
Range: 21.7 mi
Speed: 1.2 Mach maximum
Guidance: inertial and infrared terminal
Warhead: 265 lb, semi armor piercing

The Penguin was first deployed with the USN in 1993.

Phoenix

The AIM-54 Phoenix is a long-range air-to-air missile, carried in clusters of up to six on the F-14 Tomcat. The navy's only long-range air-to-air missile, the AIM-54 is an airborne weapon control system with multiple-target handling capabilities, capable of killing multiple air targets with conventional warheads. The newest Phoenix, AIM-54C, has an improved capability of countering projected threats from tactical aircraft and cruise missiles.

General characteristics of the Phoenix include:

Contractors: Hughes Aircraft Co. and Raytheon Co.
Power plant: solid propellant rocket motor built by Hercules
Length: 13 ft
Weight: 1,024 lb
Diameter: 15 in
Wing span: 3 ft
Range: 100+ nautical mi
Speed: 3,000+ mph (4,800 kmph)
Guidance system: semi-active and active radar homing
Warheads: proximity fuse, high explosive
Warhead weight: 135 lb

The system was first deployed in 1974.

Sea Sparrow

The Sea Sparrow is a highly maneuverable air-to-air missile with surface-to-air capability. The USN version is the RIM-7M Sea Sparrow, whereas the USAF deploys the AIM-7 Sparrow. Both versions are radar-guided, surface-to-air and air-to-air missiles with high-explosive warheads. The USN launches the missiles from ships as a surface-to-air antimissile defense. Both the USN and USMC also launch the missiles from aircraft.

In 2002, the Evolved Sea Sparrow Missile (ESSM) upgrade of the RIM-7 was delivered. It provides the primary air defense for capital ships of the 10 participating NATO navies.

General characteristics of the RIM-7 include:

Contractors: Raytheon Company and General Dynamics
Power plant: Hercules Mk-58 solid-propellant rocket motor
Thrust: classified
Speed: 2,660+ mph
Range: 30+ nautical mi
Length: 12 ft
Diameter: 8 in
Wingspan: 3 ft 4 in
Warhead: annular blast fragmentation warhead, 90 lb
Launch weight: about 500 lb
Guidance system: Raytheon semi-active on continuous wave or pulsed Doppler radar energy

The first version of the RIM-7 was deployed in 1976.

Sidewinder

The AIM-9 Sidewinder is a heat-seeking, short-range, air-to-air missile launched from fighter aircraft. The missile is equipped with a high-explosive warhead and an infrared heat-seeking guidance system, which enables it to home in on the engine exhaust of target aircraft.

The Sidewinder has been in the navy inventory for a long time, the first version, AIM-9A, having been test fired in September 1953. The production version, AIM-9B, became operational in 1956 and has gone through numerous improvements and alterations resulting in the current AIM-9M, deliveries of which began in 1983. The Sidewinder is the most widely used air-to-air missile among Western nations. Its general characteristics include:

Contractors: Raytheon Company, Ford Aerospace and Communications Corporation, and Loral
Power plant: Thiokol Hercules and Bermite Mk-36 Mod 11 single-stage, solid-propellant rocket motor
Length: 9 ft 6 in
Diameter: 5 in
Fin span: 2 ft 1 in
Speed: supersonic
Warhead: conventional blast fragmentation, 20.8 lb
Launch weight: 190 lb
Range: 10+ mi
Guidance system: solid-state infrared homing system

Joint Standoff Weapon (JSOW)

The JSOW is a joint USN-USAF program to develop the next-generation air-to-ground weapon system. For the USN, JSOW will provide a family of precision-guided weapons to allow aircraft to attack targets at increased standoff distances, thereby increasing aircraft survivability. Additionally, JSOW is intended to be usable in adverse weather conditions and to provide the capability of attacking multiple targets.

All JSOW variants use a common weapon body. The AGM-154A carries BLU-97 combined-effect bomblets for use against area targets. A follow-on version to this will carry a BLU-108 submunitions payload to provide anti-armor capability. A third variant is being developed to provide blast-fragmentation capability.

General characteristics of JSOW include:

Contractor: Raytheon Company
Guidance: GPS/INS
Length: 160 in
Diameter: box-shaped, 13 in on a side

Weight: 1,065 lb to 1,500 lb, depending on payload, sensor, and propulsion used
Wingspan: 106 in
Range: low-altitude launch, 12 nautical mi; high-altitude launch, 40 nautical mi
Warhead: BLU-97, combined-effect bomblets; BLU-108, sensor-fused weapon; BLU-111, 500-lb general-purpose warhead

The JSOW may be launched from the F/A-18 Hornet, F-16, AV-8B, and P-3 Orion aircraft. The weapon system was first deployed in January 1999.

Surface-Launched Missiles

Aegis Weapons System

This surface-launched missile is used against targets from wave top (antiship) to overhead (antiaircraft and anticruise missile). Usable in all weather conditions, the Aegis Weapons System operates effectively even in chaff and jamming environments. The system was developed in the late 1960s chiefly to defend against antiship cruise missiles. In this role, Aegis frees up fighter aircraft to concentrate on the outer air battle while cruisers and destroyers, equipped with the Aegis system, provide battle group area defense.

The Aegis system is based on an automatic detect and track, multifunction phased-array radar (AN/SPY-l), which performs search, tracking, and guidance functions and can track more than 100 targets simultaneously. The system was designed especially to be used in *Spruance*-class DESTROYERS. Later versions were designed for the smaller DDG-51 class destroyers.

Harpoon

The AGM-84D Harpoon is an all-weather, over-the-horizon, antiship missile featuring active radar guidance and a low-level, sea-skimming cruise trajectory. The missile may be launched from surface ships, submarines, or (minus booster) aircraft. Its general characteristics include:

Contractor: Boeing Company
Power plant: Teledyne Turbojet and solid propellant booster for surface and submarine launch

Thrust: 660 lb
Length: 12 ft 7 in air launched; 15 ft surface and submarine launched
Weight: 1,145 lb air launched; 1,385 lb submarine or ship launched from box or canister launcher
Diameter: 13.5 in
Wing span: 3 ft with booster fins and wings
Range: 60+ nautical mi
Speed: high subsonic
Guidance: sea-skimming cruise monitored by radar altimeter; active radar terminal homing
Warhead: penetration high-explosive blast

The missile was first deployed in 1985.

Rolling Airframe Missile (RAM)

The RIM-116A Rolling Airframe Missile (RAM) is a lightweight quick-reaction high-firepower anti-ship weapon system jointly developed by the U.S. and German governments. The system combines the infrared seeking of the Stinger missile and the warhead, rocket motor, and fuse of the Sidewinder missile. With its radio-to-infrared frequency guidance system, the RAM requires no shipboard support after launching. Plans call for installing the system on 83 USN and 28 German navy ships. Platforms include AMPHIBIOUS ASSAULT SHIPS, DOCK LANDING SHIPS, FRIGATES, and destroyers.

General characteristics of the RAM include:

Contractor: Raytheon
Power plant: solid-propellant rocket
Length: 9.2 ft
Launch weight: 162 lb
Diameter: 5 in
Wingspan: 1.4 ft
Speed: supersonic
Warhead: 25 lb, conventional

The RAM system began deployment in 1993.

Standard Missile

Standard Missile 2 (SM-2) is a medium-long-range shipboard surface-to-air missile defensive weapon that is part of the Aegis Weapon System (AWS) aboard *Ticonderoga*-class CRUISERS and *Arleigh*

Burke–class destroyers (DD/DDG). The primary mission of the SM-2 is fleet area air defense and ship self defense; however, it may also be used for extended-area air defense and as an antisurface ship weapon.

SM-2s maneuver using tail controls and are propelled by a solid-fuel rocket motor. Extended-range missiles also incorporate a booster with thrust vector controls. Guidance and propulsion are controlled by inertial navigation and midcourse commands from Aegis. Semi-active radar or an infrared sensor is used for terminal homing.

General characteristics of the SM-2 Block III/IIIA/IIIB medium-range missile include:

Contractors: Raytheon and others
Power plant: dual-thrust, solid-fuel rocket
Length: 15 ft 6 in
Weight: 1,558 lb
Diameter: 13.5 in
Wing Span: 3 ft 6 in
Range: 40–90 nautical mi
Guidance system: semi-active radar homing (IR in Block IIIB)
Warhead: radar and contact fuse, blast frag ment warhead
Date deployed: 1981 (SM-2 MR)

General characteristics of the SM-2 Block IV Extended-Range missile include:

Contractors: Raytheon and others
Power plant: two-stage solid-fuel rockets
Length: 21 ft 6 in with booster
Weight: 3,225 lb
Diameter: 21 in (booster)
Wingspan: 3 ft 6 in
Range: 100–200 nautical mi
Guidance system: semi-active radar homing
Warhead: radar and contact fuse, blast-fragment warhead
Date deployed: 1998

Tomahawk Cruise Missile

This long-range, subsonic cruise missile is launched from surface ships and submarines against land targets. Like other cruise missiles, it is designed to fly at extremely low altitudes piloted over an evasive route by an array of mission-tailored guidance systems. The Tomahawk was first deployed in the PERSIAN GULF WAR of 1991. Its general characteristics include:

Contractor: Raytheon Systems Company
Power plant: Williams International F107-WR-402 cruise turbo-fan engine; CSD/ARC solid-fuel booster
Length: 18 ft 3 in; with booster: 20 ft 6 in
Weight: 2,900 lb; 3,500 lb with booster
Diameter: 20.4 in
Wingspan: 8 ft 9 in
Range: 870 nautical mi
Speed: about 550 mph
Guidance system: TERCOM, DSMAC, and GPS (Block III version only)
Warheads: 1,000 lb or conventional submunitions dispenser with combined-effect bomblets

Air-, Surface-, or Submarine-Launched Missile

Standoff Land Attack Missile-Expanded Response (SLAM-ER)

The Standoff Land Attack Missile-Expanded Response (SLAM-ER) missile is an upgrade to the SLAM day/night, adverse weather, over-the-horizon, long-range, air-, surface-, or submarine-launched precision land-attack cruise missile. SLAM-ER features a highly accurate GPS-aided guidance system and is the first weapon with "Automatic Target Acquisition" (ATA), a technology that both automates and improves target acquisition in cluttered areas, while overcoming most countermeasures.

General characteristics of the SLAM-ER include:

Contractor: Boeing Company
Power plant: Teledyne Turbojet and solid propellant booster for surface and submarine launch
Thrust: greater than 600 lb
Length: 14 ft 4 in

Weight: 1,400 lb
Diameter: 13.5 in
Wingspan: 7.158 ft
Range: over-the-horizon, in excess of 150 nautical mi
Speed: high subsonic
Guidance: ring laser gyro inertial navigation system (INS) with multichannel GPS; infrared seeker for terminal guidance; Automatic Target Acquisition (ATA)
Date deployed: mid-1999

Strategic Missiles

Trident II D5 Ballistic Missile

The Trident II is an intercontinental ballistic missile launched from SUBMARINES. It is the most recent type of submarine-launched ballistic missile (SLBM) used by the U.S. Navy. The first, Polaris (A1), was introduced in 1956 and evolved through Polaris (A2), Polaris (A3), Poseidon (C3), and the current Trident I (C4) and Trident II (D5).

Trident I was deployed beginning in 1979 and will be phased out before 2010. Trident II, first deployed in 1990, will be deployed past 2020. Both the Trident I and Trident II missiles are deployed in Ohio-class (Trident) submarines, each of which carries 24 missiles.

Trident II is a three-stage, solid-propellant, inertially guided missile with a range of more than 4,000 nautical miles (4,600 statute miles). Trident II is more sophisticated than Trident I and has a greater payload capability. The newer missile incorporates lighter, stronger, stiffer graphite epoxy materials for all three stages, and an aerospike, a telescoping outward extension, reduces frontal drag by about 50 percent, thereby extending the missile's range.

Contractor: Lockheed Martin Missiles and Space, Sunnyvale, California
Propulsion: three-stage solid-propellant rocket
Length: 34 ft
Weight: 73,000 lb
Diameter: 74 in
Range: 4,000 nautical mi
Guidance system: inertial

Warhead: nuclear MIRV (Multiple Independently Targetable Re-entry Vehicle)

General characteristics of the Trident II include:

Contractor: Lockheed Missiles and Space Company, Sunnyvale, California
Power plant: three-stage solid-propellant rocket
Length: 44 ft
Weight: 130,000 lb
Diameter: 83 in
Range: 4,000+ nautical mi
Guidance system: inertial
Warheads: nuclear MIRV (Multiple Independently Targetable Re-entry Vehicle)

Mitscher, Marc Andrew (1887–1947) *navy admiral and naval aviation pioneer*

Mitscher was a naval aviation pioneer. He was born in Hillsboro, Wisconsin, and graduated from the UNITED STATES NAVAL ACADEMY in 1910. His first assignments were aboard armored cruisers, and in April 1914 he took part in the landings at Veracruz, Mexico. In 1915, he took flight training at Naval Air Station Pensacola, earning his wings in June 1916. After advanced flight training at Pensacola, Mitscher served aboard the attack cruiser *Huntington,* performing balloon and aircraft catapult experiments during April 1917.

When the United States entered WORLD WAR I, Mitscher served on ships performing convoy escort duty in the Atlantic. Before the war ended, he was posted to Naval Air Station Montauk Point on Long Island, New York, then was appointed to command NAS Rockaway, Long Island, in February 1918. In 1919, he was transferred to command of NAS Miami. In May of that year, Mitscher attempted to fly across the Atlantic, but made it only as far as the Azores, an achievement for which he received the Navy Cross. In the winter of 1920, he transferred to the Pacific as commander of the PACIFIC FLEET's air unit based in San Diego, California, then returned to the East Coast to take command of NAS Anacostia in Washington, D.C.

Marc Mitscher (center) with other USN aviators
(U.S. Navy)

During 1922–26 he also served with the Plans Division of the Bureau of Aeronautics. In 1922, he led the USN team at the international air races at Detroit and, in 1923, at St. Louis.

From July to December 1926, Mitscher served aboard USS *Langley*, the USN's first AIRCRAFT CARRIER. He transferred to the *Saratoga* for precommissioning duty and was appointed the ship's air officer when she entered the fleet in November 1927. Promoted to commander in October 1930, Mitscher returned to shore duty in Washington at the Bureau of Aeronautics, serving until 1933, when he was named chief of staff to the Base Force commander, Admiral Alfred W. Johnson, and served aboard the seaplane tender *Wright* for a year before being appointed executive officer of the *Saratoga* in 1934. Once again, Mitscher returned to the Bureau of Aeronautics as leader of the Flight Division from 1935 to 1937.

Mitscher was given command of USS *Wright* late in 1937 and was promoted to captain the following year. He then took command of Patrol Wing 1, operating out of San Diego and was subsequently appointed assistant chief of the Bureau of Aeronautics. He served in this post from 1939 until the eve of World War II, when he was given command of the new aircraft carrier USS *Hornet* in July 1941. Mitscher was in command when Colonel Jimmy Doolittle (USAAF) used the carrier to launch 16 B-25 bombers on his celebrated raid against Tokyo in April 1942. Mitscher also commanded the *Hornet* at the make-or-break Battle of Midway during June 3–6, 1942, and was promoted to rear admiral and commander of Patrol Wing 2 in July. In December, he was appointed commandant of Fleet Air, based on the Pacific island of Noumea, and when U.S. forces took Guadalcanal, he moved his base there in April 1943. Mitscher next directed combined USA, USN, and USMC operations during the Solomons campaign before assuming command of the Fast Carrier Task Force, which operated against Japanese positions in the Marshall Islands, Truk, and New Guinea from January to June of 1944.

Promoted to vice admiral in March 1944, Mitscher took charge of carrier operations at the Battle of the Philippine Sea and succeeded in decimating the Japanese carrier force in the celebrated "Marianas Turkey Shoot" of June 19–21. His next assignment was in support of amphibious landings at the Bonins and Palau during August and September. From here, he assumed command of air operations covering the landing at Leyte, Philippines, in October. During the Battle for Leyte Gulf (October 24–26), Mitscher directed carrier operations that resulted in the destruction of most of the remaining Japanese carriers. At Iwo Jima and Okinawa, in February and April 1945, Mitscher played a supporting role, and in the Battle of the East China Sea, on April 7, his carriers sank the battleship *Yamato* and most of her escorts.

In July 1945, Mitscher returned to Washington, D.C., as deputy chief of naval operations (air). Shortly after the war, in March 1946, he was promoted to admiral and given command of the Eighth Fleet. This assignment was cut short by his death, at age sixty, from illness.

Moffett, William Adger (1869–1933) *navy aviator*

Moffett was an early supporter of naval aviation and the first chief of the Bureau of Aeronautics. Born in Charleston, South Carolina, he graduated from the UNITED STATES NAVAL ACADEMY in 1890 and saw action in the SPANISH-AMERICAN WAR at the Battle of Manila Bay. As the first chief of the Bureau of Aeronautics, he ensured that aviation would play a significant role in the USN. With tragic irony, Moffett died in the crash of the dirigible *Akron* (ZRS-4) in a storm.

Moorer, Thomas Hinman (1912–   ) *chief of naval operations*

The 18th CHIEF OF NAVAL OPERATIONS, Moorer held that post during key years of the VIETNAM WAR, from August 1, 1967, to July 1, 1970. He was a vigorous opponent of the limited war strategy pursued by Secretary of Defense Robert S. McNamara and President Lyndon B. Johnson and advocated no halt to aerial bombardment and the thorough mining of Haiphong Harbor.

An Alabaman, Moorer graduated from the UNITED STATES NAVAL ACADEMY in 1933, served in various assignments during WORLD WAR II, and graduated from the NAVAL WAR COLLEGE in 1953. When he was promoted to rear admiral in 1957, Moorer was the youngest officer ever to hold that rank. He was appointed CNO after having commanded both the Pacific and Atlantic fleets. In 1971, Moorer was named chairman of the Joint Chiefs of Staff. He retired in July 1974.

Multi-Purpose Tween Decker (T-AK)   See HOSPITAL SHIPS.

museums, naval

There are a great many maritime museums in the United States. The following, listed by state, are those either maintained by or directly relevant to the U.S. Navy:

Alabama
Mobile: *Alabama* (BB-60), *Drum* (AGSS-228), LST-325, and other naval exhibits at the City of Mobile Museum

Alaska
Kodiak: Kodiak Military History Museum, Miller Point, Ft. Abercrombie, WORLD WAR II coastal defense exhibit

California
Alameda: Aircraft Carrier Hornet Foundation, *Hornet* (CVS-12)

Camp Pendleton: Assault Amphibian Vehicle Museum

Los Angeles: Los Angeles Maritime Museum, largest maritime museum on the West Coast, includes many USN models and exhibits; also USS *Los Angeles* (CA-135)

Port Hueneme: Seabee Museum at the Naval Construction Batalion Center

Richmond: Richmond Museum, SS *Red Oak Victory* Liberty ship

Rio Vista: American Patrol Boats Museum, includes PT boat and other patrol craft

San Diego: San Diego Aircraft Carrier Museum, USS *Midway* (CV-41)

San Francisco: National Liberty Ship Memorial, *Jeremiah O'Brien* Liberty ship

San Francisco: Treasure Island Museum, museum of USN World War II action in the Pacific

Santa Monica: Coastal defense fort, on ramp to Santa Monica pier

San Pedro: *Lane Victory* operational Victory ship

Vallejo: Mare Island Historic Park, former naval shipyard

Connecticut
Essex Village: Connecticut River Museum, includes replica of the *Turtle* submarine of the AMERICAN REVOLUTION.

Groton: Nautilus Memorial and Submarine Force Museum, *Nautilus* (SSN-571) and other submarines

District of Columbia
Navy Museum, Washington Navy Yard, includes *Barry* (DD-933), a collection of minisubs, and other exhibits

Naval Historical Center, Washington Navy Yard, a source for scholars

The Smithsonian Institution, includes various maritime exhibits

Florida
Fort Pierce: UDT-Seal Museum

Pensacola: National Naval Aviation Museum, at Pensacola Naval Air Station

Tampa: The American Victory Mariners Memorial and Museum Ship, *American Victory* Victory ship

Georgia
Athens: Naval Supply Corps Museum

Columbus: Civil War Naval Museum/Port Columbus Civil War Naval Center, includes remains of Civil War ironclads CSS *Jackson* and CSS *Chattahoochee* and other exhibits

Hawaii
Honolulu, Oahu: USS *Bowfin* Submarine Museum and Park, includes a Japanese midget submarine and a Regulus I missile

Pearl Harbor, Oahu: *Arizona* Memorial. *Missouri* is moored at the other end of Battleship Row from *Arizona;* also visit *Utah* Memorial, Ford Island.

Illinois
Chicago: Museum of Science and Industry, includes captured World War II German submarine *U-505* and many naval models

Kansas
Olathe: Old Olathe Naval Air Museum, preserves history of Olathe NAS

Kentucky
Louisville: Naval Civil War Museum of the Western Theater, includes USS *Louisville* (ironclad) replica

Louisiana

Baton Rouge: Louisiana Naval War Museum, includes USS *Kidd* (DD-661) and other exhibits

Lockport: LCVP KA 33-21 Association, includes Higgins boat replica

Maryland

Annapolis: UNITED STATES NAVAL ACADEMY, including many artifacts and a museum run by the U.S. Naval Institute

Baltimore: USS *Constellation;* also, Baltimore Maritime Museum, includes *Torsk* (AGSS-423) and *Taney* (WHEC-37), the last remaining armed ship afloat from the PEARL HARBOR attack; also, Project Liberty Ship, includes *John M. Brown* Liberty ship #312

Massachusetts

Boston: Boston National Historical Park, includes USS *CONSTITUTION* (still under USN commission) and *Cassin Young* (DD-793)

Fall River: Battleship Cove, includes *Massachusetts* (BB-59), *Joseph P. Kennedy, Jr.* (DD-850), *Lionfish* (SS-298), *Hiddensee* (corvette), PT-796, PT-617, and an LCM

Quincy: U.S. Naval and Shipbuilding Museum, includes USS *Salem* (CA-139) and other exhibits and archives

Michigan

Muskegon: Great Lakes Naval and Maritime Museum, includes *Crockett* (PG-88), *Silversides* (SS-236), and LST-393

Mississippi

Vicksburg: *Cairo* ironclad riverboat; also, Gray and Blue Naval Museum, includes models of Civil War gunboats and a diorama of the siege of Vicksburg

Nebraska

Omaha: Omaha Military Historical Society, includes *Marlin* (SST-2), *Hazard* (AM-240), and LSM-45

Nevada

Laughlin: Museum, includes KOREAN WAR, VIETNAM WAR, and PERSIAN GULF WAR ship models

New Hampshire

Portsmouth: Port of Portsmouth Maritime Museum, includes *Albacore* (AGSS-569)

New Jersey

Camden: *New Jersey* (BB-62)

Hackensack: New Jersey Naval Museum, includes *Ling* (AGSS-297), Vietnam War PBR, Japanese *Kaiten* suicide torpedo, German *Seehund* torpedo, and Regulus, Talos, and other missiles

Lakehurst: NAWC Lakehurst, Visitor's Center, history of USN AIRSHIPS

Lower Township: NAS Wildwood Naval Aviation Museum, includes HH-52A, T-33, A-4, Stearman, and MiG-15

Paterson: Great Falls Historic District, Paterson Museum, includes *Boat #1* (first JOHN HOLLAND submarine), and *Fenian Ram* (the second Holland submarine)

Pine Bluff: Farragut Marine Museum, Admiral Farragut Academy

Sandy Hook: Naval defense batteries

Sea Girt: New Jersey National Guard Militia Museum, includes *Intelligent Whale* (early submarine)

New York

Albany: USS *Slater* (DE-766)

Buffalo: Buffalo and Erie County Naval and Servicemen's Museum, includes *Little Rock* (CLG-4), *The Sullivans* (DD-537), *Croaker* (SS-246), and PTF-17

New York (The Bronx, Fort Schuyler): Maritime Industry Museum, SUNY Maritime College, includes large-scale model of Brooklyn Navy Yard at the end of World War II

New York (Manhattan): *Intrepid* Sea-Air-Space Museum, includes *Intrepid* (CV/CVA/CVS-11), with many naval aircraft, and *Edson* (DD-943), *Growler* (SSG-577), and other exhibits

Whitehall: Skenesborough Museum, includes exhibits on early USN history on Lake Champlain and the upper Hudson River

North Carolina

Kingston: Caswell-Nuese State Historical Site, includes *Neuse,* Confederate ironclad ram

Wilmington: Eagle Island, *North Carolina* (BB-55)

New Hanover: New Hanover County Museum, includes Civil War blockade and blockade-running

Ohio
Cleveland: *Cod* (SS-224), World War II submarine

Oklahoma
Muskogee: USS *Batfish* Park, *Batfish* (AGSS-310)

Oregon
Astoria: Columbia River Maritime Museum, includes artifacts from battleship *Oregon,* the bridge of *Knapp* (DD-563), artifacts from *Rasher* (SS-269), and other exhibits

Hammond: Fort Stevens State Park Museum, site of attack by Japanese submarine I-25 during World War II

Portland: Oregon Museum of Science and Industry, includes *Blueback* (SS-581), last diesel submarine produced for the USN

Pennsylvania
Erie: Erie Maritime Museum, includes rebuilt *Niagara*, OLIVER HAZARD PERRY'S WAR OF 1812 flagship

Philadelphia: Independence Seaport Museum, includes *Olympia* (CL-15), Admiral GEORGE S. DEWEY's flagship during the SPANISH-AMERICAN WAR; *Becuna* (SS-319)

Pittsburgh: Carnegie Science Center, includes *Requin* (AGSS/SSR-481)

Willow Grove/Hatboro: Willow Grove NAS, includes naval aircraft

Rhode Island
Newport: NAVAL WAR COLLEGE Museum, exhibits on the evolution and technology of sea warfare

Providence: USS *Saratoga* Museum Foundation, USS *Saratoga* (CV-60) and other vessels

South Carolina
Charleston (Mt. Pleasant, near Charleston): Patriots Point Naval and Maritime Museum, includes *Yorktown* (CV-10), *Laffey* (DD-724), and *Clam-*

agore (SS-343), as well as the Congressional Medal of Honor Museum

South Dakota
Sioux Falls: Battleship *South Dakota* Memorial, artifacts from the ship

Tennessee
Germantown: PT Boats, Inc., artifacts from World War II PT boats

Memphis: Mud Island, includes Civil War naval exhibits

Texas
Corpus Christi: Lexington on the Bay Museum, USS *Lexington* (CV/CVA/AVT-16).

Fredericksburg: CHESTER NIMITZ Museum of the Pacific War, includes HA-19 (Japanese midget submarine) and various warship interior sections

Fredericksburg: Defenders of America Naval Museum, includes PT-309, PT-305, LCP(L)

Galveston: Seawolf Park, includes *Cavalla* (AGSS-244) and *Stewart* (DE-238)

Houston area: San Jacinto Battleground Historical Complex, includes *Texas* (BB-35)

Orange: Southeast Texas War Memorial, destroyer *Orleck*

Rio Hondo: LPH USS *Iwo Jima*

Vermont
Vergennes: Lake Champlain Maritime Museum, includes replica of gunboat *Philadelphia*

Virginia
Dahlgren: Naval Surface Warfare Center

Norfolk: Hampton Roads Naval Museum and Nauticus, the National Maritime Center, includes *Wisconsin* (BB-64) and other exhibits

Portsmouth: Portsmouth Naval Shipyard Museum, America's first naval shipyard

Yorktown: Yorktown Victory Center, includes naval exhibits relating to the American Revolution

Washington
Bellingham: Whatcom Museum of History and Art, includes H.C. Hanson Naval Architecture Col-

lection (architect of USN and other military vessels)

Bremerton: Bremerton Boardwalk, *Turner Joy* (DD-951)

Keyport: Naval Undersea Museum, includes *Trieste II* (DSV-1) and other exhibits

Seattle: Submarine Attractions, Inc., Foxtrot-class submarine

West Virginia
Keyser: USS *Barr* World War II Collection, Mary F. Shipper Library, Potomac State College

Wisconsin
Manitowoc: Wisconsin Maritime Museum, includes *Cobia* (AGSS-245)

N

Narwhal (SSN-671)   See SUBMARINES.

National Defense Reserve Fleet (NDRF)

The NDRF was created pursuant to the Merchant Ship Sales Act of 1946 to maintain and administer a fleet of inactive but militarily useful merchant ships to meet national contingencies. Currently, the U.S. Department of Transportation's Marine Administration (MARAD) maintains inactive merchant ships and naval auxiliaries in three reserve fleet sites: 98 vessels at Ft. Eustis, Virginia, 49 at Beaumont, Texas, and 84 at Suisun Bay, California. Additionally, a Ready Reserve Fleet, established in 1976, consists of vessels maintained in a high state of readiness and strategically positioned to provide very rapid deployment of military equipment. In 1984, this was renamed the READY RESERVE FORCE (RRF).

National Museum of Naval Aviation

The 37-acre National Museum of Naval Aviation is located at Naval Air Station Pensacola, Florida, and is the second largest aviation museum in the United States, with more than 140 aircraft, other exhibits, and an extensive research library. The collection tells the story of USN, USMC, and USCG aviation, from its beginnings to the present.

The museum was opened on June 8, 1963, and is privately funded through the Naval Aviation Museum Association, which was established on December 5, 1966.

See also MUSEUMS, NAVAL.

National Naval Medical Center

Located just outside of Washington, D.C., at Bethesda, Maryland, the National Naval Medical Center calls itself the "Flagship of Navy Medicine." Its mission is to provide primary care and specialty services for active and retired uniformed services personnel and their families. Additionally, the center is a teaching institution, which provides graduate and undergraduate medical education and professional development for staff members. The center provides medical care for the leaders of the nation, including the president and vice president, their families, members of Congress, justices of the Supreme Court, and other beneficiaries as designated by the SECRETARY OF THE NAVY. NNMC Bethesda complex is a very large hospital, staffed by some 5,000 USN and civilian personnel.

The first naval medical facility in the Washington, D.C., area was established near the WASHINGTON NAVY YARD during the WAR OF 1812. Another facility at the Navy Yard was subsequently established and then, in 1843, the hospital was transferred to the Marine Barracks at 8th and I Streets. During the CIVIL WAR a temporary naval hospital was established at the Government Hospital for the Insane. After the war, in 1866, Congress appropriated funds to build a 50-bed naval hospital on Pennsylvania Avenue SE, in Washington, D.C., and in October 1906, a new Naval Hospital was built at 23rd and E Streets (present site of the USN Bureau of Medicine and Surgery), which became the Naval Medical Center in 1935, home of the Naval Hospital and the Naval Medical School. In 1938, Congress appropriated funds for the acquisition of land at Bethesda, Maryland, and the new center opened on February 5, 1942. The center has been expanding ever since.

National Naval Officers Association (NNOA)

NNOA is an organization of active duty, reserve, and retired USN officers, midshipmen, and cadets, as well as interested civilians. With members of all ranks and ethnicities, NNOA actively supports the sea services in the recruitment, retention, and career development of minority officers. NNOA is sanctioned by the SECRETARY OF THE NAVY and the secretary of transportation.

Founded in 1972, NNOA is headquartered at National Naval Officers Association, Inc., P.O. Box 10871, Alexandria, VA 22310–0871 (703–997–1068; nnoa@nnoa.org) and has 42 chapters nationwide.

See also AFRICAN AMERICANS IN THE U.S. NAVY.

Naval Aerospace Medical Research Laboratory

Located at Naval Air Station Pensacola, Florida, the Naval Aerospace Medical Research Laboratory conducts research and development in aviation medicine and allied sciences to enhance the health, safety, and readiness of USN and USMC flight personnel. Areas of particular research interest include spatial orientation, human performance, aeromedical standards, and aviation medicine. Laboratory facilities are designed to investigate acoustical, visual, vestibular, cognitive, psychopharmacological, and thermal-stress factors. The laboratory maintains three operational mobile field laboratories as well as the world's most important set of acceleration-research devices.

The predecessor to this laboratory was established at the Pensacola Naval Air Station Medical Department in 1939.

Naval Air Reserve Force

The Naval Air Reserve Force consists of 39 squadrons equipped with current USN combat and other aircraft. The entire USN logistics airlift mission is currently flown by the Naval Air Reserve. Reserve combat search-and-rescue and naval special operations squadrons are mobilization ready, and at least one Reserve airborne early warning squadron routinely engages in counterdrug missions. Naval Reserve Intelligence is also part of the Naval Air Reserve Force.

The Reserve Aviation Force consists of USN and USMC reserve units and is staffed by citizen-sailors. The force is always on mobilization-ready status. One Reserve Air Wing (CVWR), a Reserve Helicopter Wing, two Reserve Patrol Wings, and a Reserve Marine Aircraft Wing (MAW) represent most of the Reserve's warfighting capability, while a Fleet Logistics Support Wing provides airlift support for the entire USN.

The Naval Air Reserve Force was established on August 29, 1916, as the Naval Reserve Flying Corps by the Naval Reserve Appropriations Act. In 1946, the Naval Air Reserve Training Command was established at Naval Air Station Glenview, Illinois, and in 1973, the air and surface training commands were combined in New Orleans, under the chief of naval reserve. In 1983, the Naval Air Reserve Force was established as a separate command within the Naval Reserve.

Naval Air Systems Command

NAVAIR provides advanced warfare technology through work in six categories of naval aviation technology: sensors, aircraft, weapons, training, launch and recovery, and communications. NAVAIR employs about 28,000 people at eight principal continental U.S. sites and two principal sites overseas. NAVAIR headquarters is at Patuxent River, Maryland. At each NAVAIR site, engineering, development, testing, and management capabilities are integrated to deliver superior airborne weapons systems.

NAVAIR Cherry Point, North Carolina: Provides maintenance, engineering, and logistics support for a variety of aircraft, engines, and components for all services.

NAVAIR China Lake, California: home of the Naval Air Warfare Center Weapons Division; supplies the fleet with high-speed weapons, network-centric warfare, unmanned aviation, and homeland defense/counterterrorism capabilities; works with Point Mugu operations to research, develop, test, and engineer support for guided missiles, free-fall weapons, target droves, support equipment, crew systems, and electronic warfare systems.

NAVAIR Jacksonville, Florida: Performs a complete range of depot-level rework operations on designated weapon systems, accessories, and equipment; manufactures parts and assemblies as required; provides engineering services in the development of changes in hardware design; and furnishes technical and other professional services on aircraft maintenance and logistic problems.

NAVAIR Lakehurst, New Jersey: Aircraft Platform Interface (API) provides the facilities and services necessary to permit fixed- and rotary-wing aircraft to operate safely and effectively from ships at sea and from austere expeditionary airfields; designs, prototypes, tests, and contracts catapults, arresting gear, visual landing aids, flight deck marking/lighting systems, aircraft and weapons handling equipment, aircraft servicing and maintenance equipment, unique avionics testing equipment, aircraft engine test equipment, and shipboard aircraft fire trucks.

Naval Air Pacific Repair Activity, Naval Air Facility Atsugi, Japan: Performs depot-level rework on designated weapon systems, support equipment, and associated components in support of USN and USMC aircraft in the Western Pacific and Indian Ocean theaters.

Naval Air Mediterranean Repair Activity, Naples, Italy: Performs depot-level repair within the Mediterranean and Navy Central Command area of responsibility.

NAVAIR North Island, California: Partners with industry to develop, acquire, and support naval aeronautical and related technology systems.

NAVAIR Orlando, Florida: Training Systems Division serves as the principal USN center for research, development, test, evaluation, acquisition, and product support of training systems.

NAVAIR Patuxent River, Maryland: Home to the Naval Air Systems Command headquarters and the Naval Air Warfare Center Aircraft Division (NAWCAD), USN's principal research, development, test, evaluation, and engineering activity center for manned and unmanned aircraft, engines, avionics, aircraft support systems, and ship/shore/air operations.

NAVAIR Point Mugu, California: Shares the Weapons Division responsibilities with China Lake and oversees the sea test range, including San Nicolas Island, 60 miles off the California coast. Supplies fleet support for electronic attack aircraft, high-speed weapons, network-centric warfare, unmanned aviation, and homeland defense/counterterrorism capabilities.

Naval Audit Service

The Naval Audit Service is led by the auditor general of the navy and the deputy auditor general of the navy and provides independent, professional internal audit services to promote improvement in efficiency, accountability, and program effectiveness. Audits ensure that USN information is reliable, that resources have been safeguarded, that funds have been expended consistent with laws, regulations, and policies, that resources have been managed economically and efficiently, and that desired program performance has been achieved.

The Central Office of the Naval Audit Service is housed in the WASHINGTON NAVY YARD, Washington, D.C., with area offices in Virginia Beach, Virginia, and San Diego, California.

Naval Aviation Schools

Headquartered at Naval Air Station Pensacola, Florida, the Naval Aviation Schools are responsible for training in all aspects of naval aviation. The heart of the operation is the Aviation Training School. Staffed by 27 officers, five enlisted sailors, and four civilians, ATS consists of four divisions: Aviation Preflight Indoctrination, Flight Instructor Training Course, Aircrew Coordination Training, and International Military Training. ATS directs the development, operation, and administration of academic programs of instruction to support approved curricula for aviation preflight indoctrination; aircrew coordination training; international military training; and the flight instructor training course.

Naval Center for Cost Analysis

Located in Washington, D.C, the Naval Center for Cost Analysis guides, directs, and strengthens cost analysis within the DEPARTMENT OF THE NAVY to ensure the preparation of credible cost estimates of the resources required to develop, procure, and operate military systems and forces in support of planning, programming, budgeting and acquisition management. Specifically, NCCA advises the SECRETARY OF THE NAVY and CHIEF OF NAVAL OPERATIONS on matters relating to weapons system cost estimates and analysis for planning, financial management, and negotiation of major limited competition contracts. NCCA leads Department of the Navy in issues of cost policy and policy implementation; prepares independent cost estimates; and conducts economic analyses of weapon system and equipment acquisition.

Naval Center for Space Technology

NCST conceives, develops, and demonstrates space and aerospace systems and technology to meet USN, Department of Defense, and other national needs. NCST provides comprehensive systems engineering and analysis, technology development and exploitation, risk-reduction prototyping, transition to industry, and warfighter support. Activities extend from basic and applied research through advanced development in all areas of interest to the USN space program, including developing spacecraft, systems using spacecraft, and ground command and control stations.

Naval Criminal Investigative Service

The Naval Criminal Investigative Service is a worldwide federal law enforcement organization staffed exclusively by civilian special agents who provide law enforcement and counterintelligence services to the USN and USMC. About half of the 850 NCIS special agents investigate general crimes, such as homicide, rape, burglary, robbery, child abuse, arson, and theft of government property. Other agents conduct a counterdrug program and investigate sophisticated "white collar" crime, especially procurement fraud. Computer crime, counterintelligence, and protective services are also part of the NCIS mission.

NCIS is headquartered at the WASHINGTON NAVY YARD, Washington, D.C., with field offices at Newport, Rhode Island; Norfolk, Virginia; Pensacola, Florida; Camp Lejeune, North Carolina; Mayport, Florida; Los Angeles (Upland), California; San Diego, California, Bangor, Washington; Pearl Harbor, Hawaii; Naples, Italy; Yokosuka, Japan; and Manama, Bahrain.

Naval District Washington

NDW encompasses some 4,000 square miles, including the District of Columbia; the Maryland counties of Calvert, Charles, Montgomery, Prince George's, and St. Mary's; the northern Virginia counties of Loudoun, Fauquier, Fairfax, Prince William, Stafford, King George, Westmoreland, and Arlington; and the cities within their outer boundaries—a total of 400 commands and activities and more than 67,000 military and civilian employees. NDW is nicknamed the "Quarterdeck of the Navy," because it is here that most of the central command function is handled.

In addition to the WASHINGTON NAVY YARD and the Naval District Washington Anacostia Annex, Naval District Washington includes: NATIONAL NAVAL MEDICAL CENTER (Bethesda), the Nebraska Avenue Complex, U.S. NAVAL OBSERVATORY, the Potomac Annex, Arlington Service Center, NAVAL RESEARCH LABORATORY, National Maritime Intelligence Center, Naval Air Facility Washington, and NRC Solomons.

Naval Facilities Engineering Command (NAVFAC)

NAVFAC manages the planning, design, and construction of shore facilities for USN activities around the world. Staffed by 16,000 civilian and military personnel, NAVFAC's mission encompasses base development, planning, and design; military construction; public works; utilities and energy services; base realignment and closure; environmental programs; weight handling; military operations and contingency engineering; acquisition; real estate; family and bachelor housing; ocean engineering; and transportation planning and management. NAVFAC is headquartered at the WASHINGTON NAVY YARD in Washington, D.C., and has 11 engineering field divisions and engineering field activities located across the United States and Europe.

Naval Fleet Auxiliary Force (NFAF)

Operated by the MILITARY SEALIFT COMMAND, NFAF consists of 35 ships that provide fuel, food, ammunition, spare parts, and other supplies for the UNDERWAY REPLENISHMENT of the combat fleet. Ocean tugs, fast combat support ships, oilers, combat stores ships and ammunition ships, and two hospital ships make up NFAF; the ships, although government owned, are crewed by civil service mariners.

NFAF was established in 1972 after tests demonstrated that civilian crews could operate USN support ships more efficiently (at reduced cost) than USN sailors.

Naval Health Research Center

Located in San Diego, California, the center conducts research programs in human performance, modeling and simulation, field medical technologies, and behavioral science and epidemiology. The center also administers the Department of Defense Center for Deployment Health Research.

Naval Historical Center

The official history program of the DEPARTMENT OF THE NAVY, the Naval Historical Center is located at the WASHINGTON NAVY YARD, Washington, D.C. Its origin was in the founding of the Navy Department Library by President John Adams in 1800, and, today, the center encompasses a museum, an art gallery, a research library, and archives.

The Naval Historical Center is organized into branches according to the following specialized subject areas:

◆ Navy Museum: houses exhibits relating to U.S. naval history, 1775–present
◆ Navy Department Library: collections relating to naval and maritime history
◆ Operational Archives: contains USN records on operations, policy, and strategy, from 1946 to the present, as well as personal papers from 1900 to the present
◆ Curator Branch and Photographic Section: houses naval artifacts, including uniforms, armament, photographs, and artwork
◆ Navy Art Collection: exhibitions of the work of naval combat artists
◆ Ships History Branch: maintains histories of individual navy ships, 1775–present
◆ Naval Aviation History: holds documents and collections relating to naval aviation, 1911–present
◆ *Naval Aviation News* magazine: a professional magazine for active duty naval aviation personnel
◆ Early history: fosters research and writing on USN history 1775–1918

- Contemporary history: focuses on research and writing on USN history, 1945–present
- Underwater Archaeology Branch: advises on underwater archaeology issues
- Naval Historical Center Detachment Boston: maintains, repairs, and restores USS *Constitution*

Naval Meteorology and Oceanography Professional Development Center

The USN maintains the center at Gulfport, Mississippi, for the educational and professional guidance of USN and USMC meteorology and oceanography professionals. The center emphasizes the latest scientific advances in these fields.

Naval Network and Space Operations Command

NNSOC was formed in July 2002 by the merger of elements of Naval Space Command and Naval Network Operations Command to operate and maintain the USN's space and global telecommunications systems and services, support warfighting operations and command and control of naval forces, and promote innovative technological solutions to warfighting requirements. The mission of NNSOC is to enable naval forces to use information and space technologies to achieve and maintain the knowledge superiority necessary for dominating the "battle space," the entire field of battle in all its dimensions.

Operational space support to USN and USMC forces is coordinated and disseminated through the Naval Space Operations Center located at Dahlgren, Virginia. NAVSPOC monitors the status of all space systems as well as the location and operations of naval units, providing space-related operational intelligence to deployed units through various tactical communications channels. NAVSPOC also functions as the Alternate Space Control Center (ASCC) for U.S. Space Command's primary center located at Cheyenne Mountain Air Force Base, Colorado. As ASCC, the center's missions include operational direction of the global

Space Surveillance Network for U.S. Strategic Command, as well as the monitoring of the space environment to inform owners and operators of U.S. and allied space systems of potential threats to their assets.

Naval Oceanographic Office

The Naval Oceanographic Office conducts multidisciplinary ocean surveys; collects and analyzes all-source oceanographic data; provides global, numerical, oceanographic observations and products; tests and implements numerical techniques to solve oceanographic analytical and forecasting problems; and generates strategic, operational, and tactical oceanographic and geospatial products to meet the USN and Department of Defense safe navigation and weapon/sensor performance needs. NAVOCEANO is comprised of some 1,000 military and civilian personnel and maintains a fleet of forward-deployed survey vessels, which collect data worldwide. Additional data is collected by airborne and subsurface platforms, as well as by remote-sensing satellites and seaborne buoys. NAVOCEANO is located at the John C. Stennis Space Center in southern Mississippi near the Gulf of Mexico.

Naval Operational Medicine Institute

NOMI is headquartered at Pensacola, Florida, and is the principal training and consultive center for USN operational medicine. NOMI's origins may be traced to 1921, when the training of USN medical officers as flight surgeons was conducted at the U.S. Army School of Aviation Medicine, Mitchell Field, Long Island, New York. In 1939, the Medical Department of Naval Air Station Pensacola, Florida, assumed responsibility for the training of USN flight surgeons, and in 1965 the U.S. Naval School of Aviation Medicine became the U.S. Naval Aerospace Medical Institute. In 1992, the institute became the Naval Aerospace and Operational Medical Institute, and in 1996 assumed its present designation as the Naval Operational Medicine Institute, which reflects its expanded role as a research and teaching institute addressing all aspects of operational medicine, not just aviation medicine.

Naval Orientation and Recruiting Unit

The primary mission of NORU is to train personnel in support of recruitment, retention, and readiness. The unit consists of three major operations:

Enlisted Navy Recruiting Orientation (ENRO) is the basic enlisted recruiter orientation training conducted at NORU in Pensacola, Florida. The 25-day course allows students to learn, practice, and develop competence in professional selling skills, prospecting, paperwork and processing, marketing, public speaking, recruiter incentives and quality of life, and integrity and professionalism.

The Navy Recruiting Leadership Academy (NRLA) provides advanced training in recruitment and retention.

The National Training Team (NTT) assists the commander, Navy Recruiting Command, to identify operational and leadership trends that affect general recruiting productivity.

Naval Pacific Meteorology and Oceanography Center

Based in San Diego, California, the Naval Pacific Meteorology and Oceanography Center gathers, analyzes, and distributes meteorological and oceanographic data to USN and USMC units in support of ship, aircraft, and other operations.

Naval Packaging, Handling, Storage, and Transportation Center

Located at Colts Neck, New Jersey, the PHST Center is responsible for identification of life-cycle requirements, conception, design, development, prototype fabrication, test and evaluation, production acquisition, and documentation of ordnance containers and handling equipment for the USN. The center ensures that hazardous ordnance is handled and transported safely and efficiently.

Naval Postgraduate School

Located in Monterey, California, the Naval Postgraduate School is an academic institution offering study and research programs relevant to the interests of the USN and other service arms. The 627-acre campus has been home to NPS since 1947 and includes laboratories, academic buildings, a library, housing, and recreational facilities. About 1,500 students attend NPS, drawn from all U.S. uniformed services and with officers from some 30 other countries. Graduate education is fully funded, with enrollment based on outstanding professional performance as an officer, promotion potential, and strong academic background.

Naval Research Laboratory

NRL was created in 1992 as the result of the consolidation of the Navy Research, Development, Test and Evaluation Engineering facilities and Fleet Support facilities. NRL is aligned with the Office of Naval Research, the Naval Air Warfare Center, Naval Command Control and Ocean Surveillance Center, NAVAL SURFACE WARFARE CENTERS, and NAVAL UNDERSEA WARFARE CENTER. NRL's mission is to conduct a program of scientific research and advanced technological development directed toward maritime applications of new and improved materials, techniques, equipment, and systems, and ocean, atmospheric, and space sciences and related technologies. The laboratory is located in Washington, D.C.

Naval Reserve

The Naval Reserve, or U.S. Naval Reserve Force, provides mission-capable units and individuals to the USN and USMC during peace as well as war. Currently, the Naval Reserve represents 20 percent of total USN assets.

The Naval Reserve Force, numbering more than 690,000, consists of the Ready Reserve, the Standby Reserve, and the Retired Reserve. The Ready Reserve is made up, in turn, of a Selected Reserve and Individual Ready Reserve. The Selected Reserve is the primary USN source of immediate mobilization manpower. SELRES personnel are paid, either as weekend drillers or as full-time support personnel in the Training and Administration of the Reserves (TAR) program. Individual Ready Reserve (IRR) is a manpower pool in the Ready Reserve, consisting primarily of persons who have had training, who have served previously in the Active component or the Selected Reserve, and who have some period of a military obligation remaining. Although IRR members are in Ready Reserve status, they do not perform regularly scheduled training.

The Standby Reserve maintains USN affiliation without being in the Ready Reserve. Members are generally subject to involuntary active duty under full mobilization.

Retired Reserve are USN officers and enlisted personnel who receive retired pay, are under 60 years of age, and have not elected discharge. They may be ordered to active duty whenever required.

In 1887, the DEPARTMENT OF THE NAVY created a plan under which the SECRETARY OF THE NAVY was given authority to lend each state having a naval militia one of the USN's older ships, as well as equipment, to "promote drills and instruction." This precursor of the Naval Reserve was formalized by a 1915 act of Congress, creating a Federal Naval Reserve. On August 29, 1916, Congress passed the Naval Reserve Appropriations Act, which established the Naval Reserve Flying Corps. Subsequent legislation expanded the Naval Reserve to all components of the USN.

Naval Reserve Medal   See DECORATIONS AND MEDALS.

Naval Reserve Meritorious Service Medal
See DECORATIONS AND MEDALS.

Naval Reserve Officers' Training Corps (NROTC)
The mission of the NROTC program is to educate and train young men and women for service as commissioned officers in the USN or USMC. It is currently the largest single source of officers in these services.

Currently 69 colleges and universities operate a total of 57 NROTC units or consortiums. The program is available at more than 100 institutions. Annually, the USN seeks to commission 1,050 NROTC graduate officers. Selected NROTC applicants are awarded scholarships and receive full tuition and other financial benefits.

The NROTC was established in 1926 at the University of California at Berkeley, Georgia Institute of Technology, Northwestern University, University of Washington, and Harvard and Yale Universities. The first 126 midshipmen graduated in 1930 and received commissions in the U.S. Navy. The USMC entered the NROTC Program in 1932.

In 1968, Prairie View A&M became the first historically black college to host an NROTC program. In 1972, the SECRETARY OF THE NAVY authorized 16 women to enroll in the NROTC; women now participate in the program while attending any NROTC-affiliated college or university. In 1990, the NROTC Scholarship Program was expanded to include applicants pursuing a four-year degree in nursing, leading to a commission in the Navy Nurse Corps.

Naval Reserve Sea Service Ribbon   See DECORATIONS AND MEDALS.

Naval School of Health Sciences (NSHS)
Based at the NAVAL HEALTH RESEARCH CENTER in Bethesda, Maryland, NSHS offers programs in professional development; graduate medical education; continuing medical education; clinical investigation; clinical management; joint medical executive skills development; executive management education; physician assistant; and education and training governance. There is also a Medical Enlisted Commissioning Program.

Naval Sea Systems Command
NAVSEA, the largest of the U.S. Navy's five systems commands, engineers, builds, and supports the

USN fleet and USN combat systems. Its activities account for almost one-fifth of the USN budget. NAVSEA manages more than 130 acquisition programs, and the command consists of 50,000 men and women in four major shipyards, the undersea and surface warfare centers, and at various shipbuilding locations.

NAVSEA facilities are located worldwide; headquarters is at the WASHINGTON NAVY YARD.

Naval Special Warfare Command

NSWC was commissioned on April 16, 1987, at the Naval Amphibious Base in Coronado, California, and serves as the USN component of the United States Special Operations Command, headquartered in Tampa, Florida. The commander, Naval Special Warfare Command, prepares Naval Special Warfare (NSW) forces to carry out assigned missions and develops maritime special operations strategy, doctrine, and tactics.

NSW mission areas include unconventional warfare, direct action, combating terrorism, special reconnaissance, foreign internal defense, information warfare, security assistance, counter-drug operations, personnel recovery, and hydrographic reconnaissance. NSW units operate in maritime as well as riverine environments and are deployed in small units worldwide in support of fleet and national operations. Major operational components of NSWC include Naval Special Warfare Group ONE and Special Boat Squadron ONE in San Diego, California, and Naval Special Warfare Group TWO and Special Boat Squadron TWO in Norfolk, Virginia. Both of these components deploy SEAL teams worldwide.

Naval Supply Systems Command

NAVSUP provides USN forces with supplies and services, delivering information, material, services, and quality of life products. A workforce of nearly 24,000 employees manages logistics programs in supply, contracting, resale, fuel, transportation, security assistance, conventional ordnance, food service, and other quality of life programs.

The Naval Inventory Control Point (NAVICP) exercises centralized control over 350,000 different line items of repair parts.

The Navy Exchange Service Command (NEXCOM) includes 110 navy exchanges, 41 navy lodges, and 186 ships' stores. Sales exceed $2 billion annually and generate over $67 million in profits that support morale, welfare and recreation programs ashore and afloat.

The Fleet and Industrial Supply Centers (FISCs) provide a variety of logistics support services, including material management, contracting, transportation, fuel services, customer service, hazardous materials management, household goods movement support, consolidated mail services, and supply consultation.

The Navy Supply Information Systems Activity (NAVSISA) designs, develops, and maintains information systems supporting logistics, transportation, finance and accounting, and inventory math modeling.

The Naval Ammunition Logistics Center (NALC) provides centralized inventory management for the USN's non-nuclear ordnance stockpile.

The Naval Petroleum Office (NAVPETOFF) operates five major fuel depots and functions as technical adviser to the USN on petroleum matters.

The Naval Transportation Support Center (NAVTRANS) handles the transportation of USN material.

The Fitting Out and Supply Support Assistance Center (FOSSAC) provides USN forces and other federal agencies with logistics, engineering, training, and other support services.

Naval Surface Force, U.S. Atlantic Fleet

The Naval Surface Force, U.S. ATLANTIC FLEET, COMNAVSURFLANT (commander, Naval Surface Force, U.S. Atlantic Fleet), was established in 1975 as a consolidation of the Cruiser-Destroyer, Amphibious, Service and Mine Forces, U.S. Atlantic Fleet. Homeported in Norfolk, Virginia, the force encompasses 116 ships in addition to special mission and fleet support units, which make up, in total, more than 70 commands staffed by 35,000 sailors stationed variously in the United States (from Bath, Maine, to Corpus Christi, Texas) and on the high seas (from the Norwegian Sea in the Atlantic Ocean to the Persian Gulf of the Arabian Sea in the Indian Ocean).

NAVSURFLANT units include Destroyer Squadron 2, Destroyer Squadron 18, Destroyer Squadron 22, Destroyer Squadron 24, Destroyer Squadron 26, Combat Logistics Squadron 2, Carrier Group 2, Carrier Group 6, Carrier Group 8, Cruiser Destroyer Group 2, Cruiser Destroyer Group 8, Cruiser Destroyer Group 12, Surface Group 2, Surface Group MED, Amphibious Group 2, Mine Warfare Command, and Explosive Ordnance Disposal Group 2.

Naval Surface Force, U.S. Pacific Fleet

The Naval Surface Force, U.S. PACIFIC FLEET, COMNAVSURFPAC (commander, Naval Surface Force, U.S. Pacific Fleet), is headquartered in San Diego, California. The command ensures that surface ships of the Pacific Fleet are properly trained, maintained, and crewed for deployment over 102 million square miles of the Pacific and Indian Oceans.

Units include Destroyer Squadron 1; Destroyer Squadron 7; Destroyer Squadron 15; Destroyer Squadron 21; Destroyer Squadron 23; Destroyer Squadron 28; Carrier Group 1; Carrier Group 3; Carrier Group 5; Carrier Group 7; Cruiser Destroyer Group 1; Cruiser Destroyer Group 3; Cruiser Destroyer Group 5; Surface Group PAC-NORWEST; Surface Group MIDPAC; Logistics Group WESTPAC; Amphibious Group 1; Amphibious Group 3; and Explosive Ordnance Disposal Group 1.

Naval Surface Reserve Force

The Naval Surface Reserve Force maintains personnel and equipment in a state of readiness for rapid deployment as may be required.

The origin of the reserve force may be traced back to 1887, when the DEPARTMENT OF THE NAVY created a plan in which each state that maintained a naval militia was given one of the USN's older ships, as well as equipment, for drill and training purposes. The Federal Naval Reserve, direct precursor of the Naval Surface Reserve, was created in 1915.

Today's Naval Surface Reserve Force consists of 10 regional Naval Reserve Readiness Commands in addition to Naval Reserve Force ships, Mobile Inshore Undersea Warfare units, Naval Reserve Cargo Handling Battalions, Naval Reserve Fleet Hospitals, Special Boat Units, and other units.

Naval Surface Warfare Centers

NSWC operates the U.S. Navy's research, development, test and evaluation, engineering, and fleet support facilities for ship hull, mechanical, and electrical systems; surface ship combat systems; coastal warfare systems; and other offensive and defensive systems associated with surface warfare. The centers provide expertise in surface warfare modeling and analysis; surface ship combat and combat control systems; surface ship electronic warfare; surface ship electromagnetic and electro-optic reconnaissance, search, and track systems; surface ship weapons systems (including shipboard missile integration); surface ship vulnerability and survivability; ship active and passive signatures; surface and undersea vehicle hull, machinery, propulsors, and equipment; platform systems integration; strategic targeting support (including fire control, targeting, and reentry systems); amphibious warfare systems; special warfare systems; warheads; and mine countermeasure and mine clearance systems. The center's divisions include Naval Surface Warfare Center, Washington, D.C.; Naval Surface Warfare Center, Carderock Division, Hydromechanics Directorate; Naval Surface Warfare Center, Corona Division; Naval Surface Warfare Center, Crane Division; Naval Surface Warfare Center, Dahlgren Division; Naval Surface Warfare Center, Indian Head Division; and Naval Surface Warfare Center, Port Hueneme Division.

Naval Training Center Great Lakes

Located north of Chicago on Lake Michigan, NTCGL is home to the Great Lakes Naval Recruit Training Command (RTC) and is the central processing location for USN recruits, some 50,000 of whom pass through Great Lakes RTC annually. About 15,000 are onboard at any time, making the installation the third largest base in the USN. Great Lakes Service School Command (SSC), housed here, is the central training location for USN enlisted students. New recruits are onboard RTC for about nine weeks for basic training. SSC students are onboard from two weeks to 14 months, depending on the curriculum.

The center is operated by Naval Station Great Lakes (NAVSTA), which is staffed by 403 civilians and 198 military personnel. The base encompasses 1,628 acres.

The center was established in 1911 and has, since then, trained more than two million new sailors. Significantly, Great Lakes pioneered the racial integration of the USN. In 1942, Doreston Carmen, Jr., reported as the first African American for training in a general rating. Since 1994, RTC Great Lakes has been the only RTC in the USN, the only facility to offer basic training.

Naval Transportation Support Center

Located in Norfolk, Virginia, the NTSC is part of NAVAL SUPPLY SYSTEMS COMMAND and is responsible for all aspects of USN freight transportation.

Naval Treaty Implementation Program

The USN plays an important role in ensuring adherence to a variety of international arms control treaties and agreements. The Naval Treaty Implementation Program (NT 00) develops plans and procedures to ensure compliance with nonstrategic treaties and agreements. The program is staffed by senior military and civilian personnel with expertise in treaty implementation and compliance planning, policy, and preparation for treaty verification activities. The program provides information and assistance to other USN program managers, operating forces, and shore facilities regarding treaty requirements and verification activities.

Naval Undersea Warfare Center

NUWC was established on January 2, 1992, as the USN's research, development, test and evaluation, engineering and fleet support center for submarines, autonomous underwater systems, and offensive and defensive weapon systems associated with undersea warfare. The center consists of two major divisions, Division Newport located in Newport, Rhode Island, and Division Keyport located in Keyport, Washington. In addition, NUWC maintains several detachments from Andros Island in the Bahamas to Lualualei, Hawaii, and from San Diego, California, to Nanoose, British Columbia.

Naval Vessel Register

The NVR contains information on the ships and service craft of the USN inventory from the time of a vessel's authorization through its life cycle and disposal. The NVR also includes ships that have been stricken but not disposed. Although ships and service craft disposed of prior to 1987 are currently not included in the NVR, an ongoing program is gradually adding this data. The NVR may be accessed online at: www.nvr.navy.mil/.

Naval War College

The mission of the NWC is "to enhance the professional capabilities of its students to make sound decisions in command, staff, and management positions in naval, joint, and combined environments." NWC curriculum seeks to provide a sound understanding of military strategy and operational art and to "instill . . . joint attitudes and perspectives." Additionally, the NWC serves as a center for research and wargaming to develop advanced strategic, warfighting, and campaign concepts.

The NWC was established on October 6, 1884, at Coaster's Harbor Island, Newport, Rhode Island.

From the beginning, faculty included naval officers as well as officers from other services and civilian scholars. In 1981, the Center for Naval Warfare Studies was established within the NWC to bring together the related research programs of the Advanced Research Program for students, the War Gaming Department, and the Naval War College Press. Since the establishment of the center, the Naval War College has hosted the CHIEF OF NAVAL OPERATIONS' Strategic Studies Group, a cadre of USN and USMC officers selected by the CNO and the commandant of the Marine Corps to conduct original research.

navigation research/missile range instrumentation ship (T-AG)

Operated as a SPECIAL MISSION SHIP by the MILITARY SEALIFT COMMAND, USNS *Vanguard* (T-AG-194) is currently the navy's only navigational test launch ship, which performs tests related to research on various missile navigational systems.

Vanguard Class (T-AGM-19 / T-AG-194)

This class originally consisted of two ships, *Vanguard* (T-AGM-20 / T-AG-194) and *Redstone* (T-AGM-20); *Redstone* was decommissioned in 1993.

Missile range instrumentation ships (T-AGM) were designed to perform tracking, telemetry, and communication functions for the *Apollo* lunar landing missions during the late 1960s and 1970s. During the launch phase and Earth-orbit insertion phase, it was these ships that filled the gaps beyond the range and capability of land-tracking facilities. With the end of the *Apollo* era, the array of antennas and associated communications gear were removed from the ships, and equipment for testing different modes of submarine navigation installed. *Redstone* was decommissioned on August 6, 1993, and *Vanguard* was reclassified as a navigational test launch ship (designated T-AG-194) in September 1980. *Vanguard's* test equipment was upgraded in May 1997 to enable it to serve as a range instrumentation ship in support of the fleet ballistic missile program.

Specifications of this class include:

Builder: Marine Ship Corporation, Sausalito, California
Power plant: turbo-electric, two boilers, eight Westinghouse turbo-generators, 10,000 horsepower, one motor, one shaft
Length: 595 ft
Beam: 75 ft
Displacement: 24,761 tons full load
Speed: 14 knots
Crew: 45 civilian mariners, 18 scientists, plus 141 spare personnel

Navy Arctic Service Ribbon   See DECORATIONS AND MEDALS.

Navy Crane Center

The center provides engineering, acquisition, technical support, training, and evaluation services for USN "weight handling" programs. The center is headquartered in Lester, Pennsylvania, and maintains field offices at Portsmouth, New Hampshire; Norfolk, Virginia; Bremerton and Poulsbo, Washington; San Diego, California; and Pearl Harbor, Hawaii.

Navy Cross   See DECORATIONS AND MEDALS.

Navy Environmental Health Center

Headquartered in Portsmouth, Virginia, the NEHC works to promote health and prevent disease in the USN and USMC. The center coordinates and provides centralized support for issues relating to occupational health, environmental health, and preventive medicine. NEHC also administers USN Drug Screening Laboratories.

Navy Expeditionary Medal   See DECORATIONS AND MEDALS.

Navy Experimental Diving Unit

Located in Panama City, Florida, NEDU tests and evaluates diving, hyperbaric, and other life-support systems and procedures, and conducts research and development in biomedical and environmental physiology for divers. The unit consists of about 160 military divers and support personnel and serves such USN personnel as SEALs, Explosive Ordnance Disposal (EOD), salvage, saturation, and SEABEES personnel, and undersea medical officers (UMO). Facilities include the Ocean Simulation Facility (OSF), a chamber that simulates ocean conditions to a maximum pressure equivalent of 2,250 feet of seawater (fsw) and at any salinity level; the Unmanned Test Facility, used to gather equipment performance data without risking lives; and the Test Pool, used to evaluate manned diving equipment and small submersible vehicles.

Navy Flight Test

The USN flight test organization supports the development and acquisition of naval aeronautical and related technology systems by providing the personnel and facilities for extensive testing of aircraft and other flight-related systems. Flight test programs test and evaluate air vehicles, avionics, electronic warfare and sensor systems, mechanical and cargo systems, propulsion systems, ship suitability, and weapons systems. Principal testing facilities are located at China Lake, California, and Patuxent River, Maryland.

Navy Manpower Analysis Center

NAVMAC is located in Millington, Tennessee, and serves as the USN's central manpower organization, using industrial engineering methods to assess and determine the composition of billets (positions) required to run the USN most efficiently. NAVMAC defines "Occupational Standards" for all USN jobs and monitors training, making recommendations for training needs.

Navy/Marine Corps Achievement Medal
See DECORATIONS AND MEDALS.

Navy/Marine Corps Commendation Medal   See DECORATIONS AND MEDALS.

Navy/Marine Corps Medal   See DECORATIONS AND MEDALS.

Navy/Marine Corps Overseas Service Ribbon   See DECORATIONS AND MEDALS.

Navy Occupation Service Medal   See DECORATIONS AND MEDALS.

Navy Personnel Research, Studies, and Technology

NPRST is the DEPARTMENT OF THE NAVY's personnel research and development laboratory, which conducts research and development to improve the performance of individuals, teams, and organizations within the USN and USMC. NPRST is staffed by civilian researchers, military experts, university consultants, and commercial contractors with the aim of improving personnel planning, testing, recruiting, selection, classification, training, utilization, motivation, organization, and management. NPRST encompasses five research institutes: Institute for Personnel Planning and Policy Analysis, which conducts research and develops new technologies and methods for managing the USN workforce through planning and policy development; Institute for Distribution and Assignment, which researches and develops new technologies and methods of distributing and assigning personnel to billets to improve military readiness while better managing careers and control costs; Institute for Selection and Classification, which researches and develops technologies and procedures for recruiting, selecting, and classifying enlisted personnel to reduce attrition while improving satisfaction, performance, and retention; Institute for Organizational Assessment, which conducts research and development to improve USN understanding of its diverse workforce; and Institute for Enabling Technologies, which assesses new and emerging technologies for their potential application to manpower and personnel research and studies.

NPRST is located in Millington, Tennessee.

Navy Petroleum Office

NAVPETOFF is a field activity of the NAVAL SUPPLY SYSTEMS COMMAND and acts as a technical and functional manager for all petroleum programs in the DEPARTMENT OF NAVY. Located at the Defense Logistics Agency (DLA) Headquarters Complex Building, Fort Belvoir, Virginia, NAVPETOFF encompasses the Petroleum Systems Division, which addresses all matters relating to petroleum systems, petroleum policy, and fiscal and administrative functions; the Facilities Engineering Division, which provides technical support and engineering services for fuel-related military construction projects; the Fuel Management Division, which oversees all USN fuel programs and provides contractual and technical assistance; and the Resource Management Division, which oversees the fiscal resourcing and administration of NAVPETOFF.

Navy Primary Standards Laboratory

The Navy Primary Standards Laboratory is staffed by professional metrologists and is charged with maintaining and disseminating standard, accurate physical units of measurement within the USN. A major laboratory activity is providing the means and methods for precise instrument and other calibration. The Navy Primary Standards Laboratory is located at the Naval Aviation Depot complex on Naval Air Station North Island, California.

Navy Public Works Centers

The Navy Public Works Centers provide utilities, facilities maintenance, family housing services, transportation support, engineering services, and shore facilities planning support to USN afloat and ashore operating forces and other activities. The centers provide base support to military, federal, state, and local activities located within nine regional areas. Included is support to Department of Defense, USA, USAF, USMC, USCG, NASA, and a variety of state and federal activities in addition to support to USN activities.

Navy Recruiting Command

Headquartered at Millington, Tennessee, the Navy Recruiting Command is charged with recruiting men and women for enlisted, officer candidate, and officer active duty status in the regular and reserve components of the USN. The command is staffed by highly screened volunteers, most of whom have chosen recruiting as a career.

The origin of the command may be traced to 1775 when, during the AMERICAN REVOLUTION, the Continental Congress established a Marine Committee, which appointed a single recruiter. Later, the SECRETARY OF THE NAVY had direct responsibility for recruiting. Later still, the Bureau of Construction and Repair took charge, and then the Bureau of Navigation. During WORLD WAR II, in 1942, the function was assigned to the BUREAU OF NAVAL PERSONNEL. On April 6, 1971, the secretary of the navy approved the establishment of the Navy Recruiting Command.

Navy Region Hawaii

Navy Region Hawaii is the largest and most strategic USN island base in the Pacific, extending over more than 12,600 acres of land and water, and serving as the headquarters of five major fleet commands, including commander, U.S. PACIFIC FLEET (PACFLT). Commander, Navy Region Hawaii (COMNAVREG), serves as the regional coordinator for all shore-based USN personnel and shore activities in Hawaii, Midway Island, Kure Island, and the islands of Wake, Johnston, Palmyra, and Kingman Reef—a total land and water area of about 59,516 acres. The most important mission of

COMNAVREG is coordinating USN local support of the Pacific Fleet, including port and housekeeping services for more than 40 surface ships and submarines homeported in Pearl Harbor, and more than 70 shore commands and activities.

Navy Region Northeast

Navy Region Northeast consists of Naval Submarine Base New London, Connecticut; Naval Air Station Brunswick, Maine; Portsmouth Naval Shipyard, Kittery, Maine; Naval Weapons Station, Earle, New Jersey; and Naval Station Newport, Rhode Island. Under the commander in chief, U.S. ATLANTIC FLEET, commander Navy Region Northeast (COMNAVREG NORTHEAST) commands and supports the bases and facilities in the region and also serves as commander, Submarine Group TWO.

Navy Region Northwest

Navy Region Northwest is regional coordinator for the USN in Washington, Oregon, Idaho, and Alaska. The command also serves as the authority responsible for reporting to (senior) the commander in chief, U.S. PACIFIC FLEET (headquartered in Hawaii), for Naval Air Station Whidbey Island, Naval Station Everett, Naval Station Bremerton, Submarine Base Bangor, and Naval Magazine Indian Island. Most of the region's commands are along Puget Sound, which is the USN's third largest fleet concentration area, its installations and facilities occupying more than 28,000 acres and employing 26,000 active duty members, 16,000 civilian employees, and 6,000 drilling reservists.

Navy Region Southeast

Commander, Navy Region Southeast (COMNAVREGSE), leads the coordinated work of 14 commands and activities supporting the fleet in the southeastern United States and the Caribbean. The region includes Naval Air Station Jacksonville, Florida; Naval Air Station Key West, Florida; Naval Station Mayport, Florida; Naval Station Roosevelt Roads, Puerto Rico; Naval Station Pascagoula, Mississippi; Naval Base Guantánamo Bay, Cuba; Submarine Base Kings Bay, Georgia; Naval Weapons Station Charleston, South Carolina; Naval Construction Battalion Center Gulfport, Mississippi; Public Works Center Jacksonville, Florida; Naval Hospital Charleston, South Carolina; Naval Hospital Jacksonville, Florida; and Navy Dental Center, Jacksonville, Florida.

Navy Region Southwest

Navy Region Southwest encompasses USN facilities and activities in California, Arizona, and Nevada, coordinating base operating support functions for operating forces throughout this region. The command is also regional coordinator for the commander, U.S. Pacific Fleet, headquartered in Hawaii. Bases included in Navy Region Southwest are Naval Station San Diego, California; Naval Base Point Loma, California (formerly SUBASE San Diego); Naval Base Coronado, California; Naval Air Facility El Centro, California; Naval Air Station Lemoore, California; Naval Base Ventura County, California; Naval Weapons Station Seal Beach, California; and Naval Air Station, Fallon, Nevada.

Navy Unit Commendation   See DECORATIONS AND MEDALS.

Nimitz, Chester William (1885–1966) *navy admiral*

Commander of the U.S. PACIFIC FLEET during WORLD WAR II, Nimitz was born in Fredericksburg, Texas, and graduated from the UNITED STATES NAVAL ACADEMY in 1905. After serving as an ensign on the China station, he transferred to the SUBMARINE *Plunger*. Promoted to lieutenant in 1910, he took command of the submarine *Skipjack*. Two years later, he assumed command of the Atlantic Submarine Flotilla. Sent to Germany and Belgium in 1913 to study diesel engine design, Nimitz returned to the United States to direct construction of the USN's first diesel ship engine.

Admiral Chester Nimitz   *(National Archives and Records Administration)*

Promoted to lieutenant commander in 1916, Nimitz was appointed chief of staff to the commander of the ATLANTIC FLEET's submarine division following U.S. entry into WORLD WAR I in 1917. After the war, Nimitz was promoted to commander (1921) and attended the NAVAL WAR COLLEGE (1922–23). From 1923 to 1925, he was attached to the staff of the commander in chief, Battle Fleet, then, during 1925–26, served on the staff of the commander in chief, U.S. Fleet. After this, he organized the first training division for naval reserve officers at the University of California and served as administrator of this program from 1926 to 1929. Promoted to captain (1927), he was assigned command of Submarine Division 20 from 1929 to 1931.

Nimitz took command of the CRUISER USS *Augusta* in 1933, leaving this command in 1935 to become assistant chief of the Bureau of Navigation. After promotion to rear admiral in 1938, he took command of a cruiser division and then a battleship division. In 1939, he returned to the Bureau of Navigation as its chief.

Following the relief of Admiral HUSBAND E. KIMMEL on December 17, 1941 (10 days after the Japanese attack on Pearl Harbor), Nimitz was promoted to admiral and, on December 31, named to replace Kimmel as commander in chief of the Pacific Fleet. The new commander vigorously reorganized the defenses of the Hawaiian Islands and ramrodded the rebuilding of the shattered Pacific Fleet. On March 30, 1942, he was assigned unified command of all forces, sea, land, and air, in the Pacific Ocean Area. Exploiting superb naval intelligence, Nimitz checked Japanese operations against Port Moresby at the Battle of the Coral Sea on May 7–8, 1942, then at the make-or-break Battle of Midway during June 2–6, 1942. Nimitz was also largely responsible for the grand Allied strategy of "island-hopping," the selective conquest of Japanese-held islands, which served to destroy forces that were attacked while totally isolating forces that were bypassed.

Nimitz took personal command of campaigns in the Gilbert Islands (November 20–23, 1943) and the Marshalls (January 31–February 23, 1944), but, more characteristically, delegated tactical authority to trusted subordinates. One of his greatest strengths was the ability to lead and to inspire. During June 14–August 10, 1944, Nimitz personally directed the advance into the Marianas and then into the Palaus from September 15 to November 25. Simultaneously, he coordinated with General Douglas MacArthur the invasion of Leyte in the American return to the Philippines on October 20, 1944.

On December 15, 1944, Nimitz was promoted to the newly created rank of fleet admiral, then commanded the capture of Iwo Jima during February 19–March 24, 1945 and Okinawa (April 1–June 21, 1945). From January to August 1945, he also directed operations against the Japanese home islands. The Japanese surrender, on September 2, 1945, took place on Nimitz's flagship, USS *Missouri.*

After the war, Nimitz served as CHIEF OF NAVAL OPERATIONS from December 15, 1945, to December 15, 1947, and was then appointed special assistant to the SECRETARY OF THE NAVY, serving in this capacity during 1948–49. Appointed United Nations commissioner for Kashmir, he served from 1949 to 1951, then retired to write (with E. B. Potter) *Sea Power: A Naval History,* published in 1960.

NR-1 Naval Research Vessel See SUBMARINES.

O

oceanographer of the navy

The oceanographer of the navy is the resource sponsor for the Naval Meteorology and Oceanography Command in the Office of the CHIEF OF NAVAL OPERATIONS and is headquartered at the John C. Stennis Space Center near Bay St. Louis, Mississippi.

Oceanography studies the nature and behavior of the oceans, including such critical factors as temperature, salinity, and the influence of pressure at various depths. All of this information is vital to USN operations. Additionally, the oceanographer studies sea ice for its influence on ocean acoustics and the potential hazards it presents to navigation.

Oceanographic Surveillance Ships (T-AGOS)   See RESEARCH SHIPS.

Oceanographic Survey Ships (T-AGS)   See RESEARCH SHIPS.

Ohio Class (SSBN-726)   See SUBMARINES.

Oliver Hazard Perry Class (FFG-7)   See FRIGATES.

operating forces

Operating forces are those having as their primary mission participation in combat or the integral support of combat. U.S. Navy operating forces commanders report administratively to the CHIEF OF NAVAL OPERATIONS and provide, train, and equip naval forces. Operationally, they provide naval forces and report to the appropriate unified combatant commanders. USN operating forces include NAVAL RESERVE FORCES; Operational Test and Evaluation Forces; NAVAL SPECIAL WARFARE COMMAND; UNITED STATES NAVAL FORCES EUROPE; NAVAL FORCES CENTRAL COMMAND; MILITARY SEALIFT COMMAND; ATLANTIC FLEET; and PACIFIC FLEET.

See also ORGANIZATION.

organization

The U.S. Navy was founded on October 13, 1775, and the DEPARTMENT OF THE NAVY was created on April 30, 1798. The department is composed of three main components: the Department of the Navy itself, with offices principally in Washington, D.C.; the Operating Forces (which includes the U.S. Marine Corps and, in war, the U.S. Coast Guard); and the Shore Establishment. Overall, the SECRETARY OF THE NAVY is the executive of the USN. Directly reporting to him or her is the CHIEF OF NAVAL OPERATIONS, who exercises direct control over the Operating Forces and the Shore Establishment. Also directly reporting to the secretary of the navy is the commandant of the Marine Corps, who directly controls USMC Operating Forces.

With the Secretariat—the office of the secretary of the navy—are a host of commanders and administrators, the most important of whom are the undersecretary of the navy, four assistant secretaries (Research, Development, and Acquisition; Manpower and Reserve Affairs; Financial Management and Comptroller; and Installations and Environment), and the general counsel of the Department of the Navy.

The chief of naval operations (CNO), senior military officer of the USN, is responsible to the secretary of the navy for the command, utilization of resources, and operating efficiency of the Operating Forces and the Shore Establishment. The major administrators who report directly to the CNO include the director, Navy Staff; five deputy chiefs of naval operations—DCNO Manpower and Personnel; DCNO Plans, Policy, and Operations; DCNO Fleet Readiness and Logistics; DCNO Warfare Requirements and Programs; and DCNO Resources, Requirements, and Assessments—and the director of Naval Intelligence. Also reporting to the CNO are the director of test and evaluation and technology requirements, the surgeon general of the navy, the director of the NAVAL RESERVE, the OCEANOGRAPHER OF THE NAVY, and the CHIEF OF NAVY CHAPLAINS.

Commanders in the Operating Forces have a dual chain of command. Administratively, they report to the CNO, and, operationally, they provide naval forces and report to the unified combatant commanders. The Operating Forces include Naval Reserve Forces, Operational Test and Evaluation Forces, NAVAL SPECIAL WARFARE COMMAND, UNITED STATES NAVAL FORCES EUROPE, UNITED STATES NAVAL FORCES CENTRAL COMMAND, and MILITARY SEALIFT COMMAND. Also under the Operational Forces are the ATLANTIC FLEET (including Fleet Marines) and PACIFIC FLEET (including Fleet Marines). The Fleet Forces Command coordinates the two fleets. Within the fleets, (commanders responsible for particular types of forces, such as naval air force, submarine force, and surface force) administer major force components.

The Shore Establishment supports the Operating Forces, which are often collectively called "the fleet," providing facilities for the repair of machinery and electronics; for communications centers; training areas and simulators; ship and aircraft repair; intelligence and meteorological support; storage areas for repair parts, fuel, and munitions; medical and dental facilities; and air bases.

The major departments of the Shore Establishment include: BUREAU OF NAVAL PERSONNEL, BUREAU OF MEDICINE AND SURGERY, and Office of the Chief of Naval Operations. The major commands and centers active in the Shore Establishment are the NAVAL SEA SYSTEMS COMMAND; SPACE AND NAVAL WARFARE SYSTEMS COMMAND; NAVAL AIR SYSTEMS COMMAND; Strategic Systems Programs; NAVAL FACILITIES ENGINEERING COMMAND; UNITED STATES NAVAL ACADEMY; NAVAL SUPPLY SYSTEMS COMMAND; Naval Education and Training Command; Naval Meteorology and Oceanography Command; Naval Legal Service Command; Office of Naval Intelligence; UNITED STATES NAVAL OBSERVATORY; Naval Strike and Air Warfare Center; Naval Safety Center; and Naval Security Group Command.

On the operational level, the USN is organized very differently from the USA and USMC. Such units as the division, corps, brigade, battalion, company, and platoon, universal in the USA and USMC, are not used in the USN, except in a few special instances. Generally, USN operational organization is based on department and function rather than on a traditional or generic unit. This is most apparent aboard ship, in which officers and sailors are assigned to the Navigation Department, the Operations Department, the Supply Department, the Engineering Department, the Weapons and Combat Systems Department, and other departments as appropriate to a particular ship. Within each department are several divisions, their number and function depending on the size and mission of the department and the ship. Each division is headed by a division officer. The USN considers the division to be the basic unit of shipboard organization. The division, however, is itself divided into watches or sections or both. Personnel in these subdivisions are assigned to specific duties and/or time-delimited shifts within the division.

The organization of USN aircraft squadrons differs somewhat from shipboard organization. A squadron typically has a single or primary mission (combat, rescue, transport, for example), and each squadron is divided into departments, always including an Administrative Department and a Safety Department and usually also including an Operations Department and a Maintenance Department. Additionally, depending on the mission of the squadron, there may also be a Training Department, a Photographic Department, an Intelligence Department, and others, as appropriate. Each department is usually divided into divisions. For example, the Administrative Department typically includes a Personnel Division (sometimes called an Office), an Educational Services Division (Office), a Public Affairs Division (Office), and a Legal Division (Office); the Safety Department usually includes a Ground Safety Division, an Aviation Safety Division, and a Naval Air Training and Operating Procedures Standardization (NATOPS) Division. In turn, divisions may be further divided into branches, the officers and enlisted personnel of which are assigned specific responsibilities within the division's functions.

Two or more USN air squadrons may be grouped together into wings. In the USAF, squadrons are usually made up of four flights, which are typically units of three to five aircraft. In the USN, however, a flight is any group of aircraft engaged in a common mission. Some flights may be functionally subdivided into elements, which consist of two or more aircraft.

Occasionally, the USN uses such terms as battalion and brigade. However, in contrast to the USA and USMC, in which these terms are associated with a particular position in the organizational hierarchy and imply a specified number of personnel, level of commander, and types of equipment, the USN uses these terms to identify units that have a specific mission—for example, a SEABEE battalion. Another special case is the SEALs, in which the basic organization is the SEAL platoon.

Osprey Class (MHC 51)   See MINESWEEPERS, COASTAL MINEHUNTERS, AND MINE COUNTERMEASURES SHIPS.

P

Pacific Fleet

The Pacific Fleet covers more than half of the Earth's surface, some 100 million square miles. The fleet operates about 200 ships and 2,000 aircraft; its personnel number more than 239,000 sailors, marines, and civilians. The fleet is active in the Indian and Arctic Oceans as well as the Pacific.

Pacific Fleet staff report administratively to the CHIEF OF NAVAL OPERATIONS and operationally to the U.S. Pacific Command. Reporting to fleet are type commanders, numbered fleet commanders (and operational commanders), and regional commanders. Type commanders include commander, Naval Air Force, U.S. Pacific Fleet (COMNAVAIRPAC); commander, Naval Surface Force, U.S. Pacific Fleet (COMNAVSURFPAC); commander, Submarine Force, U.S. Pacific Fleet (COMSUBPAC); commander, Third Naval Construction Brigade (COMTHIRDNCB); and Marine Forces Pacific (MARFORPAC). Numbered fleet and operational commanders include commander, Third Fleet (COMTHIRDFLEET); commander, Seventh Fleet (COMSEVENTHFLT); commander, Task Force 12 (CTF-12); commander, Task Force 14 (CTF-14); commander, Maritime Defense Zone Pacific (MARDEZPAC); and Pacific Fleet regional coordinators. Regional coordinators include commander, Naval Forces, Japan (COMNAVFORJAPAN); commander, Naval Forces, Korea (COMNAVFORKOREA); commander, Naval Forces, Marianas (COMNAVMARIANAS); commander, Navy Region Southwest; commander, Navy Region Northwest; and commander, Navy Region Hawaii.

Pathfinder Class (T-AGS 60)   See RESEARCH SHIPS.

patrol coastal ships (PC)

All operational navy PC craft arc of the *Cyclone* and *Tornado* classes, their mission to perform coastal patrol and interdiction surveillance. They are especially well suited to the maritime homeland security mission and are deployed jointly with the USCG to protect America's coastline, ports, and waterways from terrorist attack.

Cyclone Class (PC)

The *Cyclone* class of patrol coastal ships (PC) perform coastal patrol and interdiction surveillance. The ships also provide full mission support for SEALs and other special operations forces. The *Cyclone*-class ships are assigned to NAVAL SPECIAL WARFARE COMMAND, with nine operating out of Naval Amphibious Base Little Creek, Virginia, and four out of Naval Amphibious Base Coronado, California. The lead ship of the class, *Cyclone* (PC 1), was decommissioned and turned over to the U.S. Coast Guard in February 2000.

General specifications of the *Cyclone* class include:

Builder: Bollinger Shipyards, Inc.
Length, overall: 169 ft 4.25 in
Beam, maximum: 25 ft
Length, waterline: 157 ft 5.75 in
Draft above bottom of keel corresponding to full load
Displacement: 315.32 tons full load
Height (highest projection above baseline to lowest projection below baseline): 58 ft 3.75 in
Superstructure material: 5086 aluminum
Fuel capacity: 12,620 gal
Fresh water capacity: 1,242 gal
Lubricating oil: 150 gal
Boats: one 20-foot RIB, two Combat Rubber Raiding Craft (Large)
Crew: 30
Capacity (including crew): 39 persons
Maximum speed: 35 knots
Cruising speed: 25 knots
Minimum maneuvering speed: 3 knots
Seaworthiness: survives through sea state 5
Range: 2,000 nautical miles at most economical speed over 12 knots
Endurance: 10 days
Propulsion: four Paxman, Type Valenta 16CM Diesel, Model 16RP200M, rating 3,350 base horsepower at 1,500 engine rpm
Propellers: five-bladed fixed-pitch nickel aluminum bronze
Generators: two Caterpillar Model 3306 DITA, rating 150 kilowatts at 1,800 rpm
Air conditioning plants: 83.33 kilowatt (23.7 tons) total
Desalinators: reverse osmosis desalinators, 400 gallons per day

Ships of the class include *Cyclone* (PC 1, decommissioned and turned over to the USCG in 2000), *Tempest* (PC 2), *Hurricane* (PC 3), *Monsoon* (PC 4), *Typhoon* (PC 5), *Sirocco* (PC 6), *Squall* (PC 7), *Zephyr* (PC 8), *Chinook* (PC 9), *Firebolt* (PC 10), *Whirlwind* (PC 11), *Thunderbolt* (PC 12), and *Shamal* (PC 13).

Tornado Class (PC)

Launched in 1999, *Tornado* (PC 14) is at present the only PC ship of its class. Its mission is to conduct coastal patrol, surveillance, and interdiction, and to support navy special warfare forces (SEALs) in their various areas of responsibility.

General specifications of the *Tornado* class include:

Overall length: 179 ft
Extreme beam: 25 ft
Maximum navigational draft: 9 ft
Displacement: 387 tons full load
Dead weight: 35 tons
Hull material: steel
Superstructure material: aluminum
Propulsion: diesel engines
Number of propellers: four
Maximum speed: 35 knots
Cruising speed: 25 knots
Crew: officers, four; enlisted, 24; SEALs, nine; reserve, two

Pearl Harbor, Japanese attack on

WORLD WAR II began in Europe on September 1, 1939, when Germany invaded Poland. Although the United States remained neutral, the administration of President Franklin D. Roosevelt increasingly provided arms and other aid to the Allies fighting Nazi and fascist aggression. In the Pacific and Asia, Japan was allied with Germany and Italy, and, throughout the 1930s, relations between Japan and the United States deteriorated. Since the early 1930s, Japan had been waging war against China, in violation of the U.S.-designed "Open Door" policy, which guaranteed Chinese independence. In an effort to pressure Japanese withdrawal from China, the Roosevelt administration embargoed a host of raw material exports to Japan. The Japanese recognized that the shortages thereby created might soon force a withdrawal from China; however, the militarists who controlled the Japanese government resolved not to back down or withdraw, but, rather, to move so swiftly and aggressively throughout Asia and the Pacific that the

United States would be overwhelmed into helplessness. Moreover, the Japanese expected that the United States would inevitably join the war in Europe and would thereby be disabled from fighting a simultaneous war on the Pacific front.

Operating according to this aggressive policy, at 7:55 A.M. (local time), December 7, 1941, approximately 200 carrier-launched dive bombers and torpedo planes attacked navy and army facilities at Pearl Harbor, Territory of Hawaii. Although the military had been warned to expect war, last-minute peace talks were under way in Washington, D.C., even as the attack began, and, through a complex combination of poor planning, lack of coordination between the navy and army, failure to exercise intelligence assets and to heed them, complacency, and just plain disbelief, the Japanese attack was virtually unopposed. The results were devastating. The battleships *Arizona, Oklahoma,*

California, Nevada, and *West Virginia* were sunk, and three other battleships, three CRUISERS, three DESTROYERS, and other vessels were severely damaged. On the ground, 180 U.S. aircraft were destroyed. Casualties totaled more than 3,400 persons, including more than 2,403 killed. In contrast, Japanese losses were light: 29 to 60 planes shot down, five midget submarines and possibly one or two fleet submarines lost. Total deaths among Japanese sailors and airmen were fewer than 100. The one piece of good fortune the PACIFIC FLEET had was that its AIRCRAFT CARRIERS were at sea during the attack and, therefore, escaped damage. It was these vessels that would carry the brunt of the Pacific naval war, especially during its first months.

On December 8, 1941, President Roosevelt asked Congress for a declaration of war. Because of Japan's alliance with Italy and Germany, the decla-

The ammunition magazine of a USN battleship explodes after a direct hit by Japanese aircraft.   *(Arttoday)*

A survivor is rescued near the USS *West Virginia* during the Japanese attack on Pearl Harbor, December 7, 1941.   *(Naval Historical Foundation)*

ration was also a de facto declaration against those nations.

Tactically, the attack on Pearl Harbor was a stunning Japanese triumph. Strategically, however, it was a disaster of such magnitude that, as historian Samuel Eliot Morison wrote, "one can search military history in vain for an operation more fatal to the aggressor." Pearl Harbor instantly galvanized vacillating and isolationist Americans into resolute warriors. Although other U.S. holdings in the Pacific fell in rapid succession, American military mobilization, already underway before the attack, kicked into high gear. Japan, which spent the early months of the war marching from one victory to another, was doomed.

Peary, Robert Edwin (1856–1920) *navy engineer and explorer*

Peary was the first man to reach the North Pole, on April 6, 1909, a feat for which he was promoted to rear admiral. Born in Cresson, Pennsylvania, he joined the USN as an engineer in 1881, then became interested in Arctic exploration. In 1886 he led a reconnaissance expedition of the Greenland icecap, and in 1891 was chief of a USN Arctic expedition. His second Arctic voyage came in 1893–95 and a third in 1898–1902. It was on his fourth expedition that he, plus a member of his USN crew and four Eskimos, reached the North Pole.

Pegasus Class (PHM 1) See HYDROFOILS.

Penguin missile See MISSILES.

Permit Class (SSN-594) See SUBMARINES.

Perry, Matthew Calbraith (1794–1858)
navy commodore

This USN officer is most famous for his 1852–54 naval expedition to Japan, during which he negotiated the Treaty of Kanagawa, which opened the long-isolated country to Western commerce.

He was born in Rocky Brook, Rhode Island, and joined the navy as a midshipman in 1807. He served in the BARBARY WARS during 1815–16, and in 1826 was promoted to master commandant and assigned to command the New York Navy Yard. In this post he was a champion of the USN adoption of steam propulsion.

Perry was promoted to captain in 1837 and to commodore in 1841. He worked with Secretary of the Navy George Bancroft to create the curriculum for the new UNITED STATES NAVAL ACADEMY at Annapolis, Maryland. With the outbreak of the U.S.-MEXICAN WAR, Perry participated in the naval blockade of Mexico's east coast, led an expedition up the Tabasco River in 1846, and in 1847 supported General Winfield Scott's assault on and capture of Veracruz. After the war, Perry supervised construction of mail steamers, then, in 1852, assumed leadership of a squadron that visited Japan to establish diplomatic and commercial relations with that country. By opening Japan to the West, the expedition had a momentous effect on Japanese culture.

Perry, Oliver Hazard (1785–1819) *navy captain*

One of the U.S. Navy's greatest heroes, Perry's remarkable victory at the Battle of Lake Erie helped turn the tide in the WAR OF 1812. He was born at Rocky Brook, Rhode Island, and was the older brother of MATTHEW C. PERRY. Joining the navy in 1799 as a midshipman under his father, Christopher R. Perry, captain of the 28-gun frigate USS *General Greene,* he was promoted to lieutenant in 1802 while serving against the Tripolitan corsairs during the BARBARY WARS. During 1804–06, Perry commanded the 12-gun schooner *Nautilus* in the Mediterranean.

After his return to the United States, Perry was assigned to supervise the building of GUNBOATS for the USN, and also led patrols to enforce the provisions of the Embargo Act during 1807–09. His career was threatened in 1811, when his command, the 12-gun USS *Revenge,* ran aground in Newport Harbor. Perry was court-martialed for negligence, but, after acquittal, was assigned to command the Newport gunboat flotilla as the War of 1812 began.

Perry was sent to Lake Erie to serve under Commodore Isaac Chauncey on February 17, 1813. Arriving at Presque Isle (modern Erie,

Commodore Oliver H. Perry, 1813, in dress uniform; an engraving by Henry Meyer from an original painting by John W. Jarvis *(Naval Historical Foundation)*

Pennsylvania), he discovered that there were no American ships on the lake. Perry improvised and quickly built a flotilla of gunboats, completing nine by the early summer of 1813, mounting a total of 54 guns. On May 27, Perry and Chauncey supported Colonel Winfield Scott in the capture of Fort George, Ontario. After this, Perry slipped his gunboat flotilla out of Presque Isle harbor during August 1–4 and, on September 10, engaged the British blockading fleet on Lake Erie. Despite initial reversals, Perry prevailed, defeating a stunned British fleet, and sending to General William Henry Harrison one of history's most famous military messages: "We have met the enemy and they are ours. Two ships, two brigs, one schooner, one sloop." Perry then went ashore to serve under Harrison in the ensuing Battle of the Thames, a key American victory in a war that, for the most part, had proved disastrous for the United States.

In January 1814, Perry was promoted to captain. After the war, he was given command of the 44-gun frigate *Java* in the Mediterranean during 1816–17. In 1819, while leading a diplomatic mission to the new republic of Venezuela, he contracted yellow fever and succumbed to it.

Persian Gulf War

On August 2, 1990, Saddam Hussein, dictator of Iraq, invaded the small nation of Kuwait, which he claimed as an Iraqi province. The United States, together with much of the rest of the world, feared that Iraq would move next against Saudi Arabia, giving Saddam control of much of the planet's oil supply. President George H. W. Bush froze Iraqi assets in U.S. banks, cut off trade with the country, and obtained United Nations resolutions condemning the invasion and supporting military action against it. The Bush administration assembled a coalition among 48 nations, 30 of which contributed military forces, while 18 provided economic, humanitarian, and other noncombat assistance, to fight what was then the fourth largest army in the world.

Operation Desert Shield, a massive buildup of U.S. and coalition forces in the Middle East, began on August 7, 1990. By January 15, 1991—the UN deadline for Iraqi withdrawal from Kuwait—approximately 450,000 coalition troops were in place. This included a very large USN contingent. The six ships of the Middle East Force, already on station in the Persian Gulf, were soon joined by the *Independence* battle group and the *Eisenhower* battle group. When UN trade sanctions were imposed, the USN commenced interception operations against ships headed to and from Iraq and Kuwait.

During Operation Desert Shield, more than 9,200 merchant ships were challenged by USN vessels, and more than 1,200 were boarded for inspection. About 67 were diverted for carrying prohibited cargo. Also during this period, the USN was responsible for strategic sealift of forces into the area. MILITARY SEALIFT COMMAND delivered 3.4 million tons of cargo and 6.8 million tons of fuels.

On January 16, with Iraqi invaders still in Kuwait, Operation Desert Shield became Operation Desert Storm—the Persian Gulf War—and for the next five weeks, the coalition, led by the United States, conducted an air war of more than 88,000 missions with losses of only 22 coalition aircraft. One-third of all air-strike sorties were flown by USN and USMC aircraft. Six aircraft carrier battle groups and two battleships were simultaneously engaged. CRUISERS, DESTROYERS, battleships, and SUBMARINES launched more than 288 Tomahawk cruise missiles from the Red Sea and Persian Gulf against heavily defended, key Iraqi facilities. USN forces completely destroyed the small Iraqi navy of more than 100 vessels. USN craft served as platforms for amphibious forces, which conducted a series of raids and feints, a successful deception operation that greatly facilitated the main ground assault. In addition, USN vessels conducted extensive antimine operations in the northern Persian Gulf.

After weeks of air and naval assault, the coalition launched a ground offensive at 4 A.M. on February 24, 1991. Within 100 hours, a cease-fire was declared, at 8 A.M. on February 28, after Iraq had agreed to U.S.-dictated terms. Kuwait was liberated, and the Iraqi armed forces decimated. Incredibly, however, the regime of Saddam Hussein proved resilient, remaining in power until a second

Gulf war, Operation Iraqi Freedom, was launched during March and April 2003 by order of George H. W. Bush's son, President George W. Bush. Saddam Hussein was captured in the course of this operation.

petty officer   See RANKS AND GRADES.

Phalanx Weapon System

A fast-reaction, rapid-fire 20-mm gun system, Phalanx provides USN ships with a "last-chance" defense against antiship missiles and littoral warfare threats that have penetrated other fleet defenses. The system automatically detects, tracks, and engages such threats as antiship missiles and aircraft. The latest version, Block 1B, includes a "man-in-the-loop" system to counter littoral warfare threats, including small high-speed surface craft, small terrorist aircraft, helicopters, and surface mines. Phalanx incorporates an advanced search and track radar system integrated with a forward looking infra-red (FLIR) detector. The Block 1B version uses "Optimized Gun Barrels," which provide improved barrel life, improved round dispersion, and increased engagement ranges. Phalanx is the only close-in weapon system capable of autonomously performing its own search, detection, evaluation, tracking, engagement, and kill assessments.

The system underwent operational tests and evaluation onboard USS *Bigelow* in 1977, and production began the following year.

General characteristics of the Phalanx CIWS (close-in weapon system) include:

Contractor: Raytheon Systems Company
Weight: 12,500 lb; later models, 13,600 lb
Range: classified
Gun type: M-61A1 Gatling
Type of fire: 3,000 rounds/min; later models, 4,500 rounds/min
Magazine capacity: 989 rounds; later models, 1,550 rounds
Caliber: 20 mm
Ammunition: armor piercing discarding sabot (APDS) depleted uranium subcaliber penetrator; penetrator was changed to tungsten in 1988; Block 1B incorporates Enhanced Lethality Cartridge with a heavier penetrator
Sensors: self-contained search and track radar with integrated FLIR

The system was first deployed in 1980 aboard USS *Coral Sea*. Block 1B was first deployed in 1999 aboard USS *Underwood*.

Phoenix missile   See MISSILES.

Pistol Marksmanship Medal   See DECORATIONS AND MEDALS.

Porter, David Dixon (1813–1891) *navy admiral*

Porter served with great distinction in the U.S.-MEXICAN WAR and the CIVIL WAR. He was born in Chester, Pennsylvania, the third of 10 children of David Porter, and was a foster brother to DAVID G. FARRAGUT. Porter accompanied his father to the West Indies aboard the frigate *John Adams* in 1824; however, he began his formal naval career not in the U.S. Navy, but as a midshipman in the Mexican navy, after his father accepted an appointment as commander in chief of that force in August 1826. The younger Porter was captured by Spanish forces in 1828, but was soon released. He returned to the United States and, in February 1829, became a USN midshipman.

Porter's first assignment was in the Mediterranean; later, he served in the Coast Survey during 1836–45. After receiving promotion to lieutenant in February 1845, he was assigned to recruiting duty in New Orleans the following year. With the outbreak of the U.S.-Mexican War, he served aboard the navy steamer *Spitfire* and participated in the naval bombardment of Veracruz led by Commodore MATTHEW C. PERRY in March 1847. During the second Tabasco campaign (June 14–22,

1847), Porter led a detachment of 70 men against the main Mexican fort there. This earned him command of *Spitfire* for the rest of the war.

After the war, Porter returned to the Coast Survey and then to a shore assignment at the UNITED STATES NAVAL OBSERVATORY. Eager to return to the sea, Porter took a leave of absence to command passenger and cargo steamers during 1849–55, returning to the navy as captain of USS *Supply*. This assignment ended before the Civil War, and, confined once again to duty ashore, Porter contemplated resigning his commission. However, at the start of war, Porter received command of USS *Powhatan* and was tasked to relieve Fort Pickens, off Pensacola, Florida, in April 1861. Promoted to commander, he was assigned to blockade duty on the Gulf coast and was instrumental in planning a major naval offensive against New Orleans during November 1861–April 1862. He led a flotilla of 20 mortar boats in support of the capture of that city on April 27. With David Farragut, he also participated in the capture of Forts St. Philip and Jackson two days later.

Later in 1862, Porter sailed under Farragut in operations against Vicksburg. In October, he was jumped in rank—over some 80 senior officers—to acting rear admiral and was assigned to open a Mississippi River shipyard at Cairo, Illinois. There Porter built a river fleet of some 80 vessels, the Mississippi Squadron, which he led in support of land operations during January 10–11, 1863. During the night of April 16–17, he led much of the squadron under the Vicksburg batteries and, on April 29, sailed past the guns at Grand Gulf (below Vicksburg) to cover Ulysses S. Grant's crossing of the Mississippi on April 30–May 1.

Following Vicksburg, Porter supported General Nathaniel P. Banks's misguided Red River campaign during March 12–May 13, 1864, and nearly lost his ships. Despite the collapse of this campaign, Porter was appointed commander of the North Atlantic Blockading Squadron in October 1864, and during December 24–25, mounted a massive bombardment of Fort Fisher, North Carolina, with a fleet of 120 ships. Unfortunately, General Benjamin Butler failed to coordinate the land

component of the attack with Porter's bombardment, and Porter had no choice but to withdraw. After General Alfred H. Terry replaced Butler, Porter made a second attempt against Fort Fisher during January 13–15, 1865; following a costly land battle, Fort Fisher fell. Subsequent to this action, in April 1865, Porter led a gunboat squadron up the James River in Virginia, which forced Confederate admiral RAPHAEL SEMMES to scuttle his fleet.

Following the war, Porter was appointed superintendent of the UNITED STATES NAVAL ACADEMY. He served until 1869 and, in July 1866, was promoted to vice admiral. Named adviser to the SECRETARY OF THE NAVY in 1869, Porter soon became de facto commander in chief of the USN following the death of his father. Promoted to admiral, Porter was appointed head of the Board of Inspections in 1877 and continued on active duty until his death in 1891.

Portsmouth Naval Shipyard

Located about 50 miles north of Boston, Massachusetts, at the southernmost tip of Maine, the Portsmouth Naval Shipyard is one of only four remaining publicly owned shipyards in the United States. It occupies Seavey Island, at the mouth of the Piscataqua River and opposite Portsmouth, New Hampshire. The shipyard specializes in submarine design, construction, modernization, and maintenance, and plays an important role in very-deep ocean submersible and special operations. Currently, the principal mission of the shipyard is overhaul, repair, modernization, and refueling of *Los Angeles*–class SUBMARINES.

The shipyard is staffed by 32 USN officers, 72 enlisted sailors, and about 4,300 civilians.

Powhatan Class (T-ATF 166)   See FLEET OCEAN TUGS.

Preble, Edward (1761–1807) *navy captain*
One of the early heroes of the U.S. Navy, Preble was born in Falmouth (modern Portland), Maine, and,

during the AMERICAN REVOLUTION, enrolled as a midshipman, not in the fledgling Continental navy but in the state navy of Massachusetts, one of several navies raised by the states during the conflict. He rose to lieutenant in this service and, after the war, shipped out with the merchant marine. When the QUASI-WAR WITH FRANCE heated up in 1798, Preble joined the USN and, the following year, was promoted to captain. As skipper of the USS *Essex*, he led an expedition to Batavia, Dutch East Indies. and his ship became the first USN vessel to show the flag beyond the Cape of Good Hope.

With the outbreak of the BARBARY WARS, Preble commanded a squadron against the Tripolitan raiders and against Tripoli itself. He enjoyed great success during 1804, then returned to the United States, where he took charge of the construction of a much-needed fleet of GUNBOATS.

Prepositioning Program

The MILITARY SEALIFT COMMAND is responsible for a Prepositioning Program, which enables the rapid deployment of large U.S. military forces anywhere in the world. "Afloat prepositioning" puts into place in key ocean areas military equipment and supplies ready for use when needed. The Prepositioning Program supports army, USAF, and USMC operations, with MARITIME PREPOSITIONING SHIPS remaining at sea, ready to deploy with essential equipment, fuel, and supplies for the initial support of military forces. The Prepositioning Program consists of 33 at-sea ships plus two aviation support ships, which are maintained in reduced operating status.

The Prepositioning Program began in the early 1980s; today, prepositioning ships are located in such areas as the Mediterranean Sea, the Indian Ocean, the Persian Gulf, and Guam. Aviation logistics ships are berthed on the East and West Coasts of the United States.

The Prepositioning Program consists of three major divisions: the Combat Prepositioning Force, the Maritime Prepositioning Force, and the logistics prepositioning ships serving the USN, army, USAF, and USMC, as well as the Defense Logistics Agency. Operational elements include Maritime Prepositioning Ship Squadron One; Maritime Prepositioning Ship Squadron Two; Maritime Prepositioning Ship Squadron Three; Afloat Prepositioning Ship Squadron Four; Combat Prepositioning Force; Maritime Prepositioning Force; Logistics Prepositioning Force; and the Afloat Prepositioning Force. This last element was established in the early 1980s to provide intertheater mobility and reduce response time for the delivery of urgently needed military equipment and supplies to a theater of operations in times of contingency. Sixteen maritime prepositioning ships carry equipment and supplies for the USMC, 13 combat prepositioning ships carry equipment and supplies for an army heavy brigade and combat support/combat service support elements; 13 logistics prepositioning ships (mostly tankers and dry cargo ships) are loaded primarily with Defense Logistics Agency fuels, USAF ammunition, USMC aviation support equipment, and USN munitions.

prepositioning ships   See COMBAT PREPOSITIONING SHIPS; LOGISTICS PREPOSITIONING SHIPS; MARITIME PREPOSITIONING SHIPS; PREPOSITIONING PROGRAM.

PT boat

The PT—patrol torpedo—boat was a product of WORLD WAR II and was designed as a small, light, and fast antiship weapon. Hundreds were built, mostly between 1942 and 1945 by Elco Naval Division of the Electric Boat Company at Bayonne, New Jersey. The Elcos were wooden-hulled and 80 feet long, with a beam of 20 feet 8-inches. They were powered by three 12-cylinder Packard gasoline engines for a total of 4,500 horsepower, which made 41 knots. Full-load displacement was 56 tons. Crews varied from 12 to 14 and included three officers.

The first Elco boats carried two 20-mm guns, four .50-caliber machine guns, and two or four 21-inch torpedo tubes. Some boats were equipped with depth charges or mine racks. Later boats had a single 40-mm gun and four torpedo launching racks. Others were retrofitted on site with antiaircraft guns and even rocket launchers.

In addition to 80-foot Elco boats, the USN also used British-designed 70-foot Vosper boats, firing 18-inch torpedoes. Elco also produced a 77-foot boat, which was used early in the war. The Huckins Yacht Company of Jacksonville, Florida, built a small number of 78-foot boats, but Higgins Industries (New Orleans, Louisiana) built far more boats of this design, which shared most specifications with the 80-foot Elco boats.

For the general public, the PT boat was made famous in World War II by the daring evacuation from the Philippines of Douglas MacArthur and his family and the exploits of John F. Kennedy, who commanded the ill-fated PT-109, saving most of its crew after it was rammed and cut in two by a Japanese warship.

Q

Quasi-War with France

The United States and France, boon allies during the AMERICAN REVOLUTION, rapidly drifted apart after that war. In the wake of its own revolution, the French government became increasingly wary of America's movement toward reconciliation with England, while many Americans did indeed draw back from a France they perceived as dangerously radical. In 1797, President John Adams authorized a commission consisting of Charles Cotesworthy Pinckney, John Marshall, and Elbridge Gerry to improve Franco-American relations by negotiating a new treaty of commerce and amity with France. The commissioners were met by three agents of French foreign minister Charles Maurice de Talleyrand-Périgord, who informed them that, before a treaty could be discussed, the United States would have to "loan" France $12,000,000 and pay Talleyrand a personal bribe of $250,000.

On April 3, 1798, President Adams presented to Congress the commission's correspondence, which did not list the French agents by name but by the letters X, Y, and Z. An outraged Congress published the correspondence to the American people, who now buzzed with talk of the "XYZ Affair." It was sufficient to mobilize Americans for war against France. By this time, French naval operations against the British in the West Indies were interfering as well with American commercial shipping. In response, Congress authorized the rush completion of three frigates, the *United States, Constellation,* and USS *Constitution,* as well as the arming and training of some 80,000 militiamen and the commissioning of a thousand privateers. George Washington was recalled from retirement to command the army, and, on May 3, 1798, in direct response to the French threat, Congress formally created the DEPARTMENT OF THE NAVY.

War was never declared, but the "Quasi-War" consisted of a number of sharp engagements in which the brand-new U.S. Navy distinguished itself. In July 1798, STEPHEN DECATUR, skipper of the sloop *Delaware,* captured the French schooner *Croyable* off the New Jersey coast. Renamed the *Retaliation,* this vessel was retaken by the French in November 1798 off Guadeloupe. However, on February 9, 1799, the USS *Constellation,* newly built, triumphed over the French frigate *Insurgente* and took it as a prize. These were the principal battles of the war, which continued sporadically through 1800, mainly in the Caribbean. Of 10 engagements, the French recapture of *Retaliation* was the only defeat the USN suffered.

The conflict was brought to a close not by American arms, but by Napoleon's decision to seek reconciliation. Bonaparte had seized the French government in a coup d'état of November 9, 1799. Seeking diplomatic recognition from neutral Denmark and Sweden, he was anxious to demonstrate his government's respect for the rights of neutrals, including the United States. Hostilities were officially ended in 1800 by the *Convention between the French Republic and the United States of America.*

R

Radford, Arthur William (1896–1973) *navy admiral*

Chicago-born Arthur Radford was one of the architects of the so-called revolt of the admirals, the protest by a cadre of high-ranking USN officers over the cancellation of construction of the supercarrier *United States* in 1949, apparently in favor of the expansion of the USAF B-36 bomber program. With other WORLD WAR II–era admirals, including ERNEST J. KING, CHESTER NIMITZ, WILLIAM F. HALSEY, and RAYMOND SPRUANCE, Radford supported Chief of Naval Operations Louis E. Denfield in appealing to Congress for reconsideration and in defense of the USN's rightful role in the nation's military.

Radford was a UNITED STATES NAVAL ACADEMY graduate (1916) and served in WORLD WAR I aboard the battleship *South Carolina*. After the war, he was trained as a naval aviator and early in World War II was promoted to rear admiral and given command of Carrier Division II.

Following the war, Radford was appointed vice chief of naval operations. From 1953 to 1957, he was chairman of the Joint Chiefs of Staff.

ranks and grades

"Rank" refers to a person's official position within the military hierarchy. "Grade" is an alphanumeric symbol associated with rank, which is keyed to pay level (and is therefore often called "pay grade").

Officer grades range from O-1 to O-10 and enlisted grades from E-1 to E-9. For basic pay associated with these grades.

USN ranks and grades fall into two groups: commissioned officers and enlisted personnel.

Officer Ranks (in descending order)

Fleet Admiral (O-10)
The highest rank in the USN, fleet admiral is rarely bestowed, and only in wartime. The army and USAF have equivalent ranks, general of the army and general of the air force. The insignia is a cluster of five stars. Five stripes, one wide closest to the cuff and four narrow above it, surmounted by a star, are displayed on the sleeve.

Admiral (O-10)
Except for the rarely bestowed fleet admiral, this is the highest command rank in the USN. The army, USAF, and USMC equivalent is general, and the insignia is a row of four stars. Four stripes, one wide closest to the cuff and three narrow above it, surmounted by a star, are displayed on the sleeve.

Vice Admiral (O-9)
The rank below admiral and above rear admiral (upper), the vice admiral is a USN officer equivalent in rank to a USAF, army, and USMC lieutenant general. Insignia of the rank is a row of three stars. Three stripes, one wide closest to the cuff and two

narrow above it, surmounted by a star, are displayed on the sleeve.

Rear Admiral (Upper) (O-8)
The rank below vice admiral and above rear admiral (lower), this officer is the equivalent in rank of a USAF, army, and USMC major general. Insignia of rank is a row of two stars. Two stripes, one wide closest to the cuff and one narrow above it, surmounted by a star, are displayed on the sleeve.

Rear Admiral (Lower)/Commodore (O-7)
The rank below rear admiral (upper) and above captain, this officer is equivalent in rank to a USAF, army, and USMC brigadier general. Insignia of rank is a single star. A single broad stripe surmounted by a star is displayed on the sleeve.

The rank of commodore was at one time used in lieu of rear admiral (lower) for an officer who commanded a squadron, division, naval group, or detachment. The term is obsolete and is no longer used as an official title, although it is sometimes still applied, unofficially, as a courtesy.

Captain (O-6)
The USN captain holds a rank above commander and below rear admiral (lower). The army, USAF, and USMC equivalent rank is colonel, and the insignia is an eagle. Note that the commander of any USN ship is addressed as "captain" while on board regardless of rank. Four narrow stripes surmounted by a star are displayed on the sleeve.

Commander (O-5)
This rank is below captain and above lieutenant commander. The insignia is a gold oak leaf, and the army, USAF, and USMC equivalent is lieutenant colonel. Three narrow stripes surmounted by a star are displayed on the sleeve.

Lieutenant Commander (O-4)
A rank below commander and above lieutenant, the lieutenant commander is equivalent in rank to a USAF, army, and USMC major. The insignia is a gold oak leaf. Two narrow stripes with a thinner stripe between them, the three surmounted by a star, are displayed on the sleeve.

Lieutenant (O-3)
A lieutenant ranks below lieutenant commander and above lieutenant junior grade. Equivalent to a USMC, army, and USAF captain, the insignia is two vertical silver bars. Two narrow stripes surmounted by a star are displayed on the sleeve.

Lieutenant Junior Grade (Lieutenant j.g.) (O-2)
The lieutenant j.g. ranks below lieutenant and above ensign. The equivalent army, USAF, and USMC rank is first lieutenant, and the insignia is a single vertical silver bar. A narrow stripe below a thinner stripe surmounted by a star is displayed on the sleeve.

Ensign (O-1)
The ensign ranks below lieutenant junior grade and is the lowest-ranking commissioned rank in the navy. Army, USAF, and USMC equivalent rank is the second lieutenant, and the insignia is a single vertical gold bar. A single narrow stripe below a star is displayed on the sleeve.

Enlisted Ranks (in descending order)

Master Chief Petty Officer of the Navy (E-9)
The highest-ranking noncommissioned officer in the USN, the master chief petty officer of the navy holds a unique rank and is in direct charge of matters relating to all enlisted USN personnel. Emblem of rank features three inverted chevrons below an inverted rocker with a star centered above the chevrons, an eagle above the inverted rocker, and a row of three stars above that. The army equivalent is sergeant major of the army; USAF equivalent is chief master sergeant of the air force; and USMC equivalent is sergeant major of the Marine Corps.

Master Chief Petty Officer (E-9)
Except for master chief petty officer of the navy, master chief petty officer is the highest noncommissioned rank in the USN. The emblem of rank features three inverted chevrons below an inverted rocker, with a ship's wheel centered above the chevrons. An eagle is above the inverted rocker, and a star is above each of the eagle's wingtips. The army equivalent rank is command sergeant major; USAF equivalent is command chief master sergeant; and

USMC equivalent is sergeant major. (Note that the army rank of sergeant major is also designated E-9, as are the USAF's chief master sergeant and the USMC's master gunnery sergeant.)

Senior Chief Petty Officer (E-8)

The rank below master chief petty officer and above chief petty officer, senior chief petty officer is equivalent to the army's first sergeant, the USAF's senior master sergeant, and the USMC's first sergeant. (Note that the army and Marine Corps master sergeant ranks are also designated E-8.) Emblem of rank features three inverted chevrons below an inverted rocker, with a ship's wheel centered above the chevrons. An eagle is centered above the inverted rocker, with a single star centered above the eagle.

Chief Petty Officer (E-7)

The CPO ranks below senior chief petty officer and above petty officer first class. The equivalent army rank is sergeant first class; equivalent USAF rank is master sergeant; and equivalent USMC rank is gunnery sergeant. The emblem of rank features three inverted chevrons beneath an inverted rocker. A ship's wheel is centered above the chevrons. An eagle is centered above the inverted rocker.

Petty Officer First Class (E-6)

A noncommissioned rank below chief petty officer and above petty officer second class, the petty officer first class is equivalent to an army staff sergeant, a USAF technical sergeant, and a USMC staff sergeant. The emblem of rank features three inverted chevrons beneath crossed anchors, which are centered under an eagle.

Petty Officer Second Class (E-5)

This noncommissioned rank is below petty officer first class and above petty officer third class. The equivalent army rank is sergeant; the USAF equivalent is staff sergeant; and the USMC equivalent is sergeant. The emblem of rank features two inverted chevrons below crossed anchors. An eagle is centered above the anchors.

Petty Officer Third Class (E-4)

This noncommissioned rank is below petty officer second class and above seaman. The army equiva-

lent is corporal; the USAF equivalent is senior airman; and the USMC equivalent is corporal. Emblem of rank features one inverted chevron below crossed anchors; an eagle is centered above the anchors.

Seaman (E-3)

This enlisted rank is below petty officer third class and above seaman apprentice. The army equivalent is private first class; USAF equivalent is airman first class; and USMC equivalent is lance corporal. The emblem of rank features three diagonal hash marks.

Seaman Apprentice (E-2)

The second lowest enlisted rank in the USN, below seaman and above seaman recruit, the seaman apprentice is equivalent to the army's private, the USAF's airman, and the USMC's private first class. The emblem of rank features two diagonal hash marks.

Seaman Recruit (E-1)

The entry-level enlisted rank in the USN, seaman recruit is below seaman apprentice and is the equivalent of the army private recruit, the USAF airman basic, and the USMC private. Emblem of rank is a single diagonal hash mark.

Ready Reserve Force

The RRF, which provides immediate sealift support for the rapid deployment of U.S. military forces, was created on February 14, 1977, and is a group of ships within the NATIONAL DEFENSE RESERVE FLEET (NDRF) including militarily useful cargo ships, barge carriers, auxiliary crane ships (ACSs), tankers, and troop ships capable of handling bulky, oversized military equipment. The vessels are all modern and maintained in a high state of readiness.

rear admiral   See RANKS AND GRADES.

repair ships (AR)

The *Vulcan* class was the only class of repair ship (AR); the functions of this class were largely taken over by DESTROYER TENDERS (AD).

Vulcan Class (AR)

The *Vulcan* class were repair ships designed to carry out battle damage repair, maintenance, and logistics support in a wartime environment for ships at anchor or moored to a pier. All four ships of this class were built and commissioned during WORLD WAR II, and all four were decommissioned during 1989–95. They were capable of repairing many vessels and could be forward deployed in time of conflict.

General specifications of the class included:

Builder: AR-5, New York Shipbuilding; AR-56–8, Los Angeles Shipbuilding and Drydock, San Pedro, California
Power plant: four boilers, steam turbines, two shafts, 11,000 shaft horsepower
Length: 529 ft
Beam: 73 ft
Displacement: 16,270 tons full load
Speed: 19.2 knots
Crew: 1,004
Armament: four 5-inch/.38-caliber guns; eight 40-mm guns

Ships of the class included: *Vulcan* (AR-5), *Ajax* (AR-6), *Hector* (AR-7), and *Jason* (AR-8).

rescue and salvage ships (ARS, ATS, ASR, DSRV)

The navy's principal rescue and salvage ships are designated ARS, ATS, ASR, and DSRV. The rescue and salvage ships designated ARS perform four salvage missions for the navy: They debeach stranded vessels, they provide heavy lift to retrieve objects from ocean depths, they tow other vessels, and they provide platforms for manned diving operations. For rescue missions, ARS vessels are equipped with fire monitors forward and amidships to deliver firefighting foam or seawater. The ships are also outfitted with equipment to provide assistance to other vessels in dewatering, patching, and supply of electrical power and other essential services. All operational ARS vessels are of the *Safeguard* class.

ATS ships serve as rescue and salvage craft, designed to save battle-damaged combat ships from further damage by towing them to safety. The ships also perform rapid fire fighting, pumping, and battle damage repair.

ASR ships provide surface support for SUBMARINE rescue operations.

DSRV craft are Deep Submergence Rescue Vehicles, which perform submerged submarine rescue.

ARS Ships

Safeguard Class (ARS)

The navy's newest—and only operational—class of rescue and salvage ships, the *Safeguard* class consists of four ships commissioned during 1985–86 and scheduled to remain in service far into the 21st century. The vessels are tasked with saving battle-damaged combat ships from further damage by towing them to safety. The ships also perform rescue, rapid fire fighting, pumping, and battle damage repair.

General specifications of the *Safeguard* class include:

Power plant: geared diesel engines, two propellers
Overall length: 255 ft
Waterline length: 240 ft
Extreme beam: 51 ft
Waterline beam: 50 ft
Maximum navigational draft: 17 ft
Draft limit: 18 ft
Displacement: 3,181 tons full load
Dead weight: 699 tons
Crew: seven officers, 92 enlisted personnel

Ships of the class include: *Safeguard* (ARS-50), *Grasp* (ARS-51), *Salvor* (ARS-52), and *Grapple* (ARS-53).

Bolster Class (ARS)

The seven ships of the *Bolster* class were commissioned at the end of World War II and were all decommissioned during 1993–94. They served as rescue and salvage ships, tasked with saving battle-damaged combat ships from further damage by towing them to safety and by effecting rescue operations and damage control, including rapid fire fighting, pumping, and battle damage repair.

General specifications of the class included:

Power plant: diesel-electric, two shafts, 3,060 shaft horsepower
Length: 213 ft
Beam: 44 ft
Draft: 15 ft
Displacement: 2,045 tons full load
Speed: 14.8 knots
Armament: two 20-mm guns
Crew: 106

Ships of the class included: *Bolster* (ARS-38), *Conserver* (ARS-39), *Hoist* (ARS-40), *Opportune* (ARS-41), *Reclaim* (ARS-42), and *Recovery* (ARS-43).

ATS Ships

Edenton Class (ATS)

The three ships of this class, commissioned during 1971–72, were decommissioned in 1996. General specifications of the class included:

Power plant: diesel engines
Overall length: 283 ft
Waterline length: 264 ft
Extreme beam: 50 ft
Waterline beam: 50 ft
Maximum navigational draft: 17 ft
Draft limit: 17 ft
Displacement: 3,496 tons full load
Dead weight: 881 tons
Crew: 10 officers, 96 enlisted personnel

Ships of the class included *Edenton* (ATS-1), *Beaufort* (ATS-2), and *Brunswick* (ATS-3).

ASR Ships

Chanticleer Class (ASR)

The eight ships of the *Chanticleer* class, commissioned between 1943 and 1950 and decommissioned during 1974–94, were built as surface support ships for submarine rescue operations. They operate the McCann rescue chamber as well as support deep-sea diving operations down to 300 feet. The ships can support divers indefinitely, low-ering them to the ocean floor in pressurized transfer chambers for periods of open-sea work. In addition to rescue operations, the ships of this class served as platforms for the conduct of deep-sea salvage operations.

General specifications of the class included:

Builders: ASR-9, Moore Shipbuilding and Drydock; ASR-13–16, Savannah Machine and Foundry
Power plant: diesel electric, one shaft
Length: 251 ft
Beam: 42 ft
Displacement: 2,320 tons full load
Speed: 15 knots
Crew: 111

Ships of the class included: *Chanticleer* (ASR-7), *Coucal* (ASR-8), *Florikan* (ASR-9), *Greenlet* (ASR-10), *Kittiwake* (ASR-13), *Petrel* (ASR-14), *Sunbird* (ASR-15), and *Tringa* (ASR-16).

Deep Submergence Rescue Vehicles (DSRV)

The navy's two DSRVs, *Mystic* (DSRV-1) and *Avalon* (DSRV-2), perform rescue operations on submerged, disabled submarines. The craft are designed for quick worldwide deployment and may be transported by truck, aircraft, ship, or by specially configured attack submarine. Once at the accident site, the DSRV works with either a surface mother ship or a mother submarine, diving, conducting a sonar search, and attaching itself to the disabled submarine's hatch. A DSRV can embark up to 24 personnel at a time for transfer to the mother vessel.

In addition to its evacuation capability, the DSRV is equipped with an arm to clear hatches on a disabled submarine and a combined gripper and cable cutter. General characteristics of the DSRVs include:

Builder: Lockheed Missiles and Space, Sunnyvale, California
Power plant: electric motors, silver/zinc batteries, one shaft, 15-shaft horsepower, four thrusters, 7.5 horsepower.

Length: 49 ft
Beam: 8 ft
Displacement: 38 tons
Speed: 4 knots
Maximum depth: 5,000 ft
Sonar: search and navigation
Crew: two pilots, two rescue personnel, and capacity for 24 passengers

Deep Drone 7200 Remotely Operated Vehicle

The Deep Drone ROV is a deep-ocean recovery vehicle, capable of working down to 7,200 feet. A remote operator controls the ROV in all six degrees of freedom, and auto-control functions are provided for depth, attitude, and heading. The ROV uses electric propulsion, carries a target-locating sonar, and has two manipulators, which can work with tools. The vehicle is also equipped with a 35-mm still camera and television cameras.

General characteristics of the vehicle include:

Length: 9 ft 3 in
Width: 4 ft 7 in
Height: 6 ft 2 in
Propulsion: electrical
Maximum operating depth: 7,200 ft
Lift capacity: 3,200 lb
Payload: 300 lb
Speed: 3 knots

research ships

Naval research ships are especially equipped to conduct measurements, surveys, and other research that contribute to the navy's missions. The vessels include:

Acoustic Research Ship (T-AG)

USNS *Hayes* is one of 28 SPECIAL MISSION SHIPS operated by the MILITARY SEALIFT COMMAND to furnish services for such USN customers as the NAVAL SEA SYSTEMS COMMAND, SPACE AND NAVAL WARFARE SYSTEMS COMMAND, and the OCEANOGRAPHER OF THE NAVY.

USNS *Hayes* is equipped to conduct acoustic surveys in support of the submarine noise reduction program and to carry out acoustic testing. The ship features a catamaran design, which provides an especially stable platform, large deck availability, and allows installation of a center-line well, essential to acoustic survey work. USNS *Hayes* was laid down on November 12, 1969, and launched July 2, 1970; in 1992, it was converted for acoustic research and reclassified T-AG 195.

NR-1 Naval Research Vessel

The NR-1 naval research vessel is the U.S. Navy's smallest SUBMARINE. It was designed for research and performs underwater search and recovery, oceanographic research missions, and installation and maintenance of underwater equipment to a depth of almost half a mile. The nuclear-powered vessel is capable of such ocean search missions as locating and identifying objects or ships lost at sea and recording ocean topographic and geological features. The principal mission of NR-1 is to work near or even on the seabed, performing sample gathering, recovery, implantation of objects on the bottom, or deep ocean repair. Launched at Groton, Connecticut, on January 25, 1969, NR-1 is the first deep submergence vessel to use nuclear power. The vessel is now homeported at Naval Submarine Base New London.

NR-1 has a maximum speed of 4 to 6 knots on the surface and is always tended by its surface support ship. Maneuvering is accomplished with four ducted thrusters, two in the front and two in the rear. There are also planes mounted on the sail, as well as a conventional rudder.

NR-1 is equipped with three viewing ports, exterior lighting fixtures, and television and still cameras for color photographic studies. The lighting suite consists of 19 250-watt gas-discharge lights and eight 1,000-watt and two 500-watt incandescent lights. There are 16 different low-light TV cameras variously positioned. The submarine carries a full range of advanced electronics and computers to aid in navigation, communications, and object location and identification. The submarine has no radar for surface navigation, but it does have a very sensitive sonar system.

NR-1 is fitted with a hydraulically powered manipulator arm, which is attached at the bow and can pick up objects weighing up to a ton. The manipulator can be rigged with various gripping and cutting tools as well as a work basket, which can be used in conjunction with the manipulator to deposit or recover items in the sea. Two retractable, rubber-tired, extendable bottoming wheels provide a fixed distance between the keel and the seabed.

NR-1's nuclear propulsion system enables the vessel to remain on the sea floor for extended periods. Following the loss of the Space Shuttle *Challenger* in 1986, the NR-1 was used to search for, identify, and recover critical parts of the *Challenger* craft.

General specifications of the NR-1 include:

Length: 145 ft 97/16 in
Pressure hull length: 96 ft 1 in
Diameter: 12 ft 6 in
Maximum beam (at stern stabilizers): 15 ft 10 in
Maximum navigational draft: 15 ft 1 in
Power plant: one nuclear reactor; one turboalternator; two motors (external); two propellers; four ducted thrusters (two horizontal, two vertical)
Design operating depth: 2,375 ft
Displacement, submerged: 366 long tons
Speed, surfaced: 4.5 knots
Speed, submerged: 3.5 knots
Mean draft: 15 ft 0.75 in
Crew: two officer, three enlisted, two scientists
Endurance: 210 man-days (nominal); 330 man-days (maximum)

Dolphin (AGSS-555)

Dolphin, homeported at the Naval Research and Development facility in San Diego, has the distinction of being the modern navy's only operational diesel-electric deep-diving research and development submarine. It is capable of carrying scientific payloads in excess of 12 tons, a much greater capacity than any other deep diving research vessel operating today. The boat can also maintain quite extensive onboard laboratory facilities, certainly more extensive than smaller deep submersible vessels. *Dolphin* is used as a platform to test advanced submarine structures, sensors, weapons, communications, and machinery systems, including advanced engineering design features, weapons, launcher and fire control systems, and deep ocean acoustics. Much of this work is classified.

The vessel is capable of operations at unprecedented depths, greatly exceeding those of any known operational submarine. The submarine is equipped with an extensive instrumentation suite designed to support multiple missions. Commissioned in 1968, *Dolphin* established a still unbroken world depth record for an operational submarine: 3,000+ feet.

General specifications of this unique submarine include:

Length: 165 ft
Beam: 18 ft
Displacement, submerged: 950 tons
Propulsion: diesel-electric—two GM 12 cylinder, 425 horsepower engines
Power: battery
Operating depth: 3,000+ ft
Speed, submerged: 10 knots (short duration), 3–4 knots (sustained)
Scientific payload: 12+ tons
External mounting pads: six port, six starboard, forward and aft of sail
Crew: five officers, 46 enlisted
Operational endurance: >15 days

Oceanographic Surveillance Ships (T-AGOS)

The mission of ocean surveillance ships is to gather underwater acoustical data in support of antisubmarine warfare. The vessels are designed to tow various underwater listening devices and to process and transmit the acquired data via satellite to shore stations. Together, these devices are called the Surveillance Towed Array System (SURTASS).

There are three classes of T-AGOS ships. The *Victorious*-class ocean surveillance ships are built on a small waterplane twin hull ("SWATH"), which provides enhanced stability at slow speeds in high latitudes and under adverse weather conditions. The *Impeccable* class are built on a similar hull, while ships of the *Stalwart* class have conventional hulls and are also used in counter-drug operations. SURTASS patrols are routinely conducted for 60 to 90 days.

Construction of the first *Victorious*-class ship began in 1986, and the first *Impeccable* in 1993.

General characteristics of the *Stalwart* class include:

Builder: Tacoma Boatbuilding, Tacoma, Washington
Power plant: diesel-electric; four Caterpillar D 398 diesel generators, 3,200 horsepower; two motors, 1,600 horsepower; two shafts; bow thruster; 550 horsepower
Length: 224 ft
Beam: 43 ft
Displacement: 2,262 tons full load
Speed: 11 knots, 3 knots when towing array
Crew: 18 civilian mariners, five technicians, and up to 15 USN personnel

Ships of the class are USNS *Prevail* (T-AGOS-8) and USNS *Assertive* (T-AGOS-9).

General characteristics of the Victorious class include:

Builder: McDermott Marine, Morgan City, Louisiana
Power plant: diesel-electric; four Caterpillar 3,512 diesel generators; two GE motors; twin-screw 1,600 shaft horsepower; two bow thrusters, 2,400 horsepower
Length: 234.5 ft
Beam: 93.6 ft
Displacement: 3,396 tons full load
Speed: 10 knots, 3 knots when towing array
Crew: 19–22 civilian mariners, five technicians, and up to 15 USN personnel

Ships of the class are USNS *Victorious* (T-AGOS-19), USNS *Able* (T-AGOS-20), USNS *Effective* (T-AGOS-21), and USNS *Loyal* (T-AGOS-22).

General characteristics of the *Impeccable* class include:

Builder: Tampa Shipyard/Halter Marine
Power plant: diesel-electric; three diesel generators; two Westinghouse motors, 5,000 horsepower, twin-screw shaft; two omni-thruster hydrojets, 1,800 horsepower
Length: 281.5 ft
Beam: 95.8 ft
Displacement: 5,370 tons full load
Speed: 13 knots, 3 knots when towing
Crew: 20 civilian mariners, five technicians, and up to 20 USN personnel

The *Impeccable* (T-AGOS-23) is the only ship of this class.

Oceanographic Survey Ships (T-AGS)

Oceanographic survey ships administered by the Military Sealift Command perform acoustical, biological, physical, and geophysical surveys to provide the military with needed information on the ocean environment. One of the principal purposes of gathering accurate oceanographic and hydrographic data is to improve technology in undersea warfare and enemy ship detection. Two ships, USNS *John McDonnell* (TAGS-51) and USNS *Littlehales* (TAGS-52), are specially designed to survey the sea bottom continuously in order to chart the world's coastlines and thereby make it easier to navigate unfamiliar shipping routes.

Ships of the *Silas Bent* class are designed specifically for surveying. They feature a bow propulsion unit that enables precise maneuverability and station keeping. Another type of ship, the *John McDonnell* class, carries 34-foot survey launches for data collection in coastal regions with depths between 33 and 2,000 feet and in deep water to 13,000 feet. *Pathfinder*-class ships carry three multipurpose cranes and five winches in addition to a range of oceanographic equipment, including multibeam echosounders, towed sonars, and expendable sensors.

Silas Bent Class

General characteristics of the *Silas Bent* class include:

> **Builders:** American Shipbuilding Company, Lorain/Christy Corporation, Sturgeon Bay, Wisconsin
>
> **Power plant:** diesel-electric; two Alco diesel generators; one Westinghouse/GE motor, 3,600 horsepower (2.69 megawatt); one shaft; bow thruster, 350 horsepower (261 kilowatt)
>
> **Length:** 285.3 ft
>
> **Beam:** 48 ft
>
> **Displacement:** 2,550 to 2,843 tons full load
>
> **Speed:** 15 knots when towing
>
> **Crew:** 31 civilians (12 officers) plus 28 scientists

The ships of this class are USNS *Silas Bent* (T-AGS-26) and USNS *Kane* (T-AGS-27).

John McDonnell Class

General characteristics of the *John McDonnell* class include:

> **Builder:** Halter Marine, Moss Point, Mississippi
>
> **Power plant:** one GM EMD 12-645E6 diesel, 2,500 horsepower (1.9 megawatt) sustained; one auxiliary diesel, 230 horsepower (172 kilowatt); one shaft
>
> **Length:** 208 ft
>
> **Beam:** 45 ft
>
> **Displacement:** 2,054 tons full load
>
> **Speed:** 12 knots (13.8 mph)
>
> **Crew:** 22 civilians plus 11 scientists

The ships of this class are USNS *John McDonnell* (T-AGS-51) and USNS *Littlehales* (T-AGS-52).

Pathfinder Class

General characteristics of the *Pathfinder* class include:

> **Builders:** Halter Marine, Moss Point, Mississippi
>
> **Power plant:** diesel-electric; four EMD/Baylor diesel generators, 11,425 horsepower (8.52 megawatt); two GE CDF 1944 motors, 8,000 horsepower (5.96 megawatt) sustained, 6,000 horsepower (4.48 megawatt); two Lips Z drives; bow thruster, 1,500 horsepower (1.19 megawatt)
>
> **Length:** 328.5 ft
>
> **Beam:** 58 ft
>
> **Displacement:** 4,762 tons full load
>
> **Speed:** 16 knots (18.4 mph)
>
> **Crew:** 28 civilians plus 27 scientists

The ships of this class are USNS *Pathfinder* (T-AGS-60), USNS *Sumner* (T-AGS-61), USNS *Bowditch* (T-AGS-62), USNS *Henson* (T-AGS-63), and USNS *Bruce C. Heezen* (T-AGS-64).

research submarine (T-AGSS)   See SUBMARINES.

Rickover, Hyman (1900–1986) *navy admiral* Hyman George Rickover, the father of the American nuclear navy and, in particular, the nuclear-powered submarine force, was born in Russia and raised in Chicago. He graduated from the UNITED STATES NAVAL ACADEMY in 1922 and went on to graduate work in electrical engineering at Columbia University (M.S., 1929). After this, he attended submarine school at New London, Connecticut, and saw pre–WORLD WAR II service on submarines and on the battleship USS *New Mexico*. In 1937, he assumed command of the minesweeper USS *Finch,* but in 1939 was assigned to the Electrical Section of the USN's Bureau of Ships. During the war, he served as head of the section.

In June 1946 Rickover received instruction in nuclear physics and engineering at Oak Ridge, Tennessee, in continuation of the Manhattan Project, which had developed the atomic bombs dropped on Japan. After his return to the Bureau of Ships in September 1947, he assumed leadership of the USN's nuclear-propulsion program. Rickover was a man of great vision, energy, and personal charisma who commanded absolute commitment and loyalty from his nuclear development team. The first fruit of their labors was the SSN *Nautilus,* the world's first nuclear-powered submarine—

indeed, the first nuclear-powered vessel of any kind. It was launched on January 21, 1954, and became the core of a great fleet of nuclear-powered submarines. Today, the entire USN submarine fleet is nuclear powered.

While still a USN rear admiral, Rickover assumed directorship of research on reactor development for the Atomic Energy Commission, a civilian agency, and was instrumental in developing the first full-scale, civilian-use nuclear power plant in the United States at Shippingport, Pennsylvania, during 1956–57. Well after reaching mandatory retirement age, Rickover, who had been exempted from retirement by an act of Congress, finally retired from the navy in 1982, having been promoted to admiral nine years earlier.

Rifle Marksmanship Ribbon   See DECORATIONS AND MEDALS.

rigid hull inflatable boat (RHIB)

The RHIB performs short-range insertion and extraction of special operations forces (SOF) as well as SOF coastal resupply and coastal surveillance missions. The boats have a range of 200 nautical miles at 32 knots, with a top speed of 45 knots. Capacity is eight passengers or 3,200 pounds. The RHIB may be transported via C-130 Hercules aircraft. The first boats were delivered to the USN in 1997.

General characteristics include:

Builder: U.S. Marine, Inc., New Orleans, Louisiana
Length: 36 ft
Capacity: eight passengers or 3,200 lb payload
Top speed: 45 knots

Rodgers, John (1771?–1838) *navy commander*

A civilian merchant master, Rodgers joined the USN and served on the *Constellation* during the QUASI-WAR WITH FRANCE in 1799, then saw service in the BARBARY WARS. Rodgers was a senior commander during the WAR OF 1812, then headed the Board of Navy Commissioners after the war. He served as acting SECRETARY OF THE NAVY in 1823.

Rolling Airframe Missile (RAM)   See MISSILES.

Roll-on/Roll-off Container Ships (T-AK)

See CARGO, FUEL, AND REPLENISHMENT SHIPS.

Roll-on/Roll-off Heavy Lift Ships (T-AK)

See CARGO, FUEL, AND REPLENISHMENT SHIPS.

S

Safeguard Class (ARS-50)   See RESCUE AND
SALVAGE SHIPS.

Sampson, William Thomas (1840–1902)
navy admiral

Born in Palmyra, New York, Sampson served in the
USN during the CIVIL WAR and, during 1886–90,
was superintendent of the UNITED STATES NAVAL
ACADEMY. From 1893 to 1897, he served as chief of
the Bureau of Ordnance and was responsible for
major improvements in naval gunnery. Sampson
earned national prominence as president of the
board of inquiry on the destruction of the battleship *Maine* in Havana harbor in 1898, the single
most prominent precipitating incident of the SPAN-
ISH-AMERICAN WAR. At the outbreak of that war,
Sampson was appointed commander of the North
Atlantic squadron and led the blockade of Cuba
and the attack on San Juan. Sampson's reputation
was somewhat tarnished when he loudly claimed
credit for the destruction of the Spanish fleet at
Santiago de Cuba, even though he was not present
for most of the battle. Sampson claimed that Winfield Scott Schley, the subordinate who actually led
USN forces there, was merely following general
instructions Sampson had laid down for the attack.
Sampson's unseemly behavior turned public opin-
ion against him and, in fact, deprived him of a substantial measure of the credit he doubtless
deserved.

Sampson was promoted to rear admiral in 1899
and commanded the Boston Navy Yard until his
death.

San Antonio–class amphibious transport dock   See AMPHIBIOUS TRANSPORT DOCK (LPD) SHIPS.

Seabees

The name *Seabees* was formed as a phonetic pun
on "CBs," which stands for "Construction Battalions" of the Civil Engineer Corps of the U.S. Navy,
conceived in October 1941 by Rear Admiral Ben
Moreell, chief of the USN Bureau of Yards and
Docks. After the December 7, 1941, attack on Pearl
Harbor, Moreell was given the green light to create
what became the Seabees.

The first Seabees were recruited from the civilian construction trades and were put under the
immediate command of the Civil Engineer Corps.
In contrast to the general population of the USN,
which was very young, the first Seabees, recruited
for their construction experience and skill, aver-
aged a mature age 37. A joke soon made the
rounds: "Never hit a Seabee. He may be your
grandfather."

As WORLD WAR II progressed, the Seabees
grew in number, 325,000 ultimately serving
before the war ended. They built all manner of

USN Seabees at work in Iraq during Operation Iraqi Freedom, May 2003 *(U.S. Navy)*

structures and facilities both in the rear and in the very front lines; hence the Seabee motto, "We build, we fight." During the war, Seabees served on six continents and more than 300 islands, constructing airstrips, bridges, roads, warehouses, hospitals, gasoline storage tanks, housing, and the like.

After World War II, the Seabees were reduced to a mere 3,300 men by 1950. Between 1949 and 1953, Seabees were reorganized into two types of unit: Amphibious Construction Battalions (PHIBCBs) and Naval Mobile Construction Battalions (NMCBs). This was just in time for the KOREAN WAR, which swelled the depleted ranks of the Seabees to more than 10,000 men. Once again, the construction units often found themselves in the front lines. Seabee contingents even accompanied the first assault troops at Inchon.

After the Korean War, Seabee units were called on to assist in relief efforts following a massive earthquake in Greece in 1953. During the 1950s and 1960s, Seabees were assigned to provide construction work and training in underdeveloped countries. During the cold war period, they often acted as the "Navy's Goodwill Ambassadors." During the VIETNAM WAR, Seabees were an important element of civic action teams, troops whose work was designed to win the hearts and minds of the people.

In 1971, the Seabees began their largest peacetime construction project on Diego Garcia, a strategically located Indian Ocean atoll. Over an 11-year period, the Seabees built a complex to accommodate the USN's largest ships and the USAF's largest military cargo jets. During the PERSIAN GULF WAR, more than 5,000 Seabees served in the Middle East, building camps and facilities for aircraft.

Sea Cadets, Naval

In 1958, at the request of the DEPARTMENT OF THE NAVY, the Navy League of the United States created the Naval Sea Cadet Corps (NSCC) and Navy League Cadet Corps (NLCC) with the objectives of helping young Americans become more patriotic and responsible citizens and helping them to understand the role of the maritime services in national defense and in maintaining the economic viability of our nation. NSCC was federally incorporated by Congress under Public Law 87–655 as a nonprofit civilian education organization separate from the Navy League on September 10, 1962. Currently, the NSCC accepts young men and women from ages 13 to 17, and the NLCC, now run under NSCC auspices, accepts members between 11 and 13.

SEALs

SEAL is an acronym for SEa-Air-Land teams, USN commando units that are the most elite special forces among the U.S. services and, by common consensus, among the armed services of the world.

The SEALs were created in 1962 by President John F. Kennedy as a maritime counterpart to the U.S. Army Special Forces, the "Green Berets"; however, their USN origins may be traced to the special Underwater Demolition Teams (UDTs), which operated as maritime commandos during WORLD WAR II and the KOREAN WAR.

Today's SEALs are trained to operate in small units, consisting of anywhere from a single person to a platoon strength of 16. Most often, they work in squads of eight or fewer. The typical SEAL mission is clandestine, with emphasis on meticulous planning and swift, stealthy execution.

The SEALs' first combat experience came during the VIETNAM WAR, in which SEAL Teams One and Two achieved a combined kill ratio of 200:1. SEALs have been deployed in Operation Urgent Fury (the 1983 U.S. intervention in Grenada),

Members of SEAL Team Two conduct SEAL Delivery Vehicle training in the Caribbean, 1997. *(U.S. Navy)*

Operation Just Cause (the 1989 invasion of Panama in pursuit of Manuel Noriega), and in the PERSIAN GULF WAR of 1991. In that conflict, SEALs executed 200 combat missions without a single casualty. SEALs were also deployed in Operation Restore Hope in Somalia (1992–94) and in Operation Enduring Freedom, the U.S. antiterrorist campaign in Afghanistan, beginning in 2001 and still under way as of mid-2004. SEALs have played a key special forces role in Operation Iraqi Freedom, the U.S.-U.K. invasion of Iraq, which began in March 2003.

In an age of so-called asymmetrical warfare, warfare in which small, weak powers use unconventional and terrorist tactics against major military powers such as the United States, it is almost certain that special operations forces like the SEALs will assume an increasingly important role.

seaman   See RANKS AND GRADES.

Sea Service Deployment Ribbon   See DECORATIONS AND MEDALS.

Sea Shadow experimental ship

Sea Shadow is a craft built to test the potential of "stealth" technology applied to warships. It was developed in a combined program of the Advanced Research Projects Agency (ARPA), the USN, and Lockheed Martin Missiles and Space Company beginning in the mid-1980s. The general characteristics of the ship include a diesel-electric powerplant, a length of 164 feet, beam of 68 feet, draft of 14.5 feet, and displacement of 560 tons fully loaded. It is crewed by 10. The vessel's appearance is radically unconventional and intended to control "signature"—that is, visibility and evidence of its presence. It is designed to present virtually no radar, sonar, visual, or acoustic signature.

Sea Sparrow missile   See MISSILES.

Seawolf **Class**   See SUBMARINES.

Second Fleet

In December 1945, after WORLD WAR II, the U.S. Eighth Fleet was formed and, in January 1947, was renamed Second Task Fleet. In February 1950, the command was again redesignated, this time as U.S. Second Fleet.

Commander Second Fleet is responsible for battle force operations in the Atlantic in support of designated unified or allied commanders. The commander is also a key member of the chain of command of NATO Supreme Allied Command Atlantic (SACLANT); in this capacity, the commander serves as commander Striking Fleet Atlantic, a multinational force that includes Belgium, Canada, Denmark, Germany, Netherlands, Norway, Portugal, Spain, the United Kingdom, and the United States. It was the Second Fleet that carried out the "quarantine" of Cuba during the CUBAN MISSILE CRISIS of October 1962.

Second Fleet staff is embarked aboard the command ship USS *Mount Whitney* (LCC/JCC 20), equipped with a cutting-edge communications suite. Major operational Second Fleet units are the following task forces: CTF-20, CTF-21, CTF-22, CTF-23, CTF-24, CTF-25, CTF-26, and CTF-28. The fleet's home is Norfolk, Virginia.

secretary of the navy

Under Title 10 of the United States Code, the secretary of the navy (SECNAV) is responsible for, and has the authority to conduct, all the affairs of the DEPARTMENT OF THE NAVY, including recruiting, organizing, supplying, equipping, training, mobilizing, and demobilizing. (The Department of the Navy encompasses the USN and USMC.) Additionally, SECNAV oversees the construction, outfitting, and repair of USN ships, equipment, and facilities. SECNAV has overall responsibility for formulating and implementing policies and programs consistent with the national security policies and objectives established by the president and the secretary of defense. By law a civilian, SECNAV is appointed by the president with the advice and consent of the Senate.

Semmes, Raphael (1809–1877) *navy commander*

Semmes was the most important naval commander of the Confederate states during the CIVIL WAR. He was a brilliant seaman, who, as captain of the commerce raider CSS *Sumter,* captured 18 prizes (vessels) and, while commanding CSS *Alabama,* captured 64 more.

Semmes was a native of Charles County, Maryland, and enrolled in the USN as a midshipman in 1826. He served in the U.S.-MEXICAN WAR and, by 1855, achieved the rank of commander. At the start of the Civil War, Semmes promptly resigned his USN commission and assumed command of CSS *Sumter* and, subsequently, CSS *Alabama.* Under Semmes, the *Alabama* became the most famous of the rebel commerce raiders. After a remarkable career during 1863–64, *Alabama* was finally defeated by USS *Kearsarge* off the French coast. Semmes escaped, however, and reentered the Confederacy by way of Mexico. In January 1865, he took command of the James River Squadron. His final maritime duty was to scuttle the squadron to prevent its capture; he was then appointed brigadier general, but soon surrendered in the capitulation of Confederate forces.

Semmes settled in Louisiana after the war, taught at Louisiana State Seminary (today the Louisiana State University), and subsequently became a newspaper editor.

Senior Enlisted Academy

Located at Naval Station Newport, Rhode Island, the Senior Enlisted Academy is the most advanced educational facility for enlisted USN personnel. Through a nine-week course, it prepares noncommissioned officers to assume duties as chief of the boat or command master chief petty officer.

Captain Raphael Semmes on the CSS *Alabama,* 1863   *(Naval Historical Foundation)*

The ranks of senior chief petty officer and master chief petty officer were established by Congress in 1958; however, as it became apparent that senior and master chiefs were given little additional responsibility beyond that accorded chief petty officers, the CHIEF OF NAVAL OPERATIONS, in 1979, took steps to expand the role of these ranks, elevating them from senior technicians to mid-level managers. In 1981, the USN opened the Senior Enlisted Academy to provide the additional education necessary to facilitate performing the new responsibilities.

The nine-week SEA curriculum includes communications skills, national security affairs, USN programs, and physical readiness training. Currently, SEA graduation is a requirement before assuming the positions of command master chief or chief of the boat.

Seventh Fleet

The Seventh Fleet was activated in 1943 and is now the USN's largest forward-deployed fleet, consisting of 40 to 50 ships, 200 aircraft, and some 20,000 USN and USMC personnel. The fleet operates in the Western Pacific, Indian Ocean, and Arabian Gulf, more than 52 million square miles of ocean, extending from the International Date Line to the east coast of Africa, and from the Kuril Islands in the north to the Antarctic in the south. Commander Seventh Fleet is embarked in USS *Blue Ridge* (LCC-19) and forward deployed to Yokosuka, Japan.

Eighteen of the fleet's ships operate from U.S. bases in Japan and Guam as the most forward-deployed elements of the force. Other ships are deployed on a rotating basis from bases in Hawaii and on the U.S. West Coast.

Established on March 15, 1943, during WORLD WAR II as a result of the redesignation of the Southwest Pacific Force, the Seventh Fleet fought in major Pacific campaigns. Following the war, on January 1, 1947, its name was changed to Naval Forces Western Pacific and, two years later, was designated as U.S. Seventh Task Fleet. On February 11, 1950, the unit was again designated the United States Seventh Fleet.

Shallow Water Intermediate Search System (SWISS)

SWISS is a dual-frequency side-scan shallow-water search sonar system, which is mounted inside a torpedo-shaped tow body for towing behind a vessel. The sonar signals are processed to produce an analog and a digital display of features on the ocean bottom. These displays may be interpreted to identify potential targets.

shore establishment

The shore establishment supports the OPERATING FORCES, also referred to as "the fleet," by providing facilities for the repair of machinery and electronics; communications centers; training areas and simulators; ship and aircraft repair; intelligence and meteorological support; storage areas for repair parts, fuel, and munitions; medical and dental facilities; and air bases. Shore establishment organizations, all of which report to the CHIEF OF NAVAL OPERATIONS, include Office of the Chief of Naval Operations, BUREAU OF NAVAL PERSONNEL, BUREAU OF MEDICINE AND SURGERY, NAVAL SEA SYSTEMS COMMAND, NAVAL AIR SYSTEMS COMMAND, NAVAL FACILITIES ENGINEERING COMMAND, NAVAL SUPPLY SYSTEMS COMMAND, SPACE AND NAVAL WARFARE SYSTEMS COMMAND, Strategic Systems Programs, UNITED STATES NAVAL ACADEMY, Naval Education and Training Command, Naval Meteorology and Oceanography Command, Office of Naval Intelligence, Naval Strike and Air Warfare Center, Naval Security Group Command, Naval Legal Services Command, UNITED STATES NAVAL OBSERVATORY, and Naval Safety Center.

See also ORGANIZATION.

shore patrol

"Shore Patrol"—SP—is the general term for any USN unit or personnel assigned to act as military police on shore.

Sims, William Snowden (1858–1936) *navy admiral*

As a U.S. Navy vice admiral, Sims commanded U.S. naval operations during WORLD WAR I. Born in Port Hope, Ontario, Sims moved with his family to Pennsylvania in 1872. After graduating from the UNITED STATES NAVAL ACADEMY in 1880, Sims saw service in the Atlantic and Pacific, as well as in Asian waters from 1880 to 1897, when he was appointed naval attaché in Paris and St. Petersburg. During the SPANISH-AMERICAN WAR in 1898, Sims coordinated U.S. intelligence activities in Europe.

While sailing on the battleship USS *Kentucky* (BB-6) beginning in November 1900, Sims learned of the then-new British method of "continuous firing," which greatly improved gunnery accuracy. Sims became an enthusiastic champion of the new technique and wrote to President Theodore Roosevelt about it in 1901. This breach of the chain of command was rewarded with a posting as inspector of gunnery training and a promotion to lieutenant commander in November 1902. Under Sims's direction, firing time for large-caliber guns was reduced from five minutes to 30 seconds, with a significant increase in accuracy.

During the Russo-Japanese War, Sims was dispatched to Asia as an observer and made important studies of the effect of modern guns on armor plate, as well as the effectiveness of battleships against smaller vessels. After promotion to commander in July 1907, Sims became naval aide to President Roosevelt and, in 1909, was assigned command of the USS *Minnesota* (BB-22). He was promoted to captain in March 1911 and was appointed instructor at the NAVAL WAR COLLEGE, which he left in 1913 to take command of the Atlantic Torpedo Flotilla through 1915. Here Sims formulated tactical doctrine for destroyers.

From November 1915 to January 1917, Sims commanded USS *Nevada* (BB-36). He was then appointed president of the Naval War College and commander of the Second Naval District and promoted to rear admiral. With American entry into World War I, he assumed command of all U.S. destroyers, tenders, and auxiliaries operating from British bases. In May he was promoted to vice admiral and, the next month, was named commander of U.S. Naval Forces Operating in European Waters.

Sims skillfully coordinated USN efforts with the British Admiralty to protect Allied shipping against U-boat attack. In recognition of his work, he was promoted to admiral in December 1918, but reverted to rear admiral shortly after his return to the United States and resumption of his duties as president of the Naval War College in April 1919.

Sims's battles did not cease with the Armistice. He was an eloquent voice of institutional criticism, declaring the USN incapable of fighting a major opponent. Although his remarks prompted a congressional investigation, his ongoing feud with Secretary of the Navy Josephus Daniels during 1920–21 was far less productive. Sims retired in October 1922, but continued to criticize naval policy. Despite this, he was promoted to admiral on the retired list in June 1930. Still an unorthodox voice, he began advocating the development of naval aviation in the belief that the airplane had made the battleship obsolete.

Sixth Fleet

Homeported in Gaeta, Italy, the U.S. Sixth Fleet conducts operations in and over the Mediterranean Sea, its approaches, adjacent inland areas, and the Black Sea. Commander Sixth Fleet reports to the commander in chief, U.S. Naval Forces, Europe (CinCUSNavEur) and to CinCSouth when the fleet operates as part of NATO as StrikFor-

South. Sixth Fleet striking power consists principally of AIRCRAFT CARRIERS and aircraft, SUBMARINES, and a reinforced battalion of marines deployed from amphibious ships on the Mediterranean. Some 40 ships, 175 aircraft, and 21,000 people make up the fleet.

Subordinate Sixth Fleet commands include Task Force 502 (Carrier Forces), Task Force 503 (Amphibious Forces), Task Force 504 (Landing Forces), Task Force 505 (Logistics Forces), and Task Force 506 (Special Operations Forces). The composition of the fleet proper consists of CTF 60 (Battle Force), CTF 61 (Amphibious Force), CTF 62 (Landing Force), CTF-63 (Logistics), CTF-64 (Submarines), CTF 67 (Maritime Surveillance), and CTF-69 (Submarines).

Space and Naval Warfare Systems Command (SPAWAR)

Using information technology and space systems, SPAWAR develops and delivers integrated command, control, communications, computer, intelligence, and surveillance systems to provide warfighters with knowledge superiority.

The DEPARTMENT OF THE NAVY established the Naval Electronic Systems Command on May 1, 1966, to provide the USN and USMC with state-of-the-art command, control, and communications electronic systems. At the time of its establishment, the command was designated NAVELEX. In May 1985, NAVELEX became Space and Naval Warfare Systems Command (SPAWAR), established under the CHIEF OF NAVAL OPERATIONS. In addition to the command, control, and communications mission, SPAWAR was charged with developing undersea surveillance and space systems programs. To carry out this mission, SPAWAR became manager of eight USN laboratories and four university laboratories, as well as seven engineering centers geographically dispersed throughout the country.

In 1995, pursuant to a directive from the Base Closure and Realignment Commission (BRAC), SPAWAR moved its headquarters staff to San Diego, California, from Arlington, Virginia. As of

October 1, 1997, SPAWAR was headquartered in San Diego with three systems centers operating in four major locations worldwide. At present, SPAWAR is staffed by some 7,500 military and civilian employees.

Spanish-American War

The USN played a leading role in the Spanish-American War, which came about in a climate of growing tension between the United States and Spain over Spain's tyrannical control of its colony, Cuba. The American government announced its support of the Cuban independence movement and, early in 1898, sent the battleship *Maine* to Havana harbor to protect American interests (which were extensive) on the island. On February 15, the *Maine* exploded, with the loss of 266 crewmen; a naval court of inquiry concluded that the ship had struck a Spanish mine (most modern analysts believe the ship's powder magazine exploded spontaneously and through no hostile action). The loss of the *Maine* ignited American war fever, and, although Spain accelerated its ongoing withdrawal from the island, President William McKinley asked

Congress to authorize an invasion. Congress did this and also voted a resolution to recognize Cuban independence from Spain. In response, Spain declared war on the United States on April 24, 1898.

While American ground forces were ill prepared for the conflict, the USN had recently undergone an expansion program, which included the construction of modern battleships and the training of an excellent officer corps. To buy time for the mustering and training of troops, U.S. military planners began the war with a naval blockade of Cuba. If naval commanders had had their way, the blockade would have been the principal war strategy, but politicians demanded immediate land action. At the time, the USN had adequate combatant ships, but few transports, and sealift to Cuba was slow and inefficient.

Nevertheless, it was the combat preparedness of the USN that averted disaster in the war. Soon after the war began, rumors circulated of the approach of a Spanish fleet under Admiral Pascual Cervera y Topete, headed for the Atlantic coast. Rear Admiral William T. SAMPSON detached several ships from the Cuban blockade squadron and put them under

USS *Maine*, an armored cruiser   *(Naval Historical Foundation)*

the command of Commodore Winfield S. Schley to guard against the approach of Cervera.

As this action took place, the USN put into operation its plan, formulated as early as 1895–97, to make a preemptive attack against Spanish ships stationed in the Philippine Islands. The objective was to destroy the ships, take Manila, and blockade the Philippine ports, thereby crippling Spain by cutting off a vital source of its revenue. Additionally, possession of the Philippines would put the United States in a powerful negotiating position to compel Spain to agree to Cuban independence. In January 1898, before the United States even began to plan for war, acting SECRETARY OF THE NAVY Theodore Roosevelt sent war preparation instructions to USN commanders, including Commodore GEORGE DEWEY. Dewey's Asiatic Squadron (five CRUISERS and two GUNBOATS) assembled in Hong Kong, then sailed to the Philippines. Dewey located the Spanish fleet at Cavite on May 1 and attacked the vessels of Admiral Patricio Montojo: four cruisers, three gunboats, and three decrepit auxiliary ships. Superior in numbers but outgunned, the Spanish fleet was sunk within a few hours; 381 Spanish sailors were killed or wounded, whereas Dewey did not lose a single man.

Having destroyed the fleet, Dewey neutralized the Spanish shore batteries, took possession of Cavite, then blockaded Manila in anticipation of the arrival of land forces to occupy the city, which fell on August 13.

In the meantime, back in the Caribbean, USN ships searched for Admiral Cervera and his fleet, which, having slipped through the Cuban blockade, had put in at the bay of Santiago de Cuba. Admiral Sampson attempted to blockade the fleet in the harbor. When this failed, during May, he coordinated with U.S. Army forces to neutralize Spanish forts and batteries, then Sampson landed marines carried aboard his squadron of five battleships, two armored cruisers, and assorted lesser vessels. The marines overran the Spanish defenders of Guantánamo Bay and established a base of operations there.

On June 20, the first army contingents began major operations on Cuba. Admiral Sampson wanted the army to land at Santiago Bay and storm the fort there. This done, Sampson could clear the bay of mines and enter it to fight Cervera's fleet. General William Shafter, having failed to transport heavy artillery, did not believe he could take the fort and therefore landed instead at Daiquirí, east of Santiago Bay. Thus, Sampson had to delay action against the Spanish fleet. Although American land forces made good progress against the Spanish, disease, especially yellow fever, took its toll of the Americans. By this time, however, the will of the Spanish defenders was breaking. As the Spanish abandoned the stronghold of Santiago, Admiral Cervera decided that he, too, needed to make a run out of the port and, on July 3, began to move out. Admiral Sampson at this time was ashore in conference with General Shafter. In his absence, Commodore Schley gave pursuit and, in only two hours, destroyed Cervera's fleet. Four Spanish cruisers and a destroyer were severely damaged and ran aground; another destroyer was sunk. Cervera lost 474 killed or wounded; 1,750 Spanish sailors were taken prisoner. Schley lost one U.S. sailor killed and another wounded. (Subsequently, an unseemly dispute developed between Schley and Sampson, who wanted to claim credit for the victory.)

The defeat of Cervera prompted Spanish officials at Santiago to surrender, and a cease-fire was effected on July 16, 1898.

Following this came a successful U.S. invasion of Puerto Rico and, in the Philippines, the fall of Manila, an operation greatly aided by Dewey's naval bombardment. On August 14, the Spanish surrender of the Philippines was formalized, and the Treaty of Paris, ending the Spanish-American War, was concluded on December 10, 1898.

special mission ships

The MILITARY SEALIFT COMMAND operates 26 ships in its Special Missions Program to provide operating platforms and services for unique U.S. military and federal government missions. Special mission ships are used for such missions as oceanographic and hydrographic survey, cable laying, missile range instrumentation, ocean surveillance, counterdrug operations, deep water search, deep water rescue, and USN submarine test support escort. Most of the special mission ships are crewed by civilians employed by companies under contract to Military Sealift Command. The technical work, research, and communications involved in the missions are conducted by military personnel as well as military-employed civilian scientists and technicians.

The MSC's special mission ships include:

USNS *Able:* oceanographic surveillance ship
USNS *Assertive:* oceanographic surveillance ship
USNS *Bold:* oceanographic surveillance ship
USNS *Bowditch:* oceanographic survey ship
USNS *Capable:* oceanographic surveillance ship
SSV *C-Commando:* submarine support vessel
MV *Carolyn Chouest:* submarine support vessel
MV *Cory Chouest:* ocean surveillance ship
MV *Dolores Chouest:* submarine support vessel
MV *Kellie Chouest:* submarine support vessel
USNS *Effective:* ocean surveillance ship
USNS *Hayes:* range instrumentation ship
USNS *Bruce C. Heezen:* oceanographic survey ship
USNS *Henson:* oceanographic survey ship
USNS *Impeccable:* ocean surveillance ship
USNS *Invincible:* dual-band radar ship
USNS *Loyal:* ocean surveillance ship
USNS *John McDonnell:* oceanographic survey ship
USNS *Observation Island:* missile range instrumentation ship
USNS *Pathfinder:* oceanographic survey ship
USNS *Prevail:* ocean surveillance ship
USNS *Mary Sears:* oceanographic survey ship
USNS *Sumner:* oceanographic survey ship
USNS *Victorious:* ocean surveillance ship
USNS *Waters:* range instrumentation ship
USNS *Zeus:* cable repair ship

See also CABLE REPAIR SHIP; MISSILE RANGE INSTRUMENTATION SHIPS; RESEARCH SHIPS.

Sprague, Clifton Albert Furlow (1896–1955) *navy admiral*

During WORLD WAR II, Sprague earned renown for his victory over the Japanese Central Force at the Battle of Leyte Gulf. Commanding an inferior force, Rear Admiral Sprague nevertheless destroyed the superior Japanese fleet of Admiral Kurita, thereby preventing it from destroying U.S. amphibious forces in Leyte Gulf in October 1944.

Born in Dorchester, Massachusetts, Sprague graduated from the UNITED STATES NAVAL ACADEMY in 1917. After Leyte Gulf, he went on to command the Alaskan Sea Frontier as commandant of the 17th Naval District. He retired with the rank of vice admiral in 1951.

Spruance, Raymond Ames (1886–1969) *navy admiral*

Spruance was born in Baltimore and graduated from the UNITED STATES NAVAL ACADEMY in 1906. He served with Admiral GEORGE DEWEY in the voyage of the Great White Fleet around the world, then served both at sea and on staff assignments during WORLD WAR I. Promoted to rear admiral in 1939, Spruance was given command of the 10th Naval District and the Caribbean Sea Frontier on the eve of WORLD WAR II. At the outbreak of the war, he was in command of Cruiser Division 5 of the PACIFIC FLEET. When Admiral WILLIAM F. HALSEY fell ill in June 1942, Spruance assumed temporary command of the Pacific Fleet and was instrumental in the American victory at the Battle of Midway, a turning point in the Pacific war.

Following Midway, Spruance was named chief of staff under Admiral CHESTER NIMITZ and deputy commander of the Pacific Fleet. Promoted in 1943 to vice admiral, he directed assaults on Tarawa, Makin, Eniwetok, Kwajalein, and Truk. In February 1944, he was promoted to admiral and commanded USN forces in the Battle of the Philippine Sea in June 1944. The following year, he directed USN operations at Iwo Jima and Okinawa.

Spruance was appointed president of the NAVAL WAR COLLEGE after the war, serving in that post

Admiral Raymond A. Spruance, April 1944 *(Naval Historical Foundation)*

until his retirement from the U.S. navy in 1948. He served as ambassador to the Philippines from 1952 to 1955.

Stark, Harold Raynsford (1880–1972) *chief of naval operations*

Stark served as eighth CHIEF OF NAVAL OPERATIONS from 1939 to 1942, when he became commander of U.S. Naval Forces, Europe, for the duration of WORLD WAR II.

He was born in Wilkes-Barre, Pennsylvania, and graduated from the UNITED STATES NAVAL ACADEMY in 1903. In 1917, during WORLD WAR I, Stark was appointed aide to Admiral WILLIAM S. SIMS, overall commander of U.S. naval forces in the war. After the war, Stark served in a variety of ordnance commands and, in 1928, became chief of staff to the commander, Destroyer Squadrons, Bat-

tle Fleet. During 1933–34, he commanded USS *West Virginia* (BB-47), from 1934 to 1937 was chief of the Bureau of Ordnance, and during 1937–38 commanded Cruiser Division, U.S. Fleet. During 1938–39, he commanded Cruisers, Battle Force, leaving this post to serve as CNO. In 1946, after his World War II service, Stark retired.

Stoddart, Benjamin (1751–1813) *secretary of the navy*

The nation's first SECRETARY OF THE NAVY, Stoddart was a native of Charles County, Maryland, and served as a captain of militia during the AMERICAN REVOLUTION. In 1779, he became secretary to the Board of War, serving until 1781. He was appointed navy secretary on May 18, 1798, and presided over the initial expansion of the newborn USN, authorizing construction or purchase of 50 warships and construction of major navy yards.

Submarine Force Atlantic Fleet

SUBLANT numbers 40 SUBMARINES and more than 15,000 U.S. Navy and civilian personnel, who provide submarine support to the Atlantic, Arctic, Eastern Pacific, and Indian Oceans, as well as the Mediterranean Sea. The fleet consists of ballistic missile submarines (SSBN) as well as attack submarines (SSN). The SSBNs carry Trident II D-5 missiles and are a key component in the nation's strategic deterrent, whereas the attack submarines perform antisubmarine warfare, intelligence gathering, insertion of special forces, Tomahawk strike missions, mining, and search and rescue.

SUBLANT is headquartered in Norfolk, Virginia, and is supported by submarine groups based in Groton, Connecticut; Kings Bay, Georgia; and Naples, Italy.

Submarine Force Pacific Fleet

Homeported at Pearl Harbor, Hawaii, SUBPAC includes ballistic missile submarines (SSBN) as well as attack submarines (SSN). The SSBNs carry Trident II D-5 missiles and are a key component in the nation's strategic deterrent, whereas the attack submarines perform antisubmarine warfare, intelligence gathering, insertion of special forces, Tomahawk strike missions, mining, and search and rescue.

The fleet consists of more than 40 submarines and auxiliary vessels. Commands include Submarine Squadron One, Submarine Squadron Three, Submarine Squadron Seven, Submarine Group Seven, Submarine Group Nine, Submarine Squadron Eleven, Submarine Squadron Fifteen, Submarine Squadron Seventeen, and Development Squadron Five, an intelligence-gathering organization.

submarines

In addition to some RESEARCH SHIPS and the research submarine (T-AGSS) USS *Dolphin,* the navy currently operates three major types of submarine: attack submarines (SSN), ballistic missile submarines (SSBN), and guided missile submarines (SSGN), in addition to the specially modified *Benjamin Franklin* class. The navy's combat submarine fleet is all nuclear powered. The first nuclear-powered submarine was the USS *Nautilus* (SSN-571), launched in 1954.

Attack Submarines (SSN)

Attack submarines are designed to seek and destroy enemy submarines and surface ships. Secondarily, SSNs engage in intelligence-collection missions and special forces delivery.

Operational SSN classes include *Los Angeles*–class submarines, *Seawolf*-class submarines, and the newest, *Virginia*-class submarines.

Los Angeles class

The most numerous class of attack submarines.

The general characteristics of the *Los Angeles* class include:

Builders: Newport News Shipbuilding Company and General Dynamics Electric Boat Division

Virginia (SSN-774) is christened, August 16, 2003. *(General Dynamics Electric Boat)*

Power plant: one nuclear reactor, one shaft
Length: 360 ft
Beam: 33 ft
Displacement: Approximately 6,900 tons submerged
Speed: 20+ knots
Crew: 13 officers, 121 enlisted
Armament: Tomahawk missiles, VLS tubes (SSN-719 and later), Mk-48 torpedoes, four torpedo tubes

Los Angeles, lead ship of the class, was deployed on November 13, 1976.

Seawolf Class

Seawolf (SSN-21) was the first vessel of this class and completed its initial sea trials in July 1996. Other *Seawolf*-class submarines are USS *Connecticut* (SSN-22) and USS *Jimmy Carter* (SSN-23). Submarines of this class share the following general characteristics:

Builders: General Dynamics Electric Boat Division
Power plant: one nuclear reactor, one shaft
Length: 353 ft
Draft: 35 ft
Beam: 40 ft
Displacement: 8,060 tons surfaced; 9,150 tons submerged
Speed: 25+ knots
Cost: about $2.1 billion each
Crew: 13 officers, 121 enlisted
Armament: Tomahawk missiles, and Mk-48 torpedoes in eight torpedo tubes

Virginia Class

The newest class of attack submarines (SSN), the *Virginia* class began construction in 1998. *Virginia* (SSN-774) was christened on August 16, 2003, and *Texas* (SSN-775) is scheduled for completion in 2005, *North Carolina* (SSN-777) in 2006, and *Hawaii* (SSN-776) in 2007. All the submarines share the following general characteristics:

Builders: General Dynamics Electric Boat Division and Newport News Shipbuilding
Power plant: one nuclear reactor, one shaft

Length: 377 ft
Beam: 34 ft
Displacement: approximately 7,800 tons
Speed: 25+ knots
Cost: about $1.65 billion each
Crew: 134
Armament: Tomahawk missiles, VLS tubes, Mk-48 torpedoes (four torpedo tubes), advanced mobile mines, and unmanned undersea vehicles

Skipjack Class (SSN-585)

The boats of the *Skipjack* class were attack submarines (SSN) of revolutionary design and were the second generation of nuclear-powered submarine after the *Nautilus.* The *Skipjack* class combined nuclear propulsion with an innovative teardrop-shaped hull, introduced in the conventionally powered *Albacore* in 1958. The new hull design reduced underwater resistance and allowed greater submerged speed and maneuverability. Another *Skipjack* innovation was its single shaft and placement of the bow planes on the sail, which greatly reduced flow noise at the bow-mounted sonar. The new reactor design, designated S5W, allowed for deep diving and high speeds and was the USN standard until the *Los Angeles* class, introduced in the mid-1970s.

One boat of the *Skipjack* class, *Scorpion* (SSN-589), was lost on May 22, 1968, with 12 officers and 87 enlisted men, probably the result of a mechanical failure and explosion, which caused a leak that flooded the submarine.

Commissioned between 1959 and 1961, the boats were decommissioned during 1986–91.

General specifications of the *Skipjack* class include:

Displacement: 3,070 tons surfaced
Displacement: 3,513 tons submerged
Length: 252 ft
Beam: 31 ft
Speed, surfaced: 15 knots
Speed, submerged: 29 knots
Test depth: 700 ft
Power plant: one nuclear reactor, two steam turbines, one shaft

Boats of the class included: *Skipjack* (SSN-585), *Scamp* (SSN-588), *Scorpion* (SSN-589), *Sculpin* (SSN-590), *Shark* (SSN-591), and *Snook* (SSN-592).

Permit Class (SSN-594)

The 14 attack submarines (SSN) of the *Permit* class were commissioned between 1961 and 1968 in response to the navy's Project Nobska, a scientific program to produce a new generation of deeper-diving, ultraquiet nuclear-powered submarines equipped with long-range sonar. The *Permit*-class boats featured a high degree of hull streamlining, reduction in sail dimensions by approximately 50 percent, quieting of the propulsion plant, and an increase in test depth, all of which contributed to advances in operational capabilities and stealth. Thus the *Permit* class is considered the world's first modern, quiet, deep-diving fast attack submarine.

Other innovations introduced with the *Permit* class include: hulls constructed of High Yield-80 (HY-80) steel alloy, which allowed operations at greater depths than previous submarines; raft mountings for turbines, motors, and other equipment, allowing quieter operations; and bow-mounted sonar, requiring the installation of torpedo tubes amidships. Larger than the earlier *Skipjack* class (SSN-585), they were just as fast.

The *Permit* class was originally designated the *Thresher* class, but the designation was changed when *Thresher* (SSN-593) was lost 200 miles off the coast of New England on April 10, 1963, apparently the result of a broken seawater pipe in the aft engine spaces. The loss of *Thresher* resulted in the incorporation of various new structural features in the later boats of the *Permit* class. All *Permit*-class submarines were decommissioned during 1989–96.

General specifications of the *Permit* class included:

Builders: SSNs 594, 595, Mare Island Naval Shipyard; SSNs 596, 607, 621, Ingalls Shipbuilding; SSNs 603, 604, 612, New York Shipbuilding; SSNs 605, 606, Portsmouth Naval Shipyard; SSNs 613–615, General Dynamics Electric Boat Division

Displacement: 4,200 tons submerged
Displacement: 3,540 tons surfaced
Length: 278 ft (SSN 605: 297 ft; SSNs 613–615, 292 ft)
Beam: 32 ft
Maximum navigational draft: 28 ft
Speed, official: 20+ knots
Speed, actual submerged: 30 knots
Speed, actual tactical: 15 knots
Operating depth, official: 400 ft
Operating depth, actual test depth: 1,300 ft
Operating depth, actual collapse depth: 1,900 ft
Construction: High Yield-80 (HY-80) steel alloy
Power plant: one S5W nuclear reactor, two steam turbines, one shaft, 15,000 shaft horsepower
Armament: Mk-48 torpedoes, four torpedo tubes; UUM-44A SUBROC UGM-84A/C Harpoon; Mk-57 deep water mines; Mk-60 CAPTOR mines
Sensors: BQQ-5 bow-mounted sonar; TB-16 towed sonar array
Crew: 143

Submarines of the class included: *Thresher* (SSN-593), *Permit* (SSN-594), *Plunger* (SSN-595), *Barb* (SSN-596), *Pollack* (SSN-603), *Haddo* (SSN-604), *Jack* (SSN-605), *Tinosa* (SSN-606), *Dace* (SSN-607), *Guardfish* (SSN-612), *Flasher* (SSN-613), *Greenling* (SSN-614), *Gato* (SSN-615), and *Haddock* (SSN-621).

Sturgeon Class (SSN-637)

Commissioned between 1966 and 1975 and decommissioned during the 1990s, the 37 attack submarines (SSN) of the *Sturgeon* class were built for antisubmarine warfare. Nuclear powered, they were larger than their predecessors *Skipjack* class (SSN-585) and *Permit* class (SSN-594) and so sacrificed some speed for increased combat capabilities. The boats were equipped to carry the Harpoon missile, the Tomahawk cruise missile, and Mk-48 torpedoes—the latter in tubes located amidships to accommodate the advanced bow-mounted sonar. Sail-mounted dive planes rotated to a vertical position for breaking through the ice when surfacing in Arctic regions.

Beginning with *Archerfish* (SSN-678), the submarines of this class were designated "long hulls" because of the 10 feet added to the hull to give them more living and working space. Additionally, six *Sturgeon*-class submarines were modified during 1982 and 1988–91 to carry the SEAL Dry Deck Shelter (DDS): SSNs 678–680, 682, 684, and 686. These boats had as their primary mission the covert insertion of special forces troops from the attached Dry Deck Shelter, a submersible launch hanger with a hyperbaric chamber that attaches to the submarine's weapon shipping hatch. All of the *Sturgeon* class were phased out by the 1990s and replaced by submarines of the *Los Angeles* and *Seawolf* classes.

General specifications of the *Sturgeon* class include:

Builder: SSNs 637, 650, 667, 669, 673–676, 678, 679, 681, 684, General Dynamics Electric Boat Division; SSNs 638, 649, General Dynamics Quincy Shipbuilding Division; SSNs 639, 647, 648, 652, 680, 682, 683, Ingalls Shipbuilding; SSNs 646, 660, Portsmouth Naval Shipyard; SSNs 662, 665, 666, 672, 677, San Francisco Naval Shipyard; SSNs 651, 653, 661, 663, 664, 668, 670, 686, 687, Newport News Shipbuilding

Displacement: 4,250 tons surfaced; SSNs 678–687, 4,460 tons

Displacement: 4,780 tons submerged; SSNs 678–687, 4,960 tons

Length: 292 ft; SSNs 678–687, 302 ft

Beam: 32 ft

Draft: 28.8 ft

Speed, official: 20+ knots

Speed, actual: 25 knots

Operating depth, official: "greater than 400 ft"

Operating depth, actual test depth: 1,300 ft

Operating depth, actual collapse depth: 1,900 ft

Power plant: one S5W nuclear reactor, two steam turbines, 15,000 shaft horsepower, one shaft

Armament: Mk-48 torpedoes, four torpedo tubes; UUM-44A SUBROC UGM-84A/C Harpoon; Mk-57 deep water mines; Mk-60 CAPTOR mines

Radars: BPS-14/15 surface search

Sonars: BQQ-5 multifunction bow mounted; BQR-7 passive in submarines with BQQ-2; BQR-26 in SSN-666; BQS-6 active in submarines with BQQ-2; BQS-12 active on SSNs 637–664; BQS-13 active on SSNs 665–687; TB-16 or TB-23 towed array

EW systems: WLQ-4(V); WLR-4(V); WLR-9

Narwhal (SSN-671)

Commissioned in 1969 and decommissioned in 1999, the attack submarine (SSN) *Narwhal* was, at the time of her launching, the quietest submarine ever built. This was the result of using a revolutionary natural circulation reactor design. Built as the prototype platform for an ultraquiet natural circulation reactor design, the boat was modified for special missions and was also fitted to sail as a Remotely Operated Vehicle. The natural circulation reactor design allows for operation with the large water circulating pumps—a major source of radiated noise—fully secured. The design pioneered in this boat was used in the later *Los Angeles* and *Ohio* classes.

Many of *Narwhal*'s missions remain classified, but it has been reported that the submarine was fitted with a special structure, called a "turtleback" forward of her rudder. It is believed that this was part of the radio equipment used to remote-control underwater vehicles.

General specifications of *Narwhal* included:

Builder: General Dynamics Electric Boat Division

Displacement: 5,350 tons submerged

Length: 314 ft

Beam: 38 ft

Speed: 20+ knots

Power plant: one S5G nuclear reactor, two steam turbines, one shaft, 17,000 shaft horsepower

Armament: torpedoes in four torpedo tubes; Harpoon missiles, Tomahawk missiles

Crew: 141

Parche (SSN-683)

Although classified as an attack submarine, the *Parche,* whose keel was laid in December 1970 at the Ingalls Shipbuilding Division of Litton Industries, Pascagoula, Mississippi, underwent an extended overhaul at Mare Island Shipyard from 1987 to 1991. The submarine was refueled and modified for "research and development." Modification included the addition of a 100-foot extension to the hull just forward of the control room and sail, bringing her total length up to just over 401 feet and submerged displacement to 7,800 tons. The new mission of the modified *Parche* was assignment to Submarine Development Squadron 5, homeport at Naval Submarine Base Bangor, Washington. The boat was tasked with intelligence gathering and underwater salvage. *Parche* supports covert intelligence-gathering operations and is equipped with a remote grapple that, extended through a hatch in the keel, can salvage such small items from the ocean floor as missiles, nuclear warheads, satellites, and so on.

Parche is a modified member of the now-obsolete *Sturgeon* class and shares with the class an ice-strengthened hull and reinforced sail, which incorporates diving planes capable of pivoting 90 degrees (vertical) to avoid damage when the boat crashes through ice to surface. In addition to bow-mounted sonar (located there to isolate it at the maximum distance from the boat's screw), *Parche* mounts short-range navigational sonars (both upward and forward facing) and armored spotlights and closed-circuit television cameras for under-ice operations. Self-defense capability includes four 21-inch-diameter torpedo tubes (two to a side, amidships, angled out from the centerline) capable of firing Mk-48 torpedoes or Harpoon or Tomahawk antiship missiles.

General specifications of *Parche* include:

Builder: Ingalls Shipbuilding, Pascagoula, Mississippi

Length: 401 feet, 5 1/8 inches

Displacement: 7,800 tons submerged

Submerged speed: >20 knots

Diving depth: >400 ft

Crew: 22 officers, 157 enlisted

Propulsion: nuclear reactor plant, single propeller

Glenard P. Lipscomb (SSN-685)

Of special historical importance is the *Glenard P. Lipscomb* (SSN-685), which was a prototype navy attack submarine (SSN) commissioned in 1974 and decommissioned in 1989. Nuclear powered, it used an innovative turbo-electric power plant known as a Submarine Turbo-Electric Drive (TEDS) rather than the conventional geared drive. In other respects, it was essentially a *Sturgeon*-class (SSN-637) submarine. The *Glenard P. Lipscomb* was intended to test the potential advantages of the new propulsion system to provide quieter operations. While the boat did prove quieter, the heavier TEDS machinery resulted in slower speeds. This, coupled with certain issues of reliability, led to the decision against using the design on the follow-on *Los Angeles* class, and *Glenard P. Lipscomb* remained a one-of-a-kind submarine. Specifications included:

Builder: General Dynamics Electric Boat Division

Displacement: 6,480 tons submerged

Length: 365 ft

Beam: 32 ft

Speed: 20+ knots

Power plant: one nuclear reactor, turbine-electric drive, one shaft

Armament: torpedoes in four torpedo tubes; Harpoon missiles, Tomahawk missiles

Crew: 141

Ballistic Missile Submarines (SSBN)

The navy's currently operational SSBNs, nuclear-powered submarines armed with long-range strategic missiles intended for the deployment of strategic (nuclear) weapons, are all of the *Ohio* class, the first of which, USS *Ohio* (SSBN-726), was deployed on November 11, 1981.

Ohio Class

The *Ohio*-class ballistic missile submarines (SSBN) were commissioned during 1981–84 to replace the aging fleet of ballistic missile submarines, most of which were built in the 1960s. The 18 *Ohio*-class submarines each carry 24 Trident missiles, accounting for half of the total U.S. strategic warheads. These weapons have no pre-set targets, but each SSBN is capable of rapidly targeting its missiles via sophisticated at-sea communications links.

The submarines are designed with a cylindrical pressure hull structure of HY-80 steel enclosed within a streamlined outer hull, which permits the submarine to move at high speeds quietly through the water. The *Ohio*-class boats were designed expressly for extended deterrent patrols. Their endurance is enhanced by three large logistics hatches, which provide large-diameter resupply and repair openings. Overhauls are scheduled at greater than 15-year intervals, and each *Ohio*-class submarine is intended to be at sea at least 66 percent of the time.

A Trident II is launched from a USN submarine.   *(U.S. Navy)*

The first eight *Ohio*-class submarines were equipped with Trident I C-4 missiles. Newer ships, beginning with the USS *Tennessee* (SSBN-734), were equipped with the Trident II D-5 missile system as they were built. On September 18, 1994, it was decided to withdraw four *Ohio*-class submarines from the strategic nuclear role and assign them to other missions. Redesignated as SSGNs, the four modified submarines would carry 154 Tomahawk missiles and Special Forces (SEALs) units and would be used for SEAL deployment. Each boat could carry up to 66 SEALs or other commandos, and a minisub (currently under development) would be affixed to the bow. The submarines chosen for conversion are *Ohio, Michigan, Florida,* and *Georgia*.

The *Ohio*-class shares the following general characteristics:

Builders: General Dynamics Electric Boat Division
Power plant: one nuclear reactor, one shaft
Length: 560 ft
Beam: 42 ft
Displacement: 16,764 tons surfaced; 18,750 tons submerged
Speed: 20+ knots (23+ mph 36.8+ kph)
Armament: 24 tubes for Trident I and II missiles; Mk-48 torpedoes have four torpedo tubes
Crew: 15 officers, 140 enlisted

The 18 *Ohio*-class submarines are USS *Michigan* (SSBN-727), slated for SSGN conversion, October 2003; USS *Georgia* (SSBN-729), slated for SSGN conversion, 2004; USS *Henry M. Jackson* (SSBN-730); USS *Alabama* (SSBN-731); USS *Alaska* (SSBN-732); USS *Nevada* (SSBN-733); USS *Pennsylvania* (SSBN-735); and USS *Kentucky* (SSBN-737). All of these vessels are homeported at the Naval Submarine Base, Bangor, Washington. Homeported at Naval Submarine Base Kings Bay, Georgia, are USS *Tennessee* (SSBN-734); USS *West Virginia* (SSBN-736); USS *Maryland* (SSBN-738); USS *Nebraska* (SSBN-739); USS *Rhode Island* (SSBN-740); USS *Maine* (SSBN-741); USS *Wyoming* (SSBN-742); and USS *Louisiana* (SSBN-743). As of mid-

2003, the USS *Ohio* (SSBN-726) and USS *Florida* (SSBN-728) were undergoing conversion to SSGNs.

George Washington Class (SSBN-598)

The *George Washington* (SSBN-598) was the world's first nuclear-powered ballistic missile submarine (SSBN). The submarines of this class, commissioned between 1959 and 1961 and decommissioned during 1981–85, constituted one of the most important weapons of the 20th century, perhaps of all time. The *George Washington* class gave the United States a stealthy and highly survivable platform from which a major thermonuclear attack could be launched.

The first two boats of the class, *George Washington* and *Patrick Henry,* had been planned as attack submarines (SSN), but were extended with a 130-foot missile compartment, nicknamed "Sherwood Forest" because of its 16 vertically mounted Polaris launch tubes.

In the early 1980s *George Washington* (SSBN-598), *Patrick Henry* (SSBN-599), and *Robert E. Lee* (SSBN-601) had their missiles removed and were reclassified as attack submarines.

General specifications of this very important class of submarine included:

> **Builders:** General Dynamics Electric Boat Division; Newport News Shipbuilding; Mare Island Naval Shipyard; Portsmouth Naval Shipyard
> **Power plant:** S5W pressurized water nuclear reactor, two geared turbines at 15,000 shaft horsepower to one shaft
> **Length:** 381.6 ft
> **Beam:** 33 ft
> **Displacement:** 5,959–6,019 tons surface
> **Displacement:** 6,709–6,888 tons submerged (approximate)
> **Speed, surfaced:** 20 knots
> **Speed, submerged:** 25 knots
> **Test depth:** 700 ft
> **Armament:** 16 tubes for Polaris missiles; six torpedo tubes

Submarines of the class included: *George Washington* (SSBN-598), *Patrick Henry* (SSBN-599),

Theodore Roosevelt (SSBN-600), *Robert E. Lee* (SSBN-601), and *Abraham Lincoln* (SSBN-602).

Ethan Allen Class (SSBN-608)

The lead ship of this class of ballistic missile submarines (SSBN), *Ethan Allen* (SSBN-608), fired, on May 6, 1962, the only nuclear-armed Polaris missile ever launched. This was during the 1962 atomic tests and, to date, is the only complete proof test of a U.S. strategic missile. Given the international ban on atmospheric testing of nuclear and thermonuclear weapons, it is highly unlikely that another test will ever be performed.

Commissioned between 1961 and 1963, all five submarines of this class were decommissioned during 1983–92 in compliance with Strategic Arms Limitation Treaty (SALT) agreements—although some vessels, their missiles removed, were reclassified as attack submarines (SSN).

General specifications of the *Ethan Allen* class included:

> **Builders:** General Dynamics Electric Boat Division; Newport News Shipbuilding
> **Power plant:** S5W nuclear reactor, two geared steam turbines, one shaft
> **Speed:** 20+ knots
> **Armament:** 16 tubes for Polaris missiles; six torpedo tubes

Submarines of the class included: *Ethan Allen* (SSBN-608), *Sam Houston* (SSBN-609), *Thomas A. Edison* (SSBN-610), *John Marshall* (SSBN-611), and *Thomas Jefferson* (SSBN-618).

Benjamin Franklin–Class Submarines

Originally commissioned as ballistic missile submarines (SSBN), there were one dozen vessels of this class, the first of which, *Benjamin Franklin,* was commissioned in 1963. All but two of the class were decommissioned by the mid-1990s; the USS *Kamehameha* (SSBN/SSN-642) and the *James K. Polk* (SSBN/SSN-645) were converted to drydeck shelter/swimmer delivery platforms for support of special warfare operations, chiefly the delivery and deployment of navy SEALs. The former missile spaces were converted to accommodations, storage, and recreation spaces.

On January 8, 1999, *James K. Polk* was inactivated, leaving *Kamehameha* as the navy's only SSBN equipped with dry deck shelters.

Guided Missile Submarines (SSGN)

Four *Ohio*-class ballistic missile submarines (SSBN) previously scheduled for inactivation during 2003–04 were slated instead for conversion to guided missile submarines (SSGN) over a five-year period ending in 2008. The primary missions of these converted ships will be land attack and Special Operations Forces (SOF) insertion and support. Secondary missions will be the traditional attack submarine roles of intelligence, surveillance, and reconnaissance (ISR), battle space preparation, and sea control. Each nuclear-powered submarine will be armed with up to 140 Tomahawk or Tactical Tomahawk land-attack missiles and will have the ability to carry and support a team of 66 SOF personnel for up to 90 days. SOF-outfitted attack submarines (SSN) can support a team for no more than 15 days.

The ships undergoing conversion are USS *Ohio* (SSBN-726), USS *Michigan* (SSBN-727), USS *Florida* (SSBN-728), and USS *Georgia* (SSBN-729). The general characteristics of these vessels include:

Builders: General Dynamics Electric Boat Division
Power plant: one nuclear reactor, one shaft
Length: 560 ft
Beam: 42 ft
Displacement: 16,764 tons surfaced; 18,750 tons submerged
Speed: 20+ knots
Armament: up to 140 Tomahawk missiles
Crew: 15 officers, 140 enlisted

Research Submarine (T-AGSS)

The USS *Dolphin* (AGSS-555) is the navy's only diesel-electric deep-diving research and development submarine. Deployed on August 15, 1968, USS *Dolphin* quickly set a world depth record for operational submarines and has since engaged in scientific and military work in acoustic deep-water and littoral research, near-bottom and ocean surveys, weapons launches, sensor trials, and engineering evaluations. Designed expressly as a test platform, USS *Dolphin* can be readily modified both internally and for installation of up to 12 tons of research and test equipment.

General characteristics of the ship include:

Builder: Portsmouth Naval Shipyard
Power plant: diesel/electric; two GM 12-cylinder, 425 horsepower engines
Length: 165 ft
Displacement: 950 tons full load
Diameter: 18 ft
Operating depth: 3,000 ft
Crew: five officers, 46 enlisted, and up to five scientists
Armament: none

submarine tenders (AS)

Today's submarine tenders furnish maintenance and logistic support for nuclear attack SUBMARINES (SSN). Submarine tenders are the largest of the navy's active auxiliaries. Their crews are made up mostly of technicians and repair personnel. Unlike the smaller SSNs, the current generation of ballistic missile submarines (SSBN) are sufficiently self-sustaining not to require tenders.

SSN Tenders

Emory Land Class
The *Emory Land* class, three ships commissioned in the late 1970s and early 1980s, include the newest navy submarine tenders (AS), specifically designed to service *Los Angeles*–class attack submarines. *Emory Land*–class ships provide food, electricity, water, consumables, spare parts, medical, dental, disbursing, mail, legal services, ordnance, and parts or equipment repair that the submarines require. These large vessels have 53 specialized shops for servicing up to 12 nuclear-powered submarines simultaneously. Service capability includes nuclear system repair and testing, electrical and electronic

repair, hull repair, sheet metal and steel work, pipe fabrication, foundry, woodworking, underwater diving and rescue, and hazardous material management. Routine services include steam, diesel fuel, water, and electricity. The ships of this class can store and handle the USN's tactical submarine-launched weapons, including Mk-48 torpedoes, mines, and Tomahawk cruise missiles. Also on board are full medical and dental facilities, laundry and dry cleaning plants, data processing equipment, and large storage areas for refrigerated and dry cargo food. Cranes, elevators, and conveyors move material on and off the ship as well as between decks.

General specifications of the class include:

Builder: Lockheed Shipbuilding and Construction Company, Seattle, Washington
Length: 644 ft
Beam: 85 ft
Displacement: 23,000 tons full load
Draft: 26 ft full load
Speed: 20 knots
Armament: four 20-mm guns; two .50-caliber guns; two 40-mm grenade launchers
Specialized shops: 53
Decks/levels: 13
Crew: 1,351, mostly technicians and specialists
Departments: Administrative, Chaplain, Communications, Deck, Dental, Engineering, Legal, Maintenance, Medical, Ops/Nav, Safety, Supply, and Weapons

Ships of the class include *Emory S. Land* (AS-39), *Frank Cable* (AS-40), and *McKee* (AS-41).

Proteus (AS-19)

Commissioned during WORLD WAR II in 1944 and not decommissioned until 1992, *Proteus* was a submarine tender (AS), its mission to repair and resupply submarines at sea. In 1959–60, *Proteus* underwent a major overhaul and reconfiguration to serve as a submarine tender to ballistic missile submarines (SSBN). In 1981, the ship was again refitted as an attack submarine (SSN) tender, in which capacity she served until her decommissioning.

General specifications of *Proteus* included:

Builder: Moore Shipbuilding and Drydock
Displacement: 19,200 tons full load
Length: 575 ft
Beam: 73 ft
Speed: 15.4 knots
Armament: four 20-mm guns
Crew: about 557, mostly technicians

L.Y. Spear Class

Commissioned in 1970 and 1971 and decommissioned in 1995 and 1996, the *L.Y. Spear* class consisted of two submarine tenders (AS). The ships of the class were designed to service attack submarines (SSN), up to four of them simultaneously, moored alongside the tender.

General specifications of the class included:

Builder: General Dynamics Quincy Shipbuilding Division
Displacement: 23,396 tons full load
Dead weight: 9,034 tons
Overall length: 643 ft
Waterline length: 620 ft
Extreme beam: 85 ft
Waterline beam: 85 ft
Maximum navigational draft: 29 ft
Draft limit: 29 ft
Speed: 20 knots
Power plant: two boilers, steam turbines, one shaft
Armament: two 40-mm guns, four 20-mm guns
Crew: 87 officers, 1,235 enlisted, mostly technicians and specialists

Ships of the class included *L.Y. Spear* (AS-36) and *Dixon* (AS-37).

SSBN Tenders (All Decommissioned)

Simon Lake Class

The two *Simon Lake*–class ships were commissioned in 1964 and 1965 and decommissioned in 1999 and 1994, respectively. They were specifically configured to service ballistic missile submarines (SSBN) and served as at-sea repair, weapons handling, and supply bases for submarines as well as other ships. The *Simon Lake* class had extensive repair facilities and was crewed by specially trained personnel skilled in such specialties as pattern making, carpentry, nuclear repair, gyro repair, interior communications, periscope and optical repair, refrigeration and air conditioning, diving and underwater hull repair, fire control repair, torpedo overhaul, instrument repair, electronics repair, chemical analysis, and other specialties. Also important was the supply function of the class. Each of these ships carried about 52,000 general and technical supply items. The ships also provided fresh water, fuel oil, lube oil, oxygen, nitrogen, antisubmarine weapons, pyrotechnics, distilled battery water, food, electrical power, small boats, and crane services. Also on board was a complement of chaplains, physicians, a medical treatment room, operating room, and X-ray facilities. The ships had disbursing facilities, barber shops, laundry and dry cleaning plants, a soda fountain, uniform shop, and a self-service ship's store.

General specifications of the class included:

Builders: Puget Sound Naval Shipyard (AS-33); Ingalls Shipbuilding (AS-34)
Displacement: 20,088 tons (AS-33) full load
Dead weight: 6,291 tons (AS-33)
Displacement: 20,922 tons (AS-34) full load
Dead weight: 6,606 tons (AS-34)
Overall length: 644 ft
Waterline length: 620 ft
Extreme beam: 85 ft
Waterline beam: 85 ft
Maximum navigational draft: 27 ft
Draft limit: 30 ft
Power plant: two boilers, steam turbines, one shaft
Armament: four 20-mm guns
Crew: 601, including mainly technicians and specialists

Ships of the class included *Simon Lake* (AS-33) and *Canopus* (AS-34).

Hunley Class

The *Hunley* class of submarine tenders (AS) consisted of two ships commissioned in 1962 and 1963 and decommissioned in 1994 and 1996. The vessels were configured specifically to service ballistic missile submarines (SSBN).

General specifications of the class included:

Displacement: 17,640 tons full load
Dead weight: 4,788 tons
Length: 599 ft
Beam: 83 ft
Speed: 19 knots
Power plant: diesel electric, one shaft
Armament: four 20-mm guns
Crew: 603, mainly technicians

Ships of the class included *Hunley* (AS-31) and *Holland* (AS-32).

DSRV Tenders

Pigeon Class

The two ships of the *Pigeon* class, commissioned in 1973 and decommissioned in 1992 and 1995, were designed as surface support ships for deep submergence rescue vehicles (DSRVs) used during submarine rescue operations (see RESCUE AND SALVAGE SHIPS). The ships conducted rescue operations using the McCann rescue chamber and also supported deep sea diving operations. They were capable of transporting, servicing, lowering, and raising two DSRVs and supporting diving operations to depths of 850 feet. The ships could support divers indefinitely, lowering them to the ocean floor in pressurized transfer chambers for intervals of open-sea work. Also, the ships could serve as operational control vessels during deep-sea salvage operations.

The *Pigeon*-class ships were the first in the world built specifically for the submarine rescue mission. Except for one MILITARY SEALIFT COMMAND ship, they are also the first catamaran-hull ships built for the navy since Robert Fulton's *Demologos* in 1812.

General specifications of the class included:

Builder: Alabama Drydock and Shipbuilding
Power plant: four diesels, two shafts
Overall length: 251 ft
Waterline length: 230 ft
Beam: 86 ft

Maximum navigational draft: 26 ft
Draft limit: 26 ft
Displacement: 4,954 tons full loaded
Dead weight: 835 tons
Speed: 15 knots
Crew: ship's company, 240; submersible operations, 24
Helicopter: helipad for landing

Ships of the class included *Pigeon* (ASR-21) and *Ortolan* (ASR-22).

Sullivan, John L. (1899–1982) *secretary of the navy*
Sullivan left Dartmouth College in December 1918 to enlist in the USN just after WORLD WAR I, but returned to college after a three-month tour. Taking a law degree at Harvard Law School, he practiced law until 1939, when he became assistant to the commissioner of internal revenue. Subsequently, he was appointed assistant secretary of the treasury. With the death of FDR, Sullivan returned to his law practice, but soon came back to Washington as assistant SECRETARY OF THE NAVY in July 1945. In 1946, he was named undersecretary, then, in September 1947, he became secretary. Two years later, on May 24, 1949, he resigned in protest of a presidential order cancelling construction of the major AIRCRAFT CARRIER *United States* during the so-called "revolt of the admirals."

Supervisors of Shipbuilding, Conversion, and Repair (SUPSHIP)
SUPSHIP works with private contractors to acquire, maintain, and modernize affordable and operationally superior ships for the U.S. Navy. SUPSHIP supervises execution of new construction, repair, and modernization. Facilities include:

- SUPSHIP Bath (Maine): Provides technical, contract, and program management functions, especially in conjunction with the Bath Iron Works Corporation.
- SUPSHIP Groton (Connecticut): Liaison between the DEPARTMENT OF THE NAVY and Electric Boat Corporation, which designs, builds, repairs, and modernizes nuclear-powered submarines.
- SUPSHIP Jacksonville (Florida): A major repair facility.
- SUPSHIP New Orleans: Provides technical, contract, and program management functions.
- SUPSHIP Newport News (Virginia): Administers shipbuilding, design, conversion, and repair contracts with Newport News Shipbuilding and Dry Dock Company and other assigned contractors.
- SUPSHIP Pascagoula (Mississippi): Provides technical, contract, and program management functions.
- SUPSHIP Portsmouth (Virginia): Provides for planning, procurement, and administration of ship repair/maintenance contracts in the Mid-Atlantic Region.
- SUPSHIP Puget Sound (Washington): Responsible for procurement and administration of new construction and ship repair contracts with private sector shipyards in the Pacific Northwest.
- SUPSHIP San Diego: Administers shipbuilding, design, conversion, and facility contracts at assigned private shipyards; also develops specifications and procures and administers contracts for overhauls, repairs, alterations, activations, and inactivations.

Surface Combat Systems Center
Surface Combat Systems Center, Wallops Island, Virginia, provides testing facilities for deployed USN surface combat systems as well as advanced systems under development. The facility provides a full maritime test environment, including an operational team and combat systems to conduct realistic test events.

Surface Warfare Officers School Command
The Surface Warfare Officers School Command, located in Newport, Rhode Island, provides professional education and training in support of USN

requirements to prepare officers to serve in surface ships at sea. The school consists of the following departments:

- Command Training Department: Provides for Naval Surface Warfare forces officers who are professionally qualified to serve as commanding officers and executive officers of seagoing and special mission units.
- Damage Control Training Department: Provides active and reserve, naval and Coast Guard officers instruction and training in damage control for surface ships.
- Department Head Training Department: Prepares mid-grade surface warfare officers to confidently and competently manage departments and direct underway operations.
- Division Officer Training Department: Prepares newly commissioned ensigns, enroute to their first tour as division officers afloat, to stand inport and underway watches, and to manage the administrative duties of the division officer afloat.
- Engineering Specialty Training Department: Prepares surface warfare officers to manage the operation and maintenance of shipboard propulsion plants and auxiliaries.
- Communications School Training Department: Prepares officers to manage the operation and maintenance of shipboard information technology and communications equipment.

Swift Boats

Officially designated Fast Patrol Craft (PCF), Swift Boats were deployed by the navy during the VIETNAM WAR for riverine operations. Some 650 Swift Boats patrolled the rivers of South Vietnam, constituting what sailors called the "brown water navy."

Swift Boats were 51 feet in length and were constructed with aluminum hulls. Armament consisted of three .50-caliber machine guns (one single mount and one twin mount) and one 81-mm mortar. Crew consisted of a single officer and five enlisted sailors. The basic design was adapted from oil rig crew boats used to support offshore drilling rigs in the Gulf of Mexico.

Two generations of Swift Boats were produced, the Mk-I and Mk-II. Specifications for both were similar and included the following:

Displacement: 22.2 tons full load
Length: 51 ft
Beam: 15 ft
Draft: 3.5 ft
Propulsion: two 12V71N diesels (General Motors); 960 bhp; two shafts
Speed: 28 knots
Range: 350 nautical miles at 28 knots
Crew: one officer, five enlisted
Weapons: one 81-mm mortar; three .50-caliber machine guns (one single mount, one twin mount)

T

Tactical Training Group Pacific, San Diego (TTGP)

TACTRAGRUPAC provides advanced tactical training to USN personnel and personnel from other services in order to improve proficiency in warfighting and joint operations. The object of the training presented is not to teach basic proficiencies, but how to integrate a given platform into the total force. Courses include:

- Joint Force Air Component Commander (JFACC) Augmentation Staff Course (JASC): Emphasizes joint air operations planning and execution and Theater Battle Management Core System (TBMCS) skill refinement.
- Joint Maritime Tactics Course: Provides senior command and staff officers tactical training to improve proficiency in warfighting in joint combat and naval expeditionary operations.
- Mission Distribution System Staff Employment Course (MDS): Provides staff Tomahawk Land Attack Missile (TLAM) strike officers and their assistants hands-on instruction in the use of Tomahawk missile systems.
- Staff Tactical Watch Officer: Provides mid-grade warfare specialty officers with the tactical and procedural skills required to perform duties as a task force/group tactical watch officer in a multithreat expeditionary force/group.
- TLAM Tactical Commander Course: Instructs senior tactical commanders and their staffs in

capabilities and employment considerations for the Tomahawk Land Attack Missile (TLAM).

Tailhook Association

Representing about 16,000 USMC and USN aviators, the association was created to provide a forum for discussing the future of USMC and USN military aviation. Unfortunately, the name "Tailhook" was badly tarnished by the scandal that broke out as a result of behavior ranging from sexual harassment to rape at the 35th Annual Tailhook Convention in Las Vegas in September 1991. A Department of Defense investigation found that 83 women and seven men had been victims of "indecent assault." Some 140 USN and USMC officers were investigated, the SECRETARY OF THE NAVY, H. Lawrence Garrett, resigned, and the CHIEF OF NAVAL OPERATIONS, Admiral Frank B. Kelso, took early retirement as a result of the scandal.

Third Fleet

With the SEVENTH FLEET, Third Fleet makes up the PACIFIC FLEET. Third Fleet covers about 50 million square miles of the eastern and northern Pacific Ocean, including the Bering Sea, Alaska, the Aleutian Islands, and a portion of the Arctic. Its principal mission is conflict deterrence.

Third Fleet was created during WORLD WAR II on March 15, 1943, under the command of Admiral WILLIAM F. HALSEY and played a key role in many major campaigns. Halsey's Third Fleet flagship, USS *Missouri* (BB-63), hosted the Japanese signing of the instrument of surrender ending World War II, on September 2, 1945.

On October 7, 1945, Third Fleet was designated a reserve fleet and decommissioned from active status. It was not recommissioned until February 1, 1973, pursuant to a reorganization of the Pacific Fleet. Currently, in addition to its peacetime mission of deterrence, Third Fleet trains naval forces for overseas deployment and evaluates state-of-the-art technology for fleet use. Since November 26, 1986, the flagship of the fleet has been USS *Coronado* (AGF-11).

Tomahawk Cruise Missile   See MISSILES.

torpedoes

Modern torpedoes are self-propelled guided projectiles that operate underwater and that detonate on contact or in proximity to a target. They may be launched from SUBMARINES, surface ships, helicopters, and fixed-wing aircraft. Some are actually parts of other weapons; for example, the Mk-46 lightweight torpedo becomes the warhead section of the ASROC (Anti-Submarine ROCket), and a captor mine employs a submerged sensor platform that releases a torpedo when a hostile contact is detected.

Currently, the USN inventory includes three major torpedoes: the Mk-48 heavyweight torpedo, the Mk-46 lightweight, and the Mk-50 advanced lightweight torpedo.

Mark-46 Lightweight Torpedo

The Mk-46 is designed to attack high-performance submarines and is currently designated the NATO standard torpedo. The Mk-46 Mod 5 is the mainstay of the USN's antisubmarine warfare lightweight torpedo inventory and is slated to remain in service until 2015. The Mk-46 may be launched from ships or aircraft.

General characteristics of the Mk-46 Mod 5 include:

Contractor: Alliant Techsystems
Power plant: two-speed, reciprocating external combustion; mono-propellant-fueled (Otto fuel II)
Length: 102.36 inches in tube-launch configuration
Weight: 517.65 lb (warshot configuration)
Diameter: 12.75 in
Range: 8,000 yards
Depth: 1,200+ ft
Speed: 28+ knots (32.2+ mph)
Guidance system: active or passive/active acoustic homing in homing mode, or snake or circle search in launch/search mode
Warhead: 98 lb of PBXN-103 high explosive

Mod 0 was deployed in 1966, and Mod 5 in 1979.

Mark-48 Heavyweight Torpedo

The Mk-48 torpedo is designed to target fast, deep-diving nuclear submarines and high-performance surface ships. USN submarines are equipped with the torpedo or with an improved version, Mk-48 ADCAP. The Mk-48 has been operational since 1972, and the Mk-48 ADCAP since 1988.

General characteristics of the Mk-48 and Mk-48 ADCAP include:

Contractor: Gould, Inc.
Power plant: piston engine; pump jet
Length: 19 ft
Weight: Mk-48, 3,434 lb; Mk-48 ADCAP, 3,695 lb
Diameter: 21 in
Range: 5+ mi
Depth: 1,200+ ft
Speed: 28+ knots
Guidance system: wire guided, with passive/active acoustic homing
Warhead: 650 lb high explosive

Mark-50 Advanced Lightweight Torpedo

The Mk-50 is designed for use against state-of-the-art submarines, which are faster, deeper-diving, and generally more sophisticated than conventional submarines. The weapons can be launched from all antisubmarine warfare-capable aircraft, as well as from torpedo tubes on surface ships. Eventually, the Mk-50 will completely replace the Mk-46 lightweight torpedo.

General characteristics of the Mk-50 include:

Contractor: Alliant Techsystems and Westinghouse
Power plant: stored chemical energy propulsion system
Length: 112 in
Weight: 750 lb
Diameter: 12.75 in
Speed: 40+ knots
Guidance system: active/passive acoustic homing
Warhead: about 100 lb high explosive in a shaped charge

Tracy, Benjamin F. (1830–1915) *secretary of the navy*

An upstate New York attorney, Tracy became a major force in organizing the state's Republican Party during the years leading up to the CIVIL WAR. Vigorous in raising and leading two volunteer regiments during the war, he performed with such heroism at the Battle of the Wilderness that he was awarded the Medal of Honor. President Benjamin Harrison appointed him the nation's 32nd SECRETARY OF THE NAVY in 1889. With his customary vigor, Tracy reformed the navy, generally raising the standard of its personnel and creating a naval militia.

transport oilers/tankers (T-AOT)   See CARGO, FUEL, AND REPLENISMENT SHIPS.

Trident II D-5 Ballistic Missile   See MISSILES.

U

underway replenishment

Underway replenishment (UNREP) is the general term for methods by which provisions, ammunition, and fuel are transferred from one ship to another at sea. The technique of replenishment at sea enables a fleet or naval formation to remain at sea for prolonged periods of time.

There are two major methods by which UNREP is carried out:

Connected Replenishment (CONREP): The replenishment ship maintains a steady course and speed, while the receiving ship comes alongside at 80 to 200 feet. The replenishment ship can service two ships at a time, one on either side. Depending on what is being transferred, the ships are connected together with wires through which fuel hoses or trolley devices are passed. Fuel is trans-

An underway replenishment oiler prepares to transfer jet fuel for the aircraft of the USS *Enterprise* (CVN-65). *(U.S. Navy)*

ferred through hoses; other goods are palletized and sent over via trolley to the receiving ship.

Vertical Replenishment (VERTREP): Helicopters are used to transfer prepositioned palletized supplies from the flight deck of the replenishment ship to the flight deck of the receiving ship.

underway replenishment oilers (T-AO)

See CARGO, FUEL, AND REPLENISHMENT SHIPS.

uniforms

In contrast to the uniforms of the other services, USN uniforms have historically reflected general seafaring and naval traditions rather than any distinctively national style. Traditionally, USN uniforms have most resembled those of Britain's Royal Navy, not only in general appearance and cut, but also in color: dark blue for winter, white for summer.

The uniform prescribed for officers of the Continental navy during the AMERICAN REVOLUTION was a blue coat faced in red. In 1802, gold lace was added to officers' uniforms. By the mid-19th century, the prescribed officer's uniform was a blue jacket, which evolved into a long, double-breasted coat by later in the century.

Before 1841, USN officers wore the cocked hat traditional with Royal Navy officers. After 1841, this was replaced by a cloth cap for regular duty. The current USN emblem was displayed on the cap beginning in 1883, and officers adopted a gold-embroidered visor just before the SPANISH-AMERICAN WAR, in 1897. For summer wear, a white coat featuring shoulder marks denoting rank was adopted in 1901. It was not until 1941, the beginning of WORLD WAR II, that officers wore loose, comfortable khaki uniforms as shipboard working dress. This reflected the general trend in the U.S. military to provide separate nonbattle and "working" battle uniforms.

Except for senior petty officers, enlisted sailors dressed from the earliest days of the USN in open-neck clothing well suited to the physically demanding occupation of the seafarer. During the first two-thirds of the 19th century, USN sailors wore "slops"—wide-legged breeches, blue jackets, vests, black neckerchiefs, and canvas hats. By 1879, the jacket was replaced by a frock or jumper featuring a deep collar edged with white tape. In 1885, sailors were issued overcoats—the familiar short pea coat, which was borrowed from Dutch maritime tradition. This gradually replaced the blue jacket.

In 1902, the USN adopted the familiar blue bell-bottomed trousers, the fly of which closed with 13 buttons, signifying the original 13 states. In 1885, the familiar stitched white canvas cap began to replace the blue cloth "flat hat" cap, which had been adopted in 1859.

As World War II brought utilitarian changes in officers' working uniforms, so it introduced changes in what enlisted sailors wore. Blue chambray shirts and denim dungarees were worn by hard-working sailors on ship and while on fatigue duty ashore. In other than working situations, World War II sailors wore the so-called Cracker Jack uniform—bell bottoms, loose blouse, neckerchief, open collar, and white "sailor cap"—which resembled the sailor trademark on boxes of Cracker Jack snack food. This uniform remained unchanged during the postwar years until 1975, when a dark blue (nearly black) coat and tie replaced the "sailor suit." However, by 1978, the sailors themselves clamored for a return to the traditional bell-bottomed uniform, which was soon readopted.

United States Naval Academy (Annapolis)

The USN came into being as the Continental navy with the AMERICAN REVOLUTION, was disbanded in 1785 by an economy-minded Congress, then reconstituted in 1794, principally to combat piracy. In 1825, President John Quincy Adams asked Congress to establish a naval academy, but to no avail. It took a crisis in 1842 to move the government to action. The brig USS *Somers* was used to train teenage naval apprentices for careers in the USN. Discipline among the raw youngsters was lacking, however, and a mutiny ensued, but was quickly put down. Three midshipmen were hanged in connection with the *Somers* incident, which moved Secretary of the Navy George Bancroft to establish a Naval School, even without congressional funding. He was determined not to send untrained young men to sea again.

The school was opened on a U.S. Army post, Fort Severn in Annapolis, Maryland, on October 10, 1845, with a class of 50 midshipmen and seven professors, who administered a curriculum consisting of mathematics, navigation, gunnery, steam propulsion, chemistry, English, natural philosophy, and French. Five years later, the Naval School officially became the United States Naval Academy. The curriculum was expanded and regularized as roughly the equivalent of a four-year college education, with shipboard training during the summers. It was not until 1933 that the U.S. Congress authorized the academy to award formal bachelor of science degrees.

While standards have remained rigorous at the academy and enrollment is limited to a brigade (4,000) of midshipmen, the curriculum has become increasingly flexible. The core curriculum is now supplemented by 18 major fields of study and a variety of electives. In 1976, Congress authorized the admission of women to all of the service academies, and women presently make up 13 to 14 percent of entering plebes (freshmen).

In addition to a four-year character development program, midshipmen study a core curriculum that includes courses in engineering, science, mathematics, humanities, and social science. After completing core requirements, midshipmen choose advanced study in a major field. In addition, the academy provides professional and leadership training, which includes assignments with actual USN and USMC units. Physical training is a major component of the academy curriculum and includes team sports as well as fitness training.

Graduates of the Naval Academy are commissioned USN ensigns or USMC second lieutenants.

United States Naval Forces Central Command

Central Command consists typically of a force of more than 20 ships, manned by 15,000 personnel (with another 1,000 ashore) and consisting of a carrier battle group, amphibious ready group, combat aircraft, and other support units and ships. Units of the FIFTH FLEET are the principal constituents of the command and are available for immediate response to emerging crises in the waters adjacent to the Middle East. The Fifth Fleet consists of forces rotationally deployed from either the PACIFIC FLEET or the ATLANTIC FLEET. Central Command naval forces typically account for as much as 80 percent of all U.S. military forces in this theater.

Central Command seeks to deter conflict by reassuring friends of a continued U.S. commitment to the region while demonstrating to would-be adversaries the resolve to do whatever is necessary to maintain or restore peace.

United States Naval Forces Europe

The area of responsibility of United States Naval Forces Europe includes 89 countries with a combined population of more than one billion—some 14 million square miles of land on three continents. Maritime coverage extends over the Mediterranean, Black Sea, and Baltic Sea, as well as a large portion of the Atlantic Ocean. USNAVEUR is divided into six maritime regions: Black Sea; Levant/East Mediterranean; Maghreb and North Africa; Northern Europe and Baltic; Northern Mediterranean; and Sub-Saharan Africa. Naval bases used by the forces include Naval Station Rota, Spain; Naval Support Activity Naples, Italy; Naval Air Station Sigonella, Sicily; Naval Support Activity Gaeta, Italy; Naval Support Activity La Maddalena, Sardinia; and Naval Support Activity Souda Bay, Crete. Ten thousand sailors and marines are stationed on USNAVEUR bases, and 12,000 are aboard deployed USNAVEUR ships.

United States Naval Observatory

Located in northwest Washington, D.C., at Observatory Circle, between Wisconsin and Massachusetts Avenues, the U.S. Naval Observatory carries out a scientific mission for the United States, the

Department of Defense, and the U.S. Navy. This mission includes determining the positions and motions of the Earth, sun, moon, planets, stars, and other celestial objects; providing astronomical data; determining precise time; measuring the Earth's rotation; and maintaining the Master Clock for the United States. The astronomical and timing data are essential for accurate navigation and the support of communications on Earth as well as in space.

The observatory was founded in 1830 as the Depot of Charts and Instruments. Originally, its primary function was the calibration of ship's chronometers, which was accomplished by timing the transit of stars across the meridian. Accurate chronometers were vital to accurate navigation. In 1844, the depot was reestablished as the U.S. Naval Observatory and was moved to a hill north of the present location of the Lincoln Memorial. It remained there for almost 50 years, during which USNO astronomers carried out pioneering measurements of the speed of light and studied the phenomena associated with solar eclipses and the transit of Venus. In 1855, the observatory began to issue astronomical and nautical almanacs. In 1877, USNO astronomer Asaph Hall discovered the two satellites of Mars.

In 1893, the USNO moved to its present location and is today considered a preeminent authority on timekeeping and celestial observation.

United States Navy Band

The United States Navy Band consists of 163 enlisted musicians and three officers in seven major performing units. The Concert Band is the major USN musical unit in Washington, D.C., and has toured worldwide. The Ceremonial Band performs at official military ceremonies and special events and is staffed, depending on performance requirements, by 15 to 99 musicians. The Commodores is an 18-member jazz orchestra. Chamber groups include a host of small wind ensembles. Country Current is a six-member country music ensemble. Sea Chanters is a 19-voice chorus. Cruisers is a five-member band that specializes in a variety of music ranging from classic rock and rhythm and blues, to today's top 40.

The first official USN band was created in 1916 when a 16-piece band from the battleship USS *Kansas* was ordered to the WASHINGTON NAVY YARD to augment a 17-piece band aboard the presidential yacht *Mayflower*. The combined unit became the Washington Navy Yard Band and came to occupy the yard's Sail Loft, the building that still serves as its headquarters and rehearsal hall.

In 1925, the unit was officially designated as the U.S. Navy Band. The Sea Chanters chorus was created in 1956, the Commodores jazz ensemble in 1969, the Country Current group in 1973, and the Cruisers pop/rock ensemble in 1999.

unmanned aerial vehicle   See AIRCRAFT: VIETNAM WAR AND AFTER.

Upshur, Abel P. (1791–1844) *secretary of the navy*

Upshur served in the Virginia House of Delegates from 1812 to 1813 and from 1825 to 1827. From 1826 to 1841, he sat on the Supreme Court of Virginia. President John Tyler appointed him the nation's 13th SECRETARY OF THE NAVY in 1841 and then secretary of state in 1843. While touring the USS *Princeton* on February 28, 1844, Upshur was killed by the explosion of a new naval gun—the "Peacemaker"—during a demonstration.

U.S.-Mexican War

After Congress voted, on March 1, 1845, to admit the Republic of Texas into the Union, the Mexican government, which had repudiated the Treaty of Velasco by which Texas independence had been recognized in 1836, severed diplomatic relations with the United States. As Mexican-American relations deteriorated, on July 4, President James K. Polk ordered Brigadier General Zachary Taylor to take up a position on or near the Rio Grande River to repel an anticipated Mexican invasion of Texas. On April 25, 1846, Mexican troops under

General Mariano Arista invaded, and the war began.

It would be primarily a land war, with American armies advancing west to seize New Mexico, Arizona, and California, and south into Mexico. However, the USN played an important role in General Winfield Scott's amphibious invasion of Veracruz in April 1847. On March 9, 1847, Commodore David Connor landed 8,600 troops at Veracruz in the first amphibious assault in U.S. military history. This put Scott in position to advance on and capture Mexico City, thereby bringing the war to an end. Connor also supported the landing with naval bombardment.

Additionally, on May 13, 1846, the day war was declared, Connor led a highly successful naval blockade of the Mexican Gulf Coast. Not a single Mexican naval vessel left port during the entire war, and ships of the blockade also succeeded in seizing several merchant ships that tried to run the blockade.

USN ships were also used to bombard Gulf of Mexico ports in support of U.S. land operations, and it was a navy commodore, John D. Sloat, who captured Monterey and San Francisco, California, in July 1846. That same month, Sloat's successor, Commodore Robert F. Stockton, coordinated with army Captain John C. Frémont to capture San Diego.

In October 1846, Commodore MATTHEW C. PERRY led a squadron up the Tabasco River and, in November, took Tampico, an important port. In April 1847, Perry steamed up the Tuxpan River and took the city of Tuxpan, which, however, could not be held because of an epidemic of yellow fever. In November, landing parties from the USS *Congress,* the USS *Independence,* and the sloop *Cyane* assaulted and took Mazatlán on the Pacific coast. These were the last significant naval operations of the war.

USS *Constitution* (Old Ironsides)

The USS *Constitution* is the oldest commissioned ship in the USN. Built at Edmund Hartt's shipyard, Boston, the vessel was made from some 2,000 trees, armed with cannon cast in Rhode Island, and fitted with copper fastenings provided by Paul Revere. Launched on October 21, 1797, *Constitution* put to sea the following year.

The *Constitution* was built pursuant to the Naval Act of March 1794, which called for the construction of a half-dozen frigates, including the 44-gun *Constitution, United States,* and *President,* and the 36-gun *Congress, Constellation,* and *Chesapeake.*

The six frigates were designed by Joshua Humphreys, who made them larger and more heavily armed than standard frigates. The *Constitution* first saw action during the QUASI-WAR WITH FRANCE, then served in the BARBARY WARS. Most famously, *Constitution* served during the WAR OF 1812, in which she bested the British 49-gun frigate *Guerriere* on August 19, 1812. Because British cannonballs seemed to bounce harmlessly off *Constitution*'s hull, she was nicknamed "Old Ironsides."

In 1830, naval inspectors declared "Old Ironsides" unfit for sea and recommended scrapping her. The public outcry, rallied in part by a stirring poem of Oliver Wendell Holmes, Sr., "Old Ironsides," prevented this. She was, however, decommissioned in 1882 and served as a receiving ship at Portsmouth, New Hampshire, returning to Boston in 1897 to celebrate her centennial. When talk of scrapping began again, the public protested, and in 1925 the vessel was restored in a program financed by donations of schoolchildren and patriotic groups. The restored *Constitution* was recommissioned in 1931. Ten years later, she was placed in permanent commission, and, in 1954, an act of Congress gave the SECRETARY OF THE NAVY direct responsibility for her continued upkeep. The ship is moored at Boston, is manned by USN personnel, and is open to the public for tours.

USS *George Washington* (CVN-73)   See
AIRCRAFT CARRIERS.

USS *Harry S. Truman* (CVN-75)   See
AIRCRAFT CARRIERS.

USS *Iwo Jima* (LHD-7)   See AMPHIBIOUS
ASSAULT SHIPS.

USS *John C. Stennis* (CVN-74)   See
AIRCRAFT CARRIERS.

USS *Nautilus* (SSN-571)

USS *Nautilus* was the navy's—and the world's—first nuclear-powered submarine, driven by an on-board, pressurized-water nuclear reactor plant. Her keel was laid on June 14, 1952, at Electric Boat Division in Groton, Connecticut, by President Harry S. Truman; she was launched on January 21, 1954, and commissioned on September 30, 1954. *Nautilus* was largely the brainchild of Captain (later Admiral) HYMAN G. RICKOVER, the father of the modern nuclear navy. He understood that nuclear power would enable submarines to remain submerged for weeks at a time even longer, as long as provisions and oxygen held out—instead of having to surface every couple of days to recharge batteries, as conventional diesel-electric boats had to do. This capability radically transformed submarine warfare, ultimately making submarines the third leg of the so-called trident nuclear deterrent strategy, consisting of nuclear-armed strategic bombers, land-based intercontinental ballistic missiles (ICBM) with nuclear warheads, and submarines armed with ICBMs.

Although fully combat capable, *Nautilus* served essentially as a testbed for nuclear submarine technology. Her first tour, which began on January 17, 1955, broke all endurance records for submerged passage. Her most famous voyage, dubbed Operation Sunshine, began on July 28, 1958, when *Nautilus* left Pearl Harbor for the Bering Strait and the Arctic ice pack. After diving under the ice near Point Barrow, Alaska, on August 1, she became the first ship to reach the geographic North Pole, passing beneath it on August 3. She surfaced in the Greenland Sea two days later after traveling 1,830 miles under the ice in 96 hours. The ship was awarded the Presidential Unit Citation (the first such award in peacetime) and her commanding officer, Commander William R. Anderson, received the Legion of Merit.

By September 1966, when *Nautilus* was decommissioned, she had completed 300,000 miles of steaming on nuclear power, more than 250,000 of which were submerged. The ship was declared a National Historic Landmark on May 20, 1982.

General characteristics of *Nautilus* include:

Builders: Electric Boat, Groton, Connecticut
Dimensions: 319 ft, 4 in by 27 ft, 6 in, by 22 ft
Displacement: 3,764 tons surfaced; 4,040 tons submerged
Power plant: one S2W PWR reactor with two steam turbines providing a total of 15,000 shaft horsepower on two shafts
Maximum speed: 20 knots surfaced, 22.5 knots submerged
Armament: six 21-inch bow torpedo tubes; total capacity, 24 torpedoes
Electronics: radar and sonar, including BQS-4 active bow mounted and BQR-2C passive bow mounted
Crew: 111

V

vice admiral See RANKS AND GRADES.

Vietnam War

Vietnam had been under French colonial control before WORLD WAR II, but fell under Japanese control during the war. The United States aided the indigenous leader of an independence movement, Ho Chi Minh, in resisting the Japanese; however, when World War II ended, the United States withdrew its support of Ho, a communist, and instead moved to prop up the weakening French regime that had been restored. Although President Harry S. Truman was opposed to colonialism, he deemed it preferable to the spread of communism in Southeast Asia. Nevertheless, despite American aid, the French lost the make-or-break Battle of Dien Bien Phu in 1954, and Vietnam became independent as well as bitterly divided between a communist North and a pro-Western South. A bitter civil war commenced.

During the administration of John F. Kennedy, direct aid to South Vietnam, in the form of "military advisers" (who, in fact, often served in combat), was steadily increased. Under JFK's successor, Lyndon B. Johnson, the U.S. military involvement in the country became even greater. On August 7, 1964, the U.S. Senate passed the Gulf of Tonkin Resolution after the DESTROYER USS *Maddox*, conducting electronic espionage in international waters in the Gulf of Tonkin, was reportedly fired at by North Vietnamese torpedo boats on two separate occasions (the second time reputedly in company with the destroyer *C. Turner Joy*). The resolution authorized the president to expand the war as he might see fit. (Years later, in June 1971, the *New York Times* published a series of articles on a secret government study, popularly called *The Pentagon Papers*. Among many other things, the document revealed that the Tonkin Gulf Resolution had been drafted months in advance of the attack on the destroyer *Maddox* and the reputed attack on the *C. Turner Joy*.) In the wake of the resolution, the war rapidly escalated. One hundred thousand combat troops were in country by July 1965; by the beginning of 1966, there were 250,000; by 1968, 550,000 U.S. military personnel were committed to the war, including 38,000 USN personnel.

Most of the war was fought on the ground by USA and USMC combat troops; however, the USN supplied sealift and naval bombardment (using the reactivated battleship *New Jersey* and other craft). Most of all, Task Force 77, lying some 100 miles offshore at Yankee Station in the Gulf of Tonkin, supplied carrier-launched air power. The USN mission included close air support as well as bombing of industrial targets (chiefly in the North Vietnamese capital of Hanoi) and tactical missions against guerrilla supply lines, vehicles, and the like.

Additional USN duties included extensive minesweeping and the operation of a variety of small patrol craft, especially on the rivers of the Mekong Delta. The so-called brown-water navy executed a most hazardous mission in these always treacherous waters (see SWIFT BOATS).

Like the KOREAN WAR, the Vietnam War was fought with the limited objective of "containing" the spread of communism. There was a great wariness of expanding the war in such a way as to provoke the overt intervention of China and/or the Soviet Union. Not only were the war objectives limited, it soon became apparent that the South Vietnamese forces were poorly led and poorly motivated. In the United States, popular opposition to the war in Vietnam increased, especially after the Tet Offensive at the beginning of 1968. This massive communist attack on many fronts was, in fact, a costly tactical defeat for North Vietnam, but its scope and daring were such as to persuade many Americans that the war was unwinnable. From 1968 on, President Johnson and his successor, Richard M. Nixon, embraced a course of "Vietnamization," withdrawing U.S. ground troops and turning over to the South Vietnamese themselves more and more of the responsibility for prosecuting the war. These forces, however, proved hopelessly inadequate to the job, and, as the U.S. withdrawal continued, South Vietnam fell to the North in 1975.

W

War of 1812

Early in the 19th century, despite the Treaty of Paris, ending the AMERICAN REVOLUTION, and Jay's Treaty, resolving certain territorial disputes, British fur trappers and traders repeatedly "invaded" U.S. territory on the western frontier. British interests also incited Indian hostility in the West in an effort to push American traders out of the frontier region. Also during this period, the Royal Navy routinely impressed (abducted for service in the Royal Navy) American merchant sailors that British boarding officers determined to be either deserters from His Majesty's navy or British subjects. These three circumstances created growing hostility between Britain and America during the first decade of the century. Added to this was the new republic's insatiable land hunger. In 1812, Spanish Florida extended as far west as the Mississippi River; since Spain was an ally of Great Britain against Napoleon, American "War Hawks" (pro-war legislators) believed that victory in a war against Britain would result in the acquisition of its ally's territory, which would be joined to the vast western territories that had been acquired by the recent Louisiana Purchase. In this climate, President James Madison secured from Congress a declaration of war against Britain in June 1812.

The American army was tiny and ill-prepared to fight a major power like Britain. It suffered one disastrous reversal after another, beginning with the loss of Fort Michilimackinac on July 17, 1812;

the loss of Fort Dearborn on August 12; the loss of Detroit on August 16; and the costly collapse of an American invasion of Canada on November 23. The year 1813 began badly as well, when William Henry Harrison suffered a major defeat along Lake Erie on January 21.

While U.S. land forces compiled a miserable record during the first year of the war, the small USN performed remarkably well. The British brought to bear 1,048 Royal Navy vessels to blockade U.S. naval and commercial shipping, whereas the USN has only 14 seaworthy craft in addition to the services of a miscellaneous array of privateers. Against all odds, American frigates triumphed in a series of notable single-ship engagements, the most famous of which were the battles between the USS *CONSTITUTION* and the British frigate *Guerrière,* off the coast of Massachusetts on August 19, 1812, and between USS *Constitution* and *Java,* off the Brazilian coast on December 29, 1812. Despite such victories, the Royal Navy blockade easily held, and the United States edged toward economic collapse. After the January 1813 disaster at Fort Malden, William Henry Harrison rebuilt his army, even as the young USN officer OLIVER HAZARD PERRY built, from scratch, an inland navy. Beginning in March 1813, he directed construction of an armed flotilla at Presque Isle (present-day Erie), Pennsylvania, while simultaneously training his sailors in artillery practice. In August, he sailed onto Lake Erie, and, on September 10, engaged the British

Engagement between USS *Chesapeake* and HMS *Shannon,* June 1, 1813   *(Naval Historical Foundation)*

squadron in a fierce battle, during which he was forced to transfer his flag from the severely damaged brig *Lawrence* to the *Niagara.* Perry destroyed Britain's Lake Erie squadron and dispatched to General Harrison one of the most famous messages in American military history: "We have met the enemy and they are ours." The victory severed British supply lines, forcing the abandonment of Fort Malden and a British evacuation from the Detroit region. On October 5, 1813, Harrison overtook the retreating British columns and their Indian allies at the Battle of the Thames and defeated them.

Although the victories at the Battles of Lake Erie and the Thames were crucial, the abdication of Napoleon on April 4, 1814, freed more British troops for service in North America. British forces under Major General Robert Ross defeated a small, mixed American force at the Battle of Bladensburg, Maryland (August 24, 1814), then stormed Washington, D.C., and burned most of the public buildings, including the Capitol and the White House,

forcing President Madison and most of the government to flee. Ross next advanced on Baltimore, bombarding Fort McHenry, in Baltimore Harbor, during September 13–14, 1814. The fort held, inspiring one witness, a Baltimore lawyer named Francis Scott Key (1779–1843), to write the song "Star-Spangled Banner."

In the meantime, some 10,000 British troops advanced into the United States from Montreal. The U.S. land force opposing them was far smaller, but, on September 11, 1814, Captain Thomas McDonough (USN) engaged the British squadron on Lake Champlain and destroyed it. This cut off the invaders from their line of supply and prompted the retreat of the army. McDonough's victory at the Battle of Lake Champlain strengthened the hand of American treaty negotiators, which resulted in the Treaty of Ghent, signed on December 24, 1814, ending the war and restoring the status quo antebellum. The subsequent victory of General Andrew Jackson in the Battle of New Orleans (January 8, 1815) came after the treaty was

The Battle of Lake Erie, shown near the end of the engagement, September 10, 1813; lithograph from a painting by R. M. Chauncey *(Naval Historical Foundation)*

signed but before news of it reached the opposing armies. Although the War of 1812 cost the United States much and benefited it little, Jackson's triumph made it feel like a victory. As for the USN, the war served to enhance the prestige of this fledgling service and continues to figure as a proud part of naval heritage.

warships: 18th and 19th century

The following classes of vessel and individual vessels are typical of warships during the U.S. Navy's first two centuries. They are listed in alphabetical order:

Alabama: Typical mid-19th-century sidewheel steamer, built 1851. Length, 214 ft 4 in Beam, 35 ft 2 in; Maximum speed, 9 knots; Armament, eight 32-pound guns.

Alaska: Early wooden screw gunboat, built 1869. Length, 250 ft 6 in; Beam, 38 ft; Maximum speed, 11.5 knots; Armament, one 11-inch gun, six 8-inch guns.

Albany: Sloop of war commissioned in 1846 and used in the U.S.-MEXICAN WAR, built 1851. Length, 147 ft 11 in; Beam, 38 ft 6 in; Maximum speed, 13 knots; Armament, 22 guns.

Alfred: Frigate built in 1774. Displacement, 200 tons; Armament, 20 9-pounders, 10 6-pounders. Used by the Continental navy in the AMERICAN REVOLUTION.

Alligator: Schooner built in 1821. Length, 86 ft; Beam, 24 ft 7 in; Maximum speed, 8 knots; Armament, 12 6-pounders. Attached to the AFRICAN SLAVE TRADE PATROL.

America: Ship-of-the-line launched 1782. With 74 guns, this was the largest ship type used by the Continental navy during the American Revolution.

Andrew Doria: Typical brig of the Continental navy, commissioned 1775. Armed with 14 4-pounders.

Argus: Early 19th-century brig, launched 1803. Length, 94 ft 6 in; Beam, 28 ft 2 in; Armament, two 12-pounders, 16 24-pound carronades. Used in the BARBARY WARS and WAR OF 1812.

Cairo-class ironclads: These were shallow-draft ironclads, mounting 13 guns, that were extensively employed by the USN's Mississippi River Squadron during the CIVIL WAR.

Canonicus-class monitors: Civil War single-turret monitors, which improved on the *Passaic* class. The nine ships of this class were laid down in 1862 and completed in 1863 and 1864. Displacement, 2,100 tons; Length, 225 ft; Beam, 43 ft; Maximum speed, 8 knots; Armament, two 15-inch Dahlgrens.

Casco-class ironclads: Single-turret, shallow-draft, twin-screw ironclads designed in 1862 for use on the Mississippi River. Eight were built. Displacement, 1,175 tons; Length, 225 ft; Beam, 45 ft 6 in; Maximum speed, 5–9 knots; Armament, single-turret gun.

Columbia-class cruisers: Two ships commissioned in 1894 and designed as commerce raiders. Displacement, 7,375 tons; Length, 413 ft; Beam, 58 ft 2 in; Maximum speed, 23 knots; Armament, one 8-inch gun, two 6-inch guns, eight 4-inch guns.

Constitution: See USS CONSTITUTION.

Cyane: Sloop commissioned in 1838 and used in the U.S.-Mexican War. Armed with 20 32-pounders.

Demologos: A unique catamaran steam FRIGATE, designed by Robert Fulton, and launched in 1814, too late for use in the War of 1812. Length, 156 ft; Beam, 56 ft; Maximum speed, 6 knots; Armament, 24 32-pound carronades.

Dolphin (PG24): Typical GUNBOAT of the era of the SPANISH-AMERICAN WAR, built 1885. Displacement, 1,486 tons; Length, 256 ft 6 in; Beam, 32 feet; Maximum speed, 16 knots; Armament, two 4-inch guns and five 3-pounders.

Galena: Ironclad screw steamer commissioned in 1862 and used in the Civil War. Length, 210 ft; Beam, 36 ft; Maximum speed, 8 knots; Armament, four 9-inch and two 100-pounders.

Hannah: This schooner, commissioned on August 24, 1775, was the first ship of the Continental navy during the American Revolution.

Hornet: Brig launched in 1805 and used in the War of 1812.

Indiana-class battleships (BB): Considered the first three modern USN battleships, commissioned 1895–96. Four 12-inch guns, eight 8-inch guns, four 6-inch guns. Top speed about 16 knots. All decommissioned 1919.

Java: Typical frigate of the War of 1812 era, although completed after the war, in 1815. Used in the Barbary Wars. Length, 175 ft; Beam, 44 ft 6 in; Armament, 33 32-pounders, 20 42-pounders.

Kalamazoo-class ironclads: Four large ironclads built during the Civil War, but completed too late to be used. Displacement, 5,600 tons; Length, 345 ft 5 in; Beam, 37 ft 6 in; Maximum speed, 10 knot; Armament, four 15-inch Dahlgrens. All four ships were deliberately destroyed during 1874–84 because of faulty construction.

Monitor: With the Confederate *Alabama* (formerly USS *Merrimack*), the most famous ship of the Civil War. Built by JOHN ERICSSON with five layers of iron plating over a wooden backing and incorporating two 11-inch Dahlgren guns in a rotating turret of unprecedented design, *Monitor* revolutionized naval warfare. Length, 172 ft; Beam, 41 ft 6 in; Maximum speed, 6 knots.

Passaic-class ironclads: Ten Civil War ironclads launched during 1862–64. Displacement, 1,875 tons; Length, 200 ft; Beam, 46 ft; Maximum speed, 7 knots; Armament, typically one 11-inch Dahlgren and one 15-inch Dahlgren.

Powhatan: Mid-century USN sidewheel steamer. Displacement, 3,765 tons; Length, 253 ft 8 in; Beam, 45 ft; Maximum speed, 11 knots; Armament, one 11-inch Dahlgren, 10 9-inch Dahlgrens, five 12-pounders.

Roanoke: Civil War–era screw frigate. Displacement, 4,772 tons; Length, 263 ft 8 in; Beam, 52 ft 6 in; Maximum speed, 11 knots; Armament, two 10-inch guns, 28 9-inch guns, 14 8-inch guns.

Wampanoag-class cruisers: Four Civil War–era steam-powered, wooden cruisers. Displacement, 4,215 tons; Length, 135 ft; Beam, 54 ft 2 in; Maximum speed, 17.5 knots; Armament, 10 9-inch Dahlgrens, three 60-pounders.

warships: Korean War, Vietnam War, and After

The following classes of vessels and individual vessels are typical of USN warships during the KOREAN WAR, VIETNAM WAR, and after.

Albany-class guided missile cruisers (CG): Three were converted from World War II–era heavy cruisers. Displacement: 13,700 tons; Length, 674 ft; Beam, 71 ft; Maximum speed, 31.5 knots; Armament, two 5-inch guns, eight SAMs, one ASROC.

Belknap-class guided missile cruisers (CG): Nine ships built between 1964 and 1967 to screen aircraft carriers in battle groups. Inactivated by 1992. Displacement, 7,930 tons; Length, 547 ft; Beam, 55 ft; Maximum speed,

Turret of the USS *Monitor* in a photo taken after the battle with the USS *Virginia*. Note dents made by enemy fire in the turret next to the gun ports.   *(Naval Historical Foundation)*

33 knots; Armament, 60 SAMs, eight Harpoon missiles, one 5-inch gun, ASROCs.

Boston-class guided missile cruisers (CAG): Two conversions from World War II heavy cruisers, made during 1952–56. Displacement, 13,300 tons; Length, 674 ft; Beam, 71 ft; Maximum speed, 33 knots; Armament, six 8-inch guns, 10 5-inch guns, 8–12 3-inch guns, four SAMs.

Bronstein-class guided missile frigates (FFG): Two ships completed during the early 1960s. Displacement, 2,360 tons; Length, 372 ft; Beam, 41 ft; Maximum speed, 24 knots; Armament, ASROCs.

Brooke-class guided missile frigates (FFG): Six ships built in the mid-1960s. Displacement, 2,643 tons; Length, 425 ft; Beam, 44 ft; Maximum speed, 27 knots; Armament, one Mk-22 Tartar launcher, two Mk-25 stern torpedo tubes.

California-class guided missile cruisers (CGN): Two nuclear-powered ships built in 1974 and 1975. Although both ships remain in commission, no additional nuclear-powered ships of this class are contemplated. Displacement, 9,561 tons; Length, 595 ft; Beam, 61 ft; Maximum speed, 30+ knots; Armament, SAMs, eight Harpoon missiles, one 5-inch gun, two 20-mm PHALANX guns, one ASROC, four torpedo tubes.

Charles F. Adams–class guided missile destroyers: Twenty-three ships of this class were built between 1960 and 1964; none are currently in commission. Displacement, 3,370 tons; Length, 437 ft; Beam, 47 ft; Maximum speed, 31.5 knots; Armament, Standard missiles, ASROCs, six 12.75-inch torpedo tubes, Harpoon missiles.

Charleston-class attack cargo ships: Five ships built between 1968 and 1970 and now decommissioned. Displacement, 18,600 tons; Length, 576 ft; Beam, 62 ft; Maximum speed, 20+ knots; Armament, six 3-inch guns and two 20-mm Phalanx guns.

Coontz-class guided missile destroyers (DDG): Ten ships built between 1959 and 1961. Displacement, 4,700 tons; Length, 513 ft; Beam, 53 ft; Maximum speed, 33 knots; Armament, Standard missiles, ASROC, eight Harpoon missiles.

Decatur-class guided missile destroyers: Four ships built between 1956 and 1959. Displacement, 4,150 tons; Length, 418 ft; Beam, 45 ft; Maximum speed, 32.5 knots; Armament, Standard missiles, Harpoon missiles, ASROC.

Ethan Allen–class submarines (SSBN, SSN): Five nuclear-powered submarines built between 1959 and 1963 and designed to fire Polaris missiles. Displacement, 6,995 tons; Length, 411 ft; Beam, 33 ft; Maximum speed, 25 knots; Armament, four 21-inch torpedo tubes and Polaris missiles. None are currently in commission.

Farragut-class guided missile destroyers (DDG): Ten ships commissioned between 1989 and 1992. Displacement, 4,700 tons; Length, 512 ft 6 in; Beam, 52 ft 6 in; Maximum speed, 33 knots; Armament, Standard missiles, Harpoon missiles, ASROC, six 12.75-inch torpedo tubes. No longer in commission.

Forrestal-class aircraft carriers: Four ships built in the 1950s and used during the cold war and Vietnam War periods. Displacement, 79,000 tons; Length, 1,046 ft; Beam, 130 ft; Armament, Sea Sparrow launchers, three Phalanx guns, 85 aircraft.

Forrest Sherman–class destroyers (DD): Fourteen ships built between 1955 and 1959. Displacement, 2,800 tons; Length, 418 ft; Beam, 45 ft; Maximum speed, 32.5 knots; Armament, ASROCs, four 21-inch torpedo tubes. None are currently in commission.

Garcia-class frigates (FF): Ten ships built between 1963 and 1968. Displacement, 2,620 tons; Length, 415 ft; Beam, 44 ft; Maximum speed, 27 knots; Armament, ASROCs, two 5-inch guns, six 12.75-inch torpedo tubes.

George Washington–class submarines (SSE, SSBN): Five completed between 1959 and 1963. Displacement, 6,955 tons; Length, 411 ft; Beam, 33 ft; Maximum speed, 25 knots; Armament, four 21-inch torpedo tubes, Polaris missiles.

Iwo Jima–class amphibious assault ships (LPH): Seven ships built between 1961 and 1970. Displacement, 18,300 tons; Length, 602 ft; Beam, 83 ft 8 in; Maximum speed, 20 knots; Armament, two Sea Sparrow launchers, four 3-inch machine guns, two Phalanx guns.

Kidd-class guided missile destroyers (DDG): Four vessels also called "Ayatollah class" because they were originally to be transferred to the shah of Iran, but were preempted by the USN after the Iranian revolution of 1979. All four were commissioned during 1981–82. Displacement, 8,140 tons; Length, 563 ft 8 in; Beam, 55 ft 1 in; Maximum speed, 30 knots; Armament, two Standard missile launchers, one ASROC launcher, eight Harpoons, two Phalanx guns, six torpedo tubes.

Kitty Hawk–class aircraft carriers: Three ships built in the 1960s. Displacement, 80,800 tons; Length, 1,047 ft; Beam, 129 ft 11 ins; Maximum speed, 30+ knots; Armament, three Sea Sparrow launchers, three Phalanx guns, 85 aircraft.

Knox-class destroyer escorts (DE): Forty-six ships commissioned between 1969 and 1974. Displacement, 3,077 tons; Length, 438 ft; Beam, 46 ft 9 in; Maximum speed, 27 knots; Armament, one 5-inch gun, four torpedo tubes.

Knox-class fast frigates (FF): Forty-six ships designed for antsubmarine warfare and commissioned between 1969 and 1974. Displacement, 4,250 tons; Length, 438 ft; Beam, 46 ft 9 in; Maximum speed, 27+ knots; Armament, Harpoon missiles, Phalanx gun, four torpedo tubes.

Lafayette-class ballistic missile submarines (SSBN): Thirty-one submarines built between 1963 and 1967 with 16 tubes for Poseidon or Trident missiles. Displacement, 7,250 tons; Length, 425 ft; Beam, 33 ft; Maximum speed, 25 knots. No longer in commission.

Leahy-class guided missile cruisers: Nine ships commissioned between 1962 and 1964 and now decommissioned. Displacement, 5,670 tons; Length, 533 ft; Beam, 53 ft 6 in; Maximum speed, 34 knots; Armament, two Standard missile launchers, eight Harpoon missiles, Phalanx guns, ASROC, six torpedo tubes.

Los Angeles–class submarine. See SUBMARINES.

Nautilus (SSN-571): The world's first nuclear-powered submarine, commissioned September 30, 1954. Displacement, 2,975 tons surfaced, 3,747 tons submerged; Length, 323 ft 9 in; Beam, 27 ft 8 in; Maximum speed, 18 knots; Armament, six 21-inch torpedo tubes.

Newport-class landing ships, tank (LST): Twenty ships built between 1969 and 1972. Displacement, 8,342 tons; Length, 562 ft; Beam, 70 ft; Maximum speed, 20 knots; Armament, four 3-inch guns, one Phalanx gun.

Nimitz-class aircraft carriers. See AIRCRAFT CARRIERS.

Ohio-class ballistic missile submarines. See SUBMARINES.

Oliver Hazard Perry–class guided missile frigates (FFG): Fifty ships built from 1977 into the 1980s. Displacement, 3,658 tons; Length, 445 ft; Beam, 45 ft; Maximum speed, 28+ knots; Armament, Standard missiles, Harpoon missiles, one 3-inch Mk-75, one Phalanx gun, six torpedo tubes.

Oregon City–class heavy cruisers (CA): Two ships commissioned in 1946. Displacement, 13,700 tons; Length, 674 ft 11 in; Beam, 70 ft 10 in; Maximum speed, 33 knots; Armament, nine 8-inch guns, 12 5-inch guns.

Patrol Boat, River (PBR): A small water-jet propelled boat used on rivers in the Vietnam War. First deployed in 1966.

Raleigh-class amphibious transport ships, dock (LPD): Three ships commissioned during the 1960s. Displacement, 16,900 tons; Length, 570 ft; Beam, 84 ft; Maximum speed, 20 knots; Armament, three 4-inch guns.

Seawolf-class attack submarines. See SUBMARINES.

Skipjack-class submarines: Five nuclear-powered submarines built during 1959–61 and featuring a radical teardrop-shaped configuration. Displacement, 3,075 tons; Length, 252 ft; Beam, 32 ft; Maximum speed, 30+ knots submerged; Armament, six torpedo tubes.

Spruance-class destroyers: Thirty-one ships built during 1975–80. Displacement, 7,800 tons; Length, 563 ft; Beam, 55 ft; Maximum speed, 30+ knots; Armament, eight Tomahawk missiles, ASROCs, six torpedo tubes.

Sturgeon/Narwhal-class submarines: Thirty-seven nuclear-powered attack submarines completed between 1967 and 1975. Displacement, 3,640 tons; Length, 292 ft; Beam, 32 ft; Maximum speed, 30 knots; Armament, four torpedo tubes, Harpoon missiles, Tomahawk missiles.

Swift boats: Fifty-foot fast patrol craft used on rivers in the Vietnam War. Three .50-caliber machine guns were standard, as was a single 81-mm mortar.

Tambor-class submarines: Twelve built in 1939. Displacement, 1,475 tons; Length, 307 ft 3 in; Beam, 27 ft 3 in; Maximum speed, 20 knots surfaced, 8.75 knots submerged; Armament, one 3-inch gun, 10 torpedo tubes.

Tarawa-class amphibious assault ships (LHA): Five ships built in the late 1970s. Displacement, 39,400 tons; Length, 820 ft; Beam, 126 ft; Maximum speed, 24 knots; Armament, two Sea Sparrow launchers, three 5-inch guns, 30 helicopters or Harrier VTOL jets.

Thomaston-class landing ships, dock (LSD): Eight ships built 1954–57. Displacement, 6,880 tons; Length, 510 ft; Beam, 84 ft; Maximum speed, 22.5 knots; Armament, six 3-inch guns.

Ticonderoga-class guided missile cruisers (CG): Twenty-seven ships built during the 1980s. Displacement, 9,500 tons; Length, 565 ft 10 ins; Beam, 55 ft; Maximum speed, 30+ knots; Armament, two to four Standard missiles, two Tomahawk launchers, eight Harpoon launchers, two 5-inch guns, two Phalanx guns, six torpedo tubes.

Tullibee/Permit (Thresher)-class submarines: Thirteen nuclear-powered submarines built between 1960 and 1968. Displacement, 2,640–3,750 tons; Length, 279–297 ft; Beam, 32 ft; Maximum speed, 30 knots; Armament, Harpoon missiles, SUBROC missiles, four torpedo tubes. No longer in commission.

Virginia-class guided missile cruisers (CGN): Four nuclear-powered cruisers commissioned in 1976–80. Displacement, 11,300 tons; Length, 585 ft; Beam, 63 ft; Maximum speed, 30+ knots; Armament, two Standard missile launchers, 16 Harpoon missile launchers, two 5-inch guns, two Phalanx guns, ASROC, six torpedo tubes.

Wasp-class amphibious assault ships (LHD): Six ships built in the 1980s and 1990s. With the *Tarawa* class, the largest amphibious ships ever built. Displacement, 40,530 tons; Length, 844 ft; Beam, 106 ft; Maximum speed, 22+ knots; Armament, two Sea Sparrow launchers, three Phalanx guns.

Whidbey Island landing ship, dock (LSD): Eight ships completed in 1984. Displacement, 11,140 tons; Length, 609 ft; Beam, 84 ft; Maximum speed, 20 knots.

warships: World War I

The following classes of vessel and individual vessels are typical of USN warships during WORLD WAR I. They are listed in alphabetical order:

Arkansas-class battleships: Two built in 1912. Displacement, 26,100 tons; Length, 562 ft; Beam, 106 ft; Maximum speed, 20 knots; Armament, 12 12-inch guns, 16 5-inch guns.

California-class armored cruisers: Six ships built between 1905 and 1907 and used during World War I. Displacement, 13,400 tons; Length, 502 ft; Beam, 70 ft; Maximum speed, 22 knots; Armament, four 8-inch guns, 14 6-inch guns, 18 3-inch guns, 12 3-pounders, two 18-inch torpedo tubes.

Chester-class scout cruisers (CL). Three ships commissioned in 1908 and decommissioned in 1930. Displacement, 3,750 tons; Length, 423 ft 1 in; Beam, 47 ft 1 in; Maximum speed, 24+ knots; Armament, two to four 5-inch guns, two to six 3-inch guns, two 21-inch torpedo tubes.

Clemson-class DESTROYERS (DD). Built between 1918 and 1922, the class included 155 ships —"four pipers"—20 of which were transferred to Britain in 1940 as part of the LEND-LEASE program. Displacement, 1,190 tons; Length, 314 ft 5 in; Beam, 31 ft 8 in; Maximum speed, 35 knots; Armament, four to eight 4-inch guns, one to three 3-inch guns, 6–12 21-inch torpedo tubes.

Connecticut-class battleships: Six ships commissioned between 1906 and 1908. Displacement, 16,000 tons; Length, 456 ft 4 in; Beam, 76 ft 10 in; Maximum speed, 18+ knots; Armament, four 12-inch guns, eight 8-inch guns, 12-20 3-inch guns.

Denver-class light cruisers: Six ships built in the years before World War I and used in that war. Displacement, 3,100 tons; Length, 309 ft; Beam, 44 ft; Maximum speed, 16.5 knots; Armament, eight 5-inch guns, eight 6-pounders.

Holland: Commissioned in 1900, this was the first SUBMARINE accepted by the USN. Displacement, 64 tons; Length, 53 ft 10 in; Beam, 10 ft 3 in; Maximum speed, 8 knots surfaced, slower submerged; Armament, four torpedo tubes. Never used in combat.

Illinois-class battleships (BB): Three ships commissioned 1900–01. Armed with 14 6-inch guns, four 3-inch guns, and capable of 17+ knots. Decommissioned in 1920.

Kansas-class battleships (BB): Four vessels built 1907–08. Displacement, 16,000 tons; Length, 450 ft; Beam, 77 ft; Maximum speed, 18 knots; Armament, four 12-inch guns, eight 8-inch guns, 12 7-inch guns, 20 3-inch guns, four torpedo tubes.

Kearsarge-class battleships: Two launched in 1898 and used during World War I. Displace-ment, 11,540 tons; Length, 375 ft 4 in; Beam, 72 ft+; Maximum speed, 16.8 knots; Arma-ment, four 13-inch guns, four 8-inch guns, 14 5-inch guns.

Langley (CV1): The first USN AIRCRAFT CARRIER, converted from a collier in 1920. Converted to a seaplane tender in 1937, it was sunk dur-ing WORLD WAR II while delivering P-40 fighter planes to a USAAF base in Java.

Maine-class battleships: Three ships built between 1902 and 1904. Displacement, 12,500 tons; Length, 388 t; Beam, 72 ft 3 in; Maximum speed, 18 knots; Armament, four 12-inch guns, 16 6-inch guns, six 3-inch guns, eight 3-pounders, two torpedo tubes.

Maryland-class battleships: Three ships com-missioned between 1920 and 1921. Displace-ment, 13,400 tons; Length, 502 ft; Beam, 70 ft; Maximum speed, 22 knots; Armament, four 8-inch guns, 14 6-inch guns, 18 3-inch guns, 12 3-pounders, two 18-inch torpedo tubes.

Mississippi-class battleships: Two vessels launched in 1905 and sold by the USN to the Greek navy in 1914. Sunk by German air attack in 1941.

Nevada-class battleships: Two vessels com-pleted in 1916 and used in World War I. Displacement, 29,900 tons; Length, 583 ft; Beam, 95 ft+; Maximum speed, 20.5 knots; Armament, 10 14-inch guns, 12 5-inch (.51-caliber) guns, eight 5-inch (.25-caliber) guns.

New Mexico–class battleships: Three ships launched in 1917. Displacement, 30,800 tons; Length, 600 ft; Beam, 97 ft+; Maximum speed, 21 knots; Armament, 12 14-inch guns, 12 5-inch guns, eight 3-inch guns, two torpedo tubes. Used in World War I and World War II.

O-11-class submarines: Six submarines com-missioned in 1918. Displacement, 491 tons; Length, 175 ft; Beam, 16 ft 4 in; Maximum speed, 14 knots surfaced, 11 knots sub-merged; Armament, one 3-inch gun, four torpedo tubes.

Pennsylvania-class battleships: Two ships completed in 1916. Used in World War I. *Pennsylvania* also fought in World War II, and *Arizona* was sunk at Pearl Harbor (see PEARL HARBOR, JAPANESE ATTACK ON). Displacement, 32,100 tons; Length, 608 ft; Beam, 97 ft 5 in; Maximum speed, 21 knots; Armament, 12 14-inch guns, 14 5-inch guns, eight 3-inch guns, two torpedo tubes.

R-1-class submarines: Twenty submarines laid down in 1917–18 and commissioned in 1918–19, too late to be used in World War I, for which they had been intended. Displacement, 569 tons; Length, 186 ft 2 in; Beam, 18 ft; Maximum speed, 13.5 knots surface, 10.5 knots submerged; Armament, four torpedo tubes.

R-21-class submarines: Seven laid down in 1917 for use in World War I; commissioned in 1919 and scrapped in 1930. Displacement, 495 tons; Length, 175 ft; Beam, 16 ft 8 in; Maximum speed, 14.5 knots surfaced, 11 knots submerged; Armament, one 3-inch gun, four torpedo tubes.

St. Louis–class semi-armored cruisers: Three completed during 1905–06. Displacement, 9,700 tons; Length, 423 ft; Beam, 65 ft; Maximum speed, 22 knots; Armament, 14 6-inch guns, 18 3-inch guns, 12 3-pounders.

South Carolina–class battleships: Two ships, the first USN dreadnoughts, launched in 1910 and used in World War I. Displacement, 16,000 tons; Length, 450 ft; Beam, 80 ft 3 in; Maximum speed, 18.5 knots; Armament, eight 12-inch guns, 14 3-inch guns, two torpedo tubes.

Subchasers: Small, wooden-hulled surface ships for antisubmarine warfare, used mostly in World War I. Displacement, 75 tons; Length, 110 ft; Maximum speed, 15 knots; Armament, one 3-inch gun, one Y gun for depth charge launch, stern depth-charge rack.

T-class submarines: Three authorized during World War I but not completed until 1920–22. Displacement, 1,106 tons; Length, 268 ft 9 in; Beam, 22 ft 4 in; Maximum speed, 20 knots. surfaced, 10.5 knots submerged; Armament, one 4-inch gun, four torpedo tubes.

Texas-class battleships: Two ships completed in 1914. Displacement, 27,000 tons; Length, 573 ft; Beam, 106 ft; Maximum speed, 21 knots; Armament, 10 14-inch guns, 16 5-inch guns, eight 3-inch guns.

Utah-class battleships: Two dreadnoughts launched in 1911 and used in World War I. Displacement, 21,825 tons; Length, 510 ft; Beam, 88 ft 3 in; Maximum speed, 20.75 knots; Armament, 10 12-inch guns, 16 5-inch guns, two 3-inch guns, two torpedo tubes.

V-1-class submarines: Nine built during World War I. Displacement, 2,000 tons; Length, 341 ft 6 in; Beam, 27 ft 6 in; Maximum speed, 18.71 knots surfaced, 11 knots submerged; Armament, one 5-inch or 3-inch gun, six torpedo tubes.

Virginia-class battleships: Five ships commissioned during 1906–07 and used in World War I. Obsolete after the war, they were used either as targets or scrapped.

Wickes-class destroyers (DD): Thirty-eight ships laid down during WORLD WAR I (1917–18) and commissioned in 1918–19. Some were transferred to Great Britain as part of the World War II Lend-Lease program. Others remained in the USN during World War II. Displacement, 1,154 tons; Length, 314 ft 5 ins; Beam, 31 ft 8 ins; Maximum speed, 35 knots; Armament, three to six 4-inch guns; one to three 3-inch guns, 6–12 torpedo tubes.

warships: World War II

The following classes of vessel and individual vessels are typical of USN warships during WORLD WAR II. They are listed in alphabetical order:

Atlanta-class light cruisers (CL): Eight built during World War II, 1941–45. Displacement, 6,000 tons; Length, 541 ft; Beam, 53 ft; Maximum speed, 32.5 knots; Armament, eight–16 5-inch guns, eight 20-inch torpedo tubes.

Bagley-class destroyers: Eight built in 1935–37. Displacement, 1,500 tons; Length, 341 ft 4 in; Beam, 35 ft 5 in; Maximum speed, 35.5 knots; Armament, four 5-inch guns, 16 21-inch torpedo tubes.

Balao-class submarines: 119 built 1942–45, one of the most important submarine types of World War II. Displacement, 1,525 tons; Length, 311 ft 9 ins; Beam, 27 ft 3 in; Maximum speed, 20.25 knots surfaced, 8.75 knots submerged; Armament, one 4-inch gun, one 5-inch gun, 10 torpedo tubes. Many of these durable submarines were used until the 1960s.

Baltimore-class heavy cruisers (CA): Fourteen built during World War II from 1943 to 1946. Displacement, 13,600 tons; Length, 674 ft; Beam, 70 ft 10 in; Maximum speed, 33 knots; Armament, nine 8-inch guns, 10 12.5-inch guns, 12–20 3-inch guns.

Benham-class destroyers: Ten built during 1939 and used in World War II. Displacement, 1,500 tons; Length, 341 ft; Beam, 35 ft; Maximum speed, 36.5 knots; Armament, four 5-inch guns, 8–16 21-inch torpedo tubes.

Benson-class destroyers: Thirty of this type built between 1940 and 1943 and used extensively in World War II. Displacement, 1,620 tons; Length, 348 ft; Beam, 36 ft; Maximum speed, 36.5 knots; Armament, four to five 5-inch guns, 5–10 21-inch torpedo tubes.

Brooklyn-class light cruisers: Two completed in 1938 and used throughout the war. Displacement, 9,650 tons; Length, 600 ft; Beam, 69 ft; Maximum speed, 32.5 knots; Armament, 15 6-inch guns, eight 5-inch guns, 28 40-mm guns, 24 20-mm guns.

Casablanca-class auxiliary ("escort") aircraft carriers (AVG, ACV, CVE): Fifty of these escort carriers were built during World War II. Displacement, 7,800 tons; Length, 512 ft 3 in; Beam, 65 ft 2 in; Maximum speed, 19 knots; Armament, one 5-inch gun and 28 aircraft.

Cleveland-class light cruisers (CL): Thirty-six ships commissioned between 1942 and 1944. Displacement, 10,000 tons; Length, 610 ft; Beam, 66 ft 6 in; Maximum speed, 32.5 knots; Armament, 12 6-inch guns, 12 5-inch guns.

Des Moines–class cruisers: Twelve ships were ordered during World War II, but only four were begun before the end of the war; three were completed and commissioned during 1948–49. Displacement, 17,000 tons; Length, 716 ft 6 in; Beam, 76 ft 4 in; Maximum speed, 33 knots; Armament, nine 8-inch guns, 12 5-inch guns, 8–20 3-inch guns.

Essex-class aircraft carriers: Ten ships built between 1942 and 1944. The last served until 1989. Displacement, 33,292 tons; Length, 856 ft; Beam, 93 ft; Maximum speed, 33 knots; Armament, 20 5-inch guns; 8–12 3-inch guns, 82+ aircraft.

Fargo-class light cruisers: Thirteen ships planned in World War II; only two commissioned during 1945–46. Displacement, 10,000 tons; Length, 611 ft 2 in; Beam, 66 ft 6 in; Maximum speed, 32.5 knots; Armament, 12 6-inch guns, 12 5-inch guns.

Fletcher-class destroyers (DD): One hundred twenty-five ships built during 1942–45. Displacement, 2,050 tons; Length, 376 ft; Beam, 40 ft; Maximum speed, 38 knots; Armament, two to five 5-inch guns, four to five 3-inch guns, five 21-inch torpedo tubes.

Gato-class (G-class) submarines (SS): Seventy-seven vessels built during World War II. Displacement, 1,526 tons; Length, 311 ft 9 in; Beam, 27 ft 3 in; Maximum speed, 20.25 knots surfaced, 8.75 knots submerged; Armament, one 3-inch gun, 10 torpedo tubes.

Gearing-class destroyers (DD): One hundred two built at the end of World War II. Displacement, 2,425 tons; Length, 390 ft; Beam, 41 ft; Maximum speed, 35 knots; Armament varied, since many were converted to a variety of purposes after the war.

Gleaves-class destroyers (DD): Sixty-six vessels built between June 1940 and April 1943. Displacement, 1,630 tons; Length, 348 ft; Beam, 36 ft+; Maximum speed, 37 knots; Armament, four to five 5-inch guns.

Gridley-class destroyers (DD): Four ships commissioned in 1937 and 1938. Displacement, 1,500 tons; Length, 341 ft+; Beam, 35 ft 6 in; Maximum speed, 35 knots; Armament, four 5-inch guns, 18–16 21-inch torpedo tubes.

Iowa-class battleships (BB): The four last battleships commissioned by the USN and representing the height of battleship design. All built during World War II. Displacement (*Iowa*), 43,785 tons; Length, 887 ft; Beam, 108 ft 2 in; Maximum speed, 33 knots; Armament, nine 16-inch guns, 20 5-inch guns. Decommissioned after the war, but some recommissioned during the KOREAN WAR, VIETNAM WAR, and PERSIAN GULF WAR.

Juneau-class light cruisers (CL): Three ships intended for use in World War II, but not commissioned until 1946. Displacement, 6,000 tons; Length, 53 ft 2 in; Beam, 53 ft 2 in; Maximum speed, 30 knots; Armament, 12 5-inch guns, up to 14 3-inch guns.

New Orleans–class CRUISERS (CL, CA): Seven ships commissioned between 1934 and 1937. Three sunk in World War II; four decommissioned in 1959.

North Carolina–class battleships (BB): Six ships completed during 1941–43. Displacement, 35,000 tons; Length, 750 ft; Beam, 108 ft; Maximum speed, 28 knots; Armament, nine 16-inch guns, 20 5-inch guns.

Omaha-class light cruisers (CL): Ten ships completed between 1923 and 1925 and used in World War II. Displacement, 7,050 tons; Length, 550 ft; Beam, 55 ft; Maximum speed, 33 knots; Armament, 12 6-inch guns, four 3-inch guns, six torpedo tubes.

Pensacola-class light cruisers (CL): Two ships completed in 1929. Displacement, 10,000 tons; Length, 570 ft; Beam, 64 ft; Maximum speed, 32.5 knots; Armament, 10 8-inch guns; four 5-inch guns, six torpedo tubes.

Perch (P)-class submarines: Six submarines built during the 1930s. Last USN submarines with riveted hulls. Displacement, 1,130 tons; Length, 300 ft 7 in; Beam, 25 ft 1 in; Maximum speed, 18.8 knots surfaced, 8 knots, submerged; Armament, six torpedo tubes.

Porpoise (P)-class submarines: Two submarines built during the 1930s. Displacement, 1,310 tons; Length, 301 ft; Beam, 24 ft 11 in; Maximum speed, 18 knots surfaced, 8 knots, submerged; Armament, six torpedo tubes.

Portland-class light cruisers (CL): Two ships built during the 1930s. Displacement, 10,000 tons; Length, 610 ft 3 in; Beam, 66 ft 1 in; Maximum speed, 32.7 knots; Armament, nine 8-inch guns, eight 5-inch guns, eight .50-caliber guns.

S-1-class submarines: Twenty-five submarines built 1920–24. Displacement, 854 tons; Length, 210 ft 3 ins; Beam, 21 ft; Maximum speed, 14.5 knots surfaced, 10.5 knots submerged; Armament, one 4-inch gun, four torpedo tubes.

S-3-class submarines: Eleven submarines commissioned 1919–23. Displacement, 876 tons; Length, 231 ft; Beam, 21 ft 10 in; Maximum speed, 15 knots surfaced, 11 knots submerged; Armament, one 4-inch gun, four to five torpedo tubes.

S-14-class submarines: Four submarines commissioned 1920–21. Displacement, 876 tons; Length, 231 ft; Beam, 21 ft 10 in; Maximum speed, 15 knots surfaced, 10.5 knots submerged; Armament, one 4-inch gun, four torpedo tubes.

S-42-class submarines: Six submarines commissioned 1924–25. Displacement, 906 tons; Length, 225 ft 3 in; Beam, 20 ft 8 in; Maximum speed, 14.5 knots surfaced, 11 knots submerged; Armament, one 4-inch gun, four torpedo tubes.

S-48-class submarines: Four submarines commissioned in 1922. Displacement, 993 tons; Length, 240 ft; Beam, 21 ft 10 in; Maximum speed, 14.5 knots surfaced, 11 knots submerged; Armament, one 4-inch gun, five torpedo tubes.

St. Louis–class light cruisers (CL): Two ships commissioned in 1939. Displacement, 10,000 tons; Length, 608 ft 4 ins; Beam, 61 ft 8 ins; Maximum speed, 32.5 knots; Armament, 15 6-inch guns, eight 5-inch guns.

Salmon-class submarines: Six built in the late 1930s. Displacement, 1,435 tons; Length, 308 ft; Beam, 261 ft 2 in; Maximum speed, 21 knots surfaced, 9 knots submerged; Armament, eight torpedo tubes.

Sargo-class submarines: Six built in the late 1930s. Displacement, 1,450 tons; Length, 310 ft 6 in; Beam, 27 ft 1 in; Maximum speed, 20 knots surfaced, 8.75 knots submerged; Armament, one 3-inch gun, eight torpedo tubes.

Seadragon-class submarines: Four built in 1938. Displacement, 1,450 tons; Length, 310 ft 6 in; Beam, 27 ft 1 in; Maximum speed, 20 knots surfaced, 8.75 knots submerged; Armament, one 3-inch gun, eight torpedo tubes.

Shark-class submarines: Two built in 1934. Displacement, 1,316 tons; Length, 298 ft 1 in; Beam, 25 ft 1 in; Maximum speed, 18 knots surfaced, 8 knots submerged; Armament, one 3-inch gun, six torpedo tubes.

Sims-class destroyers (DD): Twelve ships commissioned during 1939–40. Displacement, 1,570 tons; Length, 347 ft 7 in; Beam, 36 ft 1 in; Maximum speed, 37 knots; Armament, four to five 5-inch guns, 8–12 torpedo tubes.

Somers-class destroyers (DD): Five commissioned during 1937–39. Displacement, 1,850 tons; Length, 380 ft 11 in; Beam, 36 ft 7 in; Maximum speed, 37.5 knots; Armament, eight 5-inch guns, 12 torpedo tubes.

South Dakota–class battleships (BB): Four ships commissioned in 1942. Displacement, 34.044 tons; Length, 680 ft; Beam, 108 ft; Maximum speed, 27 knots; Armament, nine 16-inch guns.

Sumner-class destroyers (DD): Seventy commissioned 1944–46. Displacement, 2,200 tons; Length, 376 ft; Beam, 41 ft; Maximum

USS *St. Louis* (CL-49), 1939   *(Naval Historical Foundation)*

speed, 34 knots; Armament, six 5-inch guns, five torpedo tubes.

V-4/Argonaut-class submarine: One submarine built in 1931 to lay mines. Displacement, 2,710 tons; Length, 381 ft; Beam, 33 ft 10 in; Maximum speed, 15 knots surfaced, 8 knots submerged; Armament, two 6-inch guns, six torpedo tubes.

V-5/N-class submarines: Two boats (V-5, V-6) built in 1931. Displacement, 2,730 tons; Length, 370 ft 1 in; Beam, 33 ft 3 in; Maximum speed, 17.44 knots surfaced, 8 knots submerged; Armament, two 6-inch guns, six torpedo tubes.

V-8-class submarines: Two boats launched in the 1930s. Displacement, 1,110 tons; Length, 271 ft 11 in; Beam, 24 ft 11 in; Maximum speed, 16.5 knots surfaced, 8 knots submerged; Armament, one 3-inch gun, six torpedo tubes.

Worcester-class cruisers (CL, CA): Four ships planned during World War II; two built but not commissioned until 1948 and 1949. Displacement, 14,700 tons; Length, 679 ft 6 in; Beam, 70 ft 8 in; Maximum speed, 33 knots; Armament, 12 6-inch guns, 22–24 3-inch guns.

Yorktown-class aircraft carriers: Three ships built in the late 1930s. *Yorktown* and *Hornet* were both sunk in combat; *Enterprise* was decommissioned in 1956. Displacement, 19,800 tons; Length, 809 ft 6 in; Beam, 83 ft 1 in; Maximum speed, 32.5 knots; Armament, eight 5-inch guns, 90 aircraft.

Washington Navy Yard

The Washington Navy Yard serves as the headquarters for the NAVAL DISTRICT WASHINGTON, which is nicknamed the "Quarterdeck of the Navy." Additionally, the Washington Navy Yard serves as the ceremonial gateway to the nation's capital for many diplomats and other officials.

The Washington Navy Yard was authorized in 1799 by the first secretary of the navy, BENJAMIN STODDART, and is the oldest USN shore establishment. It occupies a site along the Anacostia River in southeast Washington. During its early years, it functioned as a naval base as well as the USN's largest shipbuilding and shipfitting facility. In 1815, the Board of Naval Commissioners limited the facility to shipbuilding and technology, and by the 1850s, the primary function of the yard became ordnance production. During WORLD WAR II, the Navy Yard became the largest naval ordnance plant in the world and, in 1945, was renamed the U.S. Naval Gun Factory.

Ordnance work was phased out in 1961, and in 1964 the facility was redesignated the Washington Navy Yard. Buildings were converted to office space.

Wasp Class (LHD-1)   See AMPHIBIOUS ASSAULT SHIPS.

Welles, Gideon (1802–1878) *secretary of the navy*

Welles was born and raised in Connecticut and, in 1826, became part owner and editor of the *Hartford Times*. He was active in state politics, then advanced to the federal government in 1846 when he was appointed chief of the USN Bureau of Provisions and Clothing. In 1861, President Abraham Lincoln named Welles 24th SECRETARY OF THE NAVY, a post Welles would hold, under Andrew Johnson, until 1869. Welles was a brilliant administrator who did much to expand the navy during the Civil War. His advocacy of new technology ensured that the USN acquired advanced naval artillery and developed such ironclads as USS *Monitor*.

Women Accepted for Voluntary Emergency Service (WAVES)

The WAVES—Women Accepted for Voluntary Emergency Service—was established on July 30, 1942, under the command of Lieutenant Commander Mildred H. McAfee (appointed August 2).

WAVES filled clerical positions ashore, thereby freeing men for sea and combat duty. It was not until October 1944 that the USN began accepting African-American women as WAVES. During the war, more than 100,000 women served in the WAVES before the service was disbanded in 1945.

World War I

World War I began in Europe early in August of 1914. The government of the United States, under President Woodrow Wilson, endeavored to remain neutral. Despite these efforts, anti-German feeling steadily increased in the United States, especially after Germany resumed its early policy of unrestricted submarine warfare, which resulted in the violation of the rights of the United States as a neutral. Additionally, the publication early in 1917 of the so-called Zimmermann telegram, in which the German foreign minister, Alfred Zimmermann, authorized Germany's ambassador to Mexico to induce that nation to make war on the United States, created great public outrage. In April 1917, President Wilson no longer believed he could keep America out of the war. He requested a declaration from Congress, which complied.

Even during the long period of neutrality, Wilson had successfully lobbied Congress for naval expansion. The Naval Act of 1916 authorized construction of 156 new ships. Despite this, the pacifist leanings of Secretary of the Navy Josephus Daniels tended to retard expansion; when it entered the war, the U.S. Navy was ill prepared to deal effectively with submarine warfare. Nevertheless, Admiral WILLIAM S. SIMS recognized that it was precisely for the conduct of antisubmarine warfare that the navy was most urgently needed. German U-boats were decimating Allied shipping, and there was a very real danger that England and France would starve. Sims called for every available U.S. DESTROYER to patrol British waters. Sims was also instrumental in persuading the British and the French to organize escorted convoys, and USN ships of all kinds were assigned to escort duty. At Sims's insistence, the USN also

ordered construction of small, wooden-hulled submarine chasers and rushed into operation with newly developed depth charges and contact mines, which soon proved highly effective against the U-boats. It was largely USN ships that sowed a minefield across the North Sea, creating a formidable barrier against U-boat incursion. In this "North Sea Mine Barrage," the USN laid some 56,000 mines, compared to the 13,000 laid by the Royal Navy.

The USN also contributed combat vessels to the Royal Navy offensive fleets. Five USN dreadnoughts—the most advanced battleships in the fleet—were put at the disposal of the commander of the British Grand Fleet. Three more battleships were deployed defensively, patrolling the North Sea outlets of Germany's U-boat navy.

The USN also contributed to Allied air power as early as June 1917, long before an effective U.S. presence had hit the ground. Some 500 USN aircraft, including AIRSHIPS, and a total of 6,000 naval aviators operated on the Western Front. USN artillery was commandeered for use as heavy railway guns.

Finally, the USN also played a vital role in American home waters, defending against U-boat attacks, which, however, never materialized.

World War II: Atlantic Theater

For the origins of World War II, the preparedness of the U.S. Navy, and the beginning of U.S. involvement in the war, see WORLD WAR II: PACIFIC THEATER.

The United States declared war on Japan on December 8, 1941, the day after Pearl Harbor (see PEARL HARBOR, JAPANESE ATTACK ON), and Germany and Italy declared war against the United States on December 11; however, the navy had been engaged in Atlantic combat well before the declaration. World War II began in Europe on September 1, 1939, when Germany invaded Poland. The very next month, the United States and 21 Latin American countries jointly issued the Declaration of Panama, creating in the hemisphere a 300-mile "neutrality zone" off limits to all belligerents. In June 1940, the Declaration of Havana reasserted the Monroe Doctrine, declaring that each signatory would regard an attack against any nation in the hemisphere as an attack on itself. USN ships were dispatched to patrol the neutrality zone. In September 1940, the United States and Great Britain concluded a LEND-LEASE agreement by which the USN traded DESTROYERS for bases, and early in 1941, the neutrality patrol was extended to 2,000 miles from the U.S. coast. USN ships also began escorting convoys partway to Britain. The result was an undeclared naval war with Germany, and on September 4, 1941, the destroyer USS *Greer* was attacked by a German submarine. On October 15, the USS *Kearny* was similarly attacked, and on October 31, the *Reuben James* was sunk.

By this time, the Battle of the Atlantic, primarily a German campaign of unrestricted submarine warfare against Allied warships and commercial shipping, was well under way. German submarine commanders had developed the tactics of submarine raiding far beyond the state of the art as it had existed in WORLD WAR I. German submarines now worked in "wolf packs," using multiple boats to coordinate attacks on poorly defended convoys. The submarines posed a grave threat to the very survival of Britain, let alone its ability to continue to prosecute the war. When the United States entered the war, therefore, antisubmarine warfare in the Atlantic became a prime objective along with convoy escort duty.

In response to America's entry into the war, German admiral Karl Dönitz launched Operation Drumroll (*Paukenschlag*), which dispatched submarines into the coastal waters of the United States. By early 1942, the waters off the East Coast became a killing field, as more than a half-million tons of U.S. and Allied shipping were sunk. The joint British and American development of sonar (then called Asdic) enabled easier detection of submarine activity, and USN coastal patrols proved increasingly effective against German submarines in U.S. waters.

In the open sea, the U.S. Navy and the Royal Navy steadily developed more effective antisubmarine warfare and convoy escort tactics, so that, by April 1943, the Allies had evened the score: The number of German submarines sunk equaled the number of Allied ships sunk, a 1-to-1 ratio. By the end of the Battle of the Atlantic, the German navy had lost 781 submarines out of a force of 1,175; 191 of these kills were the work of the USN. Seventy-five percent of Germany's submariners died in World War II.

The USN role in the Atlantic theater was not limited to defensive operations and antisubmarine warfare. The USN was instrumental in Operation Torch, the November 1942 amphibious invasion of North Africa. USN ships participated in landing troops and in covering the landings. In July 1943, Operation Husky supported the invasion of Sicily from North Africa. The USN and USCG operated landing craft for the Sicilian invasion and USN warships provided much-needed heavy naval bombardment. Operation Husky was followed in due course by Operation Avalanche, the invasion of the Italian mainland, commencing on September 3, 1943. The USN provided a large amphibious transport force and, again, supplied heavy bombardment in support of the landings.

Of course, the most massive use of USN assets in the Atlantic came with Operation Overlord, the "D-day" invasion of Normandy, which stepped off on June 6, 1944. The USN component of Operation Overlord was dubbed Operation Neptune and involved a total of 2,700 Allied vessels, including three USN battleships, three heavy CRUISERS, and a vast number of landing craft. During the first phase of the invasion, throughout June, 929,000 men were landed on Normandy beaches, along with 177,000 vehicles and almost 600,000 tons of supplies.

As the forces of the Normandy invasion broke out from the beachheads and began their advance into and across France, Operation Anvil was launched on August 15, 1944, in southern France, with USN-supported landings between Toulon and Cannes. By this time, the Battle of the Atlantic was

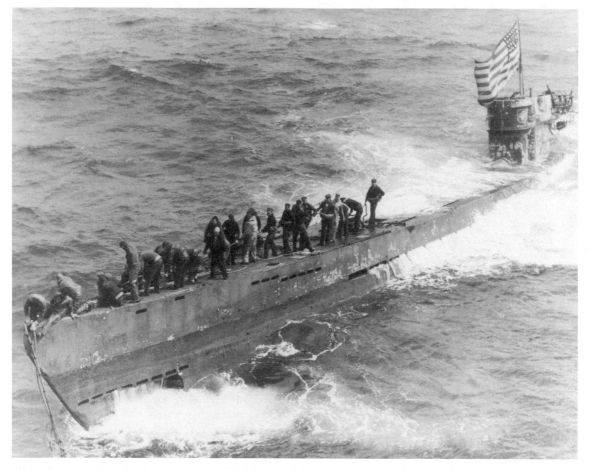

A boarding party from the destroyer escort USS *Pilsbury* (DE-133) secures a tow line to the newly captured submarine U-505 on June 4, 1944. This was the only German submarine captured at sea during the war. Since 1954, it has been on exhibit at the Museum of Science and Industry, Chicago.   *(U.S. Navy)*

all but over, and USN operations in the waters of southern France were the concluding naval actions of war in the Atlantic theater.

World War II: Pacific Theater

As with WORLD WAR I, World War II began as a European conflict (on September 1, 1939, with the German invasion of Poland) in which the United States endeavored to remain neutral. However, the alliance of Japan with Germany and Italy (the so-called Berlin-Rome-Tokyo Axis) ensured that the

war would become global. The administration of President Franklin D. Roosevelt increasingly reshaped American neutrality, fashioning a policy of "armed neutrality," in which military and other material aid was given to Great Britain and other nations aligned against Germany and Italy (see LEND-LEASE). With regard to Japan, the United States sought to curb Japanese aggression against China by placing an embargo against a host of raw materials exports in an effort to diminish Japan's ability to prosecute war. President Roosevelt saw this policy as an effective alternative to outright war with Japan. Effective it proved to be, but it was hardly an alternative to war. Instead, it provoked Japan to attack the United States at Pearl Harbor on December 7, 1941 (see PEARL HARBOR, JAPANESE ATTACK ON). On the next day, President Roosevelt secured from Congress a declaration of war against Japan, which, given its alliance with Italy and Germany, quickly led to war against those nations. The United States was fighting a world war on two fronts. (Also see WORLD WAR II: ATLANTIC THEATER.)

The catastrophe at Pearl Harbor may give the impression that the United States was thrust into war unprepared. While it is true that the navy and army installations at Pearl Harbor were caught by surprise, the nation had been preparing for war since at least 1940, when President Roosevelt authorized the first peacetime military draft in American history. Although the USN inventory of ships had been reduced after World War I and under the provisions of the Washington Naval Treaty of 1922, a second treaty, the London Naval Agreement of 1936, provided more leeway, and the USN began to rebuild to the strength specified in that document. During the later 1930s, as war clouds gathered, the USN was expanded even further, and in 1940 the so-called Two-Ocean Navy Act authorized a 70 percent increase in the fleet to ensure that it would be a viable Atlantic and Pacific force.

In a single blow, the attack on Pearl Harbor devastated the PACIFIC FLEET, sinking or severely damaging eight battleships, three CRUISERS, three DESTROYERS, and four other vessels as well as some 180 aircraft (mostly on the ground). More than 2,000 sailors and marines were killed and another 700 wounded. (Army losses were far lighter—more than 200 killed and about 400 wounded.) Fortunately, the large AIRCRAFT CARRIERS stationed at Pearl were at sea during the attack and were thus spared. They would become the nucleus around which the USN would regroup in the Pacific.

The USN began a crash expansion program. In the meantime, the Japanese executed their strategy of expansion with terrifying speed. Their objective was twofold: first, to occupy key Pacific islands and Asian countries that would constitute both an empire and a vast buffer zone against foreign aggression, and, second, to stun the United States into concluding a nonaggression pact that would give Japan a free hand in its program of conquest. The attack on Pearl Harbor, however, did not stun America, but instead galvanized its resolve, motivating a war effort of unprecedented proportions and dooming the Japanese to certain defeat.

At first, the news from the Pacific was all bad. The American-held islands of Guam and Wake fell almost immediately. British-held Hong Kong, the Malay peninsula, Singapore, and the Dutch East Indies also quickly collapsed. American and Filipino forces were able to mount a vigorous defense of the Philippines, which made Japanese conquest of those islands very costly; however, the archipelago fell to the Japanese in April 1942.

Although American military planners agreed to devote the majority of the country's resources to the war in Europe, at least initially, the USN (and the American public) was anxious to "avenge" Pearl Harbor and the other losses in the Pacific. Accordingly, USN Pacific strategy called for assuming an offensive posture as soon as possible, and in February 1942 a carrier task force led by USS *Enterprise* raided the Japanese-held Marshall and Gilbert Islands. In March, a two-carrier task force, led by *Lexington* and *Yorktown*, hit New Guinea. Even more spectacularly, on April 18, 1942, Lieutenant Colonel Jimmy Doolittle (USAAF) led a radically unconventional bombing raid against Tokyo itself. Sixteen B-25 bombers were launched from the deck of USS *Hornet*. Damage inflicted by these medium bombers was quite limited, but the raid on the Japanese capital profoundly shocked the Japanese government and military. It forced the Japanese to keep a large number of aircraft in and around Japan for defensive purposes. Even more important, the Doolittle raid, along with the two island raids that preceded it, worked wonders for American morale.

In strictly military terms, it was the Battle of the Coral Sea (May 7–8, 1942) that represented the first U.S. strategic victory. The Japanese were prevented from invading Port Moresby, which would have been a stepping-off place for an invasion of Australia. The cost of this victory was great—including the loss of USS *Lexington*—but the battle halted the Japanese juggernaut. This was followed during June 3–6, 1942, by the even more momentous (and even more costly) victory at the Battle of Midway. The small island of Midway served as a precious American toehold in the Pacific. The Japanese intended to take Midway and, in the process, lure the U.S. fleet to its destruction. Although the USN lost the carrier *Yorktown* and a large number of aircraft in the battle, the Japanese lost four carriers and one heavy cruiser as well as 322 aircraft. It was a devastating blow from which the Imperial Navy was never able to recover. From Midway on, the USN assumed the offensive and the Japanese were forced to respond. Although the costliest battles had yet to be fought, Midway was the turning point in the Pacific war.

Led by the USN, Allied command adopted an offensive strategy of "island hopping," targeting for invasion only certain Japanese-held islands, while leaving others untouched. By taking the strategically situated islands, American forces isolated Japanese forces on the other islands, rendering them useless as well as cutting them off from supply or retreat.

The island-hopping campaign began with the USN support of the amphibious assaults on Guadalcanal and Tulagi in August 1942. This initiated a series of hard-fought battles in the Solomons, which would not be fully secured until the beginning of 1944. In the meantime, the grand Allied strategy in the Pacific became a two-pronged campaign. Forces under General Douglas MacArthur and Admiral WILLIAM F. HALSEY proceeded up from Australia and New Guinea, converging on the East Indies and Philippines, while CHESTER W. NIMITZ commanded forces from Hawaii, which advanced through the Gilbert, Marshall, Caroline, and Mariana Islands. The ultimate objective of both prongs of the Pacific campaign was convergence on the Japanese home islands and an invasion of Japan that would end the war.

Aircraft carrier USS *Lexington* burning during the Battle of the Coral Sea. *(Naval Historical Foundation)*

U.S. submarine on patrol in the Pacific, 1945 *(National Archives)*

After the Solomons fell to American forces early in 1944, the Marshall Islands were targeted and seized. Next came the Marianas, including the islands of Saipan, Guam, and Tinian. Simultaneously, MacArthur took northern New Guinea and used it to launch a massive offensive against the Philippines. This provoked the titanic Battle of the Philippine Sea (June 19–20, 1944), which proved one of the great Japanese failures of the war. More than 300 Japanese aircraft were lost in an exchange that was dubbed the "Marianas Turkey Shoot." Beyond the loss of so many aircraft, the worst consequence for the Japanese was that American capture of the Marianas provided air bases from which USAAF B-29s could stage unrelenting raids against the Japanese homeland.

That homeland was already suffering from the effects of USN operations against Japanese shipping. USN submarines operated in the western Pacific and very close to Japan itself, targeting Japanese warships as well as merchant shipping and tankers. Submarine operations created a highly effective naval blockade and caused critical shortages. A force of 288 USN submarines sank 276 Japanese warships and more than 4 million tons of commercial shipping.

By the summer of 1944, it was clear that the Japanese had lost the war—but they did not give up and, in fact, only fought more fiercely. Deciding to take their stand in the Philippines, the Japanese mounted a tremendous resistance, which resulted in the Battle of Leyte Gulf (October 23–26, 1944), the greatest naval battle ever fought. Japanese losses were staggering: three battleships, four carriers, nine cruisers, and 10 destroyers. If anything, however, this near-destruction of the Imperial Navy inspired even greater desperation, this time in the form of the *kamikaze.* Japanese pilots will-

Lieutenant Alex Vraciu (USN) commanded a navy air squadron that shot down 41 Japanese aircraft during the "Marianas Turkey Shoot." The Japanese lost a total of 402 aircraft in the Battle of the Philippine Sea.   *(U.S. Marine Corps)*

ingly transformed their aircraft into human-guided missiles, unleashing suicide attacks against the American ships supporting the invasion of Okinawa in April 1945. The *kamikaze* attacks were as hopeless as they were desperate; nevertheless, the USN lost 34 ships in the Okinawa campaign, and another 368 suffered severe damage. Some 10,000 sailors were killed or wounded.

The taking of Okinawa provided the major base from which the Allies intended to launch an all-out invasion of Japan itself. By any military standard, Japan had been defeated. But the Allies understood from past experience that this would only motivate even more determined and fanatical resistance. It was contemplated that the invasion of Japan would cost perhaps a half-million Allied casualties. However, the dropping of newly developed atomic bombs on Hiroshima (August 6, 1945) and Nagasaki (August 9, 1945) made an invasion unnecessary. For the first time in their history, the Japanese surrendered to a foreign power, and the war officially came to an end on September 2, 1945, with the signing of a surrender instrument aboard the battleship *Missouri* riding at anchor in Tokyo Bay.

Y

yard patrol craft (YP)

YPs are used for training and research. As training vessels, the YP is used for basic watercraft and damage control training and for instruction in basic and advanced seamanship and navigation. As research craft, the YPs are used at the Naval Undersea Warfare Center, Keyport, Washington, to measure mobile underwater target and torpedo radiated noise and ambient water noise conditions. They also serve as a platform for deployment of suspended, stationary, in-water acoustic targets during on-range torpedo proof and test operations; deployment of countermeasure emulator during torpedo operations; and deployment of oceanographic measurement instrumentation to determine seawater conductivity and temperature at various depths.

General characteristics of the YP 654 class include:

Builders: Stephens Bros., Inc., and Elizabeth City Systems
Power plant: 12V-71N Detroit diesel engines, two propellers, horsepower rating 437, shaft horsepower at 2,100 revolutions/min
Overall length: 81 ft
Waterline length: 77 ft
Beam: 18 ft
Draft: 6 ft
Displacement: 66 tons full load
Dead weight: 11 tons
Speed: 12 knots
Cruising radius: 1,800 nautical mi
Material: wood hull, aluminum superstructure
Crew: two officers, eight enlisted; total capacity, 50 persons

The general characteristics of the YP 676 and YP 696 classes include:

Builders: Peterson Builders (YP 676 through 682); Marinette Marine (YP 683 through 700)
Power plant: 12V-71N Detroit diesel engines, two propellers, horsepower rating 437 shaft horsepower at 2,100 revolutions/min
Overall length: 108 ft
Waterline length: 102 ft
Beam: 24 ft
Draft: 8 ft
Speed: 12 knots
Cruising radius: 1,800 nautical mi
Material: wood hull, aluminum superstructure
Crew: two officers, four enlisted; total capacity, 50 persons

Z

Zumwalt, Elmo Russell (1920–) *navy admiral*

Zumwalt became the 19th CHIEF OF NAVAL OPERATIONS in 1970, the youngest full admiral and CNO in USN history. His four-year term as CNO was controversial, as he worked aggressively to liberalize the USN, especially with regard to equal opportunity for minority and women sailors and officers.

Zumwalt was born in San Francisco and graduated from the UNITED STATES NAVAL ACADEMY in 1942. He served on DESTROYERS and CRUISERS during WORLD WAR II in the Pacific, then on the battleship *Wisconsin* (BB-64) during the KOREAN WAR. After attending the NAVAL WAR COLLEGE during 1952–53, Zumwalt served in the office of the SECRETARY OF THE NAVY. During the VIETNAM WAR, from 1968 to 1970, he commanded USN operations in and around Vietnam.

After completing his term as CNO, Zumwalt retired from the USN and ran unsuccessfully for the United States Senate from Virginia in 1976.

Zumwalt Class (DD 21)   See DESTROYERS.

U.S. Navy Abbreviations and Acronyms

★ ──

AAW Anti-Air Warfare (AAW)

ACE NATO Allied Command Europe

AE Ammunition Ships

AFSOUTH Commander in Chief Allied Forces, Southern Europe

AGF Command Ships

AMRAAM Advanced Medium-Range Air-to-Air Missile

AOE Fast Combat Support Ships

ARS Rescue and Salvage Ship

AS Submarine Tender

ASROC Anti-Ship (or Submarine) Rocket

ASW Anti-Submarine Warfare

ASUW Anti-Surface Warfare

BB Battleship

BUMDE Bureau of Medicine and Surgery

BUPERS Bureau of Naval Personnel

CINCLANTFLT Commander In Chief, U.S. Atlantic Fleet

CINCPACFLT Commander In Chief, U.S. Pacific Fleet

CINCUSNAVEUR Commander In Chief, U.S. Naval Forces Europe

CNATRA Chief of Naval Air Training

CNET Chief of Naval Education and Training

CNO Chief of Naval Operations

CPO Chief Petty Officer

CV Aircraft Carrier

CVN Aircraft Carrier, Nuclear

CG Cruiser

COMINEWARCOM Mine Warfare Command

COMNAVAIRPAC Commander, Naval Air Force, U.S. Pacific Fleet

COMNAVFORJAPAN Commander, Naval Forces, Japan

COMNAVFORKOREA Commander, Naval Forces, Korea

COMNAVMARIANAS Commander, Naval Forces, Marianas

COMNAVREG Commander, Navy Region Hawaii

COMNAVREG NORTHEAST Commander, Navy Region Northeast

COMNAVREG NORTHWEST Commander, Navy Region Northwest

COMNAVREGSE Commander, Navy Region Southeast

COMNAVREGSW Commander, Navy Region Southwest

COMNAVSURFLANT Commander, Naval Surface Force, U.S. Atlantic Fleet

COMNAVSURFPAC Commander, Naval Surface Force, U.S. Pacific Fleet

COMSEVENTHFLT Commander, Seventh Fleet

COMSUBPAC Commander, Submarine Force, U.S. Pacific Fleet

COMTHIRDFLEET Commander, Third Fleet

COMTHIRDNCB Commander, Third Naval Construction Brigade

CTF-12 Commander, Task Force 12

CTF-14 Commander, Task Force 14

DD/DDG Destroyer

DON CIO Department of the Navy Chief Information Officer

DSRV Deep Submergence Rescue Vehicle

EOD Explosive Ordnance Disposal

FFG Frigates

FTSCLANT Fleet Technical Support Center, Atlantic

FTSCPAC Fleet Technical Support Center, Pacific

HARM High-Speed Anti-Radiation Missile

IDF Iceland Defense Force

INSURV Board of Inspection and Survey

IRR Individual Ready Reserve

JDAM Joint Direct Attack Munition

JSF Joint Strike Fighter

JSOW Joint Standoff Weapon

LASH Lighterage Aboard Ships

LCAC Landing Craft, Air Cushioned

LCC Amphibious Command Ships

LCM Landing Craft, Mechanized

LCU Landing Craft, Utility

LHA Amphibious Assault Ship

LHD Amphibious Assault Ship

LPD Amphibious Transport Dock

LSD Dock Landing Ships

LSV Large Scale Vehicle

MARDEZPAC Commander, Maritime Defense Zone Pacific

MARFORPAC Marine Forces Pacific

MCM Mine Countermeasures Ship

MHC Minehunter, Coastal

MSC Military Sealift Command

MV Motor Vessel

NAVAIR Naval Air Systems Command

NAVFAC Naval Facilities Engineering Command

NAVMAC Navy Manpower Analysis Center

NAVMSMO Navy Modeling and Simulation Management Office

NAVOCEANO Naval Oceanic Office

NAVPETOFF Navy Petroleum Office

NAVSEA Naval Sea Systems Command

NAVSUP Naval Supply Systems Command

NAWCAD Naval Air Warfare Center, Aircraft Division

NCIS Naval Criminal Investigative Service

NCST Naval Center for Space Technology

NDRF National Defense Reserve Fleet

NDW Naval District Washington

NEDU Navy Experimental Diving Unit

NEHC Navy Environmental Health Center

NFAF Naval Fleet Auxiliary Force

NLCC Navy League Cadet Corps

NLTUC Naval Leader Training Unit Coronado

NNOA National Naval Officers Association

NNSOC Naval Network and Space Operations Command

NOMI Naval Operational Medicine Institute

NORU Naval Orientation and Recruiting Unit

NPRST Navy Personnel Research, Studies, and Technology

NPS Naval Postgraduate School

NRL Naval Research Laboratory

NROTC Naval Reserve Officers' Training Corps

NS Naval Station

NSCC Naval Sea Cadet Corps

NSGC Naval Security Group Command

NSHS Naval School of Health Sciences

NSRL Naval Submarine Medical Research Laboratory

NSWC Naval Special Warfare Command; also, Naval Surface Warfare Center

NTC Naval Training Center

NTCGL Naval Training Center Great Lakes

NTSC Naval Transportation Support Center

NUWC Naval Undersea Warfare Center

NVR Naval Vessel Register

NWC Naval War College

OJAG Office of the Judge Advocate General

PC Patrol Coastal Ship

PT Patrol Torpedo [Boat]

RAM Rolling Airframe Missile

RHIB Rigid Hull Inflatable Boat

ROV Remotely Operated Vehicle

RTC Recruit Training Command

SCSC Surface Combat Systems Center

SEA Senior Enlisted Academy

SEAL SEa-Air-Land [commando team]

SECNAV   Secretary of the Navy

SELRES   Selected Reserve

SLAM-ER   Standoff Land Attack Missile-Expanded Response

SLBM   Submarine-Launched Ballistic Missile

SM   Standard Missile

SP   Shore Patrol

SPAWAR   Space and Naval Warfare Systems Command

SSBN   Ballistic Missile Submarine

SSC   Service School Command

SSGN   Guided Missile Submarines

SSN   Attack Submarine

SUBASE   Submarine Base

SUBGRU   Submarine Group

SUBLANT   Submarine Force Atlantic Fleet

SUBPAC   Submarine Force Pacific Fleet

SUPSHIP   Supervisors of Shipbuilding, Conversion, and Repair

SWISS   Shallow Water Intermediate Search System

T-ACS   Auxiliary Crane Ships

T-AE   Ammunition Ships

T-AFS   Combat Stores Ship

T-AFT   Fleet Ocean Tug

T-AGM   Missile Range Instrumentation Ships

T-AGOS   Counter-drug Operations/Oceanographic Surveillance Ship

T-AGS   Oceanographic Survey Ship

T-AGSS   Research Submarine

T-AH   Hospital Ships

T-AK   Container Ship, including Multi-Purpose Tween Decker, Roll-on/Roll-off Container Ship, and Roll-on/Roll-off Heavy Lift Ships

T-AKE   Advanced Auxiliary Dry Cargo Ships

T-AKF   Float-on/Float-off Cargo Ships

T-AKR   Fast Sealift Ships; also applied to Large- and Medium-speed Roll-on/Roll-off Ships

TAR   Training and Administration of the Reserves

T-ARC   Cable Repair Ship

T-AVB   Aviation Logistic Ships

TACTRAGRUPAC   Tactical Training Group Pacific

T-AO   Underway Replenishment Oiler

T-AOT   Transport Oiler/Tanker

UAV   Unmanned Aerial Vehicle

UNREP   Underway Replenishment

USNAVCENTCOM   U.S. Naval Forces Central Command

USNAVEUR   U.S. Naval Forces Europe

USNS   United States Naval Ship

USS   United States Ship

WAVES   Women Accepted for Voluntary Emergency Service

YP   Yard Patrol [craft]

Bibliography
UNITED STATES ARMY

★

GENERAL WORKS

Adams, Henry. *The War of 1812.* New York: First Cooper Square Press, 1999.

Adelson, Bruce. *George Gordon Meade: Union General.* New York: Chelsea House, 2001.

Aldebol, Anthony. *Army Air Force and United States Air Force: Decorations, Medals, Ribbons, Badges and Insignia.* Fountain Inn, S.C.: Medals of American Press, 1999.

Alexander, Bevin. *Korea: The Lost War.* London: Arrow Books, 1989.

Ambrose, Stephen E. *Americans at War.* Jackson: University Press of Mississippi, 1997.

———. *Band of Brothers: E Company, 506th Regiment, 101st Airborne from Normandy to Hitler's Eagle's Nest.* Reprint ed. New York: Simon & Schuster, 2001.

———. *Citizen Soldiers.* New York: Simon & Schuster, 1997.

———. *Crazy Horse and Custer: The Parallel Lives of Two American Warriors.* New York: Bantam, 1996.

———. *D-day, June 6, 1944: The Climactic Battle of World War II.* New York: Simon & Schuster, 1994.

———. *Duty, Honor, Country: A History of West Point.* Baltimore: Johns Hopkins University Press, 2000.

———. *Eisenhower: Soldier and President.* New York: Simon & Schuster, 1991.

Anderson, Christopher J. *Screaming Eagles: The 101st Airborne Division from D-day to Desert Storm.* New York: Chelsea House, 2002.

———. *The U.S. Army Today: From the End of the Cold War to the Present Day.* London: Greenhill, 1997.

Anzuoni, Robert P. *The All American: An Illustrated History of the 82nd Airborne Division, 1917 to the Present.* Atglen, Pa.: Schiffer Publishing, 2001.

Appleman, Roy A. *Ridgway Duels for Korea.* College Station: Texas A & M University Press, 1990.

Axelrod, Alan, and Charles Phillips. *The Macmillan Dictionary of Military Biography.* New York: Macmillan, 1998.

Badsey, Stephen. *Korean War.* New York: Gallery Books, 1990.

Barrett, Stephen Melvil, and Geronimo. *Geronimo: His Own Story.* New York: Penguin USA, 1995.

Bauer, K. Jack. *Zachary Taylor: Soldier, Planter, Statesman of the Old Southwest.* Reprint ed. Baton Rouge: Louisiana State University Press, 1991.

Beckwith, Charles A., and Donald Knox. *Delta Force: The Army's Elite Counterterrorist Unit.* New York: Avon, 2000.

Berner, Brad K. *The Spanish-American War: A Historical Dictionary.* New York: Rowman & Littlefield, 1998.

Bin, Alberto, Richard Hill, and Archer Jones. *Desert Storm: A Forgotten War.* New York: Praeger, 1998.

Black, Robert W. *Rangers in Korea.* New York: Ivy Books, 1989.

Blair, Clay. *The Forgotten War: America in Korea, 1950–1953.* New York: Times Books, 1987.

Blumenson, Martin. *Mark Clark.* New York: St. Martin's Press, 1984.

Boatner, Mark. *Encyclopedia of the American Revolution.* New York: D. McKay, 1966.

———. *The Civil War Dictionary.* New York: David McKay, 1959.

Bonn, Keith E. *Army Officer's Guide.* 49th ed. Mechanicsburg, Pa.: Stackpole Books, 2002.

Boritt, Gabor S. *Lincoln's Generals.* New York: Oxford University Press, 1994.

Bowen, Richard. *Fighting with the Screaming Eagles: With the 101st Airborne Division from Normandy to Bastogne.* London: Greenhill Books, 2004.

Bradley, Omar Nelson. *A Soldier's Story.* Reprint ed. New York: Random House, 1999.

Brady, James P. *Coldest War: A Memoir of Korea.* New York: St. Martin's Press, 2000.

Brinsfield, John Wesley, W. C. Davis, Benedict Maryniak, and James I. Robertson, eds. *Faith in the Fight: Civil War Chaplains.* Mechanicsburg, Pa.: Stackpole Books, 2003.

Brooks, Noah. *Henry Knox, A Soldier of the Revolution.* New York: Da Capo, 1974.

Carp, E. Wayne. *To Starve the Army at Pleasure: Continental Army Administration and American Political Culture, 1775–1783.* Chapel Hill: University of North Carolina Press, 1984.

Clark, Maurine Doran. *Captain's Bride, General's Lady; the Memoirs of Mrs. Mark W. Clark.* New York: McGraw-Hill, 1956.

Coffman, Edward M. *The War to End All Wars: The American Military Experience in World War I.* New York: Oxford University Press, 1968.

Coles, Harry L. *The War of 1812.* Chicago: University of Chicago Press, 1965.

Colley, David P. *Blood for Dignity: The Story of the First Integrated Combat Unit in the U.S. Army.* New York: St. Martin's Press, 2003.

———. *The Road to Victory: The Untold Story of World War II's Red Ball Express.* New York: Warner Books, 2001.

Connell, Evan S. *Son of the Morning Star: Custer and the Little Bighorn.* New York: Farrar, Straus & Giroux, 1997.

Cosmas, Graham A. *An Army for Empire: The United States Army in the Spanish-American War.* Shippensburg, Pa.: White Mane, 1994.

Cray, Ed. *General of the Army.* New York: Cooper Square, 2000.

Crost, Lyn. *Honor by Fire: Japanese Americans at War in Europe and the Pacific.* Novato, Calif.: Presidio Press, 1994.

Davidson, Phillip B. *Vietnam at War: The History 1946–1975.* Novato, Calif.: Presidio, 1988.

Dear, I.C.B., and M.R.D. Foot, eds. *The Oxford Companion to World War II.* New York: Oxford University Press, 2001.

DeMontravel, Peter R. *A Hero to His Fighting Men: Nelson A. Miles, 1839–1925.* Kent, Ohio: Kent State University Press, 1998.

D'Este, Carlo. *Eisenhower: A Soldier's Life.* New York: Henry Holt, 2000.

———. *Patton: A Genius for War.* New York: HarperCollins, 1996.

Dupuy, R. Ernest, and Trevor N. Dupuy. *The Compact History of the Civil War.* New York: Warner Books, 1993.

Dupuy, Trevor N. *The Military History of World War I.* New York: Watts, 1967.

Duus, Masayo Umezawa. *Unlikely Liberators: The Men of the 100th and 442nd.* Honolulu: University of Hawaii Press, 1989.

Earley, Charity Adams. *One Woman's Army: A Black Officer Remembers the WAC.* College Station: Texas A&M University Press, 1989.

Edmonds, Anthony O. *The War in Vietnam.* Westport, Conn.: Greenwood, 1998.

Eisenhower, John S. *Agent of Destiny: The Life and Times of General Winfield Scott.* Norman: University of Oklahoma Press, 1999.

———. *So Far from God: The U.S. War with Mexico, 1846–1848.* Reprint ed. Norman: University of Oklahoma Press, 2000.

Emering, Edward J. *U.S. Navy and Marine Corps Campaign and Commemorative Medals.* Atglen, Pa.: Schiffer, 1998.

Evans, Anthony A. *Gulf War: Desert Shield and Desert Storm, 1990–1991.* London: Greenhill, 2003.

Fellman, Michael. *Citizen Sherman: A Life of William Tecumseh Sherman.* New York: Random House, 1995.

Fletcher, Marvin E. *America's First Black General: Benjamin O. Davis, Sr., 1880–1970.* Lawrence: University Press of Kansas, 1989.

———. *The Black Soldier and Officer in the United States Army, 1891–1917.* Columbia: University of Missouri Press, 1974.

Foote, Shelby. *The Civil War: A Narrative, Vol. 1, Fort Sumter to Perryville.* New York: Random House, 1958. *Vol. 2, Fredericksburg to Meridian.* New

York: Random House, 1963. *Vol. 3, Red River to Appomattox.* New York: Random House, 1974.

Foster, Frank C. *The Decorations, Medals, Ribbons, Badges and Insignia of the United States Army: World War II to Present.* Fountain Inn, S.C.: Medals of America Press, 2000.

Fowle, Barry W. ed. *Builders and Fighters: U.S. Army Engineers in World War II.* Fort Belvoir, Va.: Office of History, U.S. Army Corps of Engineers, 1992.

Fredriksen, John C. *Free Trade and Sailors' Rights: A Bibliography of the War of 1812.* Westport, Conn.: Greenwood Press, 1985.

Freeman, Douglas Southall. *George Washington.* 7 vols. New York: Scribners, 1948–1957.

Gaff, Alan D. *Bayonets in the Wilderness: Anthony Wayne's Legion in the Old Northwest.* Norman: University of Oklahoma Press, 2004.

Gilbert, Martin. *The First World War: A Complete History.* New York: Henry Holt, 1994.

Giles, Janice Holt. *The Damned Engineers.* 2nd ed. Fort Belvoir, Va.: Historical Division, U.S. Army Corps of Engineers, 1985.

Gillie, Mildred Hanson. *Forging the Thunderbolt.* Harrisburg, Pa.: Military Service Pub. Co., 1947.

Goetzmann, William H. *Army Exploration in the American West, 1803–1863.* New Haven, Conn.: Yale University Press, 1959.

Golay, Michael. *Spanish-American War.* New York: Facts On File, 2003.

Grant, Ulysses S. *Personal Memoirs.* Reprint ed. New York: Random House, 1998.

Halberstadt, Hans. *Desert Storm Ground War.* Ann Arbor, Mich.: Motorbooks International, 1991.

Hall, Mitchell K. *The Vietnam War.* New York: Longman, 1999.

Hammond, William M., George L. MacGarrigle, and William T. Bowers. *Black Soldier, White Army: The 24th Infantry Regiment in Korea.* Washington, D.C.: U.S. Government Printing Office, 1996.

Haney, Eric. *Inside Delta Force: The Story of America's Elite Counterterrorist Unit.* New York: Delacorte Press, 2002.

Heidler, David S., and Jeane T. Heidler, eds. *Encyclopedia of the American Civil War: A Political, Social, and Military History.* Santa Barbara, Calif.: ABC-CLIO, 2000.

———. *Encyclopedia of the War of 1812.* Santa Barbara, Calif.: ABC-CLIO, 1997.

Herring, George C. *America's Longest War: The United States and Vietnam, 1950–1975.* 4th ed. New York: McGraw-Hill, 2002.

Hickey, Donald R. *The War of 1812: A Forgotten Conflict.* Urbana: University of Illinois Press, 1989.

Hill, Forest G. *Roads, Rails and Waterways: The Army Engineers and Early Transportation.* Norman: University of Oklahoma Press, 1957.

Holme, John G. *The Life of Leonard Wood.* Honolulu, Hawaii: University Press of the Pacific, 2003.

Hopkins, James E. T. *Spearhead: A Complete History of Merrill's Marauder Rangers.* Baltimore, Md.: Johns Hopkins University Press, 2000.

Huntington, Samuel P. *Soldier and the State.* Cambridge, Mass.: Harvard University Press, 1957.

Hutton, Paul Andrew. *Phil Sheridan and His Army.* Norman: University of Oklahoma Press, 1999.

Karnow, Stanley. *Vietnam: A History.* New York: Viking, 1983.

Katcher, Philip. *American Soldier: U.S. Armies in Uniform, 1755 to the Present.* Buckinghamshire, U.K.: Military Press, 1991.

———. *The Mexican-American War, 1846–1848.* London: Osprey, 1989.

Keegan, John. *The First World War.* New York: Knopf, 1999.

———. *The Second World War.* New York: Viking, 1989.

Kennedy, David M. *Over Here: The First World War and American Society.* New York: Oxford University Press, 1982.

Kennett, Lee. *G.I.: The American Soldier in World War II.* New York: Charles Scribner's Sons, 1987.

Koskimaki, George E. *The Battered Bastards of Bastogne: A Chronicle of the Defense of Bastogne, December 19, 1944–January 17, 1945.* Havertown, Pa.: Casemate Publishers, 2002.

Krueger, Walter. *From Down Under to Nippon: The Story of Sixth Army in World War II.* Nashville, Tenn.: Battery Press, 1989.

Langellier, John P. *Uncle Sam's Little Wars: The Spanish-American War, Philippine Insurrection, and Boxer Rebellion, 1898–1902.* London: Greenhill Books, 1999.

Laur, Timothy M., and Steven L. Llanso. *The Army Times, Navy Times, Air Force Times Encyclopedia of Modern U.S. Military Weapons.* New York: Berkley, 1995.

Leckie, Robert. *George Washington's War: The Saga of the American Revolution.* New York: Harper Perennial, 1992.

Lee, Robert E. *The Recollections and Letters of Robert E. Lee.* New York: Barnes & Noble Books, 2003.

Lindsey, Daryl. *Gays in the Military: Don't Ask, Don't Tell, Don't Fall in Love.* New York: Salon.com, 2001.

MacArthur, Douglas. *Reminiscences.* Annapolis, Md.: United States Naval Institute Press, 2001.

Mahan, Dennis Hart. *A Complete Treatise on Field Fortification: With the General Outlines of the Principles Regulating the Arrangement, the Attack, and the Defence of Permanent Works.* Westport, Conn.: Greenwood Publishing Group, 1969.

Manchester, William. *American Caesar: Douglas MacArthur 1880–1964.* Reprint ed. New York: Laurel Leaf, 1996.

McPherson, James M. *Abraham Lincoln and the Second American Revolution.* New York: Oxford University Press, 1990.

———. *Battle Cry of Freedom.* New York: Oxford University Press, 1988.

———. *The Atlas of the Civil War.* New York: Macmillan, 1994.

Mitchell, George Charles. *Matthew B. Ridgeway: Soldier, Statesman, Scholar, Citizen.* Lanham, Md.: Stackpole Books, 2002.

Miller, David Humphreys. *Custer's Fall: The Native American Side of the Story.* New York: Meridian, 1992.

Moskos, Charles C. *All That We Can Be: Black Leadership and Racial Integration the Army Way.* New York: Basic Books, 1997.

Mrozek, Steven J. *82nd Airborne Division.* Paducah, Ky.: Turner, 1999.

Nakasone, Edwin M. *The Nisei Soldier: Historical Essays on World War II and the Korean War.* 2nd ed. White Bear Lake, Minn.: J-Press, 1999.

Neimeyer, Charles Patrick. *America Goes to War: A Social History of the Continental Army.* New York: New York University Press, 1995.

Nelson, Paul David. *Anthony Wayne: Soldier of the Early Republic.* Bloomington: Indiana University Press, 1985.

Newby, Claude. *It Took Heroes: A Cavalry Chaplain's Memoir of Vietnam.* Novato, Calif.: Presidio Press, 2003.

Palmer, Dave R. *Summons of the Trumpet: U.S.-Vietnam in Perspective.* San Rafael, Calif.: Presidio Press, 1978.

Powell, Colin L. *My American Journey.* New York: Ballantine, 1996.

Richie, Jason. *Secretaries of War, Navy and Defense: Ensuring National Security.* Minneapolis: Oliver Press, 2001.

Ridgway, Matthew B. *The Korean War.* New York: DaCapo Press, 1988.

Rimmerman, Craig A., ed. *Gay Rights, Military Wrongs: Political Perspectives on Lesbians and Gays in the Military.* New York: Garland, 1996.

Ripley, Tim. *Desert Storm Land Power: The Coalition and Iraqi Armies.* London: Osprey, 1991.

Roagan, Helen. *Mixed Company: Women in the Army.* Boston: Beacon Press, 1982.

Royster, Charles. *Revolutionary People at War: The Continental Army and the American Character, 1775–1783.* Chapel Hill: University of North Carolina Press, 1995.

Schwarzkopf, H. Norman. *It Doesn't Take a Hero: The Autobiography of General H. Norman Schwarzkopf.* New York: Bantam, 1993.

Sears, Stephen W. *George B. McClellan: The Young Napoleon.* New York: DaCapo Press, 1999.

Shallat, Todd. *Structures in the Stream: Water, Science, and the Rise of the U.S. Army Corps of Engineers.* Austin: University of Texas Press, 1994.

Sheridan, Philip Henry. *Personal Memoirs of P. H. Sheridan.* New York: DaCapo Press, 1992.

Smith, Gene. *Until the Last Trumpet Sounds: The Life of General of the Armies John J. Pershing.* New York: Wiley, 1999.

Smith, Jean Edward. *Grant.* New York: Simon & Schuster, 2002.

Sorley, Lewis. *Thunderbolt: General Creighton Abrams and the Army of His Times.* New York: Simon & Schuster, 1992.

Southworth, Samuel A., and Stephen Tanner. *U.S. Special Forces: A Guide to America's Special Operations Units—The World's Most Elite Fighting Force.* New York: DaCapo Press, 2002.

Steffan, Joseph. *Gays and the Military.* Princeton, N.J.: Princeton University Press, 1993.

Stillwell, Joseph W. *Stillwell Papers.* Reprint ed. New York: DaCapo Press, 1991.

Stokesbury, James L. *A Short History of the American Revolution.* New York: Morrow, 1991.

Tayaka, Chester. *Go for Broke: A Pictorial History of the Japanese American 100th Infantry Battalion and the 442nd Regimental Combat Team.* Novato, Calif.: Presidio Press, 1997.

Thiebes, Raquel D. *Army Basic Training: Be Smart, Be Ready.* Philadelphia: Xlibris Corporation, April 2001.

Thomas, Emory M. *Robert E. Lee: A Biography.* New York: Norton, 1997.

Thompson, James. *Decorations, Medals, Ribbons, Badges and Insignia of the United States Marine Corps: World War II to Present.* Fountain Inn, S.C.: Medals of America Press, 1998.

Thompson, Leroy. *The All Americans: The 82nd Airborne.* London: David & Charles UK, 1988.

Tolzman, Don Heinrich, ed. *The Army of the American Revolution and Its Organizer.* Bowie, Md.: Heritage Books, 1999.

Tomajczyk, S. F. *Dictionary of the Modern United States Military.* Jefferson, N.C.: McFarland, 1996.

Treadwell, Mattie E. *The Women's Army Corps.* Washington, D.C.: U.S. Government Printing Office, 1954.

Tuchman, Barbara W. *Stilwell and the American Experience in China, 1911–45.* Reprint, ed. New York: Grove Atlantic, 2001.

U.S. Department of the Army. *Religious Requirements and Practices: A Handbook for Chaplains.* Honolulu, Hawaii: University Press of the Pacific, 2001.

U.S. Department of the Army. *Serve God and Country as an Army Chaplain.* Washington, D.C.: U.S. Department of Defense, 1992.

Utley, Robert M. *Frontier Regulars: The United States Army and the Indian, 1866–1891.* Lincoln: University of Nebraska Press, 1984.

Utley, Robert Marshall, and Wilcomb E. Washburn. *Indian Wars.* Boston: Houghton Mifflin Company, 2002.

Wagner, Margaret, Gary W. Gallagher, and Paul Finkelman. *The Library of Congress Civil War Desk Reference.* New York: Simon & Schuster, 2002.

Weigley, Russell F. *The American Way of War: A History of United States Military Strategy and Policy.* Bloomington: Indiana University Press, 1977.

Weinberg, Gerhard L. *A World at Arms: A Global History of World War II.* Cambridge: Cambridge University Press, 1994.

West, Elliott. *The Contested Plains: Indians, Goldseekers, and the Rush to Colorado.* Lawrence: University Press of Kansas, 2000.

Williams, Vera S. *WACs: Women's Army Corps.* Osceola, Wisc.: Motorbooks International, 1997.

Zaffiri, Samuel. *Westmoreland: A Biography.* New York: William Morrow, 1994.

Zeeland, Steven. *Barrack Buddies and Soldier Lovers: Dialogues with Gay Young Men in the U.S. Military.* Binghamton, N.Y.: Haworth Press, 1993.

AIRCRAFT AND AVIATION

Air Force Link. "E-8C Joint Stars." Available online. URL: http://www.af.mil/factsheets/fs_100.shtml

FAS Military Analysis Network. "AH-64 Apache." Available online. URL: http://www.fas.org/man/dod-101/sys/ac/ah-64.htm

FAS Military Analysis Network. "CH-47 Chinook." Available online. URL: http://www.fas.org/man/dod-101/sys/ac/h-47.htm

Glines, Carroll V. *The Amazing Gooney Bird: The Saga of the Legendary DC-3/ C-47.* Atglen, Pa.: Schiffer Publishing, 1996.

GlobalSecurity.org. "AH-1 Cobra." Available online. URL: http://www.globalsecurity.org/military/systems/aircraft/ah-1.htm

GlobalSecurity.org. "C-23 Sherpa." Available online. URL: http://www.globalsecurity.org/military/systems/aircraft/c-23.htm

GlobalSecurity.org. "Gulfstream." Available online. URL:http://www.globalsecurity.org/military/systems/aircraft/gulfstream.htm

GlobalSecurity.org, "OH-58 Kiowa." Available online. URL: http://www.globalsecurity.org/military/systems/ aircraft/oh-58d_ahip.htm

GlobalSecurity.org. "TH-67 Creek." Available online. URL: http://www.globalsecurity.org/military/systems/aircraft/th-67.htm

Halberstadt, Hans. *Army Aviation.* Novato, Calif.: Presidio Press, 1990.

McDonnell-Douglas. "OH-6 Cayuse." Available online. URL: http://www.boeing.com/history/mdc/cayuse.htm

Siuru, Bill D. *Huey and Huey Cobra.* New York: TAB, 1987.

U.S. Army. "Aviation.Army.Mil." Available online. URL: http://www.aviation.army.mil

U.S. Army. "Fact Sheet: Blackhawk." Available online. URL: http://www.army.mil/fact_files_site/blackhawk/index.html

U.S. Department of Defense. *21st Century Complete Guide to U.S. Army Aviation at Fort Rucker, Air Defense Artillery, Army Aviation Logistics School, Army Aeronautical Services Agency.* New York: Progressive Management, 2003.

AIR DEFENSE ARTILLERY

Directory of U.S. Rockets and Missiles. "MIM-23." Available online. URL: http://www.designation-systems.net/dusrm/m-23.html

FAS Military Analysis Network. "MIM-72/M48 Chaparral Forward Area Air-Defense System [FAADS]," Available online. URL: http://www.fas.org/man/dod-101/sys/land/chaparral.htm

Hogg, Ian V. *Infantry Support Weapons: Mortars, Missiles and Machine Guns.* London: Greenhill Books, 2002.

Trewitt, Philip. *Armored Fighting Vehicles: 300 of the World's Greatest Military Vehicles.* New York: Sterling, 2001.

U.S. Army. "Fact File: Avenger." Available online. URL: http://www.army.mil/fact_files_site/avenger/index.html

U.S. Army. "Fact File: Patriot." Available online. URL: http://www.army.mil/fact_files_site/patriot/index.html

ANTIARMOR WEAPONS

Chamberlain, Peter. *Anti-Tank Weapons.* New York: Arco, 1974.

FAS Military Analysis Network. "AGM-114 Hellfire." Available online: URL: http://www.fas.org/man/dod-101/sys/missile/agm-114.htm

FAS Military Analysis Network. "M712 Copperhead." Available online. URL: http://www.fas.org/man/dod-101/sys/land/m712.htm

Gander, Terry. *Anti-Tank Weapons.* Ramsbury, U.K.: Crowood Press, 2000.

GlobalSecurity.org. "M-47 DRAGON Anti-Tank Guided Missile." Available online. URL: http://www.globalsecurity.org/military/systems/munitions/m47-dragon.htm

Norris, John, and James Marchington, eds. *Anti-Tank Weapons.* New York: Brassey's, 2003.

Secretary of the Army. "Advanced Antitank Weapon System-Medium (AAWS-M) (JAVELIN)." Available online. URL: http://www.sec.army.mil/arat/ARAT/Target_sensing_systems/Direct_Fire/javelin.htm

ARMOR

Foss, Christopher F. *Jane's Tanks and Combat Vehicles Recognition Guide.* New York: HarperCollins, 2003.

Hunnicutt, R. P. *Armored Car: A History of American Wheeled Combat Vehicles.* Novato, Calif.: Presidio Press, 2002.

———. *Half-Track: A History of American Semi-Tracked Vehicles.* Novato, Calif.: Presidio Press, 2001.

Macksey, Kenneth. *Tank: A History of the Armoured Fighting Vehicle.* London: Macdonald & Company, 1973.

———. *Tank Warfare: History of Tanks in Battle.* New York: Stein & Day, 1988.

CAVALRY

Langellier, J. Philip. *Sound the Charge: The U.S. Cavalry in the American West, 1866–1916.* London: Greenhill Press, 1998.

Selby, John Millin. *U.S. Cavalry.* London: Osprey, 1972.

Truscott, Lucian K. Jr. *The Twilight of the U.S. Cavalry: Life in the Old Army, 1917–1942.* Lawrence: University Press of Kansas, 1989.

Urwin, Gregory J. W. *The United States Cavalry: An Illustrated History, 1776–1944.* Norman: University of Oklahoma Press, 2003.

INDIRECT FIRE SYSTEMS

FAS Military Analysis Network. "M101 105-mm Howitzer." Available online. URL: http://www.fas.org/man/dod-101/sys/land/m101.htm

FAS Military Analysis Network. "M102 105-mm Lightweight Howitzer." Available online. URL: http://www.fas.org/man/dod-101/sys/land/m102.htm

FAS Military Analysis Network. "The M114 155mm Howitzer." Available online. URL: http://www.fas.org/man/dod-101/sys/land/m114.htm

FAS Military Analysis Network. "M119A1 105mm Lightweight Towed Howitzer." Available online. URL: http://www.fas.org/man/dod101/sys/land/m119.htm

FAS Military Analysis Network. "M270 MLRS Self-Propelled Loader/Launcher (SPLL)." Available online. URL: http://www.fas.org/man/dod-101/sys/land/m270.htm

Hogg, Ian V. *Infantry Support Weapons: Missiles and Machine Guns.* London: Greenhill Books, 2002.

U.S. Army. "U.S. Army Fact File: M109 Paladin." Available online. URL: http://www.army.mil/fact_files_site/paladin/index.html

U.S. Army. "U.S. Army Fact File: M198 Towed Howitzer." Available online: URL: http://www.army.mil/fact_files_site/m198/index.html

MEDICINE

AMEDD. "About AMEDD." Available online. URL: http://www.armymedicine.army.mil/default2.htm

AMEDD. "Army Medical Department Home Page." Available online. URL: http://www.armymedicine.army.mil/armymed/default2.htm

Army Nurse Corps. "Army Nurse Corps History." Available online. URL: http://history.amedd.army.mil/ANCWebsite/anchhome.html

Gillett, Mary C. *The Army Medical Department 1775–1818.* Honolulu, Hawaii: University Press of the Pacific, 2002.

———. *Army Medical Department, 1818–1865.* Washington, D.C.: U.S. Government Printing Office, 1987.

———. *Army Medical Department, 1865–1917.* Carlisle, Pa.: Center of Military History, 1995.

Sarnecky, Mary T. *A History of the U.S. Army Nurse Corps.* Philadelphia: University of Pennsylvania Press, 1999.

U.S. Army Dental Corps. "Army Dental Corps." Available online. URL: http://www.perscomonline.army.mil/OPdc/;

U.S. Army Dental Corps. "Highlights in the History of U.S. Army Dentistry." Available online. URL: http://www.dencom.army.mil/adcs/history3.asp#rev

U.S. Army. "Army Nurse Corps." Available online. URL:http://www.branchorientation.com/nurse/profile.html

U.S. Army Veterinary Service. "U.S. Army Veterinary Service." Available online. URL: http://vets.amedd.army.mil/dodvsa/.

U.S. Department of Defense. *Composition, Mission, and Functions of the Army Medical Department.* Washington, D.C.: Headquarters, Department of the Army, n.d.

TRACKED VEHICLES

Chamberlain, Peter. *British and American Tanks of World War Two.* New York: Sterling, 2000.

Defense Industries–Army web site. "M60A3 Main Battle Tank, USA." Available online. URL: http://www.army-technology.com/projects/m60/

Defense Industries–Army web site. "M1A1/M1A2 Abrams Main Battle Tank, USA." Available online. URL: http://www.army-technology.com/projects/abrams/

FAS Military Analysis Network. "M107 175-mm Self-Propelled Gun." Available online. URL: http://www.fas.org/man/dod-101/sys/land/m107-175.htm

FAS Military Analysis Network. "M113A1 Armored Personnel Carrier." Available online. URL: http://www.fas.org/man/dod-101/sys/land/m113.htm

FAS Military Analysis Network. "M548A3 Cargo Carrier." Available online. URL: http://www.fas.org/man/dod-101/sys/land/m548.htm

Ford, Roger. *The Sherman Tank.* Osceola, Wisc.: Motorbooks International, 1999.

Hunnicutt, R. P. *Bradley: A History of American Fighting and Support Vehicles.* New York: Ballantine, 1999.

Trewitt, Philip. *Armored Fighting Vehicles: 300 of the World's Greatest Military Vehicles.* New York: Sterling, 2001.

Zaloga, Stephen J. *M26/M46 Pershing Tank 1943–53.* London: Osprey, 2001.

WEAPONS, INDIVIDUAL AND CREW-SERVED

FAS Military Analysis Network. "FIM-92A Stinger Weapons System: RMP and Basic." Available online. URL: http://www.fas.org/man/dod-101/sys/land/stinger.htm

GlobalSecurity.Org. "M16 5.56mm Semiautomatic Rifle/M4 5.56mm Carbine." Available online. URL: http://www.globalsecurity.org/military/systems/ground/m16.htm

U.S. Army "U.S. Army Fact File: M4 Carbine." Available online. URL: http://www.army.mil/fact_files_site/m-4_carbine/index.html

U.S. Army. "U.S. Army Fact File: M9 Pistol." Available online. URL: http://www.army.mil/fact_files_site/m-9_pistol/index.html

U.S. Army. "U.S. Army Fact File: M19-3 40 mm Grenade Machine Gun." Available online. URL: http://www.army.mil/fact_files_site/mk19-3/index.html

U.S. Army. "U.S. Army Fact Sheet: M203/M203A1 Grenade Launcher." Available online. URL: http://www.army.mil/fact_files_site/m203/index.html

U.S. Army. "U.S. Army Fact Sheet: M240B Machine Gun." Available online. URL: http://www.army.mil/fact_files_site/m-240b/index.html

U.S. Army. "U.S. Army Fact File: M249 Squad Automatic Weapon." Available online. URL: http://www.army.mil/fact_files_site/m-249_saw/index.html

WHEELED VEHICLES

FAS Military Analysis Network. "Heavy Expanded Mobility Tactical Truck (HEMTT)." Available online. URL: http://www.fas.org/man/dod-101/sys/land/hmett.htm

FAS Military Analysis Network. "Palletized Load System (PLS)." Available online. URL: http://www.fas.org/man/dod-101/sys/land/pls.htm

FAS Military Analysis Network. "M706 / LAV-150 Commando." Available online. URL: http://www.fas.org/man/dod-101/sys/land/lav-150.htm

U.S. Army. "Fact File: Family of Medium Tactical Vehicles (FMTV)." Available online. URL: http://www.army.mil/fact_files_site/fmtv/

U.S. Army. "U.S. Army Fact File: M1070 Heavy Equipment Transporter (HET)." Available online. URL: http://www.army.mil/fact_files_site/het/index.html

MISCELLANEOUS

U.S. Army. Acquisition Support Center. Available online. URL:http://asc.army.mil/public/overview/mission/default.cfm

U.S. Army. "Adjutant General's Corps." Available online. URL:www.branchorientation.com/adjutantgeneral/profile.html

U.S. Army. Adjutant General School web site. Available online. URL: http://agsssi-www.army.mil/Default.htm

U.S. Army. Army Aviation School web site. Available online. URL: http://www-rucker.army.mil/

U.S. Army. Army Chaplain School web site. Available online. URL: http://www.usachcs.army.mil/

U.S. Army. Army Chemical School web site. Available online. URL: http://www.wood.army.mil/usacmls/jslc.htm

U.S. Army. "U.S. Army Staff." Available online. URL: http://www.army.mil/public/arstaff.htm

U.S. Army. Army Management Staff College web site. Available online. URL: http://www.amsc.belvoir.army.mil/

U.S. Army. Army Mountain Warfare School web site. Available online. URL: http://www-benning.army.mil/AMWS/

Army National Guard. "Army National Guard." Available online. URL: http://www.arng.army.mil/default.asp

U.S. Army Physical Fitness School. "Army Physical Fitness Test." Available online. URL:

http://www. benning.army.mil/usapfs/Training/APFT/

Army Materiel Command. "Army Research Laboratory." Available online. URL: http://www.arl.army.mil/main/Main/default.cfm

U.S. Army Redstone Arsenal. "Fact Sheet: Army Tactical Missile System (Block I and IA)." Available online. URL: http://www.redstone.army.mil/pub_affairs/amcom_fact/aFACTAT~1.html

U.S. Army. Army Training Support Center web site. Available online. URL: http://www.atsc.army.mil/

AUSA. "Association of the United States Army." Available online. URL: http://www.ausa.org/

Army Materiel Command. "U.S. Army Aviation and Missile Command (AMCOM)." Available online. URL:http://www2.brtrc.com/amc/hbcu_mi/amcom.htm

U.S. Army, Battle Command Battle Laboratory. Fort Leavenworth (BCBL) web site. Available online. URL: http://cacfs.army.mil/index1.htm

U.S. Army. "U.S. Army Fact File: Bayonet." Available online. URL: http://www.army.mil/fact_files_site/bayonet/index.html

U.S. Army. Benét Labs we bsite. Available online. URL: http://www.benet.wva.army.mil/

U.S. Army. "The Caissons Go Rolling Along." Available online. URL: http://www.bragg.army.mil/history/Commanders/Commanders%20Pages/Gruber/CaissonsGoRollin g.htm

Center for Army Lessons Learned (CALL). Center for Army Lessons Learned (CALL) web site. Available online. URL: http://call.army.mil/

U.S. Army. "Chemical Corps." Available online. URL: http://www.branchorientation.com/chemical/profile.html

FAS Military Analysis Network."Table of Organization and Equipment." Available online. URL: http://www.fas.org/man/dod-101/army/unit/toe/toenum.htm

U.S. Army. Coastal and Hydraulics Laboratory CHL. Available online. URL: http://chl.wes.army.mil/

U.S. Army. Cold Regions Research and Engineering Laboratory (CRREL) web site. Available online. URL: http://www.crrel.usace.army.mil/welcome/welcome.html

FAS Military Analysis Network. "Combined Arms Center." Available online. URL: http://www.fas.org/irp/agency/army/tradoc/cac/

CASCOM. "United States Army Combined Arms Support Command." Available online. URL: http://www.cascom.army.mil/index.htm

Command and General Staff College. "Command and General Staff College." Available online. URL: http://www-cgsc.army.mil/

GlobalSecurity.org. "Communications-Electronics Command (CECOM)." Available online. URL: http:// www.globalsecurity.org/military/agency/army/cecom.htm

U.S. Army. "Forts and Installations." Available online. URL: http://www.army.mil/installations/forts.htm

U.S. Army. Joint POW/MIA Accounting Command (JPAC) web site. Available online. URL: http://www.cilhi.army.mil/eBrochure.htm

U.S. Army. "U.S. Army Fact File: Joint Service Lightweight Integrated Suit Technology." Available online. URL: http://www.army.mil/fact_files_site/jslist/index.html

U.S. Army. Judge Advocate General's Corps. "Judge Advocate General's Corps." Available online. URL: http://www.jagcnet.army.mil/

U.S. Army. "U.S. Army Fact File: M40/M42 Field Protective Mask." Available online. URL: http://www.army.mil/fact_files_site/m40/index.html

U.S. Army. "U.S. Army Fact File: Nuclear, Biological, and Chemical Reconnaissance System (M93/M93A1)." Available online. URL: http://www.army.mil/fact_files_site/nbcrs/index.html

U.S. Army. "U.S. Army Fact File: M256A1 Chemical Agent Detector Kit." Available online. URL: http://www.army.mil/fact_files_site/m256a1/index.html

U.S. Army. "U.S. Army Fact File: Joint Service Lightweight Integrated Suit Technology." Available online. URL: http://www.army.mil/fact_files_site/jslist/index.html

FAS Military Analysis Network. "Table of Organization and Equipment." Available online. URL: http://www.fas.org/man/dod-101/army/unit/toe/toenum.htm

U.S. Army. "U.S. Army Bands." Available online. URL: http://www.bands.army.mil/

U.S. Army Criminal Investigation Command. "The United States Army Criminal Investigation Command." Available online. URL: http://www.cid.army.mil

U.S. Army. "U.S. Army Materiel Command." Available online. URL: http://www.amc.army.mil/

U.S. Army Military History Institute. "About MHI." Available online. URL: http://www.carlisle.army.mil/usamhi/1aboutmhi.html#Mission

U.S. Army Space and Missile Defense Command. "U.S. Army Space and Missile Defense Command." Available online. URL: http://www.smdc.army.mil/

U.S. Army War College. "U.S. Army War College." Available online. URL: http://www.carlisle.army.mil/stratplan.asp#mission

Bibliography
UNITED STATES AIR FORCE

GENERAL WORKS

Aldebol, Anthony. *Army Air Force and United States Air Force: Decorations, Medals, Ribbons, Badges and Insignia*. Fountain Inn, S.C.: Medals of America Press, 2003.

Anderton, David A. *Strategic Air Command: Two-thirds of the Triad*. London: Allan, 1975.

Angelucci, Enzo. *Encyclopedia of Military Aircraft: 1914 to the Present* London: Book Sales, 2001.

Bacevich, A. J. *The Pentomic Era: The U.S. Army between Korea and Vietnam*. Washington, D.C.: Office of Air Force History, 1986.

Barnaby, Frank. *The Automated Battlefield*. New York: Free Press, 1986.

Betts, Richard K. *Cruise Missiles: Technology, Strategy, Politics*. Washington, D.C.: Brookings Institution, 1982.

Bond, Charles, and Terry Anderson. *A Flying Tiger's Diary*. College Station: Texas A&M Press, 1984.

Bowers, Ray L. *The Air Force in Southeast Asia: Tactical Airlift*. Washington, D.C.: Office of Air Force History, 1983.

Bowman, Martin. *The USAF: 1947–1999*. Newbury Park, Calif.: Haynes, 2000.

Bright, Charles D., ed. *Historical Dictionary of the U.S. Air Force*. Westport, Conn.: Greenwood Press, 1992.

Byrd, Martha. *Chennault: Giving Wings to the Tiger*. Tuscaloosa: University of Alabama Press, 1987.

Campbell, Christopher. *Air Warfare: The Fourth Generation*. New York: Arco, 1984.

Chandler, Charles deForest, and Frank P. Lahm. *How Our Army Grew Wings: Airmen and Aircraft before 1914*. New York: Ronald Press, 1943.

Chinnery, Philip D. *Air Commando: Fifty Years of the USAF Air Commando and Special Operations Forces, 1944–1994*. New York: St. Martin's Press, 1997.

Clark, Jerome. *The Emergence of a Phenomenon: UFOs from the Beginning through 1959*. Detroit: Omnigraphics, 1992.

Coffey, Thomas M. *HAP: The Story of the U.S. Air Force and the Man Who Built It—General H. "Hap" Arnold*. New York: Viking, 1982.

———. *Iron Eagle: The Turbulent Life of General Curtis LeMay*. New York: Crown, 1986.

Cole, John H., and Michael F. Monaghan. *Top Cover for America: The Air Force in Alaska, 1920–1983*. Anchorage, Alaska: Anchorage Chapter-Air Force Association; Missoula, Mont.: Pictorial Histories Pub. Co., 1984.

Copp, DeWitt S. *A Few Great Captains: The Men and Events That Shaped the Development of U.S. Air Power*. Garden City, N.Y.: Doubleday, 1980.

Crouch, Tom D. *The Bishop's Boys: A Life of Wilbur and Orville Wright*. New York: Norton, 1989.

Dalfiume, Richard M. *Desegregation of the U.S. Armed Forces: Fighting on Two Fronts, 1939–1953*. Columbia: University of Missouri Press, 1969.

Davis, Burke. *The Billy Mitchell Affair*. New York: Random House, 1967.

Davis, Reed E. *From Aviation Section Signal Corps to United States Air Force*. New York: Vantage, 1984.

Doolittle, James H. (with Carroll V. Glines). *I Could Never Be So Lucky Again.* Reprint ed. New York: Ballantine, 2001.

Dorr, Robert F. *Fighters of the United States Air Force.* New York: Crown, 1990.

———. *Korean War Aces: Aircraft of the Aces.* London: Osprey, 1995.

Drendel, Lou. *Aircraft of the Vietnam War.* Ipswich, UK: Aero, 1980.

Farr, Finis. *Rickenbacker's Luck: An American Life.* Boston: Houghton Mifflin, 1979.

Flammer, Philip. *The Vivid Air: The Lafayette Escadrille.* Athens: University of Georgia Press, 1981.

Ford, Daniel. *Flying Tigers: Claire Chennault and the American Volunteer Group.* Washington, D.C.: Smithsonian Institution Press, 1991.

Foulois, Benjamin D., and Carroll V. Glines. *From the Wright Brothers to the Astronauts: The Memoirs of Major General Benjamin D. Foulois.* New York: McGraw-Hill, 1968.

Francis, Charles E. *The Tuskegee Airmen: The Men Who Changed a Nation.* Boston: Branden, 1997.

Frater, Michael, and Michael Ryan. *Electronic Warfare for the Digitized Battlefield.* Boston: Artech House, 2001.

Freeman, Roger A. *The Mighty Eighth: Units, Men, and Machines.* London: Macdonald and Co., 1970.

Frisbee, John L. *Makers of the United States Air Force.* Washington, D.C.: Office of Air Force History, 1987.

Futrell, Robert F., Riley Sunderland, and Martin Blumenson. *The Air Force in Southeast Asia: The Advisory Years, to 1965.* Washington, D.C.: Office of Air Force History, 1980.

Getz, C. W. "Bill," ed. *The Wild Blue Yonder: Songs of the Air Force,* vol. 1. Burlingame, Calif.: Redwood Press, 1981.

Glines, Carroll V. *The Compact History of the United States Air Force.* New York: Hawthorne Books, 1963.

Goodall, James C. *America's Stealth Fighters and Bombers.* Osceola, Wisc.: Motorbooks International, 1992.

Gordon, Michael R., and Bernard E. Trainor. *The Generals' War: The Inside Story of the Conflict in the Gulf.* Boston: Little, Brown, 1995.

Gorn, Michael H. *Vulcan's Forge: The Making of an Air Force Command for Weapons Acquisition, 1950–1986.* Andrews AFB, Md.: Office of History, Headquarters, Air Force Systems Command, 1986.

Gray, Colin S. *Missiles for the Nineties: ICBMs and Strategic Policy.* Denver: Westview, 1984.

Gregory, Shaun R. *Nuclear Command and Control in NATO: Nuclear Weapons Operations and the Strategy of Flexible Response.* London: Palgrave Macmillan, 1996.

Gropman, Alan L. *The Air Force Integrates, 1945–1964.* Washington, D.C.: Office of Air Force History, 1978.

Gross, Charles J. *The Air National Guard: A Short History.* Washington, D.C.: National Guard Bureau Historical Services Division, 1994.

Gunston, Bill, and Peter Gilchrist. *Jet Bombers: From the Messerschmidt Me 262 to the Stealth B-2.* Osceola, Wisc.: Motorbooks International, 1993.

Hallion, Richard P. *Strike from the Sky: The History of Battlefield Air Attack, 1911–1945.* Washington, D.C.: Smithsonian Institution Press, 1989.

———. *Test Pilots: The Frontiersmen of Flight.* Washington, D.C.: Smithsonian Institution Press, 1988.

Haydock, Michael D. *City Under Siege: The Berlin Blockade and Airlift, 1948–1949.* New York: Brassey's, 2000.

Heflin, Woodford A., ed. *The United States Air Force Dictionary.* Princeton, N.J.: Van Nostrand, 1956.

Hiscock, Melvyn. *Classic Aircraft of World War I.* London: Osprey, 1994.

Holder, Bill. *Planes of the Presidents: An Illustrated History of Air Force One.* Atglen, Pa.: Schiffer, 2000.

Holman, Lynn M., and Thomas Reilly. *Black Knights: The Story of the Tuskegee Airmen.* Gretna, La.: Pelican, 2001.

Holoway, John B. *Red Tails Black Wings: The Men of America's Black Air Force.* Las Cruces, N.M.: Yucca Tree Press, 2000.

Holsinger, Paul, and Mary Anne Schofield, eds. *Visions of War: World War II in Popular Literature and Culture* (1992).

Hudson, James J. *Hostile Skies: A Combat History of the American Air Service in World War I.* Syracuse, N.Y.: Syracuse University Press, 1968.

Hurley, Alfred F. *Billy Mitchell: Crusader for Air Power.* Bloomington: Indiana University Press, 1975.

Jackson, Robert. *Air War over Korea.* London: Allan, 1973.

———. *High Cold War: Strategic Air Reconnaissance and the Electronic Intelligence War.* Newbury Park, Calif.: Haynes, 1998.

Kenney, George C. *Dick Bong: Ace of Aces.* New York: Duell, Sloan and Pearce, 1960.

Lashmar, Paul. *Spy Flights in the Cold War.* Annapolis, Md.: U.S. Naval Institute Press, 1998.

Leyden, Andrew, ed. *Gulf War Debriefing Book: An After Action Report.* Grants Pass, Ore.: Hellgate Press, 1997.

Littauer, Raphael, and Norman Uphoff, eds. *The Air War in Indochina.* Revised ed. Boston: Beacon Press, 1972.

Lloyd, Alwyn T. *A Cold War Legacy: A Tribute to Strategic Air Command, 1946–1992.* Missoula, Mont.: Pictorial Histories, 2000.

Maurer, Maurer. *Air Force Combat Units of World War II.* Washington, D.C.: Office of Air Force History, 1983.

McDaid, Hugh, and David Oliver. *Smart Weapons.* New York: Barnes & Noble, 2001.

McGuire, Nina. *Jacqueline Cochran: America's Fearless Aviator.* Lake Buena Vista, Fla.: Tailored Tours Publications, 1997.

Meilinger, Phillip S. *Hoyt S. Vandenberg: The Life of a General.* Bloomington: Indiana University Press, 1989.

Mets, David R. *Master of Air Power: General Carl A. Spaatz.* Novato, Calif.: Presidio, 1988.

Miller, Charles E. *Airlift Doctrine.* Maxwell Air Force Base, Ala.: Air University Press, 1988.

Mondey, David. *American Aircraft of World War II.* London: Book Sales, 2002.

Mzorek, Donald J. *Air Power and the Ground War in Vietnam.* Washington, D.C.: Office of Air Force History, 1988.

Neufeld, Jacob. *Ballistic Missiles in the United States Air Force, 1945–1960.* Washington, D.C.: Office of Air Force History, 1990.

O'Leary, Michael. *High Viz: U.S. Cold War Aircraft.* London: Osprey, 1995.

Osur, Alan M. *Blacks in the Army Air Forces during World War II.* Washington, D.C.: Office of Air Force History, 1977.

Parrish, Thomas. *Berlin in the Balance, 1945–1949: The Blockade, the Airlift, the First Major Battle of the Cold War.* New York: Perseus, 1999.

Robinson, Douglas. *The Dangerous Sky: A History of Aviation Medicine.* Seattle: University of Washington Press, 1973.

Ross, Stewart Halsey. *Strategic Bombing by the United States in World War II: The Myths and the Facts.* Jefferson, N.C.: McFarland, 2002.

Rottman, Gordon. *U.S. Army Air Force Uniforms.* London: Osprey, 1998.

Shaw, Robert L. *Fighter Combat: Tactics and Maneuvering.* Annapolis, Md.: Naval Institute Press, 1985.

Smythe, Donald. *Punitive Expedition: Pershing's Pursuit of Villa, 1916–1917.* Bloomington: Indiana University Press, 1985.

Snyder, Thomas S., ed. *The Air Force Communications Command 1938–1986: An Illustrated History.* Washington, D.C.: U.S. Government Printing Office, 1986.

Stout, Joseph A. *Border Conflict: Villistas, Carrancistas and the Punitive Expedition.* Fort Worth: Texas Christian University Press, 1999.

Straubel, James H. *Crusade for Air Power: The Story of the Air Force Association.* Washington, D.C.: Aerospace Education Foundation, 1982.

Sullivan, George. *Famous Air Force Fighters.* New York: Dodd, Mead, 1985.

Taylor, Michael J. H., *Jane's Encyclopedia of Aviation.* New York: Crescent, 1989.

Thayer, Lucien. *America's First Eagles: The Official History of the U.S. Army Air Service.* Reprint ed. San Jose, Calif.: R.J. Bender Pub.; Mesa, Ariz.: Champlin Fighter Museum Press, 1983.

Tilford, Earl H., Jr. *Setup: What the Air Force Did to Vietnam and Why.* Honolulu: University Press of the Pacific, 1991.

Valey, Wayne A. *Airman's Guide.* 4th ed. Mechanicsburg, Pa.: Stackpole, 1997.

Yenne, Bill. *The History of the US Air Force.* New York: Crown, 1984.

MISCELLANEOUS

Basic Aerospace Doctrine of the United States Air Force, Air Force Manual 1-1. Washington, D.C.: Department of the Air Force, 1984.

USAF Fact Sheet. "Air Force Bands," at http://www.af.mil/news/factsheets/Air_Force_Bands.html

USAF Fact Sheet. "Air Force Center for Environmental Excellence," at http://www.af.mil/news/factsheets/Air_Force_Center_for_Environm.html

USAF Fact Sheet. "Air Force Civil Engineer Support Agency," at http://www.af.mil/news/factsheets/Air_Force_Civil_Engineer_Supp.html

USAF Fact Sheet. "Air Force Doctrine Center," available at http://www.af.mil/news/factsheets/Air_Force_Doctrine_Center_.html

U.S. Air Force. Air Force Information Warfare Center Public Web, at http://afiwcweb.lackland.af.mil/

USAF Fact Sheet. "Air Force Inspection Agency," at http://www.af.mil/news/factsheets/Air_Force_Inspection_Agency.html

Suggested reading: USAF Fact Sheet. "Air Force News Agency," available at http://www.af.mil/news/factsheets/Air_Force_News_Agency.html

U.S. Air Force. *USAF Scientific Advisory Board Charter,* at www.odam.osd.mil/omp/pdf/439.pdf

U.S. Air Force. "Air Warfare Center," at http://www.nellis.af.mil/units/awfc/

U.S. Air Force. "Organization and Lineage: Numbered Air Forces," www.au.af.mil/au/afhra/org11.htm

U.S. Air Force. "USAF Fact Sheet: Organization of the U.S. Air Force," www.af.mil/news/factsheets/usaf.html

USAF Fact Sheet. "Air Force Recruiting Service," at http://www.af.mil/news/factsheets/Air_Force_Recruiting_Service.html

USAF Fact Sheet. "Thunderbirds," at http://www.af.mil/news/factsheets/Thunderbirds.html

Air Force News Service. "Air Force Unveils New Uniform," at http://usmilitary.about.com/cs/airforce/a/newafuniform.htm

Tuskegee Airmen, Incorporated. "Who Were the Tuskegee Airmen in World War II?" at www.tuskegeeairmen.org/MainFrameset.htm

Bibliography
UNITED STATES MARINE CORPS

★ ──────────────────────────────────────

GENERAL WORKS

Adkin, Mark. *Urgent Fury: The Battle for Grenada.* Lanham, Md.: Lexington Books, 1989.

Alexander, Joseph H. *The Battle History of the U.S. Marines.* New York: HarperPerennial, 1999.

Asprey, Robert B. *At Belleau Wood.* Denton: University of North Texas Press, 1996.

Ballard, John R., and John J. Sheehan, *Upholding Democracy: The United States Military Campaign in Haiti, 1994–1997.* New York: Praeger, 1998.

Bartlett, Merrill L. *Lejeune: A Marine's Life, 1867–1942.* Annapolis, Md.: Naval Institute Press, 1996.

Belknap, Michael R., ed. *Civil Rights, the White House, and the Justice Department, 1945–1968: Integration of the Armed Forces.* New York: Garland, 1991.

Bierley, Paul E. *John Philip Sousa: American Phenomenon.* New York: Warner Books, 2001.

Bradley, James. *Flags of Our Fathers.* New York: Bantam, 2000.

Butler, Smedley D. *War Is a Racket.* New York: Round Table, 1935.

Clark, Eugene Franklin. *The Secrets of Inchon: The Untold Story of the Most Daring Covert Mission of the Korean War.* New York: Putnam, 2002.

Estes, Kenneth W. *The Marine Officer's Guide,* 6th ed. Annapolis, Md.: Naval Institute Press, 1996.

Foster, John. *Guadalcanal General: The Story of A. A. Vandegrift, USMC.* New York: William Morrow, 1966.

Frank, Richard B. *Guadalcanal: The Definitive Account of the Landmark Battle.* New York: Penguin USA, 1992.

Gailey, Harry A. *Historical Dictionary of the United States Marine Corps.* Lanham, Md.: Scarecrow, 1998.

Gamble, Bruce. *Black Sheep One: The Life of Gregory Pappy Boyington.* San Francisco: Presidio Press, 2000.

Glenn, John. *John Glenn: A Memoir.* New York: Bantam, 1999.

Hammel, Eric M. *The Root: The Marines in Beirut, August 1982–February 1984.* Pacifica, Calif.: Pacifica Press, 1993.

Hickey, Donald R. *The War of 1812: A Forgotten Conflict.* Urbana and Chicago: University of Illinois Press, 1990.

Hoffman, Jon T. *Chesty: The Story of Lieutenant General Lewis B. Puller, USMC.* New York: Random House, 2001.

Iacampo, Martin. *"Sir, Yes Sir": U.S. Marine Corps Boot Camp, Parris Island.* New York: Vantage Press, 1994.

Kawano, Kenji. *Warriors: The Navajo Code Talkers.* Flagstaff, Ariz.: Northland Publishing Company, 1990.

Lenahan, Rod. *Confrontation Zone: The Story of the 1989 U.S. Intervention into Panama: Operation Just Cause.* Charleston, S.C.: Narwhal Press, 2002.

Moran, Jim. *Peleliu 1944.* London: Osprey, 2002.

Mason, Theodore K. *Across the Cactus Curtain: The Story of Guantanamo Bay.* New York: Putnam, 1984.

Millett, Allan R. *Semper Fidelis: The History of the United States Marine Corps.* New York: Free Press, 1991.

O'Brien, Cyril J. *Liberation: Marines in the Recapture of Guam.* Collingdale, Pa.: DIANE Publishing, 1994.

Owen, Joseph R. *Colder Than Hell: A Marine Rifle Company at Chosin Reservoir.* Annapolis, Md.: Naval Institute Press, 1996.

Pisor, Robert. *The End of the Line: The Siege of Khe Sanh.* New York: Norton, 2002.

Schmidt, Hans. *Maverick Marine: General Smedley D. Butler and the Contradictions of American Military History.* Lexington: University Press of Kentucky, 1998.

Soderbergh, Peter A. *Women Marines: The World War II Era.* New York: Praeger, 1992.

Thomas, Lowell J. *Old Gimlet Eye: The Adventures of Smedley D. Butler.* New York: Farrar & Rinehart, 1933.

Tomajczyk, S. F. *Dictionary of the Modern United States Military.* Jefferson, N.C., and London: McFarland, 1996.

Turner Publishing Company Staff. *History of the Defenders of the Philippines, Guam and Wake Islands 1941–1945.* Paducah, Ky.: Turner Publishing Company, 1991.

Walsh, John E. *The Philippine Insurrection, 1899–1902: America's Only Try for an Overseas Empire.* New York: Franklin Watts, 1973.

Wright, Derek. *Tarawa 1943.* London: Osprey, 2001.

WEAPONS AND HARDWARE

AIRCRAFT, FIXED-WING

Aviation Enthusiast Corner. Available online: URL: http://www.aero-web.org.

The Aviation History Online Museum. Available online: URL: http://www.aviation-history.com

Bowers, Peter M. *Curtiss Aircraft, 1907–1947.* Annapolis, Md.: Naval Institute Press, 1979.

Glines, Carroll V. *The Amazing Gooney Bird: The Saga of the Legendary DC-3/C-47.* Atglen, Pa.: Schiffer Publishing, 2000.

Hukee, Byron E. *The A-1 Skyraider Combat Journal.* Available online: URL: http://skyraider.org/hook/index.htm

Naval Historical Center. "U.S. Navy Aircraft, 1922–1962 Designation System." Available online: URL: http://www.history.navy.mil/photos/ac-usn22/ac-usn22.htm

Redding, Robert, and Bill Yenne. *Boeing: Planemaker to the World.* San Diego, Calif.: Thunder Bay Press, 1997.

Squadron 235 web site. "The F8U-Crusader." Available online: URL: http://www.vmf235.com/crusader.html

Tillman, Barrett. *The Dauntless Dive Bomber of World War Two.* Annapolis, Md.: Naval Institute Press, 1976.

U.S. Air Force Museum. "Northrop P-61C 'Black Widow.'" Available online: URL: http://www.wpafb.af.mil/museum/air_power/ap25.htm

U.S. Marine Corps. "Aircraft, Fixed Wing." Available online: URL: http://www.hqmc.usmc.mil/factfile.nsf/AVE?OpenView&Start=1&Count=1000&Expand=1#1

Warbird Alley. Information on various historical aircraft. Available online: URL: http://www.warbirdalley.com/index.htm

AIRCRAFT, ROTARY-WING

Aviation Enthusiast Corner. Information on various historical and current aircraft. Available online: URL: http://www.aero-web.org

Bell Helicopter-Textron. "AH-lJ SeaCobra." Available online: URL: http://www.paxmuseum.com/ah1/AH1.htm

FAS Military Analysis Network. "V-22 Osprey." Available online: URL: http://www.fas.org/man/dod-101/sys/ac/v-22.htm

GlobalSecurity.Org. "VH-60 Marine-1." Available online: URL: http://www.globalsecurity.org/military/systems/aircraft/vh-60.htm

The Rotorhead. "HH-1H Iroquois." Available online: URL: http://www.rotorhead.org/military/usiroquois.asp

U.S. Marine Corps. "USMC Fact File: CH-53E Super Stallion Helicopter." Available online: URL: http://www.hqmc.usmc.mil/factfile.nsf/7e931335d515626a8525628100676e0c/8a583a9bef2c6f8d8525626e0048f5fc

U.S. Marine Corps. "USMC Fact File: Tactical Bulk Fuel Delivery System, CH-53E (TBFDS, CH-53E)." Available online: URL: http//:www.hqmc.usmc.mil/factfile.nsf/7e931335d515626a852562

8100676e0c/1ce24aa4f7e1ad7485256289005a0d
d8?OpenDocument

U.S. Navy. "Fact File: CH-46D/E Sea Knight." Available online: URL: http://www.chinfo.navy.mil/navpalib/factfile/aircraft/air-ch46.html

U.S. Navy. "Fact File: CH-53D Sea Stallion." Available online: URL: http://www.chinfo.navy.mil/navpalib/factfile/aircraft/air-ch53d.html

U.S. Navy. "Fact File: VH-3D Sea King." Available online: URL: http://www.chinfo.navy.mil/navpalib/factfile/aircraft/air-vh3d.html

AIR DEFENSE ARTILLERY

FAS Military Analysis Network. "FIM-92A Stinger Weapons System: RMP & Basic." Available online: URL: http//:www.fas.org/man/dod-101/sys/land/stinger.htm

FAS Military Analysis Network. "HAWK: FAS Special Weapons Monitor." Available online: URL: http://www.fas.org/spp/starwars/program/hawk.htm

U.S. Army. "Avenger Low-Level Air Defense System, USA." Available online: URL: http://www.army-technology.com/projects/avenger/

U.S. Marine Corps. "USMC Factfile: Stinger Weapons System: RMP and Basic." Available online: URL: http://www.hqmc.usmc.mil/factfile.nsf/7e93133 5d515626a8525628100676e0c/526d081005e561f 58525626e00495937?OpenDocument

AIR-LAUNCHED WEAPONS

FAS Military Analysis Network. "AGM 114." Available online: URL: http://www.fas.org/man/dod-101/sys/missile/agm-114.htm

FAS Military Analysis Network. "AGM 122." Available online: URL: http://www.fas.org/man/dod-101/sys/missile/agm-122.htm

FAS Military Analysis Network. "AGM 123." Available online: URL: http://www.fas.org/man/dod-101/sys/smart/agm-123.htm

U.S. Air Force. "USAF Fact Sheet: AIM-7 Sparrow." Available online: URL: http://www.af.mil/factsheets/factsheet.asp?fsID=77

U.S. Marine Corps. "USMC Factfile: AGM-65E Maverick Missile." Available online: URL: www.hqmc.usmc.mil/factfile.nsf/7e931335d515626a8 525628100676e0c/65173baa6a6abb6d852 5626d00776f15?OpenDocument

U.S. Marine Corps. "USMC Factfile: AIM-9 Sidewinder Missile." Available online: URL: www.hqmc.usmc.mil/factfile.nsf/7e931335d515626a8 525628100676e0c/75b0842883e0798f852 5626e0048ad88?OpenDocument

U.S. Marine Corps. "USMC Factfile: AGM-45 Shrike." Available online: URL: www.hqmc.usmc.mil/factfile.nsf/7e931335d515626a8525628100676e0 c/fdce85522304f1328525626d00774d9d?Open-Document

AMPHIBIOUS VEHICLES

Friedman, Norman. *U.S. Amphibious Ships and Craft: An Illustrated Design History.* Annapolis, Md.: Naval Institute Press, 2002.

Kutta, Tim. *DUKW in Action.* Carrollton, Tex.: Squadron/Signal Publications, 1997.

U.S. Marine Corps. "Refurbished Amtrack Makes Debut at AAS Battalion," in *Marine Corps News* (July 17, 1999), www.fas.org/man/dod-101/sys/land/docs/990717-aav7.htm

U.S. Marine Corps. "USMC Factfile: Assault Amphibian Vehicle Command Model 7A1 (AAVC7A1)." Available online: URL: www.hqmc.usmc.mil/factfile.nsf/7e931335d515626a8525628100676e0 c/523659798f90c04f852562cf00555fb5?Open-Document

U.S. Marine Corps. "USMC Factfile: Assault Amphibian Vehicle Recovery Model 7A1 (AAVR7A1)." Available online: URL: www.hqmc.usmc.mil/factfile.nsf/7e931335d515626a8525628100676e0 c/faeb17a7dedc9541852562cf005117b4?Open-Document

U.S. Marine Corps. "USMC Factfile: Light Armored Vehicle-Recovery (LAV-R)." Available online: URL: www.hqmc.usmc.mil/factfile.nsf/7e931335 d515626a8525628100676e0c/1cd7d76d126168ca 852 562830059f59f?OpenDocument

U.S. Marine Corps. "USMC Factfile: Light Armored Vehicle-Command and Control (LAV-C2)." Available online: URL: www.hqmc.usmc.mil/factfile.nsf/7e931335d515626a8525628100676e0 c/e84e5e3ba0614f318525628300594bda?Open-Document

U.S. Marine Corps. "USMC Factfile: Light Armored Vehicle-Logistics (LAV-L)." Available online: URL: http://www.hqmc.usmc.mil/factfile.nsf/

7e931335d515626a8525628100676e0c/e40973a9
5e34cc1 5852562830058 9234?OpenDocument

U.S. Marine Corps. "USMC Factfile: Light Armored Vehicle-Mortar (LAV-M)." Available online: URL: www.hqmc.usmc.mil/factfile.nsf/7e93133 5d515626a8525628100676e0c/d988382d9ecb3ff d8525 62830059c0e0?OpenDocument

Zaloga, Steven. *Amtracs: U.S. Amphibious Assault Vehicles.* London: Osprey, 1999.

ANTIARMOR WEAPONS

Chamberlain, Peter. *Anti-Tank Weapons.* New York: Arco, 1975.

FAS Military Analysis Network. "M-47 DRAGON Anti-Tank Guided Missile." Available online: URL: www.fas.org/man/dod-101/sys/land/m47-dragon.htm

Redstone Arsenal. "TOW." Available online: URL: www.redstone.army.mil/history/systems/TOW.html

U.S. Army. "Javelin Anti-Armour Missile, USA." Available online: URL: http://www.armytechnology.com/projects/javelin/

U.S. Marine Corps. "USMC Factfile: AT-4 Light Antiarmor Weapon." Available online: URL: www.hqmc.usmc.mil/factfile.nsf/7e931335d515626a8 525628100676e0c/5fa1f5a45c4e0ebe8525627a00 7227ef?OpenDocument

U.S. Marine Corps. "USMC Factfile: Dragon Weapon System." Available online: URL: www.hqmc.usmc.mil/factfile.nsf/7e931335d515626a852562 8100676e0c/8d198eb6ac07b33b8525627b00567 d5e?OpenDocument

U.S. Marine Corps. "USMC Factfile: Saboted Light Armor Penetrator (SLAP) Ammunition." Available online: URL: www.hqmc.usmc.mil/factfile.nsf/ 7e931335d515626a8525628100676e0c/63aadbd3f 593b0378525628100774353?Open Document

U.S. Marine Corps. "USMC Factfile: Tube Launched, Optically Tracked, Wire Guided (TOW) Missile Weapon System." Available online: URL: www.hqmc.usmc.mil/factfile.nsf/7e931335d515626a8 525628100676e0c/4ba8f1e3958ca16d852 5628100789abb?OpenDocument

COMMUNICATIONS EQUIPMENT

U.S. Marine Corps. "USMC Factfile: AN/TTC-42 (V) Automatic Telephone Central Office." Available online: URL: http://www.hqmc.usmc.mil/factfile.

nsf/7e931335d515626a8525628100676e0c/ d195194b9ab01fbb8525626e0048bc24?Open Document

U.S. Marine Corps. "USMC Factfile: SB-3865 Automatic Telephone Switchboard." Available online: URL: www.hqmc.usmc.mil/factfile.nsf/7e931335 d515626a8525628100676e0c/cd1ea3ce7b847efc8 525 626e00494c2c?OpenDocument

U.S. Marine Corps. "USMC Factfile: Single Channel Ground and Airborne Radio System (SINC-GARS)." Available online: URL: www.hqmc.usmc.mil/factfile.nsf/7e931335d515626a852562 8100676e0c/06c6b4fed8a1e97a8525627a0069a60 5?OpenDocument

DECORATIONS AND MEDALS

Aldebol, Anthony. *Army Air Force and United States Air Force: Decorations, Medals, Ribbons, Badges and Insignia.* Fountain Inn, S.C.: Medals of America Press, 1999.

Emering, Edward J. *U.S. Navy and Marine Corps Campaign and Commemorative Medals.* Atglen, Pa.: Schiffer, 1998.

Foster, Frank C. *The Decorations, Medals, Ribbons, Badges and Insignia of the United States Army: World War II to Present.* Fountain Inn, S.C.: Medals of America Press, 2000.

Thompson, James. *Decorations, Medals, Ribbons, Badges and Insignia of the United States Marine Corps: World War II to Present.* Fountain Inn, S.C.: Medals of America Press, 1998.

INDIRECT FIRE SYSTEMS

Hogg, Ian V. *British and American Artillery of World War II.* London: Greenhill Books, 2002.

Raytheon, Inc. "Advanced Field Artillery Tactical Data System." Available online: URL: www.raytheon.com/c3i/c3iproducts/c3i060/c3i060.htm

U.S. Marine Corps. "USMC Factfile: AN/TPQ-36 Firefinder Radar." Available online: URL: www.hqmc.usmc.mil/factfile.nsf/7e931335d515626a8 525628100676e0c/9904f05d636d7a91852 5627a006fd82b?OpenDocument

"USMC Factfile: AN/USQ-70 Position Azimuth Determining System." Available online: URL: www.hqmc.usmc.mil/factfile.nsf/7e931335d515 626a8525628100676e0c/19487d2e7e24303a8525 627a0071af0a?OpenDocument

U.S. Marine Corps. "USMC Factfile: M49 Telescope." Available online: URL: www.hqmc.usmc.mil/factfile.nsf/7e931335d515626a852562810067 6e0c/095a68c9bdaa831c8525627b006d56b4? OpenDocument

U.S. Marine Corps. "USMC Factfile: M101A1 105mm Light Howitzer, Towed." Available online: URL: www.hqmc.usmc.mil/factfile.nsf/7e931335d515 626a8525628100676e0c/58188e8bf0819ae4852 5627b006250dc?OpenDocument

U.S. Marine Corps. "USMC Factfile: M198 155mm Medium Howitzer, Towed." Available online: URL: www.hqmc.usmc.mil/factfile.nsf/7e931335 d515626a8525628100676e0c/d9d52bbe851eee6c 852 5627b006595b2?OpenDocument

U.S. Marine Corps. "USMC Factfile: M224 60mm Lightweight Mortar." Available online: URL: www.hqmc.usmc.mil/factfile.nsf/7e931335d515 626a8525628100676e0c/a072707cfe330d3b852 5627b006b6e36?OpenDocument

U.S. Marine Corps. "USMC Factfile: M252 81mm Medium Extended Range Mortar." Available online: URL: www.hqmc.usmc.mil/factfile.nsf/ 7e931335d515626a8525628100676e0c/969a278b 663f5cbc852 5627b006c5d03?OpenDocument

U.S. Marine Corps. "USMC Factfile: M94 Muzzle Velocity System (MVS)." Available online: URL: www.hqmc.usmc.mil/factfile.nsf/7e931335d515 626a8525628100676e0c/d681328f75b18de9852 5627b0077e113?OpenDocument

U.S. Marine Corps. "USMC Factfile: M90 Radar Chronograph." Available online: URL: www. hqmc.usmc.mil/factfile.nsf/7e931335d515626a8 525628100676e0c/b25ec569febe8ee58525 627b007685de?OpenDocument

LANDING CRAFT

U.S. Marine Corps. "U.S. Marine Corps Factfile: Riverine Assault Craft (RAC)." Available online: URL: www.hqmc.usmc.mil/factfile.nsf/7e931335 d515626a8525628100676e0c/d4cbb0016e10fe5e 852 562810074c922?OpenDocument

Alaska Hovercraft, Inc. "LACV-30." Available online: URL: http://www.ahv.lynden.com/ahv/lacv-30. html

FAS Military Analysis Network. "Landing Craft, Air Cushion (LCAC)." Available online: URL: www. fas.org/man/dod-101/sys/ship/lcac.htm

Friedman, Norman. *U.S. Amphibious Ships and Craft: An Illustrated Design History.* Annapolis, Md.: Naval Institute Press, 2002.

PERSONAL AND MISCELLANEOUS EQUIPMENT

U.S. Marine Corps. "USMC Factfile: AN/PSN-11 Precision Lightweight GPS Receiver (PLGR)." Available online: URL: www.hqmc.usmc.mil/factfile. nsf/7e931335d515626a8525628100676e0c/7c932 96961c94c378525627a006b173a?OpenDocument

U.S. Marine Corps. "USMC Factfile: AN/PSS-12 Metallic Mine Detector." Available online: URL: www.hqmc.usmc.mil/factfile.nsf/7e931335d515 626a8525628100676e0c/3bf67fa6e2a110538525 62830054d19c?OpenDocument

U.S. Marine Corps. "USMC Factfile: Diver Propulsion Device (DPD)." Available online: URL: www. hqmc.usmc.mil/factfile.nsf/7e931335d515626a8 525628100676e0c/e35f778d99c25556852 5627b0052bf09?OpenDocument

U.S. Marine Corps. "USMC Factfile: Extreme Cold Weather Tent (ECWT)." Available online: URL: www.hqmc.usmc.mil/factfile.nsf/7e931335d515 626a8525628100676e0c/c7ee72d573aa709f852 5627a006751f5?OpenDocument

U.S. Marine Corps. "USMC Factfile: Field Pack, Large, with Internal Frame (FPLIF)." Available online: URL: www.hqmc.usmc.mil/factfile.nsf/7e931335 d515626a8525628100676e0c/1745728ff3abbd33 852 5627a00634955?OpenDocument

U.S. Marine Corps. "USMC Factfile: Improved ECWCS Fiberpile Shirt and Trousers." Available online: URL: www.hqmc.usmc.mil/factfile.nsf/ 7e931335d515626a8525628100676e0c/7dc31a7b b22666af852 5627a00647730?OpenDocument

U.S. Marine Corps. "USMC Factfile: Individual Tactical Load Bearing Vest (ITLBV)." Available online: URL: www.hqmc.usmc.mil/factfile.nsf/7e931335 d515626a8525628100676e0c/1ca315bbf3c1d761 852 5627a0068fd32?OpenDocument

U.S. Marine Corps. "USMC Factfile: Infantry Shelter." Available online: URL: www.hqmc.usmc. mil/factfile.nsf/7e931335d515626a85256281006 76e0c/7235b654d0c2e0b88525627a005e4599? OpenDocument

U.S. Marine Corps. "USMC Factfile: MC-5 Static Line/Free-Fall Ram Air Parachute System (SL/FF RAPS)." Available online: URL: www.hqmc.

usmc.mil/factfile.nsf/7e931335d515626a852562
8100676e0c/2b633bc0dcbcc88d852
5627c0064d965?OpenDocument

U.S. Marine Corps. "USMC Factfile: Modular Sleeping Bag (MSB)." Available online: URL: www.hqmc.usmc.mil/factfile.nsf/7e931335d515626a8525628100676e0c/3b45959ec48b4327852 5627a0058c062?OpenDocument

U.S. Marine Corps. "USMC Factfile: Oxygen Transfer Pump System." Available online: URL: www.hqmc.usmc.mil/factfile.nsf/7e931335d515626a8525628100676e0c/f33ae91af995b0018525 6281005bede9?OpenDocument

TRACKED VEHICLES

U.S. Marine Corps. "USMC Factfile: M1A1 Main Battle Tank." Available online: URL: www.hqmc.usmc.mil/factfile.nsf/7e931335d515626a852562 8100676e0c/9e6cdb7ba648f1388525627b0065de 66?OpenDocument

U.S. Marine Corps. "USMC Factfile: M1 Mine Clearing Blade System." Available online: URL: www.hqmc.usmc.mil/factfile.nsf/7e931335d515626a8 525628100676e0c/84c7f670fca3dc0e8525627b00 61fa5d?OpenDocument

U.S. Marine Corps. "USMC Factfile: M-9 Armored Combat Earthmover (ACE)." Available online: URL: www.hqmc.usmc.mil/factfile.nsf/7e931335 d515626a8525628100676e0c/5dda17f09fae8b18 8525 6289005a2c7c?OpenDocument

U.S. Marine Corps. "USMC Factfile: M60A1 Armored Vehicle Launched Bridge (M60A1 AVLB)." Available online: URL: www.hqmc.usmc.mil/factfile.nsf/7e931335d515626a8525628100676e0c/ ecc79c2c4fee4df08525627b006d8c75?Open Document

U.S. Marine Corps. "USMC Factfile: Mobile/Unit Conduct of Fire Trainer (M/U-COFT)." Available online: URL: www.hqmc.usmc.mil/factfile.nsf/ 7e931335d515626a8525628100676e0c/f826275c0 6a5a228525 6281005b79ae?OpenDoc ument

WEAPONS, INDIVIDUAL AND CREW-SERVED

FAS Military Analysis Network. "Browning Automatic Rifle (BAR)." Available online: URL: www.fas.org/man/dod-101/sys/land/m1918.htm

FAS Military Analysis Network. "Machine Gun, Cal. .30, M1919A4/M1919A6." Available online: URL:

www.fas.org/man/dod-101/sys/land/m1919.htm

FAS Military Analysis Network. "Machine Gun, Cal. .30, M1941, Johnson." Available online: URL: www.fas.org/man/dod-101/sys/land/m1941.htm

FAS Military Analysis Network. "M82A1A .50 Caliber Special Application Scoped Rifle." Available online: URL: www.fas.org/man/dod-101/sys/land/ m82.htm

FAS Military Analysis Network. "Submachine Gun, Cal. .45, M1928A1, Thompson Submachine Gun, Cal. .45, M1/M1A1 Thompson." Available online: URL: www.fas.org/man/dod-101/sys/ land/m1928.htm

Global Security.Org. "M60 7.62mm Machine Gun." Available online: URL: www.globalsecurity.org/ military/systems/ground/m60e3.htm

Kortegaard Engineering. "M1917A1 .30 Caliber Water-Cooled Machine Gun." Available online: URL: www.rt66.com/~korteng/SmallArms/30calhv.htm

Long, Duncan. *Complete AR-15/M16 Sourcebook: What Every Shooter Needs to Know.* Boulder, Colo.: Paladin Press, 2002.

U.S. Marine Corps. "USMC Factfile: M1911A1 .45 Caliber Pistol." Available online: URL: www.hqmc.usmc.mil/factfile.nsf/7e931335d515626a8 525628100676e0c/7322d78f08368e19852 5627b00654175?OpenDocument

U.S. Marine Corps. "USMC Factfile: AN/TVS-5 Crew Served Weapon Night Sight." Available online: URL: www.hqmc.usmc.mil/factfile.nsf/7e931335 d515626a8525628100676e0c/5d5f801a85a1bc68 525 627a0070e5a0?OpenDocument

U.S. Marine Corps. "USMC Factfile: M203 40mm Grenade Launcher." Available online: URL: www.hqmc.usmc.mil/factfile.nsf/7e931335d515 626a8525628100676e0c/d50a120f00de543d852 5627b006b1fec?OpenDocument

U.S. Marine Corps. "USMC Factfile: AN/PAQ-3 Modular Universal Laser Equipment (MULE)." Available online: URL:www.hqmc.usmc.mil/factfile.nsf/7e931335d515626a8525628100676e0c/3e647 6bafdce8a068525627a006c7d23?OpenDocument

U.S. Marine Corps. "USMC Factfile: Joint Service Combat Shotgun." Available online: URL: www.hqmc.usmc.mil/factfile.nsf/7e931335d515626a8 525628100676e0c/5ee9a6e9c96be5658525627b0 060500c?OpenDocument

U.S. Marine Corps. "USMC Factfile: M14 7.62mm Rifle." Available online: URL: www.hqmc.usmc. mil/factfile.nsf/7e931335d515626a85256281006 76e0c/6563e355ce34af538525627b0062a577? OpenDocument

U.S. Marine Corps. "USMC Factfile: AN/PVS-7B Night Vision Goggles (NVG)." Available online: URL: www.hqmc.usmc.mil/factfile.nsf/7e931335 d515626a8525628100676e0c/dd0d434bc4d6f3c8 525 627a006de64a?OpenDocument

U.S. Marine Corps. "USMC Factfile: AN/PVS-5 Night Vision Goggles (NVG)." Available online: URL: www.hqmc.usmc.mil/factfile.nsf/7e931335d515 626a8525628100676e0c/94d7168bba349f00852 5627a006d9c30?OpenDocument

U.S. Marine Corps. "USMC Factfile: AN/PVS-4 Individual Weapon Night Sight." Available online: URL: www.hqmc.usmc.mil/factfile.nsf/ 0/28a82b359e9bf7858525627a006d6992?Open Document

U.S. Marine Corps. "USMC Factfile: AN/PAQ-4A/4C Infrared Aiming Light." Available online: URL: www.hqmc.usmc.mil/factfile.nsf/7e931335d515 626a8525628100676e0c/2ae6b3135944b7bc852 5627a006d06da?OpenDocument

U.S. Marine Corps. "USMC Factfile: Laser Rangefinder AN/GVS-5." Available online: URL: www. hqmc.usmc.mil/factfile.nsf/7e931335d515626a8 525628100676e0c/1c2a810cbff00ef68525627b00 610852?OpenDocument

U.S. Marine Corps. "USMC Factfile: MK19 40mm Machine Gun, MOD 3." Available online: URL: www.hqmc.usmc.mil/factfile.nsf/7e931335d515 626a8525628100676e0c/9867a7c6f72a0ad0852 5627c006cb4ef?OpenDocument

U.S. Marine Corps. "USMC Factfile: MEU (SOC) Pistol." Available online: URL: www.hqmc.usmc.mil/ factfile.nsf/7e931335d515626a8525628100676e 0c/d6a3fc7de02523fe8525627c006c5814?Open-Document

U.S. Marine Corps. "USMC Factfile: MP-5N Heckler and Koch 9mm Submachine Gun." Available online: URL: www.hqmc.usmc.mil/factfile.nsf/ 7e931335d515626a8525628100676e0c/20324744 eaf1aba3852 56281005b3593?OpenDocument

U.S. Marine Corps. "USMC Factfile: Revolver, .38 Caliber." Available online: URL: www.hqmc.usmc. mil/factfile.nsf/7e931335d515626a85256281006

76e0c/1b3878907cb0168b852562810073ceb0? OpenDocument

U.S. Marine Corps. "USMC Factfile: Shoulder-Launched Multipurpose Assault Weapon (SMAW)." Available online: URL: www.hqmc. usmc.mil/factfile.nsf/7e931335d515626a852562 8100676e0c/57c7ea3d1a309a1d8525628100779b 0c?OpenDocument

U.S. Marine Corps. "USMC Factfile: 12-Gauge Shotgun." Available online: URL: www.hqmc. usmc.mil/factfile.nsf/7e931335d515626a852562 8100676e0c/047150249be0bf6c8525627a006c3e 30?OpenDocument

WHEELED VEHICLES

U.S. Marine Corps. "USMC Factfile: KLR 250-D8 Marine Corps Motorcycle." Available online: URL: http://usmilitary.about.com/library/milinfo/mar inefacts/blmotorcycle.htm

U.S. Marine Corps. "USMC Factfile: MK48-14 and Container Transporter Rear Body Unit." Available online: URL: http://usmilitary.about.com/ library/milinfo/marinefacts/blmk48-14.htm

U.S. Marine Corps. "USMC Factfile: MK48 Power Unit and MK15, Recovery/Wrecker Rear Body Unit." Available online: URL: http://usmilitary. about.com/library/milinfo/marinefacts/blmk 48-15.htm

U.S. Marine Corps. "USMC Factfile: "MK48 Power Unit and MK16, Fifth-Wheel Semi-trailer Adapter Rear Body Unit." Available online: URL: http://usmilitary.about.com/library/milinfo/mar inefacts/blmk48-16.htm

U.S. Marine Corps. "USMC Factfile: MK155 Mine Clearance Launcher." Available online: URL: www.hqmc.usmc.mil/factfile.nsf/7e931335d515 626a8525628100676e0c/6b234caa30de31c1852 5627a004df31a?OpenDocument

U.S. Marine Corps. "USMC Factfile: MK48 Power Unit and MK18 Self-loading Container and Ribbon Bridge Transporter." Available online: URL: www.usmilitary.about.com/library/milinfo/ marinefacts/blmk48-18.htm

MISCELLANEOUS

United States Marine Corps History and Museums Division. "Lieutenant Colonel William Ward Burrows, USMC (Deceased)." Available online: URL:

http://hqinet001.hqmc.usmc.mil/HD/Historical/ Whos_Who/Burrows_WW.htm

U.S. Marine Corps. "U.S. Marine Corps Factfile: Close Quarters Battle/Direct Action Program." Available online: URL: www.hqmc.usmc.mil/factfile. nsf/7e931335d515626a8525628100676e0c/d33e6 04ca949c175852 5627a00726280?OpenDocument

U.S. Marine Corps. "Marine Corps Combat Service Support Schools." Available online: URL: www. lejeune.usmc.mil/mccsss/schools.htm

United States Marine Corps. History and Museums Division. "General Robert E. Cushman, Jr., USMC (Deceased)." Available online: URL: http:// hqinet001.hqmc.usmc.mil/HD/Historical/Whos_ Who/Cushman_RE.htm

United States Marine Corps. History and Museums Division. "Sergeant Major Daniel ('Dan') Daly, USMC (Deceased)." Available online: URL: http:// hqinet001.hqmc.usmc.mil/HD/Historical/Whos_ Who/Daly_DJ.htm

U.S. Marine Corps. "U.S. Marine Corps Factfile: Diver Propulsion Device (DPD)." Available online: URL: www.hqmc.usmc.mil/factfile.nsf/7e931335 d515626a8525628100676e0c/e35f778d99c25558 52 5627b0052bf09?OpenDocument

United States Marine Corps. History and Museums Division, "General Wallace M. Greene, Jr., USMC (Deceased)." Available online: URL: http://

hqinet001.hqmc.usmc.mil/HD/Historical/Whos _Who/Greene_WM.htm

U.S. Marine Corps. "United States Marine Corps (Ret.) Lieutenant General Victor H. Krulak." Available online: URL: www.usmc.mil/genbios 2.nsf/0/e504ddb58bac48d685256a4000718813

U.S. Marine Corps. "Marine Aviation Weapons and Tactics Squadron One." Available online: URL: www.tecom.usmc.mil/mawts1/

U.S. Marine Corps. "U.S. Marine Corps Factfile: Marine Corps Combat Identification Program (MCBIP)." Available online: URL: www.hqmc. usmc.mil/factfile.nsf/7e931335d515626a852562 8100676e0c/5d819ccea84e560d8525627c006861 d8?OpenDocument

U.S. Marine Corps. "U.S. Marine Corps Factfile: Tactical Petroleum Laboratory, Medium (TPLM)." Available online: URL: www.hqmc.usmc.mil/ factfile.nsf/7e931335d515626a8525628100676e0 c/4f9646f0cbc30af6852562830055e7fb?Open-Document

U.S. Marine Corps. "U.S. Marine Band." Available online: URL: www.marineband.usmc.mil/

U.S. Marine Corps. "Mountain Warfare Training Center." Available online: URL: www.mwtc.usmc. mil/

Spec War Net. "United States Marine Corps Reconnaissance Battalions." Available online: URL: www.specwarnet.com/americas/recon.htm

Bibliography
UNITED STATES NAVY

★ ───

GENERAL WORKS

Abbott, Henry L. *Beginning of Modern Submarine Warfare, under Captain-Lieutenant David Bushnell, Sappers and Miners, Army of the Revolution.* North Haven, Conn.: Shoe String Press, 1966.

Adkin, Mark. *Urgent Fury: The Battle for Grenada.* Lanham, Md.: Lexington Books, 1989.

Allison, Graham T. *Essence of Decision: Explaining the Cuban Missile Crisis.* New York: Addison-Wesley, 1999.

Althoff, William F. *Sky Ships: A History of the Airship in the United States Navy.* Pacifica, Calif.: Pacifica Press, 1994.

Anderson, Bern. *By Sea and by River: The Naval History of the Civil War.* New York: Knopf, 1962.

Beach, Edward Latimer. *Scapegoats: A Defense of Kimmel and Short at Pearl Harbor.* Annapolis, Md.: Naval Institute Press, 1995.

Buell, Thomas B. *Master of Sea Power: A Biography of Fleet Admiral Ernest J. King.* Annapolis, Md.: Naval Institute Press, 1995 (reprint).

De Kay, James Tertius. *Monitor: The Story of the Revolutionary Ship and the Man Whose Invention Changed the Course of History.* New York: Walker, 1997.

Dewey, George. *Autobiography of George Dewey, Admiral of the Navy.* Annapolis, Md.: Naval Institute Press, 1992 (reprint).

Eller, Ernest M., and Dudley W. Knox. *The Civil War at Sea.* Washington, D.C.: Naval Historical Foundation, 1961.

Emering, Edward J. *U.S. Navy and Marine Corps Campaign and Commemorative Medals.* Atglen, Pa.: Schiffer, 1998.

Farr, James Barker. *Black Odyssey: The Seafaring Traditions of Afro-Americans.* New York: P. Lang, 1989.

Field, Edward. *Esek Hopkins, Commander-in-Chief of the Continental Navy during the American Revolution.* St. Clair Shores, Mich.: Somerset, 1998.

Field, James A., Jr. *History of United States Naval Operations: Korea.* Washington, D.C.: Department of the Navy, 1962.

Fowler, William M. *Under Two Flags: The American Navy in the Civil War.* New York: Norton, 1990.

Friedman, Norman. *U.S. Small Combatants, Including PT-Boats, Subchasers, and the Brown-Water Navy: An Illustrated Design History.* Annapolis, Md.: Naval Institute Press, 1987.

Friedman, Norman, Alan Raven, and A. D. Baker. *U.S. Battleships: An Illustrated Design History.* Annapolis, Md.: Naval Institute Press, 1985.

Goodspeed, M. Hill, *Rick Burgess, and Richard R. Burgess, eds. U.S. Naval Aviation.* Pensacola, Fla.: National Museum of Naval Aviation, 2001.

Handlin, Lilian. *George Bancroft: The Intellectual as Democrat.* New York: HarperCollins, 1984.

Hoopes, Townsend, and Douglas Brinkley. *Driven Patriot: The Life and Times of James Forrestal.* Annapolis, Md.: Naval Institute Press, 2000.

Kelly, Mary Pat. *Proudly We Served: The Men of the USS Mason.* Annapolis, Md.: Naval Institute Press, 1995.

Kitzen, Michael L. S. *Tripoli and the United States at War: A History of American Relations with the Barbary States, 1785–1805.* Jefferson, N.C.: McFarland, 1993.

Long, David Foster. *Sailor-Diplomat: A Biography of Commodore James Biddle, 1783–1848.* Boston: Northeastern University Press, 1983.

Miller, Nathan. *Sea of Glory: A Naval History of the American Revolution.* Mount Pleasant, S.C.: Nautical and Aviation Publishing Company of America, 2000 (reprint).

Morison, Samuel Eliot. *John Paul Jones: A Sailor's Biography.* Annapolis, Md.: Naval Institute Press, 1999 (reprint).

Morris, James M., and Patricia M. Kearns. *Historical Dictionary of the United States Navy.* Lanham, Md.: Scarecrow Press, 1998.

Potter, Elmer Belmont. *Bull Halsey.* Annapolis, Md.: Naval Institute Press, 1985.

Roosevelt, Theodore. *Naval War of 1812.* New York: DaCapo, 1999 (reprint).

Schneller, Robert. *A Quest for Glory: A Biography of Rear Admiral John A. Dahlgren.* Annapolis, Md.: Naval Institute Press, 1995.

Schneller, Robert John. *Farragut: America's First Admiral.* New York: Brassey's, 2002.

Silverstone, Paul H. *The Sailing Navy 1775–1854.* Annapolis, Md.: Naval Institute Press, 2000.

Skaggs, David Curtis. *Thomas Macdonough: Master of Command in the Early U.S. Navy.* Annapolis, Md.: Naval Institute Press, 2002.

Stillwell, Paul. *The Golden Thirteen: Recollections of the First Black Naval Officers.* Annapolis, Md.: Naval Institute Press, 1993.

Sweetman, Jack. *American Naval History.* Annapolis, Md.: Naval Institute Press, 1991.

Taylor, Theodore. *The Magnificent Mitscher.* Annapolis, Md.: Naval Institute Press, 1991.

Tolley, Kemp. *Yangtze Patrol: The U.S. Navy in China.* Annapolis, Md.: Naval Institute Press, 2000.

Tucker, Spencer C. *Andrew Foote: Civil War Admiral on Western Waters.* Annapolis, Md.: Naval Institute Press, 2000.

Wheeler, Gerald E. *Kinkaid of the Seventh Fleet: A Biography of Admiral Thomas C. Kinkaid, U.S. Navy.* Annapolis, Md.: Naval Institute Press, 1996.

MISCELLANEOUS

Department of the Navy. *Standard Organization and Regulations of the U.S. Navy* (OPNAV Instruction 3120.32C, April 11, 1994), at http://neds.nebt.daps.mil/312032.htm; Department of the Navy, "Navy Organization," at www.chinfo.navy.mil/navpalib/organization/org-over.html

U.S. Navy. "Fact File: Aircraft Carriers, CV, CVN," at www.chinfo.navy.mil/navpalib/factfile/ships/ship-cv.html

U.S. Navy Air War College. "Aegis Weapons System," at www.au.af.mil/au/awc/systems/dvic389.htm

U.S. Navy. "United States Navy Chaplain Corps," at www.chaplain.navy.mil/index.asp

U.S. Navy. "Fact File: Cruisers," at www.chinfo.navy.mil/navpalib/factfile/ships/ship-cru.html

U.S. Navy. "Fact File: Landing Craft, Air Cushioned—LCAC," at www.chinfo.navy.mil/navpalib/factfile/ships/ship-lcac.html

Department of the Navy. "Naval Historical Center," at www.history.navy.mil/

U.S. Navy. "Naval Vessel Register," at www.nvr.navy.mil/

Index

Page numbers in **boldface** indicate primary discussions. Page numbers in *italic* indicate illustrations.

AIR FORCE

MARINES

A

NAVY